Demographic Behavior in the Past

Cambridge Studies in Population, Economy and
Society in Past Time 6

Series Editors:

PETER LASLETT, ROGER SCHOFIELD and
E. A. WRIGLEY

ESRC Cambridge Group for the History of Population and
Social Structure

and DANIEL SCOTT SMITH

University of Illinois at Chicago

Recent work in social, economic and demographic history has revealed much that was previously obscure about societal stability and change in the past. It has also suggested that crossing the conventional boundaries between these branches of history can be very rewarding.

This series will exemplify the value of interdisciplinary work of this kind, and will include books on topics such as family, kinship and neighbourhood; welfare provision and social control; work and leisure; migration; urban growth; and legal structures and procedures, as well as more familiar matters. It will demonstrate that, for example, anthropology and economics have become as close intellectual neighbours to history as have political philosophy or biography.

Demographic behavior in the past

A study of fourteen German village populations in the eighteenth and nineteenth centuries

JOHN E. KNODEL

Population Studies Center
University of Michigan

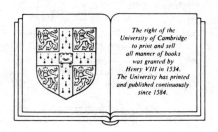

The right of the
University of Cambridge
to print and sell
all manner of books
was granted by
Henry VIII in 1534.
The University has printed
and published continuously
since 1584.

CAMBRIDGE UNIVERSITY PRESS

Cambridge
New York   New Rochelle   Melbourne   Sydney

Published by the Press Syndicate of the University of Cambridge
The Pitt Building, Trumpington Street, Cambridge CB2 1RP
32 East 57th Street, New York, NY 10022, USA
10 Stamford Road, Oakleigh, Melbourne 3166, Australia

First published 1988

Printed in Great Britain at the University Press, Cambridge

British Library cataloguing in publication data
Knodel, John E.
Demographic behavior in the past: a study
of 14 German village populations in the
eighteenth and nineteenth centuries. –
(Cambridge studies in population, economy
and society in past time, 6).
1. Villages – Germany – History 2. Germany
– Population, Rural – History
I. Title
304.6'2'0943 HB2475

Library of Congress cataloguing in publication data
Knodel, John E.
Demographic behavior in the past: a study of 14 German village
populations in the eighteenth and nineteenth centuries / John E.
Knodel.
p.   cm. – (Cambridge studies in population, economy, and
society in past time, 6)
Bibliography: p.
Includes index.
ISBN 0 521 32715 6
1. Germany – Population – History – 18th century. 2. Germany –
Population – History – 19th century. 3. Villages – Germany
History – 18th century. 4. Villages – Germany – History – 19th
century. 5. Germany – Population, Rural – History – 18th century.
6. Germany – Population, Rural – History – 19th century. I. Title.
II. Series.
HB3595.K53 1988
304.6'0943 – dc 19 87–20601 CIP

ISBN 0 521 32715 6

0008094

301·32
KNO

wv

Contents

v

Tables

ix

Figures

Acknowledgements

The research on which this book is based grew out of my participation in the Princeton European Fertility Project. In 1967, Ansley Coale, the director of that project, encouraged me to explore the possibility of obtaining individual-level data from parish records in Germany in order to examine birth intervals in areas with radically different breastfeeding patterns. In the course of that work, I learned about the existence of the village genealogies on which this book is based. The value of these genealogies as a source of family reconstitution data through which demographic behavior in the past could be studied was immediately evident and, as what might be thought of as a pilot project, I did some analysis of the genealogy for the village of Anhausen which resulted in the publication of an article on that village in *Population Studies* in 1970.

Since that time, a number of persons and organizations have been instrumental in encouraging and supporting me in further and more extensive work in historical demography that utilizes the village genealogies as the basic source of material. E. A. Wrigley, on behalf of the Cambridge Group for the Study of Population and Social Studies, kindly agreed to host a six-month visit to Cambridge during the first half of 1974. My stay there was supported through a research fellowship from the Population Council. During that time, I explored more fully the quality of village genealogies as a source of demographic data and benefited greatly not only from the facilities of the Cambridge Group and Cambridge University but also from the stimulating interactions with Tony Wrigley and his colleagues.

At more or less the same time, Edward Shorter invited me to join him in a research project to do a more systematic analysis of German demographic history based on the village genealogies. As part of an initial project funded by a grant from the Canada Council, we collaboratively explored further the quality of both the genealogies themselves, and the parish registers upon which they were based. Working together with Edward Shorter in this effort was always a stimulating and entertaining experience. Although our work resulted in a relatively favorable evaluation of the village genealogies, Edward Shorter eventually decided that his interests were best served by pursuing other areas of inquiry and left the analysis of the village genealogies for me to pursue on my own. Nevertheless, he consistently maintained interest in my work and provided me with enthusiastic encouragement and useful comments throughout the subsequent years.

During 1976 through 1978, funding from the National Institute for Child Health and Human Development permitted coding and computerization as well as analysis of a number of the village genealogies which constitute the sample on which this book is based. The sample was supplemented by additional villages, which were coded in Toronto in connection with work under Edward Shorter, who kindly made the data available to me. A research fellowship from the Rockefeller Foundation permitted me to spend the academic year of 1979–80 back with the Cambridge Group, when again the excellent environment facilitated considerable progress on analysis of the data set, which by this time had grown to 14 villages.

While attending a seminar on historical demography being held in Norway in the fall of 1979, Eugene Hammel suggested the idea of bringing together the various articles and papers that were emerging from my research based on the German village genealogies into a single and more integrated volume. I am deeply indebted to him for his initial suggestion and subsequent encouragement along these lines. Indeed, I had originally hoped to publish the book in a series that he was editing for Academic Press, but the series was discontinued prior to the completion of the research.

The preparation of the data was aided considerably by personal correspondence, and in some cases discussions, with several German genealogists. In particular, Albert Köbele, Rudolph Manger, Frederick Sauer, and Lorenz Scheuenpflug all generously provided information and answers concerning questions about the village genealogies they had themselves compiled. In addition, Barbara Heller and Walter Schaub were very helpful in providing more general information concerning the data sources on which village genealogies are based and in helping interpret various occupational and other terms, many of which are no longer in common usage, in their historical context.

A number of chapters in the present volume draw on earlier articles which have been published elsewhere. In several cases, these articles were co-authored with colleagues. I am particularly grateful to Susan De Vos, who collaborated in research on sex differentials in mortality; Albert Hermalin, who worked with me on analyses of the influences of maternal age, birth order and sibship size on infant and child mortality; Hallie Kintner, who collaborated on research concerning the age pattern of infant and child mortality; Katherine Lynch, who collaborated on research concerning marital dissolution and remarriage; and Chris Wilson, who collaborated on research dealing with trends in the underlying level of natural fertility and its components.

Although in no case do any of the chapters simply represent re-publication of a previously published article without at least some modification, several chapters resemble earlier publications relatively closely. In particular, Chapter 7 draws heavily from an article published in the *Journal of Family History*, Chapters 10 and 14 draw heavily from articles published in *Population Studies*, and Chapters 11 and 12 draw heavily from articles published in *Demography*.

Several colleagues have either read most or all of earlier drafts of this book and have provided helpful advice and comments. Ernest Benz deserves to be singled out as having provided more detailed and useful comments on various versions of this book than I could ever have expected from anyone. His intimate familiarity with archival material for several of the villages included in the sample, as well as his own work utilizing village genealogies in connection with his dissertation, placed him in an unusually favorable position to provide insightful reactions and suggestions for improving and correcting the analyses at many different points. Others who have also provided very helpful comments include Barbara Anderson, Eugene Hammel, Katherine Lynch, and Tony Wrigley.

The many exchanges with the persons mentioned above, as well as with many other colleagues, have helped make this research endeavor a rewarding experience. I am grateful and indebted to all of them for this.

PART I

Introduction

1

Family reconstitution and the historical study of demographic behavior

European historical demography was revolutionized in the 1950s by the pioneering analyses of Louis Henry using data assembled through the technique of family reconstitution.[1] The technique involves a process through which individual records of births, deaths, and marriages (or baptisms, burials, and weddings) contained in parish registers are linked together into histories of vital events for individual families. The resultant micro-level set of linked information permits a far greater depth of analysis than is possible through earlier conventional approaches utilizing parish registers.

The earlier techniques relied primarily on simple aggregative counts of vital events. Thus the information available to the analyst was typically limited to annual or monthly time series of births, deaths, and marriages. These were used primarily to examine short-term fluctuations and their interrelationships. However, there was usually no basis to calculate demographic rates because, given the rarity and imperfections of census-like documents for much of the period covered by parish records, counts of the population at risk were generally

---

[1] Henry, *Anciennes familles génévoises*; Gautier and Henry, *Population de Normande*. For a discussion of the importance of family reconstitution to the development of historical demography, see Wrigley, *Population and history*; Flinn, *European demographic system*, Chapter 1; and Sharlin, 'Historical demography.' Probably the earliest study to make extensive use of family reconstitution data for demographic analysis was by Roller (*Einwohnerschaft der Stadt Durlach*) for the town of Durlach in southern Germany shortly after the turn of the century. Indeed, the value of family reconstitution data for demographic analysis was recognized in Germany considerably earlier than elsewhere and a number of historical demographic studies based on this technique were actually carried out. This work, however, had little impact outside of Germany at the time and has gone largely unnoticed by present-day demographers (Imhof, *Einführung*, pp. 20–29). Thus the credit for the breakthrough in the use of family reconstitution in modern historical demography belongs largely to Louis Henry and his associates.

unknown. Among other things, this seriously hampered longer-range comparisons. To put it simply, traditional aggregative counting techniques provided information on the flow of events but not the stock that gave rise to them.[2]

The strengths of family reconstitution

Since family reconstitution establishes linkages between events happening to the same individual, or to members of the same family, far more demographic information is available for an individual or family than would otherwise be the case. Since families and their members do not necessarily live out their entire lives in the same village, and hence under the jurisdiction of a particular set of parish registers, the extent to which specific families can be reconstituted varies. The more fully a particular family can be reconstituted, the greater the information that can be derived. For example, by linking a woman's birth date to her date of marriage, it is possible to know her age at marriage. If the date of her first birth is further linked to her record, not only is the age at which she first gave birth known, but also the interval between marriage and first birth, which among other things indicates whether or not she was pregnant as a bride. If her death date is also linked to her record, the total duration of her marriage can be determined as can her age at death. If her record is also linked to the birth and death dates of her husband, the gap between her age and that of her husband's is known as well as whether or not she died a widow. Moreover, if reconstituted family histories of vital events are then linked to other nominal records about the family or its members, such as wills or tax lists, a great deal about their socio-economic situation can be learned and related to their demographic behavior.[3]

Equally significantly, since family reconstitution does not depend on counting events but on the linkages between them, it circumvents the problem of missing information on the population at risk that severely hampers the earlier aggregative counting approach. The ability to calculate appropriate rates from family reconstitution data requires an understanding of the crucial concept of 'presence in observation.' If this concept is properly applied, it is possible to derive the equivalent of the stock and flow type of information needed for the calculation of

---

[2] Wrigley, 'Source material.'

[3] Correct record linkage is essential for the validity of family reconstitution. The methodology for achieving this is an important concern within the field of historical demography. For a useful discussion of these isues, see Wrigley, *Identifying people*, especially the introductory chapter.

demographic rates, which today is provided by a combination of census and vital statistics, with the former yielding the number at risk and the latter the number of events. Family reconstitution can provide information both on the number of events and the number of years of exposure to risk, which for the purpose of demographic measurement can serve as the population at risk. For example, by abstracting, from the individual family histories of linked events, the total number of years a married woman lived and the number of births she experienced during particular age intervals within the reproductive age span, and summing the results, age-specific marital fertility rates can be calculated comparable to those produced from combining census and vital registration information.[4]

Henry's contribution was not only to demonstrate the potential analytical value of reconstitution data but also to formulate an appropriate set of rules for guiding the analysis, based on the concept of presence in observation.[5] These rules define for each individual within a reconstituted family the period of time that he or she can properly be regarded as at risk of experiencing a particular type of event. They explicitly take into account the fact that families differ in the extent to which their vital histories can be reconstituted. Henry framed these rules such that a variety of potential biases, some straightforward, some subtle, could be avoided or minimized.[6]

As an example, consider a case in which the date of marriage and the dates of death of both spouses are known, and there are no indications of births having occurred outside the parish (such as the death of a child whose birth is not included in the registers). For the purpose of calculating marital fertility rates, the family can be considered to enter observation at the time of marriage and to exit at the time the first of the two spouses dies. All intervening births between marriage and when the couple passes out of observation can be considered present in observation. The number of years between marriage and when the wife reaches the end of the reproductive age span, or when the marriage ends by death if that occurs earlier, can be considered as the number of years of exposure.

For contrast, consider a couple for whom the death date but not the marriage date is known and to whom a number of births in the parish register have been linked. This couple cannot be included in the calculation of an unbiased set of marital fertility rates because it would

---

[4] Wrigley, 'Source material.'
[5] See, for example, Fleury and Henry, *Nouveau manuel*; and Henry, *Manuel de démographie historique.*
[6] Wrigley, 'Population history in the 1980s.'

not be possible to know when the couple entered into observation for the purpose of fertility measurement. To take the date of the first recorded birth to the couple as a delimiter of the period of observation would risk disproportionately including fertile couples in the measurement of fertility and distorting the results, since childless couples with a missing marriage date would always be excluded.

These examples illustrate the general principle that presence in observation must be determined by events independent of the particular phenomenon being measured. Since marriage is independent of giving birth, it can be used to determine entrance into observation for the measurement of marital fertility. However, since bearing a child is not independent of fertility, it cannot be used.

The determination of the period for which someone is to be considered present in observation is not always straightforward. Even for the examples just cited, some qualifications need to be added. Thus, in the first case, if the first spouse to die is the husband, and the wife is still within the reproductive age span, an additional nine months needs to be added to the period of exposure to allow for the gestation period of a birth conceived just prior to the husband's death. In addition, if a prenuptial pregnancy prompts the marriage, the marriage is not strictly independent of the impending birth and, for certain purposes, an adjustment should be made.

In brief, the introduction of family reconstitution as a technique to assemble data has vastly expanded the horizons of historical demography. Provided appropriate care is taken when analyzing family reconstitution data, a far wider range of demographic behavior can be explored than was previously possible. While important new techniques are being developed in the continually evolving field of historical demography, including ones which make far more powerful use of aggregative counts than the earlier conventional approach,[7] family reconstitution remains central to research into the demographic behavior of the past.

The study of demographic transition

Historical population research has also received an important impetus from increased interest in recent decades in the study of the demographic transition, defined as the shift from past high levels of fertility and mortality to modern low levels. Interest in this phenomenon stems not only from its fundamental importance for so many aspects of

---

[7] See especially, Lee, R., 'Introduction'; and Wrigley and Schofield, *Population history of England.*

human life but also from a sense of urgency arising from concern over recent unprecedented levels of world population increase and the particularly rapid growth rates in less developed countries. A common hope is that, by better understanding the demographic behavior of past generations, we will increase our ability to deal with the demographic behavior of the present and future generations.

Most studies of the demographic transition as it occurred historically in Europe and the rest of the developed world, and especially studies concerned with the transformation of reproductive behavior, have been based on data derived from published census and vital statistics reports. The study of the secular decline in European fertility from the nineteenth century to World War II, sponsored by the Office of Population Research at Princeton University, is a prime example of this type of historical population research.[8] Published census and vital statistics have the important advantage of covering large populations and wide geographical areas. Nevertheless, they have two major disadvantages in comparison to family reconstitution data derived from parish registers. First, for many European countries, reliable censuses and vital registration systems providing comprehensive information date only from the latter half of the nineteenth century. They are therefore unsuited for depicting the onset and early stages of demographic transition and the prior situation from which it emerged, both of which are critical for a fuller understanding of the transition process.

Second, while census and vital statistics were ultimately derived from individual entries in the vital registers or census enumerators' books, the data reported in the published sources are already aggregated from the individual records on which they are based. Hence the published data do not provide information for individuals as such but rather for population aggregates, typically administratively defined geopolitical units such as districts, provinces, and nations. The researcher, therefore, is unable to deal with individuals as the units of analysis when relying on such data. This severely limits the extent and nature of analyses that can be undertaken. The flexibility to aggregate individual data in ways the researcher judges to be most suitable for addressing the issues at stake is lost. Moreover, only macro-level relationships between population aggregates can be explored. This risks the well-known 'ecological fallacy' inasmuch as macro-level relationships do not necessarily mirror the micro-level relationships that exist among individuals.[9]

[8] See, for example, Coale and Watkins, *Decline of fertility.*
[9] See Robinson, 'Ecological correlations.'

In contrast to published data from census and vital statistics reports, family reconstitution data refer to individuals and, as a result of the record linkage process involved, to families. Each linked record for a family or family member potentially contains extensive information of demographic relevance, hence permitting extensive investigation of relationships at the micro-level. Moreover, the period covered by parish registers, from which family reconstitution data are usually drawn, often includes the eighteenth, and in some cases the seventeenth or even parts of the sixteenth centuries.

Despite their potential for illuminating the process of demographic transition, however, most historical micro-level studies of demographic behavior involving family reconstitution data have been restricted to the period prior to the onset of the secular decline of fertility. As a result, they have had limited implications for our understanding of this critical stage of the demographic transition.[10] There are exceptions, although in some cases the studies are limited to elite groups whose fertility behavior changed in advance of the general populace or to unusual religious groups whose experience may not be typical.[11] Moreover, because of the tedious nature and enormous amount of work involved in family reconstitution, many studies have been limited to a single and often small-sized village or parish, severely restricting the ability to generalize the results. Thus our knowledge of the transformation of reproductive behavior during the demographic transition has been largely limited to those aspects which can be appropriately addressed by macro-level analysis.

The scope and organization of the study

The present study explores demographic behavior based on family reconstitution data for a sample of 14 German villages spanning a period from the eighteenth to the early twentieth century. It incorporates the type of micro-level analysis possible with family reconstitution data for a period leading to and encompassing the early stages of the demographic transition, including the initial onset of fertility decline.

[10] For an extensive review of results from a large number of family reconstitution studies, see Flinn, *European demographic system*. One factor contributing to the lack of micro-level studies covering the period of the fertility transition has been the legal restrictions in many countries on access to registers containing individual-level records for the more recent period. These restrictions are motivated by a desire to protect the privacy of living individuals or immediate descendants.

[11] For example, Henry, *Anciennes familles génévoises*; and Lévy and Henry, 'Ducs et pairs.' See, however, Andorka, 'Family reconstitution and household structures'; Imhof, 'Auswertung der Kirchenbücher', Skolnick *et al.*, 'Mormon demographic history I'; and Mineau, Bean and Skolnick, 'Mormon demographic history II.'

The analysis can thus explore aspects of demographic behavior which have had to be largely ignored by previous macro-level studies of the demographic transition and have generally not been treated in micro-level studies because of the earlier termination of the period to which they referred.

While the scope of this study is not limited to issues directly connected to the demographic transition, much of the analysis is oriented toward exploring questions which relate to behavioral changes associated with it. Moreover, since the ultimate source of the data for this study is parish records, results relating to the transition can be placed in a longer historical perspective than has generally been possible from studies based only on published vital statistics and census results.

The approach followed in this study is almost exclusively demographic. Attempts to link demographic behavior and changing demographic patterns to their social, cultural, and political context are made only sparingly. When explanations are offered, they are usually posited in terms of a relatively self-contained demographic framework. This restricted focus on demographic analysis is well suited to exploit the strengths of family reconstitution data, which are themselves largely limited to demographic events. As described in Chapter 2, the reconstituted family histories on which this study is based have generally not been linked to records outside the parish registers, although these records potentially could provide additional socio-economic information about the families. Nevertheless, as the results show, a great deal of informative analysis can take place within the demographic paradigm and raise many interesting questions for the study of social history. The results should serve as a useful starting point for more broadly based research into the causes and consequences of demographic behavior in the past.

The chapters in this book are organized into six major sections: an introductory section, four substantive sections corresponding to the main topics of the study, and a concluding section. The following chapter, which concludes the introductory section, describes the nature of village genealogies – the primary source of data used – and presents selected information on the 14 villages which constitute the sample on which this study is based.

Substantive analysis begins with the second section, comprising three chapters dealing with mortality, one of the two major demographic processes involved in the demographic transition. The first, Chapter 3, deals with levels and trends of infant and child mortality as well as differential mortality risks associated with the socio-economic position of the parent and the age and sex of the child. In addition, the seasonal pattern of infant deaths is examined. Chapter 4 focuses on the influence of maternal age, birth order, sibship size, and the birth interval on infant and child mortality risks, a topic for which the family reconstitution data used in this study are particularly well suited. The results help shed light on the extent to which child neglect might have served as a means to regulate family size during times when fertility control was minimal. Chapter 5 concludes the section by dealing with maternal mortality, one of the areas of interface between mortality and reproduction.

The third part of the book deals with family formation as broadly defined. It considers both nuptiality, an aspect of demographic behavior that has an extremely important bearing on fertility through determining the period during which a couple's marital reproduction can occur, and non-marital childbearing and its links to marriage. Chapter 6 under this section describes age at marriage, age differences between spouses, and the seasonal pattern of marriage. This is followed by Chapter 7, which treats marital dissolution and remarriage. The next two chapters treat the phenomena of non-marital childbearing and bridal pregnancy, both of which also have an important bearing on the family formation process. More specifically, Chapter 8 deals with trends and levels of illegitimacy, patterns of legitimization through the subsequent marriage of the parents, and the phenomenon of repetitive illegitimacy. Chapter 9 focuses on the phenomena of bridal pregnancy and births born prior to a couple's marriage. Consideration is given to the links between births born or conceived prior to marriage and women's subsequent reproductive careers. The data are also examined for what they imply about the circumstances of non-marital sexual activity. This section sets the stage for an examination of reproductive activity within marriage.

The fourth part of the book consists of three chapters organized around the topic of marital reproduction, the primary component of the fertility side of the demographic transition. Its major focus is on the behavioral changes involved in the shift from a situation in which couples apparently did little to deliberately limit their fertility to one characterized by the substantial practice of family limitation. Chapter 10 deals with the concept of natural fertility and documents the apparent increase in the underlying natural fertility level that took place during the period under observation, including an analysis of the major components of this phenomenon. Chapter 11 examines the onset of family limitation, the major behavioral change associated with the fertility transition. Chapter 12 concludes this section by examining the relative importance, during the early stage of the fertility transition, of changes in the starting ages of childbearing, the spacing pattern between births, and attempts to stop childbearing prior to the end of the reproductive age span.

The last analytical part of the book consists of two chapters dealing with interrelationships among different types of demographic behavior during the period under observation, with particular attention to issues relevant to our understanding of the demographic transition. Chapter 13 focuses on nuptiality and fertility interrelationships, considering both family size and marital fertility rates as measures of reproduction. Chapter 14 deals with the influence of child mortality on reproductive behavior and thus examines the relationship between the fertility and mortality components of the demographic transition. Both the impact of infant and child mortality on birth intervals and the emergence of behavior indicative of child replacement efforts are explored in some detail.

The final section consists of a single concluding chapter which reviews the major findings in a manner that underscores the distinctive value of micro-level analyses based on family reconstitution data for historical population studies, and in particular for furthering our understanding of the demographic transition. It thus brings us back to the general introductory points made in this chapter about the importance of family reconstitution studies for furthering our understanding of demographic behavior in the past.

2

The source and the sample

Although family reconstitution represents a new technique for organizing demographic data, the approach has been central to the work of genealogists for centuries. Genealogical studies are often based on the same parish records used by historical demographers, but for a number of reasons these studies are of limited value as data for historical demography. Perhaps the overriding limitation is that the genealogist usually chooses the families to be included in his study on the basis of common ancestry or descent; they thus constitute a selective sample which is not likely to be representative of the general population, or even of any clearly defined substrata.[1] Moreover, since most genealogies are based on scattered sources, they are unlikely to be a complete compilation of vital events even for the family units included.

Sources of data: village genealogies

One unusual but relatively unknown exception is the *Ortssippenbuch* (literally 'book of local kinsmen'), or village genealogy, which serves as the major source of data for this study.[2] Genealogies of this type are unique to Germany. Unlike most genealogies, in which the births,

---

[1] Hollingsworth, *Historical demography*, pp. 199–200; Knodel and Espenshade, 'Genealogical studies.'

[2] More specifically, data are drawn from 14 different village genealogies: Brezing, *Dorfsippenbuch Öschelbronn*; Hauf, *Ortssippenbuch Gabelbach*; Janssen, *Familien der Kirchengemeinde Middels* and *Familien der Kirchengemeinde Werdum*; Janssen and Manger, *Familien der Kirchengemeinde Werdum*; Köbele, *Sippenbuch der Stadt Herbolzheim, Dorfsippenbuch Kappel am Rhein, Ortssippenbuch Rust,* and *Ortssippenbuch Grafenhausen*; Sauer, *Höringhausen*; Scheuenpflug, *Ortssippenbuch Anhausen*; Verein für bäuerliche Sippenkunde und bäuerliches Wappenwesen, *Dorfsippenbuch Kreuth* and *Dorfsippenbuch Vasbeck*; and Wetekam, *Massenhausen* and *Braunsen*.

deaths, and marriages of a particular family line are traced regardless of where various branches of the family may have moved, the village genealogy encompasses the vital events of all families that ever resided in a particular village insofar as these events are recorded in the local records. They are based largely on parish records and, for more recent times, often draw on civil registers. In some cases, the genealogist–compiler also took advantage of other records, such as occasional listings of the population, to add information about individuals or families, but this was not a routine procedure.

The village genealogies generally cover whatever period the available material permits, extending back in some cases to the late sixteenth century. The data are organized in the form of family histories of individual nuclear family units in virtually the identical manner that historical demographers using family reconstitution organize data for analysis. The main advantage of village genealogies is that they spare the demographer the tedious and time-consuming initial task of the actual reconstitution. In addition, they often include sections on the local history of the village and other information which can be useful as background information for demographic analysis.

The initial series of village genealogies was a by-product of National Socialism's racial policies and ideology. Their systematic production and publication were sponsored by a party organization established for that purpose. The series was seen as serving both practical and ideological purposes. On the practical side, the village genealogies were considered an important aid for persons such as farmers and civil servants who were required by law to establish their 'Aryan' descent. Furthermore, they were seen as a way of preserving the content of parish registers in case of the loss or destruction of the originals. They were also considered to be valuable as data for the natural and social sciences, particularly genetics, sociology, and demography.

Ideologically, village genealogies were seen primarily as helping forge a feeling of national unity among the German people and fostering the key concepts of a blood and folk community (*Blut- und Volksgemeinschaft*). By demonstrating the common heritage linking Germans of all classes and walks of life to their peasant and rural origins, they were intended to form a bridge between urban and rural, employer and employee, rich and poor, and thereby undermine social and class conflict.[3]

Plans were made to compile approximately 30,000 *Ortssippenbücher* over a period of several decades but work was interrupted by the

---

[3] Kopf, 'Von Wesen und Ziel.'

outbreak of war.[4] In the initial series, only 30 volumes in all had been issued when publication was suspended in 1940.[5]

After the war, interest in compiling village genealogies continued among a number of genealogists, some of whom had been part of the original but by then defunct operation. Several private genealogical organizations began sponsoring a new series. The rationale given for compiling them differed from that put forth during the National Socialist period; they were portrayed instead as a type of basic genealogical research and as a contribution to local historical studies.[6] Their value as a means of preserving parish registers was still emphasized. Their practical value as an aid to genealogists and others interested in 'family research' was stressed much as it was during the 1930s, but without emphasizing its use in proving 'Aryan' descent. Their value for other fields – sociology, genetics, and demography – was reasserted, but most emphasis was given to their contribution to local history. Descriptive sections on the history of the village, which were not characteristic of the initial series, were commonly incorporated into volumes published in the post-war era.

It is notable that both in the pre-war and post-war periods, manuals on how to compile village genealogies stressed the need for accuracy, care, and completeness, and suggested strict systems of checks.[7] The standards of work proposed are quite impressive. Indeed, one of the reasons given for compiling village genealogies in the first place, both now and then, is the higher degree of accuracy that their adherents believe is possible through a complete and systematic processing of registers in a given parish, in contrast to research on individual family lines.

The basic family unit used to organize the vital events covered in the village genealogy is the couple and their children, if any. Non-marital unions are also included if any births resulted. The families are normally ordered alphabetically by surname without consideration of kindred affinity. Within the same name, the families are chronologically ordered according to the couple's marriage date. The families are consecutively numbered, so that each unit has a unique identification number which can be referred to when indicating links between units. The following information, when possible, is given for each family:

(a) Date and place of marriage.

[4] Rechenbach, 'Aufgaben und Ziele.'
[5] Schaub, 'Dorfsippenbücher–Ortssippenbücher.'
[6] Compare with Hofmann *et al.*, *Von der Kirchenbuchverkartung*, pp. 4–5.
[7] Demleitner and Roth, *Volksgenealogie*; Hofmann *et al.*, *Von der Kirchenbuchverkartung*. See also Wülker, 'Dorfsippenbücher.'

(b) Husband's name, parental family number, number of his previous and subsequent marital and non-marital unions, occupation, place and date of birth and death. If the husband comes from a family not included in the book or had marriages or non-marital unions which are not covered, then the available relevant information is included with the current family history.

(c) The same information for the wife. Rarely is an occupation mentioned for the wife, however.

(d) Each child's name, place and date of birth (or baptism), non-marital unions, date and place of marriage, name of spouse, occupation, place and date of death (or burial). If the child's own marital or non-marital union is included in the book, then only the child's first name and new family number are given under the parents. Occasionally other relevant information is included, such as the fact that the couple moved away, the last known residence of a child where its death is not recorded in the village, or uncertainties in the reconstitution of the particular family.

For many families, some items are missing, and for some events only an estimated year of occurrence rather than the exact date is known. Yet for most families enough data are available to be useful for demographic analysis. Examples of several consecutive family history units from one of the village genealogies included in the present study are presented in Figure 2.1. The organization of data is typical of that included in village genealogies in general. Conventional genealogical symbols are used.

The data contain information relevant to the study of a wide array of demographic behavior. Variables such as birth intervals, family size, age at marriage, infant and child mortality, and marital fertility schedules can readily be calculated from such data. In addition, as a result of a variety of recently developed indirect methodologies as well as techniques especially designed to take advantage of family reconstitution data, a great deal of less obvious information can be extracted. Since the data are at the micro-level, all the variables can be related to each other.

As with virtually all family reconstitution data sets for village populations based on local parish records, the one major aspect of demographic behavior for which the village genealogies are particularly ill-suited is migration. Although scattered references to migratory moves are found in them, no systematic investigation of migration is possible. The absence of information, such as birth or death dates for individuals, makes it clear that substantial migration occurred, but generally it is unknown just when a family as a whole or its individual

16 Introduction

Figure 2.1. Four family units from a village genealogy

251 ○○ 22.1.1759: *Bartholomäus Brugger* (später Brucker) ⟨S.d. Michael B., Bürger in Hausen vor Wald, Kr. Donaueschingen, u.e. Elisabetha geb. Fischer⟩, Zimmerman, +Grafenhausen 15.8.1818. u. *Salomea Duffner* ⟨aus 525⟩, *20.9.1731, +4.6.1809.
11 Kdr: Johann Nikolaus 6.12.1759, +18.4.1836. −Anna Maria (Zw) 5.4.1761, +15.4.1761. −Katharina (Zw) 5.4.1761, +16.4.1761. −Franz Anton 24.6.1762, +6.3.1779. −Alexander ⟨252⟩. −Katharina ⟨253, 1482⟩. −Maria Theresia (Zw) 4.3.1768, +12.3.1768. −Franz Joseph (Zw) 4.3.1768. −Mädchen +*5.2.1769. −Franz Joseph 5.7.1770, +8.3.1779. −Maria Helena 24.5.1773, +4.11.1773.

252 ○○ 11.5.1789: *Alexander Brucker* ⟨aus 251⟩, Zimmerman, *22.6.1764, +18.7.1824, u. *Katharina Köbele* ⟨aus 1725⟩, *11.8.1763, +15.11.1834.
6 Kdr: Landolin 22.9.1790, +23.5.1791. −Katharina 13.12.1792, +28.6.1831. −Rosa 4.3.1796. −Cäcilia ⟨3508, 1980⟩. −Maria Anna ⟨3292⟩. −Peter Alexander ⟨256, 257⟩.

253 ○−○: *Katharina Brucker* ⟨aus 251; ○○ s. 1482⟩, *26.11.1766, +21.2.1834.
1 Kd: Gertrud ⟨255⟩.

254 ○−○ *Wallburga Brucker* ⟨T.d. Joseph B., in Forchheim, Kr. Emmendingen, u.d. Barbara geb. Lösch⟩ ⟨○○ s. 2455⟩, +Grafenhausen 1.12.1840.
1 Kd: Mechtildis 29.3.1817, +17.9.1817.

Source: Albert Köbele, *Ortssippenbuch Grafenhausen* (Grafenhausen, 1971), p. 328.

Symbols:
  ○○=Marriage
  ○−○=Non-marital union resulting in an illegitimate birth
  *=Birth
  +=Death
  +*=Stillbirth

Explanation: The family identification numbers run from 251 to 254. The information listed for family 251 indicates that on 22.1.1759 a marriage took place in Grafenhausen (unless otherwise stated, the place of each event listed takes place in the local village) between Bartholomaeus Brugger (later known as Brucker) and Salomea Duffner. The groom's parents were Michael Brugger, a Buerger in Hausen vor Wald in the district of Donaueschingen, and Elisabetha Brugger, whose maiden name was Fischer. Bartholomaeus was a carpenter and died in Grafenhausen on 15.8.1818. His birth date is not given (probably because he was born in Hausen vor Wald). His wife, who stems from family 525 in the genealogy was born in Grafenhausen on 20.9.1731 and died there on 4.6.1809.

Eleven children were born to the couple. The first, Johann Nikolaus was born on 6.12.1759 and died (apparently single) on 18.4.1836. The next two children were twins who died 10 and 11 days after their birth. The fourth child was born on 24.6.1762 and died (apparently single) on 6.3.1779. The fifth child, Alexander, marries and forms the family identified as number 252, which is the immediately following family unit. Information on his birth and death is given under his marriage. The next child born, Katharina, was given the same name as an earlier sibling who died and has both a non-marital and a marital union listed in the genealogy. The non-marital union is identified as number 253 and is the next unit listed after her brother Alexander's marriage. Her marriage forms family unit number 1482 and is not shown in Figure 2.1 but can be found further on in the genealogy. Information on her birth and death are included under both her unions. Her birth is followed by another set of twins who die very early. The next child is stillborn and therefore is not named but only listed as a girl. The last two children are listed with their birth and death dates, the next to last also being given the name of an earlier sibling who had died.

The next two family units, as already indicated, are formed by children from the family unit just described. Number 252 results from the marriage of son Alexander with Katharina Koebele, who stems from family 1725. Their six children are listed. Number 253 represents the non-marital union of Alexander's sister, Katharina, which resulted in one child, Gertrud. The father of the child is apparently not known. Katharina later marries and forms family 1482. Finally, family 254 represents another non-marital union resulting in one child which dies as an infant. The mother, whose name is also Brucker, has no apparent relationship to the family Brucker described in the units 251–53 but comes from Forchheim in the district of Emmendingen. She also marries later, forming family unit 2455 listed further on in the book.

members moved in or out of the parish. Indeed, this is one of the chief reasons for having strict rules based on other indirect evidence to determine presence in observation.

Selection of families and quality of data

In any demographic study based on family reconstitution data, only a certain proportion of families (or individuals) can be appropriately included in any particular analysis. One obvious reason for this is that for some families critical information necessary for particular calculations is missing. For example, the age at marriage can be calculated only for individuals for whom both the date of birth and date of marriage are known. A less obvious reason, as discussed in Chapter 1, is that for some reconstituted families the partial information available is insufficient for specifying the period of time that particular family members can properly be regarded as present in observation with respect to the local parish recording system. This prevents accurate determination of the duration during which the individual in question can be considered at risk of a particular vital event. Without such a determination, rates cannot be accurately calculated and serious biases can distort the results.

A detailed description of the rules followed for making an initial selection of families from the village genealogies for inclusion in the present study, and the rationale for such rules, is provided in Appendix A. Since reproductive behavior is the focus for much of the study, the basic strategy followed was to include only married couples for whom the available information was sufficient to permit its use for fertility analysis. For eight of the fourteen villages included in the present study, only preselected couples married before 1900 and conforming to the initial selection rules specified in Appendix A were coded; for the other six villages, both married couples and non-married couples with illegitimate births were coded, including those married after 1900, using a more extensive scheme. In this study, however, only the subset of couples from the fully-coded villages which meet the same preselection criteria applied to the other villages are included in most analyses. Several special analyses, however, which either require additional information coded only for the fully-coded villages, or which would be seriously biased by the preselection process, are based on only the six fully-coded villages.

While the village genealogies generally cover whatever period the available records permitted, and in some cases extend from the late sixteenth century to the time of compilation, the analysis in this study is limited, with rare exceptions, to couples married during the eighteenth and nineteenth centuries.[8] Although reproductive histories of couples married from 1900 on are excluded, births occurring after 1899 to couples married before 1900 are not. Hence the time period covered by the study extends into the early part of the twentieth century with the exception of one village, Werdum, for which the genealogy is based only on records up to 1900. Most couples in Werdum who married toward the end of the nineteenth century were excluded from the analysis since their complete reproductive histories were not known.

The decision to limit the analysis to couples married during the eighteenth and nineteenth centuries follows from both practical and theoretical considerations. On the practical side, only two of the village genealogies on which the present study is based incorporate information from parish records prior to 1700 (see Table B.4 in Appendix B). Thus any analyses based on couples married before the eighteenth century would have to be based on only a few of the 14 villages and would not be comparable to later analyses based on all villages. Indeed, for many villages, only part of the eighteenth century is covered since the parish records extant at the time of the compilation of the genealogy begin sometime after the turn of the century, although in most cases before mid-century. For this reason some analyses in fact exclude couples married prior to 1750. Moreover, for analyses related to infant and child mortality, the period of time for some villages is even more circumscribed because of obvious deficiencies in local death registration during part or all of the eighteenth century. Couples married during the twentieth century are generally excluded, since information such as death dates of spouses is often lacking, and this information is essential for determining whether or not the couple is in

---

[8] When the unit of analysis is the child, such as in analyses of infant and child mortality, births occurring in the eighteenth century to couples married before 1700 are also included, provided the couple meets the usual selection criteria (and, in the case of mortality analyses, that the registration of child deaths is judged to be complete during the early eighteenth century – see Appendix B).

observation during their entire reproductive span. In addition, by stopping with couples married before 1900, we largely eliminate problems of interpretation of results based on individual reproductive histories affected by the disruptions associated with two World Wars.

On the theoretical side, the period chosen is well suited for the study of important demographic change. Whereas there is virtually no evidence that the demographic transition, either in terms of mortality or fertility, had begun before the eighteenth century, aggregate level data make clear that in most German provinces both had begun to decline by the end of the nineteenth century.[9] For many of the sample villages only the beginning of the fertility decline will be captured in our data, but, given the apparent irreversibility of the fertility transition, its inception and initial spread are the most interesting phases.[10]

In addition to the appropriateness of the techniques of analysis used, the validity of any study of demographic behavior in the past will depend heavily on the accuracy and completeness of the sources on which it is based, and thus, in this study, on the quality of data contained in the genealogies for the 14 villages which constitute the sample. This issue is discussed in detail in Appendix B.

In general, the family reconstitution done by the compilers of the German village genealogies appears to be quite reliable and the overall quality of the data appears to be high. Indeed, the data contained in the village genealogies appear in most cases to be of equal quality to those analyzed by historical demographers who do their own reconstitution. One serious problem encountered for some villages, however, is an obvious deficiency in the registration of deaths of infants and children during part of the eighteenth century and, in one case, through the first decade of the nineteenth century. Rather than attempt to adjust the different infant and child mortality data, where relevant, analyses are limited to those periods for which death registration is judged complete.

A note on the presentation of results

In connection with issues regarding the selection of cases and data quality, several points should be noted about the results presented in the tables included in subsequent chapters. First, when the focus is on the husband, wife or couple, as in most discussions of nuptiality and fertility, results typically refer to marriage cohorts, that is to couples who marry within particular periods. Most such tables are limited to

---

[9] Knodel, *Decline of fertility.*   [10] Knodel, 'Family limitation.'

couples marrying between 1700 and 1899 and results are usually shown by year of marriage, grouped into 25- or 50-year spans. If the focus is on the children, as in most analyses of infant and child mortality, results typically refer to birth cohorts of children and thus are shown by year of child's birth. Most such tables are limited to children born between 1700 and the early twentieth century. For the early periods, however, years for which registration of infant and child deaths is judged to be deficient (see Table B.4 in Appendix B) are omitted and, for the twentieth century, only births to couples married before 1900 are considered.

A second point is that the specific couples or children included in any particular analysis, and thus the number of cases on which it is based, vary depending on the specific restrictions imposed on the cases to be included. As described in Appendix A, there are two types of restrictions: those generally applied in the initial selection of cases for coding (or used to select cases from the fully-coded villages for inclusion in the study) and additional restrictions imposed on particular analyses.[11] The general restrictions can be assumed to apply to all analyses unless otherwise specified. The additional restrictions that are imposed on a particular analysis, however, vary and are therefore footnoted in each table reporting results. Code numbers are used to indicate the most common of these additional restrictions. An explanation of each code is provided in Table A.1 in Appendix A.

Third, a word of caution is in order with respect to the potential role of random fluctuation in results based on small numbers of cases. Demographic behavior is the product of both systematic and random components, that is it has both a probabilistic and a deterministic aspect. The smaller the number of cases on which any analysis is based, the greater the potential contribution of random components to the specific findings and the less likely a meaningful interpretation can be made with confidence. The total sample consists of over 11,000 couples and over 55,000 children. Nevertheless, when results are presented for individual villages or regional groupings, or for marriage or birth cohorts, or if other detailed breakdowns of the sample are presented, the number of cases involved in some specific categories can be quite small.

A variety of statistical procedures exist for determining confidence intervals of estimates based on samples. By and large, such procedures are not utilized in this study. Typically, they are based on the assump-

---

[11] A few analyses based only on the six fully-coded villages are not subject to the same general restrictions, but these are exceptional and thus will always be explicitly indicated.

tion of probabilistic sampling, a condition clearly not met by the data set being used. Attention is instead focused on overall patterns of results whose meaning should either be apparent or not, without the need to determine the statistical precision of specific figures based on an arbitrarily chosen level of statistical significance. The number of cases is also not reported in any detail for specific tables. However, when results for a particular category are based on relatively few cases (typically less than 50), they are usually noted by placing them in parentheses, and if the number of cases is very small (typically less than 20), the category is combined with an adjacent one or else completely suppressed.

Finally, when results refer to the combined sample of all villages, the totals are generally self-weighted. Since the weight of each village is proportional to the number of cases selected from it for inclusion in the particular analysis, the proportionate share of total cases attributable to the different villages is not identical over time or across analyses. Compositional shifts, therefore, can influence the combined sample results. This is particularly true during the eighteenth century since the extant parish registers begin at different times for different villages. In the case of infant and child mortality analyses, the compositional shift over the eighteenth century is even more pronounced since periods of deficient death registration are excluded on a village-specific basis. During the nineteenth century, compositional shifts are less marked, although toward the end the contribution of the village of Werdum declines sharply since, as explained above, the genealogy is based only on records up to 1900. For analyses in which compositional shifts are believed to have an important bearing on the interpretation of results, this is explicitly mentioned in the text and in some instances additional controls are introduced. Otherwise self-weighted totals are presented without specific comment.

The sample villages

The period spanned by the present study, from the early eighteenth to the early twentieth century, is one characterized by major social, economic, cultural, and political changes in Germany and elsewhere. Although extensive or systematic explorations of the links between demographic behavior and the socio-economic, cultural, or political situation are beyond the scope of this study, some background information on the sample villages and the areas in which they are located can be of value. Occasionally, this information is referred to when particularly pertinent to specific analyses. A discussion of the general characteristics, population size and growth, occupational distributions, and potential representativeness of the villages is presented here. Additional details about a variety of social, economic, and historical conditions specific to each village, gleaned primarily from the introductions in the genealogies, are provided in Appendix C.

General characteristics
The location of the 14 villages comprising the sample is indicated on a map of present-day Germany in Figure 2.2, and selected descriptive information is provided in Table 2.1. The villages are located within five different areas of Germany. The four villages in the former Grand Duchy of Baden are all close to each other and each shares a common boundary with at least one other. Two of them, Grafenhausen and Kappel, were recently administratively amalgamated. They are on the Rhine Plain close to the western edge of the Black Forest. Both Kappel and Rust are directly on the banks of the Rhine. The village of Öschelbronn is in the former Kingdom of Württemberg, near the eastern edge of the Black Forest in the present-day district of Böblingen. The two Bavarian villages of Anhausen and Gabelbach are located in the Swabian area of Bavaria within about 20 kilometers of each other and both belong to the present-day district of Augsburg, not far from the city of that name. The third Bavarian village, Kreuth, is located about 100 kilometers to the southeast in the mountainous terrain near the Austrian border in the district of Miesbach in Upper Bavaria. The four villages within the geographical boundaries of the former principality of Waldeck (now the district of Waldeck) in central Germany are all within 20 kilometers of each other. Höringhausen, however, was formerly an enclave that administratively belonged to Hesse-Darmstadt and later to the Prussian province of Hesse-Nassau, although geographically it was deep within Waldeck. The two villages in East Friesland, an area in the northwest corner of Germany that belonged at times to Prussia and at others to the former independent Kingdom and later Prussian Province of Hanover, are also relatively close to each other, being separated by less than 20 kilometers. Middels is located in the present-day district of Aurich, and Werdum in the neighboring district of Witmund.

   The four villages in Baden and the three in Bavaria are predominantly Catholic, while the other seven villages are predominantly Protestant. The Baden villages and the village in Württemberg are located in areas characterized by partible inheritance patterns, while the others are located in areas where impartible inheritance pre-

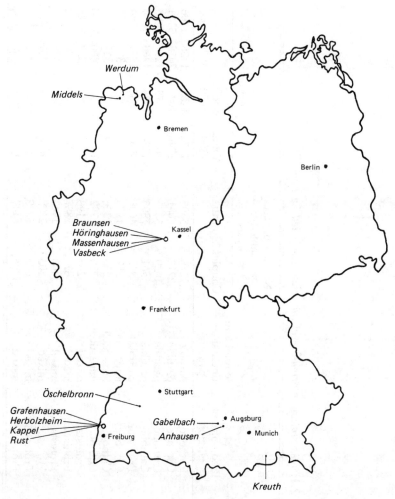

Figure 2.2. *Location of sample villages within the boundaries of present-day Germany*

dominated or where there was a mixed pattern with some tendency toward impartibility.

The number of families and children analyzed from each genealogy varies considerably for the individual villages. In order to avoid the problems associated with excessively small numbers of cases, the three Bavarian villages as well as the four Waldeck villages are each combined into single data sets in many of the analyses. Occasionally for this reason, but more commonly when interest centers around

Table 2.1. *Descriptive information of the villages selected for analysis*

Village	State or area[a]	Predominant religion	Predominant inheritance pattern[b]	Number of cases available for analysis[c]		Population size[d]			
				Couples	Births	About 1800	About 1850	1900	1933
Grafenhausen	Baden	Catholic	partible	1276	5885	1272	1462	1438	1406
Herbolzheim	Baden	Catholic	partible	2213	10,081	1746	1988	2018	3141
Kappel	Baden	Catholic	partible	1029	5335	670	1373	1297	1485
Rust	Baden	Catholic	partible	1561	7895	1394	1926	1768	1844
Öschelbronn	Württemberg	Protestant	partible	842	4606	n.a.	886	1051	954
Anhausen	Bavaria	Catholic	impartible	287	1373	n.a.	290	305	351
Gabelbach	Bavaria	Catholic	impartible	256	1326	227	264	311	362
Kreuth[e]	Bavaria	Catholic	impartible	210	792	n.a.	220[e]	400[e]	500[e]
Braunsen	Waldeck	Protestant	mixed	265	1198	239	267	233	228
Höringhausen	Waldeck	Protestant	mixed	627	2887	700[f]	762	730	892
Massenhausen	Waldeck	Protestant	mixed	460	1942	n.a.	463	413	358
Vasbeck	Waldeck	Protestant	mixed	503	2378	n.a.	429	459	465
Middels	East Friesland	Protestant	mixed	695	3229	n.a.	n.a.	n.a.	906
Werdum	East Friesland	Protestant	mixed	1498	5144	n.a.	n.a.	n.a.	698

n.a. = not available

[a] These designations, except in the case of Höringhausen, Middels, and Werdum, refer to the state as defined during the period under study rather than to current states of the Federal Republic of Germany. Höringhausen, while administratively part of Hesse-Darmstadt and later Hesse-Nassau, was geographically an enclave within the area of the principality of Waldeck. The area of East Friesland in which Middels and Werdum are located was administratively part of Hanover. In terms of present-day states, Baden and Württemberg have been merged to form the state of Baden-Württemberg, Bavaria remains a state, Waldeck is a district in the state of Hesse, and East Friesland is in Lower Saxony.

[b] In most areas, actual inheritance practices were undoubtedly complex, involving a variety of arrangements, and thus the designation here is only intended to be a rough characterization. The areas classified as mixed generally had a tendency towards impartibility.

[c] The numbers refer to couples married between 1700 and 1899 selected for inclusion and their children. The exact period covered depends on when the extant parish registers began (see Appendix B). The general criteria for selection are described in Appendix A. Most analyses included in the present study are based on more restrictive criteria, and thus on somewhat smaller numbers of cases than indicated here. The exact number depends on the particular analysis.

[d] Derived from various sources including data provided in the introductions to the village genealogies.

[e] The village genealogy refers only to the ecclesiastically defined parish of Kreuth, which is smaller than the civilly defined *Gemeinde* to which census statistics refer. In 1939, the parish included 516 persons while in 1933 the *Gemeinde's* population was 1325. Based on these figures, the population of the parish has been estimated from censuses at the dates shown.

[f] Estimated from the number of houses.

regional differences, the four villages in Baden and the two in East Friesland are combined to form single data sets.

Population size and growth
The villages range in population size from only a few hundred to close to two thousand in the mid-nineteenth century. One of the places listed (Herbolzheim) gained legal status as a town in 1810 and, since the beginning of the nineteenth century has had the largest population of the 14 places included in the sample. For convenience, Herbolzheim is referred to as a village in this study even though from 1810 onward it was officially a small town.

Information on population size is provided for several of the villages in the genealogies. Unlike estimates for the nineteenth century and later periods, which are usually based on state censuses, these earlier figures are typically derived from some special source whose accuracy or precise reference group is uncertain. Based on the ecclesiastical visitation reports (*Visitationsberichte*), the 1692 population (literally called 'souls') is given as 201 for Grafenhausen, as 450 or 480 for Herbolzheim (depending on the specific source), as 118 for Kappel, and as about 200 for Rust.[12] If these figures are accurate, they would imply very substantial population growth in all three places during the eighteenth century: more than a six-fold increase for Grafenhausen between 1692 and 1813; almost a six-fold increase for neighbouring Kappel between 1692 and 1803; over a three-and-a-half-fold increase for Herbolzheim between 1692 and 1810; and an almost seven-fold increase in Rust between 1692 and 1815.

There is considerable reason to doubt, however, that the comparison between the 1692 and early nineteenth-century figures reflects an accurate picture of actual population growth. Figures from ecclesiastical visitations in 1702 indicate that the number of 'communicants' (presumably persons receiving sacraments at Easter time) was as follows: Grafenhausen, 333; Herbolzheim, 700; Kappel, 220; and Rust, 379. All figures are substantially above the 1692 estimates. Moreover, since 'communicants' are presumably at least 14 years old, and possibly limited to those attending Easter service, the total population would be substantially larger. The 1692 figures may be accurate but unrepresentative in the sense that they may reflect a temporary situation of reduced population associated with the War of the Palatinate Succession, which was being fought during this period. Many

---

[12] Personal communication from Ernest Benz.

former residents may have temporarily sought refuge elsewhere, returning only after hostilities ceased.[13]

An examination of changes in the number of marriages taking place also suggests that the actual population increased, especially for Grafenhausen and Kappel, but more modestly than comparisons between the 1692 and early nineteenth-century figures imply. Presumably the number of marriages should increase in roughly the same proportion as does the population. The total number of locally recorded marriages in Grafenhausen increased from 75 in 1690–1709 to 173 in 1800–19, or only by 2.3 times. In Kappel, the number of local marriages increased only by 14 percent, from 132 during the first two decades of the eighteenth century (the extant parish registers date from 1700) to 151 during the first two decades of the nineteenth century. In Rust, the number of marriages increased by about 1.6 times between 1690–1709 and 1800–19, indicating substantial but not spectacular growth. In Herbolzheim, a sample check of local marriages indicates a doubling between the first two decades of the eighteenth and nineteenth centuries respectively. Thus the marriage counts suggest that the 1692 population figures may be underestimated (or, less likely, that the early nineteenth-century figures are overestimated) and that the population increase was not as large as that indicated by a comparison of the population counts in 1692 and the early nineteenth-century figures.

Further evidence that a substantial population increase occurred during the eighteenth century, in Grafenhausen and Kappel, even if not the six-fold increase indicated by the population figures, is provided by reports presented by local authorities to the representative of the lord whose jurisdiction included the villages. Grafenhausen authorities presented a petition in 1763 stating that 'the village was already so severely overcrowded that it would be impossible to tolerate more and went on to request that, in view of the many persons who intended to settle in Grafenhausen, anyone intending to marry and settle in the village be required to pay a fee to both the village and the lord.[14] Likewise, in 1782, the mayor of Kappel reported that 'as a result of the sharp increase in current inhabitants over several years, much new construction has been done.'[15]

Based on the number of communicants, the population of Gabelbach is estimated as between 160 and 180 inhabitants in 1677. This would

---

[13] Personal communication from Ernest Benz.

[14] Köbele, *Ortssippenbuch Grafenhausen*, p. 33.

[15] Köbele, *Dorfsippenbuch Kappel am Rhein*, p. 65.

imply some modest population growth between then and 1810, when a population of 227 is given. Counts of vital events provided in the village genealogy, however, indicate considerably fewer marriages and births occurring during the early decades of the nineteenth century than during the last third of the seventeenth century, casting doubt on the validity of the population estimates. Late seventeenth- or early eighteenth-century estimates of population are not available for the other villages, at least not from the information included in the village genealogies.

Figures indicating drastic previous declines in the population associated with the Thirty Years War (1618–48) are provided for several villages: a decline from 700 to 50 in Herbolzheim between 1600 and 1648; a decline from 650 to 150 in Rust between 1629 and 1642; a decline from 540 to 220 in Öschelbronn between 1621 and 1640; and a decline from 270 to 76 in Vasbeck between 1620 and 1640. The Massenhausen genealogy indicates that only a few residents survived the war. Again, the accuracy of such figures is unknown and difficult to judge, although the effect of the Thirty Years War on many of the villages was undoubtedly devastating. With the exception of East Friesland,[16] the areas where the sample villages are located were ravaged by the Thirty Years War. Specific references to the plundering, destruction, and hardship are made in all the village genealogies except those for the two East Frisian villages and for the Bavarian village of Kreuth (for which only a brief descriptive section is contained in the genealogy).

During the nineteenth century, many of the villages experienced substantial emigration to the New World as well as out-migration to elsewhere in Germany, especially to cities. Specific mention of substantial emigration, particularly in the nineteenth century, but sometimes in the eighteenth, usually to the New World but also elsewhere, is also found in the village genealogies for each of the four Baden villages, and for Öschelbronn, Höringhausen, Massenhausen, and Vasbeck. Emigration may have been substantial in the remaining sample villages as well, but it was not commented on in the (sometimes very brief) introductory sections of the genealogies. In general, many of the villages were under considerable population pressures during much of the period covered. This is spelled out quite explicitly in several of the genealogies, and out-migration, particularly emigration, as well as the intensification of agriculture, are mentioned as primarily adjustments to these pressures.

---

[16] Mayhew, *Rural settlement and farming*, pp. 120, 149.

Table 2.2. *Percent of couples married 1700–1899 for which husband's occupation is known, and the percent distribution of known occupations*

| | % with occupation known[b] | % Distribution of known occupations[a] | | | | | |
| | | Proletarians | | | Artisans, businessmen, professionals | Mixed, other | Total |
		Farmers	Cottagers	Laborers, unskilled			
Grafenhausen	99	46	0	20	28	6	100
Herbolzheim	97	23	0	27	40	10	100
Kappel	99	29	0	27	28	16	100
Rust	94	19	0	25	41	15	100
Öschelbronn	93	33	0	16	35	16	100
Anhausen	85	14	25	27	21	14	100
Gabelbach	77	9	22	24	37	8	100
Kreuth	76	28	21	7	22	22	100
Braunsen	89	20	6	26	33	14	100
Höringhausen	65	24	2	26	38	10	100
Massenhausen	62	22	12	24	25	17	100
Vasbeck	91	46	12	11	22	10	100
Middels	98	34	33	11	8	14	100
Werdum	96	24	16	34	19	7	100
All villages	92	28	6	24	30	12	100

Note: Based only on couples selected for analysis (see Appendix A). Persons with occupations in two different groups were assigned to the mixed category. The occupations scheme is described in Appendix D.
[a] As percent of couples with known occupations only; the total may not add exactly to 100 because of rounding.
[b] As percent of couples with known and unknown occupations.

Occupational distributions

Additional information on the character of the sample villages is provided in Table 2.2, which presents summary information on the occupational distribution of husbands for couples included in the present study. Also indicated is the percentage of couples for whom occupational information is available among those families preselected for analysis. The occupational classification scheme is described in detail in Appendix D. The difficulties involved in such an undertaking are substantial and the resulting distribution for any particular village should be considered only a very rough guide to its occupational structure. In addition to the fact that the groupings are rather crude and involve a fair amount of arbitrary judgment, the distribution of occupations of the husband in couples preselected for analysis for whom the occupation was stated in the genealogy is unlikely to be a random sample of the total occupational distribution within the village. Not only are men who never married not represented, but it is also likely that husbands for whom occupational data are missing, as well as husbands in the couples who did not meet the criteria necessary for inclusion in this study, are distributed differently from husbands included with known occupations (see Appendix A).

For most of the villages, at least some information on a husband's occupation was available for the large majority of preselected couples, although for several data sets information was lacking for a substantial proportion of the couples, particularly during the eighteenth century (see Appendix D). Moreover, despite the problems involved with interpreting these results, it seems reasonably safe to assume that the diversity in occupational structure evident in Table 2.2 reflects genuine diversity among the villages included in the sample. For instance, the absence of cottagers in the four villages in Baden and in Öschelbronn undoubtedly reflects the prevailing patterns of impartible inheritance in these villages.[17] A more detailed breakdown of the occupational distribution for both the eighteenth and nineteenth centuries is provided in Appendix D (Table D.3) and highlights additional differences between the villages, such as the considerable number of fishermen in Kappel and Rust, both located on the banks of the Rhine, and the substantial number of sailors in Werdum, located near the North Sea coast.

As Blum notes, from medieval times to the nineteenth century, when the majority of Europeans lived in villages and drew their livelihood from rural pursuits, the village community

regulated the collective life of their residents according to rules understood and

---

[17] *Ibid.*, pp. 125–35.

accepted by all the villagers. The extent of the collective discipline exercised by each community varied widely. The differences among them, however, were of degree and not kind. Each imposed some form of limitation upon the activities of all its residents in the presumed interest of the group as a whole, and each engaged to a greater or lesser extent in some form of collective economic activity that usually involved the management and use of land communally.[18]

The villagers under study are unlikely to be exceptions and in a broad sense share common features that derive from the general conditions and developments in rural Germany, indeed rural Europe, during the two-century period under study. During all or most of the period, the large majority of the rural population derived its livelihood from agriculture, if not directly as farmers or cottagers, then as agricultural laborers or as artisans providing services or producing wares for those in agriculture. Thus most were one way or another part of the peasantry as broadly defined and as such their fates were intimately intertwined.

By any reasonable standard of today, most villagers during the period under study lived in conditions of considerable poverty and deprivation.[19] They were also affected by the major changes in agriculture that occurred, including changes in techniques and crops, as well as the series of reforms constituting the emancipation of the peasants.[20] Such was undoubtedly the case for the sample villages, whether explicitly stated and detailed in the village genealogy introductions or not, and these factors should be considered as part of the setting in which local demographic behavior occurred.

Representativeness of the villages
No claim can be made that the 14 villages included in the present study form a representative sample of the rural population of Germany in the eighteenth and nineteenth centuries. The choice of sample villages was limited to somewhat more than the 100 villages for which genealogies were published. A study of the extent to which such villages covered the diversity of German villages in the past was relatively

---

[18] Blum, 'Village as community,' p. 157.
[19] Nevertheless, contemporary diversity is likely to have been an important aspect of village life, even if all villagers were poor relative to the situation today. One illustration that social elites were not entirely absent from the villages is provided by research currently being undertaken by Ernest Benz on the four villages in Baden. At least seven members of these villages either served as deputies to the Baden legislature or were candidates for this office (personal communication from Ernest Benz).
[20] Blum, *Old order.*

favorable in its assessment.[21] Villages for which genealogies exist are found in most regions (although with several distinct concentrations), cover a reasonably representative range in terms of population size (but exclude large towns and cities), and include a diverse range of social and economic conditions.

The villages incorporated in the present study, however, were not randomly selected from all those with village genealogies. The criteria used for selection were in part arbitrary and in part purposive, although some attempt was made to select genealogies which were of better quality and which represented a diverse group of areas. Nevertheless, as the information provided in this chapter and in Appendix C indicates, and as information on inter-village differences in child mortality, marital fertility levels, and age at marriage suggests, the sample villages represent an interesting variety of social, economic, and demographic settings in which to explore demographic behavior in the past. Moreover, since the social and economic lives of the rural population were for the most part rather locally circumscribed for much of the eighteenth and nineteenth centuries, and in many essential respects regulated and controlled by the village community,[22] the village is a particularly appropriate context in which to explore the demographic behavior of individuals.

[21] Knodel, 'Ortssippenbücher als Quelle.'
[22] Berdahl, 'Christian Garve'; Blum, 'Village as community,' and 'Internal structure.'

PART II

Mortality

3

Infant and child mortality: levels, trends and seasonality

Our exploration of demographic behavior in the sample villages begins with an examination of mortality, one of the two core elements of the demographic transition. The determination of adult mortality is difficult with family reconstitution data because of problems associated with the determination of the period at risk for persons whose history of vital events is known only incompletely. At best, the level of adult mortality can be estimated only within some plausible range.[1] Precise estimates of infant and child mortality are far more readily obtained. In this study, analysis of mortality experience is limited primarily to the risks of dying in infancy or childhood and to the special case of maternal mortality; assessment of general adult mortality itself is not attempted, although indications of overall life expectancy are derived indirectly from the infant and child mortality estimates.

Following a discussion of data quality issues and problems of measurement as they relate to estimating mortality, the current chapter presents findings on levels and trends in infant and child mortality, including an examination of neonatal and post-neonatal mortality risks. Estimates of overall life expectancy are derived from the level and age patterns of mortality under age 10. Finally, the seasonal patterns of infant mortality are examined. Chapter 4 then investigates socio-economic and demographic differences in infant mortality, including a detailed examination of the association of infant and child mortality with maternal age, birth order, sibship size, and birth intervals. Chapter 5 concludes the section on mortality by focusing on risks of death to the mother associated with childbirth.

---

[1] Wrigley, 'Mortality in pre-industrial England.'

Data quality and problems of measurement

Obtaining accurate estimates of mortality from family reconstitution data depends not only on following procedures for determining the period of risk that minimize possible biases but also on the completeness of death registration in the source on which the family reconstitution is based. As detailed in Appendix B, the inclusion of infant and child deaths in the parish registers in a number of the sample villages was deficient for at least some of the period covered by this study. With the exception of one village, these problems seem to be limited to the eighteenth century and appear largely to be related to the fact that deaths to children prior to first confirmation were treated separately from deaths to adults. Since the periods during which incomplete registration of infant and child deaths appear to be a serious problem can be reasonably clearly identified, they have been excluded from the analyses focusing on infant and child mortality.

Besides the wholesale omission of infant and child deaths in the parish registers during certain periods for some of the villages, two additional problems relating to the nature of the data involved in infant and child mortality analysis merit attention. The first problem concerns the practice, in the Bavarian villages of Anhausen and Gabelbach during the latter part of the eighteenth century, whereby the exact death date of children was not noted but simply designated by a cross following the birth entry in the parish registers and transcribed as such in the village genealogies. As discussed in Appendix B, such cases apply to children who died at ages prior to first confirmation and thus can be considered to be largely limited to the deaths of children within the first decade of life. In analyses in which the age structure of infant and child mortality is critical, periods during which child deaths are commonly indicated only by a cross following a birth date, without noting the exact death date, are excluded for the two villages in which this practice occurred. In other analyses, where the focus is not on the age structure of mortality, deaths indicated by a cross without an exact death date in these two villages have been distributed to age groups under age 10 in proportion to the age distribution of known deaths under ten during the period 1800–49 in the two villages combined.[2]

---

[2] As indicated in Appendix B, the practice of indicating a child death by a cross without an exact death date was common in Anhausen until about 1798 and in Gabelbach until about 1811. A few cases are also present later than these years but they are exceptional. Thus periods starting with 1798 in Anhausen and 1811 in Gabelbach have been included in all mortality analyses even when the focus is on the age structure of death. In such cases the few deaths designated only by a cross are distributed in the same way

The second problem deals with the treatment of stillbirths. As discussed in Appendix B (Table B.6), the level of stillbirths as recorded in the village genealogies varies considerably from village to village. It seems likely that much of the inter-village variation is due primarily to differences in the extent to which stillbirths were recorded in the parish registers and differences in the way in which stillbirths were defined. The evidence presented in Appendix B strongly suggests that some stillbirths appear as early infant deaths, and possibly vice versa, and that the extent to which this happens differs among the village genealogies. For this reason, stillbirths are included as part of infant mortality in most of the analyses.[3]

Finally, before discussing the findings of the analysis of infant and child mortality, several features about the sample of births on which the analysis is based, and the methodology used to compute the mortality risks, should be noted, as they differ to some extent from the usual procedures in most historical demographic studies based on family reconstitution data. As noted in Appendix A, this study is based largely on samples of couples and their children preselected in such a way as to maximize the proportion that will be included in fertility analyses. One result of the selection criteria applied is that illegitimate children other than those born to couples who later marry are excluded. Also, because the analyses generally include only births to couples married prior to 1900, those births that occur after 1900 will be to women who are older and have been married longer than would be typical of all mothers giving birth during the same years following 1900.[4] These births are concentrated in the years immediately following 1900, although some occur as late as in the 1920s.

In calculating the mortality risks during infancy and childhood, children within the selected families for whom a birth date but no

as they are for earlier periods, that is proportionally according to the distribution of deaths with known death dates in the villages during the period 1800–49.

The proportional distribution used to distribute deaths marked only by a cross in Anhausen and Gabelbach is as follows:

Stillbirths   .04
Under 1   .80
Ages 1–4   .11
Ages 5–9   .05

[3] Exceptions to this practice are made when comparisons with figures from other sources which explicitly exclude stillbirths are presented. It should be recognized that complete comparability cannot be ensured, given the probable lack of uniformity in the treatment of stillbirths in the parish registers and hence the genealogies. In addition, results in several analyses are shown both including and excluding stillbirths.

[4] For example, women married in 1899 who gave birth in 1910 will be older on the average than women married in 1909 who gave birth in 1910. Only births to the former, however, are included in the sample.

death date or additional information was provided were assumed to have survived to at least age 15. A few of these children are likely to have died prior to age 15 without their deaths being registered in the parish records, even during periods of complete death registration, due to migration of the family, or even of the child independently of the family, prior to the child's death. Given the way in which the families were preselected for inclusion in this study, this bias is probably minimal, especially for death risks at younger ages. Since only families for which the death rate of at least one of the married couple is known were selected, and in the vast majority of cases the death of the parent occurred within the parish, there are unlikely to be many cases in which the family left the parish within the first few years following birth. This problem could be more serious for deaths to children in the later childhood ages. The implications for the calculation of infant and child mortality are discussed in detail in Appendix E.

When an analysis focuses on mortality risks past age 1, an additional control is usually introduced which restricts calculations to couples for whom the death dates of both spouses are known and the end of the marital union occurred within the local village. This further increases the probability that the family remained 'in presence of observation' at least until the end of the union. Nevertheless, a few cases undoubtedly remain in which children who were under age 15 when the union ended left the village prior to age 15 and thus are not under observation for the full first 15 years of life.

Any such bias as might exist presumably would have little if any effect on trends, unless it changed substantially over time. Moreover, as shown in Appendix E, mortality risks as calculated in this study, based on the simplifying assumption that children with unknown death dates in the preselected families survive at least to age 15, actually yield slightly *higher* estimates of mortality risks than when more complicated standard procedures for determining the period of risk are followed. Thus in this study, given the initial selection of cases, the simplified procedure utilized may actually be preferable to the standard but more complicated procedure generally followed in the analysis of family reconstitution data. In any event, the mortality estimates by both procedures are very close and thus differences in the results they yield are of little substantive importance.

As also indicated in Appendix E, the exclusion of illegitimate births not followed by a marriage exerts a modest downward bias on the infant and child mortality rates based only on the preselected families. Mortality risks are usually higher for illegitimate than for legitimate children and the evidence suggests that German village populations in the eighteenth and nineteenth centuries were no exception. Moreover, as discussed in Chapter 8, illegitimate births that survived were more likely than those that died to be followed by the marriage of the parents, or at least to be linked to the parents' marriage in the course of family reconstitution, and thus to be included in the data for the preselected families. Hence the infant and child mortality rates calculated in this study are somewhat lower than if the analysis included all illegitimate births rather than just those followed or linked to a subsequent marital union. Historical demographic studies of infant and child mortality based on family reconstitution data often exclude illegitimate births and therefore the resulting mortality rate data are biased downward. This study deviates from the more usual practice by including premarital births to couples who eventually marry, and may compound the downward bias to a modest extent.

Trends and levels of infant and child mortality

National life tables providing detailed information on age-specific levels of mortality are available for Germany only after 1870. Several German states produced life tables for earlier years although only exceptionally for periods prior to the mid-nineteenth century. Likewise, estimates of infant mortality at the national level only start with the last third of the nineteenth century although infant mortality rates for individual German states are more numerous for earlier periods than are full life tables.

In general, the available official statistics indicate little evidence of any sustained decline in infant mortality prior to the end of the nineteenth century, and in some states not until even later.[5] Time-series data on infant mortality based on local studies of cities, towns, and villages, covering in many cases the eighteenth century and even earlier, show that the average level of infant mortality in these locations either increased or remained roughly constant until the late nineteenth century, when a decrease is first noticeable.[6]

Information on child mortality above age 1 is considerably scarcer. A steady and substantial decline is evident during the last third of the nineteenth century, when the first national life tables were compiled.[7] There is little evidence available from official statistics to determine how long this trend had been under way. Given the different implica-

---

[5] Knodel, *Decline of fertility*, Chapter 4.
[6] Kintner, 'Infant mortality,' Chapter 1; Lee, W. R., 'Germany'; Imhof, 'Unterschiedliche Säuglingssterblichkeit.'
[7] Knodel, *Decline of fertility*.

tions of different sequences in fertility and mortality decline for understanding the demographic transition, and the real possibility that infant and child mortality trends may have differed substantially, information on long-term trends prior to the period covered by official statistics takes on added importance.[8]

The probabilities of dying before age 1 ($_1q_0$), between exact ages 1 and 5 ($_4q_1$), and between exact ages 5 and 15 ($_{10}q_5$), are shown in Figure 3.1 for the period from the mid-eighteenth century to the early twentieth century for the combined sample as well as for regional groupings of villages. While the combined sample is clearly composed of a non-random selection of German villages, the results for the end of the nineteenth century correspond reasonably closely to the national levels of infant and child mortality indicated by official statistics.[9] At a more local level, both the level and trend of infant mortality indicated for the four Baden villages, during the last half of the nineteenth century, correspond closely to the official statistics at the district level.[10]

The most striking feature of the results is the indication that infant and child mortality generally follow divergent paths from the end of the eighteenth to the beginning of the twentieth century. For the sample as a whole, infant mortality is highest during the third quarter of the nineteenth century and declines only moderately by the start of the twentieth century. In contrast, the probabilities of dying between ages 1 and 5 and between ages 5 and 15 decline almost steadily from the mid-eighteenth century. The pronounced rise in infant mortality during the third quarter of the nineteenth century, evident for the sample as a whole, is absent in the Waldeck and East Frisian villages. The modest fall in infant mortality for births from 1900 onward for the combined sample is the result of a slight increase in infant mortality in the Baden villages combined with a sharp drop everywhere else.

[8] Matthiessen and McCann, 'Mortality.'

[9] For the period 1875–99, our combined sample yields the following values: $_1q_0$ (excluding stillbirths) = .226; $_4q_1$ = .095; and $_{10}q_5$ = .039. This compares to an unweighted average of the three-decade estimates at the national level for the period 1871–1900 as follows: $_1q_0$ = .226; $_4q_1$ = .117; and $_{10}q_5$ = .053.

[10] The most appropriate comparison appears to be with the district of Ettenheim. Grafenhausen, Kappel, and Rust were all located in the district of Ettenheim during the last half of the nineteenth century. Herbolzheim also belonged to Ettenheim during the mid-part of the period, but due to redistricting was part of two other districts at other times within the 50-year span. Excluding stillbirths, $_1q_0$ in the four Baden villages was .246 during the period 1850–74 and .243 during the period 1875–99. In comparison, the infant mortality rate (infant deaths per 1000 live births) in the district of Ettenheim was as follows: 248 in 1856–63, 248 in 1864–69, 244 in 1875–80, 257 in 1885–90, and 213 in 1891–95 (from *Beiträge zur Statistik der inneren Verwaltung des Grossherzogthums Baden*, 46).

The general pattern of an earlier decline in child mortality than in infant mortality holds for most of the regional groupings, with the main exception being the Bavarian villages. For these villages, however, equivalent indices are shown only from 1800 on because of the lack of exact death date information for many of the infant and child deaths prior to that time. For the East Frisian villages, the trends in infant and child mortality are more parallel than elsewhere. Given that infant mortality is higher than child mortality, even parallel declines would reflect greater proportionate reductions in the latter than in the former.

The slowness of the decline in infant mortality relative to improvements in mortality at childhood ages above 1 is not unique to Germany but appears rather to be a common feature of the demographic transition in much of Europe.[11] One possible contributory factor to the decline of child mortality, particularly at ages immediately following infancy, was the introduction of smallpox inoculation, which became compulsory in a number of German states very early in the nineteenth century.[12]

A realistic assessment of the linkages between changes in mortality and fertility associated with the demographic transition clearly needs to incorporate measures of mortality which go beyond just the first year of life. In the case of Germany, judging from the results for the combined sample of all villages, improvements in child mortality were cancelled out to some extent by rising infant mortality during parts of the eighteenth and nineteenth centuries. The result is that the probability of surviving to age 15 fluctuated within a relatively narrow range until the beginning of the twentieth century.

Trends in the probability of surviving to age 5 during the eighteenth and nineteenth centuries are shown in Table 3.1 for the individual villages along with summary information on infant and early-child mortality for the entire period combined. In most of the villages, the risk of dying before age 5 fluctuated within a relatively narrow range during much of the period under observation. With the exception of Rust, and to a lesser extent Middels, child mortality declined between the third and fourth quarters of the nineteenth century and, where sufficient data are available, can be seen to continue to decline during the early twentieth century. The actual decline in the early part of the twentieth century is most likely greater than indicated by this study because, as mentioned above, only births to couples married before 1900 are included in the analysis, and the mortality of children born to

[11] Wrigley, *Population and history*; Matthiessen and McCann, 'Mortality.'
[12] Lee, W. R., 'Germany,' and 'Mortality change.'

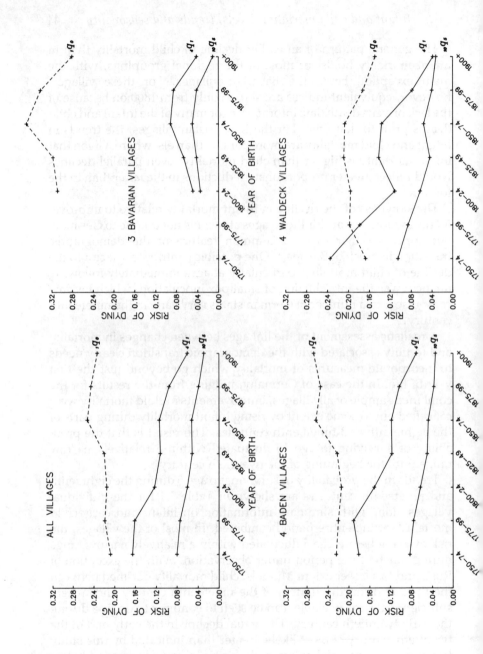

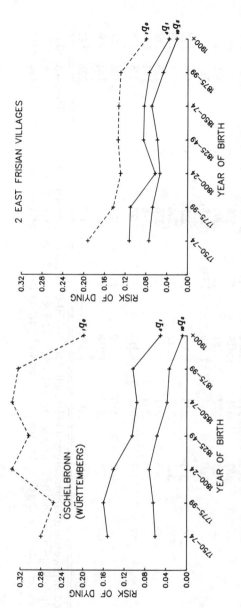

Figure 3.1. *Trends in infant and child mortality*. The calculations of $_1q_0$ include stillbirths. Results are subject to restrictions 2, 3, 6 and 7 (see Table A.1)

Table 3.1. *The probability of dying before age 5 ($_5q_0$) by year of birth and village of residence, and the probabilities of dying before age 1 ($_1q_0$) and between ages 1 and 5 ($_4q_1$), by village*

	$_5q_0$ by year of birth							All years of birth	
	1700–49	1750–99	1800–24	1825–49	1850–74	1875–99	1900+	$_1q_0$	$_4q_1$
Grafenhausen	.414	.365	.350	.325	.374	.309	.310	.254	.123
Herbolzheim	.424	.358	.375	.370	.377	.333	.258	.236	.163
Kappel	—	—	.268	.265	.326	.285	.244	.204	.102
Rust	—	.388	.289	.268	.319	.371	.414	.243	.120
Öschelbronn	.403	.382	.430	.377	.399	.395	.240	.300	.129
3 Bavarian villages	—	.380	.342	.362	.426	.397	.311	.321[a]	.069[a]
Anhausen	—	.482	.371	.419	.472	.458	—	.381[a]	.083[a]
Gabelbach	—	.405	.377	.381	.458	.398	(.310)	.348[a]	.085[a]
Kreuth	—	.260	.244	(.219)	(.233)	(.235)	—	.211	.039
4 Waldeck villages	.297	.351	.285	.321	.314	.237	.181	.188	.142
Braunsen	.330	.342	.215	.315	.314	.206	—	.171	.136
Höringhausen	.315	.343	.241	.313	.288	.276	.188	.175	.142
Massenhausen	—	.354	.302	.346	.337	.178	—	.194	.147
Vasbeck	.276	.362	.351	.310	.321	.228	—	.208	.135
Middels	—	.208	.185	.160	.182	.189	.111	.122	.067
Werdum	.327	.278	.182	.238	.238	.212	—	.167	.108
All villages	.362	.342	.311	.307	.337	.317	.279	.228	.124

Note: Results based on fewer than 50 births are omitted; results based on 50–99 births are shown in parentheses. The calculations of $_1q_0$ and $_5q_0$ include stillbirths. Results are subject to restrictions 2, 3, 6, and 7 (see Table A.1).
[a] Excluding periods (in Anhausen and Gabelbach) when a cross without an exact date of death was commonly used to indicate a child death.

them after 1900 is probably higher than of all infants born during the same period. In most villages, the risk of death for young children was quite high, even at the end of the nineteenth century, and the improvement during the last half of the nineteenth century was quite modest.

Substantial differences in the levels of infant and child mortality for the various villages are also apparent. One potentially important determinant of these differences, especially in infant mortality, is the variation in the prevailing infant-feeding practices, especially with regard to the prevalence and duration of breastfeeding. For this reason, and also because of the potential influence breastfeeding can exert on fertility, evidence on regional and local variations in infant-feeding practices is reviewed in Appendix F. The evidence indicates that the three Bavarian villages are located in areas where it was not common to breastfeed at all or, where breastfeeding was practiced, for only very short durations. In areas where the other sample villages are located, breastfeeding appears to have been common but differences with respect to duration were probably substantial. Fairly prolonged breastfeeding appears to have been most common in Waldeck and East Friesland, while more moderate breastfeeding characterized the areas where the sample villages in Baden and Württemberg are located.

The evidence presented in Appendix F suggests that differences in infant-feeding practices account for much of the variation observed in infant mortality among the villages. In particular, the highest infant mortality rates are found for two of the three Bavarian villages, both located in areas where breastfeeding was known to be relatively rare, at least during the nineteenth century. The lowest infant mortality was found for Middels and Werdum, the two East Frisian villages, where breastfeeding was probably most extensive.

Support for the suggestion that infant-feeding practices played an important role in accounting for the observed differences in infant mortality levels is provided by the high negative correlation between the village infant mortality levels and the two measures, designed to reflect the extent of breastfeeding in the villages (see Table F.1), presented in Appendix F. With the village as the unit of analysis, infant mortality as indicated by $_1q_0$ in Table 3.1 correlates $-.85$ with one estimate of the extent of breastfeeding (Estimate A in Table F.1) and $-.84$ with the other (Estimate B in Table F.1).

Interestingly, the risk of dying in the first four years following infancy is relatively low in the Bavarian villages, perhaps reflecting a selection process in which only the hardier infants survived the high mortality before age 1. However, contrary to this interpretation, early-childhood mortality among the three Bavarian villages themselves is lowest in Kreuth which is also characterized by the lowest infant mortality.[13] One possible mechanism accounting for the relatively low early-childhood mortality in the Bavarian villages might be the absence of weaning diarrhea, a likely important factor leading to death during these ages elsewhere, given that many children in the Bavarian villages were either not breastfed at all or were weaned long before the end of the first year of life. In other villages, where a substantial proportion of children might have been breastfed for longer than a year, the increased risk of mortality following weaning might contribute to the early child mortality rate.

Neonatal and post-neonatal mortality

Within infancy and childhood, the risk of mortality varies substantially with age. This is already clearly evident in the results on mortality before age 1, between age 1 and age 5, and between age 5 and age 15. Furthermore, within the first year of life sharp differences in mortality risks exist according to age, with the probability of dying being far higher in the first month of life than at any other time.

Death very early in infancy is attributable not only to high vulnerability to infectious diseases but also to causes preceding or associated with birth, such as obstetrical trauma, congenital defect, and functional inadequacy. Mortality due to such factors is commonly referred to as 'endogenous,' while those associated with the postnatal environment, such as lack of hygiene, poor nutrition, infection, or accident, are referred to as 'exogenous.' Progress in reducing mortality during much of the period of secular decline has been disproportionately attributable to the control of environmental factors and thus to exogenous causes.[14]

---

[13] Given the extremely low level of breastfeeding indicated by the survey in the early 1900s reported in Appendix F for the subdistrict (*Amtsgerichtsbezirk*) in which Kreuth is located, the level of infant mortality appears to be quite low. This raises a question about the accuracy of either the infant mortality results or the appropriateness of the survey results for the subdistrict for judging the extent of breastfeeding in Kreuth. It is worth noting that in 1900–04 official statistics indicate an infant mortality level of only 220 infant deaths per 1000 live births in the district (*Amtsbezirk*, today called *Kreis*) in which Kreuth is located. This is relatively low compared to most other districts with similarly low levels of breastfeeding. For example, infant mortality during the same years, according to official statistics, was 343 and 272 for the districts of Augsburg and Zumarshausen, to which Anhausen and Gabelbach respectively belonged at the time (Groth and Hahn, 'Säuglingsverhältnisse').

[14] United Nations, *Population trends*, p. 122.

Since deaths due to endogenous causes are limited mainly to very early infancy, a distinction is frequently made between 'neonatal mortality' and 'post-neonatal mortality,' with the dividing line typically set at one month or earlier. Post-neonatal mortality is almost entirely attributable to exogenous causes, while neonatal mortality will include deaths due both to endogenous and exogenous causes. Since deaths shortly before and shortly after birth are unlikely to differ in their underlying causes, late fetal deaths and stillbirths are sometimes combined with deaths during the first month of life to constitute collectively what has been termed 'perinatal mortality.'[15] In this analysis, the term 'neonatal mortality' is used to refer to deaths occurring prior to one month of life both when stillbirths are included or excluded; in either event the treatment of stillbirths is clearly indicated. 'Post-neonatal mortality' is used to refer to deaths occurring after the first month of life but before the end of the first year of life.

The overall levels in neonatal and post-neonatal mortality, as well as the proportion of deaths occurring in the first year of life, are shown in Table 3.2 for the sample villages during the entire period under observation. For neonatal mortality, results are shown both including and excluding stillbirths. Inter-village differences in post-neonatal mortality are greater than in neonatal mortality. If stillbirths are included, neonatal mortality varies from a low of approximately 7 percent in Middels to a high of 19 percent in Anhausen, whereas post-neonatal mortality varies from a low of approximately 6 percent in Middels to a high of almost 25 percent in Gabelbach. Thus much of the inter-village variation in infant mortality is due to variation in post-neonatal mortality.

It is interesting to note that exceptionally high neonatal mortality rates are found in the three Bavarian villages (whether or not stillbirths are included). Evidence on breastfeeding patterns for the early twentieth century, reviewed in Appendix F, indicates that a very high proportion of children were either not breastfed or were weaned prior to one month old, which may account for the unusually high neonatal mortality rates. Two of the three Bavarian villages also experienced the highest post-neonatal mortality rates, again perhaps reflecting the lack of protection in these two villages compared with that provided by breastfeeding in other villages, at least for part of the post-neonatal period. The relatively low post-neonatal mortality rate in the Bavarian village of Kreuth is somewhat puzzling since, according to an infant-

---

[15] *Ibid.*

Table 3.2. *Neonatal mortality, post-neonatal mortality, and deaths in first month as percent of deaths in first year, by village*

	Neonatal mortality			Deaths in first month as % of deaths in first year	
	Including stillbirths	Excluding stillbirths	Post-neonatal mortality	Including stillbirths	Excluding stillbirths
Grafenhausen	.120	.098	.150	48	42
Herbolzheim	.098	.087	.153	41	38
Kappel	.094	.084	.122	46	43
Rust	.110	.081	.146	46	38
Öschelbronn	.161	.110	.166	54	43
Anhausen[a]	.189	.165	.234	50	46
Gabelbach[a]	.138	.132	.247	39	38
Kreuth	.136	.129	.087	64	63
Braunsen	.088	.049	.090	52	36
Höringhausen	.080	.054	.100	47	36
Massenhausen	.095	.059	.109	49	37
Vasbeck	.118	.070	.096	58	44
Middels	.067	.031	.063	53	34
Werdum	.093	.050	.075	58	41
All villages	.108	.081	.129	48	40

Note: Neonatal mortality refers to the risk of dying during the first month of life; post-neonatal mortality refers to the risk of dying between the end of the first month and the first year of life. Results are subject to restrictions 6 and 7 (see Table A.1).
[a] Excluding periods when a cross without an exact date of death was commonly used to indicate a child death.

feeding study in the early twentieth century, Kreuth was in an area where breastfeeding was as uncommon as for the areas in which the other two Bavarian villages are located.

Among the other villages in the sample, the four villages in Baden and Öschelbronn in Württemberg show fairly similar levels of post-neonatal mortality, and all five are consistently higher than the four villages in Waldeck and the two in East Friesland. This is roughly consistent with the evidence regarding infant-feeding practices reviewed in Appendix F. The four Baden villages and Öschelbronn appear to be characterized by earlier weaning, with a substantial proportion of children probably weaned prior to the end of the first year of life, while longer breastfeeding and later weaning appear to characterize the Waldeck and East Frisian villages. In this connection, it is interesting that the contrast between the four Baden villages and

Öschelbronn, on the one hand, and the Waldeck and East Frisian villages, on the other, is largely absent with respect to mortality in the early-childhood ages following infancy (see the $_4q_1$ values in Table 3.1), when presumably the protection provided by breastfeeding would no longer be a factor.

Trends in neonatal and post-neonatal mortality for the combined sample and regional groupings of villages are shown in Figure 3.2. In general, neonatal mortality shows greater stability during the period under observation than post-neonatal mortality. The rise in infant mortality during the third quarter of the nineteenth century for the sample as a whole (see Figure 3.1) appears to be entirely attributable to a sharp increase in post-neonatal mortality during that period and is largely limited to the four Baden and the three Bavarian villages. Neonatal mortality during that period remained relatively constant or even declined in several places. Given the different aggregate causes of death that characterize neonatal and post-neonatal mortality, it is perhaps not surprising that there is greater fluctuation in the latter since exogenous causes are more likely to vary over time.

Bourgeois-Pichat determined that in many populations there is an essentially linear relationship between age and the cumulative infant death rate after the first month of life, provided that age is expressed as the function $[\log(n+1)]^3$, where n is age in days since birth.[16] This relationship can then be used to separate infant deaths attributable to endogenous causes from those associated with exogenous causes. This is possible provided the assumptions are made that few, if any, endogenously caused deaths occur beyond the end of the first month and that exogenous deaths during the first month follow the same pattern as those in later months.

The level of endogenous mortality can be estimated simply by extrapolating to age 0 the straight line formed by the cumulative mortality after month 1 and accepting that value as representing endogenous mortality. By simply subtracting the estimated endogenous mortality from all mortality during the first month, exogenous mortality during the first month can be estimated. Note that neonatal mortality is attributable to both endogenous and exogenous causes, and that this technique permits the division of first-month mortality into each of these two components. The technique, labeled the 'biometric analysis of infant mortality,' is also useful for examining the age pattern of mortality during the first year of life, particularly since deviations from the postulated straight-line relationship after month 1

[16] Bourgeois-Pichat, 'Infant mortality.'

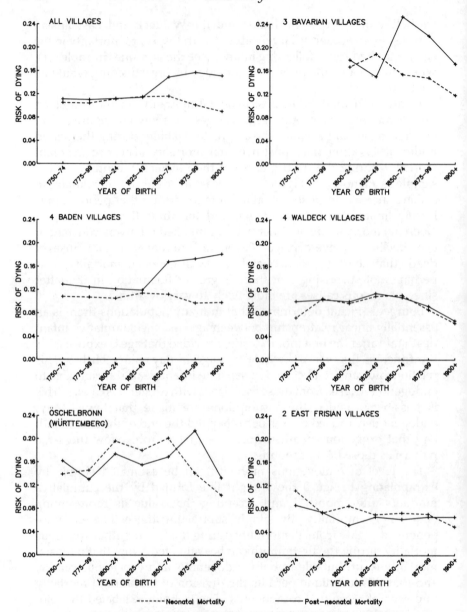

Figure 3.2. *Trends in neonatal and post-neonatal mortality.* Neonatal mortality refers to the risk of dying during the first month of life and includes stillbirths. Post-neonatal mortality refers to the risk of dying between the end of the first month of life and the end of the first year of life. Results are subject to restrictions 6 and 7 (see Table A.1)

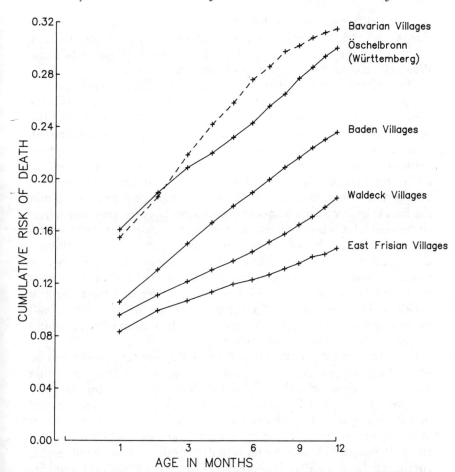

Figure 3.3. *Cumulative proportion dead by age in months within the first year of life.* The cumulative proportion dead includes stillbirths. Results are subject to restrictions 6 and 7 (see Table A.1)

are sensitive to infant-feeding patterns characterizing the population.[17]

    The cumulative proportion of deaths is plotted in Figure 3.3 by age in months within the first year of life after transforming age according to the formula incorporated in the biometric model. Despite substantial differences in the levels of mortality, in general a roughly linear pattern is found, although some deviation is evident. In particular, the

[17] Knodel and Kintner, 'Breast feeding patterns'; Pressat, *Demographic analysis*; Bourgeois-Pichat, 'Infant mortality.'

Bavarian villages show a pattern in which mortality rises more steeply during the early months of infancy and less steeply during the later months, so that the curve is slightly convex in shape, while the Waldeck villages show the opposite pattern.

The pattern characterizing the Waldeck villages represents a relatively common exception to the posited linear relationship and is generally interpreted as resulting from 'excess mortality' during the remainder of the first year of life, attributable to digestive impairments associated with weaning and artificial feeding.[18] Thus the upturn evident in the cumulative rates for the Waldeck villages in the second half of the first year of life may reflect a pattern in which a substantial proportion of infants were weaned at those ages. It is interesting that the East Frisian villages do not show a similar upturn. This may reflect somewhat later weaning in those villages, with significant concentrations occurring only after age 1 or being more evenly distributed during the first year of life. Some of the evidence on infant-feeding practices reviewed in Appendix F suggests that the East Frisian villages may have been characterized by longer breastfeeding than those in Waldeck. The differences in the age pattern of infant mortality, as well as the lower level of infant mortality in the East Frisian villages, would be consistent with such a difference.

In contrast, the very different pattern in the Bavarian villages may be attributable to the lack of breastfeeding or the very early weaning that appears to characterize them. Mortality rises steeply during the early months of life, probably because of the lack of the protection that breastfeeding would otherwise provide and the heightened dangers associated with artificial feeding. By the later months of infancy, the curve flattens out because weaker children or those in more vulnerable circumstances have already died and because the situation resembles more closely those in other places where, by the later ages of infancy, a substantial proportion of children are already weaned.

As indicated above, endogenous mortality can be estimated according to the biometric method by extrapolating back to age 0 the straight line fitting the data points represented by cumulative infant mortality and the logarithmic transformation of age past the first month (i.e. by the Y-intercept). Given the deviations from linearity which are especially evident during the last half of the first year of life in several villages, only data points for ages one through six months were used to estimate endogenous mortality. The best fit was determined by linear regression, with the implied Y-intercept taken as indicating the endo-

---

[18] Pressat, *Demographic analysis*; Bourgeois-Pichat, 'Infant mortality.'

genous mortality level. According to these calculations, the following rates of endogenous infant mortality (per 1000 births including still-births) resulted: 72 in the four Baden villages, 131 in Öschelbronn, 104 in the three Bavarian villages, 77 in the four Waldeck villages, and 69 in the two East Frisian villages.[19]

In general, we would expect endogenous mortality to be relatively uninfluenced by infant-feeding practices since its causes originate from inherent fetal weaknesses or conditions surrounding the birth. While not too much weight should be placed on the results, given the approximate nature of the biometric technique for deriving estimates of endogenous mortality, it is reassuring that rather similar estimates of the level of endogenous mortality are indicated for all but Öschel-bronn and the three Bavarian villages. Even the Bavarian villages, with their much higher infant mortality, have just slightly higher than average endogenous mortality according to this estimate. Only Öschelbronn appears to be truly deviant in the level of endogenous mortality indicated. This may in part be due to a particularly diligent recording of stillbirths (see Table 13.1), since stillbirths are included in the calculation.

Implied life expectancy

As already indicated, the estimation of adult mortality from family reconstitution data is considerably more problematic than the calcula-tion of infant and child mortality. Without information on mortality risks at all ages, it is not possible to calculate a complete life table and thus not possible to calculate directly an estimate of life expectancy at birth. One alternative is to indirectly estimate life expectancy through the application of model life tables (i.e. generalized hypothetical life tables embodying typical age patterns of mortality risks at different overall levels of mortality). All that is required is to determine which model life table embodies the mortality risks in infancy and childhood that match most closely those of the observed population. The life expectancy at birth indicated in that model life table is then taken as the life expectancy corresponding to the observed data. While the pro-

---

[19] As discussed in Appendix B, the definition of stillbirths apparently varies among the villages, with the possibility that some early-infant deaths are actually stillbirths and vice versa. Hence, the endogenous mortality rates have been estimated including stillbirths. It is possible to exclude stillbirths from the estimates and, when this is done, the following rates (per 1000 live births) result: 53 in the Baden villages, 79 in Öschelbronn, 90 in the Bavarian villages, 39 in the Waldeck villages, and 29 in the East Frisian villages. The high value for the Bavarian villages might be due to the apparent tendency to consider some stillbirths as if they were live births.

cedure is relatively simple, the validity of the results is uncertain and they can therefore be considered only as rough estimates, especially when they refer to periods or regions other than those on which the construction of the model life tables is based. Indeed, the use of model life tables within historical demography has not been without criticism.[20]

Probably the best-known and most widely used model life tables are the regional model life tables developed at Princeton University by Coale and Demeny.[21] They are based on over 300 actual life tables thought to be of reasonable accuracy. Most of these life tables refer to European populations, or populations settled by Europeans overseas, and date from the last third of the nineteenth century through to the period after World War II. Four different regional 'families' of model life tables were created. The West tables cover much of western Europe as well as overseas European settlements and other non-European populations. The East tables cover mainly central European countries and draw heavily on German life tables. The North and South tables are derived mainly from life tables from Scandinavian and southern European countries respectively. The East, North and South groups are separated out because they reveal age patterns with substantial and significant deviations from the world average, while the West pattern is in a sense a residual one thought to have the most general applicability.

The four regional model life table families differ with respect to the age structure of mortality within infancy and childhood as well as with respect to the relationship of infant and child mortality to adult mortality. Since German life tables, including a number from the late nineteenth century, were an important component of those determining the East model, we might expect the East model to fit the experience of the sample villages most closely. In actuality, the situation is more complicated both because there were substantial variations regionally within the sample in the age pattern of mortality during the first years of life (see Table 3.1) and because trends in infant and child mortality diverged during the period under observation (see Figure 3.1). The result is that the model life table family which best fits the age pattern of mortality in infancy and childhood differs both over time and across regional groupings of villages.

The values of $_1q_0$, $_4q_1$, and $_5q_5$, as observed in the entire sample over time and in several regional groupings of villages for selected periods, are compared in Figure 3.4 with the equivalent model life table values

---

[20] For example, see Schofield, 'Statistical problems.'
[21] Coale and Demeny, *Life tables* and *Life tables*, 2nd edn.

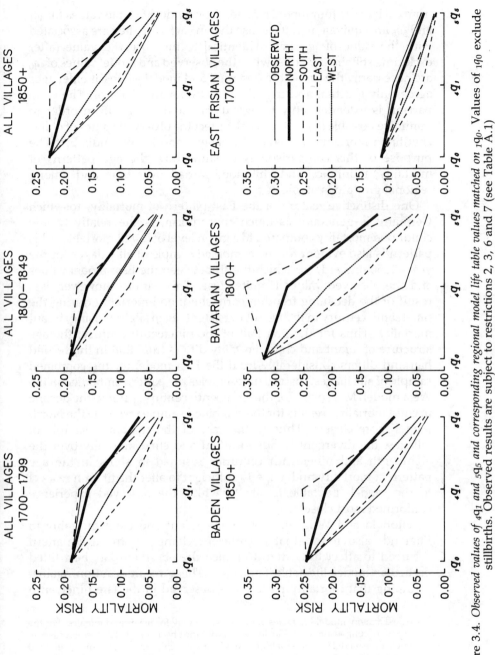

Figure 3.4. Observed values of $_4q_1$ and $_5q_5$ and corresponding regional model life table values matched on $_1q_0$. Values of $_1q_0$ exclude stillbirths. Observed results are subject to restrictions 2, 3, 6 and 7 (see Table A.1)

from each of the four model families. The model life table values for $_4q_1$ and $_5q_5$ are equivalent in the sense that in each case they are associated with the value of $_1q_0$ that is identical to the observed value (after excluding stillbirths). Thus, while the observed and model values of $_1q_0$ are necessarily the same, the observed and model values at older ages agree only if actual and model age patterns are identical. The comparison is extended only to age 10 rather than age 15 in order to minimize possible biases that might affect the observed values of older-childhood mortality, as referred to above and in Appendix E.[22] The purpose of this comparison is to show how the age patterns of mortality in infancy and childhood varied over time and among regional groupings of villages.

One distinctive feature of the East pattern of mortality, to which Germany is generally assumed to conform, is the relatively low childhood mortality compared to a given level of infant mortality. This pattern is also evident for the combined sample of all villages for the years 1850 onward, for which the fit between the East model values and the observed values is quite close. This pattern, however, is a result of the declining trend in early-childhood mortality during the nineteenth century in the face of persistent, even slightly rising, infant mortality. Thus for the first half of the nineteenth century, the age structure of infant and child mortality differs from that in the second half and differs considerably from the East model for the combined sample of all villages. Instead, it resembles the pattern embodied in the West model. Moreover, for the eighteenth century, prior to the decline in child mortality, results for the combined sample resemble the North model more closely. Thus in the case of the combined sample of villages, the divergent trends in infant and child mortality over the eighteenth and nineteenth centuries resulted in shifts in the age pattern of mortality under age 10 sufficient to alter the fit with respect to the model life table family to which the observed experience conformed most closely.

Schofield and Wrigley, in studying infant and child mortality in England, also found that a sufficient change in the age pattern occurred to affect the extent to which the observed data best fitted particular model life table families.[23] These results caution against assuming that mortality patterns as observed in the late nineteenth

[22] Coale–Demeny model life tables are given separately for males and females. For the purpose of comparing the model life tables with the observed results, it is necessary to combine the model l_x values for both sexes. This was achieved by obtaining a weighted average of the two sexes assuming a sex ratio at birth of 105 males to 100 females.

[23] Schofield and Wrigley, 'Infant and child mortality.'

century or during the twentieth century, on which the different families of model life tables have been determined, will necessarily apply to earlier periods. In the case of Germany, it appears that as far as mortality under age 10 is concerned the distinctive East pattern only emerged toward the end of the nineteenth century, and may not have applied during earlier years.

Also shown in Figure 3.4 are equivalent comparisons for several regional groupings of villages between the observed age pattern of mortality under age 10 and the model life table values corresponding to the observed mortality risk under age 1. For the four Baden villages during the period from 1850 onward, the age pattern of mortality appears to most closely fit the East model. Although the degree of conformity is fairly close, the observed drop-off in childhood mortality compared to infant mortality is actually slightly more extreme than that embodied in the corresponding East model.

A far more pronounced example of this is provided by the Bavarian villages from 1800 onward. While the East pattern comes closest of the four model life table families to that observed in the Bavarian villages, the fit is still poor. Mortality risks between exact ages 1 and 5 and between exact ages 5 and 10 as observed are much lower relative to infant mortality risks than embodied even in the East pattern. In the cases of both the Baden and the Bavarian villages, the possible transference of some stillbirths to the early-infant death category may contribute to the exaggerated East pattern but, especially in the latter case, could hardly account for all of it.

An opposite situation characterizes the East Frisian villages from 1700 onward, where childhood mortality is relatively high compared to the observed level of infant mortality. The pattern conforms most closely to the North model, with values of $_4q_1$ and $_5q_5$ being even higher relative to $_1q_0$ than implied by the North model.

Quite possibly, differences in the infant-feeding practices account for at least part of the different age patterns of infant and child mortality observed for the regional groupings of villages as well as the deviations from the model life table patterns. The Bavarian villages represent the extreme case of little or no breastfeeding and thus the minimal amount of protection from mortality risks during infancy. At the same time, there should be an absence of problems associated with weaning later in childhood in these villages. The Frisian villages probably represent the opposite situation, or at least a marked contrast in this respect, to the Bavarian villages.

For Germany as a whole, at least during the latter part of the nineteenth century, the overall East pattern to which it conforms appears to result from a combination of patterns far more extreme than the East pattern considered separately, such as in the areas of Bavaria and elsewhere, where little breastfeeding occurred, and the reverse situation in areas such as East Friesland, where breastfeeding was extensive. Thus caution must be used when choosing a model life table family to apply to particular regional groupings of villages, given the substantial differences in the age pattern of mortality that characterize them, at least as far as mortality under age 10 is concerned.

In order to estimate life expectancy at birth (e_0) from the Coale–Demeny life tables, the corresponding life table from each of the four regional families is determined by matching the observed probability of dying before age 10 (excluding stillbirths) with the model life table characterized by that probability.[24] The results are shown in Table 3.3 for the regional groupings of villages, by year of birth of children and for each of the four families of regional life tables.

As a way to determine which of the four model families best fit the observed data, the sum of the absolute deviations from the observed values of $_1q_0$, $_4q_1$, and $_5q_5$, and those embodied in the chosen model life tables, has been calculated. The model for which the sum of the absolute deviations is a minimum is judged to be the best-fitting one and the life expectancy for that particular model is italicized in the results. These results should only be considered as rough estimates, given the uncertainties about the applicability of model life tables to historical data and particularly the possibility that the model which best fits the age pattern of infant and child mortality may not necessarily be the one that best fits the age structure of mortality over a wider age range.

If it is accepted that the appropriate model for the combined sample as a whole shifts from North to West to East, a moderate but steady increase in life expectancy of about five years is indicated over the span covered by this study. If, on the other hand, we were to assume that the East model, or for that matter any of the other three models, is the most appropriate throughout the period, a more modest increase in life expectancy would be indicated. Indeed, a slight reduction in life expectancy between the first and second halves of the nineteenth century is implied by all but the West model. Regardless of the trend in life expectancy indicated, the results are fairly consistent in indicating that during most of the period under study life expectancy at birth was in the range of 35 to 40 years.

[24] Model life table values of $_{10}q_0$ were estimated for the two sexes combined as indicated in note 22. A simple arithmetical average of male and female life expectancy was used to represent the combined sex life table at any given level.

Table 3.3. *The observed probability of dying before age 10 (excluding stillbirths) and corresponding life expectancy at birth (e_0) according to Coale–Demeny regional model life tables, by year of birth and regional grouping of villages*

	Observed $_{10}q_0$	e_0 according to model			
		North	South	East	West
4 Baden villages					
pre-1800	.404	32.3	*34.0*	34.0	31.1
1800–49	.330	38.4	40.3	40.0	*40.0*
1850+	.345	37.1	39.0	*38.8*	39.6
Öschelbronn					
pre-1800	.378	34.4	*36.2*	36.1	33.1
1800–49	.384	33.8	35.6	*35.5*	32.6
1850+	.359	35.9	37.8	*37.6*	36.3
3 Bavarian villages					
1800–49	.357	36.1	38.0	*37.8*	36.8
1850+	.410	31.8	33.5	*33.5*	30.6
4 Waldeck villages					
pre-1800	.366	*35.3*	37.2	37.0	34.6
1800–49	.294	41.6	*43.6*	43.0	40.3
1850+	.259	45.0	*47.0*	46.1	43.6
2 East Frisian villages					
pre-1800	.277	*43.1*	45.1	44.5	41.8
1800–49	.190	*51.6*	54.2	52.5	50.4
1850+	.189	*51.7*	54.3	52.6	50.5
All villages					
pre-1800	.364	*35.5*	37.3	37.2	35.1
1800–49	.311	40.1	42.0	41.6	*38.7*
1850+	.323	39.0	41.0	*40.6*	39.4

Note: The corresponding regional model life table was determined by matching the observed value of $_{10}q_0$. Italicized values of e_0 are from the regional model judged to best fit the observed values of $_1q_0$, $_4q_1$, and $_5q_{10}$ determined by the minimum sum of the absolute differences between the observed and model life table values.

Substantial variation according to the regional grouping of the villages is suggested by the results. If we accept the estimate corresponding to the best-fitting model for each time period, the following results are indicated: there appears to be little improvement in life expectancy in Öschelbronn; a worsening of life expectancy in the Bavarian villages; some improvement in the Baden villages between the eighteenth and early nineteenth centuries but not *during* the nineteenth century; and a substantial improvement of almost twelve years of life expectancy in the Waldeck villages, and over eight years in the East Frisian villages. In the latter case, all the improvement occurred between the eighteenth and early nineteenth centuries and none between the first and second halves of the nineteenth century. Thus, while the results cannot be taken as precise estimates of life expectancy at birth, the contrasts between the regional groupings of villages are pronounced enough to suggest strongly that mortality conditions and improvements were substantially better in some than in others.

Seasonality of infant mortality

It has long been recognized that mortality risks are higher at some times of the year than at others. Seasonal fluctuations of mortality have frequently been a topic of research in historical demographic studies. A common approach to investigating the seasonality of mortality is simply to examine monthly fluctuations in the number of deaths. A difficulty with this approach when it is applied to mortality during the first year of life is created by the fact that the monthly number of infant deaths will be influenced by monthly variations in the number of births, thus complicating interpretation. Since a high proportion of infant deaths occur within a few weeks after birth, the extent of the influence of monthly fluctuations of births on monthly fluctuations in infant deaths can be substantial.

The most common way to cope with this problem is to assess the extent of the influence in an impressionistic manner and decide whether or not genuine monthly fluctuations in mortality still remain to be explained.[25] Some researchers simply ignore the problem,[26] while others limit their consideration to the death rate during the first month of life (neonatal mortality) and thus minimize the problem.[27] Since seasonal fluctuation in post-neonatal mortality is of at least as great an interest as that of neonatal mortality, limiting investigation only to the latter is far from a fully satisfactory situation.

In this study, a more rigorous approach is followed, taking advantage of the fact that with family reconstitution data it is possible to calculate risks of death by months of age for births grouped by calendar month of occurrence. These death risks can then be combined to estimate seasonal fluctuations in the infant mortality rate (or mortality

---

[25] Schofield and Wrigley, 'Infant and child mortality'; Lithell, 'Breastfeeding.'
[26] Imhof, 'Unterschiedliche Säuglingssterblichkeit.'
[27] Brändström and Sundin, 'Infant mortality.'

between any two exact ages in months) which are completely
independent of monthly fluctuations in the number of births. A minor
problem with this approach is that the calculated mortality risks do not
refer to precise calendar months but rather to overlapping spans
covering approximately two calendar months. For example, infants
born in April who die prior to reaching the exact age of one month
include some children who die in April itself and others who die in
May, while those April births that die between exact ages one and two
months will include some who die in May and some who die in June,
and so on.[28] Nevertheless, the ambiguity created by the overlapping
two-month span is not a very serious impediment for examining
seasonal fluctuations in infant mortality and permits us to eliminate
completely the much more serious and distorting influence of seasonal
fluctuations in births on the results. For the sake of convenience, the
overlapping two-month spans will be referred to simply as months in
the following discussion.

The monthly rates of neonatal, post-neonatal, and overall infant
mortality as calculated by the approach described above are presented
in Figure 3.5 for the total sample of villages for all periods combined.
The results indicate a general picture of higher mortality risks during
late winter, and even more so during the late-summer months, with
more moderate rates prevailing in spring and late fall. It is also clear
that the seasonal fluctuations in infant mortality are due by and large to
seasonal fluctuations in post-neonatal mortality. In contrast to the
distinct seasonal pattern of mortality during the post-neonatal months
of life, neonatal mortality shows much less marked seasonal variation,
although some rise in neonatal mortality during the summer months is
also apparent. The general pattern probably reflects different conditions operating during the year on the survival chances of infants.
Without information on cause of death, it is difficult to determine with
certainty which factors were responsible for the observed seasonal
pattern of infant mortality. Quite likely the harsh, cold weather of the
late-winter months and diseases such as dysentery resulting from
contaminated food in the hot summer months are important con-
tributors to the pattern. As indicated below, regional differences in the
seasonal pattern of infant mortality correspond roughly with differences in infant-feeding practices and thus support the suggestion

[28] For the purpose of calculating seasonal infant mortality, age at death was calculated in
days and divided by 30.43 (365.25/12) to determine age in completed months. The
probability of dying between any two exact ages in months was calculated for the first
year of life for infants born in a particular calendar month by the usual life table
techniques. This yields a matrix of mortality risks by month of age for infants grouped
according to month of birth (for a combined period of years).

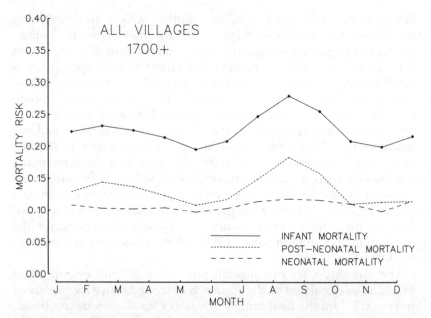

Figure 3.5. *Neonatal, post-neonatal and infant mortality risks by approximate calendar month.* Results refer to the combined sample of all villages. Calculations of neonatal and infant mortality include stillbirths. Results are subject to restrictions 6 and 7 (see Table A.1)

that food contamination was important in those areas where summer mortality peaks are observed.

Index values of neonatal, post-neonatal, and infant mortality for different periods of time are presented in Figure 3.6 for the combined sample of all villages. The index values were calculated in such a way that each monthly figure is expressed as a percent of the unweighted mean of all monthly values combined. Thus an index value of 120 would indicate that mortality during that particular month was 20 percent higher than the unweighted average of all months. Values above 100 indicate above-average mortality risks and values below 100 indicate below-average risks. The most notable feature of the results is the considerably more pronounced summer mortality peak during the last half of the nineteenth century compared to the earlier periods. Indeed, mortality was so high during the late-summer months that mortality during most of the rest of the year was below average.

It is interesting to note that the increase in the relative excess of late-summer mortality is apparent for both neonatal and post-neonatal mortality although more marked for the latter. Imhof has found a

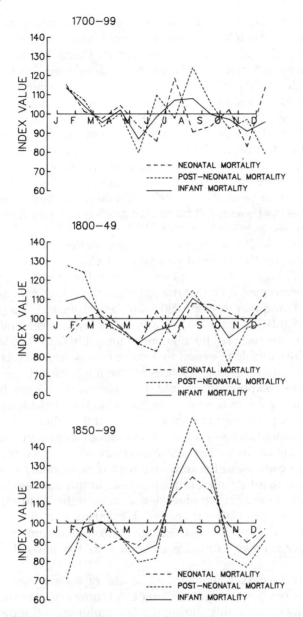

Figure 3.6. *Index of the monthly variation in neonatal, post-neonatal and infant mortality risks by year of birth.* An index value of 100 equals the unweighted average for all months combined. Calculations of infant and neonatal mortality include stillbirths. Results refer to the combined sample of all villages and are subject to restrictions 6 and 7 (see Table A.1)

similar development in the seasonal pattern of infant mortality in Berlin, with a much larger relative summer excess of mortality emerging during the late nineteenth century.[29] Precisely why the more pronounced summer peak in mortality developed during the late nineteenth century is unclear, although one possible contributing factor could be a shift toward less breastfeeding or increased supplemental feeding among breastfeeding mothers. As reviewed in Appendix F, direct evidence of a change in breastfeeding patterns during the late nineteenth century is generally not available, although there is some indication that in Berlin a rapid change was occurring, at least toward the end of the century. Indeed, data for Berlin indicate that the summer peak of mortality was far more substantial for children reported as not breastfed at the time of death than is true for those who were reported as being breastfed.[30]

Considerable differences in the seasonal pattern of infant mortality are evident for the regional groupings of villages, as can be seen in Figure 3.7. Again, the results are presented in the form of indexed values constructed such that the unweighted average over all months equals 100 and monthly mortality rates are expressed as a percent of the unweighted average. While a variety of influences undoubtedly operate on the seasonal fluctuations in mortality risks during infancy, it seems reasonable to expect that these factors will interact with the prevailing infant-feeding practices.[31] One might expect, for example, that where weaning occurs late the children would not be greatly exposed to infections from contaminated food or drink until they were well into, or past, their first year of life, and thus that excess summer mortality would be less pronounced or absent. Schofield and Wrigley interpret the relatively low *infant* mortality rates during the summer months in contrast to the relatively high *child* mortality rates during those same months, in an English parish, in this manner.[32] It is thus particularly interesting to observe that in both the Waldeck and East Frisian villages the late-summer peak in infant mortality, during the neonatal as well as the post-neonatal period, is entirely lacking and that above-average mortality is limited to the late-fall or winter months.

The seasonal pattern of infant mortality for the other regional groupings of villages is quite different. All show to some extent above-average infant mortality during the late summer, and indeed this is true for both the neonatal and post-neonatal period of infancy. As

[29] Imhof, 'Unterschiedliche Säuglingssterblichkeit.'
[30] Imhof, 'Remarriage.'   [31] Lithell, 'Breastfeeding.'
[32] Schofield and Wrigley, 'Infant and child mortality.'

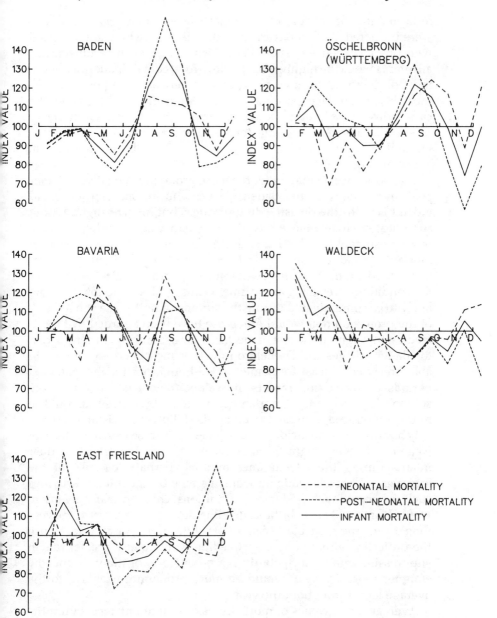

Figure 3.7. *Index values of the monthly variation in neonatal, post-neonatal and infant mortality.* An index value of 100 equals the unweighted average for all months combined. Calculations of neonatal and infant mortality include stillbirths. Results are subject to restrictions 6 and 7 (see Table A.1)

indicated in Appendix F, the evidence suggests that very few infants were breastfed at all in Bavaria and the minority who were breastfed were often weaned very shortly after birth. Under such circumstances, all infants would be highly susceptible to food contamination. Thus the most pronounced summer peak, both in neonatal and post-neonatal mortality, might be expected for the Bavarian villages. This is not the case, however. Although both post-neonatal and neonatal mortality do show an above-average rate for the late-summer months, it is not as marked as in the Baden villages or in Öschelbronn (located in Württemberg).

One possible explanation for the more pronounced relative summer peak in mortality in the Baden villages and in Öschelbronn could indeed lie with the breastfeeding practices but involve slightly more complicated circumstances. In the Bavarian villages, where infants were presumably not breastfed during any season, absolute levels of mortality could be, and in fact were, high throughout the year, undoubtedly reflecting the devastating effect of artificial feeding under the conditions prevailing at the time. While food is undoubtedly more likely to be contaminated during the summer months, the general lack of the protection that would otherwise have been afforded by breast-feeding throughout the rest of the year was also lacking. In contrast, in the Baden villages and Öschelbronn, where most children were prob-ably breastfed at least for some time although not for the extended periods characterizing infants in Waldeck and East Friesland, the seasonal impact on infant mortality as related to breastfeeding could be more pronounced, provided weaning also followed a seasonal pattern.

While there is no evidence available on the seasonal pattern of weaning, women might be more likely to cease breastfeeding their infants during the late-summer months, perhaps because of the increasing demands made on women's time by agricultural activities such as harvesting.[33] Under such conditions, children at any given age would be more likely to be breastfeeding during other times of the year than during the particularly active part of the agricultural cycle. Hence the protection afforded by breastfeeding would play a greater role in suppressing infant mortality during other times of the year and the summer mortality peak would be more pronounced relative to the average level throughout the year.

Average index values of mortality risks at different ages within the first two years of life, during the late-summer and early-fall months, the period corresponding roughly to the harvest season, are shown in

---

[33] Golde, *Catholics and Protestants.*

Table 3.4 *Average index value of mortality risks at different ages during the three two-month spans from July/August to September/October, by regional grouping of villages*

	Age in completed months			
	0	1–5	6–11	12–23
4 Baden villages	113	157	111	98
1 Württemberg village	114	151	74	91
3 Bavarian villages	112	110	58	98
4 Waldeck villages	87	98	88	99
2 East Friesland villages	98	95	70	82
All villages	108	142	96	96

Note: Mortality during the first month of life includes stillbirths. Results are subject to restrictions 6 and 7 (see Table A.1).

Table 3.4 for the regional groupings of villages. An interesting pattern appears. The sharp seasonal excess of infant mortality during these months in the Baden villages and in Öschelbronn is limited largely to children in the range of one to five months. Except for the Baden villages, mortality risks are below average during this calendar period for infants in the second half of their first year of life and, for all regional groupings, mortality risks during the second year of life are close to or below average for this period. Such a pattern could be consistent with the interpretation provided above of the possible role of a seasonal pattern of weaning, provided that most infants in the Baden villages and Öschelbronn were normally weaned at close to six months of age during much of the year but were weaned considerably earlier during the busy harvest season. Moreover, contaminated food and the resulting diarrhea may be much more likely to be fatal among young infants than older ones, thus making the results of the (postulated) loss of protection from breastfeeding for young infants during the summer months in these villages particularly devastating. Even if a seasonal pattern of weaning existed in the Waldeck or East Frisian villages, provided it affected only older infants or children over age 1, the consequences for increasing mortality during the summer months might be minimal, especially compared to mortality risks during the harsh winter months.

Naturally, without direct evidence on seasonal weaning patterns, and indeed on causes of death, such an explanation must remain speculative. The fact that there were regional differences in the seasonal variation of infant mortality, as well as in the overall level, seems reasonably clear. Confirmation of the regional differences as implied for the villages in this study is provided in part by results presented by Imhof.[34] The seasonal pattern of infant deaths (although without control for the seasonal pattern of births) for the small Baden town of Philippsburg, located further north on the Rhine Plain, is very similar to that found for the Baden villages in the present sample. Likewise, the seasonal pattern of infant deaths in the East Frisian village of Hesel closely resembles the seasonal pattern of infant mortality for the two East Frisian villages in the present sample. While factors other than differences in infant-feeding practices quite likely play a part, feeding practices are certainly one important potential source of regional variation.

Conclusions

In this chapter, substantial variations in the levels of infant and child mortality have been identified. They appear to be related to differences in the prevailing infant-feeding practices, although other factors undoubtedly also played a part. Considerable regional variation in the seasonality of infant mortality is evident and may in part also be linked to infant-feeding practices. The degree of seasonality increases over time and is quite pronounced by the last half of the nineteenth century.

For the overall sample, the child mortality rate shows a moderate and steady decline from the mid-eighteenth to the turn of the twentieth century, while trends in infant mortality show that levels were highest during the third quarter of the nineteenth century and that the secular decline leading to low modern levels starts only toward the end of the nineteenth century. Even within the first year of life, these differences in the trends in neonatal and post-neonatal mortality are evident, with the former showing considerably greater stability over time. The rise in infant mortality during the last quarter of the nineteenth century results from an increase in post-neonatal risks of death. The divergent paths followed by infant mortality and early-childhood mortality result in overall mortality risks under age 5 showing little consistency in terms of long-term trends. During most of the period under observation, the probability of dying before age 5 fluctuated around a level of 30 percent.

Life expectancy at birth can be estimated from infant and child mortality rates with the use of model life tables. However, the difference in trends between infant and child mortality creates difficulties

----

[34] Imhof, 'Unterschiedliche Säuglingssterblichkeit.'

for determining which specific model is most appropriate. Regardless of the particular model used, life expectancy at birth remained within the range of 35–40 years during most of the period under observation. In addition, a moderate but steady increase in overall life expectancy seems likely during this period.

4

Infant and child mortality: socio-economic and demographic differentials

In the previous chapter, inter-village differences in mortality were examined and found to be substantial, especially along regional lines. Differences in mortality risks by age, both within the first year of life and within the childhood ages, and shifts in these differences over time were also analyzed. This chapter continues the examination of infant and child mortality by focusing on the differential risks associated with socio-economic status and demographic characteristics. Owing to the limited amount of information contained in the village genealogies, the examination of socio-economic differentials relates only to the occupation and village leadership status of the child's father. However, a far more extensive analysis of demographic differentials is possible because of the considerable information on demographic characteristics that results from the record linkage involved in the family reconstitution process. Analyses of demographic differentials in this chapter focus on infant and child mortality risks associated with the sex of the child, maternal age, birth order, sibship size, and birth interval.

A particularly interesting consideration in the study of infant and child mortality in the past is the possibility that child neglect or abusive child-care practices served as a way of limiting family size prior to the widespread use of contraception or abortion.[1] While infanticide immediately following birth was not unknown in eighteenth- and nineteenth-century Europe, it was probably limited largely to desperate unwed mothers and was rare among married couples. However, there is some evidence emerging from studies by social historians and others suggesting that traditional practices of infant hygiene and childrearing in parts of Europe contributed substantially to high rates

[1] Scrimshaw, 'Infant mortality'; Knodel and van de Walle, 'Lessons from the past.'

of infant and child mortality and constituted what present-day as well as contemporary commentators consider as child neglect. Such practices included sending the baby out to a wet nurse, dosing the infant with gin or opiates to keep it quiet, sleeping in the same bed with the baby and thus risking 'overlaying' and consequently suffocating it, leaving the infant unattended lying in its own filth – often in stifling swaddling clothes – for hours on end, feeding the baby unwholesome 'pap' from an early age instead of breastfeeding it, and rocking the infant violently in its cradle until it was virtually knocked into a sleep of insensibility. Collectively these practices probably helped contribute to the high infant and child mortality that characterized much of Europe in the eighteenth and nineteenth centuries. Not all these practices were common everywhere and there is no direct evidence that they were practiced in the sample villages. There are scattered references to at least some of them being prevalent in various areas of Germany.[2] In this chapter, particular attention is given to the implications of demographic differentials for possible patterns of child neglect that might have served as a means for adjusting the sex composition of the family or of limiting family size when birth control practices were uncommon.

Occupational and status differentials

Based on the occupational classification scheme described in Appendix D, we can examine differentials in child mortality by occupational groups of the child's father. The probability of dying before age 5 is presented in Table 4.1 for the major occupational groups for the combined sample of all villages as well as the separate regional groupings of villages. As the results show, differentials in child mortality among broad occupational groups were rather modest and far less pronounced than differences across villages or regional groupings of villages.

In the East Frisian villages, where mortality is generally low, it is low for all major occupational groupings; in Öschelbronn and the Bavarian villages, where child mortality is generally high, it is high regardless of occupational grouping. A slight tendency is evident for children with fathers in proletarian occupations to experience above-average risks of dying, although this is neither pronounced nor consistent across village groupings or over time within groupings. There are also no clear differentials in the trend of child mortality according to the broad occupational groups, nor is there any evidence of a substantial

[2] Shorter, *Modern family*, pp. 168–204; Shorter, 'Die grosse Umwälzung'; Langer, 'Infanticide'; deMause, 'Psychospeciation.'

Table 4.1. *The probability of dying before age 5 ($_5q_0$), by occupational group, year of birth, and regional grouping of villages*

	Farmers	Proletarians	Artisans and skilled	Mixed, other, unknown	Total
4 Baden villages					
Pre 1800	.364	.411	.367	.378	.376
1800–49	.317	.332	.328	.297	.322
1850+	.320	.369	.337	.333	.337
Total	.328	.361	.339	.331	.340
Öschelbronn (Württemberg)					
Pre-1300	.385	.391	.363	.420	.389
1800–49	.357	.436	.439	.386	.402
1850+	.417	.362	.369	.358	.382
Total	.390	.393	.389	.391	.390
3 Bavarian villages					
Pre-1800	(.517)	.449	.334	.352	.381
1800–49	(.403)	.350	.371	.316	.351
1850+	.351	.424	.389	.408	.400
Total	.390	.400	.371	.355	.379

4 Waldeck villages					
Pre-1800	.306	.389	.295	.357	.337
1800–49	.311	.282	.320	.303	.304
1850+	.264	.298	.254	.263	.271
Total	.291	.310	.284	.324	.303
2 East Frisian villages					
Pre-1800	.258	.267	.335	.272	.274
1800–49	.143	.223	.198	.157	.195
1850+	.183	.189	.230	.177	.189
Total	.209	.230	.267	.208	.226
All villages					
Pre-1800	.329	.350	.350	.361	.346
1800–49	.300	.320	.332	.295	.309
1850+	.308	.331	.329	.316	.321
Total	.311	.324	.335	.326	.324

Note: Results in parentheses are based on less than 100 cases. Results are subject to restrictions 2, 3, 6 and 7 (see Table A.1).

improvement in child mortality during the second half of the nineteenth century compared to earlier years.

Given the broad definition of the occupational categories in Table 4.1, it is possible that they obscure sharper differentials existing among more homogeneous socio-economic groups in the population. It is thus instructive to examine child mortality differentials by a more detailed occupational breakdown. The probability of dying before age 5 is shown in Table 4.2 according to detailed occupational subcategories, as well as according to whether or not the child's father was a village leader (village leadership status is also described in Appendix D).

With few exceptions, occupational differentials in child mortality based on the more detailed scheme are also remarkably modest. For example, couples in which the husband fell in the relatively unambiguous category of day laborer were undoubtedly among the poorest in the village and yet their children show no consistent tendency to experience substantially higher-than-average mortality. Couples in which the husband fell in the professional category were probably among the better-off families in the village. While their children appear to have experienced considerably lower-than-average child mortality in the three Bavarian and the four Waldeck villages, this is not so in the Baden villages. Interestingly, the small group of families for which the husband was designated as a village leader of one sort or another in the genealogies did not experience mortality that was noticeably different from that of the vast majority of families, for which no leadership role was indicated.

In brief, the results suggest that socio-economic position, at least as indicated by occupation or status as a village leader, made little difference in the mortality risks experienced by children in the families. The relatively homogeneous levels of mortality across different socio-economic groupings within the villages may reflect the pervasive poverty that characterized villagers in general, even those that were relatively better off. The fact that all social strata within the village appear to have shared a more or less common risk of child loss suggests that child mortality was largely determined by exogenous forces beyond the control of individual families, at least to the extent that their behavior was bound to local regional customs such as infant-feeding practices or customs concerning child care that could influence infant and child mortality.

Table 4.2. The probability of dying before age 5 ($_5q_0$), occupational subcategory, status in village, and regional grouping of villages

	Number and regional location of villages					
	4 in Baden	1 in Württemberg	3 in Bavaria	4 in Waldeck	2 in East Friesland	All villages
Occupational subcategory						
Farmer	.382	.390	.390	.291	.209	.311
Cottager	—	—	.368	.375	.221	.283
Day laborer	.368	.345	.450	.264	.242	.328
Other unskilled	.338	.390	.363	.297	.219	.316
Sailor	—	—	—	—	.225	.225
Weaver	.301	.426	.519	—	(.323)	.373
Other home industry	.387	—	—	—	(.216)	.369
Artisan	.340	.387	.386	.289	.273	.336
Fisherman	.325	—	—	—	—	.325
Businessman	.341	.367	.364	.318	.276	.339
Professional	.353	—	(.254)	.168	—	.307
Farmer–artisan, etc.	.325	.463	—	—	.209	.329
Farmer–proletarian	.303	.318	(.324)	.243	.182	.291
Proletarian–artisan, etc.	.390	.426	.344	(.242)	.173	.334
Other	(.200)	—	(.455)	.365	—	.351
Unknown	.348	.356	.355	.326	.368	.338
All sub-categories	.340	.390	.379	.303	.226	.324
Status in village						
Village leader	.341	.398	(.362)	.321	.206	.326
Non-leader	.339	.389	.380	.302	.227	.324

Note: Calculations of ($_5q_0$) include stillbirths. Results based on fewer than 50 cases are omitted; results in parentheses are based on 50–99 cases. Results are subject to restrictions 2, 3, 6 and 7 (see Table A.1).

Sex differentials

In modern European populations including Germany, mortality risks are higher for males at every age, including infancy and childhood, than they are for females. This has not necessarily been the case in the past, and indeed there is considerable evidence that in many countries the female advantage in mortality has increased substantially during the twentieth century.[3]

Sex differentials in infant and child mortality are of particular interest because of their potential to reflect preferential treatment of one sex over the other, although interpretation of mortality results in this connection is not a straightforward matter.[4] As described above, traditional child-care practices in parts of Europe in the past probably contributed to infant and child mortality. In the absence of birth control, selective neglect could potentially serve both as an effective substitute for family limitation practices and as a way to adjust the sex composition of the family.

Even if traditional child-care practices were unrelated to such motivations about family size, provided there were strong preferences for children of one sex over the other, those of the preferred sex might receive better treatment, such as receiving more and better food or better-quality care. This could lower mortality rates for children of the preferred sex relative to those of the less favored sex. Such is apparently the case today in much of South Asia, where the main factors behind the excessive female mortality at young ages appear to be worse nutrition and generally preferential treatment of sons.[5] Favored treatment of sons is also thought to account for excess mortality among daughters in nineteenth-century Ireland.[6] There, girls under age 5 averaged just slightly lower mortality than boys (although not as low as might have been expected if no favoritism had been shown to boys), while in later childhood boys had the clear advantage.

One problem with examining sex differentials in infant and child mortality is the possible existence of differences in the completeness of birth and death registration by sex of child. This is examined in some detail in Appendix B. In brief, evidence from the sex ratio at birth suggests births of both sexes were registered with equal frequency. Evidence on the completeness of death registration is inconclusive and

[3] United Nations, *Population trends*, p. 116.   [4] Wall, 'Neglect of females.'
[5] Cassen, *India*, pp. 56–57, 114; Chen, Huq, and D'Souza, 'Sex bias'; El-Badry, 'Mortality.'
[6] Kennedy, *Irish emigration*, pp. 51–65.

neither rules out nor substantiates some minor differential under-registration of deaths for female infants and children..

Child mortality under age 5 for the sample villages is compared, in Table 4.3, for male and female children over the period under study. The overall picture suggests that, in most places at most times, girls under age 5 experienced lower mortality than males on average, with several exceptions. For example, in Grafenhausen, Herbolzheim, and the Waldeck villages, there appears to be a trend from close to equal mortality risks by sex to a female advantage by the second half of the nineteenth century. For the sample as a whole, the female advantage remains relatively constant over the period covered.

Lower mortality among young girls does not necessarily imply that female children were given preferential treatment, since there appears to be a biologically innate female advantage that is evidenced in virtually all low-mortality populations today.[7] For example, in both East and West Germany around 1970, $_5q_0$ for females was only 77–78 percent as high as for males. Thus while lower male than female mortality is highly suggestive of favored treatment of sons, lower female mortality might simply reflect no preferential treatment of either sex. In fact, if the female mortality advantage is very small, this could still indicate worse treatment for girls. The relevant question is whether the female advantage is more or less than might be expected from biological factors alone. Unfortunately, this is a difficult area for making firm judgments.[8]

In a study of mortality in modern populations, Preston finds that females have a greater mortality advantage in low-mortality populations than in high-mortality populations.[9] In a substantial number of the latter, females actually experience higher death rates than males. The relationship between sex differentials and mortality level is probably due in part to a positive association between level of mortality and the extent of preferential treatment. But there are undoubtedly other factors underlying the relationship as well. For example, the importance of relatively sex-neutral infectious diseases is greater at higher levels of mortality.[10] Thus there is reason to expect that, independent of sex-discriminatory practices, females would not experience as great a relative advantage in high-mortality situations, such as in the sample villages during the eighteenth and nineteenth centuries, as would be found in low-mortality situations, such as in Germany today. If innate biological factors alone were to be operative, however, female children should still experience at least some modest advantage. Judging from

[7] Preston, *Mortality patterns*, pp. 121–26.
[8] Wall, 'Neglect of females.'
[9] Preston, *Mortality patterns*, pp. 121–24.
[10] *Ibid.*, p. 153.

Table 4.3. *Child mortality ($_5q_0$) by sex of child and ratio of female to male mortality, by year of birth and village*

	Pre-1800	1800–49	1850+	Total
Grafenhausen				
Males	.369	.347	.352	.354
Females	.369	.327	.326	.336
Ratio	1.00	0.94	0.93	0.95
Herbolzheim				
Males	.377	.384	.357	.372
Females	.371	.359	.325	.349
Ratio	0.98	0.93	0.91	0.94
Kappel				
Males	—	.277	.307	.295
Females	—	.255	.289	.276
Ratio	—	0.92	0.94	0.94
Rust				
Males	.415	.299	.352	.342
Females	.358	.247	.361	.321
Ratio	0.86	0.83	1.02	0.94
Öschelbronn				
Males	.397	.396	.396	.396
Females	.339	.405	.365	.369
Ratio	0.85	1.02	0.92	0.93
3 Bavarian villages				
Males	.317	.397	.443	.411
Females	.230	.299	.344	.313
Ratio	0.73	0.75	0.78	0.76
4 Waldeck villages				
Males	.328	.306	.292	.308
Females	.333	.292	.243	.288
Ratio	1.01	0.95	0.83	0.93
Middels				
Males	.229	.189	.186	.196
Females	.184	.153	.160	.163
Ratio	0.80	0.81	0.86	0.83
Werdum				
Males	.301	.216	.234	.264
Females	.265	.202	.221	.238
Ratio	0.88	0.93	0.94	0.94
All villages				
Males	.348	.321	.334	.333
Females	.324	.293	.305	.306
Ratio	0.93	0.91	0.91	0.92

Note: Results are subject to restrictions 2, 3, 6 and 7 (see Table A.1).

the $_5q_0$ values, clear discriminatory behavior is not evident in the German villages. In general, girls under age 5 experienced a mortality advantage which seems to be at least close to what might reasonably be expected in the absence of any preferential treatment of children of either sex.

Even in high-mortality populations, where unequal treatment of sons and daughters is known to exist, it is often only after infancy that females experience a clear mortality disadvantage. This is apparent from relatively recent data from Ceylon, Pakistan, and Bangladesh, and historically in Ireland.[11] Apparently, the innate biological advantage plays a more important role in determining sex differentials during the first year of life than in subsequent childhood years. Boys may be particularly disadvantaged with respect to neonatal mortality, an important component of overall infant mortality.[12] Moreover, mortality differences due to discriminatory feeding might be evident only after a child is weaned, since breast milk has the same content whether being fed to a boy or a girl.

A detailed age breakdown of infant and child mortality is presented in Table 4.4. This focuses on the results for the villages collectively, and shows that the female mortality advantage under age 5 noted above appears to be the result of a more pronounced advantage under age 1 combined with a slight advantage between ages 1 and 2 and a disadvantage between ages 2 and 5. The combination of a small advantage for girls during the second year of life and a small disadvantage during the next three years results in essentially equal probabilities of dying between exact ages 1 and 5 ($_4q_1$) for both sexes. Furthermore, the risk of dying between exact ages 5 and 15 ($_{10}q_5$) is also close to equal for males and females. In infancy, girls show the greatest advantage during the first months of life and the least advantage toward the end of the first year. The decreasing advantage of girls probably reflects in part the increasing importance of the relatively sex-neutral infectious diseases. Nevertheless, the lack of any advantage after the second year of life, and indeed even a small disadvantage between ages 2 and 5, might reflect possible discriminatory child-care practices favoring sons, but if so, only to a modest extent.

Results for the separate villages or village groups are generally similar. The Bavarian villages appear the most exceptional, with a substantial female advantage persisting through age 5 but reversing between 5 and 15, during which ages male mortality appears to be unusually

[11] El-Badry, 'Mortality'; Curlin, Chen, and Hussain, *Demographic crisis*; Kennedy, *Irish emigration*, pp. 59–60.
[12] Naeye *et al.*, 'Neonatal mortality.'

Table 4.4. *Infant and early-childhood mortality by sex of child and ratio of female to male mortality, by village*

| | $_1q_0$ | $_4q_1$ | $_{10}q_5$ | Probability of dying between exact ages | | | | | | |
				0 & 1 month	1 & 3 months	3 & 6 months	6 & 9 months	9 & 12 months	1 & 2 years	2 & 5 years
Grafenhausen										
Boys	.266	.120	.057	.126	.064	.050	.035	.023	.056	.068
Girls	.240	.126	.049	.113	.050	.041	.036	.024	.058	.072
Ratio	0.90	1.05	0.86	0.90	0.79	0.82	1.04	1.03	1.04	1.07
Herbolzheim										
Boys	.252	.160	.057	.109	.053	.057	.032	.029	.075	.092
Girls	.220	.166	.061	.088	.049	.042	.033	.029	.071	.102
Ratio	0.87	1.04	1.07	0.81	0.92	0.75	1.02	1.01	0.95	1.11
Kappel										
Boys	.214	.103	.057	.103	.047	.041	.023	.019	.047	.058
Girls	.194	.102	.046	.089	.035	.032	.032	.020	.044	.061
Ratio	0.91	0.99	0.82	0.86	0.76	0.78	1.44	1.06	0.93	1.04
Rust										
Boys	.257	.115	.048	.125	.052	.048	.037	.023	.086	.062
Girls	.225	.125	.049	.092	.044	.052	.034	.026	.058	.071
Ratio	0.87	1.09	1.00	0.73	0.85	1.08	0.90	1.12	1.04	1.14
Öschelbronn										
Boys	.309	.127	.056	.170	.053	.036	.55	.035	.059	.072
Girls	.271	.134	.047	.132	.057	.049	.36	.029	.061	.076
Ratio	0.88	1.06	0.84	0.78	1.08	1.34	0.66	0.83	1.03	1.06

3 Bavarian villages[a]

Boys	.359	.082	.035	.176	.092	.085	.042	.022	.037	.047
Girls	.270	.059	.043	.125	.058	.068	.034	.017	.034	.026
Ratio	0.75	0.72	1.24	0.71	0.62	0.80	0.81	0.78	0.93	0.55

4 Waldeck villages

Boys	.196	.140	.067	.098	.029	.027	.029	.028	.065	.080
Girls	.169	.143	.067	.085	.026	.025	.020	.024	.062	.086
Ratio	0.86	1.02	1.01	0.86	0.90	0.95	0.69	0.86	0.96	1.07

Middels

Boys	.138	.067	.047	.75	.024	.018	.014	.015	.030	.038
Girls	.104	.067	.051	.055	.014	.010	.018	.011	.024	.043
Ratio	0.75	1.00	1.09	0.74	0.56	0.55	1.30	0.73	0.81	1.14

Werdum

Boys	.166	.117	.076	.095	.031	.022	.014	.014	.045	.076
Girls	.154	.099	.075	.083	.031	.019	.012	.017	.044	.057
Ratio	0.93	0.84	0.99	0.87	1.01	0.87	0.85	1.24	0.98	0.75

All villages

Boys	.239	.124	.057	.117	.048	.042	.031	.024	.057	.071
Girls	.207	.125	.056	.095	.041	.037	.028	.023	.056	.073
Ratio	0.87	1.01	0.98	0.81	0.85	0.89	0.90	0.97	0.97	1.04

Note: Calculations of $_1q_0$ and the probability of dying between exact ages 0 and 1 month include stillbirths. The ratio of female to male mortality was calculated before rounding mortality rates as shown. Results are subject to restrictions 2, 3, 6 and 7 (see Table A.1).

[a] Excluding periods (in Anhausen and Gabelbach) when a cross without an exact date of death was commonly used to indicate a child death.

low.[13] In all villages or village groups, female infant mortality is lower than male, although in each of the four Baden villages the female advantage disappears during the later months of infancy. In addition, mortality between ages 2 and 5 was higher for girls, with only the exceptions of the Bavarian villages just noted and Middels.

One potentially important influence on infant mortality in the past was the prevailing infant-feeding practices. There is substantial evidence to show that, throughout the early months of life, infants who were weaned typically experienced higher mortality than those still being breastfed.[14] Thus the variation in the age pattern of sex differentials in mortality among the different villages found in Table 4.4 might be explained by differences in breastfeeding customs. Moderate breastfeeding durations, as indicated in Appendix F for the Baden villages, might also account for the loss of a female advantage during the later months of infancy if the sex-neutral protection of breastfeeding gave way to preferential treatment of boys. However, in the Bavarian villages, where any breastfeeding was uncommon, the pronounced female advantage during the first half year of life suggests that the artificial feeding practices, at least in those villages, did not discriminate against daughters.

Differences in the age at weaning between girl and boy infants could also contribute to sex differentials in mortality. It is possible to test indirectly for sex differentials in this respect by comparing the length of birth intervals following the birth of sons and daughters. As discussed in Appendix F, breastfeeding typically delays conception. Thus, in the absence of birth control, the length of the birth interval tends to be directly proportional to the duration of breastfeeding. Even during periods of family limitation, the length of birth intervals would reflect the extent of breastfeeding if birth control was practiced primarily to stop childbearing rather than to space children.

A comparison of the average interval following the birth of boys and of girls is provided in Table 4.5. Since there are sex differentials in infant mortality, and since infant deaths typically shorten birth intervals by curtailing breastfeeding and thus shortening the period of postpartum amenorrhea, the average interval following births of children surviving to at least age 1 is shown in addition to all intervals. The results are clear in indicating only minimal, statistically non-

---

[13] Statistics for all of Bavaria show a similar strong female advantage in infant mortality. For example, from 1835–36 to 1868–69, the infant mortality rate for the entire kingdom averaged 41.2 per 100 live births for males and 35.7 for females (Lee, W. R., *Population growth*, p. 6).

[14] Knodel and Kintner, 'Breast feeding patterns.'

Table 4.5. *Average interconfinement interval (in months) by sex of the child born at the onset of the interval, for intervals following all births and intervals following births surviving to at least age 1, by village*

	Intervals following all births			Intervals following surviving births of		
	Boys	Girls	Difference[a]	Boys	Girls	Difference[a]
Grafenhausen	28.7	28.6	0.1	31.0	30.2	0.8
Herbolzheim	28.1	28.3	-0.2	30.1	30.1	0.0
Kappel	28.4	28.2	0.2	29.7	29.5	0.2
Rust	27.7	27.4	0.3	29.7	29.0	0.7
Öschelbronn	26.4	26.2	0.2	29.0	28.3	0.7
3 Bavarian villages	22.8	22.9	-0.1	23.7	23.7	0.0
4 Waldeck villages	31.3	31.2	0.1	33.7	33.2	0.5
Middels	34.0	35.2	-1.2	35.7	36.9	-1.2
Werdum	33.2	33.1	0.1	35.3	35.1	0.2
All villages	29.0	29.0	0.0	31.2	30.9	0.3

Note: In cases where the confinement starting the interval resulted in a multiple birth, the sex of the last-born of the multiple birth was assigned to the confinement. Results subject to restrictions 2, 3, 6, and 7 (see Table A.1).
[a] None of the differences are statistically significant at the .05 level.

significant, differences in the subsequent birth intervals according to
the sex of the child. Little difference in birth intervals following births
of boys and girls would be expected in Bavaria, where breastfeeding
was rare. It is more notable that in the Waldeck and East Frisian
villages, where breastfeeding was probably most extensive, there is
also no indication that boys were breastfed to a later age than girls.
Apparently, sons and daughters were treated similarly with regard to
breastfeeding throughout Germany as far as our sample villages
suggest. This agrees with direct evidence from Berlin, where census
tabulations from 1885 to 1905 indicate essentially equal proportions of
boys and girls being breastfed.[15]

Wall has suggested that any neglect of female children during the
period prior to deliberate family limitation should show up more
strongly in, or perhaps be entirely limited to, children of higher birth
ranks.[16] He argues that the first few children will undoubtedly be
wanted, regardless of sex, since families want heirs even if there is no
real property to transmit, and that, at least in the European case,
daughters will suffice when there are no sons. He therefore suggests
examining sex differentials in infant and child mortality according to
birth rank. His own evidence in several English parishes points to
excess female mortality in infancy being more common among higher-
order births, although his findings are not conclusive.

To examine the possibility of such a relationship, Table 4.6 shows the
ratio of female to male mortality in infancy and childhood in the sample
villages. In brief, there appears to be little systematic relationship
between sex differentials in mortality and birth rank, and no consistent
pattern of excess female mortality among higher birth ranks. Based on
these findings, it seems reasonably safe to conclude that any neglect of
female infants that may have existed was as likely to manifest itself
among earlier births as it was among later births.

Maternal age, birth order, sibship size, and birth intervals

Considerable interest and research have focused on the association
between infant mortality on the one hand, and maternal age, birth
rank, sibship size (ultimate number of births), and birth spacing on the

---

[15] For example, in 1885, 55.0 percent of male infants were reported as breastfed
compared to 55.5 percent of females; in 1905, the proportion of male and female
infants breastfed was each 31 percent. Thus, in the intervening 20 years, although the
practice of breastfeeding declined substantially, it did so equally with regard to sons
and daughters. (Calculations from the Berlin censuses were kindly provided by Hallie
Kintner.)

[16] Wall, 'Neglect of females.'

Table 4.6. *The ratio of female to male mortality in infancy and childhood according to birth rank and regional grouping of villages*

	Birth rank				
	1–2	3–4	5–6	7+	Total
4 Baden villages					
$_1q_0$	.86	.85	.88	.92	.88
$_4q_1$	1.03	1.14	1.09	.90	1.04
$_{10}q_5$	.98	1.07	.92	.86	.97
Öschelbronn					
$_1q_5$	.93	.74	.90	.92	.88
$_4q_1$	.97	1.07	.98	1.17	1.06
$_{10}q_5$	1.05	.79	.64	.80	.84
3 Bavarian villages					
$_1q_0$	.67	.70	.79	.85	.75
$_4q_1$	.65	.97	.85	.49	.72
$_{10}q_5$	1.99	1.97	.51	1.19	1.24
4 Waldeck villages					
$_1q_0$	.88	.85	.94	.80	.87
$_4q_1$	1.12	.82	1.05	1.21	1.02
$_{10}q_5$	.91	.88	1.70	.88	1.02
2 East Frisian villages					
$_1q_0$	.94	.80	.75	.91	.86
$_4q_1$	.82	.96	.81	1.07	.88
$_{10}q_5$	1.04	1.17	.71	1.06	1.01
All villages					
$_1q_0$	.87	.83	.87	.91	.87
$_4q_1$	1.00	1.04	1.02	.97	1.01
$_{10}q_5$	.99	1.04	.96	.90	.98

Note: Results are subject to restrictions 2, 3, 6 and 7 (see Table A.1).

other. Concern about the possible higher mortality risks associated with late or very early childbearing, as well as higher mortality among children of high birth rank, among children in large families, and among those born after short birth intervals, has served as part of the rationale for providing family-planning services both in developed and developing countries in the second half of the twentieth century. Furthermore, assumptions about the relationship of infant and child mortality with these factors have been suggested as the basis through which declines in fertility can contribute to reduced infant and child mortality.[17]

[17] For example, see Taucher, 'Infant mortality levels.'

Interpretation of the results of studies on the relationship between infant and child mortality and these factors is complicated for a number of reasons: some of these factors are highly associated with each other; in populations where deliberate fertility control within marriage is common, the decision to continue childbearing is to some extent contingent on the outcome of previous pregnancies; cross-sectional data or truncated longitudinal data are sometimes used to make inferences which are more appropriately based on complete reproductive histories; and both fertility patterns and infant mortality are frequently associated with socio-economic status, an association that leads to possible spurious correlations.

Family reconstitution data from earlier periods, such as those for the 14 villages on which this study is based, avoid or at least minimize several of these problems. In particular, completed reproductive histories are known for all families; deliberate family limitation within marriage was either largely absent or at only moderate levels during the period under observation; and socio-economic differentials in infant mortality (as well as fertility, as discussed in Chapter 11) are not very pronounced.

One potential complication is the possibility that child neglect or abusive child-care practices were used as a means of limiting family size, as discussed above. If such practices acted in the same way as deliberate birth control to limit family size, as some contemporary commentators suggest,[18] they could have influenced the association between infant and child mortality on the one hand, and maternal age, birth rank, or total number of births on the other. Under such circumstances we would expect relative underinvestment in child-care efforts for children of high birth rank, and thus higher mortality for higher birth orders and advanced maternal age (which would be highly correlated with birth rank). Other behavioral factors may also be involved in the relationships since even in populations where deliberate birth control within marriage is absent, behavioral as well as biological mechanisms influence fertility (see the discussion in Chapter 10).

Overall patterns
Neonatal, post-neonatal, infant, and early-childhood mortality (infant mortality being defined as the risk of dying between birth and exact age 1, or $_1q_0$, and early-childhood mortality as the risk of dying between exact ages 1 and 5, or $_4q_1$) are each shown in Figure 4.1 according to

---

[18] For example, see Kull, 'Beitraege zur Statistik,' pp. 143–50.

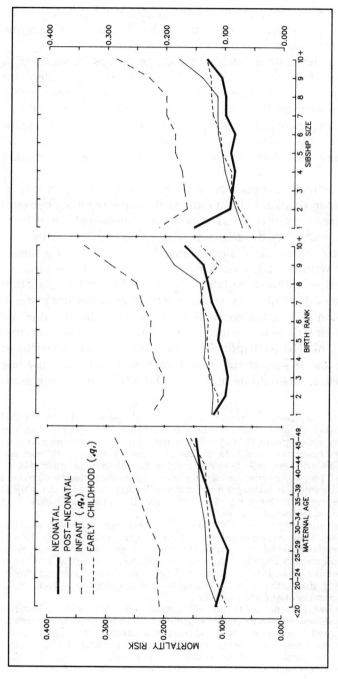

Figure 4.1. *Neonatal, post-neonatal, infant and early-childhood mortality by maternal age, birth rank, and sibship size*. All results refer to the combined sample of all villages, are subject to restrictions 6 and 7, and exclude prenuptial births. Results for birth rank are based only on first marriages of the mothers; results for sibship size are based only on first marriages of the mothers, and are additionally subject to restriction 4 (see Table A.1)

maternal age, birth rank, and final number of births, separately. Note that sibship size is defined in terms of the final number of births regardless of the survival status of the births.[19]

In general, mortality in each of these age groups increases with maternal age after age 25. A slight J-shaped curve is evident for neonatal mortality, with infants to mothers under age 20 experiencing modestly higher mortality rates than those to mothers in their twenties. In contrast, there is essentially a monotonic increase with age for post-neonatal mortality and early-childhood mortality, with the youngest age group of mothers experiencing the lowest rates of child loss.

Neonatal as well as overall infant mortality also show a modest J-shaped curve in relation to birth rank, with mortality falling between the first and second birth orders but increasing fairly steadily with birth rank from the third birth order on, with an acceleration in the rise apparent after birth order 6. Post-neonatal mortality shows a similar pattern but with mortality risks for the first three births virtually identical. Early-childhood mortality, however, shows little association with birth rank. Post-neonatal and early-childhood mortality increase fairly monotonically according to sibship size, with the extent of the differences being more pronounced than in either the case of maternal age or birth rank. Neonatal mortality shows a U-shaped relationship to sibship size and is particularly high in families which had only one birth. However, it should be noted that the results for the one-birth

---

[19] All results exclude prenuptial births to the couples since these would be concentrated at younger maternal ages and lower birth orders, and because the evidence indicates that mortality among prenuptial births to married couples is biased downward, as discussed in Appendices B and E. In the case of results referring to birth order and sibship size, only first marriages to women are considered since the number of births born during a previous marriage is often unknown. In addition, results referring to sibship size are limited to marriages which remained intact until the end of the wife's reproductive years. Thus the results of analyses of the different factors are usually not based on identical subsets of couples.

The overall mortality rate for children born to first marriages differs little from that to all marriages. However, children born to marriages remaining intact until the wife reaches the end of the childbearing years tend to have slightly lower mortality risks. This occurs presumably for two reasons. First, an infectious disease may affect more than one member of the family at a time and hence the death of a parent may be associated with the death of a child. Second, the loss of a parent may decrease the quality and quantity of care and provision.

One other feature about the analysis relating infant and child mortality to maternal age, birth rank, and sibship size deserves mention. The usual practice of imposing restrictions 2 and 3 (see Table A.1) on the analysis of mortality above age 1 was not followed in this case since most of the focus is on mortality below age 1, and a further reduction in the number of cases was deemed more undesirable than the slight downward bias this might introduce on mortality between exact ages 1 and 4.

Table 4.7. *Infant mortality ($_1q_0$) by length of interval to current birth and fate of previous birth*

Interval in months to current birth	Fate of previous birth					
	Survived infancy		Died in infancy		All fates	
	$_1q_0$	N	$_1q_0$	N	$_1q_0$	N
Less than 12	.403	460	.379	714	.388	1174
12–17	.294	4298	.293	3488	.293	7786
18–23	.216	5970	.251	1991	.225	7961
24–29	.183	6836	.267	792	.192	7628
30–35	.170	5115	.286	396	.178	5511
36–47	.166	4382	.320	377	.178	4759
48+	.175	2968	.316	297	.188	3265

Note: Results refer to the combined sample of all villages and are limited to births of second and higher birth rank, exclude prenuptial births, and are subject to restrictions 6 and 7 (see Table A.1). In the case of a multiple birth, only the first-born is considered.

family are based on far fewer cases than any of the others and thus the unusually high neonatal mortality rate for single-child families may be partially a result of statistical fluctuation.

There is considerable evidence that the mortality risk of a given child is substantially higher if the child is born after a brief interval than after a longer one.[20] The relationship between infant mortality and the length of the previous birth interval based on the experience of women in the present sample is addressed in Table 4.7 according to the survival status of the previously born child.

The results reveal a strongly and largely inverse relationship between the risk of infant mortality and the length of the previous birth interval when the fate of the prior birth surviving infancy is not taken into consideration. Infant mortality declines sharply as the birth interval extends from a brief to a more moderate length but is only minimally affected thereafter. The lowest mortality risks are associated with intervals of two and a half to four years in length, with a slightly higher mortality being associated with intervals of four years or longer. This relationship is essentially the same for infants following the birth of an immediately previous child who survived infancy, but is considerably weaker and less regular for children whose birth followed the birth of an immediately previous child who died in infancy. Regardless

[20] Maine, *Family planning*; Wray, 'Population pressure'; Knodel, 'Infant mortality and fertility'; United Nations, *Foetal, infant, and early childhood mortality*.

of the length of the interval to the current birth, infant mortality is higher when the previous child died than when it survived, although the difference is far more pronounced following longer intervals than it is following shorter ones.

A variety of reasons may underlie the relationship between previous birth interval and risk of infant death. The especially high mortality associated with intervals of less than a year is undoubtedly in part a result of a disproportionate share of such births involving short gestational periods and thus being premature. Since it is impossible with family reconstitution data based on birth registers to measure the length of the pregnancy, the importance of this factor cannot be assessed precisely. However, it is interesting to note that the proportion of stillbirths following short birth intervals is above average: 3.4 percent following birth intervals of less than 12 months and 2.8 percent following intervals of 12–17 months, compared to 2.4 percent following all longer intervals combined. Nevertheless, the main explanation must lie elsewhere. Two or more births in rapid succession might weaken the mother. This could affect the physical constitution of a new child, or perhaps a physically weak mother is less capable of giving adequate care to a child during the critical period of infancy. Independently of the physical condition of the mother, it is possible that the presence of a second young child in the household at the time of a birth would reduce the amount of care and attention the mother could afford to give to the newborn infant.

The fact that the relationship between the preceding birth and infant mortality is more pronounced when the previous child survived than when it died supports the hypothesis that a second infant or young child in the household consumes some of the care that the mother would otherwise be devoting to the newborn infant. When the preceding child is older, that is the birth interval is longer, the mother need not give as much attention to it and is able to give greater care to the newborn infant, thus enhancing its chances for survival. Where the preceding child died before the next birth, two infants would not be present at the same time to compete for their mother's care and thus the relationship no longer holds. It is not surprising that the overall infant mortality is higher for births following infant deaths than for births terminating intervals during which the preceding infant survived, since it is likely that mortality risks among siblings are positively correlated.

Maternal age

Given the close association between maternal age and birth rank, it can be instructive to examine the relationship between infant mortality and maternal age, controlling for birth order. Such a comparison is complicated, however, by the operation of a selection process which strongly biases the relationship at higher birth orders. The reason for this is that women who bear higher-order children at young ages are selected for rapid childbearing, which itself is strongly associated with increased infant mortality. The basis of the selection process is twofold. First, in populations where at least some children are breastfed and where deliberate birth spacing through other means is not common, the death of a child shortens the birth interval. Thus women who experience infant deaths will tend to arrive at a given parity at a younger age than women whose previous births survive infancy. Second, children born after brief intervals experience higher mortality than those born after moderate or longer intervals. The extent of this bias when examining the relationship between maternal age and infant mortality at higher birth ranks is strong enough to affect the apparent relationship substantially, such that younger women experience unusually high rates of child loss.

Comparison of the relationship between maternal age and neonatal, post-neonatal, total infant, and early-childhood mortality is presented in Figure 4.2 for birth ranks 1 through 3. Results for higher birth ranks are not shown because of the substantial bias, already discussed, that would influence the results. Strictly speaking, only results for first births are totally free of this bias. For this reason a dotted line is used to represent the relationship between maternal age and the mortality measure prior to age 30 for birth orders 2 and 3.

In general, the results point to an increase in neonatal mortality with maternal age, especially during the later part of the reproductive span. For first births, the only exception to rising neonatal mortality with age is the slightly higher rate experienced by mothers under 20 compared to those aged 20–24. The slight declines in neonatal mortality with age during the early part of the reproductive span may be an artifact of the bias described above. In contrast to neonatal mortality, little association with maternal age is evident for post-neonatal mortality. Thus the relationship between total infant mortality and maternal age largely resembles that of neonatal mortality. Early-childhood mortality, like post-neonatal mortality, shows little association with maternal age, although a modest increase is evident for all three birth ranks between the two oldest age groups shown. Thus, in general, the results suggest that maternal age is of some importance for mortality soon after birth

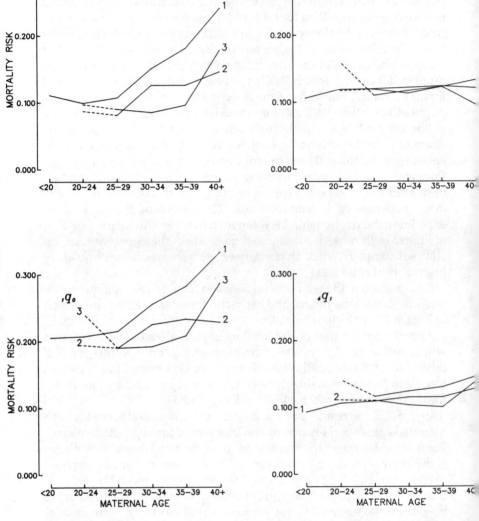

Figure 4.2. *Neonatal, post-neonatal, infant and early-childhood mortality by maternal age for birth ranks 1, 2 and 3*. Results refer to the combined sample of all villages, are based on first marriages of the mothers, and are subject to restrictions 6 and 7 (see Table A.1); prenuptial births are excluded. Results based on fewer than 100 births are not shown

when endogenous causes are important, but of little importance for children who survive the first month.

Birth rank and sibship size

A number of studies have pointed out that data on infant mortality and birth rank based on all women combined regardless of the final number of births they eventually achieve can provide a very different impression of the association between infant mortality and birth rank within given sibship sizes. The reason for this is that mortality risks for children at all birth ranks are frequently higher within families with a large number of births than are mortality risks for families with a smaller number of births. At least in part, the reason is that a woman must experience more rapid childbearing over the reproductive years if she is to have a large number of births than if she is to have fewer births. This is relevant because mortality risks following short birth intervals are typically higher than those following moderate or longer birth intervals. Although women with a final number of births of any number contribute to births of rank 1, and those with two or more children contribute to birth rank 2, only those with a large final number of births can contribute to high birth ranks. Thus, even if within any given sibship size there is no association between birth rank and mortality risks, if women who bear large numbers of children generally experienced greater rates of child loss, there would be a rising mortality rate associated with birth rank for results based on a combined population of all sibship sizes. Cross-sectional studies of the relationship between infant mortality and birth rank typically suffer from this problem.

When complete reproductive histories for women are known, as happens with family reconstitution data, mortality risks can be examined by birth rank for different sibship sizes separately. Results of such a comparison based on the infant mortality rate ($_1q_0$) are shown in Figure 4.3 for the combined sample of all villages. Some irregularity in the results is to be expected given the reduced number of cases for each birth rank category and for each sibship size category. Nevertheless, the results are reasonably clear. In general, there is little evidence of a consistent relationship between birth rank and infant mortality once sibship size is controlled for.

These findings imply that to the extent underinvestment in child care or abusive practices contributed to infant mortality, they did not appear to be specific to birth rank and thus were not used to limit family size in the same way as modern birth control is. In the latter case, efforts are typically made to stop childbearing toward the end of

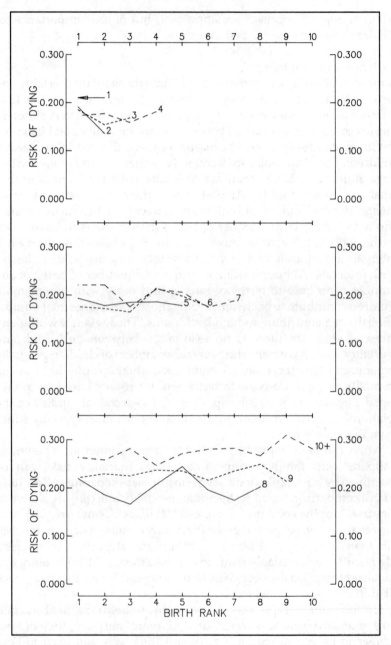

Figure 4.3. *Infant mortality ($_1q_0$) by birth rank and sibship size.* Results refer to the combined sample of all villages, are based on first marriages of the mothers, and are subject to restrictions 4, 6 and 7 (see Table A.1); prenuptial births are excluded

the reproductive span once the desired number of children is attained. This point is discussed in detail in the section of this book on marital reproduction.[21] Since it seems reasonable to assume that most couples wanted at least some children, if child neglect or abusive child-care practices were used to limit family size, they should appear to be more pronounced at higher parities.[22] It is all too easy to mistake the rise in infant mortality with higher birth orders that is usually evident when different sibship sizes are combined as supporting a birth-rank-specific underinvestment in child care, even if no such association may actually exist within given sibship sizes.[23]

Additional evidence that underinvestment in child care, to whatever extent it existed, was not more common among children of higher birth rank is provided by the results in Table 4.8, which indicate early-childhood mortality by birth rank within given sibship sizes. The most consistent finding is that, with one exception (sibship size 5–6), it is children of birth ranks 1 and 2 combined who experience low early-childhood mortality risks compared with higher-order births. However, there is clearly no monotonic increase with birth rank, and

[21] While it might seem that a more appropriate way to test if later-born children tend to be neglected more than earlier children would be to examine mortality risks in relation to the number of previous children *still surviving*, rather than simply to birth rank without regard to the survival status of the previous births, the results would be confounded by the tendency for infant and child mortality to 'run in families.' In other words, there is a positive association between the probability of successive children surviving or dying early.

[22] Indeed, a frequently cited quotation from the early nineteenth century which would lead us to expect this is from Joseph Hazzi (*Statistische Aufschlüsse*, Vol. II, p. 182), who, in commenting on conditions in Bavaria, indicated:

> The peasant is glad when his wife brings him the first rewards of love and he is also pleased with the second and third, but not so for the fourth. He regrets being a father of many children as his wealth is too modest to permit him to have favorable expectations for them. He regards all subsequent children as hostile elements which take bread out of the mouths of himself and his present family. Even the tender heart of the mother is indifferent to the fifth child and for the sixth she wishes loudly for its death or that the child (as it is locally expressed) should go to Heaven.

Interestingly, when infant mortality is examined by birth rank within given sibship sizes separately for the Bavarian villages as a group, some tendency is evident that births of higher orders experienced greater mortality risks, but this is generally not the case for the combined sample of all villages. For example, in the three Bavarian villages taken together, the following $_1q_0$ values were found:

| | Sibship size | | |
Birth rank	6–7	8–9	10+
1–5	.279	.303	.280
5+	.307	.355	.361

[23] See, for example, Imhof, 'Unterschiedliche Säuglingssterblichkeit.'

Table 4.8. *Early-childhood mortality ($_4q_1$) by birth rank and sibship size*

Birth rank	Sibship size					
	1–2	3–4	5–6	7–8	9–10	11+
1–2	.070	.080	.111	.110	.105	.121
3–4		.098	.107	.129	.134	.142
5–6			.096	.124	.122	.153
7–8				.122	.131	.150
9–10					.106	.125
11+						.134

Note: Results refer to the combined sample of all villages, are based on first marriages for the mothers, and are subject to restrictions 4, 6, and 7 (see Table A.1); prenuptial births are excluded.

the risks among higher birth ranks for larger sibship sizes differ little from those found for lower birth ranks. Indeed, even for all sibship sizes combined, there appears to be little association between early-childhood mortality and birth rank (see Figure 4.1).

It is interesting to compare the results from the present study with those based on births for a recent period. Bakketeig and Hoffman analyzed data based on several hundred thousand mothers in Norway who gave birth to one or more children during 1967–73.[24] Information on successive births was linked to each mother for those who gave birth to more than one child during that period. They found that, for all births combined, perinatal mortality decreased slightly between birth ranks 1 and 2 but increased thereafter through birth rank 4 (virtually no mothers gave birth to more than four children during the seven-year period under observation). In contrast, when perinatal mortality was related to birth rank after controlling for attained sibship size, the perinatal mortality decreased with increasing birth rank. This was obscured in the combined results because of the positive association between mortality and sibship size.

In their analysis, Bakketeig and Hoffman overlook the problem created by the fact that in a population where contraception is widespread, such as modern Norway, pregnancy outcomes influence whether or not couples continue to have additional children: couples are more likely to stop having children after a successful pregnancy than after one resulting in an infant death. Even in the total absence of any association between mortality risks and birth rank a distinct decline in mortality with birth rank would appear within given sibship

[24] Bakketeig and Hoffman, 'Perinatal mortality.'

sizes, provided that couples were more likely to stop childbearing when a pregnancy resulted in a surviving child and were more likely to continue if the pregnancy resulted in an infant death. Such is likely to be the case in modern populations where contraception is common.

The impact of infant and child mortality on reproductive behavior, based on the sample of German villages, is analyzed in considerable detail in Chapter 14. In the present context, however, it is useful to point out that the amount of family limitation characterizing couples in our sample is quite modest compared with modern European populations, and thus the results of the relationship of infant mortality with birth rank within given sibship sizes suggest that the findings based on the modern Norwegian data may well be an artifact of reproductive decison-making rather than a reflection of a biological process through which parity and infant survival chances are linked.

While birth order seems to have little consistent effect once sibship size is controlled for, the converse is not true. There is a steady increase in both infant and child mortality rates at most birth orders with increasing sibship size, an increase which is gradual over much of the range, but accelerates at the highest sibship sizes.

The finding that sibship size is more strongly related to infant mortality than birth rank is requires explanation; the ultimate number of children cannot be a direct determining factor since a subsequent birth can affect the infant mortality risk of a previous one to only a limited degree – through competing for the attention and care of the parents. The observed pattern of rising infant mortality by sibship size – particularly among families with nine or more births – probably arises from the interplay of fertility and mortality. Mothers with a large number of births will tend to have shorter birth intervals and be subject to a number of other characteristics, such as a shorter breastfeeding period and more pressure on limited resources, that contribute to higher infant and child mortality. At the same time, those women with biological and behavioral characteristics that lead to unsuccessful outcomes will experience more rapid childbearing and a large number of births. Thus, women with the largest number of births are highly selected for characteristics that contribute to high levels of mortality among their offspring.

Family reconstitution data permit a direct assessment of only some of the factors implicated. Table 4.9 examines the degree to which differentials in birth interval and the survival of the previous birth account for differentials in the infant mortality rates of the indexed birth among different sibship sizes. For every category of birth interval, the highest infant mortality is still found among births from the

Table 4.9. *Infant mortality ($_1q_0$) by sibship size, birth interval, and survival status of the previous birth*

Birth interval (months)	Survival status of previous birth[a]	Sibship size		
		2–6	7–9	10 or more
All intervals	Died	.24	.27	.31
	Survived	.16	.18	.27
	Total	.17	.20	.28
Less than 12	Died	.26	.35	.42
	Survived	.37	.32	.42
	Total	.31	.34	.42
12–17	Died	.24	.27	.32
	Survived	.22	.27	.33
	Total	.23	.27	.33
18–23	Died	.22	.24	.26
	Survived	.18	.20	.26
	Total	.19	.21	.26
24–29	Died	.19	.25	.29
	Survived	.14	.17	.22
	Total	.15	.18	.23
30–35	Died	.25	.27	.33
	Survived	.14	.16	.23
	Total	.15	.16	.24
36–47	Died	.28	.29	.31
	Survived	.13	.15	.24
	Total	.14	.16	.24
48 or more	Died	.33	.28	.56
	Survived	.15	.19	.24
	Total	.17	.20	.27

Note: Results refer to the combined sample of all villages, exclude prenuptial births, are based on first marriages of mothers, and are subject to restrictions 4, 6, and 7 (see Table A.1). In the case of a multiple birth, only the first-born is considered.
[a] Survival status refers to whether or not the previous birth died in infancy.

largest sibship sizes. Also noticeable is the much higher infant mortality at very short intervals (less than 12 months) of birth in large sibships, a feature that is possibly due to the higher proportion of premature births among mothers who have many births. In addition, there is an upturn in mortality at the longest intervals (48 months or more) which might be attributable to a maternal age effect.

To probe the factors underlying the relationship of infant mortality

Table 4.10. *Infant mortality ($_1q_0$) among birth ranks 2 through 5 for sibships of five or more by sibship size, unadjusted and adjusted in various combinations for maternal age, region, previous birth interval and the number of infant deaths among the first five births excluding the indexed birth*

| Adjustment variables | Sibship size | | | Difference between 5–7 and 10+ |
	5–7	8–9	10+	
No adjustments	.181	.201	.254	.073
Maternal age	.172	.207	.269	.097
Region	.187	.200	.242	.055
Previous interval	.189	.200	.237	.048
Other infant deaths	.186	.201	.243	.057
Region, previous interval, other infant deaths	.192	.200	.229	.037
Maternal age, region, previous interval, other infant deaths	.185	.205	.241	.056

Note: Results refer to the combined sample of all villages, are based on births to first marriages of mothers, and are subject to restrictions 4 and 7 (see Table A.1). Prenuptial births and families with multiple births among the first five births are excluded. Adjustment is made by multiple classification analysis.

to sibship size further, the rates for different sibship size categories were statistically adjusted for the effect of several factors likely to be involved. To eliminate any possible confounding influence of birth rank, and to permit a measure of birth interval and each woman's endogenous proclivity for infant loss to be measured, the analysis is limited to births of ranks 2 through 5 among sibships of five or more. The factors for which the infant mortality rates are adjusted, in various combinations, are maternal age (at the time of the birth), previous birth interval, region, and the number of infant deaths among the first five births excluding the indexed birth. This last variable takes into account the tendency of some women to be more prone, either through genetic or behavioral reasons, to the loss of children through infant and child mortality. Region is assumed to serve as a rough indicator of breast-feeding prevalence. The results are shown in Table 4.10. Sibship sizes have been grouped into three categories, and the difference between the largest (10+) and smallest (5–7) categories is shown so as to facilitate comparison of the impact of sibship size on infant mortality for each particular combination of adjustments.

Prior to adjustment for any contributing factor, the probability of dying before age 1 for the subset of births analyzed was .181 among sibships of 5–7 births and .254 for births of sibships of at least 10; this yields a difference of 73 more infant deaths per 1000 births for the larger sibship category compared to the smaller one. Adjustment for maternal age alone serves to increase the impact of sibship size. The reason for this is that, on the average, mothers of large sibships are younger at any given birth rank (in this case, the second through fifth ranks) than mothers of smaller sibships. Since infant mortality risks generally rise with mother's age during much of the reproductive span, the younger maternal age at ranks 2 through 5 for mothers of large sibships helps lower their associated infant mortality rate. When adjustment is made for this, the relation of sibship size and infant mortality becomes even stronger. The other three factors each help contribute to the positive association of sibship size and infant mortality, and thus adjustment for them reduces the degree of association. Each of the factors – region, previous interval, and other infant deaths – has about the same strength of association when considered individually.

Since adjustment for maternal age operates in the opposite direction, an assessment needs to consider the extent to which the three other factors account for the positive association between sibship size and infant mortality. In the absence of an adjustment for maternal age, the three other factors taken together reduce the difference between the larger and smaller sibship size categories by about half (from .073 to .037). When adjustment is made for maternal age and the three other factors simultaneously, the difference is reduced by only about a quarter (from .073 to .056), but a more relevant comparison is with the results adjusted for maternal age alone, in which case the other three factors again reduce the difference by almost half (from .097 to .056). Thus a sizable proportion of the relationship between sibship size and infant mortality is accounted for by the variables available. The fact that a relationship persists even after adjustment suggests that some of the difference is attributable to other factors not included in the analysis, as well as to possibly imprecise measurement of the included factors, particularly the very rough indicator of the extent of breastfeeding.

Conclusions

Family reconstitution data permit a detailed examination of the risks of infant mortality according to a number of attributes of the father, mother, or the child. In contrast to the sharp regional differences in infant and child mortality, socio-economic differences, at least as indicated by the occupation or village leadership status of the father, show little association with the mortality risks experienced by the children. The fact that all social strata within a village appear to have shared a more or less common risk of child loss is consistent with the possible importance of local or regional infant-feeding customs, common to all classes, as a key determinant of infant mortality.

Little support is provided by the evidence from the sample villages that traditional child-care practices, detrimental as they might have been, were used to adjust the sex composition of the family or served as a means of limiting the number of offspring on a parity-specific basis. Perhaps in some villages, a preference was shown to sons in terms of child care, but there is little to indicate that such preferential treatment was extreme enough to have had much of a detectable impact on sex differences in mortality risks.

Examination of the association of infant mortality with birth rank and sibship size indicates that there appears to be little association between birth order and mortality risk within particular sibship sizes. In contrast, the total number of children born to a mother *is* related to infant mortality, regardless of the child's birth rank. For large sibships infant mortality is high for children of all birth orders, while for smaller sibships infant mortality is lower regardless of birth rank. These findings reveal that a misleading impression can result from examining the association between birth order and mortality risk when families of different sibship sizes are aggregated together. The results generally undermine the view that the higher infant and child mortality for births of higher orders, observed when sibship size is not controlled for, is evidence of the existence of 'infanticide by neglect,' through underinvestment in the care of children of higher birth ranks.

5

Maternal mortality

Calculation of adult mortality from family reconstitution data is problematic because of the difficulty of determining with any precision, for those individuals for whom a death date is unknown, the period during which they are present in observation and hence at risk of dying. In the special case of maternal mortality, provided it is defined as the risk of dying during or shortly after confinement and is expressed as a rate relative to the number of confinements, this problem is essentially absent. The beginning of the period of risk is clearly defined by the birth of a child and ends, according to different definitions, within a few weeks or months following confinement. Since it is unlikely that many women migrate out of a village shortly after giving birth, and that those few who do are unlikely to have died in some other village within the specified period, women for whom no death date is known can be safely assumed to have survived the critical period after confinement.

Issues of measurement and definition

In measuring maternal mortality from reconstituted family histories, there are special problems that are essentially inherent to the parish register sources on which these histories are typically based.[1] The most important one is the fact that maternal mortality may be associated with miscarriages and undelivered pregnancies, which are often not recorded at all, or with stillbirths, which are less than fully recorded in the registers (see Appendix B). In such cases, the woman's death does not appear to follow a reproductive event in the reconstituted family

[1] Dobbie, 'Maternal mortality'; Wrigley and Schofield, 'Population history from family reconstitution.'

102

history and thus is not classified as a maternal death. To the extent that this occurs, maternal mortality is underestimated.

A special problem particular to this study is created by the fact that the preselection of couples included the criterion that the death date of at least one of the spouses be known. This tends to bias estimates of maternal mortality upward because, in the case of couples in which the wife died at or shortly following childbirth, her death date is almost certain to be known. But, as indicated in Appendix A, for 6 of the 14 villages included in this study (Braunsen, Kappel, Massenhausen, Middels, Öschelbronn, and Rust) all the couples in the village genealogy were coded. By going back to the fully-coded data of these villages, it is possible to calculate maternal mortality for all women and thus avoid the biases that would result from examining maternal mortality based on those selected solely according to the specific criteria for inclusion in this study.

In order to determine the extent of the bias, maternal mortality rates have been calculated for both the preselected women on which most of the study is based and for all women for the six fully-coded villages. Based on confinements for the years 1700–1899 to legitimate unions (including premarital births to couples who eventually marry), and using the most common definition of a maternal death as one occurring within six weeks of confinement, maternal mortality, as expressed per 1000 confinements, is found to be 9.25 when based on all confinements and 10.46 when based on confinements selected according to the specific criteria for determining inclusion in the present study. Although the bias is fairly modest, inflating the rates for the restricted sample of women by about 13 percent, it could differ over time and across groups. The difference is actually less than it might be because the restricted sample includes prenuptial births to couples who eventually marry, but not illegitimate births that were not followed by the parents' marriage. In the former case, the mother obviously would have had to survive to marry. To avoid the biases created by the preselection process, the following analysis of maternal mortality is based on all women in the 6 fully-coded villages rather than on the more restricted sample of women in all 14 villages.[2] Consideration is

---

[2] In a recent study of maternal mortality in a French village from 1680 to 1814, based on family reconstitution data, Bideau ('Accouchement') compares rates based on families for whom the end of the marital union is known with rates based on families including those for whom the end of the union is unknown. He finds that the rates based only on cases for which the end of the marital union is known were 27 percent higher (23.6 versus 18.6 per 1000 confinements) than when women for whom the end of the marital union is unknown are included. Surprisingly, he chooses to base much of his analysis only on women in marital unions with a known end.

limited, however, to mortality following local confinements (i.e. those occurring in the village) and for which an exact date of confinement is known.

In both historical and contemporary studies of maternal mortality, a variety of definitions appear to be used in practice. Some studies provide statistics on maternal mortality which are based on causes of death rather than simply on time since confinement. While a definition based on cause of death would be more precise, it is obviously impractical for most historical studies, where such information is lacking. It is also impractical for use in many developing countries today, where cause-of-death information is incomplete or faulty. Thus a number of other studies simply classify deaths to women within some period following the birth of the last child as constituting a maternal death. This risks misclassifying some deaths occurring shortly after childbirth, but unrelated to it, as maternal mortality, and missing others which in fact result from childbirth but which occur past the time span used for determining maternity-related deaths.

Even when the definition is based on the length of time following childbirth, the period chosen is not uniform in all studies and may involve deaths up to three months following confinements. Based on the six fully-coded villages, maternal mortality rates, expressed as maternal deaths per 1000 confinements, are presented in Table 5.1 according to different durations of periods following confinement. Probably the most common definition involves deaths within the first six weeks following childbirth. This is the definition recommended by the International Federation of Gynecology and Obstetrics, in a qualified form by the World Health Organization, and by the American College of Obstetrics and Gynecology.[3] The latter also recommends distinguishing between maternal deaths occurring within the first 7 days and those occurring between 8 and 42 days following termination of pregnancy. Clearly, the first week following confinement is the most dangerous period of time and, as indicated by our results, involves roughly half of all the deaths occurring within 42 days of delivery, during most time periods.

Using a definition of maternal mortality based on all deaths within 42 days of delivery probably results in including more deaths unrelated to childbirth than in excluding deaths attributable to childbirth but which occur after 42 days. The net effect of this bias, combined with the undercount of maternal deaths associated with undelivered pregnancies, miscarriages or stillbirths not recorded in the registers, is

[3] Schofield, 'Maternal mortality'; Hughes, *Obstetric–gynecologic terminology*, p. 454.

Table 5.1. *Maternal deaths per 1000 confinements according to different definitions of maternal death, and percent of deaths in first 42 days following confinement that occur in first 7 days, by year of confinement*

	Maternal deaths per 1000 confinements, in days following confinement				Of deaths in first 42 days, % in first 7 days	Number of confinements
	7	42	60	90		
1700–49	5.4	9.5	10.3	10.8	57	3888
1750–99	4.3	7.6	8.3	9.1	57	6048
1800–24	4.2	7.8	8.2	9.4	55	4257
1825–49	6.9	11.3	11.7	11.7	61	5389
1850–74	5.6	10.8	11.0	12.3	52	5381
1875–99	4.0	9.7	10.2	10.8	42	5476
1900–24	1.9	4.1	4.9	5.1	47	4679
1925–49	0.3	0.9	0.9	0.9	—[a]	1699

Note: This table is limited to the six fully-coded villages (Kappel, Rust, Öschelbronn, Braunsen, Massenhausen, and Middels). Results are based on local confinements for which an exact date of confinement is given. Women with unknown death dates are assumed to have survived past stated reference periods.
[a] Fewer than 10 deaths in first days.

probably negligible, at least judging from the levels that might reasonably be expected.[4]

Trends

Since all couples, including those married after 1900, were processed in the fully-coded villages, trends through the first half of the twentieth century can be examined. Moreover, since an examination of individual villages did not reveal lower maternal mortality during periods when the registration of infant and child deaths was deficient (see Appendix B), these periods are not excluded. The results suggest that little improvement in maternal mortality occurred prior to the turn of the twentieth century and indeed that conditions during the mid-nineteenth century may have been somewhat worse than during previous periods. It is difficult to know how general the trends based

---

[4] The number of maternal deaths per 1000 confinements for the restricted sample of women for the 14 villages combined were: 12.1 for 1700–49, 11.8 for 1750–99, 10.0 for 1800–24, 12.3 for 1825–49, 11.6 for 1850–74, and 10.1 for 1875–99. These are biased upward as indicated in the text.

on our sample of six villages are. Results for the restricted sample of women from all 14 villages combined also show a higher maternal death rate during the middle two quarters of the nineteenth century than in the first or last quarter.[5] Moreover, in a study of maternal mortality in three other German villages and a small German town between 1780 and 1899, Imhof found that maternal mortality was also higher in the mid-nineteenth century than in either the early or late nineteenth century, although it was highest during the first three decades of the period he investigated.[6]

One possible explanation for a rise in maternal mortality during the middle of the nineteenth century, if indeed such an increase is genuine, could lie in the initial increase in total demand for labor, necessitated by agricultural reforms, which is thought to have been met in part by an extended workload for peasant women. Apparently, there was generally hardly any period of rest either during pregnancy or immediately after childbirth for women in rural society in Germany at the time.[7] However, in an extensive review of maternal mortality statistics from a variety of sources, including a number referring to German populations, Shorter discerns no consistent evidence of an increase in maternal mortality during the mid-nineteenth century.[8] Data he presents for Prussia covering the years 1816 through 1894 indicate fairly steady maternal mortality, ranging from 7.6 to 9.5 maternal deaths per 1000 deliveries until the end of the third quarter of the century and then somewhat lower rates than that for the last quarter of the century.

It is noteworthy that the general level of maternal mortality indicated for Prussia was of the same order of magnitude as that indicated by our

[5] Schofield, 'Maternal mortality.'

[6] Imhof ('Women, family, and death,' Table 5.4) found the following maternal mortality rates per 1000 births for the three villages and one small town combined: 13.1 for 1780–1809, 7.5 for 1810–39, 9.8 for 1840–69, 8.1 for 1870–99, and 9.2 for all time periods combined. It is unclear from the article if the time period refers to year of marriage of the mother or year of confinement. While the overall rate is very close to the rate found in this study for the equivalent time period, the results are not strictly comparable. Imhof limits consideration to couples for whom the exact date of death of at least one spouse is known. This would bias the rates upward in the same way as discussed for the restricted sample in the present study. He also gives no indication that he excludes non-local births, of which there were undoubtedly some since his source is also village genealogies; including these would bias the rates downward (since presumably the mother would have survived long enough to move into the local village with the child and would be included in the genealogy). Moreover, his rates are ostensibly expressed per birth rather than per confinement, again slightly biasing the results downward. It is difficult to judge the net effect of all these biases combined.

[7] Lee, W. R., 'Family and modernization'; Imhof, 'Unterschiedliche Säuglingssterblichkeit'; Sabean, 'Peasant agriculture.'

[8] Shorter, 'Maternal mortality.'

sample of six villages, at least until the end of the nineteenth century. Moreover, official statistics for Germany as a whole during the first quarter of the twentieth century, as presented by Shorter, indicate a maternal mortality rate of between 3.5 and 5.0 maternal deaths per 1000 live births, a rate which is again reasonably consistent with the rates indicated by the sample of six villages. Owing to a lack of strict comparability in definitions of maternal mortality, these comparisons can be used to indicate agreement on the order of magnitude only.

The general picture presented by the data from the six villages, and confirmed by Shorter's extensive review of maternal mortality in a number of Western countries, is that childbearing throughout the eighteenth and nineteenth centuries was associated with a risk of death many times higher than that in the twentieth century and that a substantial improvement occurred only during this later period. In West Germany, childbearing carried with it a risk of only about .2 or .3 deaths per 1000 births by the late 1970s, which is only a small fraction of the levels found in our sample villages during the eighteenth and nineteenth centuries.[9] Moreover, given the far lower rate of childbearing today than in the past, a maternal death has become a very rare event indeed. The 1 percent or so chance of death associated with each confinement in our sample villages during the eighteenth and nineteenth centuries, in combination with considerably higher fertility, meant that a not insignificant proportion of women ended their lives as a result of their reproductive efforts. Given the average age at which women started childbearing and the average rate of childbearing, a 1 percent chance of dying at each confinement would lead to a roughly 5 percent cumulative chance of a woman dying due to childbirth before reaching the end of her reproductive span.

Differentials

Table 5.2 indicates the maternal mortality rates for the different villages, as well as for the marital status of the union, the sex of the child, and the multiple-birth status of the confinement, for confinements occurring during the eighteenth and nineteenth centuries. For the six villages combined, almost a 1 percent chance of death for the

[9] According to the 1979 *United Nations Demographic Yearbook*, maternal mortality in West Germany was 31.1 per 100,000 live births in 1977 and 23.1 per 100,000 in 1978. Apparently, a maternal death is determined by cause of death rather than time since confinement. Imhof ('Women, family, and death,' p. 161) indicates that, based on a definition of death within six weeks of pregnancy termination, the maternal mortality rate in West Germany in 1973 was 45.9 per 100,000 births. This compares with a figure based on cause of death of 37.9 for 1973, according to the UN Yearbook.

Table 5.2. *Maternal deaths within six weeks of confinement per 1000 confinements, by village, by marital status of union, by sex of child and by multiple-birth status of confinements, for confinements occurring 1700–1899*

	Maternal deaths per 1000 confinements	Number of confinements
Village		
Kappel	7.4	6487
Rust	10.3	9976
Öschelbronn	11.9	5033
Braunsen	11.0	1722
Massenhausen	10.3	2899
Middels	6.5	4322
All 6 villages	9.5	30,439
Marital status of union[a]		
Marital	9.2	28,771
Non-marital	13.2	1667
Sex of child[b]		
Boy	9.4	15,603
Girl	8.7	14,700
Multiple-birth status		
Single	9.2	29,960
Multiple	25.1	479

Note: This table is limited to the six fully-coded villages (Kappel, Rust, Öschelbronn, Braunsen, Massenhausen, and Middels). Results are based on local confinements for which an exact date of confinement is given. Women with unknown death dates are assumed to have survived past the end of the six-week reference period.

[a] Premarital confinements to women who later marry the father are included under marital unions; one confinement of a woman in a union of unknown marital status is excluded.

[b] In cases of multiple birth, the confinement is included under the sex of the first-born child; a small number of confinements for which the sex of the birth is unknown are excluded.

mother within six weeks was associated with each confinement. Some variation is evident across villages, although given the infrequent occurrence of a maternal death, some statistical fluctuation would be expected. Data presented by Shorter for East Friesland, based apparently on a larger number of cases, indicate maternal mortality that is more than twice as high as the rate characterizing the East Frisian village of Middels.[10] In addition, when maternal mortality is

---

[10] Shorter, 'Maternal mortality.'

calculated based on the restricted sample of preselected women in Werdum, and then compared to the same rates calculated for Middels based on preselected women (rather than all women), far higher rates are indicated for Werdum. Thus it does not appear that the low rate for Middels is typical for East Friesland generally.[11]

Non-marital unions are associated with higher maternal mortality than marital unions are. Part of this difference is due to confinement order, however. A substantially higher proportion of confinements associated with non-marital unions are first confinements and, as indicated below, maternal mortality associated with first confinements (11.7 deaths per 1000 confinements) is above average. Nevertheless, since non-marital maternal mortality is higher than that associated with all first confinements, this appears to be only part of the explanation, although the small number of cases on which the non-marital maternal mortality is based must be kept in mind. Indeed, the differences between non-marital and marital maternal mortality are not statistically significant at the .05 level, even without taking into account differences in confinement order.[12]

Maternal mortality associated with the birth of a boy is higher than that associated with the birth of a girl. Although the difference is small and not statistically significant at the .05 level, it is in the expected direction. Given the larger average size of newborn males, an increased risk is to be expected with the birth of boys. Far more dangerous are confinements associated with multiple births. Despite the small number of such cases in our sample, the difference in maternal mortality associated with single and multiple births is statistically significant at the .05 level.

Among the most often studied aspects of maternal mortality is its relationship to the mother's age and to the order of confinement.[13] There is general agreement that biological causes at least partly under-

---

[11] Based on the restricted sample of preselected women, the maternal death rate in Werdum per 1000 confinements was 21.4, compared to 8.3 for Middels.

[12] The results may also be biased toward inflating non-marital maternal mortality because of both the way the village genealogies are constructed and the way in which marital and non-marital confinements were defined in the data-processing. Premarital births to couples that eventually marry are listed as part of the couple's reproductive history rather than separately as products of an illegitimate union and have been considered in the present analysis of maternal mortality as confinements to marital unions. Illegitimate births to women who do not marry the father are listed separately and are treated as confinements to non-marital unions. For the mother of an illegitimate birth to eventually marry the father, she would obviously have to survive, while a woman having an illegitimate birth and dying shortly thereafter would have little possibility of converting the union from a non-marital to a marital one.

[13] Berry, 'Maternal mortality'; Nortman, *Parental age*; Bonte and Verbrugge, 'Maternal mortality.'

lie age and confinement order differences in maternal mortality, while differences in overall levels of maternal mortality are largely a result of non-biological causes such as socio-economic levels, cultural practices, and the state and accessibility of medical technology. To the extent that age at confinement and number of children ever born are associated with socio-economic status (or the other relevant characteristics), the association between maternal mortality and age of mother and con- finement order can also reflect non-biological influences. For example, if women of different socio-economic statuses start or terminate child- bearing at different ages, or if they differ with respect to their health and access to health facilities, we would expect maternal mortality rates at the extreme childbearing ages to differ from those at other ages, even in the absence of any biological effects. The same can be said for maternal mortality associated with higher-order confinements if women of different socio-economic statuses are represented in dif- ferent proportions among those who have below- and above-average numbers of births. As is the case for the analysis of infant and child mortality, one advantage of examining the association of maternal mortality with age of mother and confinement order for earlier periods, when deliberate fertility control within marriage was less common, is that the non-biological influences should be less import- ant. As indicated in the section on marital reproduction, fertility control within marriage appears to be either largely absent during most of the period covered by this study or at modest levels during the remainder.

Maternal deaths per 1000 confinements are shown in Figure 5.1 according to the age of mother at confinement and according to confinement order, based on confinements in the eighteenth and nineteenth centuries for the six fully-coded villages combined. The J- shaped relationship between maternal mortality and age which typi- fies most populations is clearly evident.

The extent to which maternal mortality is higher at the later child- bearing ages is somewhat less pronounced than is typical in most contemporary populations, including those in high-mortality develop- ing countries for which reliable data are available. Nortman points out that the age differentials typically widen as the level of mortality is reduced.[14] According to her estimates for high-mortality populations (defined as those with more than 1.0 maternal deaths per 1000 confine- ments), maternal mortality in the age group 40–44 is typically twice as high as that for the unweighted average of all age groups through age

[14] Nortman, *Parental age.*

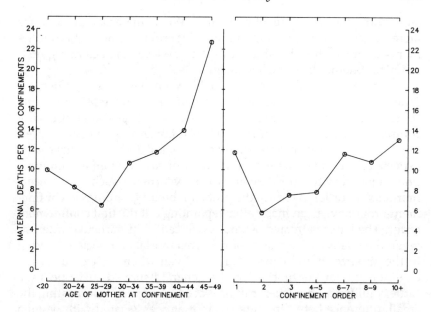

Figure 5.1. *Maternal mortality within six weeks of confinement by age of mother and confinement order, 1700–1899.* Results are limited to the six fully-coded villages only and are restricted to local confinements for which an exact confinement date is known and to first marriages of women with no previous union resulting in an illegitimate birth

group 40–44. In the results for the six German villages, the same calculation indicates that the 40–44 age group of women experienced maternal mortality rates only about 40 percent higher than the unweighted average up to that age group. Given the fact that the overall level of maternal mortality in the German villages during the eighteenth and nineteenth centuries was about four times as high as the average of Nortman's high-mortality populations, the more attenuated relationship with age observed for the German villages may simply represent a more extreme case of less-pronounced differentials occurring as the overall level of maternal mortality increases across populations. However, it may also reflect less self-selection at higher ages of women in low socio-economic categories than occurs in more modern populations.

The relationship of maternal mortality with confinement order is less pronounced than the association with maternal age. Again a J-shaped curve, although considerably flattened, roughly describes the relationship. Particularly sharp is the drop between maternal mortality rates associated with first confinements and the maternal mortality associ-

ated with the second confinement.[15] While maternal death rates
increase generally with rising confinement order, it is not until confinements of the sixth order and above that the level characterizing first-
order confinements is reached again.

Given the inevitable association between age and confinement
order, it is of some interest to examine maternal mortality while
controlling for both variables simultaneously. The results of such a
comparison are indicated in Table 5.3. Caution is required in interpreting the results because of the extent of statistical fluctuation that can be
expected, due to an insufficient number of cases, when examining a
phenomenon with a low frequency of occurrence such as maternal
mortality. In order to reduce the problem, broad groupings of confinement order have been made after separating out the first confinement
order. The latter is treated separately since it is of particular interest,
given the relatively high level of maternal mortality associated with it
in the absence of any control for age. Even when we examine only
confinements of the first order, the general J-shaped curve persists.
Little confidence, however, can be placed in the results indicating the
small difference between maternal mortality associated with women
under 20, which is based on a small number of cases, and the lower
levels found for women in their twenties.

Some limited data for other populations suggest that, for women
bearing their first child, the J-shaped relationship with age gives way to
a monotonic increase in maternal mortality with age, with women
under 20 experiencing the lowest rates.[16] Moreover, results for the
restricted sample of women for all 14 villages also indicate that the
maternal mortality rate is lowest for women under age 20.

At higher confinement orders, maternal mortality also increases
fairly steadily with age in the six fully-coded villages, at least judging
from the two broad confinement order categories into which confinements after the first have been grouped; for both categories, however,
there are insufficient cases of women under age 20 to determine their
level of maternal mortality, and in the group of sixth- and higher-order

[15] The situation described in note 12 may actually slightly bias *downward* maternal
mortality indicated for first confinements. When maternal mortality is examined by
confinement order, all women with an illegitimate union are excluded. However,
some married women with no illegitimate *union* may have had a premarital birth with
their husband, but, since they married, that birth would be considered part of a
reproductive history to a marital union. These births are predominantly first births
(although occasionally a couple has more than one premarital birth). Obviously, for
the couple to marry, the woman must have survived, thus biasing downward the
maternal mortality rate associated with first confinements as defined in the present
analysis.

[16] Nortman, *Parental age.*

Table 5.3. *Maternal deaths within six weeks*
of confinement per 1000 confinements, by age
and confinement order, for confinements
occurring 1700–1899

Age at confinement	Confinement order		
	1	2–5	6+
Under 20	(11.7)	—	—
20–24	10.5	3.2	—
25–29	8.0	4.9	(6.2)
30–34	(22.0)	8.5	12.3
35–39	(23.3)	10.1	11.0
40–44	—	(18.5)	13.2
45–49	—	—	(20.2)

Note: This table is limited to the six fully-coded villages (Kappel, Rust, Öschelbronn, Braunsen, Massenhausen, and Middels). Results are based on local confinements for which an exact date of confinement is given and are restricted to first marriages to women who had no previous unions resulting in an illegitimate birth. Women with unknown death dates are assumed to have survived past the end of the six-week reference period. Results in parentheses are based on less than 500 confinements.

confinements there are insufficient numbers of women below age 25 to make this determination. Nevertheless, the results suggest that the higher mortality of women under 20 compared to those in their twenties, when confinement order is not controlled for, is largely an artifact of the concentration of first-order confinements at younger ages. The results also reveal that once age is controlled for, first-order confinements consistently have a higher maternal mortality associated with them than higher birth orders. Indeed, without exception, for the broad confinement order groups shown, the highest maternal mortality is found for women at their first confinement.

Mortality and reproductive history

While not directly a matter of maternal mortality, an interesting issue concerns the possible association between mortality following the completion of childbearing and the number of children ever born. Do the life chances differ between women who have gone through

Table 5.4. *Age of wife at death by number of children ever born,*
unadjusted and adjusted for village of residence and year of marriage,
among once-married women who survived to at least age 45, 1700–1899

Number of children ever born	Unadjusted	Adjusted
0–2	60.7	60.7
3–5	60.5	60.3
6–8	60.1	60.2
9–11	60.3	60.6
12+	60.7	60.6
Total	60.4	60.4

Note: Results refer to the combined sample of all villages, are subject to restriction 4 (see Table A.1), and are additionally restricted to women who married under age 45. Adjustment for village of residence and year of marriage has been made through multiple classification analysis.

childbirth only a few times or not at all, compared to those who have borne many children? Bideau has explored this relationship, utilizing data from a number of family reconstitution studies done in the field of historical demography.[17] He concluded that there is at best a weak relationship between the number of children a woman has borne and her expectation of life on her 45th birthday. In particular, he found some slight evidence that the most fertile women, particularly those who have borne 12 or more children, live longer than the remainder.

It is possible to examine this issue with the data from the sample of German villages under study. The results are presented in Table 5.4, both before and after being statistically adjusted for village of residence and year of marriage. These adjustments were made in order to control for differences in mortality after age 45 which are associated with specific village conditions and with the specific time period. In general, the unadjusted and adjusted results are very similar. In both cases no clear-cut association is evident between the age at death and the number of children a woman had borne. Both the least fertile and the most fertile women are quite similar in average age at death, but in each case they lived only a few months longer than women whose fertility was moderate.

Discussion

Bearing children in past times was not without serious health risks for the mother. Family reconstitution data provide the basis for estimating

[17] Bideau, 'Fécondité et mortalité.'

the risk of maternal death associated with childbearing. Results from the sample of German villages included in this study suggest that there was a roughly 1 percent chance of maternal death associated with each confinement. This meant that the average married woman was exposed to an approximately 5 percent cumulative chance of dying as a result of her reproductive activity, before reaching the end of her childbearing span. Moreover, there were many other health risks associated with fertility, in particular infections developing after delivery that did not necessarily end in death. Such complications could well have been far more common than maternal mortality. Thus, while only a small minority of women actually died, perhaps most either experienced complications associated with delivery itself or knew someone who had either experienced such complications or had actually died in the course of childbirth. It is not implausible under such conditions that a substantial proportion of women faced an approaching delivery with some foreboding.[18] Quite possibly, such considerations were one of the factors contributing to a receptivity to family limitation, at least among women, and hence a part of the overall context that led to the fertility transition.

[18] Shorter, *Women's bodies*.

PART III

Family formation

6

Marriage

Given that reproductive activity is generally normatively sanctioned only within marital unions, nuptiality patterns can have important consequences for moderating population growth. This was recognized as such by Malthus, who placed a central importance on marriage as a 'preventive check.'[1] The extent to which delayed and foregone marriage actually contains population growth depends also on the extent that reproductive activity is restricted to marital unions. Thus the level of out-of-wedlock childbearing, and the extent and nature of its links to marriage, are important aspects of the system regulating the formation of reproductive unions within a population. The four chapters constituting this section on family formation examine nuptiality and non-marital reproductive activity as exemplified by the German village populations under study.

On the broadest level of comparison, the most distinguishing feature of demographic behavior in western Europe during the eighteenth and nineteenth centuries was a system of family formation characterized by relatively late entry into marriage for both sexes and significant proportions never marrying. The outlines and implications of this very unusual, perhaps unique, marriage pattern that characterized Europe in the past have been described in an influential essay by Hajnal.[2] Considerable evidence has accumulated since the essay's publication to confirm the general picture of a pattern of late marriage and substantial celibacy persisting for at least several centuries and extending into at least the initial decades of the twentieth century. Thereafter, substantial declines in the age at marriage and increases in the proportions ever marrying occurred throughout western Europe and in overseas areas settled predominantly by Europeans.[3] More

---

[1] Malthus, *Principle of population.*
[2] Hajnal, 'Marriage patterns.'   [3] Hajnal, 'Age and marriage.'

119

recently, the marriage age has again turned upward as part of an apparently wide-ranging transformation of marriage and cohabitation patterns. Links with the historical pattern have become increasingly ambiguous.[4] The origins of this historical pattern remain obscure but clearly predate the eighteenth century and thus the period covered in the present study.[5]

An important extension of Hajnal's original description of the western European marriage pattern has been made by Laslett, and more recently by Hajnal. Both place it within the wider context of a generalized western European family pattern or household formation system which includes as its features not only late age at marriage and substantial proportions never marrying but also a relatively narrow age gap between spouses, with substantial proportions of wives older than husbands, a predominance of nuclear-family households, and the frequent presence in households of unrelated young unmarried adults as 'life cycle' servants (i.e. participants in the institutionalized system through which young people left their parents' homes to be in service in the households of someone else). Thus the western European marriage pattern was an essential part of a broader family system prevailing in the past, which in turn has a number of wide-ranging social, economic, and psychological implications.[6]

As Hajnal also initially observed, the European marriage pattern is consonant with the demographic rates and economic structures distinguishing western Europe from other traditional societies.[7] Much of its significance lies with its unusual flexibility: since the timing of female marriage is not an immediate consequence of reaching physical maturity as it is in a number of traditional societies, and since many women never marry, marriage behavior may be responsive both over time and across communities to social and economic influences in a way that would not otherwise be possible. In this sense the western European marriage pattern may be better described as 'a repertoire of adaptable systems' than as a single pattern.[8]

Not all aspects of the western European family system described above can be suitably studied with family reconstitution data alone.[9] In

---

[4] Festy, 'Marriage.'
[5] Smith, Richard M., 'European marriage patterns.'
[6] Laslett, 'Western family'; Hajnal, 'Household formation systems.'
[7] Hajnal, 'Marriage patterns.'
[8] Wrigley, 'Marriage, fertility and growth,' p. 182. See also Hajnal, 'Household formation systems,' p. 478.
[9] The proportion who ever marry can be indirectly estimated if data on the marital status of persons dying is routinely recorded in the parish records. Under such circumstances, the proportion indicated as single among persons dying over some age after

particular, neither the proportion who ever marry nor household structure can readily be determined with any precision from such data. However, family reconstitution data do permit detailed analyses of other important aspects of nuptiality behavior. This chapter examines age at marriage, the age gap between spouses, and the seasonality of marriage. The following chapter then turns to a consideration of marital dissolution and remarriage, including descriptions of the duration of marital unions, the age at widowhood, and the incidence and timing of remarriage. The last two chapters in this section examine illegitimacy, bridal pregnancy, and prenuptial births, stressing the connections between these phenomena, and marriage patterns. Together, these four chapters present a selective but relatively detailed picture of the family formation system that was a crucial aspect of the context of the demographic transition.

It should be noted that due to the preselection of families for inclusion in this study, these analyses are sometimes based on a more restricted set of families than would have been the case had no preselection been made. However, at least with respect to the mean age at first marriage, there is little reason to expect the results to be biased because of this (see the discussion in Appendix A). Thus family reconstitution data in general, and the data set on which this study is based in particular, can provide useful insights into a number of important aspects of nuptiality in the past and enhance our understanding of the prevailing family system.

Age at marriage

Patterns and trends

As in most of western and northern Europe, entrance into marriage occurred relatively late in Germany during the eighteenth and nineteenth centuries. As is evident from Table 6.1, the ages at first marriage for both men and women in all the sample villages clearly fall within the range of European late marriage. In most cases, men married on the average around 28 or 29 for the two-century period, with the main exception being the Bavarian villages, especially Kreuth, where initial entry into marital unions began at even later ages. On the average, women entered their first marriage two to three years younger than their husbands. Their age at first marriage generally averaged close to 26 during the two-century period. The main excep-

which first marriage rarely occurs can be an approximate measure of permanent celibacy. Such information, however, is not available in the village genealogies on which this study is based.

Table 6.1. Mean age at first marriage for men and women by year of marriage

	1700–49	1750–99	1800–24	1825–49	1850–74	1875–99	1700–1899
Grafenhausen							
men	27.0	27.7	28.0	28.1	28.1	27.6	27.8
women	26.3	25.9	27.1	26.6	25.4	24.4	25.8
Herbolzheim							
men	26.3	26.7	29.2	29.3	29.3	28.0	28.2
women	24.4	24.7	27.1	26.2	27.4	26.1	26.0
Kappel							
men	26.6	27.3	27.0	27.7	28.8	28.3	27.7
women	25.2	25.0	24.8	26.6	26.0	26.1	25.6
Rust							
men	27.1	27.7	27.1	29.4	29.2	27.6	28.1
women	25.5	26.0	26.3	27.2	26.6	25.5	26.1
Öschelbronn							
men	26.4	26.5	27.7	28.9	28.7	28.6	27.8
women	24.6	24.7	25.8	26.7	27.4	26.9	26.0
Anhausen							
men	—	(29.4)	(29.0)	(32.9)	(32.4)	(31.4)	30.8
women	(27.6)	27.3	(27.4)	(30.7)	(30.5)	(27.0)	28.5
Gabelbach							
men	—	(29.1)	(28.0)	(31.6)	(32.2)	(29.8)	30.1
women	(27.9)	(28.8)	(28.7)	(29.8)	(29.7)	26.6	28.5

Kreuth							
men	—	32.5	(34.7)	(37.1)	(35.9)	(35.1)	34.7
women	—	30.5	(32.4)	(32.8)	(31.1)	(30.6)	31.2
Braunsen							
men	(31.5)	28.3	(27.0)	(29.6)	(28.9)	(27.5)	28.7
women	(25.0)	25.8	(25.1)	(26.7)	(26.9)	(23.9)	25.6
Höringhausen							
men	(31.0)	27.7	30.3	31.6	30.3	27.4	29.3
women	26.0	26.9	26.6	28.6	28.2	25.0	26.9
Massenhausen							
men	28.1	27.3	(27.1)	28.7	30.7	(28.3)	28.4
women	26.5	27.7	27.3	26.7	28.4	24.9	27.1
Vasbeck							
men	28.1	26.9	(25.5)	29.3	28.9	(28.3)	27.9
women	26.6	26.2	26.1	26.7	26.3	25.1	26.2
Middels							
men	—	28.9	27.6	29.4	29.6	28.4	28.8
women	(23.7)	22.8	23.4	25.2	24.7	23.5	23.9
Werdum							
men	29.8	29.6	29.2	29.6	29.9	(30.1)	29.6
women	24.3	25.7	25.1	26.8	26.8	(24.4)	25.7
All villages							
men	27.8	28.0	28.3	29.4	29.5	28.3	28.6
women	25.3	25.7	26.2	26.9	26.9	25.5	26.1

Note: Results based on fewer than 20 cases are omitted; results based on 20–49 cases are shown in parentheses.

tions are again the Bavarian villages, especially Kreuth, where women were noticeably older at first marriage, and Middels, where women were somewhat younger. There is no major change in age at marriage during the period, although for both men and women a pattern of gradual increase followed by a sharper decline at the end of the nineteenth century is evident for most villages.[10]

These results for the villages at the end of the nineteenth century are generally consistent with those for Germany as a whole, and indeed for much of Europe, in indicating that nuptiality changes had only a minor impact on the trend in overall fertility at that time and, if anything, were counteracting the emerging pattern of fertility decline rather than contributing to it.[11] Moreover, during the two centuries represented by the present sample of German villages, the moderate changes in the age at marriage for women could have had only a modest impact on fertility (as discussed in Chapter 13). This contrasts considerably with the experience in England, where it has recently been shown that the age at first marriage, as well as proportions ever marrying, fluctuated more substantially and account for considerable variation in the fertility level.[12]

During the nineteenth century, a number of German states enacted, or in some cases re-enacted, legislation restricting marriage, which was later repealed.[13] These laws were passed following the Napoleonic period, when Malthusian ideas were gaining acceptance within educated and influential circles. Concern about overpopulation, the growth of pauperism, and the consequent pressure on public funds for relief, as well as the perception of the poor as posing a potential threat of revolution, underlie the initial enactment of the restrictive legisla-

---

[10] The ages at marriage calculated from family reconstitution data are potentially biased downward for the initial decades following the establishment of parish registers if the age of spouses at marriage must be derived from linking a marriage entry to birth entry. The reason for this is that older persons who marry during this period will have been born prior to the start of the birth register and thus their age will not be known, while younger persons will be more likely to have been born after the start of the register. Since age was often recorded in the death entry and sometimes in the marriage entry, this problem is not severe. Nevertheless, rises in the age at marriage during the first four or five decades following the start of the birth register are potentially artifacts of the bias described. This would affect only those villages where the extant registers begin during the late seventeenth century or later (see Table B.4 in Appendix B). Interestingly, there is no consistent tendency for marked increases in age at marriage to appear in the sample villages, presumably because age was available from information other than the birth registers. Nevertheless, since age at death may not be accurate, some caution is required when interpreting the results.

[11] Knodel, *Decline of fertility*; van de Walle, 'Marriage and marital fertility.'

[12] Wrigley and Schofield, *Population history of England*; Wrigley, 'Marriage, fertility and growth.'

[13] Knodel, 'Law, marriage and illegitimacy'; Matz, *Pauperismus und Bevölkerung.*

tion that started to appear during the third decade of the century. Outside the Prussian territories, the local community rather than the state was usually responsible for granting relief to impoverished residents within its boundaries. Hence, marriage restrictions were frequently imposed through local ordinance rather than through state laws. In addition, in order to prevent an influx of indigent people through migration, many areas legislated regulations limiting the rights of residents of other regions or towns to settle within their territory. Such laws made marriage between persons from different communities difficult and narrowed the range of economic opportunities open to those wanting to establish a family.

Marriage restrictions were not uniform among the different German states nor among the various localities within any particular state. Information on specific laws in the sample of villages included in this study has not been collected. However, marriage restrictions are known to have been imposed generally throughout most of the areas in which the villages are located. Restrictive legislation was widespread in Baden, Württemberg, Bavaria, Hesse–Darmstadt (under whose administration the village of Höringhausen fell) and Hanover (under whose jurisdiction the two Frisian villages were for most of the first two-thirds of the nineteenth century).

A common feature of these restrictive laws was a regulation requiring a couple wishing to marry or settle in the community to produce evidence of having sufficient wealth or property, a secure income, or assured stable employment opportunities, in order to allay doubts about their ability to support their children. In addition, high minimum ages at marriage were sometimes imposed. Thus the impact of these laws would be expected to lead to an increase in the age at marriage. By the second half of the nineteenth century, concern about the high illegitimacy assumed to be resulting from the restrictive marriage legislation, as well as the arbitrariness with which the laws had been applied, led to pressure for their repeal. Moreover, economic conditions had changed and migration to cities, as well as emigration abroad, alleviated some of the pressures in the rural areas. Industrialization was beginning to proceed rapidly and required greater territorial and occupational mobility. Thus, starting in the early 1860s, legislative action weakened restrictions on marriage and on residence establishment. They were dealt a severe blow between 1866 and 1871, when in all states the principal restrictive provisions were repealed or greatly modified.

In order that the course of age at marriage during the nineteenth century in the sample villages can be examined in more detail, the

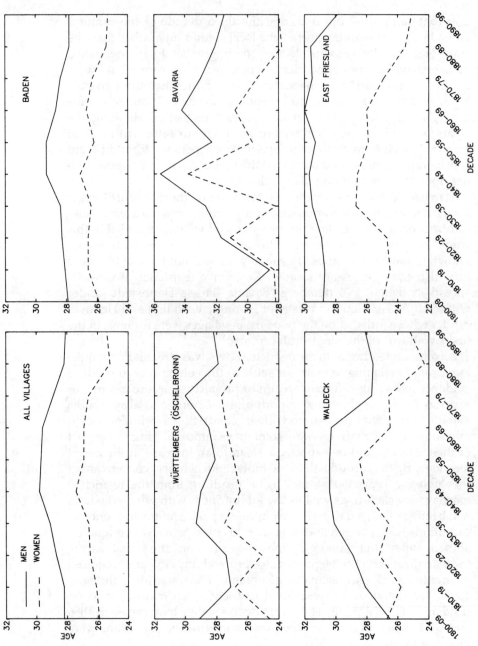

Figure 6.1 Age at first marriage by decade during the nineteenth century for regional groupings of villages

average age at first marriage is shown by decade in Figure 6.1 for regional groupings of villages. Since results for decades are based on relatively small numbers of marriages, some random fluctuation is to be expected. For Öschelbronn and the Bavarian villages, the number of marriages included in the analysis was often below 50 per 10-year period, making them especially vulnerable to this problem. Nevertheless, the results are reasonably clear. For the sample taken as a whole, and indeed for virtually all of the regional groupings, a rise in the age at marriage is evident during the first half of the nineteenth century for both men and women. Moreover, declines in the age at first marriage are generally evident toward the end of the century, with a particularly pronounced decline apparent between the decade of the 1860s and 1870s for men in the Waldeck villages. For the total sample, the extent of change is reasonably commensurate for both men and women although several exceptions are apparent. In particular, in the East Frisian villages, the age at first marriage showed considerably greater change for women than it did for men, both with respect to the increase earlier in the century and the decrease toward the end of the century. In the Waldeck villages, a more pronounced rise in the age at first marriage is evident for men in the first half of the nineteenth century, with a roughly commensurate decline evident for both sexes toward the end of the century, although not precisely at the same time.

Without more precise information on the existence and nature of restrictions in the individual villages, it is not possible to make a conclusive statement about their impact on trends in age at marriage during the nineteenth century. The general pattern of change is reasonably consistent with what would be expected if these laws were influencing the age of marriage. It seems likely that at least part of the trends apparent during the nineteenth century can be attributed to changing legal regulations.

Several measures are presented in Table 6.2 which indicate the distribution of age at first marriage for men and women in the combined sample of all villages. Teenage marriage was always uncommon for men and became virtually non-existent during the nineteenth century. For the overall period, only 1 percent of men married before reaching age 20. Even at its highest level, in the first half of the eighteenth century, less than 3 percent of grooms were under 20. Since women marry at earlier ages than men on the average, teenage marriages were somewhat more common for brides but still involved less than one in ten for the combined eighteenth and nineteenth centuries. A clear trend toward a decline in teenage marriages for women is apparent during the time span covered, with the percentage

Table 6.2. Selected measures of the distribution of age at first marriage by sex and year of marriage

	1700–49	1750–99	1800–24	1825–49	1850–74	1875–99	1700–1899
Men							
% marrying							
under 20	2.5	2.0	1.6	0.1	0.0	0.2	1.0
under 25	34.8	31.1	28.1	18.6	13.9	21.0	23.8
30 or over	26.5	26.9	28.8	35.8	32.7	24.8	29.4
40 or over	4.0	3.5	3.9	4.8	5.7	2.7	4.1
Quartiles							
First	24.0	24.3	24.6	25.8	25.9	25.3	25.0
Median	26.7	26.9	27.2	28.2	28.1	27.3	27.5
Third	30.3	30.3	30.6	31.6	31.4	29.9	30.7
Range (3rd–1st)	6.3	6.0	6.0	5.8	5.5	4.6	5.7
Women							
% marrying							
under 20	13.9	13.3	10.9	6.4	6.1	6.1	9.4
under 25	57.5	54.4	52.2	43.9	45.3	54.0	51.0
30 or over	17.3	19.2	20.3	22.6	23.3	13.7	19.5
40 or over	2.2	3.3	4.6	3.7	4.4	1.8	3.4
Quartiles							
First	21.3	21.5	21.8	22.8	22.7	22.4	22.1
Median	24.1	24.4	24.7	25.6	25.5	24.6	24.8
Third	27.7	28.4	28.7	29.5	29.5	27.3	28.5
Range (3rd–1st)	6.4	6.9	6.9	6.7	6.8	4.9	6.4

Note: Results refer to the combined sample of all villages.

of first marriages for brides occurring at ages under 20 falling by more than half from the already modest level of about 14 percent in the first half of the eighteenth century to less than half of this level by the end of the nineteenth century.

The substantial majority of first marriages for both men and women occurred during their twenties. However, close to 30 percent of men married for the first time at age 30 or over for the combined eighteenth and nineteenth centuries, while for women, approximately a fifth did so. A sharp drop in the percentage of both men and women marrying at age 30 or later is evident toward the end of the nineteenth century, falling to levels considerably below those characteristic of earlier periods. Only small proportions of men and women waited as late as their 40th birthday to initially enter marriage.

These figures, of course, tell us nothing about the proportion who never married, which it is unfortunately not possible to determine from the village genealogies. Even without such data, however, it is clear that the relatively advanced age at first marriage and the underlying distribution of age at marriage meant that for a significant number of women, a rather substantial proportion of their potentially reproductive years was spent prior to entry into a marital union. At the same time, only a small proportion postponed marriage for so long that their chances to bear any children were severely jeopardized (the relationship between childbearing and age at marriage is discussed in detail in Chapter 13).

Trends in the median age at first marriage more or less parallel those for the mean age discussed above. The median shows a modest trend of increase from the first half of the eighteenth century until well into the nineteenth century, followed by a decline of almost a full year between the last two quarters of the nineteenth century. As the information on the proportion of marriages below 20 and above 30 indicates, the sharp decline in the median is due to a reduction of late marriages rather than an increase in very young marriages. Thus only a modest decline is evident in the first quartile in contrast to a substantial decline in the third quartile.

The inter-quartile range is somewhat larger for women than for men throughout the period under observation, and for both sexes shows a substantial contraction during the last half of the nineteenth century. Some changes are evident earlier but are modest in comparison. Thus the age range within which first marriages took place became considerably more concentrated during the last quarter of the nineteenth century, largely as a result of a sharp decline in the third quartile, than at any time since the beginning of the eighteenth century. The sudden-

ness of this shift in the distribution of marriages is particularly pronounced for women. Thus, although the central tendency for age at
marriage was downward toward the end of the nineteenth century, it
resulted largely from a substantial decrease in first marriages occurring
at older ages in conjunction with the absence of any increase in
marriages occurring at particularly young ages.

Socio-economic differentials

The pattern of late marriage that characterized the village populations
as a whole was also true for different socio-economic groups, as is
evident in Table 6.3, which presents age at first marriage according to
the occupational group of the husband. It should be noted that it is not
possible to determine from the village genealogies if the husband was
already practicing the occupation listed at the time of marriage or if he
took up this occupation subsequently. The same uncertainty applies to
the attainment of village leadership status, which is examined in
relation to age at marriage in Table 6.4. Particularly in the case of the
latter, marriage may have occurred first.

Perhaps the most striking feature of the results is the similarity in age
at first marriage across occupational categories, particularly for men.
To the extent that any consistent pattern is apparent, laborers and their
wives appear to have married later than other villagers. This holds true
both for the eighteenth and nineteenth centuries. Wives of laborers are
characterized by later-than-average marriage ages in virtually all the
villages. For men, the only exception is Werdum, where laborers enter
their first marriage at a slightly younger age than is usual for the rest of
the villagers. There is little consistency in the difference in age at first
marriage between men in the farmer category and men in the
predominantly artisan category. A more consistent difference,
however, is apparent for their wives. With the sole exception of the
Bavarian villages, wives of farmers were characterized by an earlier age
at first marriage than wives of men in the artisans' group. Moreover,
without exception, farmers' wives married younger than laborers'
wives. Thus, despite the small magnitude of differences in age at first
marriage associated with the husband's occupation, the nature of
these differences is both consistent across villages and persistent
between the eighteenth and nineteenth centuries for women.

It is generally accepted that the key mechanism underlying the
relatively late age at marriage characteristic of the western European
marriage pattern was the socially imposed link between the ability to
establish an independent household and the ability to earn a livelihood

adequate to support the formation and maintenance of a family.[14] Thus it is notable that men's age at first marriage in our sample of villages appears to be less closely linked to their occupational category than is their wives' age at first marriage. This finding is consistent with observations by Wrigley, based on late nineteenth-century data, that female nuptiality patterns were much more variable than male patterns.[15] Such a finding is intriguing in terms of its implications for understanding the traditional European marriage pattern. Clearly, the wife's age at the start of reproduction is far more crucial than that of the husband's in terms of the impact on the number of children the couple eventually has, especially when deliberate attempts to limit fertility within marriage are largely absent. The actual mechanism through which men's occupations affect their wives' ages at marriage is an important area for further investigation.

The results from the German villages are also interesting in light of the recent discussions of the demographic impact of the proletarianization process that accompanied the transformation of Europe from a peasant to an industrial society.[16] While the arguments linking proletarianization to population growth involve various dynamics, they generally assume that the rural proletariat, defined in this study as including laborers, cottagers, and low or unskilled workers, married earlier than the rest of the population, both because they were relatively freer from the preindustrial social controls which regulated marriage and because their maximum earning capacity was reached at a young age.

Clearly, the results from the present sample of German villages do not conform to this expectation. The later marriage among proletarian husbands and wives may be related to the restrictive marriage legislation during the nineteenth century, since presumably such restrictions most strongly affected those with fewest resources. However, it is notable that the same pattern of later-than-average marriage characterizes proletarian couples marrying during the eighteenth century, when marriage restrictions were probably less pervasive. Moreover, somewhat similar patterns have been found for family reconstitution studies elsewhere in Europe.[17] In addition, an extensive analysis of nuptiality in the Netherlands, based on censuses, shows that agri-

---

[14] Hajnal, 'Marriage patterns'; Hajnal, 'Household formation systems'; Laslett, 'Western family.'

[15] Wrigley, *Industrial growth.*

[16] Tilly, 'Historical study'; and 'European proletariat.'

[17] See, for example, Eriksson and Rogers, *Rural labor,* p. 114; Charbonneau, *Tourouvre-au-Perche,* p. 75; and Winberg, 'Population growth and proletarianization,' p. 177.

Table 6.3. *Mean age at first marriage for men and women by year of marriage and occupational category of husband*

	Men				Women			
	Farmers	Proletarians	Artisans and skilled	All (including unknown)	Farmers	Proletarians	Artisans and skilled	All (including unknown)
Grafenhausen								
1700–99	27.1	28.3	27.4	27.5	25.4	27.2	25.8	26.0
1800–99	27.9	29.3	27.5	28.0	24.9	27.9	26.3	25.8
Herbolzheim								
1700–99	26.3	27.4	26.6	26.6	23.4	25.7	24.3	24.6
1800–99	28.9	29.5	28.6	28.9	25.5	27.7	26.3	26.6
Kappel								
1700–99	26.8	27.6	26.8	27.1	23.8	26.7	24.6	25.0
1800–99	27.6	28.9	27.7	28.0	24.4	28.4	25.2	25.9
Rust								
1700–99	27.1	28.4	26.5	27.6	23.7	27.1	25.3	25.8
1800–99	27.2	30.6	28.1	28.4	24.1	29.3	25.9	26.2
Öschelbronn								
1700–99	25.8	(28.8)	25.6	26.4	23.0	(26.4)	24.6	24.7
1800–99	28.6	29.9	28.2	28.5	25.9	28.1	27.4	26.8

3 Bavarian villages								
1700–99	—	(30.9)	(27.9)	30.1	—	(28.1)	(27.0)	28.5
1800–99	34.2	32.6	31.0	32.4	29.6	30.3	27.2	29.6
4 Waldeck villages								
1700–99	27.3	28.1	28.1	28.1	25.7	27.6	26.7	26.6
1800–99	28.3	29.6	28.8	28.9	25.1	27.6	26.6	26.6
Middels								
1700–99	28.6	29.2	—	29.0	21.7	(24.1)	—	23.0
1800–99	28.6	29.3	(28.3)	28.8	23.8	24.7	(24.0)	24.2
Werdum								
1700–99	30.5	29.2	29.7	29.6	24.0	25.9	25.1	25.3
1800–99	31.1	28.8	29.8	29.6	24.0	26.7	26.5	26.1
All villages								
1700–99	27.6	28.6	27.3	27.9	24.1	26.4	25.3	25.6
1800–99	28.6	29.7	28.5	28.9	25.0	27.7	26.3	26.4

Note: Results in parentheses are based on 20–49 cases; results based on fewer than 20 cases are omitted. Multiple-occupation husbands (with occupations in different groups) and their wives were coded in a separate mixed category not shown, but are included in the results that refer to all husbands or wives.

Table 6.4. *Mean age at first marriage by occupational subcategory of husband, status in village, and regional grouping of villages*

	4 in Baden		1 in Württemberg		3 in Bavaria		4 in Waldeck		2 in East Friesland		All villages	
	Men	Women	Men	Women	Men	Women	Men	Women	Men	Women	Men	Women
Occupational subcategory												
Farmer	27.6	24.6	27.7	25.1	33.8	29.5	28.0	25.3	29.8	23.7	28.3	24.7
Cottager	—	—	—	—	32.7	29.2	28.0	26.0	29.3	25.4	29.8	26.3
Day laborer	30.0	28.5	(29.0)	(28.7)	(33.3)	(32.9)	30.8	28.1	28.8	26.6	29.9	28.1
Other unskilled	28.6	26.9	(31.8)	(27.2)	(34.2)	(30.7)	28.8	28.4	28.3	25.5	29.2	27.5
Sailor	—	—	—	—	—	—	—	—	29.3	24.7	29.3	24.7
Weaver	28.2	27.1	28.3	27.2	(28.7)	(28.7)	—	—	(28.4)	(27.1)	28.2	27.2
Other home industry	28.5	27.3	—	—	—	—	—	—	—	—	28.8	27.4
Artisan	28.0	26.2	27.4	26.9	29.6	27.5	28.1	26.8	29.8	26.8	28.2	26.5
Fisherman	26.3	24.7	—	—	—	—	—	—	—	—	26.3	24.7
Businessman	27.7	25.1	(26.5)	25.0	(31.7)	(25.4)	(29.3)	(25.8)	29.0	23.5	28.0	25.0
Professional	29.4	24.8	(29.1)	(27.2)	—	—	(31.6)	(26.1)	(29.6)	(25.2)	29.9	25.6
Farmer–artisan, etc.	26.4	24.6	(26.0)	(25.4)	—	—	—	—	(27.7)	(23.0)	26.7	24.6
Farmer–proletarian	27.7	25.9	(28.1)	(24.9)	—	—	(26.9)	(23.3)	(28.2)	(24.0)	27.8	25.5
Proletarian–artisan, etc.	28.2	25.7	(27.2)	(26.4)	(32.5)	(31.1)	(29.9)	(28.1)	29.6	24.7	29.2	26.5
Other	—	—	—	—	—	—	28.4	26.8	—	—	29.1	26.6
Unknown	28.8	27.6	(27.2)	24.7	30.6	30.0	28.8	26.9	28.9	25.7	28.9	27.3
All subcategories	28.0	25.9	27.8	26.0	31.8	29.2	28.6	26.6	29.3	25.1	28.6	26.1
Status in village												
Village leader	25.8	23.4	25.8	25.1	—	—	27.8	24.3	28.4	23.8	26.8	24.1
Non-leader	28.1	26.0	28.1	26.2	31.8	29.3	28.7	26.7	29.4	25.1	28.7	26.2

Note: Results in parentheses are based on 20–49 cases; results based on fewer than 20 cases are omitted.

cultural laborers were distinctly less likely to marry at all than other major occupational groups in the nineteenth century.[18]

A more detailed examination of occupational differentials in age at first marriage is provided in Table 6.4, which indicates results for each of the occupational subcategories, as well as the status of the husband in the village in terms of village leadership, for the regional groupings of villages. With regard to the issue of proletarianization and age at marriage, the results for day laborers and their wives are particularly interesting since they epitomize the rural proletariat more than any other subcategory. For all regional groupings, wives of day laborers are characterized by an above-average age at first marriage and, with the sole exception of the East Frisian villages, men who are day laborers enter into marriage later than average. However, although the number of cases is often small, those day laborers who are also indicated in the genealogies as farmers (the farmer–proletarian subcategory), as well as their wives, do not marry particularly late. Interestingly, men who were or eventually became village leaders, and their wives, who presumably are at the higher end of the social-status spectrum in villages, marry at younger-than-average ages in every regional grouping where there are sufficient cases for comparison. Indeed, the contrast between leaders and non-leaders is sharper than between most occupational categories. In general, the extent of differentials across occupational subcategories is not very pronounced.

If it can be assumed that proletarian status, particularly that of a day laborer, is associated with a lack of wealth and economic security and that, in contrast, village leaders are predominantly recruited from those families which are in an economically more favorable position, the later-than-average age at marriage of spouses in the former category and the earlier age at marriage of those in the latter category may be interpretable in those terms. If the basis norm that a marital union should only be entered into when the prospects for being able to sustain a family appeared reasonable was more or less followed by all strata of society, persons in less favorable economic positions might have needed to delay marriage longer in order to accumulate sufficient savings, broadly defined in terms of the goods necessary to maintain a household. Since the wife brings such savings with her to the marriage, proletarian men may opt for women who are older, given that such women would have had a longer time to acquire these savings. Couples composed of husbands or wives from more advantaged economic backgrounds would be under less constraint in these

---

[18] Frinking and van Poppel, *Sociaal-demographische analyse.*

respects, especially if the wife is provided with a relatively decent dowry, or the husband is assured of inheriting sufficient wealth or a relatively secure source of livelihood, such as the family farm, or a share of it, or a craft shop or other business.

Hajnal has recently made a similar argument, linking the later age at marriage of laborers' wives compared to farmers' wives to longer periods of service prior to marriage. He suggests that savings accumulated by a woman during service were probably often a substantial contribution to the economic basis of her subsequent marriage and that future wives of laborers would have needed a longer period of service to accumulate the necessary savings.[19] It can be argued that, although proletarians may reach their maximum earning-power relatively early, their capacity to earn is nevertheless low. Savings would thus be harder to accumulate, especially for women, if they received lower wages. Where payment was partially in terms of room and board or in kind, saving would be all the harder. Clearly, the issue of the effect of the increasing proletarianization of the rural population needs further investigation. In all likelihood, the results will point to a more complex situation than initially anticipated.

In sum, the data on age at first marriage for the sample villages suggest that changes in nuptiality over the eighteenth and nineteenth centuries were fairly minor and thus cannot have had much impact either on trends in overall fertility for the village populations as a whole, or on fertility differentials among the major occupational subgroups. Differences across regional groupings of villages, however, are considerably larger and must be incorporated into any adequate comparison of regional contrasts in demographic regimes. Data from the village genealogies shed no light on changes in proportions married, an aspect of nuptiality which could potentially change independently of age at marriage. Census data are available for the latter part of the nineteenth century and indicate that for that part of the period under study the proportion of the population remaining permanently single was relatively stable on the national and provincial level, averaging slightly under 10 percent for men and slightly over 10 percent for women for the country as a whole.[20] Thus, with respect to the onset of the fertility transition during the nineteenth century, changes in the nuptiality component of overall fertility either played little part or operated in a direction counteracting the decline in fertility.

---

[19] Hajnal, 'Household formation systems,' p. 475.
[20] Knodel, *Decline of fertility*; Knodel and Maynes, 'Marriage patterns.'

Age differences between spouses

Not only is the age at which men and women marry of demographic and social importance, but so is the average difference between the ages of husbands and wives. In most traditional and in many modern societies, increased age carries with it increased authority, at least within much of the life span. Thus the age gap between husband and wife carries with it implications concerning familial authority. When husbands are typically much older than their wives, women are more likely to be in a more subservient position than in situations where husbands and wives are approximately equal in age or where the wife is senior to her husband. The age difference between spouses also has several important demographic implications. Not only is it a factor in determining the probability of widowhood at any given age, thus affecting the chances that a woman will complete her reproductive span within an intact marital union, but the husband's age may also have an independent impact on marital fertility rates (see Chapter 13).

The predominance of a late average age at marriage for both men and women in Europe during the last several centuries implies as a corollary that the age gap between spouses was relatively small. Laslett has stipulated that one of the distinctive features of the Western family pattern is that the age gap between spouses was minimal on average and that a substantial proportion of wives were older than their husbands.[21] It is already evident from Table 6.1 that the difference in the mean age at first marriage between men and women was of the order of a couple of years. Here the age differences between spouses is examined in some detail. Unlike the preceding analysis of age at marriage, the results presented here apply only to those couples for which both the husband's and wife's ages at marriage were known. In general, both first marriages and remarriages are considered.[22]

Patterns and trends

Table 6.5 presents the mean age difference between spouses as well as the percent distribution of age differences according to the year of marriage and also according to the regional location of the village. For the sample as a whole, the average age gap between spouses was not quite four years. Had this calculation been limited to primary marriages, that is those involving the first marriage of both husband and wife, the average age difference between spouses would be 3.2 years.

[21] Laslett, 'Western family.'
[22] In these instances, persons who remarry are therefore represented more than once in the calculations.

Table 6.5. *Mean age differences between husband and wife and percent distribution of age differences, by year of marriage and by regional grouping of villages*

	Mean age difference	Standard deviation	Difference between husband's and wife's ages (% distribution across)						
				Wife older by		Less than 1 year difference	Husband older by		
			Total	5+ years	1–4 years		1–4 years	5–9 years	10+ years
Year of marriage									
1700–49	4.2	8.6	100	10.4	9.4	18.9	19.1	22.2	20.0
1750–99	3.7	8.0	100	10.9	9.3	22.0	18.4	20.8	18.6
1800–49	3.9	7.4	100	8.3	8.9	23.2	20.9	22.5	16.2
1850–99	4.1	6.4	100	5.1	6.2	26.1	26.0	23.0	13.6
Regional location of village									
4 in Baden	3.9	7.3	100	7.4	7.4	24.9	24.2	21.4	14.7
Öschelbronn (Württemberg)	3.1	6.7	100	6.9	11.9	25.4	24.3	19.6	11.9
3 in Bavaria	3.9	7.7	100	10.7	7.9	22.7	17.6	22.7	18.4
4 in Waldeck	3.7	7.4	100	9.9	9.3	22.6	19.4	20.9	17.8
2 in East Friesland	4.8	7.3	100	7.3	7.3	19.9	18.6	26.9	20.0
All villages	3.9	7.3	100	8.0	8.1	23.5	22.0	22.3	16.2

This is approximately a year longer than the average age gap for primary marriages characterizing a sample of 13 English villages during the seventeenth and eighteenth centuries.[23]

For the sample of German villages, there is little change over time evident in the mean age difference between spouses, which is almost identical in the first half of the eighteenth century and the second half of the nineteenth century. The lack of trend in the mean age difference, however, masks a substantial shift in the distribution of age differentials between spouses. The proportion of marriages in which the husband was 10 or more years older than his wife declined substantially as did the proportion of marriages in which the wife was older than the husband by any amount. A substantial increase is apparent in the proportion of marriages in which the husband and wife were approximately the same age, that is where there is less than one year's difference, and where the husband is older than the wife by no more than four years.

The shift in the distribution of age differences is related to some extent to the increasing proportion of all marriages that involved first marriages for both the husband and wife (primary marriages), a topic which is examined further below. This accounts for only a modest share of the observed change, however, and similar shifts in distribution are evident when consideration is limited to primary marriages. For example, the mean age gap between husbands and wives in mutual first marriages shows no consistent trend, falling from 3.5 to 3.0 years between the first and second halves of the eighteenth century and increasing to 3.2 years by the latter half of the nineteenth century. At the same time, the share of primary marriages involving spouses whose ages differed by less than one year in either direction steadily increased from 24 percent to 29 percent. Thus, despite the lack of any substantial change in mean age difference between spouses, a higher proportion of marriages over the time span examined involved couples in which the husband and wife were relatively close in age.

In Table 6.5, husbands and wives who differ by less than one year have been grouped together. If, for the entire sample, we separate out from this group those in which the wife was older and combine it with the proportion of marriages in which the wife was more than one year older than the husband, approximately one-quarter of marriages during the entire time span are found to involve marriages in which the wife was senior to the husband. There was some decline in this figure during the time period involved, with the proportion of marriages in

---

[23] Wrigley and Schofield, 'Population history from family reconstitution.'

which the wife was older than the husband approaching 30 percent during the eighteenth century but falling to only slightly more than 20 percent during the last half of the nineteenth century.

Wrigley and Schofield, in their study of 13 English parishes during the seventeenth and eighteenth centuries, also find a trend toward greater equality in the ages of spouses in primary marriages and a substantial decline in both extremes of the distribution, as well as a decline in the proportion of primary marriages in which the wife is older than the husband.[24] In reviewing evidence from a number of scattered European studies, Shorter finds a similar pattern for the eighteenth and nineteenth centuries.[25]

Shorter interprets the trend toward closer equality of the ages of spouses and the decline in the proportion of marriages involving brides senior to their grooms as indicative of a shift away from instrumental considerations and toward emotional ones as determinants of the choice of a marriage partner. He argues that during this period economic considerations were of primary importance, and older women were attractive as mates because of the greater savings they would have accumulated and the greater experience they would have acquired in matters important for running a household within the context of a predominantly family economy. In addition, they would have fewer fecund years ahead to bear children, an advantage when contraception is minimal. As romantic love became more important as a basis for mate selection and companionate marriage became the more dominant model, and as techniques of family limitation diffused, such considerations would have acquired less importance and compatibility more importance, a trend that would lead to greater equality in the ages of partners.

In a similar vein, Phayer interprets the more frequent occurrence of a large age gap between a younger wife and an older husband during earlier times as a sign that familial economic considerations predominated over affective relationships in the choice of a partner.[26] The German village data clearly confirm the trend toward greater equality in ages of spouses detected elsewhere in Europe, although this in itself does not indicate that romantic love became a more important basis of mate selection.

Regional differences in the age gap between spouses are not very pronounced. Almost identical mean age differences characterize the Baden, Bavarian, and Waldeck villages. Only the two East Frisian villages show a distinctly larger age gap, and the village of Öschel-

---

[24] *Ibid.*   [25] Shorter, *Modern family*, Appendix III.
[26] Phayer, *Sexual liberation and religion*, pp. 15–16.

bronn in Württemberg shows a somewhat smaller age gap than the total sample. The close agreement in the mean age difference for several of the regional groupings of villages, however, does not imply a similar distribution of age differences. The three Bavarian villages are characterized by a higher proportion of marriages with age differences at extreme levels in both directions. The two East Frisian villages differ particularly with respect to the proportion of marriages in which the husband is substantially older than the wife rather than a lack of marriages in which the wife is older than the husband.

Socio-economic differentials

Hochstadt has pointed out that most studies show a considerably larger age difference between spouses in the nineteenth century for upper- and middle-class families than they do for the lower classes.[27] The social mechanisms determining age at marriage undoubtedly differ by class origin of the marriage partners. For the well-to-do classes, where going into service was not part of the normal life cycle, there may have been more interest in marrying a daughter earlier in order to relieve themselves of the burden of support. At the same time, interest would focus on husbands who had already shown suitability through financial success or following a period of educational preparation. Moreover, richer husbands would be able to afford to marry younger wives, whereas poorer males might need to choose women who had accumulated sufficient savings during longer periods in service.

The mean age difference between spouses is indicated in Table 6.6 by occupational group, occupational subcategory, and village leadership status, for the different regional groupings of villages. Given that the sample deals largely with rural village populations, few if any marriage partners were from the privileged classes to which Hochstadt refers. Nevertheless, we might expect to find some differential in age difference between spouses according to occupation and status within the village. For the sample as a whole, the smallest age difference between spouses is indeed found for the proletarian grouping of occupations, although this is not consistently true for each regional grouping. The largest age gap is found for the professional subcategory for the sample as a whole and this appears to be reasonably consistent across regional groupings. Likewise, couples in which the husband attains village leadership status are characterized generally by a larger age gap than other couples. Thus, to some extent, couples in

[27] Hochstadt, 'Demography and feminism.'

Table 6.6. *Mean age difference between husband and wife by occupational group, occupational subcategory, status in village, and regional grouping of villages*

	4 in Baden	1 in Württemberg	3 in Bavaria	4 in Waldeck	2 in East Friesland	All villages
Occupational group						
Farmers	4.3	3.6	5.4	4.5	6.8	4.8
Proletarians	3.0	3.0	3.5	3.5	3.9	3.4
Artisans and skilled	4.0	2.5	4.2	3.8	4.3	3.9
Mixed, other, unknown	3.9	3.6	3.4	3.2	4.4	3.7
Occupational subcategory						
Farmer	4.3	3.6	5.4	4.5	6.8	4.8
Cottager	—	—	3.3	4.4	4.3	4.1
Day laborer	3.0	(1.1)	(3.1)	4.1	3.3	3.2
Other unskilled	2.5	(4.8)	(7.1)	2.2	2.0	2.8
Sailor	—	—	—	—	5.7	5.7
Weaver	3.1	3.0	(2.0)	—	(2.8)	3.0
Other home industry	3.3	—	—	—	—	3.0
Artisan	3.7	2.2	3.1	3.3	3.4	3.4
Fisherman	3.1	—	—	—	—	3.1
Businessman	4.9	2.4	(7.1)	(3.1)	5.9	4.9
Professional	5.9	(4.8)	—	(8.3)	(5.3)	6.0
Farmer–artisan, etc.	3.6	(4.4)	—	—	(6.4)	4.1
Farmer–proletarian	3.6	(3.3)	—	(3.1)	(3.5)	3.5
Proletarian–artisan, etc.	4.3	(3.1)	(2.9)	(2.4)	4.5	3.9
Other	—	—	—	1.8	—	3.0
Unknown	4.8	4.0	2.9	3.6	3.4	3.7
Status in village						
Village leader	4.8	3.0	—	5.9	6.2	4.8
Non-leader	3.8	3.2	3.9	3.6	4.7	3.9
All couples	3.9	3.1	3.9	3.7	4.8	3.9

Table 6.7. *Mean age difference between husband and wife by age of wife at marriage and village*

	Age of wife at marriage					
	Under 20	20–24	25–29	30–34	35–39	40–49
Grafenhausen	8.0	5.2	2.9	1.5	−0.9	0.8
Herbolzheim	8.0	5.5	3.3	1.1	2.7	0.1
Kappel	7.6	5.4	2.6	0.8	1.3	(−5.5)
Rust	7.4	5.3	3.2	1.2	−0.5	1.6
Öschelbronn	6.9	5.1	2.0	−0.4	(−0.6)	(0.4)
3 Bavarian villages	—	7.0	4.7	1.6	1.3	0.1
4 Waldeck villages	8.5	5.5	2.7	1.2	0.0	0.0
Middels	10.1	6.3	3.4	(−0.1)	(−1.4)	—
Werdum	9.8	6.7	3.6	2.0	0.2	−1.3
All villages	8.4	5.6	3.1	1.2	0.5	−0.2

Note: Results based on 20–49 cases are shown in parentheses; results based on fewer than 20 cases are omitted.

which the husband is presumably of higher status do show a tendency toward a larger age difference between spouses, while couples from the poorer strata appear to show the smallest difference.

Since entry into marital unions occurs within a reasonably clearly specified range of ages, husbands who marry toward the lower end of this range necessarily marry women who are of the same age or who are older, while women who marry at the young end of the acceptable age range can only marry husbands who are of the same age or older. Thus the age difference between spouses will be associated with the age at which either sex marries. For the purpose of fertility analysis, it is of some interest that the age gap between spouses shows a clear relationship with the age of the wife at marriage. The younger the age of the wife at marriage, the older her husband tends to be relative to herself, and thus the larger the age gap. This is shown in Table 6.7 for the sample villages.

Both for the sample as a whole and for each village, women who married young tended to marry men considerably older, while women who married at older ages tended to marry husbands of similar or even younger age. This has potential implications for understanding age-specific fertility since for any given age of wife, husbands of women who marry young tend to be older than husbands who marry at more advanced ages. If the fertility of women at a given age declines with the age of the husband, this will affect the association between age at marriage and marital fertility, as examined in Chapter 13.

Seasonality of marriage

In many populations, there are preferred times of the year for marriages to take place and other times that are judged to be less desirable. Such preferences may coincide with the religious calendar and, in predominantly agricultural populations, may be related to the annual agricultural work cycle. Unlike the timing of births, especially in a population where little birth control is practiced, or of deaths, the timing of marriage is more directly under the voluntary control of the couple involved. Thus the degree and patterns of seasonality of marriage and their determinants can differ considerably from those of births and deaths. In particular, the seasonality of marriage is more likely to reflect explicit preferences than is true for the other two vital events.

In order to indicate monthly variations in the number of marriages, absolute monthly totals of the number of marriages have been converted to index figures where 100 indicates that the number occurring in the month in question is the number to be expected if marriages were evenly distributed throughout the year, taking the number of days in each month into account. Values above 100 indicate that a disproportionately high number of marriages take place in that particular month, while values below 100 indicate that disproportionately fewer marriages take place. The results are shown in Figure 6.2 for the regional groupings of villages in the sample. For all regions, considerable seasonal variation in marriages is apparent. While some common features are evident for all regions, there are also considerable differences. Thus there does not appear to be a national pattern of seasonal preferences for nuptiality that characterizes all areas of Germany.[28]

The one feature common to all regions is a relative deficit in the number of marriages during the month of March. This undoubtedly corresponds to a tendency to avoid marriage during the period of Lent. Since the ecclesiastical calendar does not coincide precisely with the secular calendar, and since seasonal variation is being represented by the latter, the extent of avoidance of marriage during Lent is probably even more pronounced than is indicated in these results. There also appears to be a common tendency for a disproportionate number of marriages to take place shortly following Lent, although the extent varies from region to region. In several of the regions, a disproportion-

---

[28] Examination of the seasonal patterns of marriages at the individual village level reveals close similarity in patterns among villages in the same region, thus justifying consideration of seasonality based on regional groupings of villages.

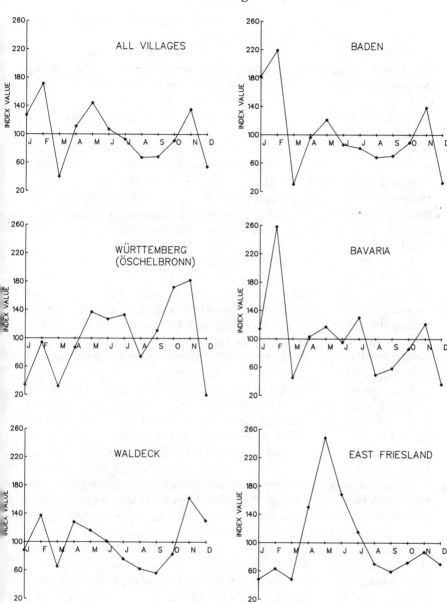

Figure 6.2. *Index values of monthly variations in marriages by regional groupings of villages*

ate number of marriages take place in February, perhaps in anticipation of the avoidance of marriages during Lent.

Another relatively common feature of the seasonal pattern of marriages is the disproportionately low frequency of marriage during the months of August and September, presumably the busiest period of the agricultural year, when harvesting is taking place. Again, this is followed in most areas by a disproportionately high number of marriages in the month of November, with again a disproportionately low frequency in the month of December, perhaps in relation to an avoidance of marriage during Advent. Avoidance of marriage during Lent and Advent was usual in much of Europe. Moreover, seasonal patterns of marriage in northwest Europe share a basic common structure reflecting the changing seasonal demand for labor in agriculture, with a trough in marriages typically evident during the summer.[29]

There are some noticeable regional variations in Germany in the seasonal pattern of marriage, indicating that further examination of this phenomenon should be done at the regional rather than at the national level. It is notable that there is only an imperfect agreement in seasonal marriage patterns according to the religious affiliation of the villages in the sample; while the two Catholic regional groupings – Baden and Bavaria – show considerable similarity, the three Protestant groupings differ considerably from each other.

A convenient way to summarize the extent of the seasonality of marriage is to calculate the average monthly absolute deviation from 100 of the index values described above. In other words, for each month the absolute difference between 100 and the actual index value is taken and then averaged over all 12 months. By taking into consideration absolute values rather than the direction of the difference, we avoid negative and positive values cancelling each other out. The result can be considered as the index of the extent of seasonality of marriage and is referred to as such. One problem with this index, and indeed with calculating index values as previously described, is that the extent of relative monthly fluctuation is sensitive to the total number of events being considered. In populations with small numbers of marriages, there is likely to be greater monthly variation simply because of random chance. Thus caution is called for when examining seasonal fluctuations based on index values of either type when the number of cases is small.

The index of the extent of seasonality of marriage is shown in Table 6.8 for the regional groupings of villages according to year of marriage,

---

[29] Wrigley and Schofield, *Population history of England*, pp. 298–303.

Table 6.8. *Index of extent of seasonality of marriage by regional grouping of villages and by year of marriage, by marriage order and by months to first birth*

	4 in Baden	1 in Württemberg	3 in Bavaria	4 in Waldeck	2 in East Friesland	All villages
All marriages	42.3	43.4	39.5	28.7	47.0	31.8
Year of marriage						
1700–49	53.3	78.8	(35.5)	37.8	47.3	39.3
1750–99	58.7	52.1	59.0	28.7	46.9	38.5
1800–49	35.5	56.8	41.9	26.0	53.2	30.5
1850–99	39.5	28.8	38.6	29.5	54.0	29.7
Marriage order						
Primary	45.3	44.2	45.6	30.7	49.3	32.9
Non-primary	35.3	49.2	32.3	22.6	38.7	29.6
Months to first birth[a]						
No birth before 9 months[b]	47.0	46.2	40.2	28.4	54.0	35.8
First birth in 7–8 months	51.2	(55.2)	—	46.2	57.1	37.8
First birth in 0–6 months	28.8	37.8	(31.8)	25.7	22.8	20.6
First birth illegitimate	23.5	(45.9)	(51.8)	31.7	—	22.8

Note: For an explanation of the method of calculation, see the text. Results in parentheses are based on 50–99 cases. Results based on fewer than 50 cases are omitted.
[a] Births to either spouse in previous marriages or illegitimate unions are ignored.
[b] Including childless couples.

marriage order, and months to first birth. As can be seen, the extent of seasonal variation in the number of marriages does vary to some extent by region, with seasonality being least pronounced in the four Waldeck villages, and most pronounced in the two East Frisian villages. It is worth noting that the index of seasonality for all villages combined is relatively low because of the partial balancing effect of differences in the seasonal patterns in the different regional groupings. Thus results for the total sample combined are not a good indication of what is happening in the individual regional groupings.

For most regional groupings, some decline in the extent of seasonality is apparent during the period under observation. The main exceptions are the East Frisian villages, where, if anything, seasonality increases slightly between the eighteenth and nineteenth centuries. The timing of the reduction in seasonality among the remaining regional groupings, however, is not uniform. For the four Baden villages, the main difference appears to be between the eighteenth and nineteenth centuries. In the Württemberg village, a sharp decline occurs both between the first and second halves of the eighteenth century and then again between the first and second halves of the nineteenth century. In the Waldeck villages, a reduction is apparent only between the first and second halves of the eighteenth century. The Bavarian villages show the lowest seasonality during the first half of the eighteenth century and the highest in the second half, with a consistent decline thereafter. Given the small number of cases on which the data for the first half of the eighteenth century are based, however, the apparent rise in seasonality of marriage between the first and second half of the eighteenth century in that regional grouping may not be reliable.

Given the fact that the timing of marriage is largely a matter of deliberate choice, the extent to which marriage is concentrated in the customarily preferred months and avoided in months considered to be less appropriate should vary with the extent of pressure under which the couple marries. For example, when there is a more urgent economic need to marry for a given couple, the pressure to marry would probably be greater and less consideration would be given to following the prevailing customs concerning the most appropriate season to wed. Thus marriages in which at least one of the couple is remarrying should conform less to the preferred seasonal pattern than would primary marriages. Presumably the partner who would be remarrying might be under considerable economic pressure to re-establish a conjugal unit so as to effectively function socially and economically within the community. Hence, in general, the extent of seasonality of primary marriages would be expected to be greater than for non-primary unions (i.e. ones in which at least one spouse is remarrying), assuming there is no great influence of any seasonal pattern of deaths on the latter. This is indeed the case for all regional groupings of villages, with the sole exception of Öschelbronn, the one Württemberg village, and is thus consistent with the presumption that remarriages are more a matter of urgency than primary marriages.

Another situation in which some unusual urgency may be felt to marry is the one in which the bride has become prenuptially pregnant. Presumably in some of these cases, the desire to legitimize the union would predominate over desires to avoid marriage during particular seasons or to marry during the preferred times of year. In Table 6.8, several different situations are distinguished. The first represents marriages in which no birth occurred prior to nine months after marriage and thus represents situations in which a pregnancy or birth did not antedate the decision to marry. The second represents cases in which the first birth occurred within seven or eight months following marriage. This situation presumably includes mainly cases in which the bride was premaritally pregnant but the couple was probably unaware or uncertain of this at the time of the wedding, given the pregnancy's short duration. Therefore they would be unlikely to have advanced the date of the wedding in response to the pregnancy. Little difference would thus be expected in the extent and pattern of seasonality between these two categories.[30]

In contrast, most couples who experienced their first birth within the first six months of marriage were almost certainly aware of the fact of a prenuptial conception. This may have prompted them to decide to marry even if the time of year was not ideal. Indeed, for all regional groupings of villages for which sufficient cases are available, the extent of seasonality of this third category is less than for the first two categories. There is a substantially smaller number of marriages in which the first birth occurred during the seventh and eighth month compared to those for which no prenuptially conceived birth occurred. Thus it is not surprising that the index of the extent of seasonality is frequently somewhat higher for the second than for the first category. But given the smaller number of cases in the third category compared to the first, it is particularly striking that such marriages are consistently characterized by a lower index value than marriages not involving a prenuptial conception.[31]

---

[30] Wrigley, 'Marriage, fertility and growth.'

[31] For the sample as a whole, the number of marriages in which the first birth occurred in the seventh or eighth month was only 12 percent as great, and the number with a first birth within zero to six months of marriage was only about one-fifth as great, as in the case of marriages not involving a prenuptial conception or birth.

A fourth category, involving marriages of couples who had an illegitimate birth prior to marriage, is more difficult to interpret since it is not easy to judge how much pressure they felt to marry in order to legitimate the child. Presumably this group is self-selected with respect to sensitivity to such matters, since by definition they resisted or were otherwise prevented from marrying during the wife's initial pregnancy. It is interesting that they are not characterized by a consistently different degree of seasonality compared to the other groups. Instead, their relative position varies with the regional grouping of the villages.

The extent of seasonality, of course, does not automatically imply similarity in the seasonal pattern itself. In order to summarize the extent of similarity in the monthly pattern, another index can be calculated in the following manner. First, monthly index values can be calculated separately for each of the four categories of marriage such that a value of 100 indicates that the number occurring in the month in question was the number to be expected if marriages were evenly distributed throughout the year (i.e. the same calculation as is shown in Figure 6.2). Then for each month the absolute difference in the value of this index for each of the second through fourth categories respectively and the value for the first category (no prenuptial conception or birth) can be calculated, summed, and averaged. The resulting values, shown in Table 6.9, express the average absolute difference and thus the degree of similarity in seasonal pattern.

The seasonal pattern of marriages in which the first birth occurred seven or eight months after marriage should more closely resemble marriages not involving a prenuptial pregnancy than marriages in which the first birth occurred zero to six months after marriage. This expected result is apparent for the Baden and East Frisian villages but not for Öschelbronn in Württemberg or the four Waldeck villages taken as a group (insufficient cases are available for the Bavarian villages to make this comparison). Moreover, in the Waldeck villages, marriages of couples who already had an illegitimate birth show a more similar seasonal pattern to marriages with no prenuptial pregnancy than either of the other two categories. These results then suggest that in addition to the different seasonality of marriages in the different regions, the nature and the social significance of the seasonal pattern may also differ.

In sum, the results presented in this chapter place German village populations squarely within the distinctive late-marrying pattern that characterized western Europe in the past. At the same time, the considerable differences apparent among the regional groupings of

Table 6.9. *Index of similarity in the monthly pattern of marriages between couples for which no birth occurred before nine months of marriage and couples which experienced a birth prior to nine months of marriage, according to number of months to first birth and regional grouping of villages*

	4 in Baden	1 in Württemberg	3 in Bavaria	4 in Waldeck	2 in East Friesland	All villages
First birth in 7–8 months	9.0	(27.3)	—	28.8	16.3	10.3
First birth in 0–6 months	27.8	11.5	(30.3)	16.6	31.8	20.7
First birth illegitimate	29.8	(33.6)	(30.9)	14.1	—	21.1

Note: For an explanation of the calculations, see the text. Results in parentheses indicate that the category being compared to marriages of non-prenuptially pregnant brides is based on 50–99 cases; results based on fewer than 50 cases are omitted.

villages underscore the point that the system was far from fixed and uniform, but notable rather for its flexibility and adaptability.

Many marriages in the sample villages involved couples in which there was only a relatively small gap between the ages of the bride and groom. In addition, it was not unusual for the wife to be older than her husband, even if such marriages were in the minority. Thus the observed age differences between spouses were consistent with the pattern that Laslett and others have stressed as another important feature of European nuptiality in the past.[32]

Seasonal variations in the number of marriages taking place were pronounced in all the sample villages although the specific pattern differed among the regional groupings. Clearly the timing of marriage was responsive to customary preferences within the community about the appropriate time during the year to wed. This seasonality reflects the fact that marriages were under a type of volition control that was largely lacking for births and deaths. In this sense, it is consistent with the view that, prior to the widespread practice of family limitation within marriage, nuptiality was the primary aspect of the demographic system through which demographic behavior could be regulated. Even if the effect of late marriage on eventual family size was not consciously considered by the individual couple when deciding on when to marry, the impact was to keep their reproductive potential, and the community's natural increase, in check.

[32] Laslett, 'Western family.'

7

Marital dissolution and remarriage

Most historical investigations of nuptiality in western Europe have focused on the relatively late entry into first marriage for both sexes and the substantial proportions never married that were typical in the past. Far less attention has been paid to the patterns of marital dissolution and remarriage that were characteristic of the prevailing socio-economic and demographic systems, despite their potential significance for the individuals and societies involved.[1]

The studies of historical patterns and trends of remarriage in Europe that have been done are usually based on data on the distribution of marriages according to the marriage order of the spouses. Results have typically revealed a substantial decline in the proportionate share of marriages involving people remarrying, and a concomitant growth in the proportion of primary marriages (those between never-married men and women). In their analysis of English trends, for example, Schofield and Wrigley argue that while 25–30 percent of those marrying in the sixteenth century were remarrying, this proportion had declined to only 10 percent by the nineteenth century.[2] Data from local family reconstitution studies in France, including those by Cabourdin and Bideau, confirm the existence of a trend, from the sixteenth to the nineteenth century, toward a decreasing proportion of remarriages.[3]

There has been considerably less work done on the actual probabilities and rates of remarriage.[4] In their history of the European family, Mitterauer and Sieder assume that the probability of remarriage underwent a 'continuous' decline over the last two centuries, although

---

[1] Baulant, 'The scattered family'; Smith, 'European marriage patterns'; Bideau, 'Widowhood and remarriage.'
[2] Schofield and Wrigley, 'Infant and child mortality,' p. 212.
[3] Cabourdin, 'Le remariage' and 'Le remariage sous l'Ancien Régime'; Bideau, 'Widowhood and remarriage,' p. 29.
[4] Compare with Livi-Bacci, *Portuguese fertility*; Dyrvik, 'Trait du remariage.'

they provide no supporting evidence.[5] In fact, the finding that remarriages became a progressively smaller proportion of total marriages does not necessarily imply that individual probabilities of remarriage also declined. If widows and widowers constituted a smaller proportion of European populations in the nineteenth century compared to those of earlier centuries, individual probabilities of remarriage could have remained unchanged, or even have increased, despite the decline in the proportion of remarriages.

This chapter examines the related phenomena of marital dissolution and remarriage, including the incidence of remarriage and probabilities of remarriage, based on the experience of the sample of German village populations under study. The results provide compelling evidence for a secular decline in the tendency to remarry. The data also show that probabilities of remarriage were inversely associated with age and number of children; and that women were far less likely to remarry than men. No clear differences in either the probability of remarriage or its tendency to decline over time is evident among major occupational groups.

Marital dissolution

In German villages during the eighteenth and nineteenth centuries, almost all marital unions persisted until the death of one of the spouses. Divorce, separation, and annulment were rare events. Because this was the case and because inclusion of couples whose marriage ended prior to the death of a spouse created problems for determining the period of risk for fertility, such couples were excluded in the course of the preselection process described in Appendix A. In none of the sample villages did more than a few couples qualify for exclusion based on this reason. Thus for the time period covered, their exclusion does little to bias the study of marital dissolution.

As indicated in Chapter 3, estimates of adult mortality from family reconstitution data are difficult. The fact that child mortality at ages above infancy declined during much of the period under study suggests that there may also have been an improvement in adult mortality. Such an improvement would affect the age at which dissolution of marriages occurred, as well as the average duration of a marital union at the time of dissolution. Of all marriages in the period 1700–1899, 48 percent ended through the death of a wife and 52 percent through the death of a husband.

---

[5] Mitterauer and Sieder, *European family*, p. 150.

The mean age of husbands and wives at the time of marital dissolution is presented in Table 7.1 for different marriage cohorts of the combined sample of all villages. These estimates are probably biased downward because they are based only on couples for whom the marriage date and both death dates are known. Since the main reason death dates would not be known is out-migration from the villages, and since the longer a couple lives the longer they are at risk of out-migration, the chance that the couple will be included in the analysis is greater the sooner after marriage a spouse dies.[6] The risk that such a bias will distort the trend over time is less serious provided major changes in the extent to which this bias operated did not occur.[7]

In Table 7.1a, age at dissolution is shown according to the survival status of each spouse at the time the union ends. The average age of a surviving wife and a surviving husband at the time of marital dissolution is quite similar. In contrast, the age of death of a wife whose own death ends a union is considerably below that of a husband whose death interrupts the marriage, perhaps reflecting the prevailing risks of maternal mortality ending a woman's life prematurely (see Chapter 5).

The average age at dissolution for both husbands and wives regardless of survival status at the time of the end of the union increases

---

[6] The age at the end of marriage for couples who move in from elsewhere should be biased in the opposite direction. However, such couples are generally excluded from the analysis since their marriage dates are unknown. Moreover, unless their age at burial or at some other event occurring in the village is given, their age at the time of marital dissolution will also be unknown.

[7] If out-migration of married persons varied over time, the trend could be affected. Another potential bias may also affect the trend. Calculations of the age at the end of union for family reconstitution data are potentially biased downward for the initial decades following the establishment of parish records, relative to later periods, if ages at death are determined solely by linking the death of a spouse to the spouse's birth date. The reason for this is that older persons marrying and dying during this period will have been born prior to the start of the birth register and thus their age will not be known, while younger persons will be more likely to have been born after the start of the register.

While part of the increase in the age at marital dissolution between the cohorts married during the first and second halves of the eighteenth century might be attributable to this bias, the rising trend is probably genuine since age at death was often included in death entries in the parish registers, thus eliminating the potential bias referred to above. In addition, for a number of the villages, birth registration began considerably before the eighteenth century, thus eliminating any problem for calculations of age at the end of the union. The problem would be more severe if the tabulations were made according to year of marital dissolution rather than by year of marriage. Since only marriages which begin from 1700 onward are considered, the analysis deals almost entirely with persons born at the earliest in the second half of the seventeenth century, and indeed predominantly those born after the third quarter of the seventeenth century.

Table 7.1a. *Mean age at dissolution of marriage by sex, survival status and year of marriage*

| | Husband | | Wife | |
	Survives	Dies	Survives	Dies
1700–49	50.2	55.8	48.7	48.1
1750–99	53.1	56.1	50.9	50.7
1800–24	52.3	56.5	51.0	50.4
1825–49	53.5	58.0	52.9	50.7
1850–74	54.7	58.9	53.8	51.9
1875–99	56.1	61.0	56.2	53.1
1700–1899	53.5	57.8	52.4	50.9

Note: Results refer to the combined sample of all villages and are restricted to couples for whom both death dates are known.

Table 7.1b. *Mean age at dissolution of marriage by sex and year of marriage for first and last marriages of surviving spouses*

| | First marriage | | Last marriage | |
	Surviving husband	Surviving wife	Surviving husband	Surviving wife
1700–49	49.3	48.1	59.3	53.7
1750–99	52.4	50.4	60.6	55.1
1800–24	51.5	50.7	59.5	54.8
1825–49	53.0	52.7	61.2	56.0
1850–74	54.1	53.7	62.5	55.8
1875–99	55.6	56.3	63.8	58.1
1700–1899	52.9	52.2	61.4	55.8

Note: Results refer to the combined sample of all villages and are restricted to couples for whom both death dates are known.

generally with successive marriage cohorts over the period studied. For surviving husbands the improvement represents a six-year increase, while for husbands whose death ends the marriage the increase is five years. For wives an increase of seven and a half years is evident in cases where the wife survives, while an increase of five years is apparent in cases where the wife's death precedes that of her husband. Most probably these results are attributable to improving adult mortality during the eighteenth and nineteenth centuries in the sample villages. Interpretation of the results in these terms, however, is complicated by the decrease in marriages in which there were large age differences between spouses (see Table 6.5).

Trends in the average age at marital dissolution shown in Table 7.1a are subject to the influence of changes in the age of entry into marriage as well as the extent of remarriage. Since age at marriage was relatively stable, as discussed in Chapter 6, it is unlikely to have exerted much influence. To eliminate the possible effect of changing probabilities of remarriage on the age at the end of the union, the age at the end of first marriage can be examined. This measure is necessarily free of any influence of remarriage. The age at the end of both first and last marriages of the surviving spouse are shown in Table 7.1b. Since first marriages that were not followed by a remarriage are at the same time also last marriages, they are included in both categories.

Changes in the age at marital dissolution for surviving spouses in first marriages differ only modestly from the results for all marriages, indicating that changing remarriage probabilities had only a moderate impact on the latter. Undoubtedly, the predominant factor responsible for the increase in the age at marital dissolution was an improvement in adult mortality.

The somewhat greater increase in the mean age at the end of first marriages compared to all marriages reflects the decline in the probability of remarriage, examined below. The reason for this is as follows. The average age at the end of remarriages is virtually always older than the average age at the end of first marriages. Since a decline in the probability of remarriage generally reduces the proportion of marriages that are remarriages, the compositional shift tends to lower the age at the end of all marriages, other things being equal. Hence changes in the probability of remarriage dampened the observed increase in the age at the end of union for all marriages.

Increases in the age at dissolution of the surviving spouse's last marriage are also of interest as they indicate the age at which permanent widowhood or widowerhood began. However, these figures are particularly sensitive to the declining chances of remarriage (especially since they include first marriages not followed by a remarriage). This explains why the age at the end of a last marriage increased somewhat less than for all marriages and considerably less than for first marriages. In contrast to the average age at the end of a first marriage, which was almost identical for surviving spouses of both sexes, surviving husbands were considerably older than surviving wives at the end of last marriages. This probably reflects the greater likelihood of husbands in last marriages to have been previously married, and thus for their last marriage to be a remarriage. For example, among all

Table 7.2. *Average duration of marital unions by age at marriage of husbands and wives and by year of marriage*

Age at marriage	Husbands				Wives			
	1700–99	1800–49	1850–99	Total	1700–99	1800–49	1850–99	Total
Under 25	26.5	27.0	29.3	27.4	25.0	26.1	29.1	26.7
25–30	24.5	25.4	28.8	26.5	22.9	23.1	27.1	24.5
30–34	23.4	22.5	26.5	24.1	18.9	20.3	22.9	20.6
35–40	19.5	21.5	22.8	21.2	16.4	19.0	19.2	18.1
40–49	16.9	15.9	18.1	16.9	14.8	15.8	16.6	15.6
50+	11.8	11.8	13.4	12.2	10.3	11.3	—	10.4
All ages	23.2	23.3	26.7	24.4	22.4	23.2	26.7	24.0

Note: Results refer to the combined sample of all villages and are subject to restriction 3 (see Table A.1). Results based on fewer than 20 cases are omitted.

last marriages during the eighteenth and nineteenth centuries, 21 percent involved remarriages for husbands compared to only 10 percent for wives. In general, the results (whether for all, first, or last marriages) indicate that over the course of the eighteenth and nineteenth centuries, both husbands and wives remained in marital unions until progressively older ages. This, in turn, had important implications for trends in remarriage.

In the absence of divorce, annulment, or separation, the average duration of a marital union at the time of dissolution is determined by the age at marriage and the age at widowhood. Since the average age at widowhood was increasing while the age at marriage was remaining relatively stable, the average duration of a marital union at the time of dissolution generally increased during the eighteenth and nineteenth centuries. This is shown in Table 7.2, which indicates the average duration of marital unions by age at marriage for both spouses. As would be expected, the average duration of a marital union at the time of dissolution is inversely related to the age of entry into the union. At the same time, for all age-at-marriage categories, the average duration of a marital union increased, for both husbands and wives, between the eighteenth and the second half of the nineteenth century.

Only rarely did both spouses die at the same time. Thus the dissolution of a marriage is typically followed by a period during which the surviving spouse lived as a widow or widower or, if remarriage occurred, as the partner of a new spouse. During this period the surviving spouse's living conditions undoubtedly changed substantially, particularly if remarriage did not occur, as he or she would no longer function as part of a conjugal unit. In cases where remarriage occurred, the period of widowhood was curtailed and the surviving spouse once again functioned as part of a single conjugal unit until the death of one of the spouses again disrupted the marriage. While family reconstitution data are not suited for determining with whom, if anybody, a widow or widower lived following the dissolution of a marriage, they can shed light on the duration of widowhood and the process of remarriage.

The mean number of additional years lived by the surviving spouse following both first and last marriages is shown in Table 7.3. The latter category includes both first marriages of persons who have married only once (since it is also their last marriage) and the last marriages of persons who have remarried. In the cases of both first and last marriages, the period of survival is simply the interval between the death dates of the two spouses. Thus, following the end of the first marriage, the survival interval includes any time spent by the surviv-

Table 7.3. *Mean number of additional years lived by the surviving spouse following first and last marriage for men and women, by year of marriage dissolution*

Year of marriage dissolution	Years between end of first marriage and death of surviving spouse[a]		Years between end of last marriage and death of surviving spouse	
	Husband survives	Wife survives	Husband survives	Wife survives
1700–49	16.5	19.0	9.5	13.9
1750–99	18.1	18.8	11.2	14.9
1800–24	17.8	17.7	11.8	14.3
1825–49	17.1	17.0	11.5	14.5
1850–74	16.6	16.4	11.2	14.7
1875–99	17.0	17.1	10.9	16.0
1700–1899	17.3	17.5	11.2	14.9

Note: Results refer to the combined sample of all villages and include marriages prior to 1700 that ended after 1700. Results are restricted to couples for whom both death dates are known.
[a] Including periods during which a remarriage may have occurred.

ing spouse in a remarriage. The number of years spent between the end of the last marriage and the death of the surviving spouse refers exclusively to a period when the surviving spouse was no longer part of a conjugal unit, but rather a permanent widow or widower until death.

As the results indicate, the surviving spouse, whether husband or wife, lived between 16 to 19 years on the average following the death of his or her first spouse. There appears to be little difference either over time or between the sexes in this respect. There is also no clear trend over time in the mean duration of survival following last marriage.

The lack of a difference between husbands' and wives' survival. interval following a first marriage is consistent with the similar average ages of surviving spouses of both sexes at the time that the first marriage ended, and indicates a similarity in the average age at death for spouses of each sex who survive their first marriage. In contrast, the average years survived by a husband following the end of his last marriage was less than that for a wife following her last marriage. This reflects differences in the average age of a widow and widower at the end of last marriages, which in turn is due to the higher propensity for men to remarry than for women (discussed below). The fact that first-marriage survivors of both sexes have similar ages of death indicates that mortality differences between the sexes are relatively unimport-ant, compared to differences in remarriage chances, in accounting for the differences in the duration of widowhood following last marriage.

Remarriage

The distribution of marriage types
The evolution over time of the distribution of marriages by marriage order combinations for the combined sample of all villages is shown in Table 7.4 along with the mean age at marriage according to the prior marital statuses of the spouses. There was a steady increase in the proportion of primary marriages (bachelors with spinsters), which rose over the eighteenth and nineteenth centuries from approximately two-thirds to four-fifths of all marriages, while the proportion of remarriages decreased, particularly those involving a widow. Since divorces are excluded from these tabulations, and indeed were virtu-ally non-existent, they have no effect on these results. As is evident from the findings presented in Table 7.4, the explanation lies in a decline in age-specific remarriage probabilities and in improving adult mortality, given that the probability of remarriage is negatively related to age at the time of marital dissolution. Throughout the period under

Table 7.4. *Percent distribution of marriages and mean age at marriage for men and women by prior marital statuses of couple and by year of marriage*

| | Prior marital status of spouses | | | | |
	Bachelor and spinster	Widower and spinster	Bachelor and widow	Widower and widow	Total
% distribution across					
1700–49	66.9	18.4	10.3	4.5	100
1750–99	72.0	15.5	8.5	4.0	100
1800–49	74.1	15.8	7.2	2.9	100
1850–99	81.4	13.2	4.0	1.4	100
1700–1899	75.2	15.2	6.8	2.8	100
Age at marriage for men					
1700–49	27.7	40.6	28.9	(47.7)	30.8
1750–99	27.8	40.6	30.1	47.9	30.6
1800–49	28.6	41.8	31.4	50.4	31.5
1850–99	28.8	40.5	32.1	51.5	30.8
1700–1899	28.4	40.9	30.9	49.4	31.0
Age at mariage for women					
1700–49	24.6	27.9	36.3	43.1	27.2
1750–99	24.9	29.5	35.5	43.9	27.3
1800–49	25.5	31.4	35.1	43.8	27.7
1850–99	25.5	30.4	34.6	41.3	26.7
1700–1899	25.3	30.1	35.3	43.3	27.2

Note: Results refer to the combined sample of all villages. Results in parentheses are based on fewer than 50 cases.

observation remarriages were more likely to involve widowers than widows, reflecting a greater tendency for men to remarry than for women.

The average age at marriage for both men and women in each of the prior marital status categories remained relatively constant over the period under observation. There was only a slight increase in the average age of men entering primary marriages and an even less pronounced increase for women entering primary marriages. For men, a slight increase in the age at marriage for other prior marital status combinations is also evident over the period covered. However, due to the increasing share of primary marriages, which occur at younger ages than other types of marriages, the average age of men for all marriages is identical for the first half of the eighteenth century and the second half of the nineteenth century. A similar modest compositional effect due to the increasing share of primary marriages affects the average age of women for all marriages, which is slightly lower at the end of the period under observation than at the beginning.

Probabilities of remarriage

Life table techniques are well suited for a detailed examination of the probability of remarriage following the dissolution of a union. To apply such techniques, information is needed on the date of the dissolution of a union, and the date of the death of the surviving spouse or the date of remarriage, whichever comes first. Although family reconstitution data typically contain such information, the date of remarriage in this study was coded only for the six fully-coded villages and not for the remaining eight, for which an abbreviated scheme was applied (see Appendix A). Thus full life table techniques can be applied only to the six fully-coded villages. Since information on whether or not a remarriage occurred was coded for the remaining villages, a somewhat less detailed analysis of remarriage is possible for all 14 villages in the sample. Before we turn to the full set of villages, a more detailed examination of the probability of remarriage is presented based on an application of life table techniques to the six fully-coded villages.

The cumulative proportions of widows and widowers remarrying, according to the number of months since marital dissolution as estimated by the life table approach, is shown in Figure 7.1 for the combined sample of the six fully-coded villages. The results clearly show a striking difference in the probability of remarriage for men and women. Widowers were far more likely to remarry than were widows. For the six villages taken together during the period of the eighteenth and nineteenth centuries, the probability of remarriage during the ten years following the end of a union was more than twice as high for men as it was for women. Moreover, those widowers who did remarry tended to do so more quickly than those widows who remarried.

For both sexes, the probability of remarriage tapers off substantially by the end of five years following marital dissolution. Thus, for men, the probability of remarriage within the first five years after the end of a previous marriage was approximately 42 percent, increasing to only 45 percent by the end of ten years. For women, the probability of remarriage within the first five years following marital dissolution was approximately 19 percent, increasing to only 20 percent by the end of ten years. Indeed, based on these life table calculations, among those husbands who had remarried by the end of ten years, more than half did so by nine months following marital dissolution. For those women

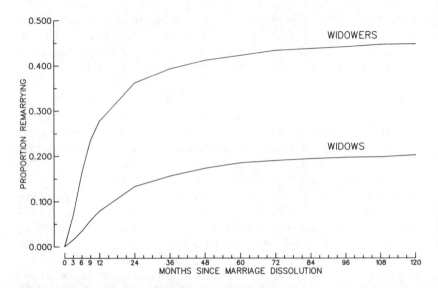

Figure 7.1. *Cumulative proportions remarrying as estimated by life table techniques, for surviving spouses of marriages ended 1700–1899.* Results are limited to the six fully-coded villages and to couples for whom both death dates are known. Marriages ending in annulment or divorce or where migration of the surviving spouse is indicated are excluded

who remarried within the first ten years, more than half remarried by the end of the first year following marital dissolution. The substantial proportions remarrying, and the rapidity with which remarriage took place, especially for men, are all the more striking in view of the generally unfavorable attitude of the Church toward remarriage.[8]

Table 7.5 indicates the probability of remarriage, estimated by the life table approach, for the six fully-coded villages according to the year of dissolution, as well as for each village separately and according to the age at dissolution. A clear time trend in remarriage probabilities is evident, with a sharp reduction in the proportions remarrying occurring from the eighteenth century onward. Since all marriages were coded for the fully-coded villages, including those occurring after 1900, the analysis can be extended into the twentieth century, although much of our discussion will focus on the eighteenth and nineteenth centuries.

It is evident that the trend that was already strongly apparent before

[8] Goody, *Family and marriage*, pp. 188–89.

Table 7.5. *Life table estimates of the proportion remarrying within selected periods of time since marriage dissolution, by year of dissolution, by village, and by age at dissolution*

	Men					Women				
	Proportion remarrying within					Proportion remarrying within				
	3 mo.	6 mo.	1 yr.	2 yr.	10 yr.	3 mo.	6 mo.	1 yr.	2 yr.	10 yr.
Year of dissolution										
1700–99	.142	.244	.398	.494	.586	.039	.085	.153	.203	.321
1800–49	.042	.148	.243	.324	.409	.005	.013	.066	.128	.210
1850–99	.033	.105	.206	.283	.365	.000	.003	.022	.047	.086
1900–24	.003	.048	.104	.162	.294	.000	.000	.003	.021	.086
1700–1899	.070	.163	.278	.362	.448	.015	.034	.079	.133	.202
Village (dissolutions 1700–1899)										
Kappel	.143	.243	.341	.391	.443	.051	.093	.146	.181	.255
Rust	.100	.241	.363	.462	.555	.014	.044	.106	.174	.253
Öschelbronn	.012	.071	.173	.232	.341	.000	.000	.020	.080	.114
Braunsen	.023	.084	.285	.431	.419	.000	.000	.056	.145	.243
Massenhausen	.024	.117	.293	.423	.502	.000	.011	.087	.143	.182
Middels	.000	.014	.085	.180	.305	.000	.000	.010	.040	.124
Age at dissolution (dissolutions 1700–1899)										
Under 30	(.077)	(.314)	(.595)	(.843)	(.955)	.016	.071	.261	.507	.777
30–39	.149	.395	.603	.741	.887	.025	.072	.184	.324	.473
40–49	.081	.200	.377	.500	.622	.019	.030	.059	.092	.137
50–59	.027	.050	.126	.175	.241	.000	.000	.003	.008	.013
60+	.007	.011	.019	.029	.034	.000	.000	.000	.000	.003

Note: This table is limited to the six fully-coded villages and to couples for whom both death dates are known. Marriages ending in annulment or divorce, or where migration of the surviving spouse is indicated, are excluded. Results in parentheses are based on fewer then 100 persons entering into the initial life table calculation.

1900 continued at least until the first quarter of the twentieth century.[9] For husbands whose marriage ended in the death of the wife during the eighteenth century, the probability of remarrying within two years following marital dissolution was almost 50 percent, and close to 60 percent by the end of ten years. In contrast, by the second half of the nineteenth century, the probability of remarrying within two years drops to less than 30 percent, and within ten years to only a little more than one out of three chances. By the first quarter of the twentieth century these probabilities had dropped substantially further.

For women, an even greater proportional decrease in the probability of remarriage is evident. For those widows whose husbands died in the eighteenth century, approximately one-fifth remarried within two years following marital dissolution, and almost a third by the end of ten years. In contrast, only 5 percent remarried within two years, and less than 10 percent by the end of ten years, by the end of the nineteenth century.

The changing nature of remarriage is also reflected in the declining pace at which remarriage occurred. During the eighteenth century, widows and widowers remarried far more rapidly than in subsequent periods. For men, the life table estimates indicate that the proportion who remarried within six months, among all who remarried within ten years following marital dissolution, declined from 42 percent in the eighteenth century to only 16 percent by the first quarter of the twentieth century. For women, an even more drastic reduction in the pace of remarriage occurred. The proportion of those women remarrying within ten years of marital dissolution who did so by the end of the first year declined from almost half in the eighteenth century to only 3 percent by the first quarter of the twentieth century. Similar declines in the pace of remarriage have been suggested by other historical studies as well.[10]

The probabilities of remarrying in the six individual fully-coded villages show considerable variation. For men, remarriage is least common and occurs at a relatively slow pace in the East Frisian village of Middels. For women, remarriage is also relatively uncommon in Middels, and a similar pattern is also evident for the village of Öschelbronn. The pace of remarriage for women is likewise very slow

[9] Given the increasing importance of divorce as a source of marital dissolution during the twentieth century, the present analysis, which is limited to studying remarriage following marital dissolution as a result of the death of a spouse, is not extended beyond the first quarter of the twentieth century, even for the fully-coded villages for which such data are available.

[10] Flandrin, *Families in former times*, pp. 115–16. Compare with Lee, W. R., 'Family and modernization,' p. 96.

in Middels relative to the other villages. It is interesting to observe that the remarriage patterns do not correspond strictly to religious differences among the villages. While both Öschelbronn and Middels, the two villages characterized by the least remarriage, are Protestant, the Waldeck villages of Braunsen and Massenhausen are also Protestant and yet are characterized by considerably higher rates of remarriage. The two Catholic villages of Kappel and Rust in Baden are also characterized by high rates of remarriage, but these are not noticeably higher than those for the two Waldeck villages.

A number of historical demographic studies have established a strong negative association between the probability of remarriage and the age of the surviving spouse at the time of marital dissolution.[11] This same relationship is clearly apparent in German villages during the eighteenth and nineteenth centuries. As indicated by the life table estimates for the six fully-coded villages, the probability of remarrying following marital dissolution declines sharply with age for both men and women. For men, the large majority who were under age 50 at the time of marital dissolution remarried within ten years, while only a small percentage did so if they were age 60 or above at the time of the death of their wife. For women, the large majority remarried only among those who were under 30 at the time of the death of their husband, although almost half of those who were in their thirties at the onset of widowhood remarried as well. Only a very small percentage of women over age 40 at the time of marital dissolution remarried, and almost none over age 50 did so.

From the point of view of the reproductive potential lost through marital dissolution, it is notable that a substantial proportion of women who became widows in their prime reproductive ages remarried, and hence had an opportunity to resume their reproductive careers. Thus the low rates of remarriage for women above age 40, while perhaps having a substantial impact on the social and economic circumstances of the women involved, have little demographic significance.

While it is not possible to apply the life table approach to calculate the full set of remarriage probabilities by duration (since marital dissolution) for the combined sample of 14 villages, the proportions that ever remarry can be estimated. As with the life table estimates for the fully-coded villages, it is necessary to restrict calculations to those couples for whom both death dates are known in order to maximize the chance that the surviving spouse was under observation for the full period between marital dissolution and death. While in some cases this

---

[11] For example, Bideau, 'Widowhood and remarriage'; and Cabourdin, 'Remarriage.'

involves surviving spouses who moved out of the village and died elsewhere, in all likelihood if the death date were available to the genealogist, information on whether or not that spouse had remarried would also have been available.

As the date of remarriage has not been coded for the full set of villages, it is not possible to calculate probabilities of remarriage net of the probability of death, as could be done with the life table approach for the six fully-coded villages. Thus results for the complete set of villages are influenced not only by the probability of remarriage but also by the probability of death.[12] In order to minimize the impact of the competing risk of death from the estimates for the full set of all villages, separate estimates of the probability of remarriage have been made for those surviving spouses who lived at least five years after marital dissolution. Results of the life table analysis of remarriage based on the subset of fully-coded villages indicate that the vast majority of remarriages take place within the first five years following marital dissolution. Thus, by restricting calculations to those who survive at least five years, a close approximation to the probability of remarrying independent of the competing probability of death is achieved.

Estimates of the proportion remarrying among all survivors and among those surviving at least five years, for both men and women, are presented in Table 7.6 for the complete set of 14 villages combined. As expected, estimates of remarriage based on spouses surviving at least five years are substantially higher than estimates of remarriage among all survivors. Given the larger number of cases available for analysis from the full set of 14 villages compared to the subset of 6 fully-coded villages, it is possible to trace the trend of the probability of remarriage in greater detail.

Whether or not we consider all survivors or only those surviving at

---

[12] Following marital dissolution, the surviving spouse is subject to the competing risks of remarriage and death. The life table approach allows for the fact that the surviving spouse is only at risk of remarriage up until the time that remarriage actually occurs or until the time at which the surviving spouse dies, whichever comes first. The surviving spouses who do not remarry prior to their death are eliminated, following their death, from the denominator of the probabilities of remarrying, while those who do remarry are eliminated from the denominator following their remarriage.

For example, imagine two populations with equal probabilities of remarriage at each duration following marital dissolution for surviving spouses, but with different probabilities of surviving to a given duration. Under such circumstances, a lower proportion of survivors at the time of dissolution would remarry in the higher-mortality population because greater proportions would die prior to having found a new marriage partner. Life table analysis would reveal that the probability of remarriage at any given duration since dissolution for those who continue to survive is equal in the two populations.

Table 7.6. *Proportion remarrying for men and women by year of marriage dissolution, among all surviving spouses and among those surviving at least five additional years*

Year of marriage dissolution	Among all survivors		Among those surviving at least 5 additional years	
	Men	Women	Men	Women
1700–49	.644	.390	.740	.446
1750–99	.536	.300	.617	.350
1800–24	.466	.227	.527	.270
1825–49	.396	.183	.462	.210
1850–74	.399	.110	.472	.128
1875–99	.334	.073	.418	.083
1700–1899	.445	.200	.521	.233

Note: Results refer to the combined sample of all villages and include marriages prior to 1700 that ended after 1700. Results are restricted to couples for whom both death dates are known.

least five years, the results indicate that the probability of remarriage for both men and women declined steadily during the eighteenth and nineteenth centuries. Since the full sample of all villages is based only on marriages occurring through 1899, estimates of the probability of remarriage during the twentieth century would be seriously biased due to sample censorship and thus are not shown.[13] Results from both the subset of fully-coded villages and the complete sample of all villages do agree, however, in indicating a very substantial reduction in the probability of remarriage during the eighteenth and nineteenth centuries. In general, the results based on the sample of all villages suggest somewhat higher probabilities of remarriage for any given period of time than do the results from the subset of six fully-coded villages. This is apparent from the fact that the proportion remarrying among those surviving at least five years, based on the combined

[13] Since only marriages prior to 1900 are included in the data set for the full sample, marriages ending during successive years in the twentieth century would be to couples that on average would be progressively older simply because couples that were younger at the time of dissolution during the twentieth century would be more likely to have also been married during the twentieth century. Given that the probability of remarriage is strongly related to the age at which marital dissolution occurs, such a selection of cases, based only on marriages contracted prior to the twentieth century, would seriously bias downward the probability of remarriage for marriages dissolving during the twentieth century. The reverse problem is not present at the beginning of the eighteenth century since the results are based on marriages regardless of whether they were contracted prior to or subsequent to the turn of the eighteenth century.

sample of all villages, is generally higher for equivalent time periods than are the estimates of the probability of remarriage within ten years following marital dissolution, based on the life table results for the fully-coded villages.[14]

The probabilities of remarrying according to the age of the surviving spouse at the time of marriage dissolution, as well as according to the year of marital dissolution are shown in Table 7.7 for the complete sample of all villages combined. Again, results are presented both for all survivors and for those who survive at least five years following the time of dissolution.

As was true for the subset of the six fully-coded villages, the results for the combined sample of all villages show a very strong relationship between age at end of union and probability of remarriage. Moreover, this is true throughout the period under observation. At any given age at the time of marital dissolution, the probability of remarriage for a man is greater than for a woman. Sex differences are particularly pronounced at the older ages. For men or women who were widowed under age 30, the vast majority remarried, although during the second half of the nineteenth century there was a noticeable decline in the probability of remarriage among widowed women under 30. For both sexes, remarriage is not common after age 60, even after controlling for the competing probability of death, by limiting consideration to those who survived at least five years. For surviving spouses who were in their forties at the time of marital dissolution, remarriage was quite common for men but relatively rare for women, except during the first half of the eighteenth century. In addition, while a significant proportion of men who were in their fifties at the time of marital dissolution remarried, only a very small minority of women of the same age did so.

As indicated above, the average age of the surviving spouse at the time of marital dissolution increased during the period under observation. Given the fact that there is a strong negative association between

---

[14] These two estimates are not precisely equivalent. Those based on the life table approach as applied to the fully-coded villages estimate the probability of remarriage only within the first ten years following marital dissolution and thus do not incorporate the fact that a small proportion of persons will remarry after ten years. In contrast, the estimates based on the set of all villages incorporate remarriages at any duration, including those occurring after ten years. On the other hand, the life table estimates eliminate from the probability of remarriage the competing risk of dying during any time prior to the ten-year period subsequent to marital dissolution, while those based on the complete set of villages eliminate only the competing risk of dying during the first five years following marital dissolution. Since little remarriage occurred after five years and even less after ten years, and since these biases are in opposite directions, it is unlikely that they have a serious effect on the comparability of the two sets of results.

Table 7.7. *Proportions remarrying for men and women by age at dissolution and year of dissolution, among all surviving spouses and among spouses surviving at least five additional years*

	Age of surviving spouse at end of union				
	Under 30	30–39	40–49	50–59	60+
Among all survivors					
Men					
1700–49	(.875)	.938	(.761)	.491	(.050)
1750–99	(.939)	.875	.696	.321	.102
1800–49	.897	.839	.635	.254	.074
1850–99	.932	.874	.582	.233	.022
1700–1899	.916	.866	.639	.275	.054
Women					
1700–49	(.800)	.707	.410	.089	.000
1750–99	.870	.631	.277	.050	.023
1800–49	.785	.536	.145	.035	.000
1850–99	.671	.307	.071	.010	.000
1700–1899	.781	.511	.184	.032	.003
Among those surviving					
at least 5 additional years					
Men					
1700–49	(.952)	.966	(.780)	(.511)	—
1750–99	.932	.899	.743	.345	.163
1800–49	.934	.868	.647	.271	.098
1850–99	.970	.897	.626	.272	.030
1700–1899	.948	.893	.671	.301	.076
Women					
1700–49	(.814)	.722	.437	.109	(.000)
1750–99	.918	.667	.289	.063	.038
1800–49	.816	.558	.159	.032	.000
1850–99	.688	.323	.074	.011	.000
1700–1899	.813	.536	.195	.035	.006

Note: Results refer to the combined sample of all villages. Results in parentheses are based on 20–49 cases; results based on fewer than 20 cases are omitted. Results include marriages prior to 1700 that ended after 1700. Results are restricted to couples for whom both death dates are known.

age at dissolution and probability of remarriage, the increased age at end of union would contribute to a decline in the overall probability of remarriage even if no changes in the age-specific probabilities of remarriage occurred. As is evident in Table 7.7, such a compositional effect can explain only a small part of the decline in the overall probability of remarriage that occurred during the eighteenth and nineteenth centuries in the sample villages. With only the exception of men under age 30, the probability of remarrying for each age group of surviving spouses declined during the period.

For both men and women, the proportionate decline in the probability of remarriage is directly related to the age of the spouse at the end of the union. A much greater proportionate decline in the probability of remarriage occurred for men and women at older ages than for those who were younger at the time of marital dissolution. For men under age 30, the probability of remarrying remained virtually unchanged during the two centuries. Moreover, there was only a modest decline for those who were in their thirties at the time of the end of the previous union. However, very substantial reductions in the probability of remarriage are evident for men who were older when their marriage ended. For women, there was a similar relationship between the proportionate decline in the probability of remarrying and the age at the time of marital dissolution, although, unlike men, women in their thirties experienced a substantial reduction in remarriage probabilities. Indeed, the proportion of women in this group remarrying during the second half of the nineteenth century was less than half of the proportion remarrying during the first half of the eighteenth century. For women above age 50, the probability of remarrying was reduced to very close to zero by the end of the nineteenth century.

The proportion remarrying among all survivors, as well as among those surviving at least five years, is presented in Table 7.8 for each of the 14 villages, as well as for the combined regional grouping of villages.[15] Some inter-village variability in the probability of remarriage for both men and women is evident, but in general it is not clearly along regional lines. When the probabilities of remarriage are compared according to regional groupings, they are rather similar. The main exception is the lower probability of remarriage for the Württemberg village of Öschelbronn. However, since Öschelbronn is the only village in Württemberg in the sample, and since considerable variation is evident among several other villages within other regional groupings, there is little basis for concluding that this reflects a regional difference, rather than simply being a peculiarity of the local village.

[15] In order to ensure comparability across all villages, results are based on cases selected according to the criteria put forth in Appendix A (with the additional restriction that the death date of both spouses is known). Thus the results in this table for the six fully-coded villages are not based on the same selection of cases as was true for the life table analysis presented in Table 7.5. Nevertheless, the results appear to be quite similar.

Table 7.8. *Proportion remarrying for men and women by region and village, among all surviving spouses and among those surviving at least five additional years, marriages ending 1700–1899*

Region and village	Among all survivors		Among those surviving at least 5 additional years	
	Men	Women	Men	Women
Baden	.486	.235	.559	.275
Grafenhausen	.454	.236	.520	.276
Herbolzheim	.514	.239	.592	.280
Kappel	.408	.234	.458	.274
Rust	.524	.228	.610	.267
Württemberg	.300	.095	.361	.108
Öschelbronn	.300	.095	.361	.108
Bavaria	.421	.197	.478	.232
Anhausen	.455	.225	.521	.264
Gabelbach	.485	.194	.561	.230
Kreuth	.277	.156	.296	.190
Waldeck	.464	.183	.544	.212
Braunsen	.417	.235	.508	.253
Höringhausen	.430	.148	.500	.178
Massenhausen	.463	.173	.550	.220
Vasbeck	.512	.201	.591	.220
East Friesland	.377	.164	.473	.190
Middels	.291	.134	.360	.150
Werdum	.414	.176	.521	.207
All villages	.445	.200	.521	.223

Note: Results refer to the combined sample of all villages and include marriages prior to 1700 that ended after 1700. Results are restricted to couples for whom both death dates are known.

Interestingly, in East Friesland the probability of remarriage for the village of Werdum was considerably higher than that for Middels. Thus the low probability of remarriage in Middels observed in connection with the detailed life table analysis did not appear necessarily to be typical for the area of East Friesland. In addition, the probability of remarriage in Kreuth was considerably lower than in the other two Bavarian villages, again suggesting that inter-village variation was greater than regional variation. In all villages, the probability of remarriage was considerably higher for men than for women, with the male probability of remarriage often exceeding the female probability by a factor of two.

Socio-economic differentials

The proportion remarrying for the combined sample of all villages among men and women surviving at least five years following the death of a spouse is shown in Table 7.9, according to the occupational group, occupational subcategory, and village leadership status of the husband. Given the strong association of remarriage probabilities with age at the time of marital dissolution, and the decline in remarriage chances over the two-century period under observation, results are shown adjusted (by use of multiple classification analysis) for both of these influences. For the four broad general occupational groupings, the probability of remarriage for both men and women was remarkably similar, whether or not adjustment is made for age at, and year of, dissolution. Even for the occupational subcategories, the probabilities of remarriage were generally fairly similar, with only a few exceptions.

Among all occupational subcategories, the unadjusted probability of a husband remarrying was at least 45 percent, and in only one subcategory did it exceed 60 percent. After results are adjusted for age at, and year of, dissolution, considerable similarity remains in the probability of remarriage, although two groups, sailors and professionals, fell below the 40 percent level. The results for sailors may be in part a result of the small number of cases involved.

Regardless of their former husband's occupation, women's probabilities of remarriage were far lower than men's. In most cases, both unadjusted and adjusted results indicate a probability of remarriage for women well below 30 percent. The most notable exception is the unusually high probability of remarriage associated with wives of fishermen, which remains higher than for other groups even after adjustment. A somewhat lower than average chance of remarriage for women in the proletarian group is partially eliminated by adjustment. Thus there appears to be little coherence in the pattern of differences in remarriage according to husband's occupation. It is worth noting that proletarian husbands did not suffer the same disadvantage as their wives in terms of chances of remarriage.

A comparison of the unadjusted probability of remarriage according to the husband's village leadership status reveals roughly similar probabilities of remarriage for those who were leaders and for those who were not, but considerably lower probabilities of remarriage for the wives of village leaders. The lower remarriage chances of wives of village leaders prior to adjustment undoubtedly reflects, in part, their more advanced age at the time of dissolution compared to wives of non-leaders (56.7 versus 49.9 respectively). Interestingly, there is far less difference in the age at the end of marriage between the village

Table 7.9. *Proportion remarrying for men and women by occupational group, by occupational subcategory, and by status in village, unadjusted and adjusted for age at dissolution and year of dissolution, among those surviving at least five additional years, marriages ending 1700–1899*

	Unadjusted		Adjusted for age at dissolution and year of dissolution	
	Men	Women	Men	Women
Occupational group				
Farmer	.50	.26	.51	.26
Proletarian	.53	.20	.52	.22
Artisans and skilled	.53	.24	.51	.23
Mixed, other, unknown	.53	.24	.51	.23
Occupational subcategory				
Farmer	.50	.26	.51	.26
Cottager	.49	.20	.51	.23
Day laborer	.55	.18	.54	.21
Other unskilled	.56	.13	.48	.15
Sailor	(.50)	(.23)	(.38)	(.13)
Weaver	.51	.23	.53	.24
Other home industry	.58	.27	.52	.30
Artisan	.53	.23	.51	.23
Fisherman	.55	.42	.54	.33
Businessman	.55	.22	.51	.20
Professional	.45	.18	.39	.17
Farmer–artisan, etc.	.58	.22	.57	.27
Farmer–proletarian	.50	.15	.49	.21
Proletarian–artisan, etc.	.62	.23	.59	.25
Other	(.54)	.19	(.52)	.17
Unknown	.49	.30	.45	.23
Status in village				
Village leader	.55	.09	.57	.18
Non-leader	.52	.24	.51	.24
All couples	.52	.23	.51	.23

Note: Results refer to the combined sample of all villages, include marriages prior to 1700 that ended after 1700, and are restricted to couples for whom both death dates are known. Results in parentheses are based on fewer than 50 cases. Adjustment for age at marital dissolution was made through multiple classification analysis and was done separately for men and women. Unadjusted results for widowers include cases in which the age at dissolution is unknown, while the adjusted results are based only on widowers for whom age at dissolution is known; in the case of widows, since age at dissolution is known for all, adjusted and unadjusted results are based on the same number of cases.

Table 7.10. *Proportion remarrying for men and women by occupational group and year of dissolution, unadjusted and adjusted for age at dissolution, for those surviving at least five additional years*

	Unadjusted for age at dissolution				Adjusted for age at dissolution			
	Farmers	Proletarians	Artisans and skilled	All (including unknown)	Farmers	Proletarians	Artisans and skilled	All (including unknown)
Widowers								
1700–49	.71	(.87)	.74	.74	(.60)	(.67)	(.57)	.61
1750–99	.59	.69	.60	.62	.59	.58	.50	.56
1800–49	.48	.52	.51	.49	.50	.51	.49	.50
1850–99	.42	.41	.48	.45	.46	.47	.51	.48
Widows								
1700–49	.45	.45	.44	.45	.39	.37	.36	.38
1750–99	.37	.33	.39	.35	.36	.29	.32	.32
1800–49	.28	.22	.27	.24	.27	.20	.23	.23
1850–99	.15	.07	.08	.11	.17	.14	.14	.15

Note: Results refer to the combined sample of all villages, include marriages prior to 1700 that ended after 1700, and are restricted to couples for whom both death dates are known. Results in parentheses are based on 20–49 cases. Husbands, and wives of husbands, with two occupations in different groups were coded in a separate mixed category not shown, but are included in the results that refer to all husbands or wives. Adjustment for age at marital dissolution was made through multiple classification analysis and was done separately for men and women. Unadjusted results for widowers include cases in which the age at dissolution is unknown, while the adjusted results are based only on widowers for whom age at dissolution is known; in the case of widows, since age at dissolution is known for all, adjusted and unadjusted results are based on the same number of cases.

leaders and non-leaders themselves if they survived their wives (52.9 versus 51.4 respectively), and adjustment has considerably less effect.

Even after adjustment, the results indicate that widows of village leaders remarried somewhat less than widows of non-leaders. Perhaps this reflects a shortage of appropriate candidates for remarriage for women in the more privileged strata of the village, if such women hesitate to marry men who are from less advantaged positions than their former husbands. In contrast, village leaders themselves may have been in a particularly favorable position to remarry, as their presumably more privileged status in the village might have made them particularly attractive candidates even when they were somewhat older.

Trends over time in the probability of remarriage also show little consistent difference by occupation. As shown in Table 7.10, the decline in the proportions remarrying occurred in each major occupational grouping. Results are shown both unadjusted and adjusted for age at dissolution. While adjusting for the changing average age at dissolution over the eighteenth and nineteenth centuries diminishes the extent of the decline in remarriage, it by no means eliminates it. For women, the adjusted results indicate a remarkably similar magnitude of decline between the first half of the eighteenth and the second half of the nineteenth centuries for all three major occupational groups.

Remarriage and the number of children
Among the circumstances that might substantially affect the chances of remarrying is the number of children that the widow or widower has at the time of widowhood. A thorough analysis of this would take into account not only the number of surviving children, but also their ages, since quite different effects on chances of remarriage might be expected if children are still young and dependent, compared to situations in which the children are already old enough to be in the labor force and thus provide support for the widowed parent.[16]

Table 7.11 shows the percent remarrying according to the number of children who survived to age 5, controlling for age at widowhood or widowerhood. Though marriage probabilities were universally higher for men than for women of the same age group and with the same number of children, a similar inverse association characterized both

---

[16] Because of the way in which the data have been coded for this study, the probability of remarriage is related in the following analyses to the number of children surviving to age 5 who had been born to the couple prior to marital dissolution. It should be noted that some of these children who were born more than five years prior to marital dissolution might have died before the end of the parents' marriage, but given the relatively low mortality of children past age 5, this number is bound to be quite small.

Table 7.11. *Proportion of widowers and widows remarrying, among those surviving at least five years after marital dissolution, by age at marital dissolution and number of children surviving to age 5, marriages ending 1700–1899*

Surviving partner and number of children	Age at time of dissolution					
	Under 30	30–39	40–49	50–59	60+	Total[a]
Widowers						
None	.97	.93	.82	.51	.29	.72
1–2	.92	.91	.67	.30	.7	.63
3–4	—	.88	.69	.27	.3	.49
5+	—	.80	.57	.22	.4	.31
Total	.95	.89	.67	.30	.8	.52
Widows						
None	.84	.72	.32	.11	.2	.31
1–2	.82	.58	.23	.4	.0	.34
3–4	.77	.51	.16	.1	.1	.22
5+		.43	.16	.2	.0	.12
Total	.81	.54	.19	.4	.1	.23

Note: Results refer to the combined sample of all villages, include marriages prior to 1700 that ended after 1700, and are restricted to couples for whom both death dates are known. Results based on fewer than 20 cases are omitted.
[a] Total for widowers includes cases in which the age at dissolution is unknown; in the case of widows, age at dissolution is known for all.

sexes in each age group. In every age group, those with no children surviving to age 5 were the most likely to remarry and indeed, except for widowers under age 40 and widows under age 30, the reduction in the chances of remarrying between those with no children and those with just one or two children is quite pronounced. It is interesting to note further that a strong negative association between age at dissolution and remarriage persists within each category of number of children.

While the age of children at the time of marital dissolution is not controlled for directly, presumably most if not all of the children of widowers or widows under age 40 would still be of dependent ages. In contrast, most of the children of parents who became widowed after age 50 would probably be old enough to make significant contributions to the support of the surviving parent, either in terms of labor to the household or through remittances if they were old enough to leave home. While the negative association between probability of remarriage and number of children holds at all ages, for both widows and

Table 7.12. *Proportion of widowers and widows remarrying, among those surviving at least five years after marital dissolution, by year of marital dissolution and number of children surviving to age 5, adjusted for age at time of dissolution*

Sex of surviving spouse and number of children	Year of marital dissolution			
	1700–49	1750–99	1800–49	1850–99
Widowers				
0	(.59)	.69	.62	.60
1–2	.52	.56	.50	.50
3–4	(.71)	.51	.48	.49
5+	(.67)	.48	.43	.40
Widows				
0	.31	.42	.30	.26
1–2	.43	.36	.28	.17
3–4	.30	.27	.22	.14
5+	.39	.24	.15	.13

Note: Results refer to the combined sample of all villages, include marriages prior to 1700 that ended after 1700, and are restricted to couples for whom both death dates are known. Results in parentheses are based on fewer than 50 cases. Adjustment for age at marital dissolution was made through multiple classification analysis, treating age as a covariate (in continuous form), and was done separately for men and women.

widowers, it is noticeably weaker for widowers under age 40 and widows under age 30.

In Table 7.12, the association between remarriage and the number of children is shown for different time periods. Given the importance of age at marital dissolution for the chances of remarrying and the fact that the age at marital dissolution increased over the time period being covered, results are presented that are statistically adjusted for age at marital dissolution. In the last three half-century periods of the eighteenth and nineteenth centuries, a substantial negative association between the number of children and the chances of remarriage is evident. In contrast, for the first half of the eighteenth century, no consistent association appears. This may imply that at that time, and perhaps earlier, having children was not a discouragement to remarriage. However, these results for the first half-century period need to be regarded with some caution since they are based on fewer cases than the subsequent half-centuries. Moreover, for each of the subsequent half-centuries, the negative association is fairly similar and there is no trend toward a strengthening relationship, as would be

Table 7.13. *Unadjusted and adjusted proportions of widowers and widows remarrying, among those surviving at least five years after marital dissolution, by year of dissolution, age at dissolution, and number of children surviving to age 5*

	Widowers		Widows	
	Unadjusted	Adjusted	Unadjusted	Adjusted
Year of marital dissolution				
1700–49	.73	.61	.45	.37
1750–99	.61	.56	.35	.32
1800–49	.49	.50	.24	.23
1850–99	.44	.49	.11	.16
Age at marital dissolution				
Under 25	(.91)	(.79)	.90	.83
25–29	.95	.88	.78	.74
30–34	.93	.90	.65	.63
35–39	.86	.85	.43	.43
40–49	.67	.67	.19	.19
50–59	.30	.31	.04	.04
60+	.08	.10	.01	.03
Number of children surviving to age 5				
0	.73	.61	.31	.31
1–2	.61	.56	.34	.25
3–4	.49	.50	.22	.21
5+	.44	.49	.12	.20

Note: Results refer to the combined sample of all villages, include marriages prior to 1700 that ended after 1700, and are restricted to couples for whom both death dates are known. Results in parentheses are based on fewer than 50 cases. Adjustment was made through multiple classification analysis, and was done separately for men and women. Adjusted results for each variable are adjusted for the other two.

expected if the nature of the relationship was evolving in a linear fashion over time.

Given these various relationships between year of marital dissolution, age at marital dissolution, and number of children at the time of marital dissolution, it is useful to examine the probability of remarriage within a limited multivariate framework incorporating all three of these variables. Table 7.13 presents the results of a multiple classification analysis in which the probability of remarrying is related to each of these three variables, adjusting for the effects of the other two. The analysis is done separately for widowers and widows. While the association between the probability of remarriage and each separate variable is reduced by statistically adjusting for the other two variables, substantial associations still persist in all three cases. Thus the probability of remarriage declines over time even after adjusting for age at marital dissolution and number of children. The inverse association between age at marital dissolution and remarriage persists after adjustment for year of dissolution and number of children; and the inverse association between remarriage and number of children is still evident after the year of, and age at, marital dissolution are controlled for.

Discussion

A number of clear and interesting results emerge from the analysis of marital dissolution and remarriage. The long-run decline in the probabilities of remarriage over the course of two centuries in the sample villages was accompanied by an increase in the average age of both husbands and wives at the time that death terminated their marriages. Since the age of entry into marriage was relatively stable, the average duration of a marital union also increased as a result. The frequency and pace of remarriage following the death of a spouse declined substantially. Moreover, pronounced age and sex differentials in the likelihood of remarriage were evident: widows were far less likely to remarry than widowers, and the probabilities of remarriage declined rapidly with age, particularly with women.

The decline in remarriage probabilities was doubtless caused in part by improvements in adult mortality, which gradually raised the ages of surviving spouses to levels at which remarriage has historically been rather unlikely. However, declines in adult mortality cannot account for the substantial declines that were also evident in age-specific probabilities of remarriage.

The fact that declines in age-specific marriage probabilities affected both men and women, as well as all occupational groups in the sample villages suggests the presence of a social change of wide scope. Previous scholars have suggested several explanations for the decline in remarriage that range from the economic to the psychological. Mitterauer and Sieder, for example, argue that declines in remarriage are linked to aggregate trends in the European economy, particularly to the decline of the family as the primary unit of production, and the advent of capitalist economies. Their analysis is based on the idea that the preindustrial, rural household was one in which the entire family formed an integral economic unit of production, and as such required that the two central adult roles, one male and one female, be filled.[17] When the unit was broken, it was difficult for the surviving spouse to continue operations effectively, especially if left with small children. Often, they hypothesize, the most realistic alternative under such circumstances was prompt remarriage.

They further argue that the pressure to remarry, for both widows and widowers, subsided as a 'consequence of the decrease in the social and economic importance of filling the central positions in the family, which has allowed for a greater number of "incomplete" families.'[18] Widow- and widower-headed families became more viable as the larger European economy changed from one based on domestic production to a more capitalistic economy based on larger units of production.

According to Mitterauer and Sieder's view, the pressure to remarry would have weighed most heavily on widows and widowers with children, especially small children. Data from the German villages, however, indicate a clear *inverse* association between the number of children and the chances of remarriage for both widows and widowers. Thus, those widowed persons who would appear in most need of a new spouse were precisely those least likely to remarry.[19] Data on remarriage by number of children suggest that understanding the possible economic or social *pressures* to remarry provides only a partial explanation of the decline in remarriage.

There may have been a growing reluctance on the part of single persons to marry widows or widowers, particularly those much older than themselves. A possible growth of sentiment in marriage and a rise in the ideal of a companionate marriage, referred to in Chapter 6, may gradually have reduced the desire of young, single people to enter into marriage with a widow or a widower. It is noteworthy that the analysis of the age gap between spouses in the sample of villages, also presented in Chapter 6, shows a considerable reduction in the proportion of marriages in which spouses were of sharply disparate ages.

Mitterauer and Sieder, as well as Jean-Louis Flandrin, have argued that the historic growth of stronger affective bonds between husbands and wives over the course of marriages that were themselves of longer duration contributed to the decline of remarriage and to the growth of intervals between widowhood and remarriage, for both men and

[17] Mitterauer and Sieder, *European family*, p. 150; Sieder and Mitterauer, 'Family life course.'
[18] Mitterauer and Sieder, *European family*, p. 150.
[19] See also Schofield and Wrigley, 'Remarriage intervals,' pp. 218–19.

women.[20] However, the growth in marriage duration over the entire period under study was rather modest for our sample village populations.

In populations where high rates of death or divorce lead to the frequent dissolution of marriage before the end of the reproductive span, remarried persons have the potential to contribute measurably to the overall level of fertility and therefore to have a noticeable, if not large, demographic impact.[21] Given the fact that remarriage in the sample villages during most of the period under observation was relatively common for women under age 40, the extent to which marital dissolution through the early death of a husband reduced the reproductive capacity of the population was moderated considerably, at least until the late nineteenth century. At the same time, the low probabilities of remarriage for women aged 40 or over had little or no impact on reproduction because such women were either already terminally sterile or past their most fecund years.

The reasons underlying the widely documented, sharp differences between widows and widowers in probabilities of remarriage clearly merit further exploration. If it is true that a substantial sexual division of labor and the typical economic functioning of rural couples during the eighteenth and nineteenth centuries required both a man and a woman to function efficiently, one might expect that women would be under the same pressures to remarry as men.[22] It may, however, have been easier for women to take on the male tasks for themselves than for men to take on the female tasks, a factor which would have lessened the pressure on women to remarry.[23]

Explaining the secular decline in remarriage itself is an even greater challenge. The continuous decline of remarriage probabilities in rural village populations seems puzzling given the relatively long persistence of domestic systems of production in such settings. In particular, peasants and artisans might be expected to be groups within which the family functioned more strongly, and persisted longer as a productive unit, in comparison to proletarians. Yet there is little difference in the levels of remarriage of these two groups. Given the fact that the changing nature of the economy must have affected occupational groups differently, their similar patterns of decline in the probabilities

---

[20] Mitterauer and Sieder, *European family*, p. 62; Flandrin, *Families in former times*, p. 115.
[21] Coale, 'Introduction.'
[22] Baulant, 'The scattered family'; Kennedy, *Irish emigration*.
[23] Segalen, 'Mentalité populaire et remariage,' p. 69.

of remarriage suggest that more than just economic changes lay behind these trends.

Finally, although a substantial decline in remarriage is evident, it should not obscure the fact that in the sample villages, and probably in preindustrial Europe generally, remarriage was relatively frequent and rapid for much of the period under study. This overall pattern can be viewed as part of the broader western European family and household formation system referred to in Chapter 6. Given the normative stress on the economic independence of single-family households, once such a household was established, there would be considerably greater need for the household to have two adults to function adequately, especially if adult married children were not present, than would be true in the case where an extended-family household was the norm.

Illegitimacy

In Germany, as indeed throughout most of Europe, the vast majority of reproductive behavior during the eighteenth and nineteenth centuries took place within the confines of marital unions as formally defined by the Church and the legal system. The discouragement of extramarital fertility was critical for the western European preindustrial demographic system, in which nuptiality was the principal mechanism through which a precarious balance between population and local resources was achieved.[1] Nevertheless, virtually nowhere was the suppression of births out of wedlock complete, and in some areas and during some periods non-marital fertility made more than a trivial contribution to overall fertility levels.[2] Moreover, while marriage often marked the beginning of a couple's reproductive career, this was by no means always the case. Prenuptial births to couples who subsequently married were not unusual, and even when a couple's first birth was postnuptial, a prenuptial conception often preceded, and in some cases may have precipitated, the marriage itself.

Births born or conceived out of wedlock are of concern not only for their demographic significance but also for what they imply about social life in the past. Their impact on the lives of the parents and children directly involved, as well as on the community at large, is a matter of historical interest. Moreover, they can serve as an imperfect indicator of premarital and extramarital sexual activity. Since sexual intercourse does not always result in a birth, the prevalence of illegitimate or prenuptially conceived births provides only a minimum

---

[1] Mackenroth, *Bevölkerungslehre*; Schofield, 'Demographic structure and environment'; Flinn, *European demographic system*.
[2] Shorter, Knodel and van de Walle, 'Decline of non-marital fertility'; Laslett *et al.*, *Bastardy*.

estimate of the extent of non-marital sexual activity. Moreover, the probability of a birth occurring is influenced by a number of intervening factors, such as fecundity, contraception, and abortion. These other factors could account for differences in out-of-wedlock or prenuptially conceived births. Nevertheless, it seems reasonable to assume that such intervening factors did not vary sufficiently during much of the period under observation and that illegitimacy and bridal pregnancy can serve at least as rough indicators of trends, and to some extent levels, of non-marital sexual activity.[3]

Considerable attention has been paid to illegitimacy and bridal pregnancy by social historians, some of whom have interpreted increases in their prevalence between the eighteenth and nineteenth centuries in western Europe as signalling a sexual revolution, with a lively debate developing over its causes and significance.[4] The mechanisms of social control influencing non-marital sexual activity are also of interest. Wrigley, for example, has recently argued that non-marital fertility and bridal pregnancy in the case of early modern England were regulated by the same social and economic forces that affected the timing and incidence of marriage proper, and in this sense were very much part of the institution of marriage more broadly defined.[5]

In this chapter, non-marital childbearing is examined to the extent permitted by the data contained in the village genealogies. In particular, the data are used to assess the levels and trends in illegitimacy, the patterns of legitimization, and the extent of repetitive illegitimacy. The next chapter then explores the phenomenon of bridal pregnancy and prenuptial births, completing the section on family formation. Before proceeding to a presentation of the substantive results, however, several issues concerning definitions and measurement require discussion. Since these issues as they refer to illegitimate and prenuptial births are closely interrelated, they are discussed in this chapter even though much of the substantive discussion of prenuptial births is deferred until the next chapter.

Issues of definition and measurement

The genealogies serving as the basis for this study encompass both legitimate and illegitimate births occurring in the villages and make it

[3] Shorter, *Modern family*, pp. 86–98.
[4] Shorter, *Modern family*; Phayer, *Sexual liberation and religion*; Laslett *et al.*, *Bastardy*.
[5] Wrigley, 'Marriage, fertility and growth.'

easy to distinguish between them. As described in Chapter 2, births to unmarried women for which there is no evidence of a subsequent marriage to the natural father are assigned to separate 'family' units designated with a special symbol reserved for non-marital unions. In cases where the evidence indicated that the parents of an illegitimate child subsequently married, the prenuptial births are attributed, along with any legitimate births, to the couple as a marital union, but can easily be distinguished from postnuptial births by a comparison of the date of birth with the date of marriage. Postnuptial births resulting from a prenuptial pregnancy are also readily identifiable through a comparison of the dates of marriage and first postnuptial birth.

Perhaps because family reconstitution lends itself so well to identifying prenuptial conceptions, historical demographic studies based on such data frequently examine bridal pregnancy in detail.[6] Illegitimacy has typically received less attention in such studies, with consideration usually limited to the proportion of total births that are born out of wedlock.[7] Only occasionally have attempts been made to exploit the potential of family reconstitution data for more intensive studies of illegitimacy, in part presumably because of a variety of methodological problems involved.[8] Indeed, non-marital unions and premarital births to couples who eventually marry are sometimes defined as outside the analytical scope of family reconstitution studies conducted within historical demography. In this study, as discussed in Chapter 2 and Appendix A, non-marital unions were coded only for the six fully-coded villages and were specifically excluded in the initial selection of couples for the remaining eight. Thus, for the complete sample of 14 villages, information is available for analysis on bridal pregnancy and prenuptial births to married couples, but not on illegitimate births that were not subsequently followed by the couple's marriage (at least as indicated in the genealogy). Examination of the full range of out-of-

---

[6] A full reconstitution is not necessary for the study of bridal pregnancy since only first postnuptial births need to be linked to marriages. Indeed, one of the most extensive studies of bridal pregnancy, in this case in England, is based on only this limited segment of the family reconstitution process (Hair, 'Bridal pregnancy in earlier centuries,' and 'Bridal pregnancy further examined').

[7] Such analyses in fact do not require family reconstitution at all since they can be based on simple counts of births by legitimacy status, which is often indicated directly in birth registers, whether parochial or civil. For example, the most extensive historical study of regional variations and trends over time in illegitimacy in England is based on counts directly from parish registers rather than from family reconstitution data (Laslett, *Family life and illicit love*, Chapter 3, and 'Illegitimacy').

[8] Some examples of the use of family reconstitution data for more detailed studies of illegitimacy can be found in Laslett *et al.*, *Bastardy*.

wedlock births must therefore be restricted to special analyses based on the subset of the six fully-coded villages.[9]

Measuring illegitimacy

Family reconstitution data are not well suited for calculating a true *rate* of non-marital fertility which would relate out-of-wedlock births to the years at risk of the exposed population of unmarried women. The problem lies in the difficulty of determining the period during which an unmarried woman can be considered present in observation. For this reason, illegitimacy is typically measured instead by the proportion of all births that are born out of wedlock, often referred to as the illegitimacy *ratio* (even though, strictly speaking, it is a proportion rather than a ratio). Since the number of total births, which serves as the denominator of this index, includes legitimate births, the index is sensitive not only to the propensity of unmarried women to have an illegitimate birth, but also to the level of marital fertility and to the proportion of women of reproductive age who are married.[10] By restricting the illegitimacy ratio to first births only, the influence of marital fertility can be minimized, but nuptiality still remains as a potentially confounding influence. The inadequacy of the illegitimacy ratio as an indicator of non-marital fertility is of some concern in the present study since both nuptiality and marital fertility differed among villages and changed moderately over time. Hence these potentially distorting influences need to be taken into account when interpreting results.

Distinguishing non-legitimized and legitimized births

Illegitimacy is a broad concept encompassing births resulting from a variety of circumstances, ranging from casual encounters to engagements to marry in which the husband-to-be prematurely died before the wedding could take place.[11] The circumstances leading to a bridal

---

[9] The subset of the 6 fully-coded villages appears to be reasonably typical of the complete sample of 14 villages, at least with respect to the overall level of bridal pregnancy and prenuptial births. For example, for couples married during the nineteenth century, 28 percent of first postnuptial births were born within the first eight months of marriage for the six fully-coded villages compared to 26 percent for the full sample. For the same couples, 12 percent of all first births preceded marriage both for the subset of 6 villages and for the complete set of 14 villages.

[10] For a fuller discussion of this issue, see Knodel and Hochstadt, 'Urban and rural illegitimacy.'

[11] See, for example, von Ungern-Sternberg and Schubnell, *Grundriss der Bevölkerungswissenschaft*; Laslett, 'Illegitimacy'; Wrigley, 'Marriage, fertility and growth'; and Shorter, *Modern family*.

pregnancy are also undoubtedly quite varied, ranging from cases where the wedding was imminent at the time that conception occurred to cases where there may have been little prior intention to marry. The genealogies contain relatively little direct information about the circumstances surrounding a particular illegitimate birth or prenuptial pregnancy. Nevertheless, through relying on indirect indicators, some limited inferences can be made.

In the case of the fully-coded villages, two categories of illegitimate births can in principle be distinguished: those for which there was an indication that they were followed by the marriage of the parents and those for which there was no such indication. In the present chapter, the former are referred to interchangeably as 'legitimized' or 'prenuptial' and the latter as 'non-legitimized' births.[12] Such a distinction, if correct, would be substantively interesting. Presumably legitimized and non-legitimized births often resulted from different types of relationships between the parents and involved different circumstances in which the child was raised. It might be expected, for example, that the nature of the parental union at the time that the birth occurred more closely resembled a marital union in cases of legitimized births than non-legitimized ones. In addition, legitimized children would generally be similar to legitimate children inasmuch as those who survived would typically grow up in a household where the natural father was present. Non-legitimized children presumably would not unless the couple were living together in a common-law union.

Although non-legitimized births can be studied only from the subset of fully-coded villages, it is still possible to distinguish prenuptial from postnuptial births for the complete set of villages and to determine if the conception of a postnuptial birth occurred before or after marriage. Moreover, prenuptially conceived postnuptial births can be further subdivided according to how advanced the pregnancy was at the time of marriage. Such a subdivision is potentially useful in distinguishing different sets of circumstances in which the marriage took place.[13] For example, in cases where the birth occurs close to nine months follow-

---

[12] Note that, as defined here, legitimized births include those which died prior to their parents' marriage so long as they are attributed to the couple's marital union. As discussed in the text and Appendix G, births to a couple prior to their marriage which died before the parents married will probably *not* be linked to the couple. Note also that the term 'prenuptial' (which is synonymous with 'legitimized' as defined here) refers only to births preceding a couple's own marriage to each other and does not encompass births to unwed mothers (or fathers) who marry a spouse other than the natural parent of the child.

[13] Imhof, 'Illegitimät,' pp. 548–50; Wrigley, 'Marriage, fertility and growth.'

ing marriage, the couple themselves may have been unaware that a pregnancy was already under way at the time of the wedding and conception is likely to have taken place during a period of betrothal. In cases where the pregnancy was advanced, not only the couple themselves but also the community at large was likely to have taken notice of it, and social pressure may have played a more important role in precipitating the marriage. In the first instance, therefore, the decision to marry is more likely to have led to the bridal pregnancy, while in the latter the pregnancy is more likely to have contributed to the decision to marry.

There is little reason to suspect that coverage of illegitimate births is unusually deficient,[14] or to doubt that legitimate and illegitimate births can be accurately distinguished on the basis of village genealogies. Illegitimate births are usually clearly designated as such in the parish registers in Germany[15] and thus the compilers of the genealogies would have had little trouble in identifying them. Less confidence, however, can be placed in the accuracy of distinctions between legitimized and non-legitimized births. Manuals on how to compile a village genealogy clearly stress the importance of linking premarital illegitimate births to the subsequent marriage of the parents,[16] and this is a standard feature of the genealogies. Nevertheless, sufficient information might not have been available to the genealogist to do this in every case. There are several potential sources of error. These are summarized below and explored in some detail in Appendix G.

One situation in which an error is likely to arise involves unwed mothers who gave birth in the village but who later married outside the village. The genealogist would generally have been unaware of such a marriage since it would not have entered the local registers. Unless he fortuitously learned about the marriage in some other connection, the birth would be attributed to a non-marital union in the genealogy even if in fact it had been legitimized later.

Another situation that could give rise to error involves cases where the father's name is not provided in the parish register entry for the illegitimate birth and the child either dies before the mother marries or is not mentioned further in the registers following the marriage. The frequency with which this situation occurred varied across villages and over time.[17] Under such circumstances, the compiler would have

---

[14] Knodel and Shorter, 'Family reconstitution data.'

[15] Demleitner and Roth, *Volksgenealogie.*

[16] Demleitner and Roth, *Volksgenealogie*; Hofmann *et al.*, *Von der Kirchenbuchverkartung.*

[17] Generally in Germany prior to the beginning of the nineteenth century, illegitimate children were routinely given the name of the father provided it was known. This changed under the influence of the Napoleonic Code, although in some places it

difficulty knowing if the woman's husband was the child's father unless some additional information were available.[18] The result would be to attribute some births that were actually prenuptial to a non-marital union of the mother (with the father unspecified) rather than to the marital union of the couple.

Both situations described above would result in understating the proportion of illegitimate births that were legitimized. This potential bias needs to be considered when interpreting results which refer to illegitimate *births* by legitimization status. An additional potential bias can affect results which focus on the proportion of *women* who experienced out-of-wedlock births, since some women's premarital reproductive histories may not be recorded in the local parish records. This problem is likely to be particularly severe for women who moved to the village at or subsequent to the time of marriage. If a non-native woman experienced an out-of-wedlock birth elsewhere, it would not be found in the local register and the compiler of the genealogy would probably be unaware of it, especially if the child died prior to the woman moving into the parish. This would bias the result toward understating the proportion of women who experienced such births. The problems of illegitimate births prior to marriage that are unaccounted for, or marriages following illegitimate births that are unaccounted for, are both related to migration and could potentially be eliminated by restricting analysis to native women who die locally, and thus are likely to have spent their entire life in the village. However, such a restriction risks introducing substantial selectivity biases since migration appears to be closely associated with the type of birth characterizing the start of a woman's reproductive career (see the discussion in Appendix G).

Measuring the prevalence of prenuptial births

Although past historical demographic studies have occasionally examined the prevalence of prenuptial births, no single standard

persisted longer than others (Demleitner and Roth, *Volksgenealogie*, p. 38). Examination of the village genealogies suggests this had a substantial influence on whether or not the father's name was included in the birth register when an illegitimate birth was entered. Indeed, the French Civil Code as promulgated at the start of the nineteenth century specifically forbade 'scrutiny as to paternity' (van de Walle, 'Illegitimacy'). The potential problems that might result from the exclusion of the father's name for determining whether an illegitimate birth is legitimized are examined in more detail in the text.

[18] In cases where the child dies after the couple marries or experiences some other event that is then recorded in the local registers, the name of the parents would often be indicated, thus enabling the genealogist to link the earlier birth entry to the marital union of the parents.

measure has been used to represent this phenomenon. It is possible, for example, to express the prevalence of prenuptial births in relation to all brides, to brides still of reproductive age only, or to fertile brides only (i.e. brides who bear at least one child either before or after marriage). In fact, the choice of denominators among those specified makes only a modest difference.[19] Thus it would be redundant to present all the alternative measures in the analysis. Since it is reasonable to assume that childlessness was largely involuntary in the village populations during the period under study, eliminating non-fertile women from the denominator of the measure of prenuptial births seems desirable. Hence in the following analysis, the prevalence of prenuptial births is usually expressed as a percentage of fertile brides, including brides who only gave birth prenuptially.

Trends and levels of illegitimacy

The trend in illegitimacy based on the combined results for the six fully-coded villages is shown in Figure 8.1a in terms of the percentage illegitimate among all births, and in Figure 8.1b among all first births. While the latter is much higher, since most out-of-wedlock births are first births, the trends are very similar. After following a rather erratic initial course, illegitimacy shows a sharp rise during the second half of the eighteenth century and the early part of the nineteenth century and then declines fairly steeply during much of the remainder of the nineteenth century. For the six villages combined, illegitimate births as a percentage of all births reaches a peak of over 13 percent for the decades of the 1820s and 1830s, while the proportion illegitimate among first births reaches a maximum of 40 percent during the 1820s. This is in sharp contrast to the far lower levels experienced during the early decades of the eighteenth century when out-of-wedlock births were at times as low as 2 percent of all births and less than 10 percent of first births. A rather rapid and substantial decline in illegitimacy is apparent throughout much of the latter half of the nineteenth century and into the first decade of the twentieth century, although an upturn is apparent in the second decade, the last period shown in the graphs.

The sharp rise in the illegitimacy ratio during the latter part of the eighteenth and the early part of the nineteenth centuries has been observed in much of northern and western Europe.[20] It is also known

---

[19] For example, among women marrying in the eighteenth and nineteenth centuries in the combined sample of all villages, 7.6 percent of all brides, 7.7 percent of brides under 50, and 8.7 percent of fertile brides experienced a prenuptial birth.

[20] Shorter, *Modern family.*

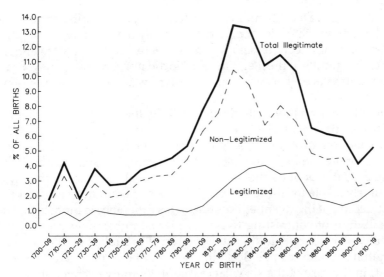

Figure 8.1a. *Trends in illegitimacy by legitimization status: illegitimate births as percent of all births*

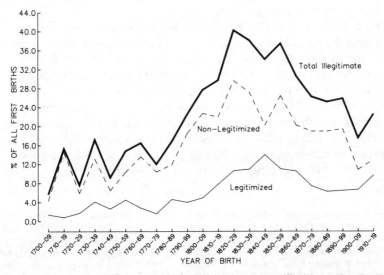

Figure 8.1b. *Trends in illegitimacy by legitimization status: illegitimate first births as percent of all first births.* Results for Figures 8.1a and 8.1b are limited to the six fully-coded villages and are restricted to local births for which an exact birth date is known. In the case of first births, the associated non-marital union or marriage must also have been local. Legitimized births refer to illegitimate births which are attributed to a couple who subsequently married

that illegitimate fertility measured in terms of a non-marital fertility *rate* declined in much of Europe, and specifically in Germany, during the latter part of the nineteenth and the early part of the twentieth centuries; trends in the illegitimacy ratio did not necessarily mirror this change, however, because marital fertility was declining at the same time.[21]

For Germany as a whole, during 1850–59, the first decade for which such statistics are available at the national level, 11.5 percent of births were born out of wedlock, a figure almost identical to the 11.4 percent found for the combined sample of six villages.[22] The similarity does not hold for later periods, however – the national illegitimacy *ratio* was relatively stable for the last several decades of the nineteenth and the first decade of the twentieth century. This difference is probably more a reflection of contrasting trends of marital rather than non-marital fertility. A moderate decline in marital fertility buoyed up the national illegitimacy ratio despite declining non-marital fertility rates. In contrast, in the case of the six villages, marital fertility changed little and hence the declining illegitimacy ratio can be taken as a sign of a decline in non-marital fertility.[23] In this sense the experience of the six villages resembles the national situation more than is apparent from an uncritical comparison of legitimacy ratios *per se*.

Figures 8.1a and 8.1b also show illegitimacy ratios separately for legitimized and non-legitimized births. As discussed in connection with measurement issues, there is reason to suspect that some apparently non-legitimized births were in fact births to couples who later married. In any event, the trends in these two components of the illegitimacy ratio more or less mirror each other during the period under observation and, to the extent that these results can be accepted, the rise and fall in total illegitimacy appears to be more a result of changes in non-legitimized than in legitimized births. A somewhat earlier peak in non-legitimized births is also evident.

[21] Shorter, Knodel and van de Walle, 'Decline of non-marital fertility'; Knodel, *Decline of fertility*.

[22] von Ungern-Sternberg and Schubnell, *Grundriss der Bevölkerungswissenschaft*, p. 216.

[23] As measured by the Coale indices of marital and non-marital fertility (I_g and I_h), marital fertility declined by 13 percent nationally between 1866–68 and 1898–1902, while non-marital fertility declined by 16 percent (Knodel, *Decline of fertility*, p. 39). Thus the decline in marital fertility almost equaled that of non-marital fertility, with the result that the latter is not evident from trends in the illegitimacy ratio. In contrast, marital fertility measured by the equivalent index for the combined total of the six fully-coded villages declined by only 2 percent between the 1860–69 and 1890–99 marriage cohorts. While an equivalent index of non-marital fertility cannot be calculated for the six fully-coded villages, unless nuptiality increased sharply, the decline in the illegitimacy *ratio* during the periods when these marriage cohorts were reproducing would reflect a decline in the *rate* of non-marital childbearing.

Trends in illegitimacy in the individual villages are shown in Table 8.1 as a percentage of total births. All villages are characterized by a rise in illegitimacy starting sometime during the eighteenth century and, with the exception of Middels, by a subsequent decline later in the nineteenth century. For all villages and all periods, non-legitimized births represent a larger component of illegitimacy than do legitimized births.

Despite the similarity between the villages in the course of illegitimacy and the importance of non-legitimized births, considerable differences in the levels are evident. During most of the period under observation, the two Waldeck villages of Braunsen and Massenhausen were characterized by the highest illegitimacy and, with the exception of the last quarter of the nineteenth century, by far the lowest level characterized the village of Middels in East Friesland. Even during the last quarter of the nineteenth century, only in Kappel does illegitimacy fall slightly below that in Middels. Considerable and persistent regional variations in non-marital fertility rates based on official statistics are evident in Germany, at least from the latter part of the nineteenth century when such statistics are first available.[24] East Friesland was characterized by one of the lowest non-marital fertility rates of any region in the country, and thus Middels is not exceptional for the area in which it is located.

As discussed in Chapter 6, legal restrictions on marriage were imposed, or in some cases reimposed, during the early nineteenth century in parts of Germany, including areas in which some of the sample villages were located. This legislation was later repealed or weakened, particularly during the 1860s and early 1870s. Indeed, one reason for the repeal was concern about the high rates of illegitimate fertility that the restrictions were thought to foster. There is some evidence suggesting that the repeal of these laws resulted in reductions in non-marital fertility in the affected areas.[25]

Without more precise information on the nature of such local regulations on marriage in the local communities under study, an exacting analysis of their possible effect on illegitimacy trends is not feasible. It seems clear, however, that marriage restrictions are unlikely to be the main explanation for the major trends in illegitimacy. Not only is the rise and fall of non-marital fertility a common feature of much of western and northern Europe, including those areas in Germany not affected by such legislation, but in the sample of the six fully-coded villages the sharpest rise in the illegitimacy ratio took place

[24] Knodel and Hochstadt, 'Urban and rural illegitimacy'; Knodel, *Decline of fertility*.
[25] Knodel, 'Law, marriage and illegitimacy.'

Table 8.1. *Illegitimate births as percent of total births by legitimization status, village, and year of birth*

	1700–49	1750–74	1775–99	1800–24	1825–49	1850–74	1875–99	Total
Kappel								
All illegitimate	2.0	1.7	3.1	5.9	9.3	7.3	2.8	5.2
Non-legitimized	1.4	1.3	4.3	4.6	5.6	5.6	1.3	3.6
Legitimized	0.5	0.5	0.9	1.3	3.7	1.7	1.4	1.6
Rust								
All illegitimate	2.5	3.0	4.4	13.6	15.6	10.3	4.6	8.7
Non-legitimized	1.9	2.2	3.8	10.7	10.9	6.3	3.3	6.2
Legitimized	0.6	0.7	0.6	2.9	4.6	4.0	1.2	2.5
Öschelbronn								
All illegitimate	2.3	4.6	4.9	5.2	7.6	15.3	11.6	7.9
Non-legitimized	1.5	3.5	3.7	4.0	5.4	11.6	8.7	5.9
Legitimized	0.9	1.0	1.2	1.2	2.1	3.7	2.9	2.0
Braunsen								
All illegitimate	6.3	5.9	2.7	14.3	23.0	16.2	8.4	11.3
Non-legitimized	4.2	4.7	2.3	11.1	17.0	11.2	6.6	8.4
Legitimized	2.1	1.2	0.5	3.3	6.1	5.0	1.8	3.0
Massenhausen								
All illegitimate	5.7	8.5	11.1	17.2	25.0	18.5	11.7	14.5
Non-legitimized	5.1	7.1	8.7	13.6	18.9	13.0	10.3	11.3
Legitimized	0.6	1.4	2.4	3.6	6.1	5.5	1.4	3.2
Middels								
All illegitimate	0.4	0.3	0.7	1.5	2.5	2.8	3.0	2.1
Non-legitimized	0.4	0.0	0.5	1.1	1.5	1.7	2.4	1.4
Legitimized	0.0	0.3	0.2	0.4	1.1	1.1	0.7	0.7

Note: Results refer to the six fully-coded villages and are restricted to births occurring in the village for which an exact birth date is known. Legitimized births refer to illegitimate births which are attributed to a couple who subsequently married.

during the first two decades of the nineteenth century, precisely when marriage restrictions were thought to be particularly liberal.[26] Moreover, the decline in illegitimacy continues long after the repeal of the most restrictive legislation, in the 1860s. The unusually sharp decline in legitimized births between the 1860s and 1870s, however, does coincide with the general repeal of marriage restrictions and may be linked to it. During the periods of restrictions, authorities may have prevented some couples from marrying initially but, after the birth of an out-of-wedlock child, may have acceded to the couple's wishes.

Regardless of the role legislative changes may have had on age at marriage or on out-of-wedlock births, changes in the age at marriage would be excepted to induce parallel changes in the illegitimacy ratio because of the nature of the measure: delayed marriage depresses the denominator of the illegitimacy ratio (if all births as opposed to only first births are included) by reducing legitimate births, and inflates the numerator by lengthening the average amount of time a single woman is exposed to the risk of an illegitimate birth. In the combined sample of the six fully-coded villages, decade averages (not shown) indicate a somewhat irregular increase in the age at first marriage for both men and women from the mid-eighteenth century until the mid-nineteenth century, an increase which was followed by a somewhat more regular decline during the remainder of the nineteenth century.[27] A similar pattern of a rise and then a fall in the ages at marriage during the nineteenth century is evident for the full sample of all villages, as indicated in Chapter 6 (see Figure 6.1).

Thus, during the period that the illegitimacy ratio was rising steeply, at least for the six fully-coded villages, an increasing age at marriage may have been contributing to it. Similarly, during part of the period when the illegitimacy ratio was declining rapidly, a falling age at marriage may have played some part. Given the rather moderate changes in age at marriage compared to the quite substantial rise and fall of the illegitimacy ratio, the influence of the shifts in age at marriage is likely to have been only modest.

---

[26] Knodel, 'Law, marriage and illegitimacy'; Matz, *Pauperismus und Bevölkerung*.

[27] Age at marriage for the six fully-coded villages has been calculated for all persons for whom at least a birth year and an exact marriage date are known. This permits the calculation to be based on more cases than when the calculation is based on only the preselected couples, such as is done in Chapter 6. A comparison of results for the six fully-coded villages indicates little systematic difference between resulting age at marriage for these two different base populations (see Appendix A, Table A.5). However, increasing the number of cases makes the decade averages more stable.

Patterns of legitimization

The simple fact that a birth occurs out of wedlock informs us little about the nature of illegitimacy in the sample villages. For this reason it is of interest to pursue more fully analyses which take advantage of the distinction that can be made with family reconstitution data between legitimized and non-legitimized out-of-wedlock births. As indicated above, results of such analyses must be interpreted cautiously because of potential biases inherent in the data which would prevent detection of the legitimization of some illegitimate births.

Despite these problems, it is still of some interest to examine the trends and patterns of legitimization, as long as the potential biases that might affect the results are kept in mind. In Table 8.2, the percentage of illegitimate births that are eventually legitimized is shown both for all births and separately by survival status to age 1. For illegitimate births in general, the percentage that are eventually legitimized is noticeably higher during the nineteenth than during the eighteenth century, with the trend continuing into the twentieth century (which can be studied with the data for the fully-coded villages). There is little reason to believe that this trend is an artifact of the problems discussed above and in Appendix G: there was no consistent trend toward an increase in the proportion of unwed mothers who died outside the village, and the inclusion of the father's name in records of illegitimate births became less common over time.

Only modest differences in the proportion of illegitimate births that were legitimized are evident among the six different villages, ranging from roughly a fifth to a third, at least as detectable in the genealogies. While it is possible that the biases mentioned above exert unequal influences in the different villages, it seems unlikely that very large differences would emerge even after these biases had been taken into account. Apparently the level of illegitimacy varies considerably more than the tendency to legitimize an out-of-wedlock birth.

The proportion legitimized is shown separately for male and female births. There is apparently little relationship between legitimization and the sex of the child. Any suspicion that there might be a greater tendency to legitimize a male child, in the interest of securing a male heir, is not borne out by these findings. Indeed, slightly more female than male out-of-wedlock births were legitimized.

For all periods, all villages, and both sexes, infants who survive to age 1 are much more likely to be legitimized than non-survivors. Clearly, this result is at least partially an artifact of the greater difficulty of linking non-survivors to the parents' subsequent marriage. Two

Table 8.2. *Legitimized births as percent of illegitimate births, by survival status to age 1 and by year of birth, by village and by sex*

	All births	Survivors to age 1[a]	Non-survivors[a]
Year of birth			
1700–49	23.9	(27.3)	—
1750–99	20.2	22.1	(12.2)
1800–49	27.2	33.3	9.4
1850–99	29.1	36.3	12.7
1900–49	46.0	51.9	21.8
1700–1899	27.0	33.4	11.8
Village (births 1700–1899)			
Kappel	30.6	36.7	20.3
Rust	28.4	38.2	6.7
Öschelbronn	25.4	30.7	15.5
Braunsen	26.1	29.0	14.3
Massenhausen	22.7	26.5	11.5
Middels	32.2	34.2	21.4
Sex (births 1700–1899)			
Male	25.7	32.0	11.3
Female	28.3	34.8	11.0

Note: Results refer to the six fully-coded villages and are restricted to births occurring in the village for which an exact birth date is known. Legitimized births refer to illegitimate births which are attributed to a couple who subsequently married. Results in parentheses are based on 20–49 births; results based on fewer than 20 births are omitted.
[a] Limited to periods when the registration of child deaths is judged to be relatively complete.

other possible factors may also be involved. First, the survivorship of an illegitimate infant might indeed increase the likelihood of marrying, possibly because of associated community pressure, a greater sense of responsibility to get married for the child's sake on the part of the couple themselves, or a combination of both. Second, unwed mothers with little prospect of marrying the father may be in a situation less favorable for caring for the infant than those who are likely to marry. Although infant mortality among illegitimate children was moderately higher than among legitimate children, it is unlikely that this second factor would account for much of the substantial difference, between surviving and non-surviving infants, in the proportion legitimized (see Appendix E, Table E.2).

Additional information on legitimization can be extracted from the data available for the complete set of 14 villages even though it does not contain information about non-legitimized births. Table 8.3 indicates

Table 8.3. *Frequency and selected characteristics of marriages preceded by a prenuptial birth, by year of marriage and regional location of village*

	% of fertile marriages with prenuptial birth	For couples with prenuptial birth		
		% with more than one such confinement	average months from first birth to marriage	% marrying within one year of first birth
Year of marriage (all villages)				
1700–49	2.2	(4)	(21)	(62)
1750–99	3.1	6	25	56
1800–24	9.1	17	33	40
1825–49	14.1	23	40	26
1850–74	14.5	25	44	30
1875–99	9.0	10	31	34
1700–1899	8.6	18	37	34
Regional location and year of marriage				
4 Baden villages	8.7	18	38	32
1700–99	2.5	(5)	(26)	(58)
1800–99	11.5	19	39	29
1 Württemberg village	10.3	15	32	40
1700–99	5.4	—	—	—
1800–99	13.2	19	30	41
3 Bavarian villages	8.6	16	37	35
1700–99	1.4	—	—	—
1800–99	12.8	(17)	40	(31)
4 Waldeck villages	14.8	23	42	29
1700–99	4.4	(11)	(27)	(41)
1800–99	21.3	25	44	27
2 East Friesland villages	2.4	(2)	(6)	86
1700–99	1.7	—	—	—
1800–99	2.9	(3)	(7)	(80)

Note: Results are subject to restriction 1 (see Table A.1). Results based on 20–49 cases are shown in parentheses; results based on

the percentage of married couples who had a prenuptial birth and, for those couples with a prenuptial birth, how common it was for more than one illegitimate confinement to be associated with marriage and how long an interval occurred between the time of the first prenuptial birth and the subsequent marriage. As discussed above and in Appendix G, not all prenuptial births to a couple are likely to be recorded as such in the genealogies. Thus the proportion of couples with prenuptial births is understated. In addition, the time between the first prenuptial birth and marriage is probably underestimated. It is more difficult to assess if the extent of repetitive prenuptial births among those with a known prenuptial birth is over- or understated, since this will depend on the particular pattern of which actual prenuptial births elude being detected as such.

The trend in the percentage of fertile marriages with at least one prenuptial birth follows quite closely the trends in legitimized births as already examined for the six fully-coded villages.[28] Only a small proportion of marriages were preceded by a birth during the eighteenth century. Prenuptial births were considerably more common during the nineteenth century, rising substantially during the first half and declining during the second half. The trends during the nineteenth century correspond roughly to what would be expected if they were influenced by the imposition and later repeal of marriage restrictions. An examination of decade averages (not shown) indicates a particularly sharp increase in the proportion of couples with a prenuptial birth between the 1810s and the 1820s and, as was also evident in Figure 8.1 for the six fully-coded villages, a particularly sharp decline between the 1860s and 1870s.

The increasing prevalence of prenuptial births among married couples between the eighteenth and nineteenth centuries is evident for all regional groupings of villages. Nevertheless, substantial differences in the overall levels existed, especially for the nineteenth century, when such differences were more pronounced. During this period, couples in the two villages in East Friesland were least likely to have had prenuptial births, and couples in the villages in Waldeck were by far the most likely.

A positive association is apparent, among couples with at least one

---

[28] The fact that the couples included in the complete sample of all 14 villages were preselected on a number of criteria not specifically relevant for the study of prenuptial births does not appear to have biased the results. This is evident from a comparison based on the six fully-coded villages. The proportion of couples married during the combined eighteenth and nineteenth centuries who experienced a prenuptial birth is almost identical, whether results are based on all couples for which the calculation can be made or only on the preselected couples.

confinement, between the overall prevalence of prenuptial births and repetitive prenuptial confinements.[29] During the first half of the eighteenth century, couples with a prenuptial birth only rarely experienced more than one confinement prior to marriage. By the third quarter of the nineteenth century, when the probability of a couple having a prenuptial birth was at its peak, fully one-quarter of those with a prenuptial birth had more than one prenuptial confinement. This drops off sharply for the last quarter of the nineteenth century as the probability of having a prenuptial birth also declined. Likewise, in the East Friesland villages, where prenuptial births were rare, of those couples who experienced a prenuptial birth, virtually none had more than one such confinement. In contrast, in the four villages in Waldeck, both prenuptial births were most common and the proportion experiencing multiple prenuptial confinements was highest.

The delay between the first prenuptial birth and marriage also seems to correspond closely to the frequency with which couples experienced prenuptial births. During the eighteenth century, the average delay was approximately two years, and more than half the couples who eventually married after an out-of-wedlock birth did so within one year. During the middle two quarters of the nineteenth century, when the highest proportions of married couples experienced prenuptial births, the delay between the birth and marriage was the greatest, averaging well over three years and with considerably less than a third marrying in the first year. Likewise, a comparison of the regional groupings of villages shows a similar relationship. In the East Frisian villages, marriage occurred very quickly after the first prenuptial birth, while in the Waldeck villages it was delayed longest.

The dramatic contrast between the eighteenth and nineteenth centuries with respect to the time between a prenuptial birth and a subsequent marriage is illustrated in Figure 8.2, which shows, for couples who eventually marry, the cumulative proportion married during the first successive 36 months following the first prenuptial birth. In the eighteenth century, over a quarter of couples who legitimized their first prenuptial birth did so within 3 months, half did so by 8 months, and two-thirds by 15 months. In sharp contrast, during the nineteenth century it took 10 months before a quarter of couples with prenuptial births married, almost two years before half of them married, and over three years before two-thirds married.

The results point to an apparent coherence in the patterns of

---

[29] Results refer to confinements rather than births to avoid having a woman who had an illegitimate multiple birth (twins or triplets), but no subsequent illegitimate births, appear as if she experienced repeated childbearing out of wedlock.

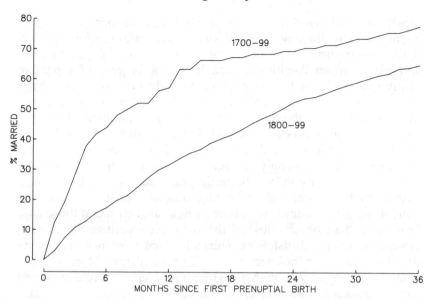

Figure 8.2. *The cumulative percent married by months since a prenuptial birth and year of marriage, among couples who eventually legitimize the birth.* Results are based on the combined sample of all villages and are subject to restriction 1 (see Table A.1)

legitimized births. During periods and in places where it was more usual for a married couple to start their reproductive career prior to marriage, there also appears to be less of an urgency to marry following the birth and a greater tolerance of having more than one birth before getting married. It is possible that the implementation and later repeal of marriage restrictions contributed to this coherence over time: if such restrictions forced couples to delay official marriage past when they wished to cohabit, the restrictions could lead to an increase in the proportion of couples with a prenuptial birth, an increase in the number of prenuptial births per couple that experienced them, and a longer wait until marriage permission was finally granted. Marriage restrictions may also help explain a similar coherence apparent in the way the pattern varied with regional location.

Repetitive illegitimacy

Recent discussions of historical trends in illegitimacy by Peter Laslett and his associates have stressed the importance of the bearing of repetitive illegitimate births by a bastardy-prone subsociety.[30] According to this view, there was a small subgroup, or subsociety as they call it, that was particularly prone to bearing illegitimate children. In times and places when illegitimacy was high, the bearing of repetitive illegitimate births by this subgroup is thought to account for a large share of all out-of-wedlock births; when illegitimacy was low, repetitive illegitimacy is thought to have been less frequent. Thus the increase in illegitimacy observed between the eighteenth and nineteenth centuries would be less the result of out-of-wedlock child-bearing spreading generally throughout the population than a product of increased activity by the bastardy-prone subsociety. Laslett also stresses that the circumstances leading to an illegitimate birth could be quite different for women who bear a single such birth and those who bear more than one.[31] Most of the work on repetitive illegitimacy examined only the British Isles. Thus it is of some interest to examine the phenomenon in the context of the German villages. Moreover, the village genealogies, although not without problems, are relatively well suited for such an analysis.[32]

The evidence presented above indicates that bearers of repetitive prenuptial births contribute disproportionately more when the overall level of prenuptial births is high than when it is low. Using data for the six fully-coded villages, this same issue can be explored with respect to non-legitimized out-of-wedlock births. In Table 8.4, which presents the results of such an analysis, the term 'bastard-bearer' is used exclusively to refer to women who give birth to non-legitimized children and does not include mothers of prenuptial births (unless they also had a non-legitimized birth). A woman is labeled as a 'repeater' if there was evidence in the genealogy that she gave birth to more than one non-legitimized child.[33]

Again, the various biases which could affect the results must be kept in mind. In addition to the biases discussed above, which could lead to a misclassification of some births as non-legitimized, although they were in fact legitimized, there is the risk that women who spent time outside the village had non-legitimized births not included in the local

[30] See, for example, Laslett, 'Bastardy prone sub-society'; McFarlane, 'Illegitimacy'; Oosterveen et al., 'Family reconstitution and bastardy.'

[31] Laslett, 'Bastardy prone sub-society.'

[32] For a discussion of the problems in detecting repeated bastard-bearing, see Laslett, 'Bastardy prone sub-society.'

[33] In this analysis results refer to births rather than confinements because of the nature of the coding of the particular data set on which this analysis is based. Thus the small number of women who gave birth to non-legitimized twins but experienced no further non-legitimized births would be counted as 'repeaters.' Given the low frequency of such cases, this has little effect on the extent of repeated bastard-bearing indicated.

Table 8.4. *Frequency of non-legitimized childbearing and repeated non-legitimized childbearing by year of first birth and by village*

	Bastard-bearers as % of fertile women	Repeaters as % of bastard-bearers	Among women who are born and die locally and survive at least 5 years past first birth	
			Bastard-bearers as % of fertile women	Repeaters as % of bastard-bearers
Year of first birth				
1700–49	9.7	12.3	4.2	—
1750–99	13.7	24.4	8.3	(33.3)
1800–24	25.0	46.7	21.0	58.4
1825–49	25.0	34.2	18.1	42.4
1850–74	23.3	33.6	14.3	40.5
1875–99	19.6	22.4	10.3	26.5
1700–1899	19.7	31.7	13.2	42.3
Village				
Kappel	13.3	34.8	8.7	49.2
Rust	21.0	32.7	16.1	39.2
Öschelbronn	23.5	32.8	16.0	36.9
Braunsen	26.9	24.3	16.5	(47.6)
Massenhausen	33.3	32.9	22.1	52.0
Middels	7.4	(15.9)	3.6	—

Note: Results refer to the six fully-coded villages and are based on women whose first birth occurs locally. A bastard-bearer is defined as a woman who experienced at least one non-legitimized illegitimate birth; a repeater is defined as a woman who experienced more than one such birth. Results in parentheses are based on 20–49 cases; results based on fewer than 20 cases are omitted.

registers. To the extent that this problem exists, it would lead to an undercount of bastard-bearers as well as repeaters. Thus, to some extent, the potential biases should counteract each other. Results are also shown separately for only those women who were born and who died in the village and who survived at least five years past their first birth. Among this subset of women, not only should the risks be minimal that a woman experienced a non-legitimized birth outside the village or later legitimized an apparently non-legitimized birth by marrying the father outside the village, but there should have been sufficient chance to have had a second birth.

Examining the results based on all fertile women, it is apparent that the proportion of women who gave birth to at least one non-legitimized child increased dramatically between the first half of the eighteenth century and the first half of the nineteenth century, by which time one out of four fertile women is classified as a bastard-bearer. This declines modestly during the second half of the nineteenth century but remains at a level far above that of the eighteenth century. The trend in the proportion of unmarried mothers who gave birth to more than one non-legitimized child corresponds reasonably closely with the overall frequency of bearing non-legitimized births. It is lowest in the first half of the eighteenth century, when barely one in eight mothers of non-legitimized births can be considered a repeater, while by the first quarter of the nineteenth century almost half of such women had more than one non-legitimized birth. Repetitive non-legitimized childbearing declines substantially during the remainder of the nineteenth century, but even by the last quarter it is well above the level evident in the first half of the eighteenth century.

There is also substantial variation among the villages with respect to the proportion of fertile women experiencing a non-legitimized birth. It is the lowest, by far, in the East Frisian village of Middels and the highest in the two villages in Waldeck. Thus, both with respect to the general trend in non-legitimized childbearing over time and in the inter-village variation, the results correspond closely with those for prenuptial births examined above. Variation among villages with respect to overall non-legitimized childbearing and repetitive non-legitimized childbearing is by no means as close as the correspondence in the trends over time in these two phenomena. In four of the villages, roughly one-third of all mothers of non-legitimized births had more than one such birth despite considerable differences in the overall level of non-legitimized childbearing. However, repetitive non-legitimized childbearing is clearly the lowest in Middels, where the overall level is also the lowest.

Results based only on women who were born and died locally and who survived at least five years past their first birth show a similar trend over time in overall non-legitimized childbearing, and a similar pattern of inter-village variation. Nevertheless, the level indicated is noticeably lower than that for all fertile women. This undoubtedly reflects the much greater tendency, discussed above, for women with non-legitimized births to migrate out of the village sometime prior to their death, and hence to be excluded from the data, compared to women who marry in the village and bear only legitimate children.[34] Thus while controlling for local birth and death probably ensures that most of the women included are under observation during their reproductive life, the selectivity with respect to non-legitimized child-bearing is sufficient to more than counteract the elimination of these other biases.

The experience of repeaters is less likely to be affected by selectivity due to migration, and indeed may give a truer picture of the extent of repetitive non-legitimized childbearing than results based on all fertile women. Indeed, the proportion of women who bore more than one non-legitimized birth is higher for this subsample of women than for all fertile women. Again, the overall trend in repetitive non-legitimized childbearing over time is similar, although there is rather more inter-village variation than in the case of all fertile women. The absolute level, however, is substantially higher, indicating that during the first quarter of the nineteenth century more than half the mothers of non-legitimized births could be classified as repeaters. In addition, in the five villages for which there were sufficient cases to calculate the extent of repetitive illegitimacy, repeaters represented between somewhat over a third to over a half of women bearing non-legitimized children. Clearly, repetitive non-legitimized childbearing was an important component of illegitimacy in German villages in the past.

In brief, there are major changes evident in the level of illegitimate childbearing, as well as in the tendency for couples to precede their marriage with a prenuptial birth, during the eighteenth and nineteenth centuries. Moreover, the tendency to have repetitive non-legitimized illegitimate births as well as repetitive prenuptial births,

---

[34] There appears to be much less selection with respect to being born in the village. Among women in the six fully-coded villages, 77 percent of women with a non-legitimized first birth were born in the village, compared to 76 percent of other fertile women.

and the waiting period between bearing a prenuptial birth and legitimizing it through marriage, shifted considerably. While numerous biases affect the various measures presented, they are unlikely to account in a major way for the observed results. A discussion of the context and social meaning of some of these results is deferred until after consideration of the related phenomenon of bridal pregnancy and fuller consideration of prenuptial childbearing, both of which are the topics of the next chapter.

9

Bridal pregnancy and prenuptial births

Much of the premarital sexual activity in German villages in the past occurred among couples who subsequently married. This is apparent not only from the statistics on prenuptial births already presented in the previous chapter but even more so from the statistics on births that, although born after a couple married, were clearly conceived prior to the wedding date. This chapter focuses on the outcome of such premarital sexual activity, examining more closely the phenomenon of prenuptial births and exploring in detail the phenomenon of bridal pregnancy. Before proceeding to the analysis of these phenomena, however, a brief discussion about several issues relevant to the measurement of bridal pregnancy is in order.

Measuring bridal pregnancy

Fewer problems are involved in the measurement of bridal pregnancy than is the case for illegitimacy and its division into legitimized and non-legitimized births, as discussed in the previous chapter. In the present study, a woman is considered to have been pregnant at marriage if she gave birth by the start of the eighth elapsed month following the wedding date. While normal variance in the biological period of gestation will result in some women being misclassified with respect to bridal pregnancy, the margin of error should be minor. The net result is probably a slight underestimation of the proportion pregnant at marriage since use of an eight-month interval errs on the conservative side, excluding more births that were actually prenuptially conceived than falsely including births postnuptially conceived.[1]

[1] For a discussion of various cut-off points for defining bridal pregnancy, see Hair, 'Bridal pregnancy in earlier centuries.' The definition employed in the present study is probably the one most commonly used in historical demographic studies. However,

Bridal pregnancy can be expressed as a percentage of all brides, of reproductive-aged brides, or of brides with at least one postnuptial birth. Since childlessness was probably involuntary, it is preferable to eliminate women who never experienced a postnuptial birth from the denominator of the measure of bridal pregnancy.[2] In addition, a combined measure of prenuptial births and bridal pregnancy is presented, expressing those who experienced either a prenuptial birth or who were pregnant at marriage as a percentage of all fertile brides. Because some brides qualify on both accounts and because the measure of prenuptial births relates to all fertile brides, while the bridal pregnancy measure relates only to postnuptially fertile brides, the combined measure of prenuptial births and bridal pregnancy is somewhat less than the simple sum of the two measures.

While it was not rare for a couple's first birth to precede their marriage, especially during the nineteenth century, generally only a modest proportion of married couples began their reproductive careers in this manner. Far more frequently, however, the first post-nuptial birth was conceived prior to marriage. When both of these modes of initiating childbearing are considered jointly, a very substantial proportion of married couples are involved. The general trends in prenuptial births, prenuptial conceptions, and their combination, are shown in Figure 9.1 for the complete sample of all 14 villages combined.

After following a somewhat erratic pattern during the first half of the eighteenth century, bridal pregnancy, as measured by the percentage of first legitimate births born within eight months of marriage, increases fairly steadily, reaching a peak of almost 30 percent by the fourth decade of the nineteenth century. Thereafter, bridal pregnancy declines to slightly less than 25 percent but rises again by the last two decades of the century to levels nearly as high as the previous peak. As is already evident from results presented in the previous chapter, the proportion of married couples with a prenuptial birth remained at low levels throughout the eighteenth century, never involving more than a small percentage of fertile married couples. A sharp rise is evident from the beginning of the nineteenth century and reaches a plateau of approximately 16 percent during the middle three decades of the

unlike many other studies, the present analysis includes stillbirths as well as live births, thus increasing the probability that some of the births occurring before the eighth full month would have been prenuptially conceived. Nevertheless, the number of such cases is undoubtedly small.

[2] The choice of denominator makes only a modest difference. For the combined sample of all villages, 19.3 percent of all brides, 19.5 percent of brides under 50, and 22.1 percent of postnuptially fertile brides were pregnant at the time of marriage.

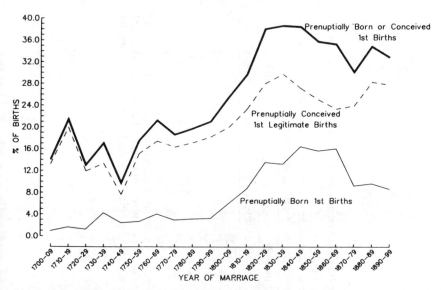

Figure 9.1. *Indices of prenuptial conceptions and prenuptial births by decade of marriage.* Results are based on the combined sample of all villages and are subject to restriction 1 (see Table A.1). In addition, couples for whom the date of the first postnuptial birth, if any, is inexact are excluded

century. This is followed by a sharp decline between the 1860s and the 1870s, perhaps in response to the repeal of marriage restrictions, and remains fairly constant at a level considerably higher than that characteristic of the previous century. Thus bridal pregnancy, prenuptial births, and illegitimacy share a common major increase between the latter part of the eighteenth and the middle of the nineteenth centuries, although they follow somewhat different paths thereafter. In particular, the subsequent declines in prenuptial births and overall illegitimacy are not replicated in the trends of bridal pregnancy during the last half of the nineteenth century.[3] The fact that earlier both illegitimacy and bridal pregnancy rose indicates that there was not simply a trade-off taking place between these two phenomena such that levels of non-marital sexual activity remained unchanged. Rather the trends suggest that a substantial increase in sexual activity outside of marriage occurred, leading to increases in both.

Taken together, a large proportion of married couples began their reproductive careers with either a prenuptial birth or conception. From

---

[3] Trends in bridal pregnancy, based on the six fully-coded villages alone, resemble closely those for the complete sample of 14 villages, and in particular show no greater tendency to decline during the last half of the nineteenth century.

Table 9.1. *Prenuptial pregnancies as percent of first legitimate births by prior experience with prenuptial births, year of marriage, and regional location of village*

| | Year of marriage and experience with prenuptial births | | | | | | | |
| | 1700–99 | | 1800–99 | | Total | |
	None	At least one	None	At least one	None	At least one
4 Baden villages	10	(5)	20	28	17	26
1 Württemberg village	23	—	33	31	29	31
3 Bavarian villages	9	—	12	(20)	11	(19)
4 Waldeck villages	17	(15)	34	39	27	36
2 East Friesland villages	26	—	36	(5)	31	(3)
All villages	16	11	25	30	22	28

Note: Results are subject to restriction 1 (see Table A.1). In addition, couples for whom the date of the first postnuptial birth, if any, is inexact are excluded. Results based on 20–49 cases are shown in parentheses; results based on fewer than 20 cases are omitted.

levels fluctuating more or less in the range of 10 to 20 percent during much of the eighteenth century, a peak of close to 40 percent is reached and sustained during the 1820s through the 1840s, and levels involving close to a third or more of married couples continue for the remainder of the nineteenth century.

Prenuptial births and bridal pregnancy are not mutually exclusive phenomena since it is possible for any given woman to experience both. Family reconstitution data allow us to determine just how common such a dual experience was. For the combined sample of 14 villages, women who both experienced a prenuptial birth and were pregnant at marriage constituted less than 1 percent of all fertile women married during the eighteenth century; this figure rose to 3 percent of women married during the nineteenth century. Thus only a small proportion of women had both experiences. However, as the results presented in Table 9.1 show, women who experienced a prenuptial birth were no less likely to be pregnant at marriage than women who had not given birth prenuptially. During the nineteenth century, bridal pregnancy for the sample as a whole was actually somewhat higher among women with a prenuptial birth than among those without. The most notable exception is found in the two East Frisian villages, where a bridal pregnancy was extremely rare among women who began their reproductive career with a prenuptial birth. This may reflect the unusually short interval between the birth of a prenuptial infant and the subsequent marriage, a pattern characteristic of East Frisian couples. For many, the intervening interval would simply not have been sufficient for another pregnancy to have taken place.

Bridal pregnancy and prenuptial births

Indices of bridal pregnancy and prenuptial births separately, as well as in combination, are shown for both the eighteenth and nineteenth centuries in Table 9.2 for the individual villages and their regional groupings. An increase between the eighteenth and nineteenth centuries in bridal pregnancy is evident for every village in the sample and is generally substantial. Likewise, an increase in the percentage of married couples whose first birth occurred prior to marriage is also evident for every village, with increases substantial in most cases. In every village during the eighteenth century, it was more common for a bride to be pregnant than to have had a prenuptial birth; and in all but two Bavarian villages, this was also the case in the nineteenth century. The combined probability that a bride either had a prenuptial birth or

Table 9.2. *Indices of bridal pregnancies and prenuptial births by year of marriage, village, and regional location of village*

	Of first legitimate births, % prenuptially conceived			Of all first births (to marriages)					
				% prenuptially born			% prenuptially born or conceived		
	1700–99	1800–99	Total	1700–99	1800–99	Total	1700–99	1800–99	Total
4 Baden villages	10	21	18	3	12	9	12	29	24
Grafenhausen	12	20	18	3	11	8	14	28	24
Herbolzheim	5	19	14	2	11	8	7	27	20
Kappel	8	20	16	2	9	7	9	25	20
Rust	18	25	23	3	15	12	22	36	32
Öschelbronn (Württemberg)	24	33	29	5	13	10	28	42	36
3 Bavarian villages	9	13	12	1	13	9	10	24	19
Anhausen	9	12	11	1	7	5	11	19	16
Gabelbach	13	13	13		13	9	15	24	21
Kreuth	4	15	11	0	21	13	4	31	21
4 Waldeck villages	17	35	28	5	21	15	21	48	38
Braunsen	27	28	27	4	17	12	30	39	35
Höringhausen	22	39	33	7	28	21	28	57	48
Massenhausen	14	39	29	7	21	15	21	50	39
Vasbeck	10	30	21	1	14	8	10	38	26
2 East Friesland villages	25	35	31	2	3	2	27	37	33
Middels	20	38	34	1	2	2	20	40	36
Werdum	27	32	29	2	3	3	29	35	32
All villages	15	26	22	3	12	9	18	34	28

Note: Results are subject to restriction 1 (see Table A.1). In addition, couples for whom the date of the first postnuptial birth is inexact are excluded.

was pregnant at the time of marriage increased substantially in every village between the eighteenth and nineteenth centuries.

Regional variation is evident in the extent of bridal pregnancy and prenuptial births. Bridal pregnancy was distinctly lowest in the three Bavarian villages, while prenuptial births were distinctly least common in the two East Frisian villages. The level of bridal pregnancy, however, is relatively high in the two East Frisian villages, suggesting that they are distinguished less by a low frequency of premarital sex than by a high probability that a prenuptial conception was followed by a marriage before birth occurred. This corresponds with the marked tendency, discussed in the previous chapter, among those few couples who did experience a prenuptial birth in these two villages, to wed relatively quickly before a second one could occur (see Table 8.3).

Among the three Bavarian villages, only in Kreuth were prenuptial births more common than the average for the combined sample of all villages. However, non-legitimized births appear to have been relatively common in Anhausen and not unusually low in Gabelbach. Although neither of these two villages was fully coded, tabulations of births by legitimacy status (but not legitimization status) are provided in the genealogies, enabling a comparison with the ratios for the six fully-coded villages. Illegitimacy ratios during the nineteenth century were relatively high in Anhausen and more or less average in Gabelbach. With above-average or average illegitimacy ratios but low proportions of legitimized births, non-legitimized births must have been relatively common.[4] Moreover, the districts and provinces in which the three Bavarian villages are located were characterized by substantial levels of illegitimacy during periods of the nineteenth century for which official statistics are available.[5] Thus in the East Frisian villages the low level of prenuptial births is compensated for in part by higher bridal pregnancy, and in the Bavarian villages the low level of bridal pregnancy is at least partially compensated for by substantial illegitimacy.

A somewhat different pattern is represented by the Waldeck villages, where *both* bridal pregnancy and prenuptial births were relatively common during the nineteenth century. When considered jointly, half the couples married during that time in Massenhausen, and more than half in Höringhausen, were characterized by either prenuptial births or bridal pregnancy. For the eighteenth and nineteenth centuries combined, of all the 14 villages, only in Anhausen

[4] The proportion of all births that were born out of wedlock during the nineteenth century was 13 percent in Anhausen and 8 percent in Gabelbach.
[5] Lindner, *Uneheliche Geburten*; Hindelang, *Fruchtbarkeit*.

was the probability less than one in four of starting out on marriage
with either a prior birth or with the bride pregnant. Clearly, premarital
sex as indicated by prenuptial conceptions and births, was a common
nineteenth-century phenomenon in German villages.

The timing of a prenuptially conceived birth relative to when the
marriage took place reflects the duration of the pregnancy at the time of
the wedding and thus provides additional information about the
nature of bridal pregnancy. Figure 9.2a shows the percentage of all first
postnuptial births that occurred at each of the first eight completed
months after marriage for couples marrying in the eighteenth and
nineteenth centuries. Although the definition of prenuptial pregnancy
used in the present study excludes births occurring during the eighth
completed month following marriage, such births are shown in
Figures 9.2a and 9.2b. This highlights the fact that there was no change
between the eighteenth and nineteenth centuries in the percent of first
postnuptial births that occurred during the seventh and the eighth
completed months.

The general rise in bridal pregnancy evident between the two
centuries resulted from increased proportions of births occurring
during the first six completed months following marriage but not by
the proportion of births occurring in the seventh and eighth completed
months. Although a large proportion of births in the latter group
would have been conceived prior to marriage, the pregnancy would
have been of such short duration at the time of the wedding that the
couple would have at most only suspected it. Such pregnancies
probably occurred as a result of sexual intercourse following betrothal,
the reading of the banns, the negotiation of a marriage contract, or
some other type of definite agreement to marry on the part of the
spouses. Unfortunately, direct evidence on the date of betrothal or the
usual interval between betrothal and marriage is unavailable for the
sample villages. Nevertheless, these data suggest that intercourse was
relatively common once the decision to marry had been made and the
ceremony was imminent, whether in the eighteenth or the nineteenth
century. The increase in prenuptial pregnancy is entirely a result of
conceptions during periods further removed from the marriage
ceremony, and perhaps from the decision to marry.

The lack of change in the proportion of births occurring during the
seventh and eighth elapsed months after marriage is evident in Figure
9.2b. In contrast, increases occurred in the proportion of births that
took place shortly after marriage (and hence for which there was a
considerable delay between the conception and the wedding), as well
as in the proportion of births occurring three to six months after

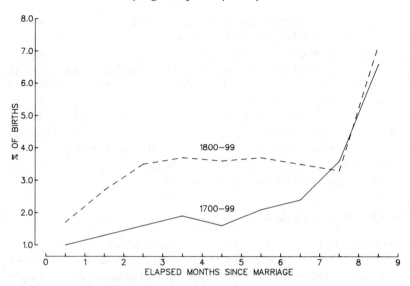

Figure 9.2a. *The timing of prenuptially conceived postnuptial births: percentage of all first postnuptial births occurring at single months since marriage, by year of marriage*

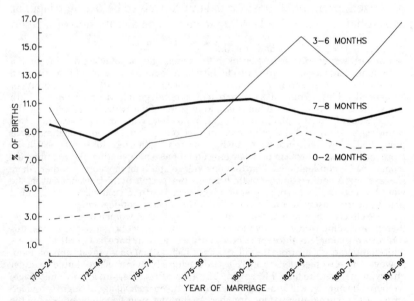

Figure 9.2b. *The timing of prenuptially conceived postnuptial births: percentage of all first postnuptial births occurring during selected intervals since marriage, by year of marriage.* Results for Figures 9.2a and 9.2b are based on the combined sample of all villages and are subject to restriction 1 (see Table A.1). In addition, couples with an inexact date of the first postnuptial birth are excluded

marriage. In the latter group, the couple was probably aware of the pregnancy but may have still been able to shield it from the community at large, while among the former group, given the advanced stage of the pregnancy at the time of marriage, this would have been unlikely. Wrigley has observed a very similar shift in the timing of births after marriage in England, a shift associated with a substantial increase in the prevalence of bridal pregnancy between the late seventeenth and early nineteenth centuries.[6] Thus in both England and Germany, increases in bridal pregnancy were not a result of increased intercourse shortly before marriage, but rather of increased sexual activity that probably began even before formal betrothal took place.

Out-of-wedlock pregnancies and their outcomes

The most complete picture of the extent of premarital sexual activity, as reflected in data on births, can be obtained for the subset of the six fully-coded villages. Since information is available for these villages with respect both to non-marital and marital unions, it is possible to determine for each fertile woman whether her first birth was non-legitimized, prenuptial, postnuptial but conceived before marriage, or postnuptial and conceived after marriage.[7] The distribution of women

---

[6] Wrigley, 'Marriage, fertility and growth.'

[7] Not all births appearing as first births in the genealogies actually are first births. If a woman had had an earlier birth outside the village that was not evident from the local records, the birth appearing as her first in the genealogy would actually be a second or higher-order birth. Thus, if a woman had a non-legitimized or prenuptial birth elsewhere and only moved to the village at the time of marriage, her first birth in the village would be postnuptial, even though in fact her actual first birth was not. This would bias downward the proportion of first births that were non-legitimized or prenuptial. However, since women who bear non-legitimized children appear to be more mobile than others, an opposite effect might also be operating. For example, if a woman had a non-legitimized birth in one village and then moved to another where she also bore a non-legitimized birth, from the perspective of the present analysis she would be counted as having a first non-legitimized birth in each village. This would tend to overrepresent women whose first birth appears non-legitimized.

These effects can be minimized by restricting analysis to women born in the village, thereby excluding women known to have migrated at least once since birth. Even this control is not complete, since some locally born women may have had a birth elsewhere while temporarily away from the village. Since such a situation is probably uncommon, however, most women born in a village and having a birth in a village should be under observation the entire time. Moreover, since a woman can be born in only one village, women who migrate will appear in the analysis only in their village of origin (provided a first birth occurred there). One drawback of limiting analysis to women born in the village is that women who migrate before their first birth will be consistently excluded, since they will not have had a birth in their village of origin. An exception to this would be women who became pregnant while elsewhere, perhaps while in service, and returned to their home village to give birth to an illegitimate child. There is clearly some risk of introducing a selectivity bias through this restriction in the analysis.

according to the status of their first birth, defined in this manner, is provided in Table 9.3 for the six fully-coded villages. During the eighteenth century, well over two-thirds of first births in the combined six villages were conceived postnuptially, but by the nineteenth century this declines to less than half. Indeed, between the eighteenth and nineteenth centuries, there is a marked increase in all the other categories of births. Relatively little difference in the distribution of first births, however, is evident between the first and second halves of each of these two centuries. During the first half of the twentieth century, a decrease in the proportion of first births that were non-legitimized was balanced by an increase in the proportion that were prenuptially conceived.

The same general shift in the distribution of first births between the eighteenth and nineteenth centuries observed for the six villages collectively is also evident for each of the individual villages. In the eighteenth century, postnuptial conceptions were the predominant mode of starting a reproductive career in all six villages, but by the nineteenth century, only in Kappel was this the case. In Massen-hausen, a postnuptial conception is not even the modal way in which to start childbearing, being considerably less common than non-legitimized first births. In nearby Braunsen, postnuptial conceptions represent only a little over one-third of all fertile women. Thus in these two Waldeck villages, the large majority of women during the nineteenth century bore or conceived their first child out of wedlock. Even in Middels, where non-legitimized and prenuptial conceptions are relatively uncommon, the high frequency of bridal pregnancies still results in less than half of fertile women during the nineteenth century beginning their childbearing experience with a postnuptial concep-tion. In brief, these results indicate quite clearly that premarital sexual activity was quite common in rural Germany during the nineteenth century. Given that such activity did not necessarily result in a birth, it is almost certain that a majority of women experienced their first intercourse out of wedlock.

Using the data for the six fully-coded villages, it is also possible to examine the marital outcome for all women whose first birth was conceived out of wedlock. The results are shown in Table 9.4. The

In fact, when analysis is restricted to women born in the village, results differ little from those shown. For the combined sample of the six fully-coded villages and the combined eighteenth and nineteenth centuries, 18 percent (compared to 19) of first births to women born in the village are non-legitimized, 8 percent (compared to 7) are prenuptially born, 19 percent (compared to 19) are prenuptially conceived, and 55 percent (compared to 55) are postnuptially conceived. Apparently, to the extent the potential biases discussed above existed, they more or less balanced each other out.

Table 9.3. *Percent distribution of first births in terms of marital outcome and timing of marriage by year of birth and village*

	Total	Non-legitimized	Prenuptial birth	Prenuptial conception	Postnuptial conception
Year of birth					
1700–49	100	9.2	2.2	16.7	71.9
1750–99	100	13.1	3.6	14.5	68.9
1800–49	100	24.3	10.0	18.8	46.8
1850–99	100	20.7	8.4	21.1	49.8
1900–49	100	9.5	8.4	28.2	53.9
1700–1899	100	19.1	7.3	18.6	55.1
Village and year of birth					
Kappel					
1700–99	100	13.0	6.3	12.3	68.5
1800–99	100	10.1	2.3	9.0	78.6
	100	14.4	8.3	14.0	63.4
Rust					
1700–99	100	20.4	8.7	16.7	54.2
1800–99	100	10.0	2.6	16.8	70.6
	100	24.7	11.2	16.7	47.5
Öschelbronn					
1700–99	100	22.2	6.0	20.8	51.0
1800–99	100	13.0	4.3	22.0	60.6
	100	26.8	6.8	20.2	46.2
Braunsen					
1700–99	100	26.5	9.6	18.8	45.0
1800–99	100	15.6	5.2	19.8	59.4
	100	32.9	12.2	18.3	36.6
Massenhausen					
1700–99	100	32.5	9.4	16.3	41.7
1800–99	100	20.5	4.1	11.8	63.6
	100	39.7	12.6	19.1	28.6
Middels					
1700–99	100	6.9	3.7	33.4	56.0
1800–99	100	1.6	0.8	15.9	81.7
	100	8.3	4.5	38.2	49.0

Note: Results refer to the six fully-coded villages and are based on women whose first birth occurred locally.

Table 9.4. *Prevalence and marital outcome of first out-of-wedlock pregnancies by year of birth and by village*

	% of all first births conceived out of wedlock	% distribution of marital outcomes			
		Couple marries before birth	Couple marries after birth	Couple does not marry	Total
Year of first birth					
1700–49	28	59	8	33	100
1750–99	31	46	11	42	100
1800–49	53	35	19	46	100
1850–99	50	42	17	41	100
1900–49	46	61	18	21	100
1700–1899	45	41	16	42	100
Village (births 1700–1899)					
Kappel	32	39	20	41	100
Rust	46	37	19	45	100
Öschelbronn	49	42	12	45	100
Braunsen	55	34	17	48	100
Massenhausen	58	28	16	56	100
Middels	44	76	8	16	100

Note: Results refer to the six fully-coded villages and are based on women whose first birth occurred locally.

percentage of all first births that are conceived out of wedlock is also indicated to provide some sense of the proportion of women involved. There is little reason to doubt on methodological grounds the accuracy of the proportion of women indicated as marrying *before* the birth. Less confidence, however, can be placed in the results referring to the estimates of the percentages marrying after the birth or not marrying at all since, as discussed in Appendix G, some of the out-of-wedlock births that were in fact followed by a marriage probably appear in the genealogies as if they were not legitimized. Thus the percentage of couples indicated as marrying after the birth should be regarded as a minimum estimate and the proportion indicated as not marrying at all as a maximum estimate.

The results indicate a substantial decline in the probability of marrying before the birth between the first half of the eighteenth century and the first half of the nineteenth century, as the overall frequency of out-of-wedlock pregnancies increased. This trend is then reversed as the frequency of out-of-wedlock pregnancies declines modestly. Part of the sharp decline between the first half of the eighteenth and the first half of the nineteenth century in the probability of marrying prior to the birth of a child conceived out of wedlock was made up by an increase in the probability of marrying after the birth occurred. Despite the tendency to underestimate the proportion who married after the birth, the results indicate that, throughout the two-and-a-half-century period under observation, the majority of women who conceived a child out of wedlock eventually married the father of the child, either before or after its birth.

Considerable variations in the outcomes of out-of-wedlock pregnancies are evident for the individual villages. In Kappel, where out-of-wedlock conceptions were least common, the probability of marrying before the birth was the lowest. Many couples, however, married after the birth. Thus of those in Kappel who did experience an out-of-wedlock pregnancy, over two-thirds eventually married the father. The other quite distinctive pattern among the six villages is found in Middels, where over three-quarters of women who experienced an out-of-wedlock pregnancy married before the birth. Of the six villages, only in Massenhausen do a majority of women experiencing an out-of-wedlock first pregnancy appear not to marry the child's father. Even here, however, this may not have been the actual case given the possibility that some subsequent marriages were not so indicated in the genealogy.

Occupational and status differentials

Social historians have generally argued that the control of sexual activity outside of marital unions is of greater importance to peasant proprietors than to the rural proletariat. Presumably, control over land led to greater concerns over inheritance and dowries and the necessity to limit offspring to legitimate issues. Moreover, marriage was virtually a prerequisite for managing a farm, given the segregation by sex of many agricultural tasks. Hence, to the extent that non-marital sexual activity threatened the solidarity of marriage, it would also threaten the economic underpinnings of peasant existence.

The rise in illegitimacy and bridal pregnancy between the eighteenth and nineteenth centuries is sometimes attributed to the growth of the proletarian class and the proletarianization of the population.[8] It is thus of interest to examine socio-economic differentials in both the prevalence and the trends of out-of-wedlock births and conceptions. Unfortunately, this is not possible with respect to overall legitimacy

---

[8] Phayer, *Sexual liberation and religion.*

because of the difficulty in determining the social class of mothers of non-legitimized births.[9] However, in the case of bridal pregnancy and prenuptial births, occupational and village leadership status information is generally available for the hubands involved and thus such an analysis is feasible. The results are shown in Table 9.5 according to the standard occupational groups and subcategories, as well as leadership status in the village.

Among broad occupational groups, both bridal pregnancy and prenuptial births were clearly highest for proletarians. This is the case both in the eighteenth and nineteenth centuries for bridal pregnancy. Prenuptial births were low for all groups in the eighteenth century, but distinct differences emerged in the nineteenth century, when proletarians experienced the highest frequency and farmers the lowest. The rise in bridal pregnancy, however, affected all the major occupational groups more or less equally. In addition, prenuptial births increased noticeably in all broad occupational groups although to an unequal extent: the rise was the smallest for farmers and the greatest for proletarians.

The increase in bridal pregnancy and prenuptial births affected every occupational subcategory with the sole exception of the small number of sailors. For the combined eighteenth and nineteenth centuries, both bridal pregnancy and prenuptial births are highest among wives of miscellaneous unskilled workers represented by the 'other unskilled' subcategory of proletarians and next highest among day laborers. At the other extreme, wives of businessmen are characterized by the lowest level of bridal pregnancy and wives of sailors by the lowest level of prenuptial births.

For no occupational subcategory is bridal pregnancy negligible. In most cases, close to a fifth or more of brides of husbands in most of the various occupational subcategories appear to have been pregnant at marriage. In relative terms, differentials with respect to prenuptial births are sharper. In several occupational subcategories prenuptial births remain quite uncommon even during the nineteenth century. Interestingly, cottagers resemble farmers rather than other proletarians in the sense that they were relatively unlikely to experience births prior to marriage. However, the fact that sailors, the subcategory with the fewest prenuptial births, and a fair proportion of cottagers are located in the East Frisian villages may help account for their low level of prenuptial births.

[9] A more complex analysis relating out-of-wedlock births to the social origins of unwed mothers is feasible with family reconstitution data but is beyond the scope of this study.

Table 9.5. *Indices of prenuptial pregnancies and births by occupational group, occupational subcategory, status in village, and year of marriage*

	Of first legitimate births, % prenuptially conceived			Of all first births (to marriages)					
				% prenuptially born			% prenuptially born or conceived		
	1700–99	1800–99	Total	1700–99	1800–99	Total	1700–99	1800–99	Total
Occupational group									
Farmers	13	21	19	2	7	5	15	27	23
Proletarians	20	31	28	3	16	12	22	42	36
Artisans and skilled	12	22	19	2	11	8	14	31	25
Mixed, other, unknown	17	30	24	4	14	9	20	38	30
Occupational subcategory									
Farmer	13	21	19	2	7	5	15	27	23
Cottager	23	27	25	1	6	4	24	32	29
Day laborer	24	34	31	4	21	17	28	48	43
Other unskilled	19	39	36	6	21	18	22	53	47
Sailor	26	(14)	21	2	(2)	2	28	(16)	23

Weaver	9	27	20	2	13	8	10	35	25
Other home industry	(21)	25	24	(5)	12	10	(26)	34	32
Artisan	12	24	20	2	13	10	14	33	27
Fisherman	11	30	21	4	13	9	15	41	29
Businessman	12	15	14	2	5	4	14	20	18
Professional	12	24	19	0	5	3	12	29	22
Farmer–artisan, etc.	14	23	20	2	6	5	14	26	22
Farmer–proletarian	18	31	27	3	11	9	21	39	34
Proletarian–artisan, etc.	21	32	28	2	14	10	23	41	35
Other	25	33	30	11	19	15	33	46	40
Unknown	15	31	20	4	22	10	20	44	27
Status in village									
Village leader	15	25	20	2	9	6	17	32	24
Non-leader	15	26	22	3	12	9	18	34	29
All couples	15	26	22	3	12	9	18	34	28

Note: Results refer to the combined sample of all villages and are subject to restriction 1 (see Table A.1). In addition, couples for whom the date of the first postnuptial birth is inexact are excluded. Results based on 20–49 cases are shown in parentheses.

The status of the husband in terms of village leadership appears to have had little impact on bridal pregnancy, but couples in which the husband was a village leader were characterized by lower levels of prenuptial births than were couples in which the husband was not a leader. Increases in bridal pregnancy and prenuptial births between the eighteenth and nineteenth centuries, however, are evident regardless of village leadership status.

Since bridal pregnancy tends to be higher among the same groups for which prenuptial births are more common, differentials are particularly pronounced when they are considered jointly. The proclivity for the day laborers and other unskilled workers to experience both leads these two subcategories to stand out. Nevertheless, the increases in bridal pregnancy and prenuptial births were pervasive. Hence, despite the distinct difference in the levels characterizing the various social strata of the village, the major changes in premarital sexual behavior between the eighteenth and nineteenth centuries were virtually universal. Proletarians may have contributed somewhat more than their proportional share, but all major segments of village society apparently participated in the increased premarital sexual activity evident in the changed levels of bridal pregnancy and prenuptial births.

Links to marriage and reproductive careers

Wrigley has raised a fundamental issue concerning the relation between marriage and non-marital sexual activity.[10] Results for early modern England suggest that whatever sanctions operated to delay or inhibit marriage were also effective in reducing fertility outside of marriage. Moreover, when entry into marriage was relatively easy, constraints on illegitimate fertility appear to have been more relaxed. Thus in the English case, trends in nuptiality, bridal pregnancy and illegitimacy were roughly parallel, at least from the end of the seventeenth to the early nineteenth century.[11] Wrigley also refers to fragmentary evidence indicating that the age at which women began their reproductive careers was similar, whether the initial event was an illegitimate or legitimate birth.

With family reconstitution data a number of linkages between nonmarital or premarital sexual activity (as reflected in evidence on births)

[10] Wrigley, 'Marriage, fertility and growth.'
[11] Because of the built-in tendency for the illegitimacy ratio and age at marriage to covary in the same direction, the fact that the English illegitimacy ratio rose while age at marriage declined is all the more striking (Wrigley, 'Marriage, fertility and growth').

and marriage and childbearing can be explored. Unfortunately, as explained in Chapter 6, a comprehensive measure of nuptiality which takes into account the proportions ever marrying as well as age at marriage cannot readily be derived from such data. Thus the correspondence between trends in overall nuptiality and those in illegitimacy and bridal pregnancy, as revealed for England, cannot be examined fully for the sample of German villages. However, trends in age at marriage can be compared with trends in these phenomena. Such a comparison indicates that to the extent there is any association, it is generally in the opposite direction from that found for England.[12] Modest increases in the age at marriage accompanied the substantial rises in illegitimacy and bridal pregnancy between the mid-eighteenth and mid-nineteenth centuries; in the latter half of the nineteenth century age at marriage declined modestly as illegitimacy fell and bridal pregnancy fluctuated. Given the only rough correspondence, it would not appear that the phenomena were closely related.

Wrigley also observed that as the marriage age fell and nuptiality became more universal in England during the eighteenth and nineteenth centuries, young brides were more likely to be pregnant at marriage than older ones, an apparent reversal of an earlier situation.[13] He interprets this as suggesting that, with the easing of constraints on marriage, couples engaged more readily in sex relations in anticipation of marriage at younger ages. In contrast, in France, where nuptialiy was decreasing during much of the same period, older brides were more likely to be pregnant.

For German village populations, as shown in Table 9.6 for the combined sample of all villages, bridal pregnancy varies little with the wife's age at marriage, both in the eighteenth and nineteenth centuries. Moreover, the substantial increase in bridal pregnancy affected brides of all ages more or less equally.

Quite a different pattern is evident with respect to prenuptial births. Particularly during the nineteenth century, there is a pronounced positive association between the probability of having a prenuptial birth and age at marriage. Almost a third of the brides over age 40

[12] Age at marriage probably underwent a greater change in England between the late seventeenth and early eighteenth centuries than was the case in Germany during the eighteenth and nineteenth centuries. Based on a pooled sample of 12 English villages for which family reconstitution data of reasonable quality are available, the age at first marriage for men declined by over two years between 1675–99 and 1800–24, while the age at first marriage for women declined by almost three years (Wrigley, 'Marriage, fertility and growth'). As indicated in Chapter 6 (see, for example, Table 6.1), changes in age at first marriage for the combined sample of German villages during the eighteenth and nineteenth centuries were more modest.

[13] Wrigley, 'Marriage, fertility and growth,' pp. 180–82.

Table 9.6. Indices of prenuptial pregnancies and birth by year of marriage, wife's age at marriage, and prior marital status of spouses

| | Of first legitimate births, % prenuptially conceived | | | Of all first births (to marriages) | | | | | |
| | | | | % prenuptially born | | | % prenuptially born or conceived | | |
	1700–99	1800–99	Total	1700–99	1800–99	Total	1700–99	1800–99	Total
Age at marriage									
Under 20	10	25	18	0	5	3	11	28	20
20–24	16	28	24	2	9	7	18	35	29
25–29	17	23	21	4	13	11	20	33	29
30–34	15	25	22	4	16	12	19	37	30
35–39	13	21	18	2	16	11	15	32	26
40+	17	22	19	6	32	21	23	43	37
Prior marital status									
Bachelor, spinster	17	28	24	3	13	10	20	37	31
Widower, spinster	9	15	13	1	5	3	11	18	15
Bachelor, widow	13	23	18	3	5	4	15	26	21
Widower, widow	17	24	20	0	4	2	17	27	22
Age difference between spouses									
Wife at least 1 year older	18	30	26	4	15	11	23	40	34
Difference less than									
1 year	16	31	27	5	19	15	21	43	37
Husband 1–4 years older	15	26	23	3	10	8	17	33	29
Husband at least 5 years older	14	21	18	1	8	6	15	27	23
All villages	15	26	22	3	12	9	18	34	28

Note: Results are based on the combined sample of all villages and subject to restriction 1 (see Table A.1). In addition, couples for whom the date of the first postnuptial birth is inexact are excluded.

during the nineteenth century had borne a child with their husband prior to marriage, while less than one out of ten brides under age 25 did so. To some extent this positive association between prenuptial births and age at marriage is to be expected, since the older a woman is at the time of marriage the longer she has been at risk of a prenuptial birth.

Furthermore, prior marital status shows an association with both bridal pregnancy and prenuptial births. Marriages involving bachelors and spinsters are most likely to involve a bridal pregnancy or a prenuptial birth, while those between a widower and a spinster are the least likely. The rapidity with which widowers remarried, discussed in Chapter 7, may have diminished the probability of a prenuptial conception or birth occurring. Nevertheless, the differences between the combinations of the prior marital status are only moderate with respect to bridal pregnancy, indicating that a number of remarriages, particularly for women, were preceded by a conception. Prenuptial births are far less common when one of the partners is remarrying, undoubtedly in part because the couple was at risk for shorter periods, assuming that sexual relations between the couple did not begin before the end of the prior marriage of the remarrying partner (or partners).

Bridal pregnancy is more common when the wife is older than the husband or both are about equal age, and least common when the husband is five or more years older. A similar relationship holds for prenuptial births. The lower levels associated with marriages in which the husband is considerably older may be due to the larger concentration of remarriages of widowers in this group and may reflect the relatively short interval to remarriage when a widower is involved.

Using data from the six fully-coded villages, it is possible to examine the age of women at their first birth according to different modes of entry into reproductive careers. The results are presented in Table 9.7. During the eighteenth and nineteenth centuries taken together, women were approximately one year younger at the onset of child-bearing if their first child was born out of wedlock than if it was born after marriage. This difference is apparent for all of the villages, except Middels in East Friesland, where illegitimacy was generally quite low. A trend over time is also evident. During the eighteenth century, women were actually slightly older at the time of first birth if the birth was born out of wedlock. This difference then reverses, increasing to the point where during the first half of the twentieth century women with a first birth out of wedlock were more than three years younger than women whose first birth occurred after marriage. However, during the period of prime concern, the eighteenth and nineteenth centuries, the difference is never very large, averaging only slightly over a year.

Table 9.7. *Age of mother at first birth by legitimacy status of first birth and year of birth and village*

	All first births	Illegitimate first birth			Legitimate first birth		
		Not legitimized	Legitimized	Total	Prenuptially conceived	Postnuptially conceived	Total
Year of birth							
1700–49	26.0	(27.4)	—	(26.3)	24.9	26.2	26.0
1750–99	25.7	26.8	(23.2)	25.8	25.0	25.9	25.7
1800–49	25.3	25.1	23.6	24.6	24.8	26.1	25.7
1850–99	25.3	24.3	24.1	24.2	24.3	26.2	25.7
1900–49	25.6	23.7	21.9	22.8	24.2	27.2	26.1
1700–1899	25.4	25.0	23.8	24.6	24.6	26.1	25.7
Village (births 1700–1899)							
Kappel	25.8	25.7	23.2	24.7	24.5	26.3	26.0
Rust	25.4	24.8	23.8	24.5	24.4	26.2	25.8
Öschelbronn	25.7	25.5	23.4	25.0	24.9	26.3	25.9
Braunsen	25.2	25.0	24.8	24.9	25.6	25.3	25.4
Massenhausen	25.5	24.2	23.2	23.9	25.4	26.8	26.4
Middels	24.7	25.1	26.4	25.6	24.3	24.9	24.6

Note: Results are based on the six fully-coded villages only and are restricted to local first births for which the exact date is known. In cases of marital unions, results are additionally restricted to local marriages for which the exact date is known. Results in parentheses are based on 20–49 births; results based on fewer than 20 births are omitted.

Within each of the broader categories of illegitimate and legitimate births, differentials in the age at first birth are also evident according to whether or not an out-of-wedlock birth was legitimized, and according to whether a postnuptial birth was conceived before or after marriage. In general, women whose first birth was out of wedlock began childbearing later in cases where their first birth is not subsequently legitimized than in cases where it is. In addition, women whose first birth was postnuptial were younger on average if that birth was conceived prior to marriage than if it was conceived after marriage. Overall, women whose first birth was prenuptial began their reproductive careers earliest, while those whose first birth was conceived after marriage began their reproductive careers latest. In general, the differences were not extremely large even between these more refined categories of mode of entry into childbearing, with the average age at first birth differing within a range of only 2 or 3 years.

While it is not possible with the complete sample of all villages to examine the age of entry into childbearing for women whose first birth was non-legitimized, a comparison can be made for both husbands and wives according to whether the first birth to their marital union occurred before marriage, was conceived before marriage but occurred after marriage, or was conceived after marriage. Moreover, it is possible to examine the age of each spouse at the time of the first postnuptial birth (regardless of whether or not there was a premarital birth), and to see whether that birth was conceived before or after marriage. The results of such a comparison are shown in Table 9.8 in relation to the first marital union of each spouse respectively. Since the prevalence of prenuptial births and bridal pregnancy varied over time, region, and occupational group, the results for the combined two-century period covered are shown in a form statistically adjusted for these factors, as well as in their unadjusted form. Statistical adjustment for these factors, however, has little impact and the overall picture remains similar to that evident prior to adjustment.

In general, both husbands and wives are youngest at the time of their first birth if that birth was prenuptial, and oldest if that birth was conceived after marriage. Both husbands and wives were also younger at the time of their first postnuptial birth if that birth was conceived prior to marriage than if it was postnuptially conceived. The direction of these differences in age at first birth and age at first postnuptial birth persisted throughout the two-century period under observation. Thus the mode in which couples first became parents appears to have had some bearing on the age at which they began their reproductive careers. However, throughout the period the contrast in mean ages

Table 9.8. *Age at first birth and age at first prenuptial birth, for husbands and wives, by the timing of the birth and year of marriage*

Spouse and timing of birth	Year of marriage					Adjusted total[a]
	1700–49	1750–99	1800–49	1850–99	Total	
Husband						
First birth						
Before marriage	(25.8)	25.7	27.0	26.2	26.5	26.4
In first 8 months	28.4	27.9	27.8	27.7	27.8	27.7
After first 8 months	29.2	29.3	29.9	30.2	29.8	29.8
Total	29.0	28.9	29.0	29.1	29.0	29.0
First postnuptial birth						
In first 8 months	28.4	27.9	28.1	27.8	28.0	27.8
After first 8 months	29.2	29.3	30.0	30.2	29.8	29.9
Total	29.1	29.0	29.5	29.6	29.4	29.4
Wife						
First birth						
Before marriage	(24.9)	25.4	24.8	24.4	24.7	24.3
In first 8 months	25.5	25.8	25.6	25.1	25.4	25.4
After first 8 months	26.2	26.4	26.9	26.9	26.7	26.8
Total	26.1	26.3	26.4	26.2	26.3	26.3
First postnuptial birth						
In first 8 months	25.5	25.8	25.9	25.3	25.6	25.6
After first 8 months	26.3	26.5	27.1	27.0	26.8	26.9
Total	26.2	26.4	26.8	26.6	26.6	26.6

Note: Results are based on the combined sample of all villages, are limited to first marriages of the wife or husband, and are subject to restriction 1 (see Table A.1). In addition, couples for whom the date of the first postnuptial birth is inexact are excluded. Results based on 20–49 cases are shown in parentheses.

[a] Adjusted by multiple classification analysis for region, year of marriage, and occupational grouping of husband.

was modest, with differences limited to within a range of a few years.

The age at first marriage for both husbands and wives in the complete sample of all villages can also be examined in relation to the timing of the first birth or first postnuptial birth. The results are shown in Table 9.9 and include summary figures for the entire two-century period under observation, statistically adjusted for year of marriage, region, and occupational grouping. In general, age at first marriage was latest both for husbands and wives when the marriage was preceded by a birth, and youngest when the first birth was postnuptial but conceived prior to marriage. Thus prenuptial births are associated with the youngest ages at first birth but the oldest ages at first marriage. Indeed, the age at first birth for those with a prenuptial birth is younger, both for men and for women, than the average age of marriage for those whose reproductive career begins with a postnuptial birth, whether or not prenuptially conceived. Apparently, the forces that determined the initiation of childbearing for those couples who experienced a prenuptial birth were different from those that determined it for others. Prenuptial births were not simply the result of marriage delayed beyond the usual age, but also of an earlier onset of reproduction.

The relationship between the age at marriage and the timing of the first postnuptial birth has implications for understanding the circumstances of bridal pregnancies. If prenuptial pregnancies are simply random occurrences resulting from normatively sanctioned sexual relations following betrothal or a commitment to marry, the age of marriage should be similar for couples whether or not the bride is pregnant prior to the wedding. If on the contrary, a prenuptial pregnancy precipitates or hastens a marriage, couples in which the bride is pregnant would be younger at marriage than those in which the bride is not pregnant. As is evident from Table 9.9, bridal pregnancy is associated with earlier marriage, both on the part of men and women, although women pregnant as brides were only moderately younger at marriage than those who conceived their first birth postnuptially. This suggests that in at least some proportion of cases, a prenuptial pregnancy may have had some effect in precipitating or advancing the wedding, but clearly the impact is modest.

Additional evidence that prenuptial pregnancies advanced the date of marriage, if not precipitating the marriage altogether, is provided by information on the month the wedding occurred. The monthly distribution of marriages, examined in Chapter 6, revealed a lower degree of seasonality for pregnant than for non-pregnant brides, suggesting that the former were under some pressure to marry quickly rather than

Table 9.9. *Age at first marriage, for husbands and wives, by the timing of the first birth and the first postnuptial birth, and year of marriage*

Spouse and timing of birth	Year of marriage					Adjusted total[a]
	1700–49	1750–99	1800–49	1850–99	Total	
Husband						
First birth						
Before marriage	(27.9)	27.5	30.2	29.3	29.5	29.4
In first 8 months	28.0	27.5	27.5	27.4	27.5	27.3
After first 8 months	27.7	27.8	28.5	28.9	28.4	28.5
Total	27.7	27.8	28.5	28.6	28.3	28.3
First postnuptial birth						
In first 8 months	28.0	27.5	27.8	27.5	27.6	27.5
After first 8 months	27.6	27.8	28.6	28.9	28.4	28.5
Total	27.7	27.8	28.4	28.5	28.2	28.2
Wife						
First birth						
Before marriage	(26.7)	27.6	28.0	27.6	27.8	27.3
In first 8 months	25.1	25.4	25.2	24.7	25.1	25.0
After first 8 months	24.8	25.0	25.6	25.6	25.3	25.4
Total	24.9	25.1	25.8	25.6	25.5	25.5
First postnuptial birth						
In first 8 months	25.1	25.4	25.6	25.0	25.3	25.2
After first 8 months	24.8	25.0	25.8	25.7	25.5	25.5
Total	24.9	25.1	25.7	25.5	25.4	25.4

Note: Results are based on the combined sample of all villages and are subject to restriction 1 (see Table A.1). In addition, couples for whom the date of the first postnuptial birth is inexact are excluded. Results based on 20–49 cases are shown in parentheses.

[a] Adjusted by multiple classification analysis for region, year of marriage, and occupational grouping of husband.

Table 9.10. *Percent of marriages occurring in most preferred months by pregnancy status of bride, by region, and by year of marriage*

	Year of marriage		
	1700–99	1800–99	Total
4 Baden villages			
Not pregnant	51	43	46
Pregnant	47	32	35
1 Württemberg village			
Not pregnant	52	37	43
Pregnant	54	35	41
3 Bavarian villages			
Not pregnant	21	20	20
Pregnant	—	(14)	15
4 Waldeck villages			
Not pregnant	30	21	25
Pregnant	27	20	22
2 East Friesland villages			
Not pregnant	42	59	51
Pregnant	38	36	37

Note: Most preferred months are those in which the proportion of marriages are more than one-third greater than would be expected if marriages were evenly distributed throughout the year. Non-pregnant brides include those who remained childless after marriage. Results are subject to restriction 1 (see Table A.1). In addition, couples for whom the date of the first postnuptial birth is inexact are excluded. Results in parentheses are based on 20–49 cases; results based on fewer than 20 cases are omitted.

to wait until a more customary month to do so. In order to examine this aspect of seasonality more directly, the percentage of couples marrying during the preferred months can be compared according to the pregnancy status of the bride. For the purpose of this analysis the customary and presumably preferred marriage months are defined as those in which the probability of marriages is more than one-third greater than would be expected if marriages were distributed evenly throughout the calendar year. The results of this comparison, presented in Table 9.10, are shown separately for each regional group of villages, since the pattern of seasonality differs considerably by region.

For the combined eighteenth and nineteenth centuries, the percentage of marriages occurring during the most preferred months is lower in each regional grouping when the bride was pregnant than when she was not. The differences are generally more pronounced during the nineteenth than during the eighteenth century. There are also considerable regional differences. As might be expected, bridal pregnancy appears to affect the timing of marriage most where seasonal peaks in marriages are clearest (see Figure 6.2). Thus in the East Frisian villages and in Baden, where peaks are pronounced, the percent who married during the preferred months is noticeably higher for non-pregnant than it is for pregnant brides. In contrast, in both Öschelbronn, the village in Württemberg, and in the Waldeck villages, where sharp seasonal concentrations of marriages are less evident, the percentages of couples marrying during the preferred months are quite similar regardless of the pregnancy status of the bride.

One factor which might affect the timing of the first birth, and particularly the occurrence of a bridal pregnancy, is the fecundity of the couple. If sexual activity were routine following betrothal or a commitment to marry, a pregnancy prior to marriage would be more likely to ensue for couples who were more fecund than for those who were less. Under such circumstances we might expect couples in which the bride was pregnant to conceive their second child more quickly than couples in which the bride was not pregnant. Indeed this seems to be the case. For couples married during the eighteenth and nineteenth centuries in the combined sample of all villages, the average interval between the first and second legitimate confinements is half a month shorter for women who were pregnant as brides than for those who were not. Statistical adjustment for year of marriage, region, husband's occupational group, and survival status of the infant to age 1, increases this difference to slightly over a month (results not shown).

In order to examine if women who were pregnant as brides experienced higher fertility in general than those who were not, age-specific marital fertility rates for each group can be compared. So as not to bias the results in favor of those who were pregnant, marital fertility rates have been calculated only for those age intervals following the one in which the first postnuptial birth occurs. The results are shown in Table 9.11 for the combined sample of all villages.

Women who were pregnant at marriage generally experienced modestly higher marital fertility rates than those who were not. This pattern is particularly consistent for women married during the nineteenth century, when bridal pregnancy was at a higher level. Thus these results also suggest that women who were pregnant as brides are selected for being more fecund than those who were not. While differences in deliberate fertility control or a number of other factors could account for the observed fertility differences between pregnant and non-pregnant brides, an interpretation in terms of fecundity

Table 9.11. *Age-specific fertility rates per 1000 married women with at least one postnuptial birth, excluding age interval in which first postnuptial birth occurs, by pregnancy status at marriage and year of marriage*

	Age					
	20–24	25–29	30–34	35–39	40–44	45–49
1700–99						
Pregnant	406	415	367	300	174	30
Not pregnant	403	410	373	311	167	25
1800–99						
Pregnant	430	415	361	298	158	19
Not pregnant	424	411	356	275	128	13
1700–1899						
Pregnant	423	415	363	298	162	22
Not pregnant	413	411	363	289	142	17

Note: Results refer to the combined sample of all women and are subject to restrictions 1, 2 and 3 (see Table A.1). In addition, couples for whom the date of the first postnuptial birth is inexact are excluded.

differences seems plausible. In any event, the differences are rather modest.

The association between the mode of entry into reproductive career and completed fertility is examined in Table 9.12 in terms of the mean number of children ever born for women who survive until the end of the reproductive age span in intact marriages. Results are adjusted statistically, first for year of marriage, region, and husband's occupational group, and then in addition for the age at first birth, and for the age at first postnuptial birth. The unadjusted results show a substantial difference in the completed fertility of women with different modes of entry into childbearing. Couples whose first birth was prenuptially born experienced slightly over one full child more than those whose first birth was conceived after marriage. Women whose first birth was postnuptial but was conceived prior to marriage fall more or less in between these two groups.

Adjustment for year of marriage, region, and husband's occupation increases these differences modestly, but when the wife's age at first birth is additionally taken into account the differentials are considerably reduced: there is almost no difference in the mean number of children ever born between couples whose first birth was prenuptially born and those whose first birth was prenuptially conceived. However, couples whose first birth was postnuptially conceived still

Table 9.12. *Mean number of children ever born, by the timing of couple's first birth and first legitimate birth, unadjusted and adjusted for selected factors*

	Unadjusted	Adjusted for year of marriage, region, and husband's occupation	Adjusted for year of marriage, region, husband's occupation and	
			Age at first birth	Age at first postnuptial birth
Timing of first birth				
Prenuptially born	6.90	7.01	6.25	—
Prenuptially conceived	6.42	6.57	6.30	—
Postnuptially conceived	5.79	5.74	5.90	—
Timing of first postnuptial birth				
Prenuptially conceived	6.56	6.70	—	6.37
Postnuptially conceived	5.90	5.86	—	5.95

Note: Results are based on the combined sample of all villages and are subject to restrictions 1, 2, 3 and 4 (see Table A.1). In addition, couples for whom the date of the first postnuptial birth is inexact are excluded. Adjustment is made by multiple classification analysis.

average somewhat fewer children ever born than the first two groups. Thus much of the higher fertility of women whose first birth predates marriage is due to an earlier start and hence longer period of exposure to childbearing. Nevertheless, the finding that women whose first birth is either prenuptially born or conceived experience slightly higher completed fertility, even after the earlier onset of childbearing is taken into account, is consistent with the suggestion that such couples are selected for somewhat higher fecundity.

If consideration is limited only to the timing of the first postnuptial birth, the more rapid pace of childbearing characteristic of women who were pregnant as brides, compared to those whose first birth was conceived after marriage, manifests itself in higher completed fertility. Part of the difference is due to the somewhat earlier start of childbearing among pregnant brides, but even after this is taken into account, such couples still average more children ever born by the end of the childbearing ages.

Discussion: the circumstances of non-marital sexual activity

The finding indicating that a large proportion of couples in the sample villages engaged in sexual activity prior to marriage during much of the period under observation raises questions about the nature and circumstances of such relationships. Did marital and non-marital reproductive unions simply differ with respect to whether or not they were officially sanctioned by the Church or were they of a fundamentally different nature? To what extent was premarital sexual activity a routine matter within the bounds of local customs and norms? Evidence of substantial non-marital sexual activity during the eighteenth and nineteenth centuries is by no means unique to German village populations, and has been indicated for much of northwestern Europe to one degree or another. Social historians have been debating the significance of such evidence ever since historical demography began to provide extensive documentation of the prevailing behavioral patterns.

The findings discussed in the previous chapter suggest that the likelihood of marriage following an out-of-wedlock birth was probably higher if the infant survived, although biases in the data prevent a definitive conclusion. If this is the case, it would suggest that some couples would not have married had the infant died early, and thus that there was not an unconditional prior commitment to marry, at least for some of these couples. Only the presence of an existing infant pressured the marriage to take place.

Table 9.13. *Mean interval between the first and second confinements according to the status of each confinement with respect to the timing of marriage, marriages 1700–1899*

Status of confinements		All first born	First born survives infancy[a]
First	Second		
Prenuptially born	Prenuptially born	40.8	42.4
Prenuptially born	Prenuptially conceived	37.7	40.2
Prenuptially born	Postnuptially conceived	38.9	40.6
Prenuptially conceived	Postnuptially conceived	25.3	27.4
Postnuptially conceived	Postnuptially conceived	25.5	27.3

Note: Results are based on the combined sample of all villages and are subject to restriction 2 (see Table A.1). In addition, couples for whom the date of the first postnuptial birth is inexact are excluded.
[a] Results subject additionally to restriction 7.

Some additional light can be shed on the nature of premarital unions by examining data on birth intervals. If couples who bore children prior to marriage were in fact cohabiting in marital-type unions virtually identical to those of couples who were already formally married, there should be little difference between them in the pace of childbearing during the initial period following the first birth. On the other hand, if cohabitation was less regular among such couples, there should be a greater delay between births than for couples already married. Table 9.13 compares the interval between the first and second confinements, according to the status of each of these confinements, with respect to the timing of marriage. Interpretation of the results is complicated by the difficulty, discussed in Appendix G, of accurately distinguishing non-legitimized from legitimized out-of-wedlock births. Particularly problematic is the likelihood that some prenuptial births may appear as non-legitimized illegitimate births in the genealogies. This is especially probable when the birth took place during a period when the father's name was not routinely included in entries for illegitimate births in the register and the infant did not survive until the parents' marriage. Since the first-born of couples who start their childbearing prior to marriage appear to be selected for surviving infancy, and since birth intervals following an infant survival are typically longer than those following an infant death, results are shown separately for intervals following surviving first-born infants.

Essentially the same pattern emerges regardless of whether intervals following all first-born or those following surviving first-born infants are considered. Intervals following a birth preceding marriage are substantially longer on average than intervals following births of children that are born postnuptially. The status of the second-born child has little impact on this pattern. Thus in cases where the first-born occurs prior to marriage, the average interval is only slightly longer if the second-born occurs prior to marriage than if the second-born is either prenuptially conceived or postnuptially conceived. Likewise, considerably shorter intervals are characteristic of births following a first child that is postnuptially born, regardless of whether it was conceived prior to marriage or after marriage. The pace of reproduction in premarital unions during the period prior to marriage thus appears to be considerably slower than that of postmarital reproduction. This difference, however, is almost certainly overstated due to the misclassification of some prenuptial births as non-legitimized illegitimate births. Thus the results should be considered only suggestive of an actual difference.

The finding that couples with a prenuptial birth eventually averaged as many or more children as did couples with a postnuptial first birth, even when age at first birth is taken into account, indicates that their pace of childbearing *after* marriage was at least as rapid as that for other couples (see Table 9.12). These results suggest that cohabitation following a prenuptial birth was probably less regular up until the time of marriage than it was following marriage. For at least some couples who initiated reproduction before marriage, the formalization of marriage was probably associated with a change in living arrangements. Unfortunately, biases in the data prevent a more conclusive judgment of this issue.

For the six fully-coded villages, it is possible to calculate the pace of childbearing for women who experienced repetitive non-legitimized births. The average interval between such births for the six villages combined during the eighteenth and nineteenth centuries together is approximately 52 months, an even longer interval than typically followed a first prenuptial birth. This may at least in part be attributable to the fact that in some cases different partners fathered successive births to the same unwed mother. Unfortunately, given the high proportion of repeat bastard-bearing for which the name of the father is not given in the records, it is not feasible to examine non-marital unions of particular sets of partners with more than one birth to determine how closely their pace of childbearing resembled that of married couples.

A fascinating set of observations about marital and non-marital sexual customs in rural Germany at the end of the nineteenth century is provided by an unusual and little known survey conducted in the mid-1890s which sheds light on the local perceptions of the phenomena under investigation.[14] Questionnaires were sent out to over 14,000 rural Protestant pastors inquiring about a range of topics dealing with sexual activity both inside and outside marriage. The response rate was low, with only about 1000 questionnaires being returned, but they did cover most areas in Germany. The results were written up in a largely narrative fashion in the form of regional reports, and compiled into two volumes. The person writing up a particular region could also add information based on his knowledge of the local situation.

For the regions represented by the sample of villages on which the present study is based, no information is provided by the survey for Waldeck – although surrounding administrative areas (*Regierungsbezirke*) are covered – and mention is made of only one of the two administrative areas in which the three Bavarian villages are located. In addition, in Baden and Bavaria, the sample villages are Catholic, while the survey is based on informants presumably more familiar with the Protestant populations. More generally, given the low response rate and the special nature of the informants, the results must be viewed cautiously. It is somewhat reassuring that the compilers of the reports were cognizant of these problems. Despite these reservations, it is encouraging that the findings fit in well with the results on the prevalence of illegitimacy and bridal pregnancy as derived from the village genealogies.

Many respondents, probably the majority, reported that premarital sexual relations were either customary or common in their local parishes. Reports specific to those areas of Baden and Württemberg in which the sample villages were located, as well as for East Friesland and the administrative areas surrounding Waldeck, all agreed in this respect. Only in the administrative area in which two of the Bavarian villages were located were reports considerably more mixed in this respect. Interestingly, data from the village genealogies showed bridal pregnancy and prenuptial births to be particularly infrequent in these villages (see Table 9.2). Mention was often made that non-marital sexual activity was more common among workers and laborers than among peasants.

A prior intention to marry was often, although not always, thought to be present among couples engaged in non-marital sexual relationships. In some cases, marriage was believed to have been precipitated by a pregnancy, and thus sexual relations to have been initiated prior

[14] Allgemeine Konferenz der deutschen Sittlichkeitsvereine, *Die geschlechtlich sittlichen Vehältnisse*.

to a firm commitment to wed. Many respondents mentioned that women were more likely to anticipate marriage when engaging in out-of-wedlock sex than were men, and some were thought to have done so in order to force a marriage. Some respondents specifically mentioned that sexual relations were considered permissible once a couple was engaged. One informant for a parish in the area of Öschelbronn indicated that engaged couples were considered the same as married couples. The right to test a woman's ability to conceive a child was also mentioned occasionally as a rationale for starting sexual relations. Respondents varied in the extent they felt premarital sex was disapproved of by the community, although it was often mentioned that attitudes were lax in this respect.

The qualitative results of this survey thus agree well with the quantitative evidence provided by the present study that bridal pregnancy was common in most of the sample villages in the nineteenth century. The higher prevalence of premarital births and bridal pregnancy found to characterize proletarians compared to farmers is also in accord with the observations of the rural pastors.

Also of interest is the substantial body of ethnographic evidence describing widespread customs and norms during preceding centuries sanctioning premarital intercourse in much of northern and central Europe.[15] These customs apparently stemmed from old patterns of nocturnal visitation which were common in some rural areas during medieval times and persisted into the eighteenth and nineteenth centuries. According to these customs, an unmarried man was permitted to sleep with an unmarried woman and, if both partners were potential spouses, to have sexual relations. However, the couple was held responsible for their offspring and marriage was expected to follow if pregnancy occurred. Whether intentional or not, such customs permitting premarital intercourse served as a way by which men tested the childbearing ability of prospective brides.[16]

Although there is no direct evidence that such customs existed in the specific sample villages, it is thought that they characterized much of Germany.[17] Such customs, however, if they were longstanding, cannot account for the large increase in prenuptial births or pregnancies that occurred in the late eighteenth and early nineteenth centuries. If they helped set the stage for premarital intercourse, it must have been in combination with changes in other influences as well.

Non-marital sexual activity in German villages during the

[15] Wickman, 'Einleitung der Ehe.'
[16] Myrdal, *Nation and family*, pp. 42–44.
[17] Wickman, 'Einleitung der Ehe,' pp. 216–43.

eighteenth and nineteenth centuries seems to have encompassed a range of circumstances. It is not clear under which circumstances, if any, out-of-wedlock sex can be considered as truly socially aberrant behavior. It does seem that much of it occurred as part of the process leading up to marriage, and was perhaps linked to engagement or some strong prior commitment to marry. Premarital sexual activity in this context was probably reasonably well tolerated, if not completely condoned, by popular attitudes, even if officially frowned upon by the ecclesiastical authorities.[18] The normalcy of bridal pregnancy by the nineteenth century is testified to by its prevalence and by the fact that it had little effect on the age at which the couple wed, most likely advancing their marriage by only a matter of months on average. Not all non-marital sexual activity falls in this category, however, as indicated by the substantial proportions of women who had out-of-wedlock births, particularly those that were not later legitimized by marriage. Some non-marital sexual encounters lacked a strong sense of commitment or obligation on the part of the partners. Moreover, when marriage did follow, the circumstances of the union probably changed, judging from the apparently quicker pace of marital as opposed to premarital childbearing.

Many questions about non-marital sexual and reproductive activity in German village populations of the past remain unanswered and cannot be appropriately addressed by the kind of analysis followed here. Exposing the behavioral patterns more fully will hopefully contribute to the shaping of the broader social historical questions to be pursued. Clearly the major changes that have been shown to have taken place during the two-century period under investigation merit continued attention beyond the more narrow realm of historical demography.

---

[18] Phayer, *Sexual liberation and religion*, p. 18.

PART IV

Marital reproduction

10

Trends in marital fertility and underlying natural fertility components

It is now well established that the reduction in fertility associated with the demographic transition in Europe was primarily a matter of changing reproductive behavior within marriage. While non-marital fertility also declined during the period of fertility change, it never constituted a large proportion of overall fertility, except in a few regions.[1] Moreover, to the extent that nuptiality changed during the period of fertility decline, it generally increased, thereby counteracting rather than facilitating the trend to lower levels of reproduction.[2]

In the sample of German villages on which this study is based, non-marital fertility has not been measured directly. However, the rise in illegitimacy ratios and their subsequent decline after the mid-nineteenth century probably reflect corresponding trends in non-marital reproduction. Even at their peak, illegitimate births never represented as much as 15 percent of all births, at least for the six fully-coded villages. Data on age at first marriage suggest that changes in nuptiality over the eighteenth and nineteenth centuries in the sample villages were fairly minor and thus cannot have had much impact, either on trends in overall fertility for the village populations as a whole, or on fertility differentials among the major occupational subgroups. No information on the proportions married, an aspect of nuptiality which could potentially change independently of the age at marriage, is available from the village genealogies. However, analysis of census data in the latter part of the nineteenth century indicates that the proportion of the population remaining permanently single was relatively stable at the national and provincial levels.[3] Thus it is the

---

[1] Shorter, Knodel, and van de Walle, 'Decline of non-marital fertility,' pp. 371–93.
[2] van de Walle, 'Marriage and marital fertility,' pp. 486–501; Watkins, 'Regional patterns of nuptiality,' pp. 199–215.
[3] Knodel, *Decline of fertility*; Knodel and Maynes, 'Marriage patterns,' pp. 129–68.

marital fertility component of overall fertility which is the proper focus of the study of the onset of the demographic transition in Germany and a key aspect of the general level of fertility during the entire period under observation.

The three chapters constituting this section focus primarily on marital reproduction. The present chapter examines the overall levels and trends in marital fertility, discusses conceptual and measurement issues related to the distinction between natural and controlled fertility, presents evidence of a secular increase in the underlying level of natural marital fertility, and examines the proximate determinants of this phenomenon. Because of the trend toward an increased reproductive capacity in married couples, change in marital fertility levels is not necessarily a sensitive indicator of an increase in deliberate attempts to limit family size. Chapter 11 provides a more detailed examination of evidence of changes in reproductive behavior that appear directed toward restricting the number of children born, and documents the onset of the transition from natural fertility to family limitation. Finally, Chapter 12 concludes this section on marital reproduction by examining the relative roles that changes in the age at which childbearing started, birth spacing, and deliberate attempts to stop childbearing, played during the initial phases of the fertility transition.

Levels and trends of marital fertility

The accuracy of an analysis of marital fertility depends on the completeness with which births to married couples were included in the local registers upon which the village genealogies are based. An assessment of the completeness of birth registration is provided in Appendix B. In general, the results are encouraging. Even during the periods when there was an obvious problem with the registration of infant and child deaths, birth registration appears to be reasonably complete. However, there is some uncertainty about how accurately stillbirths were distinguished from live births in the parish registers and hence in the village genealogies. Particularly in Catholic areas, stillbirths may have been incorrectly recorded as live births. For these reasons, analysis of fertility (as in the case of infant mortality) is based on all births, including those indicated as stillbirths.

As a summary measure of levels and trends in marital fertility, a modified version of the I_g index developed by Ansley Coale has been adopted.[4] Like the original, it indicates the ratio of observed fertility to

---

[4] Coale, 'Fertility in Europe from the French Revolution to World War II.'

the highest marital fertility on reliable record at the time the index was developed (that of Hutterite women married 1921–30). Unlike the original, however, this modified version incorporates a direct standardization for age distribution within the childbearing ages, thereby taking advantage of the availability of age-specific marital fertility rates for the village populations.[5] The number of married women by five-year age groups for all of Germany, as recorded in the 1871 census, the first census for which such data are available at the national level, is used as the basis for standardization. The modified version, labeled I_g' to differentiate it from the original index, has an advantage over a simple total marital fertility rate (which could be computed by summing the *unweighted* age-specific marital fertility rates for each five-year age group and multiplying by five) because it avoids giving undue weight to the marital fertility rates in the younger ages, when relatively few women are actually married. Moreover, it facilitates comparison with the extensive amount of previous research on the fertility transition in Europe that incorporates the Coale index of

---

[5] As defined by Coale,

$$I_g = B_L/\Sigma m_i F_i$$

where B_L is the annual number of legitimate births in the specified population, m_i is the number of married women in each five-year age interval in the reproductive span in the specified population, and F_i is the fertility of married Hutterite women in each age interval.

The modified version is defined as follows:

$$I_g' = \Sigma f_i M_i/\Sigma M_i F_i$$

where F_i is the same as above, f_i is the observed fertility rates of married women in each five-year age interval in the specified population, and M_i is the number of married women in each five-year age interval in the reproductive span in the standard population, which in this case is the number of German women as recorded in the 1871 census.

The values of M_i (stated in 100s of women) and F_i (stated per woman) used in the calculation of I_g' are as follows:

Age	M_i	F_i
15–19	282	.300
20–24	3904	.550
25–34	10,942	.447
35–39	10,336	.406
40–44	8841	.222
45–49	8058	.061

Note that F_i for ages 15–19 has been arbitrarily selected, substituting for the observed rate of Hutterite women aged 15–19 (see Coale, 'Low fertility').

A comparison between I_g and I_g' for the village populations in our sample indicates that the effect of direct standardization is small and that the two measures are typically quite close.

Table 10.1. *Age-standardized index of marital fertility* (I_g') *by year of marriage*

	1700–49	1750–99	1800–24	1825–49	1850–74	1875–99
Grafenhausen	.77	.87	.80	.75	.67	.53
Herbolzheim	.83	.82	.80	.72	.75	.74
Kappel	.77	.79	.75	.83	.82	.84
Rust	.80	.79	.84	.85	.85	.89
Öschelbronn	.72	.77	.85	.96	.91	.98
3 Bavarian villages	(.89)	.99	.90	.90	1.01	.90
4 Waldeck villages	.70	.77	.76	.83	.85	.70
Middels	—	.70	.64	.70	.63	.64
Werdum	.74	.73	.60	.67	.66	—
All villages	.77	.80	.77	.79	.79	.76

Note: Results in this table are subject to restrictions 1, 2 and 3 (see Table A.1). Results in parentheses are based on an average of 100–199 woman-years per five-year age group from 20–49; results based on fewer than 100 woman-years not shown.

marital fertility, since the value of the original and the modified indices do not differ greatly from one another under most circumstances.

Table 10.1 shows the trends and levels of marital fertility by marriage cohort for the sample villages based on the age-standardized index of marital fertility. Based on official statistics, the national level of I_g fluctuated between .76 and .73 for the late 1860s and the 1870s, the earliest period for which it can be calculated, and thus agrees well with the level of I_g' found for the 1850–74 marriage cohort in the combined sample of 14 villages.[6]

There is substantial variation among villages in the level of fertility as measured by I_g'. Women in the three Bavarian villages experienced the highest fertility for most marriage cohorts. The 1850–74 marriage cohort in these villages experienced fertility that even exceeded slightly the level of the Hutterites, which serves as the standard underlying the marital fertility index. Women in Werdum and Middels, two villages in East Friesland, typically experienced the lowest fertility, 70 percent or less of the Hutterite fertility level for most marriage cohorts. As noted above, Bavarian villages were also characterized by the highest infant mortality and the East Frisian villages by the lowest. As with the case of mortality, the differences in marital

[6] Knodel, *Decline of fertility.*

fertility levels between these sets of villages is probably related to the differences in infant-feeding practices. As discussed below, in the absence of birth control, breastfeeding can lower fertility by delaying the postpartum resumption of ovulation and hence lengthen birth intervals. Thus the relative absence of breastfeeding in the Bavarian villages probably helps to account for the unusually high fertility there, whereas the pattern of widespread, relatively longer breastfeeding probably contributed to the lower fertility in East Friesland.

Variations in trends in marital fertility among the villages are also evident. The decline in fertility, so distinctly evident at the end of the nineteenth century in national and provincial level statistics, shows considerable variation at the village level.[7] In Grafenhausen, a sustained fall in fertility appears to have started considerably earlier than the end of the nineteenth century, with I_g' declining for each successive marriage cohort during the entire century. In nearby Herbolzheim, a fertility decline early in the nineteenth century also appears to have taken place, but the level of marital fertility remains practically unchanged during the last half of the century. In contrast, in Kappel, Rust, and especially in Öschelbronn, marital fertility generally increased throughout the nineteenth century, reaching its highest level for the 1875–99 marriage cohort. In the Bavarian villages and the Waldeck villages, fertility drops fairly sharply in the last quarter of the nineteenth century, but not to levels distinctly below those of all earlier cohorts. In the East Frisian villages of Werdum and Middels, it is more difficult to judge if a decline was under way in the nineteenth century, both because I_g' fluctuates considerably and, in the case of Werdum, because there are insufficient data for the cohort married at the end of the century. Thus in terms of trends in the level of marital fertility, the village data indicate considerable diversity with respect to if and when the secular decline to modern low fertility levels started during the period under investigation.

Concepts and definitions

An important distinction for the historical study of reproductive behavior, and particularly for the study of changes in reproductive patterns associated with the demographic transition, is the one between natural and controlled marital fertility. The concept of natural fertility was developed by Louis Henry, who initially defined it as fertility in the absence of deliberate efforts to limit births, but later

[7] Knodel, *Decline of fertility.*

refined the concept to refer more specifically to fertility in the absence of *parity-dependent* birth control.[8] As he put it, natural fertility prevails when there is an *absence* of behavior to control births which is 'bound to the number of children already born and is modified when the number reaches the maximum which the couple does not want to exceed.'[9] According to this definition, natural fertility is distinguished by the lack of actions to stop childbearing at any particular parity in order to limit family size to a given number, and thus by a situation in which couples continue childbearing throughout the biologically determined reproductive span.

The concept of natural fertility, as developed by Henry and as applied in demography, explicitly recognizes that reproductive levels under conditions of natural fertility are influenced not only by purely biological factors, but also by behavioral factors and, especially because of the latter, can vary substantially despite the absence of deliberate actions to limit family size.

Behavior which affects the level of fertility through prolonging the interval between births but is independent of parity is not considered contrary to natural fertility. Examples of such behavior include breast-feeding, temporary postnatal abstinence, and short-term migration separating spouses, provided there is no association with the number of children already born. Generally, the concept of natural fertility is applied to reproductive behavior within marriage (or similarly stable sexual unions) rather than to overall fertility, since the latter is so strongly contingent on the prevailing marriage patterns.

Natural fertility no longer exists once some perceptible proportion of couples practice family limitation. As used in this study, the term 'family limitation' refers specifically to deliberate attempts to limit the number of offspring by stopping childbearing before the end of the couple's reproductive span, and assumes that couples alter their reproductive behavior once they reach the number of children they consider sufficient. It is not necessary that the couple decide on this number in advance. They need only decide at some point in their reproductive career that no additional children are wanted, and then act to prevent or slow further childbearing. Thus, when family limitation is present, reproductive behavior is affected by the number of children a couple has and fertility control is parity-dependent. Family limitation is a more specific term than 'birth control.' Whereas both terms include deliberate attempts to stop childbearing, birth control includes any deliberate spacing practices, regardless of whether they

---

[8] Henry, 'Théoriques des mesures,' pp. 135–51.
[9] Henry, 'Data on natural fertility,' p. 81.

are parity-dependent or not, while family limitation excludes spacing practices, even if deliberate, if those practices are not related to the number of children already born.

Since the concept of natural fertility is defined in terms of the absence of family limitation rather than of birth control practices in general, the potential existence of situations in which deliberate but parity-independent practices to space births are present makes a simple dichotomy that contrasts natural and controlled fertility somewhat ambiguous.[10] Henry and others have undoubtedly been led to define natural fertility in such a way that only parity-dependent practices are excluded because of the greater ease in detecting such behavior. The question of spacing versus stopping behavior during the onset of the fertility transition, for which this issue has particular relevance, is considered at length in Chapter 12. At this point, it is at least worth noting that analysis of provincial- and national-level data for a variety of populations indicates that the introduction and spread of family limitation, that is parity-dependent control, was usually a key feature of the fertility transition.[11]

It is important to note that the concept of natural fertility involves behavioral components and explicity does not refer to a purely biological definition of the ability to reproduce. For example, the frequency of intercourse and infant-feeding habits are to a large extent socially or culturally determined, yet both interact with the biological processes underlying reproduction to influence a couple's ability to bear children. The concept of natural fertility thus takes into account that, in any real population, the ability to reproduce is in fact a function of both biological and behavioral processes.

Even among populations where family limitation is commonly practiced, it is possible to view the observed fertility level as a joint product of the extent of deliberate control and an underlying level of natural fertility, where the latter refers to the level that would prevail if no deliberate family limitation were practiced but other behavioral and biological factors remained the same. The value of conceptualizing marital fertility in this way is to recognize explicitly that trends in fertility levels need not necessarily reflect trends in the prevalence of family limitation practices. It could be possible, for example, for increases in the underlying natural fertility level to offset partially, or even entirely, an increase in the practice of family limitation, such that

---

[10] The ambiguities involved in the dichotomy of natural versus controlled fertility, as defined by Henry and as typically used in the demographic literature, are discussed at some length in Knodel, 'Natural fertility: patterns, levels and trends.'
[11] Knodel, 'Family limitation,' pp. 219–49.

observed fertility levels would decline more modestly or not at all compared to the steeper declines that would have resulted had the underlying level of natural marital fertility remained unchanged.

Age patterns of natural and controlled marital fertility

Family reconstitution data lend themselves fairly readily to a variety of measures designed indirectly to detect the extent to which married couples were practicing family limitation, and hence whether or not a population is characterized by natural or controlled marital fertility. Most of these measures are based on the observation that when family limitation is common, in contrast to when natural fertility prevails, couples generally terminate childbearing at younger ages and tend to concentrate their childbearing in the earlier part of the wife's potentially fertile period.

The concept of natural fertility does not imply a particular level of fertility. However, the distinction between natural and controlled fertility has important implications both for the age of mothers at their last birth and for the age patterns of childbearing. Since couples take no deliberate actions to terminate childbearing prior to the end of the reproductive age span under conditions of natural fertility, the age at which a mother bears her last child is likely to be older on average than in populations where family limitation is common. Moreover, the specification that natural fertility be free of parity-dependent control suggests that the shape of the natural marital fertility curve over the reproductive age span will be determined primarily by the decline in the ability to bear children with age. As long as that ability remains high, fertility should as well. Only with the rapid decline of reproductive ability at older reproductive ages does fertility also decline precipitously with advancing age. In contrast, in populations where family size limitation is common, age-specific marital fertility rates tend to show a more rapid decline at earlier ages and to be particularly low at the older reproductive ages. This occurs because the proportion of couples who have reached a family size they do not wish to exceed, and who make efforts to prevent further births, increases with age. As a result, fertility is disproportionately lower at the older reproductive ages in comparison to a natural fertility situation.

Coale and Trussell have developed a standard age-specific schedule of natural marital fertility based on the average of 10 of the 13 marital fertility schedules from presumed natural fertility populations, presented in an influential article by Henry on the topic.[12] This

---

[12] Coale and Trussell, 'Model fertility schedules,' pp. 185–258; Henry, 'Data on natural fertility,' pp. 81–91.

standard is intended to embody the typical age pattern of natural fertility. In the first panel of Figure 10.1, age-specific marital fertility schedules from several of the sample villages are shown, along with the Coale–Trussell natural fertility standard. The specific examples of Middels and the Bavarian villages were chosen because they represent a considerable contrast in the level of marital fertility even prior to any signs of the fertility decline. In both cases, the marriage cohorts chosen represent the situation prior to the fertility decline. Also shown are two marriage cohorts from Grafenhausen, one for the last half of the eighteenth century before fertility declined, and the other for the last quarter of the nineteenth century, a time by which fertility in that village had already shown substantial decline.

Despite the considerable differences in fertility levels represented by the different villages, with the exception of the late nineteenth-century marriage cohort for Grafenhausen, the curves share a common convex shape along with the standard natural fertility schedule. Some irregularity in the curve for Middels is evident, with fertility being slightly lower at ages 25–29 than at ages 30–34, but this is probably attributable to the fluctuations associated with small numbers of cases. In contrast, the curve for the late nineteenth-century marriage cohort in Grafenhausen is somewhat concave, with a more rapid decline in fertility occurring at the younger age groups than is evident in the other fertility schedules.

One way to standardize for the level of fertility is to express the rate at each age as a percentage of the rate at ages 20–24. This has been done in the second panel of Figure 10.1. The results show even more clearly the similar convex shape of all the schedules except for the late nineteenth-century cohort in Grafenhausen. The similarity with respect to the age pattern of fertility of those schedules that resemble the Coale–Trussell standard implies that they are also characterized by natural fertility. In contrast, the more concave shape of the late nineteenth-century marriage cohort for Grafenhausen presumably indicates the practice of family limitation on a parity-dependent basis.[13]

The trends in the observed age-specific marital fertility rates for the combined sample of the 14 villages are presented in Table 10.2 and Figure 10.2 for couples married between 1750 and 1899, grouped into marriage cohorts by quarter-century periods. Rates for married women aged 15–19 in late-marrying populations, such as those in the

---

[13] The fact that populations characterized by natural fertility share a relatively similar age pattern of marital fertility has been found to hold for both modern and historical populations under a wide range of different conditions. See Knodel, 'Natural fertility: patterns, levels and trends.'

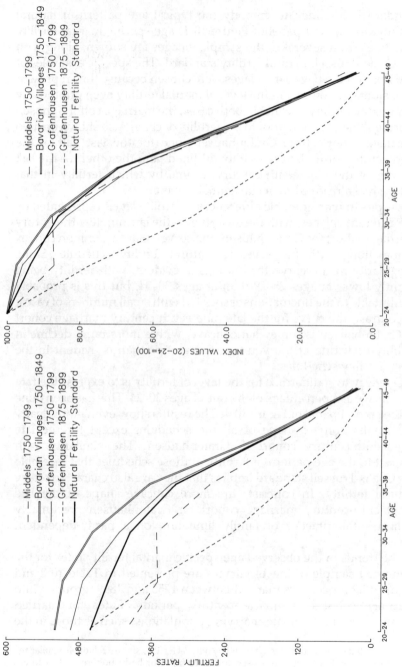

Figure 10.1. *Age-specific marital fertility schedules: rates and index values for selected villages and marriage cohorts. Results are subject to restrictions 1, 2 and 3 (see Table A.1)*

Table 10.2. *Age-specific marital fertility, the ratio of total marital fertility over 30 (TMF30+) to total marital fertility over 20 (TMF20+), the Coale–Trussell indices of natural fertility level (M) and marital fertility control (m), and mean square error (MSE) of estimates of M and m, by year of marriage*

Year of marriage	15–19	20–24	25–29	30–34	35–39	40–44	45–49	TMF30+/TMF20+	M	m	MSE
1750–74	384	439	425	374	303	173	26	.50	.95	–.03	.001
1775–99	376	455	426	376	301	155	25	.49	.99	.05	.000
1800–24	482	463	412	362	285	151	18	.48	.99	.08	.000
1825–49	473	503	430	379	286	141	15	.47	1.07	.18	.000
1850–74	486	533	450	362	288	128	15	.45	1.14	.27	.001
1875–99	483	547	462	353	247	104	6	.41	1.20	.46	.000
Percent change 1750–74/1875–99	+26	+25	+9	–6	–18	–40	–75	–18	+26	—	—

Note: Marital fertility rates are expressed per 1000 married women. Results refer to the combined sample of all villages and are subject to restrictions 1, 2 and 3 (see Table A.1).

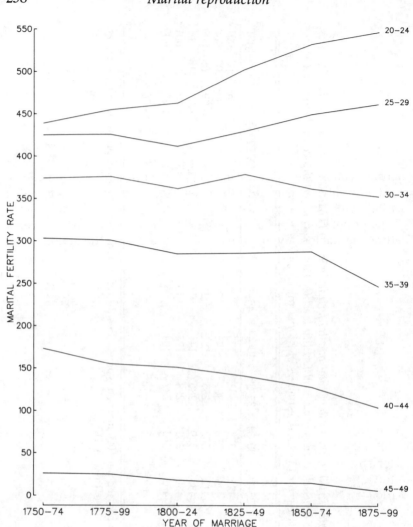

Figure 10.2. *Age-specific marital fertility rates by year of marriage*. Results are based on the combined sample of all villages and are subject to restrictions 1, 2 and 3 (see Table A.1)

sample German villages, are typically difficult to interpret, and thus are best ignored (and are omitted in Figure 10.2). The results for the other age groups, however, are of considerable interest and indicate two distinct trends: toward higher fertility among younger married women and toward lower fertility among older women. The latter trend, particularly pronounced among women in their forties, undoubtedly reflects an increasing practice of deliberate family limitation which, as described above, is expected to have a disproportionate impact at older ages.

The steady increase in fertility among women 20–24 and the less regular increase among women 25–29 are more difficult to interpret in terms of volitional control. It is generally assumed that deliberate limitation of fertility is least likely at younger ages, when the family-building process is still at an early stage, and it seems particularly unlikely that any such tendency would be strongest among the earlier marriage cohorts and weakest among the later cohorts. The increase in marital fertility of women in their twenties, plus the rising levels of marital fertility in general as measured by the I_g' index for several of the village populations, raises the possibility that the underlying level of natural marital fertility might have increased during the period under observation. Before we examine this issue more fully, it will be useful to discuss how the degree of family limitation might be succinctly measured on the basis of information on the age patterns of natural fertility.

One very simple way to summarize the age structure of marital fertility in a manner that should be sensitive to the extent of family limitation, as well as independent of the overall fertility level, is to calculate the ratio of total marital fertility over age 30 (TMF 30+) to total marital fertility over age 20 (TMF 20+). Total marital fertility over any particular age is simply the summation of the age-specific marital fertility rates from that age and above (multiplied by 5 if the age-specific rates were originally calculated for five-year age intervals). The results express the proportion of childbearing that takes place after age 30 for a hypothetical woman who married at age 20 and lived to the end of the reproductive span, and experienced the prevailing age-specific marital fertility rates. The results of such a calculation are also included in Table 10.2. The lower the ratio of TMF 30+ to TMF 20+, the faster marital fertility declines with age and thus the stronger the evidence of family limitation. The steady decline in this index, and particularly the more rapid decline during the second half of the nineteenth century, is therefore suggestive of an increased practice of family limitation in the sample as a whole.

This measure permits not only a judgment of whether the age structure of marital fertility was changing in a manner suggestive of increased family limitation, but also provides some idea of whether or not family limitation was practiced at all before any substantial change is evident. This is possible since the relationship of marital fertility with age is relatively constant for natural fertility populations, and thus the proportion of marital fertility after age 20 that occurs after age 30 is relatively fixed. According to the ten marital fertility schedules used by Coale and Trussell for constructing their standard natural fertility schedule, marital fertility after age 30 accounts for between 46 to 53 percent of marital fertility after age 20 in the absence of family limitation.[14] For all ten populations together, the average was exactly 50 percent. In contrast, in modern-day populations which practice extensive family limitation, TMF 30+ is typically below 25 percent of TMF 20+, and in some cases even below 15 percent. As is evident from Table 10.2, this ratio for the combined sample of German villages starts out at precisely the average of the ten natural-fertility populations used by Coale and Trussell and declines by the late nineteenth century to a point that is decisively below the range of the separate schedules on which the standard is based.

The Coale–Trussell indices

A more sophisticated measure summarizing the extent to which family limitation is implicit in the age structure of any particular marital fertility schedule has been developed by Coale and Trussell.[15] Their analytical model of marital fertility, when applied to an observed schedule of age-specific marital fertility rates, permits the estimation of both the extent of fertility control within marriage and a scale factor of fertility level. The index of fertility control, designated as m, indicates the extent to which the age pattern of observed marital fertility deviates from the standard age pattern of natural fertility, taking into account that such deviations would be expected to increase with age in populations practicing deliberate family limitation. Since it is predicated on the concepts of natural fertility and parity-dependent fertility control, as discussed above, and is not sensitive to non-parity-dependent efforts to space births, m can be considered more appropriately as an index of family limitation rather than of birth control in general. Nevertheless, because it is generally referred to in the literature as the Coale–Trussell index of fertility control, this terminology is retained here. The index is constructed so that it will equal zero if the shape of the observed fertility schedule in question resembles the standard natural fertility schedule. The faster fertility falls with age, the greater the amount of fertility control implied and the higher the value of the m index. If fertility falls less rapidly with age

[14] Coale and Trussell, 'Model fertility schedules,' pp. 185–258.
[15] Coale and Trussell, 'Model fertility schedules,' pp. 185–258; 'Technical note,' pp. 203–13.

than in the standard schedule, negative values result. Since m is determined entirely from the age patterns of fertility, it is independent of the level of fertility.

Small differences in the value of m are not necessarily meaningful indications of differences in the extent of family limitation. For example, among the ten empirical fertility schedules which served as the basis for determining the standard shape of natural fertility, the values of m ranged from $-.15$ to $.24$. On a cross-sectional basis, some range of differences is to be expected even when little or no family limitation is being practiced. On the other hand, modern populations in which contraception is widespread are typically characterized by m values well over 1.00. Thus moderate or large cross-sectional differences or consistent trends over time in a series of m values can be interpreted with reasonable confidence as reflections of differences in the degree of fertility control.[16]

The scale factor of fertility level, designated as M, is intended to be independent of the extent of voluntary control, as defined above, and thus can serve, under some circumstances, as an indicator of the underlying level of natural fertility. It is based on the assumption that even when family limitation is common, the fertility of younger married women is unlikely to be influenced since such women are at the early stages of family-building and have not reached the number of children they do not want to exceed. The M index is constructed so that it will equal 1.00 when the underlying level of natural fertility is the same as the level embodied in the standard natural fertility schedule. Deviations from 1.00 indicate the proportionate deviation from that level.

Since, in the Coale–Trussell model, voluntary control has been defined in the more narrow sense of parity-dependent behavior, deliberate efforts to extend birth intervals that are independent of the number of children already born can complicate the interpretation of both indices. When deliberate spacing of births independent of parity is common, the m index seriously underestimates the extent of voluntary control in its broader sense, which would include efforts to space children as well as to stop childbearing at some chosen family size. Moreover, the value of M is sensitive to deliberate birth spacing, even when spacing practices are parity-dependent. In general, deliberate spacing tends to depress the M index. In most developed countries today, where contraceptive practices and abortion are widespread, couples commonly practice birth control both for spacing and stopping

---

[16] Coale and Trussell, 'Technical note,' pp. 203–13.

purposes. In these circumstances, the M index will be depressed and cannot be taken as a reliable estimate of the underlying level of natural fertility. In addition, trends in M may not accurately reflect trends in underlying natural fertility if the extent of deliberate birth spacing is changing. For example, if birth-spacing efforts are increasing at the same time that increases in the underlying natural marital fertility level are taking place, the trend in M will understate the change in the latter.

Although values of m can be calculated for separate age groups of women, in this study a single value of m is used to characterize a given age schedule of marital fertility. The single value is arrived at through a simple least-squares regression procedure suggested by Coale and Trussell.[17] This procedure also yields a measure of how well the observed age pattern of marital fertility fits with the Coale–Trussell fertility model. Low values of the mean square error indicate that the observed schedule conforms well either to the standard natural fertility schedule or to the expected age pattern of departure when fertility is controlled. Coale and Trussell consider values of the mean square error above .005 to indicate relatively poor fits. When the estimates of M or m in this study are based on regressions for which the mean square error equals or exceeds this value, this will be so indicated.[18]

[17] Coale and Trussell, 'Technical note,' pp. 203–13.
[18] More specifically m and M are defined in the basic equation

$$r(a)/n(a) = M.e^{mv(a)}$$

where a stands for age, $r(a)$ is the observed marital fertility schedule, $n(a)$ is the empirically derived standard natural fertility schedule, M is a scale factor reflecting the population's underlying level of natural fertility measured relative to the standard, and $v(a)$ is an empirically derived function expressing the tendency for older women in populations where family limitation is practiced to effect particularly large reductions of fertility below the natural level. By taking the natural logarithms of both sides of the equation, the result is

$$1n[r(a)/n(a)] = 1n(M) + m.v(a)$$

By letting $1n[r(a)/n(a)] = y$, $1n(M) = c$, and $v(a) = x$, $1n(M)$ and m are estimated by ordinary least squares in which all points have equal weight. Only the five-year age groups from 20–24 to 40–44 are used for the estimation, since marital fertility at ages 45–49 tends to be subject to relatively greater random fluctuations because of the small number of births typically occurring in that age group. The model and the procedure for estimating it are described in detail by Coale and Trussell ('Modern fertility schedules,' p. 572; 'Technical note,' pp. 203–13).

A drawback of the procedure used in this study is that it gives equal weight to rates at all ages, even though at some ages the number of women-years of experience on which the rate is based is considerably smaller than others. A maximum likelihood procedure recently developed by James Trussell (personal communication), avoids this problem. It can be applied provided data on both the numbers of births and years of experience are available rather than only the age-specific marital fertility rates themselves. A comparison of estimates of M and m based on this new procedure and

Values of the M and m indices are included in Table 10.2. For all the marriage cohorts of the combined sample of villages, the fit between the observed and model schedules is quite good as indicated by the low values of the mean square error. The increase in marital fertility among younger married women is reflected in the substantial increase in M in successive marriage cohorts, particularly during the nineteenth century, while the shift in the age pattern of marital fertility toward a more rapid decline with age, indicative of the increasing practice of family limitation, is reflected in the rising values of m. The M index increased in value by more than a quarter between the first and last marriage cohort, while the m index rose from a level just slightly below zero, indicative of natural fertility, to a level substantially above zero, a level which is suggestive of at least some voluntary fertility control within marriage.

The relative constancy of the achieved level of overall marital fertility (as summarized by I_g' in Table 10.1) for successive marriage cohorts stands in marked contrast to the almost steady increase in the M index. The fact that marital fertility showed little change is apparently the result of substantial but countervailing decreases in fertility at older ages through family limitation and increased fertility levels at younger ages. Only between the last two marriage cohorts is the increase in the practice of family limitation large enough to more than compensate for the increasing fertility in the early years of marriage; the result is a modest decline in overall marital fertility.

These results indicate that a movement away from natural fertility toward deliberate family limitation began, at least in some parts of rural Germany, considerably before the end of the nineteenth century, the period which, on the basis of measures of aggregate fertility derived from census and vital statistics reports, has generally been accepted as marking the onset of the fertility transition in Germany.[19] Insofar as the sample of 14 villages is typical of rural Germany, the earlier onset of voluntary fertility control appears to have been masked in the measures of observed fertility by a substantial and concurrent rise in the underlying level of natural marital fertility.

on the least-squares regression technique reveals only very small differences in the results, differences which could have at most only negligible effects on any substantive interpretations. Since previous publications of results based on the German village sample have utilized the linear regression estimate technique and since there is only a modest difference in the results of the two procedures, the earlier procedure is also followed here for the sake of consistency.

[19] Knodel, *Decline of fertility*.

The overall trend in underlying natural fertility

As already noted, the increases in fertility among younger married women in the sample villages suggest that a rise in the underlying level of natural fertility took place between the second half of the eighteenth century and the late nineteenth century. Despite its drawbacks, in particular the fact that the presence of deliberate birth spacing will depress the level of M and lower the estimate of the underlying level of natural fertility, we rely on this index as a summary measure of the level of underlying natural fertility for lack of a superior alternative measure. Moreover, it also seems plausible that the problems posed by deliberate birth spacing for interpreting the M index are far less serious in populations, such as those in most of the German villages during the time period under investigation, where attempts to stop childbearing seem to predominate over attempts to space births (see Chapter 12). Nevertheless, it is important to bear in mind that if deliberate birth spacing becomes more common as attempts to limit family size through stopping behavior increase, we would expect declining values of the M index to coincide with rising values of the m index, even when there was no genuine change in the underlying level of natural fertility.[20]

A different sort of problem is presented by the fact that a potential source of distortion of levels of marital fertility, particularly among younger married women, and thus of the trend in the M index, is changing patterns of premarital sexual behavior. Prenuptial pregnancies leading to postnuptial births artificially inflate marital fertility rates in age groups where newlyweds make up a large proportion of married women. The reason for this is that, in the calculation of marital fertility rates, brides who are pregnant at the time of their wedding are treated as if they were at risk of conceiving only from the date of the wedding, when in fact they were obviously exposed to the risk of pregnancy for some period prior to marriage.[21] Given the way in

[20] The subsequent analyses of changing levels of underlying natural marital fertility exclude results for the first half of the eighteenth century in order to avoid any possible distortion in trends that would result from the large compositional changes in the combined sample of all villages, given that fertility information is not available for many of the villages for much or all of this period.

[21] The fact that some women who were not pregnant at the time of the wedding were also engaged in prenuptial sexual relationships, and hence risked pregnancy before marriage, does not bias the marital fertility rate, provided the probability of conceiving in a given month is independent of having sexual relations in a previous month. Moreover, the proportion of married women in a given age group who actually married in that age group, provided the newlywed women were not pregnant at the time of marriage, probably has little direct influence on the marital fertility rate for that

which the M index is calculated, any circumstance which disproportionately increases marital fertility rates at younger ages, all else being equal, will increase the value of M.

As shown in Table 10.3, for the combined sample of all villages, women who were pregnant at marriage bore a child on the average within four to five months following their wedding, and thus would have contributed only this amount of 'women-months of exposure,' by the time of their first legitimate birth, to the determination of the marital fertility rate in the age group in which they fell. In contrast, women who were not pregnant at marriage averaged about a year longer prior to their first postnuptial birth. Thus increases in the proportion of married women in any given age group whose marriage also occurs in that age group and who were prenuptially pregnant can inflate the age-specific marital fertility rate without any real change in the risk of childbearing. Given the trend toward increased bridal pregnancy in the sample villages during the eighteenth and nineteenth centuries, as documented in Chapter 9, it is important to explore the extent to which the observed trend in the M index is an artifact of changing patterns of premarital sexual behavior.

In order to eliminate the influence of changes in the prevalence of prenuptial pregnancy on the M index, it has been recalculated on the basis of age-specific marital fertility schedules adjusted for prenuptial pregnancies. The adjustment consists of attributing to the denominator of the age-specific marital fertility rate the same number of woman-years of exposure prior to the first legitimate birth for women who were pregnant as brides as was found for those not pregnant in that marriage cohort. Such an adjustment seems justified since, as suggested by the results presented in Chapter 9, there seems to be only a modest difference between pregnant and non-pregnant brides in terms of their fecundability. For example, the interval between the first and second postnuptial confinements is only modestly shorter, and marital fertility only slightly higher, for pregnant than for non-pregnant brides. The effect of the adjustment is to reduce the fertility rate in all age groups in which women who are pregnant at marriage married. The reduction is disproportionately large in the younger age

age group. This is indicated by the fact that the average interval from wedding to first legitimate birth among women not pregnant at marriage is about half as long as the average interval between legitimate confinements. Since, on average, women who were married before entering a five-year age group will be mid-way between their previous and next birth, they will contribute half the average inter-confinement interval to the denominator of the marital fertility rate before having a birth in the age group. This is about the same amount of exposure time that newlywed women who are not pregnant at marriage contribute before their first birth.

Table 10.3. *The interval between marriage and the first legitimate birth, by pregnancy status at marriage, and the index of natural marital fertility level (M), unadjusted and adjusted for prenuptial pregnancy*

| | Interval to first birth (in months) | | | M index | |
	Pregnant[a]	Not pregnant[b]	Difference	Unadjusted	Adjusted[c]
1750–74	5.0	17.8	12.8	.95	.92
1775–99	4.7	16.6	11.9	.99	.97
1800–24	4.3	16.2	11.9	.99	.95
1825–49	4.4	16.1	11.7	1.07	1.01
1850–74	4.2	15.8	11.6	1.14	1.08
1875–99	4.4	15.6	11.2	1.20	1.13

Note: Results refer to the combined sample of all villages and are subject to restrictions 1, 2 and 3 (see Table A.1).
[a] Refers to women who gave birth within the first eight months of marriage.
[b] Refers to women whose first birth occurred more than eight months following marriage.
[c] See text for description of adjustment.

groups, where such women form a substantially higher proportion of all married women than they do at older ages.

Both the original values of the M index and the recomputed values based on age-specific marital fertility rates adjusted for pregnancies are also shown in Table 10.3 for the combined sample of all villages. As expected, the effect of the adjustments is to reduce both the level of M for each cohort and the amount of increase in the M index for successive marriage cohorts. The amount of increase remaining, however, is still substantial. The proportionate increase in M between couples married during 1750–74 and couples married during 1875–99 is reduced only from 26 percent prior to adjustment to 23 percent after adjustment.

Adjusted values of M for 50-year marriage cohorts are presented in Table 10.4 for the individual villages. In most cases, when compared to unadjusted values (not shown), the increases in the values of M are reduced or the extent to which M decreases becomes greater. In several instances, small increases in the unadjusted values reverse to become a decrease. Nevertheless, a predominant pattern of increased underlying natural fertility remains after adjustment is made for bridal pregnancy. In all villages except Öschelbronn, M increased between the cohorts married during the first and second halves of the nineteenth century. Moreover, with only the exceptions of Grafenhausen and Werdum, underlying natural marital fertility appears to be higher for the 1850–99 marriage cohort than for the 1750–99 cohort.

There is also considerable variation among villages with respect to the levels of the M index. The Bavarian villages are consistently characterized by unusually high values, exceeded only once – by Öschelbronn for the 1800–49 marriage cohort. Middels in East Friesland consistently shows the lowest value of M, and except for the 1750–99 cohort, is followed by Werdum. These inter-village differences between the highest and lowest values of M, as well as the rough rank ordering in between, correspond roughly to the likely differences in infant-feeding practices discussed in Appendix F. Villages where breastfeeding appears to have been less common and for shorter durations tend to rank higher in terms of their underlying level of natural fertility than those in the opposite situation.

The proximate determinants of natural marital fertility

While the M index is convenient for detecting change in the overall level of underlying natural fertility (when changes in deliberate birth spacing are minimal or absent), it provides no insight into the nature of

Table 10.4. *Index of natural marital fertility level (M) adjusted for prenuptial pregnancies, by marriage cohort and village*

	Marriage cohort			Change		
	1750–99	1800–49	1850–99	1750/99–1800/49	1800/49–1850/99	1750/99–1850/99
Grafenhausen	1.06	1.00	1.05	–.06	+.05	–.01
Herbolzheim	.92	1.02	1.20	+.10	+.18	+.28
Kappel	.87	1.00	1.08	+.13	+.08	+.21
Rust	.99	.99	1.28	.00	+.29	+.29
Öschelbronn	1.01	1.18	1.17	+.17	–.01	+.16
3 Bavarian villages	1.11	1.14	1.34	+.03	+.20	+.23
4 Waldeck villages	.89	.89	1.00	.00	+.11	+.11
Werdum	.95	.86	.91	–.09	+.05	–.04
Middels	.83	.81	.89	–.02	+.08	+.06
All villages	.95	.98	1.10	+.03	+.12	+.15

Note: Results are subject to restrictions 1, 2 and 3 (see Table A.1).

the change. The actual or underlying level of natural marital fertility can be thought of as the direct product of four components: the onset of permanent sterility, fecundability, the duration of postpartum non-susceptibility, and the risk of spontaneous intrauterine mortality. Since a change in any one of these, with the others remaining constant and in the absence of deliberate control, would affect the level of marital fertility, they can be considered the proximate determinants of natural marital fertility.[22] Fortunately, family reconstitution data are well suited for exploring some of these proximate determinants in depth, through a variety of indirect measures.[23]

Permanent sterility

Couples can reproduce only if both spouses are fecund. With increasing age, the proportion of couples with at least one spouse sterile rises, reaching 100 percent by the end of the reproductive span. Thus in any reasonably large population, at the time of marriage at least a small proportion of couples are unable to bear any children because of physiological impairments to either or both of the spouses. The older the age at marriage, the higher the proportion of couples in this situation.

If we assume that voluntary childlessness was negligible in German village populations during the period under observation, then the extent of permanent sterility from the onset of marriage can be approximated by the proportion of married women who remained childless through to the end of the reproductive age span. Since this approach reflects only permanent sterility existing at the time a woman first begins sexual cohabitation, it does not answer the question of whether either spouse was previously fecund. Given the focus in the present analysis on *marital* fertility, this is not a serious drawback.

The age pattern of the proportion childless is shown in Figure 10.3 for the combined sample of all villages. The results refer only to women whose marriages remained intact until they reached the end of the reproductive age span, including women who were previously married. Thus births to women from any earlier and necessarily interrup-

---

[22] Bongaarts, 'Natural marital fertility'; Bongaarts and Potter, *Fertility, biology, and behavior.*

[23] In defining the onset of permanent sterility as one of the proximate determinants, Bongaarts and Potter (*Fertility, biology, and behavior*) consider both primary and secondary sterility (primary sterility refers to the total absence of births, while secondary sterility refers to the loss of reproductive ability following at least one birth). The present analysis ignores secondary sterility, except in cases where a prenuptial birth or a birth to a prior marriage occurred. The main reason for this is that changes in secondary sterility are difficult to examine in a context of increasing family limitation.

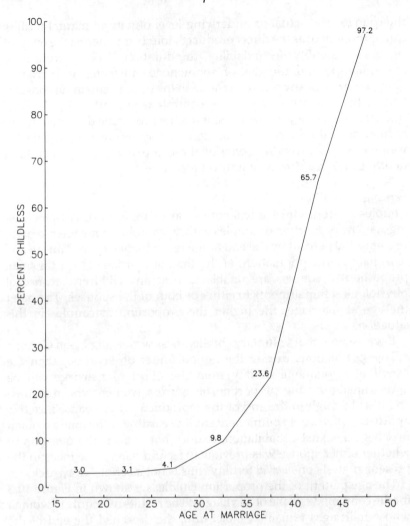

Figure 10.3. *Percent of married women remaining childless, by age at marriage.* Results refer to the combined sample of all villages and are subject to restrictions 1, 2, 3 and 4 (see Table A.1). Only postnuptial births are considered in the determination of childlessness

ted marriages are ignored. In addition, for practical purposes the age at marriage is used as the age at which sexual activity begins, and for this reason illegitimate births are also ignored.[24] Moreover, for simplicity

[24] For several reasons the age at marriage is only an approximation of the age from which permanent sterility is observed. For women who actually begin cohabiting at mar-

the proportion childless for each five-year age of marriage group is plotted at the midpoint of the age interval even though there is reason to doubt that the precise age from which subsequent sterility is being measured corresponds to the midpoint.[25] Since the main purpose of determining the variation of permanent sterility by age in this study is to provide a basis for age standardization of the percent childless over time, this need not be of much concern. The age profile of childlessness follows the expected pattern, increasing with age at marriage, at first slowly and then more rapidly.

In this analysis, the prime interest lies in changes over time in permanent sterility. Particular interest is focused on discovering if a decline in sterility might be responsible for, or have contributed to, the observed increase in the level of underlying natural fertility as indicated by the rise in the M index. Since the extent of permanent sterility among married couples is dependent upon the distribution of couples by age at marriage, it is important to adjust for changes in the age at marriage over time before assessing changes in the rate of sterility. To do this, we have calculated the percent childless standardized for age at marriage by using the marriage age distributions for couples married during the entire period 1750 to 1899 as the standard.

Both unstandardized and standardized results are presented in Table 10.5 for 25-year marriage cohorts. The two sets of figures indicate a peak in sterility for the cohort of 1800–24. The unstandardized results also show a progressive decline in sterility in subsequent cohorts. Except for the drop from the unusual peak for the 1800–24 cohort, however, this appears to be largely the result of a shift toward a younger age at marriage, as is indicated by the lack of an equivalent decline in the standardized results. Indeed, the proportions childless after standardization for age at marriage are quite similar for all cohorts except the cohort married during the first quarter of the nineteenth century.[26] While the unusually high sterility found for the cohort of

riage, we are observing permanent sterility at the mean age at which fertile couples who marry at that age have their first child, since some women will lose their capacity to conceive and carry a pregnancy to term between marriage and the time their first birth would on average occur. This results in a slight overstatement of sterility by age. A factor operating in the opposite direction is created by women who are pregnant at marriage and thus clearly begin cohabiting before their wedding date. In addition, women who have illegitimate children also clearly begin sexual relations before marriage.

[25] Leridon, 'L'estimation de la stérilité,' pp. 231–45; Trussell and Wilson, 'Sterility.'

[26] Another factor which could potentially influence the observed percentage childless is the age gap between spouses, since the cause of the couple's sterility may be the husband's inability to reproduce, which undoubtedly rises with age for men. Multiple classification analysis provides a technique for controlling for both age at marriage of wife and the age gap between spouses simultaneously. In essence, it standardizes for

Table 10.5. *Percent of married women remaining permanently childless, unstandardized and standardized for age at marriage, by year of marriage*

	Unstandardized	Standardized
1750–74	11.8	10.8
1775–99	11.9	11.3
1800–24	16.2	14.0
1825–49	13.1	11.8
1850–74	10.0	10.3
1875–99	6.7	10.5

Note: Results refer to the combined sample of all villages and are subject to restrictions 1, 2, 3 and 4 (see Table A.1). The standardization is based on the age-at-marriage distribution of all marriage cohorts combined. Only postnuptial births are considered in the determination of childlessness.

1800–24 remains puzzling, the relative constancy in childlessness for the other cohorts, after taking into account changes in age at marriage, is the more important finding in relation to the general increase in the underlying level of natural fertility and suggests that changes in permanent sterility contributed little to it.

Fecundability
The probability of conception during a menstrual cycle in the absence of contraception, known as fecundability, can be estimated indirectly from data on the interval between marriage and first birth. More precisely, an estimate can be derived from the proportion of legitimate first births that occur during months 9, 10 and 11 after excluding births that occur earlier than nine months following marriage. These proportions are converted into estimates of fecundability based on a modified mathematical model originally proposed by Bongaarts.[27] The estimates of fecundability are independent of the influence of breast-feeding since the measure is based on intervals between wedding and

both factors at the same time. The results indicate that controlling for changes in the age gap between spouses had little additional effect to controlling for age at marriage of wife separately, and thus the trend in the percentage childless adjusted for both factors was very close to the results after standardization for wife's age at marriage alone.

[27] Bongaarts, 'Estimation of fecundability.' For a description of the modification, see Knodel and Wilson ('Secular increase,' Appendix 1).

Table 10.6. *Proportion of first births occurring within 9–11 months of marriage, estimated mean fecundability, and mean interval from marriage to first birth by age at marriage, for women married 1750–1899*

Age at marriage	Proportion in 9–11 months	Mean fecundability	Interval to first birth (in months)
15–19	.342	.174	19.3
20–24	.465	.270	16.5
25–29	.473	.286	16.7
30–34	.436	.266	16.2
35–39	.298	.170	19.2
40–49	.274	.170	19.2

Note: Results refer to the combined sample of all villages and are subject to restriction 1 (see Table A.1). In addition, couples with a prenuptial birth or a postnuptial birth prior to nine months of marriage are excluded.

first birth (and couples with illegitimate births have been excluded). However, since the estimates refer to fecundability immediately following marriage, if fecundability declines with the duration of marriage, as is often assumed, then the level of fecundability in the population at large could be substantially below that indicated by this technique.

As is evident in Table 10.6, fecundability varies with age. Teenage brides show somewhat lower fecundability than women marrying in their twenties, and from age 30 onward a decline sets in which accelerates after age 35. These changes probably reflect biological changes taking place over a lifetime and correspond closely to the age-specific changes in the proportion of anovular cycles noted by Doring.[28] They may also be influenced by changing coital frequency. The estimates for the older women, especially those above age 40, are likely to be overestimates *vis-à-vis* other age groups because some women, although fecund at the time of marriage, will become sterile before conceiving. This will be particularly true of women with low fecundability, and hence with long wait times to conception; in these cases a truncation bias will be introduced. However, since the primary interest in this study is in the trend of fecundability over time rather than in the absolute level at any given time, these biases are of minor consequence for our analysis, provided they change little during the period under observation.

Given the clearly age-specific nature of fecundability, it is important to standardize the results for age at marriage. Otherwise, changes in

[28] Doring, 'Anovular cycles,' pp. 256–63.

Table 10.7. *Proportion of first births occurring within 9–11 months of marriage, estimated mean fecundability, unstandardized and standardized for age at marriage, and mean interval from marriage to first birth*

| | Proportion in 9–11 months | Mean fecundability | | Interval to first birth (in months) |
		Unstandardized	Standardized	
1750–74	.375	.204	.212	18.4
1775–99	.390	.215	.221	17.3
1800–24	.444	.260	.262	17.1
1825–49	.462	.277	.273	16.9
1850–74	.468	.283	.280	16.5
1875–99	.478	.293	.282	16.3

Note: Results refer to the combined sample of all villages and are subject to restriction 1 (see Table A.1). In addition, couples with a prenuptial birth or a postnuptial birth prior to nine months of marriage are excluded.

the latter may produce apparent changes in the fecundability index, even when the underlying age-specific fecundability has remained constant. Trends in the interval between marriage and the first legitimate birth, and the estimates of mean fecundability, both standardized and not, are presented in Table 10.7 for each 25-year marriage cohort in the combined sample of all villages. Both the unstandardized and standardized estimates indicate a substantial rise. Although standardization reduces the magnitude, the estimated increase in fecundability remains considerable: from .212 for women married in the period 1750–74 to .282 for those married in the last quarter of the nineteenth century, constituting a rise of 33 percent. A parallel decline in the interval between marriage and first birth is also evident, falling from 18.4 to 16.3 months.

The fact that the increase in fecundability was widespread can be seen in Table 10.8, which presents the estimates of mean fecundability for each 50-year marriage cohort for the separate villages or village sets, standardized for age. In all but one, mean fecundability of the 1850–99 cohort was above that of the 1750–99 cohort. While some villages evidenced only moderate changes, in most the rise was considerable, and in some cases dramatic. In both Kappel and Middels, mean fecundability rose by around 60 percent.

Postpartum non-susceptibility
Another major component of fecundity amenable to analysis using family reconstitution data is the period following a birth during which a woman is not susceptible to conception. It is now widely accepted that differences in breastfeeding practices are the major determinant of this non-susceptible period.[29] Prolonged lactation protects against pregnancy by delaying the return of ovulation, and thereby extends the postpartum non-susceptible period, during which the woman is usually amenorrheic. Moreover, the impact of breastfeeding on extending the period of postpartum amenorrhea is also influenced by the nature of the breastfeeding practices. For example, supplemental feeding of the infant with foods other than breast milk tends to reduce the impact of lactation on amenorrhea compared to situations of exclusive breastfeeding.

One simple way to estimate, from reproductive histories, the mean duration of non-susceptibility is to compare the interval between marriage and first birth (excluding intervals involving a premarital pregnancy) with the following interval between first and second births

---

[29] van Ginneken, 'Prolonged breastfeeding,' pp. 179–98; McCann *et al.*, 'Breastfeeding'; Bongaarts, 'Natural marital fertility.'

Table 10.8. *Mean fecundability, standardized for age at marriage, by year of marriage*

	Marriage cohort			Change		
	1750–99	1800–49	1850–99	1750/99–1800/49	1800/49–1850/99	1750/99–1850/99
Grafenhausen	.250	.300	.244	+.050	−.056	−.006
Herbolzheim	.246	.312	.343	+.066	+.031	+.097
Kappel	.220	.274	.341	+.054	+.067	+.121
Rust	.212	.293	.276	+.081	−.017	+.064
Öschelbronn	.290	.265	.332	−.025	+.067	+.042
3 Bavarian villages	.247	.274	.280	+.027	+.006	+.033
4 Waldeck villages	.202	.215	.227	+.013	+.012	+.025
Werdum	.183	.193	.245	+.010	+.052	+.062
Middels	.173	.203	.275	+.030	+.072	+.102
All villages	.217	.258	.283	+.041	+.025	+.065

Note: Results are subject to restriction 1 (see Table A.1). In addition, couples with a prenuptial birth or a postnuptial birth prior to nine months of marriage are excluded. The standardization was based on couples married 1750–1899 for the entire sample of all villages.

(excluding intervals following an infant death). The difference should reflect the extent to which the interval between the first and second births is extended by postpartum non-susceptibility. For several reasons, the resulting estimate is only a rough approximation. Declining fecundability with increasing duration of marriage will tend to lengthen the waiting time to conception and thus lengthen the interval following first birth relative to the interval following marriage, biasing the estimate of the non-susceptible period upward. Attempts to postpone either the first or second birth would also influence the estimate. A further drawback with a simple comparison is that the interval before a woman's last birth is often distinctly longer than other intervals, even in the absence of deliberate birth control. Where a woman has only two children, this interval may yield a poor estimate of the non-susceptible period. This problem can be avoided by basing estimates only on women with at least three legitimate confinements.

Results obtained by this method are shown in Table 10.9 as 'Estimate 1' of the non-susceptible period. They indicate an increase in non-susceptibility, peaking for the 1800–24 cohort, the same cohort for which permanent sterility was highest, followed by a steady decline in the duration for cohorts married during the remainder of the nineteenth century. It is important to note that the extent of the decline, as well as the apparent increase for couples married during the latter half of the eighteenth century, is very much determined by the unusually long estimate found for the cohort of 1800–24. While there is no reason to believe that the estimate for this cohort is less reliable than that for others, the rather approximate nature of the estimation techniques should be borne in mind.

A second way of estimating the length of the non-susceptible period is to examine the relationship between the length of birth intervals and the age at death of the child born at the beginning of the interval. An interval following the birth of a child who survived beyond the age of weaning will reflect the full influence of breastfeeding, while an interval following the death of a child who dies before being weaned will, on average, be shorter. The strength of this relationship in the aggregate depends on the proportion of infants breastfed and the average duration and intensity of breastfeeding. As with the previous estimate of the non-susceptible period, intervals between the penultimate and ultimate births are best excluded from consideration.

In interpreting the results of this second approach, it should be recognized that factors other than infant-feeding practices can exert an influence on the relation between the age of a child at death and the subsequent birth interval (see the discussion in Chapter 14). The data

Table 10.9. *Two alternative estimates (in months) of the postpartum non-susceptible period (NSP) by year of marriage*

	Estimate 1			Estimate 2		
	Interval to first birth	Interval between first and second confinements	Difference (estimated NSP)	Birth interval following infant dying in first month	Birth interval following infant surviving 1 year	Difference (estimated NSP)
1750–74	16.4	26.0	9.6	17.6[a]	29.9[a]	12.3[a]
1775–99	15.4	26.1	10.7	17.3[a]	29.6[a]	12.3[a]
1800–24	15.3	27.1	11.8	{ (17.5)[b] { 17.6	{ (29.5)[b] { 29.1	{ (12.5)[b] { 11.5
1825–49	14.7	25.8	11.1	17.8	28.4	10.6
1850–74	14.8	24.6	9.8	18.3	27.1	8.8
1875–99	15.0	22.5	7.5	19.5	25.3	5.8

Note: Results refer to the combined sample of all villages and are subject to restrictions 1 and 7 (see Table A.1). In addition, Estimate 1 is based on women with at least three postnuptial confinements and excludes women with a premarital birth or a postnuptial birth prior to nine months of marriage. Estimate 2 excludes intervals between the penultimate and ultimate confinements.

[a] Excluding Kappel and the three Bavarian villages because of obvious deficiencies in death registration or problems in distinguishing the exact age at death.

[b] The figures not in parentheses only exclude births in part of the cohort in Kappel due to obvious deficiencies in death registration; the figures in parentheses exclude all births to couples in Kappel and the three Bavarian villages to facilitate comparison with the estimates for the two earlier marriage cohorts.

on which this study is based do not permit us to distinguish the influence of breastfeeding on the length of the interval from these other mechanisms; these should, nonetheless, be borne in mind.

The results based on this second method are presented in Table 10.9 as 'Estimate 2' and point to a considerable decline in the non-susceptible period, especially during the nineteenth century. A minor problem of comparability across marriage cohorts is created by compositional shifts in terms of which villages are included as the basis of the calculations. When calculating this measure for couples married during the eighteenth century, it is necessary to exclude not only Kappel, where death registration was generally deficient during this period, but also the Bavarian villages where the exact age of death of infants cannot be determined (see Appendix B). Since the prevalence and duration of breastfeeding was unusually low for the Bavarian villages, their exclusion in the estimates referring to couples married prior to 1800 biases trends. To facilitate comparison, results for the 1800–24 marriage cohort are shown both for all villages and for only those villages which served as the basis of estimates for the earlier cohorts. When this problem is taken into consideration, there appears to be little change indicated between the 1750–74 and 1800–24 cohorts.

A problem for interpreting the results arises from the fact that the decline in the estimates during the nineteenth century is due not only to decreasing intervals following child survival, but also in part to increasing intervals after an early death, which should logically be independent of changes in breastfeeding habits. About two months of the almost six months' decline comes about in this puzzling way. One possible but purely speculative explanation of this increase is that a tendency to reduce the frequency of intercourse, or to be abstinent for some period following a birth, emerged over the period under observation, perhaps as a result of a greater concern for maternal health or attempts to space births (see, however, Chapter 12). Even if this increase in intervals following early infant deaths is discounted, however, the estimates still indicate a decline of three to four months in the length of the non-susceptible period during the nineteenth century.

Although the two estimates of the non-susceptible period are not consistent with each other regarding changes during the last half of the eighteenth century, they both point to a substantial decline during the nineteenth century. The most likely explanation for such a change, if it is indeed genuine, is a reduction in the prevalence and duration of breastfeeding. It is also possible that breastfeeding patterns changed little but that their impact on the non-susceptible period decreased because of improved nutrition. Although still controversial, some scholars argue that there is a substantial negative association between women's levels of nutrition and the extent to which breastfeeding delays the return of ovulation.[30] As noted in Appendix F, direct information on breastfeeding is rare for periods before the latter part of the nineteenth century in Germany. Annual statistics on breastfeeding collected from midwives in Baden during the last quarter of the nineteenth century and the early years of the twentieth century pointed to little change between 1882 and 1905, in the area where the four Baden villages in our sample are located, in the proportion of mothers reported as not having breastfed their children (see Appendix F). Unfortunately, no other time trend information is available.

Intrauterine mortality
Changes in intrauterine mortality will also affect the underlying natural fertility level. A decline in fetal wastage during the period under consideration could have contributed both to the observed increase in the M index as well as the increase in the index of fecundability, given that an increase in the proportion of first pregnancies coming to term would increase the proportion of intervals between marriage and first birth that occur within 9–11 months following the wedding. Data on intrauterine mortality are not provided in the village genealogies, except for indications of stillbirths. As discussed in Appendix B, the stillbirth data are probably incomplete. Moreover, the treatment of stillbirths probably differed between Catholic and Protestant parishes, with a tendency in Catholic areas to treat some stillbirths as if the infant had actually died shortly after birth.

The percent of children that were indicated as stillborn in the village genealogies is shown in Table 10.10 for different marriage cohorts. Although little confidence can be placed in these results, they do show some tendency for the stillbirth rate to decline during the nineteenth century in both the Protestant and Catholic villages, although on an absolute level the change is small. The trends in stillbirths will not affect marital fertility as measured in this study since they are included along with live births in the fertility measures. However, if the decline in stillbirths is real and mirrors a similar proportionate decline in fetal wastage, the impact on the underlying level of natural fertility could be substantial. Although little is known of the determinants of

---

[30] Frisch, 'Malnutrition,' pp. 1272–73; Anderson and McCabe, 'Nutrition and fertility,' pp. 343–63. See also Bongaarts, 'Malnutrition,' pp. 564–79; and Menken *et al.*, 'Nutrition fertility link,' pp. 425–41.

Table 10.10. *Percentage of all births that were stillbirths by predominant religion of village and parents' year of marriage*

	All villages	Catholic	Protestant
1750–74	3.2	1.7	4.6
1775–99	2.7	1.9	3.7
1800–24	3.5	2.5	5.0
1825–49	3.3	2.5	4.8
1850–74	2.8	2.1	4.0
1875–99	2.2	1.3	4.0

Note: Results refer to the combined sample of all villages and are subject to restrictions 6 and 7 (see Table A.1). Four percent of presumed infant and child deaths, indicated only by a cross but no exact death date in the villages of Anhausen and Gabelbach, were assumed to be stillbirths, based on the distribution of deaths with known dates during the period 1800–49 (see Appendix B).

intrauterine mortality, one could speculate that it might be responsive to changes in the prevalence of disease or the level of nutrition, both of which might have improved over the period covered by our analysis.

The changing seasonality of births

If the secular increase in fecundity suggested by the present analysis is indeed a genuine phenomenon, at least for much of Germany, the broader question arises as to what caused it. One intriguing and possibly related demographic finding concerns the diminishing degree of seasonality of births during the period under observation. During the latter half of the eighteenth century, births in the sample villages exhibited a marked seasonality whose most characteristic feature was a trough in births during the late spring and summer months (May through August) which corresponded to a reduction in conceptions roughly during the harvest months (August through November). If first births, which are strongly influenced by the seasonality of marriage, are eliminated, we find the number of second and higher-order births during these months was about 20 percent below the number that would be expected if births were evenly spread throughout the year. The magnitude of this deficiency progressively declines over time, so that during the last quarter of the nineteenth century births in the late spring and summer months were less than 1 percent below the expected number.

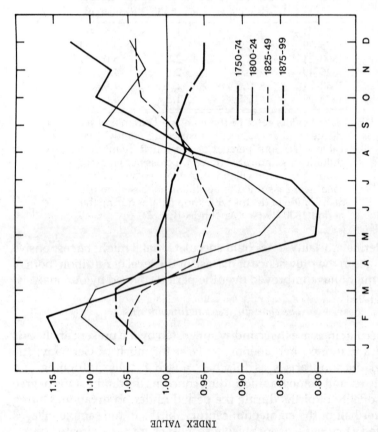

Figure 10.4. Three-month moving average of index values of the monthly variation in second and higher legitimate births by marriage year of parents. Results refer to the combined sample of all villages. The index value refers to the monthly ratio of observed births to births expected in the absence of seasonality

The steady reduction in seasonality of second and higher-order births to successive marriage cohorts is evident in Figure 10.4, which shows three-month moving averages in the ratio of actual to expected births occurring each month. While the reduction of seasonality in births does not 'explain' the observed rise in fecundity, it does suggest that a non-negligible proportion of it may be associated wth the elimination of the trough in fertility (and presumably fecundity) during May through August.[31] Clearly, the modification of the seasonal distribution of childbearing is an important element that should be taken into account in any broader explanation.

Discussion

The neglect of research on the ability to reproduce during past times is probably due in part to the prominence of nuptiality as the crucial determinant of fertility in the theoretical models of preindustrial population dynamics, the importance of voluntary control within marriage in models of the demographic transition, and the implicit assumption in much historical demographic research that underlying natural fertility was relatively constant. The unavailability of appropriate data and techniques of measurement has probably also been an important deterrent. As illustrated in this study, family reconstitution

---

[31] A rough-and-ready measure of the impact of changing seasonality can be made as follows. First, let us assume that the pattern of seasonality of births experienced by women marrying in the period 1875–99 prevailed also for those marrying at the start of our period. More exactly, let us assume that the ratio of births occurring in the four months May to August to births in the rest of the year is the same in cohort of 1750–74 as that observed for the cohort of 1875–99. Further, let us assume that the seasonal pattern of the former cohort was produced solely by a deficit of births between May and August. This deficit for the 1750–74 cohort can be estimated by subtracting the observed births occurring between May and August from the number that would have occurred had they been in the same ratio to births during the rest of the year, as found for the 1875–99 cohort.

The new level of underlying natural marital fertility which would be implied by such a decrease in the summer deficit can then be defined as the ratio of births estimated for the whole year, given the seasonality of 1875–99, to observed births for the whole year, multiplied by the initial level of M. The difference between the increase actually observed in M from the 1750–74 to the 1875–99 marriage cohort and the reduced increase after adjusting M for 1750–74 for the 1875–99 seasonality gives a rough idea of how much of the actual increase might be attributed to a reduction in seasonality. This calculation probably overestimates the contribution of reduced seasonality, since it implicitly assumes, unrealistically, that a reduction in the deficit of births between May and August would leave the number of births during the remainder of the year unchanged. Nevertheless, it can still serve as a rough guide. The calculation described above indicates that about 25 percent of the increase in M can be attributed to the reduction in seasonality. If, instead, we use the values of M adjusted for changes in the extent of prenuptial pregnancy, the increase accounted for by reduced seasonality is 30 percent.

provides useful data for indirectly estimating underlying natural fertility and its proximate determinants.

The evidence examined for the sample of German village populations suggests that the underlying level of natural fertility significantly increased between the middle of the eighteenth century and the turn of the twentieth century. Efforts to discover the components of natural marital fertility responsible for the increase, while not yielding conclusive findings, are clearest with respect to an increase in fecundability. The results were also suggestive of a reduction in the nonsusceptible period following birth. Less clear was evidence concerning reductions in permanent sterility. A reasonable guess is that changes in this component were relatively unimportant after allowing for changes in the age at marriage. Speculation on intrauterine mortality is even less secure as it can only be inferred from unreliable data concerning stillbirths.

The extent to which the underlying natural fertility level was increasing in other German villages or elsewhere in western Europe during the same period of time is uncertain, given the lack of comparable data for much of the period under examination. A review of evidence from a number of other German village studies indicates increases in the M index of the underlying natural marital fertility level in many of them.[32] There are also scattered pieces of evidence in villages outside Germany that point in both directions. In a study of an Alpine village in Switzerland, Netting detects a noticeable increase in marital fertility and the M index during the same period as covered in the present analysis.[33] He attributes this to rising fecundity but does not know what caused it. He also cites results for a number of other Swiss villages which indicate increasing marital fertility elsewhere in Switzerland between 1750–99 and 1800–49.

There is considerable evidence that the age of menarche was declining by the end of the nineteenth century in various parts of Europe, although whether it was declining throughout the century is in dispute. Shorter has recently assembled evidence suggesting that the fall in the age of menarche in France may date from the end of the eighteenth century.[34] While changes in the age of menarche are unlikely to directly influence fertility in populations where the age of marriage is as late as in western Europe, they might be symptomatic of a more general change in fecundity.

There is also considerable evidence that increases in marital fertility

[32] Knodel and Wilson, 'Secular increase,' pp. 53–84.
[33] Netting, *Balancing*.
[34] Shorter, 'L'âge des premières règles,' pp. 495–511.

have taken place in various parts of the developing world.[35] These increases in fertility undoubtedly reflect changes in underlying natural fertility and may well have important implications for understanding the demographic transition. Indeed, there is accumulating evidence that a pre-decline rise in fertility, presumably reflecting changes in natural fertility, may be a relatively common feature of both historical and contemporary fertility transitions.[36]

To attempt an explanation of the observed increase in underlying natural fertility in the sample villages beyond the exploration of the demographic components already presented would take us well beyond the data at hand and the intended scope of this study. Nevertheless, a few comments on the possible sources of such an explanation seem in order. Given the increasing interest in recent years in the relationship between nutrition and fertility, this is an obvious area that should be considered in connection with historical changes in fecundity.

Netting has singled out the introduction of potatoes into the diet of the Swiss villagers he studied as a potentially important factor responsible for their increased fertility.[37] As indicated in Appendix C, the start of potato cultivation during the period under study is specifically mentioned in several of the village genealogies. In general, potatoes became widespread in Germany during this time, and major improvements in agricultural production were taking place between the mid-eighteenth century and the end of the nineteenth century throughout western Europe.[38] There is indeed some evidence of an improvement of nutrition among the German population during the nineteenth century.[39] During at least the earlier part of this period, meat was at best a rarity in peasant diets.[40] The village genealogy for Höringhausen specifically comments on the fact that it was customary in earlier times to slaughter no more than one pig per family to last the winter.[41] Unfortunately, a consensus has yet to emerge as to the nature and extent of the link between nutrition and fecundity despite the increasing number of contemporary studies on the topic. Some researchers, most notably Frisch, have argued that nutrition is an important determinant of fertility, both in populations today where contraception is not practiced and in those in the past.[42] Others disagree.[43]

[35] Knodel, 'Natural fertility: patterns, levels and trends.'
[36] Dyson and Murphy, 'Onset of fertility transition,' pp. 399–440.
[37] Netting, *Balancing*.   [38] Blum, *Old order*.
[39] Teuteberg, 'Diet and industrialization.'   [40] Blum, *Old order*, p. 186.
[41] Sauer, *Höringhausen*, p. 80.   [42] Frisch, 'Food intake and fertility,' pp. 22–30.
[43] Bongaarts, 'Malnutrition,' pp. 564–79; Menken *et al.*, 'Nutrition fertility link,' pp. 425–41.

While most of the recent discussion centers on the physiological connection between nutrition and fertility, there are also social mechanisms that may link the two together which need to be explored. Poor nutrition could result in reduced desire for sexual intercourse. Shortages in food might have led to the temporary migration of one of the spouses. A reduction in food shortages could have reduced these periods of separation and thus increased the level of underlying natural fertility.[44]

There is consensus that infant-feeding practices are potentially an important influence on underlying natural fertility. As discussed above, only limited data are available on this factor. Thus, while changes in breastfeeding patterns remain an intriguing potential explanation for the apparent increase in the underlying level of natural marital fertility, the available data seem unlikely to settle the question definitely.

Changes in a whole range of social behavior could also have increased the underlying level of natural fertility even if the physiological mechanisms governing the ability to reproduce remained unchanged. Social historians have debated the possibility of a 'sexual revolution' which could have had a bearing on the frequency of intercourse during the same period covered by our data.[45] There is no reason to believe that the nature of relations between spouses remained static during the past, especially during the nineteenth century, when a multitude of other social changes were taking place. The possible changes in the intimate details of daily life which might have had relevance for the ability to reproduce are numerous. For example, an increased workload for women could have reduced the frequency and length of breastfeeding; changing sleeping arrangements for parents and children could have altered the frequency of intercourse. Hopefully, historical ethnology can help uncover some of these changes. Documenting them in a convincing fashion, however, is likely to be difficult; establishing empirical links with changes in the components of underlying natural fertility will probably prove even more challenging.

[44] Menken *et al.*, 'Nutrition fertility link,' pp. 425–41.
[45] Shorter, *Modern family*.

11

From natural fertility to family limitation

The decline in fertility associated with the demographic transition has been characterized as a shift from a system in which reproduction was largely controlled through social institutions and customs to a system where the private choice of individual couples plays the major role.[1] This shift of control from the societal to the family level involves the emergence and spread of a fundamentally new pattern of reproductive behavior that has been described in the previous chapter as family limitation. In brief, the fertility transition can be viewed as representing the transformation of a population's reproductive pattern from one characterized by natural fertility to one in which family limitation predominates. In this chapter, the nature and extent of marital fertility control in the sample village populations are explored, in the course of which several relevant methodological and substantive issues are addressed.

As described in the previous chapter, at the core of family limitation are attempts to stop childbearing prior to the end of the biologically defined reproductive span. This has implications for both the age at which women terminate childbearing and the age patterns of fertility. The exploration of the shift of natural fertility to family limitation begins by examining indices that utilize these implications for detecting deliberate marital fertility control. In particular, the Coale–Trussell index of fertility control (m) and the age of mothers at last birth are examined in some detail. Attention is then focused on evidence provided by parity progression probabilities. Finally, the question is addressed as to whether the alterations in the age patterns of childbearing during the initial phases of the fertility transition reflected

[1] Wrigley, 'Fertility strategy,' p. 148.

287

consideration about the number of children already born or resulted more directly from a consideration about age at childbearing itself.

Village-level trends in the index of fertility control

Values of the Coale–Trussell m index for the individual villages are presented in Table 11.1. The low values of m characterizing couples married during the eighteenth century in all the villages or village sets suggest that little if any parity-dependent control was being exercised at this time, and thus that the situation can more or less be characterized as one of natural fertility.

Noticeable contrasts in the trends in m values over time are apparent in the different villages.[2] Of particular interest is the diversity of

[2] The values shown in Table 11.1 are unadjusted for changes in the prevalence of prenuptial pregnancies. Postnuptial births that are premaritally conceived tend to artificially inflate marital fertility rates, particularly at the younger reproductive ages, where a disproportionately large share of married women are newlyweds. This influences the age pattern of marital fertility such that marital fertility declines more sharply with age when prenuptial pregnancies are common than when they are less frequent. Since the m index is based entirely on the age pattern of marital fertility, an increase in the prevalence of bridal pregnancy in itself would typically lead to some increase in the value of m.

A comparison of the trend in the unadjusted m indices with the trend in m values based on age-specific marital fertility rates, after adjustment for prenuptial pregnancy is made following the procedure described in Chapter 10, indicates that the influence of the increases in bridal pregnancy (discussed in Chapter 9) is quite modest. Several examples suffice to illustrate this point:

	Marriage cohort		
	1750–99	1800–49	1850–99
All villages			
Unadjusted m	.01	.13	.36
Adjusted m	.00	.09	.28
Grafenhausen			
Unadjusted m	.05	.18	.67
Adjusted m	.03	.14	.64
Herbolzheim			
Unadjusted m	−.11	.24	.60
Adjusted m	−.12	.20	.54
Öschelbronn			
Unadjusted m	.18	.23	.20
Adjusted m	.15	.16	.11

Thus, in the combined sample of all villages, the moderate increase in the m index persists after adjustment, although to a slightly lesser degree. In both Grafenhausen and Herbolzheim, sharp rises in m are still indicated after adjustment, and in Öschelbronn the lack of change remains a feature of the adjusted trends.

Table 11.1. *Coale–Trussell index of fertility control (m) by year of marriage*

	1700–49	1750–99	1800–24	1825–49	1850–74	1875–99
Grafenhausen	.13	.05	.01	.34	.59	.79
Herbolzheim	−.11	−.11	.10	.37	.51	.67
Kappel	−.03	−.09	.15	.10	.17	.19
Rust	.07	.11	−.07	.09	.32	.51
Öschelbronn	.28	.18	.28	.17	.13	.27
3 Bavarian villages	(−.07)	−.04	.22	.08	*.28*	.41
4 Waldeck villages	.00	−.05	.02	−.02	*.03*	.44
Middels	—	.04	.10	*.12*	*.21*	.46
Werdum	.03	.23	.25	.29	(.24)[a]	—
All villages	.04	.01	.08	.18	.27	.46

Note: Results are subject to restrictions 1, 2 and 3 (see Table A.1). Values in parentheses indicate that the results are based on an average of 100–199 woman-years per five-year age group within the 20–44 range; results based on fewer woman-years are omitted. Values of *m* shown in italics indicate that the mean square error of the regression used to estimate *m* exceeded .005.
[a] Including a small number of couples married between 1875 and 1899.

experience represented by the four villages of Baden, all of which are located quite near each other. Couples in both Grafenhausen and Herbolzheim show signs of adopting modern reproductive patterns well in advance of other villages. In Herbolzheim, a steady rise in *m* is evident for each successive marriage cohort, starting with couples married in the first quarter of the nineteenth century, and in Grafenhausen in the second quarter of the nineteenth century. In nearby Rust, *m* also increases steadily for cohorts married during the nineteenth century, but interpretation is somewhat more problematic due to the unusually low figure for the 1800–24 cohort. In contrast, in Kappel there is a noticeable absence of any substantial increase in *m* for couples married throughout the nineteenth century. While the increase in the *m* index in Kappel between couples married at the end of the eighteenth century and the 1800–24 marriage cohort may signal some early spread of family limitation, the trend clearly does not continue for subsequent marriage cohorts to any substantial extent. The striking contrasts among these four neighboring or nearby villages in Baden underscore just how localized important differences in demographic patterns could be during the preindustrial era.[3]

Contrasts among the other villages in the sample are also evident. In Öschelbronn, the trend in *m* is even less decisive than in Kappel, and

[3] Spagnoli, 'Population history.'

the value of this index, even for couples married at the end of the nineteenth century, does not rise above values characterizing earlier cohorts. In other villages, the value of *m* is typically higher for the 1875–99 marriage cohort than for any of the previous ones (excluding Werdum, for which data for this cohort are missing). Some fluctuations in the value of *m* are to be expected when calculations are based on small numbers of couples, as in this study, and this makes it difficult to distinguish genuine changes in the underlying fertility pattern from random movement. Thus it is difficult to interpret increases in *m* that are not part of a trend, such as those between the 1700–49 and 1750–99 marriage cohorts in Werdum and those between the 1750–99 and 1800–24 cohorts in the Bavarian villages. Changes of this magnitude can neither be taken as conclusive evidence of family limitation nor dismissed out of hand. We can be more confident that the increase in *m* values characterizing the fertility of couples married at the end of the nineteenth century reflected an increase in the practice of family limitation because in most cases they were distinctly higher than previous values and often represented a continuation of a rising trend.

The experience of several villages demonstrates even more clearly than results for the sample as a whole that the onset of the transition to modern reproductive patterns, as signaled by increased family limitation, may be obscured in data representing trends in marital fertility levels under circumstances where the underlying level of natural marital fertility may be increasing. Perhaps the most striking example is provided by Rust. The level of marital fertility as measured by I_g' increased for marriage cohorts during the nineteenth century (see Table 10.1), while at the same time the *m* index indicates that family limitation efforts were steadily, if slowly, increasing. Herbolzheim also provides an interesting example. In spite of the leveling-off of marital fertility as measured by I_g' in the second half of the century, the *m* index continues the trend toward higher values already established among earlier cohorts. In cases where either the natural marital fertility level is not changing or the increase in family limitation is sufficient, marital fertility should decline as attempts at fertility control increase. Grafenhausen is a clear case of concurrence in the trends of fertility and family limitation. In addition, a number of the increases in *m* between the last two marriage cohorts in several villages were also accompanied by noticeable declines in marital fertility.

The wide range in the level of marital fertility in the absence of any substantial practice of family limitation (as evident for cohorts characterized by low values of the *m* index) underscores the importance of societal-level influences on fertility in the pre-transition situation. For example, among couples married in the period 1750–99, the *m* index is virtually identical for the Bavarian and Waldeck village populations despite a large difference in marital fertility levels. While it may be convenient to infer the practice of family limitation from the levels of marital fertility, it can also be quite misleading. Very low levels of fertility usually do involve deliberate birth control of parity-dependent nature, but moderate or high levels do not necessarily rule out family limitation, as is indicated by examples from several of the Baden villages. In both Rust and Herbolzheim, for example, even the cohort married at the end of the nineteenth century is characterized by I_g' levels that are moderately high but also by values of the *m* index that clearly point to some family limitation. In contrast, I_g' in Middels for cohorts married between the mid-eighteenth and mid-nineteenth centuries is considerably lower, but is associated with very low levels of the *m* index.

Age of mother at last birth

Another measure reflective of the changing age pattern of childbearing that should be particularly sensitive to family limitation is the age at which a woman bears her last child. In populations where family limitation is common, women bear their last child at an earlier age than in populations where no deliberate attempts to stop childbearing are made. Table 11.2 presents this measure for couples in which the marriage remained intact until the end of the wife's reproductive span.

Table 11.2. *Age of mother at last birth by year of marriage*

	1700–49	1750–99	1800–24	1825–49	1850–74	1875–99
Grafenhausen	40.0	40.2	39.9	38.5	37.3	35.2
Herbolzheim	40.8	40.9	39.7	37.7	37.2	37.5
Kappel	40.2	41.1	40.2	40.4	39.2	38.9
Rust	40.1	40.1	41.4	39.8	39.2	38.6
Öschelbronn	39.0	39.1	38.3	39.0	39.3	38.6
3 Bavarian villages	(41.1)	41.2	(39.8)	40.0	40.2	38.4
4 Waldeck villages	39.9	41.0	40.2	41.0	40.7	37.5
Middels	—	40.4	(39.1)	40.4	39.1	37.8
Werdum	39.7	39.3	38.7	39.1	(37.7)[a]	—
All villages	40.0	40.3	39.8	39.3	38.8	37.7

Note: Results are subject to restrictions 2, 3 and 4 (see Table A.1). Results in parentheses are based on 20–49 women; results based on fewer than 20 women are not shown.
[a] Includes a small number of couples married between 1875 and 1899.

One striking feature of these results is the similarity in the age of mother at last birth across different villages for the earlier marriage cohorts. Prior to declines in this measure associated with the fertility transition, the average age at which women terminated childbearing was generally around 40. This corresponds to the results from other family reconstitution studies from Europe for populations assumed to be characterized by natural fertility.[4]

The trends in age of mother at last birth are reasonably consistent with trends in the values of the m index. For most villages, the age of mother at last birth is rather similar for the cohorts during the first and second halves of the eighteenth century. Sharp declines in the age of mother at last birth for the cohorts married at the end of the nineteenth century are evident for both the Bavarian and the Waldeck villages, paralleling increases in the m index. Some divergence between the trend in family limitation given by the age of the mother at last birth and the m index is apparent for Grafenhausen and Herbolzheim. In Grafenhausen, the age of mother at last birth declined steadily for each successive cohort from the end of the eighteenth century, suggesting an earlier onset of family limitation than was apparent from the m index. In Herbolzheim, the age of mother at last birth, after declining substantially for the cohorts married in the first half of the nineteenth century, levels off for cohorts married in the second half. This is in contrast to the trend in the m index, which indicates a continuing increase in family limitation for each socio-economic cohort. Even so, the age of mother at last confinement for the 1875–99 marriage cohort in Herbolzheim is substantially below the level experienced for cohorts married in the eighteenth or early nineteenth century. Some irregular downward movement in the age of mother at last birth is even evident in Kappel for couples married during the nineteenth century, a movement which resembles the trend observed for Rust, although the decline is far less decisive than that observed for the neighboring village of Grafenhausen.

Trends in the two measures of family limitation examination so far – the Coale–Trussell index of fertility control and the age of mother at last birth – are both sensitive to the disproportionate decline in fertility at older ages that characterized most of the villages at some point in the nineteenth century, although in different ways. Thus they are not independent measures. Still the two measures need not necessarily show identical trends. In addition, the age of mother at last birth is based exclusively on completed unions, while the m index is based on

[4] Smith, Daniel Scott, 'Homeostatic demographic regime'; Flinn, *European demographic system*.

couples regardless of whether their union ended before the wife completed her reproductive years. Furthermore, they can and do give somewhat different pictures of the emergence of family limitation in our sample villages. Taken together, they provide somewhat more information than either one of them does singly.

Both measures underscore the fact that the decline in fertility at the end of the nineteenth and in the early twentieth century, evident in the macro-level statistics for Germany and reflected in some of the sample villages, was the result of a fundamental transformation of reproductive behavior from a pattern characteristic of natural fertility to one indicative of deliberate attempts to stop childbearing before the end of the wife's reproductive years. Even in those villages where little or no decline in the level of marital fertility was evident at the end of the nineteenth century, there were signs that the underlying behavioral pattern was also beginning (or continuing as in the case of Herbolzheim) to change, and that the behavioral mechanisms which were eventually to reduce fertility to much lower levels were already emerging.

Beyond this, the village data reveal interesting differences in the onset of the trend toward family limitation. At the one extreme, data for Grafenhausen, Herbolzheim, and to a lesser extent Rust, all near each other, show evidence of increasing couple-level control very early in the nineteenth century. At the other extreme, Öschelbronn, and perhaps even Kappel (a neighbor of both Grafenhausen and Rust and near to Herbolzheim), both show no evidence of fertility decline and only minimal evidence of increasing family limitation even by the end of the nineteenth century. Previous analysis of aggregate data shows substantial regional variation in the fertility transition.[5] Even greater variation appears to exist among villages, including nearby ones.

Occupational differentials

Was the diversity observed in the changes in reproductive behavior among villages matched by a similar diversity within villages among different socio-economic groups? In an effort to shed some light on this question, the measures of marital fertility and family limitation examined for the village populations as a whole are produced in Table 11.3 according to the occupational category of the husband. In order to avoid the problems associated with the small numbers of cases in each category, the results are presented for only two broad marriage

---

[5] Knodel, *Decline of fertility*.

Table 11.3. *Age-standardized index of marital fertility (I_g'), index of fertility control (m), and age of mother at last birth, by year of marriage and occupational category of husband*

	I_g' index			m index			Age of mother at last birth		
	1750–1849	1850–99	Change	1750–1849	1850–99	Change	1750–1849	1850–99	Change
Grafenhausen									
Artisans, etc.	.85	.62	−.23	.15	.81	+.66	39.6	36.6	−3.0
Farmers	.77	.57	−.20	.18	.72	+.54	39.3	35.7	−3.6
Proletarians	.84	(.76)	(−.08)	.16	(.29)	+.13	40.0	(39.4)	(−0.6)
Total, inc. unknown	.81	.60	−.21	.13	.67	+.54	39.6	36.3	−3.3
Herbolzheim									
Artisans, etc.	.78	.75	−.03	.14	.61	+.47	39.2	37.2	−2.0
Farmers	.74	.66	−.08	.08	.79	+.71	39.6	36.4	−3.2
Proletarians	.77	.80	+.03	.12	.59	+.47	39.3	38.0	−1.3
Total, inc. unknown	.78	.74	−.04	.08	.60	+.52	39.6	37.5	−2.1
Kappel									
Artisans, etc.	.80	.77	−.03	.00	.17	+.17	41.0	38.1	−2.9
Farmers	.77	.82	+.05	.07	.25	+.18	39.9	38.8	−1.1
Proletarians	.79	(.87)	(+.08)	−.04	(.29)	+.33	40.9	39.8	−1.1
Total, inc. unknown	.79	.83	+.04	.03	.18	+.15	40.6	39.1	−1.5
Rust									
Artisans, etc.	.83	.86	+.03	.04	.32	+.28	40.4	39.3	−1.1
Farmers	.83	.84	+.01	−.10	.61	+.71	40.4	38.3	−2.1
Proletarians	.77	.88	+.11	.11	.46	+.35	40.4	38.8	−1.6
Total, inc. unknown	.82	.87	+.05	.05	.42	+.37	40.4	38.9	−1.5

	I_g'	m	I_g'	m	I_g'	m	Age	Age	Diff.
Öschelbronn									
Artisans, etc.	.89	−.11	1.00	.23	.11	−.12	38.8	39.4	+0.6
Farmers	.79	+.05	.84	.15	.33	+.18	38.6	38.1	−0.5
Proletarians	(.84)	—	—	(.36)	—	—	(38.5)	(40.1)	(+1.6)
Total, inc. unknown	.84	.11	.95	.19	.20	+.01	39.1	39.0	−0.1
3 Bavarian villages									
Artisans, etc.	(.94)	(+.08)	(1.02)	.31	.37	+.06	39.9	(39.5)	(−0.4)
Farmers	.79	(+.06)	(.85)	−.01	(.31)	(+.32)	(40.5)	(39.3)	(−1.2)
Proletarians	.91	+.06	.97	.08	.33	+.25	40.1	39.1	−1.0
Total, inc. unknown	.95	+.00	.95	.05	.33	+.28	40.5	39.3	−1.2
4 Waldeck villages									
Artisans, etc.	.83	−.09	.74	−.07	.28	+.35	41.1	38.7	−2.4
Farmers	.83	−.02	.81	−.13	.22	+.35	40.9	38.9	−2.0
Proletarians	.77	+.06	.83	.03	−.01	−.04	40.7	39.7	−1.0
Total, inc. unknown	.78	.00	.78	−.03	.19	+.22	40.9	39.5	−1.4
2 East Friesland villages									
Artisans, etc.	.66	—	—	.21	—	—	38.5	(39.1)	(+0.6)
Farmers	.68	−.04	.64	.18	.71	+.53	38.9	37.6	−1.3
Proletarians	.69	−.05	.64	.15	.20	+.05	39.9	38.6	−1.3
Total, inc. unknown	.68	−.03	.65	.18	.30	+.12	39.6	38.4	−1.2

Note: I_g' and m are subject to restrictions 1, 2 and 3 (see Table A.1). Values of I_g' and m based on less than an average of 100 woman-years per five-year age group within the range 20–44 omitted; values based on an average of 100–199 woman-years are shown in parentheses. Values of m shown in italics indicate that the mean square error of the regression used to estimate m exceeded .005.

The average age of mother at last birth is subject to restrictions 2, 3 and 4. Results for the age of mother at last birth based on fewer than 20 women are omitted; results in parentheses are based on 20–39 women. The category, 'Artisans, etc.' includes businessmen and professionals; the category, 'Proletarians' includes cottagers and other unskilled workers.

cohorts, couples married between the mid-eighteenth and mid-nineteenth centuries and couples married during the last half of the nineteenth century. In addition, the two East Frisian villages, as well as the three Bavarian and four Waldeck villages, have been combined into single data sets.

There appears to be little consistency among different villages with respect to occupational differentials in marital fertility. Perhaps the most striking feature for couples married between 1750 and 1849 is the general lack of any substantial difference between occupational group-ings. For the villages of Herbolzheim, Kappel, and the two East Frisian villages, virtually no occupational differences in the level of marital fertility are evident, and in the other villages there is rarely as much as a 10 percent difference between the occupational groupings with the highest and lowest rates. Clearly, occupational differences in fertility within villages are less than the differences found in the average fertility between villages.

Occupational differentials are more pronounced for couples married after 1850 because of the differences in the extent to which the various occupational groupings participated in the onset of the fertility decline toward the end of the nineteenth century, but again these contrasts defy clear-cut generalizations. In addition, since the 1850–99 cohort generally involved smaller numbers of cases, random fluctuations are more likely to affect the results. Occupational differentials with respect to changes in fertility between the two marriage cohorts also show little consistency among the different villages.

The changes in reproductive behavior that were emerging during the nineteenth century in the German villages are less evident in measures of the level of marital fertility than in the measures of family limitation, since fertility trends were confounded by the increase in the underlying natural marital fertility level, discussed in the previous chapter. Among the couples married prior to 1850, occupational differences as revealed by the index of fertility control and by the age of mother at last birth are generally minimal. For most occupational categories, the *m* index is quite low and the age of mother at last birth is quite close to age 40. The most noticeable exception is the proletarian category in Öschelbronn, which is characterized by the highest *m* value and, together with artisans in the East Frisian villages, the lowest age at last birth; this may, however, suffer from being based on a small number of cases.

Somewhat more consistency is evident in the changes in the indices of family limitation for couples married before and after 1850 than was apparent for changes in the level of marital fertility. Increases in family limitation are indicated by increases in the *m* index and decreases in the age of mother at last birth. The most common pattern was for farmers to show the greatest increase in the practice of family limitation. There were exceptions, most notably in Kappel, but also elsewhere. While occupational differentials in the increase of family limitation practices are reasonably consistent, it is also worth noting that in those villages where at least a moderate increase in family limitation is indicated for the total population, all three occupational categories seemed to have participated, at least to some extent, in altering their reproductive behavior in a manner consistent with parity-dependent control.

For some purposes in subsequent analyses presented in this and later chapters, it is useful to distinguish marriage cohorts characterized predominantly by natural fertility from those among which a noticeable amount of family limitation is practiced. For this purpose, the Coale–Trussell m index serves as a useful summary measure. As indicated in Chapter 10, the value of m for the sample as a whole is close to zero for couples married during the last half of the eighteenth century, reflecting close conformity to the standard age pattern of natural fertility. The emergence and spread of family limitation for the combined sample of all villages is signaled by the steady increase in the value of m between successive marriage cohorts during the nineteenth century. As the results clearly indicated, however, the individual villages or village sets follow rather divergent paths. For convenience, village-specific marriage cohorts that are characterized by a value of m of under .30 are considered to be predominantly natural fertility marriage cohorts, while those with high values are considered to practice more than a minimal amount of family limitation. Such a dividing line is arbitrary but has the practical advantage that in none of the individual villages is there an apparent reversion to lower levels once the .30 mark has been exceeded. The large majority of village-specific marriage cohorts that constitute the natural fertility group, according to this criterion, are characterized by m values of .20, and many by values under .10.[6]

---

[6] A minor problem is presented by Werdum, where only a small number of couples married during the last quarter of the nineteenth century qualified for inclusion in this study due to the fact that the genealogy for that village was based only on records up to 1900 (see Chapter 2). While the m value for the cohort 1850–99 is .24 and thus under the .30 level, if m is calculated based strictly on marriages between 1850–74, it is .31 and slightly over the criterion value. For classification purposes, the value of .24 for the 1850–99 cohort was used, and thus Werdum is included in the natural fertility category for the entire period under observation. The family limitation cohorts consist of the following marriage cohorts: 1825–99 in Grafenhausen and Herbolzheim; 1850–99 in Rust; and 1875–99 in each of the three Bavarian villages, each of the four Waldeck villages, and Middels. All remaining marriage cohorts constitute the natural fertility cohorts. For the combined sample of all villages, the natural fertility cohorts are characterized by a value of m of .06 compared to .48 for the family limitation cohorts.

Parity progression probabilities

The analysis has so far focused on detecting family limitation defined primarily in terms of attempts at curtailing childbearing prior to the end of the reproductive span. The assumption underlying this is that once couples reach some number of children they do not wish to exceed, their reproductive behavior changes in ways intended to prevent additional childbearing. Thus, conceptually, family limitation has been defined in terms of parity-specific behavior on the part of the couple, that is the changes in their reproductive behavior are assumed to depend on the number of children already born. However, both the Coale–Trussell index of fertility control and the age of mother at last birth, the two measures examined up to this point, are based on age rather than directly on parity. We now turn to analyses which relate reproductive behavior directly to parity, and illustrate some of the problems of such an approach. The closely related issue of whether family limitation is in fact parity-dependent or instead really age-dependent is then addressed. This is of some importance for interpreting the more conventional indices of family limitation already presented, given their reliance on age as a proxy for parity.

Given the assumption, underlying a number of measures of fertility control, that couples limit their family size through the practice of birth control on a parity-specific basis, it is of interest to explore directly the relationship between reproductive behavior and parity. There are, however, complications with such an approach. The chief difficulty arises from the fact that parity progression is a decremental process in which progressively fewer couples reach successively higher parities. This creates a problem for interpreting results, since the subset of couples who do progress are likely to differ from those that do not in ways that are related to their chances of yet further progression. For example, in comparison to couples whose childbearing stops at lower parities, couples who go on to higher parities under conditions of natural fertility are likely to be characterized by higher fecundity. In addition, in transitional populations where deliberate birth control is practiced by only a part of the population, couples going on to higher parities also tend to be disproportionately selected from those who are not attempting to limit family size or who are ineffective at it. Moreover, even in a population in which birth control is perfect, the distribution of target family sizes would influence the pattern of parity progression.[7] Hence it cannot be assumed that the presence of family

---

[7] For example, it is easy to construct a distribution of desired family sizes which, under conditions of perfect contraception, would result in identical parity progression probabilities over a wide range of parity levels.

limitation will be reflected in a simple unilinear decline in the proportion progressing to the next parity at successively higher parity levels. Nor can it be assumed that as fertility control spreads, declines in progression probabilities will be greatest at the highest parity levels.

The most straightforward measure of reproductive behavior that can be directly related to parity is the parity progression ratio, typically defined as simply the proportion of women at a particular parity who move to the next higher parity. For several reasons, this measure is not ideally suited for examining parity progression probabilities in this study. Since it refers to the *eventual* progression to the next higher parity, calculations are most appropriately limited to 'complete' families, that is to those in which the couple remains in an intact union until the wife reaches the end of the reproductive age span, in which case the number of cases on which it can be based is reduced. Moreover, the measure will be dependent on the number of fecund years remaining to the couple: the younger the age at which the wife achieves a given parity, the longer the period she is at risk of progressing to the next parity.

An alternative measure, adopted in this study, is the probability of progressing to the next parity within five years among women who remain in an intact union for at least five years following a birth and who are under age 40 at the time of the birth.[8] This measure permits inclusion of 'incomplete' unions provided they remained at risk of an additional birth for at least five years, thus expanding the number of cases that can be incorporated into the analysis.[9] A five-year cut-off point is of course arbitrary, but can be justified by the fact that almost all women who go on to have an additional birth do so within 60

[8] In the present analysis, parity is defined in terms of the number of *births*, including multiple births (twins, triplets). However, progression between parities within a multiple-birth set is ignored. Thus a woman who experienced a single birth followed by twins followed by another single birth would be considered to be at parity four. Her progression from parity 2 to parity 3, however, would be excluded from analysis since it was automatic given the fact that it was within a set of twins.

[9] Observations based on couples who do not survive in an intact union for at least an additional five years following the birth are considered 'censored' since they are not exposed to the risk of an additional birth for a full five years. Such censored observations are excluded in the approach being used and thus some loss of cases is still involved. The use of life table techniques would allow full use of all available data including censored observations (Weir, 'Fertility transition,' pp. 111–12; Rodriguez and Hobcraft, *Illustrative analysis*). The application of life table techniques, however, is considerably more complicated and would yield results reasonably similar to those from the simpler measure opted for in this study. For example, the proportions estimated as progressing from parity 3 to parity 4 within five years for successive marriage cohorts in the combined sample of all villages differ as follows according to the treatment of the censored observations (in this case, couples who do not survive a full five additional years following achievement of parity 3):

months.[10] Restricting the analysis to women who are under age 40 at the time of giving birth presumably eliminates a large share of women who become secondarily sterile prior to the end of the five-year period of observation.

The measure is also likely to be more sensitive to deliberate attempts at birth control for several reasons. First, imperfect contraceptive practices may postpone a birth for a substantial period but not permanently. Such failed contraceptive efforts would not be revealed in a standard parity progression ratio, but would be in the case of the proposed measure to the extent that delays were of at least five years' duration. In other cases, a couple may start out preventing further births but experience a change of mind, perhaps in reaction to the loss of a child, and have an additional birth. Again, the standard parity progression measure would not reflect the initial practice of birth control, while the proposed measure could.[11]

One limitation of the present analysis is that it deals with births rather than surviving children. Thus, observed relationships will be confounded by child mortality experience. Parity progression ratios based on surviving children are examined in Chapter 14 in connection

	Censored observations	
Marriage cohort	included	excluded
1750–99	.931	.909
1800–24	.917	.905
1825–49	.904	.877
1850–74	.866	.842
1875–99	.843	.820
Percent decline	9.5	9.8

In general, the life table approach, which incorporates censored events, increases somewhat the estimates of the probability of progression within five years from parity 3 to parity 4, probably because couples with censored observations involved a disproportionate number of cases of maternal mortality associated with the next birth. However, trends in parity progression probabilities, the main interest in the present analysis, are very similar whether or not censored observations are included.

[10] For example, for the combined sample of all villages, 95 percent of births that were eventually followed by another birth, and occurred to women who were under age 40 and in an intact union for at least an additional ten years, were followed by an additional birth within less than 60 months.

[11] The fact that there was greater change during the period under study in the proportion progressing to the next parity within five years compared to the proportion eventually progressing is probably due to the greater sensitivity of the former measure to increased attempts at marital fertility control. For example, for the combined sample of all villages, the probability of progressing from parity 3 to parity 4 within five years (according to the measure described in the text), declined by 9.4 percent between the 1750–99 and the 1875–99 marriage cohorts compared to a 5.1 percent decline in the proportion eventually progressing from parity 3 to parity 4 (among complete unions with at least five years of additional exposure).

with the analysis of the impact of infant and child mortality on reproductive behavior.

The potential, as well as the complexity, of utilizing parity progression measures as indications of family limitation is illustrated by the results presented in Figure 11.1, which show the probabilities of progressing from one parity to the next within five years for the entire sample of all villages. Results are shown separately for the predominantly natural fertility marriage cohorts and for those cohorts characterized by family limitation (based on the m index as explained above). For both sets of cohorts, parity progression probabilities are shown by age group of the mother at the time of the birth of the child marking the parity from which the progression occurs. Controlling for the age of the mother ensures that the number of fertile years remaining is essentially the same regardless of the parities between which the progression occurs. The importance of controlling for age is evident from the fact that for both the natural fertility cohorts and the family limitation cohorts there is an inverse relationship, at all parity levels, between age and the probability of progression to a higher parity.

For the natural fertility cohorts, there is only a weak association between the probabilities of progressing and parity level. For the two age groups under 30, the probability of progression generally increases with parity. For women in their thirties, there is a moderate curvilinear association between parity level and the probability of progression. In particular, there is a slight fall in progression probabilities with increasing parity at lower parity levels, but an increase thereafter, which is particularly pronounced for the 35–39 age group. The increase may be related to a selection process through which more fecund women, and thus women who are more likely to continue childbearing, are more likely to reach higher parities. At the same time, the practice of family limitation among a limited proportion of the couples may account for the initial decline with parity, since the natural fertility cohorts have been defined rather loosely and potentially include at least a small proportion of couples practicing deliberate birth control. Nevertheless, the general association with parity, even for this oldest age group of women, is quite modest.[12]

The experience of the family limitation cohorts contrasts with that of the natural fertility cohorts in several respects. For all age groups, the

[12] A roughly similar relationship of parity progression ratios (defined in terms of eventual progression) with age and parity is reported for a sample of English villages for couples married during the seventeenth and eighteenth centuries, when natural fertility also prevailed (Wilson, 'Natural fertility'). In particular, a modest curvilinear relationship between the proportion progressing and parity level is evident in the 35–39 age group.

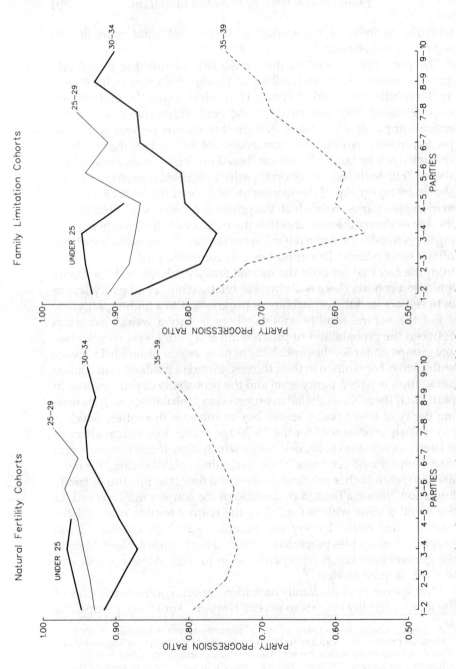

Figure 11.1. *Proportion of mothers progressing to next parity within five years by age of mother.* Results refer to the combined sample of all villages, are subject to restrictions 2, 3 and 6 (see Table A.1), and are limited to women under age 40 at the time of the initia-

progression probabilities are lower for the family limitation cohorts than they are for the natural fertility cohorts at virtually all parities. Even more striking is the greater curvilinearity of the relationship between parity level and progression probabilities for all but the youngest age group compared to their counterparts in the natural fertility cohorts: progression probabilities at first decline with parity and then increase. The initial decline with parity is particularly sharp for women in their thirties. This decline with parity within the lower range of parity levels probably mirrors the distribution of the preferred number of children: while few couples presumably wish to stop childbearing at only one child, considerably more might wish to stop at two children, and an even greater number at three. This, then, would lead to a decline in parity progression from parities 1 through 3.

Starting with parity 4, there is a substantial increase, with each successive parity level, in the probability of continuing childbearing for women aged 30–34, while for women aged 35–39 there is a substantial increase starting at parity 6. This quite likely reflects the selection processes referred to above. Not only are women selected for higher fecundity as parity increases, but they are probably also more likely to be ineffective at limiting family size or to be non-limiters, possibly because of larger family size targets. Particularly in the early stage of the fertility transition, the spread of family limitation may be incomplete within a village, and there may be only a limited proportion of couples practicing deliberate birth control.

The lower levels of parity progression found in the family limitation cohorts at virtually all parities probably reflect the practice of family limitation. Nevertheless, the extent to which limitation is evident depends very much on the parity level being compared. Moreover, selection processes affect parity progression probabilities in such a way that, despite the parity-dependent nature of family limitation at the couple level, in the aggregate, deliberate limitation is not increasingly evident as parity increases.

The extent to which progression probabilities decline with parity over the lower range of parity levels for the family limitation cohorts is less for younger women – indeed, it is irregular for those under age 25 – and is more pronounced for older women. Moreover, given the relatively late age at marriage characterizing the German village populations, increased selectivity for fecundity with increasing parity at a given age might be more severe for the younger age groups, even at relatively low parity levels, compared to their older counterparts. Thus a tendency for increased attempts to stop childbearing at parity 2 compared to parity 1, or at parity 3 compared to parity 2, among

Table 11.4. *Index values of proportion of mothers progressing to next parity, by parity and year of marriage (1750–99 = 100)*

	Year of marriage				
	1750–99	1800–24	1825–49	1850–74	1875–99
All villages					
1–2	100	96	96	96	97
2–3	100	97	95	95	94
3–4	100	98	96	93	91
4–5	100	99	93	93	89
5–6	100	101	91	95	90
6–7	100	98	99	94	93
7–8	100	99	99	96	92
8–9	100	94	99	100	91
9–10	100	103	102	94	99
Grafenhausen					
1–2	100	101	98	97	95
2–3	100	97	93	89	84
3–4	100	100	92	88	71
4–5	100	87	81	85	71
5–6	100	100	87	86	78
6–7	100	93	102	82	(74)
7–8	100	100	87	(90)	(102)
8–9	100	(96)	(86)	(103)	—

Note: Results are subject to restrictions 2, 3 and 6 (see Table A.1), and are limited to women who are under age 40 at the time of the birth initiating the progression and who remain in an intact union for at least five subsequent years. Results in parentheses are based on 20–49 cases; results based on less than 20 cases are omitted.

women aged 25 to 29, might be more than counterbalanced by a relatively pronounced selectivity for higher fecundity characterizing women at successively higher parity levels.

The probable operation of selection processes as outlined above suggests that the transition from natural fertility to family limitation might not be evident, in the form of declining parity progression ratios, at all parities. Moreover, it leaves the expectation that over the course of the fertility transition there will be increasingly greater declines in progression probabilities at successively higher parity levels only up to a certain point, after which the amount of decline will diminish and perhaps become negligible at the highest parity levels. Changes in parity progression probabilities for successive marriage cohorts are indicated in Table 11.4 by indexing the value for the 1750–99 marriage cohort as 100 and representing the value for successive marriage cohorts as a percent of the 1750–99 level. In addition to showing results for all villages, results are also shown for the village of Grafenhausen, since family limitation and fertility decline appear to have progressed furthest there, compared to any other sample village, over the period under study.

For the combined sample of all villages, modest declines in the parity progression probabilities are equally evident, but the extent of decline differs considerably according to parity level. In addition, the trend is not always consistent, although for all but the lowest and highest parities shown, the progression probabilities are lower for the 1875–99 marriage cohort than for any previous one. The most pronounced declines in progression probabilities are found following parities 3, 4 and 5. At parity 1, no trend is evident among cohorts married in the nineteenth century, although all such cohorts experienced a somewhat lower probability of continuing past the first birth than the 1750–99 marriage cohort, which serves as the point of reference. Moreover, the trend is quite erratic for progression probabilities past parities 8 and 9. Thus the increase in family limitation evident in the indices based on age patterns of fertility manifests itself in the somewhat curvilinear relationship established between declines in parity progression probabilities and parity level.

The results for Grafenhausen, although based on a considerably smaller number of cases, are nevertheless of considerable interest because of its earlier and more advanced fertility transition during the nineteenth century. Considerably sharper declines in progression probabilities at some parities are apparent for Grafenhausen couples compared to the combined sample of all villages. The most pronounced decline occurs at parities 3 and 4, with a fall of almost 30 percent between the levels characterizing the 1750–99 marriage cohort and couples married in the last quarter of the nineteenth century. In contrast, changes in progression probabilities at the higher parities are erratic and do not point to any clear evidence of decline, although a lack of sufficient cases on which to base calculations becomes a serious problem at these parities, making interpretation all the more difficult.

In brief, the results of Table 11.4 suggest that selection processes complicate the pattern of change in parity progression probabilities as family limitation spreads, and may indeed mask the transition from natural fertility to family limitation at higher parities. However, they also suggest that, at moderate parities, changed reproductive behavior is reflected in declining proportions of couples going on to have an additional birth within the period in which an additional birth would normally be expected under conditions of natural fertility.

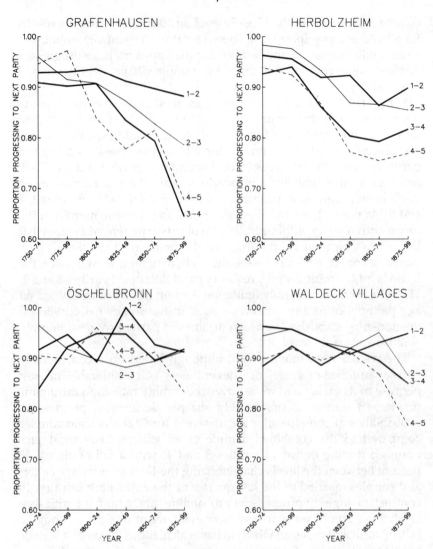

Figure 11.2. *Proportion of mothers progressing to next parity within five years by year of marriage.* Results are subject to restrictions 2, 3 and 6 (see Table A.1) and are limited to women under age 40 at the time of the initiating birth and who remain in an intact marriage for at least five subsequent years

The contrasting paths of the fertility transition for the different village populations are reflected in the parity progression data as well. In Figure 11.2, the proportion of mothers progressing to the next parity within five years is shown graphically for selected villages with quite different courses of fertility transition. Only progressions following parities 1 through 4 are shown, since they represent the range in which an increasing extent of decline is likely, associated with increasing parity levels, as family limitation spreads through the population.

The case of Grafenhausen has been discussed above and is consistent with the impression that the transition from natural fertility to family limitation began early and had advanced considerably in that village by the end of the nineteenth century. The early start to the fertility transition in Herbolzheim is also evident from the declining parity progression probabilities that start with the cohorts married at the beginning of the nineteenth century, but, unlike Grafenhausen, a leveling-off of the transition is evident for the cohorts married in the second half of the nineteenth century. Öschelbronn provides a quite different picture, indicating little evidence of any consistent trend in parity progression probabilities right up through cohorts married at the end of the nineteenth century. For couples married in the Waldeck villages, increasing attempts to terminate childbearing following parities 2 through 4 emerge only among couples married at the end of the nineteenth century.

Even in the villages where family limitation appears to have progressed the furthest by the end of the nineteenth century, the probability of progressing between the first and second birth is at most only moderately affected, suggesting that few couples made efforts to limit family size to an only child. In general, the variations in the onset and progress of the fertility transition among the different villages in the sample, as detected by the measures based on age patterns of fertility, are quite consistent with the evidence based on parity progression.

As Weir has pointed out, parity progression probabilities can be used to study time period trends as well as marriage cohort trends.[13] By grouping the probabilities according to the year of the birth initiating the potential progression, trends in fertility corresponding to specific years, rather than to specific marriage cohorts, can be obtained. Time trends in parity progression probabilities for the combined sample of all villages are presented in Figure 11.3 in terms of decades. Only progression probabilities following births 1 through 4 are shown.

Despite some irregularities in the trend, a general downward drift in the probabilities of progressing to the next parity within five years following the birth of the second through the fourth child is evident. There is little evidence of any consistent time trend, however, in the

---

[13] Weir, 'Fertility transition,' p. 113.

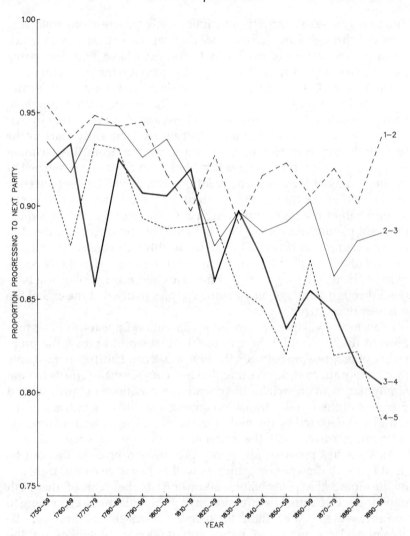

Figure 11.3. *Proportion of mothers progressing to next parity within five years by decade of child's birth.* Results are based on the combined sample of all villages, are subject to restrictions 2, 3 and 6 (see Table A.1), and are limited to women under age 40 at the time of the initiating birth and who remain in an intact marriage for at least five subsequent years

probability of progressing from the first to the second birth. Given the somewhat erratic path followed by the parity progression probabilities, it is difficult to pinpoint precisely a date for the beginning of their decline. Nevertheless, it seems fairly evident that by the mid-nineteenth century signs of the fertility transition are evident for the sample as a whole.

Parity or age dependence?

Most discussions of the emergence of family limitation assume that attempts by couples to terminate childbearing before the end of the wife's reproductive age span depend on the number of surviving children the couple already has and that family limitation is thus a parity-dependent phenomenon. Yet most indices used to detect family limitation are age-dependent. Since age and the number of surviving children are strongly correlated, the observed age dependence of family limitation is assumed to be primarily a reflection of couples reacting to the number of surviving offspring, rather than being a direct response to the wife's age. It is possible, however, that normative prescriptions regarding the proper age to have children are also important and may play some additional and perhaps even a commanding influence.[14]

In order to test if the changes in reproductive patterns observed in our sample of German villages are influenced by couples' past fertility, and thus are parity-dependent, we can examine the relationship between these changes and the wife's age at marriage. Since at any particular age, women who married younger are more likely than women who married later to have achieved a given number of offspring, and thus to have reached a family size they consider sufficient, declines in family size and increases in family limitation should be more pronounced among younger marrying wives during the onset of the fertility transition, provided their actions are influenced by their already achieved family size. If, on the other hand, attempts to stop childbearing are entirely a reaction to norms about the appropriateness of continuing childbearing at a particular age and not to the number of children already born, then age at marriage should bear little relationship to the ongoing changes in reproductive behavior. The use of age at marriage as a proxy for parity avoids the problems associated with the selection processes involved when parity is directly related to subsequent fertility. It does assume, however, that neither the number of children considered sufficient nor norms about the appropriate age to stop childbearing differ greatly by age at marriage.

The results of such an analysis are presented in Table 11.5, which indicates the changes in the total marital fertility rate above age 30, the

[14] See, for example, Bean *et al.*, 'Family limitation'; Rindfuss and Bumpass, 'Age and fertility.'

Table 11.5. *Total marital fertility above age 30 (TMF30+), number of children ever born (CEB), and age of mother at last birth (AMLB), by wife's birth year and age at marriage*

Village and wife's birth year	TMF30+			CEB			AMLB		
	<23	23–27	28–32	<23	23–27	28–32	<23	23–27	28–32
Grafenhausen									
1732–1807	4.06	4.11	4.54	8.28	6.56	4.65	38.3	39.7	(40.9)
1808–32	3.35	3.51	(4.64)	(7.21)	(6.00)	(4.67)	(37.6)	(39.7)	(40.1)
1833–67	2.27	2.46	(3.75)	5.93	4.55	(4.16)	35.7	35.9	(38.5)
Change[a]	−1.79	−1.65	−0.79	−2.35	−2.01	−0.49	−2.6	−3.8	−2.4
Herbolzheim									
1732–1807	3.83	4.25	5.01	7.51	6.53	5.10	39.2	39.7	41.1
1808–32	3.01	2.99	4.41	(6.83)	5.07	4.62	(35.4)	37.3	38.6
1833–67	2.27	2.96	4.42	6.05	5.26	4.47	34.6	36.8	39.0
Change[a]	−1.56	−1.29	−0.59	−1.46	−1.27	−0.63	−4.6	−2.9	−2.1
Kappel									
1732–1832	3.90	4.25	5.03	7.69	6.45	5.12	39.5	40.6	41.3
1833–67	3.33	4.28	(6.21)	(6.85)	6.94	5.82	37.1	39.4	41.3
Change	−0.57	0.03	1.18	−0.84	0.49	0.70	−2.4	−1.2	0.0
Rust									
1732–1832	4.31	4.27	4.73	8.09	6.46	4.76	39.5	39.8	40.4
1833–67	3.84	4.11	(4.03)	8.56	(6.66)	(4.61)	38.7	38.8	38.5
Change	−0.47	−0.16	−0.70	0.47	0.20	−0.15	−0.8	−1.0	−1.9
Öschelbronn									
1732–1832	3.81	4.39	5.66	8.03	6.76	(5.76)	37.8	39.6	40.0
1833–67	(4.68)	5.03	(5.30)	(8.55)	7.97	(5.58)	(37.8)	39.4	(39.8)
Change	0.87	0.64	−0.36	0.52	1.21	−0.18	0.0	−0.2	−0.2

1732–1832	4.63	6.11		7.82	5.61		39.5	40.8	
1833–67	4.11	5.28		(7.04)	(5.11)		(37.5)	(40.4)	
Change	−0.52	−0.83		−0.78	−0.50		−2.0	−0.4	
4 Waldeck villages									
1732–1832	4.44	4.79		8.43	6.32	5.04	41.0	40.2	41.2
1833–67	3.63	(4.75)		8.00	5.86	(4.87)	38.3	39.2	(41.1)
Change	−0.81	−0.04		−0.43	−0.46	−0.17	−2.7	−1.0	−0.1
Middels									
1732–1832	3.45	3.56		7.08	4.93		39.7	39.6	
1833–67	2.80	3.46		5.85	4.96		(37.3)	39.4	
Change	−0.65	−0.10		−1.23	0.03		−2.4	−0.2	
Werdum[b]									
1732–1832	2.88	3.24		6.32	5.07	3.99	37.7	38.9	40.0
All villages									
1732–1807	3.90	4.08	4.83	7.77	6.26	4.87	39.1	39.9	40.7
1808–32	3.53	3.75	4.87	7.40	6.02	4.99	37.9	38.8	40.2
1833–67	3.15	3.63	4.68	7.06	6.00	4.78	37.0	38.1	39.7
Change[a]	−0.75	−0.45	−0.15	−0.71	−0.26	−0.09	−2.1	−1.8	−1.0

Note: Results referring to TMF30+ are subject to restrictions 1, 2 and 3 (see Table A.1); results referring to CEB are subject to restrictions 1, 2, 3 and 4; results referring to AMLB are subject to restrictions 2, 3 and 4.

Values of TMF30+ based on an average of 100–199 woman-years per five-year age group within the 30–49 age range are shown in parentheses; all other values of TMF30+ are based on an average of 200 woman-years. Values of CEB and AMLB based on 20–49 women are based on at least an average of 200 woman-years; all other values are based on at least 50 women. In the case of the three Bavarian villages and Middels, age-at-marriage categories have been combined to avoid basing results on excessively small numbers of cases.

[a] Change in the values of all indices for Grafenhausen, Herbolzheim and the combined sample of all villages are based on a comparison of the 1732–1807 and the 1833–67 cohorts.

[b] The 1833–67 birth cohort of women for Werdum is omitted because of insufficient cases.

number of children ever born, and the age of mother at last birth according to the wife's age at marriage. The data are presented by birth cohorts of women rather than by year of marriage in order to hold constant, across different age-at-marriage categories, the years in which women in each cohort reach the end of their childbearing years. This is important since the time span covered by our observations includes the onset of the fertility transition for most of the village populations. If the preferred family size were decreasing, or if information about, or acceptability of, family limitation were increasing on a period-specific basis during the end of the period under observation, grouping the women by year of marriage would act to exaggerate the differences across age-at-marriage categories. This is because younger marrying women in a particular *marriage cohort* would reach the end of the reproductive span at a later date and at a more advanced stage of the transition than older marrying women.[15] The same is not true for a *birth cohort*.[16]

The results for the combined sample of all villages indicate that the changes in reproductive patterns differ across age-at-marriage groups in a way consistent with the assumption that couples are reacting in a

[15] For example, among women married in 1890, those who married at age 20 experienced their later childbearing years, say between 35 and 44, largely during the period 1905–14, while those who married at age 30 passed through these ages ten years earlier, in the period 1895–1904. Thus the younger marrying women experienced their later childbearing years at a more advanced point in the fertility transition, when family limitation and reduced fertility were presumably more widespread than when the older marrying women reached the end of their reproductive span, ten years earlier.

[16] An additional problem for the analysis is created by the fact that in some villages information is available only for couples married from the mid-eighteenth century on, and in all villages couples married after 1899 are excluded regardless of when they were born. Given that the analysis relates to women married up to and including age 32, all women in the sample born before 1732 or after 1867 have been excluded to avoid a truncation bias. For example, women born in 1875 who married at age 20 are included in our sample since their marriage occurred before the end of 1899, while women born in 1875 who married at age 30 are excluded from our sample since their year of marriage is after 1899.

If women in our sample born after 1867 were not excluded from the analysis, the result would be that the distribution of women by year of birth among the youngest age-at-marriage category, for women in the more (most) recent birth cohort, would be much more skewed toward women born later in the century than it would be among women in the oldest age-at-marriage category. Under such circumstances, women in the youngest age-at-marriage category would on average have reached the end of their childbearing span at a later year, and thus at a time that was further along in terms of the fertility transition, than women in older age-at-marriage categories. The converse of this problem holds for women married at the beginning of the period under observation, although the bias that would have been introduced would probably have been minimal, given the lack of evidence that reproductive changes associated with the fertility transition were under way in the eighteenth century in any of the sample villages.

parity-specific manner. Women who married at younger ages experienced larger declines in all three measures than women who married at older ages. Some differences are evident for particular villages, but generally this pattern holds in most cases. The main exceptions are Rust and Öschelbronn. For Öschelbronn, the evidence suggests that even by the end of the nineteenth century the population had yet to participate to any significant extent in the fertility transition. In the case of Rust, the situation is complicated by the apparent sharp rise in underlying natural fertility as indicated by increases in the Coale–Trussell M index (see Table 10.4).

In all villages the number of children ever born to women who married at younger ages continues to exceed the number of children ever born to women married later for the more (most) recent birth cohort of women. Such a finding is typical, even in modern populations where efficient means of contraception are almost universally practiced, and is attributable to a host of factors, including longer exposure to the risk of unwanted pregnancy, and selectivity toward both higher fecundity and higher fertility desires associated with women who marry young.[17] Thus such a relationship is not necessarily contradictory to an assumption of parity-specific fertility goals, especially in populations only in the initial stages of the transition from natural fertility to widespread family limitation. The important point is that the relationship is typically weaker in most villages for the more (most) recent birth cohort because of the inverse relationship between age at marriage and the amount of decline in children ever born.

It is interesting to note that, even for the earlier birth cohorts, there is a reasonably consistent positive association between age at marriage and both the total marital fertility rate after age 30 and the age of mother at last birth. This could be interpreted as a sign of family limitation since, under conditions where couples attempt to stop or reduce childbearing in response to having achieved a family size they consider sufficient, we would expect younger marrying wives to experience lower fertility in the later childbearing years and to cease childbearing sooner than wives who married later, as explained above. However, there are also a variety of non-volitional factors which can result in a similar relationship, and the mere existence of the relationship is thus not necessarily an indication of family limitation. Moreover, non-volitional factors would not be likely to account for differential *changes* in reproductive behavior over time by age at marriage, such as are observed in the sample villages. In Chapter 13,

[17] Rindfuss and Bumpass, 'Age and fertility.'

the relationship between age at marriage and both marital fertility and age of mother at last birth is more fully explored.

Discussion

The focus of the present chapter has been on the transformation of reproductive behavior from a situation referred to as natural marital fertility to one in which the practice of deliberate family limitation is common. The evidence documenting this shift, and the extent to which it progressed, has been derived entirely from the reconstituted reproductive histories of couples residing in the sample villages. The evidence has been quantitative and indirect, based essentially on the age patterns of childbearing and parity progression probabilities. At this juncture, it is useful to discuss the extent to which available *qualitative* data confirm or contradict the interpretation being placed on the quantitative results. In particular, does the attribution of natural fertility to marital reproductive behavior during much, or for some villages during all, of the period under investigation seem plausible in the light of qualitative evidence?

There are ample references to contraceptive methods and abortion in Western literature long before even the earliest signs of fertility limitation are evident in the quantitative data for the sample villages. The methods discussed range from the magical to the potentially effective.[18] Shorter has recently argued that a number of effective drugs for inducing abortion were available long before the emergence of more modern abortion techniques toward the end of the nineteenth century.[19] Catholic theologians have debated and denounced contraception since early times.[20] Such evidence has led some scholars to conclude that birth control must at least have been widely known, and perhaps practiced, among broad segments of the married population for a considerable period predating the modern fertility transition.[21] Others contest this view, stressing that much of the discussion of birth control was directed at its use outside of marriage and that knowledge and practice may have been restricted primarily to the privileged classes.[22] In his encyclopedic review of the history of contraception, Himes concluded that, although contraceptive practices are very old, diffused knowledge of them is relatively recent.[23] In addition, Shorter

---

[18] Himes, *Medical history*. [19] Shorter, *Women's bodies*.
[20] Noonan, *Contraception*. [21] Imhof, *Bevölkerungsentwicklung*, pp. 446–59.
[22] Knodel and van de Walle, 'Lessons from the past'; van de Walle and Knodel, 'Europe's fertility transition.'
[23] Himes, *Medical history*, p. 333.

has stressed that the dangers of abortive drugs in the pre-modern period were so high that their use was confined to truly desperate women, resulting in abortion being concentrated mainly among the unmarried.[24]

Literary evidence and scattered commentaries by contemporary observers, while suggestive, are not necessarily a reliable basis for establishing the facts about fertility control among the popular classes in the past. For this reason, the survey of rural Protestant pastors in Germany during the mid-1890s, described in Chapter 9, provides an unusually systematic and potentially valuable set of qualitative observations on a topic of particular relevance for this study. The questionnaire sent to the pastors included inquiries about the average number of children, both for laborers and peasants, and asked further if the two-child system was common, which methods were practiced to prevent births, especially among married couples, and whether having many children was considered disgraceful by the community.[25] While it is possible to argue that perhaps the pastors were unaware of what was actually happening in their community, it seems likely that they were closer to the conditions of everyday life than were many of the other observers, including the occasional traveler whose observations often serve as the basis for asserting that birth control was widespread.

The picture reflected in the pastors' responses accords well with what might be expected from the fact that by the mid-1890s, when the survey took place, sustained fertility decline was only at an initial stage in the rural areas of many provinces and had not yet begun in others.[26] The majority of respondents flatly rejected the notion that the two-child system was prevalent and denied that contraception was practiced. This was clearly the predominant view. There were also numerous exceptions, which to some extent were regionally clustered. Specific methods of birth control mentioned included abstinence (described as sleeping separately), coitus interruptus, condoms, and various forms of abortion. A number of respondents mentioned that it was difficult to know precisely the means being used since the practice of birth control was done secretly. Others mentioned that birth control, especially abortion, was associated with the unmarried.

There was considerable variation in the description of how large families were regarded in the community, although regional clustering

[24] Shorter, *Women's bodies*, p. 177.

[25] Allgemeine Konferenz der deutschen Sittlichkeitsvereine, *Die geschlechtlich sittlichen Verhältnisse*.

[26] Knodel, *Decline of fertility*.

was apparent in this respect. In some areas, having many children was described as being universally viewed in a positive way. In the majority of areas, however, the picture painted by the respondents was more mixed, with at least some indicating that many viewed large families as a burden, adding at times that this was simply seen as a matter of fate to which couples resigned themselves. Almost no respondents said that large families were considered disgraceful (as asked in the questionnaire) but rather that, if there was a negative attitude, it was more in the sense of regarding couples as unfortunate or unlucky to have a large number of children. Given that many communities had either begun or were on the threshold of fertility decline, the dissatisfaction with high uncontrolled fertility implied by the pastors' comments is not surprising.

Frequently, when limitation of family size or birth control practice within marriage was mentioned, the respondent linked it to farmers, particularly rich farmers, sometimes commenting that concern about the subdivision of property played an important role. In this respect, the qualitative material provided by this survey fits well with the quantitative evidence presented in the present chapter. Analysis of occupational differentials in marital fertility and family limitation indices indicates that such differences were minimal for couples married prior to 1850, as might be expected in a predominantly natural fertility setting. However, the increases in family limitation evident among couples married in the second half of the nineteenth century were above average for couples in which the husband was a farmer and below average for couples in which the husband was a laborer, a situation consistent with that described by the pastors.

It is also interesting to take particular note of the impressions given with respect to the specific areas in which the sample villages are located. It is somewhat reassuring, for example, that respondents from Schwarzwaldkreis, the area in which Öschelbronn is located, universally denied the presence of the two-child system and of birth control practice, thereby conforming to the indication from the analysis of family reconstitution data that natural fertility largely persisted there through to the end of the nineteenth century. Limitation of family size and practice of birth control were also uniformly denied by respondents from East Friesland, with the interesting exception of one respondent who mentioned that mothers breastfed their children for an unusually long period in order to delay their next conception.

In general, then, the qualitative evidence from the survey of rural pastors is not at odds with the picture presented by the quantitative analysis of the family reconstitution data from the sample villages. In particular, natural fertility marked by an absence of deliberate birth control practices is quite consistent with the observations of the rural pastors. Furthermore, the unfavorable attitudes toward large families described by a number of the respondents fits well with the subsequent fertility decline which engulfed all of Germany within less than two decades and which was already becoming evident in some of the villages included in this study as the nineteenth century was progressing.

The considerable diversity evident in the quantitative analysis of the different villages included in this sample underscores the danger of relying on the experience from any single village to make general points, as is sometimes done in the field of historical demography. Perhaps the most glaring example of this tendency is the frequent citation of the English village of Colyton, where Wrigley presents evidence suggesting the practice of family limitation during the seventeenth century, as indicative of a general situation in preindustrial Europe.[27] Indeed, more recent evidence for England from a sample including 13 additional villages suggests that Colyton was an anomaly even in that country. The general pattern was one of natural fertility throughout the eighteenth and nineteenth centuries.[28]

In the analysis presented in this chapter, a particularly striking feature is the substantial diversity among the small number of villages included in the sample with respect to the timing of the emergence of family limitation. In all the villages, couples who married during the last half of the eighteenth century appear to be characterized predominantly by natural fertility. However, in some, family limitation emerges shortly after the turn of the nineteenth century, whereas in others natural fertility persists, at least through to the close of the century. To some extent, this same diversity is revealed in the qualitative survey of the rural pastors, which thus gives additional support to this pattern.

---

[27] Wrigley, 'Family limitation.'   [28] Wilson, 'Natural fertility.'

12

Starting, stopping, spacing and the fertility transition

Although the concept of family limitation has been defined as a strategy of limiting births through stopping behavior, a logical alternative strategy could be the limitation of births through efforts both to deliberately prolong intervals between births and to delay the start of childbearing following marriage. A fuller understanding of behavioral changes underlying the fertility transition clearly requires assessment of the part played by birth spacing in the reproductive changes that were taking place. Moreover, since the final number of children a couple has also depends on the age at which reproduction begins, consideration needs to be given to when childbearing is initiated. This chapter starts, therefore, by examining the role of birth-spacing patterns in the shift to deliberate marital fertility control. This then leads to a more comprehensive analysis which attempts to assess, within a single integrated framework, the relative contribution of starting, spacing, and stopping behavior during the initial phases of the fertility transition. Finally, given the dominance of stopping behavior indicated by this analysis, an attempt is also made to estimate the proportion of couples who deliberately attempted to limit family size by earlier cessation of childbearing.

Birth spacing

The measures of fertility control that have been examined so far are primarily designed to detect attempts to stop childbearing, and reveal little, if anything, about birth-spacing patterns. Indeed, most historical demographic studies based on family reconstitution data, when examining evidence of deliberate marital fertility control, focus more on deliberate efforts at stopping childbearing than on efforts to space children. The main reason for this is the greater ease with which

318

deliberate stopping can be detected compared to deliberate spacing. In particular, as discussed in Chapter 10, there are reasonably clear expectations with regard to the age pattern of fertility and the age at which childbearing ceases under conditions of natural fertility, as well as how these change in response to deliberate efforts to limit family size through stopping behavior. There are no equivalent expectations concerning birth-spacing patterns.

While the age pattern of fertility and the age of mother at last birth vary only modestly under conditions of natural fertility, birth spacing can vary substantially from population to population as a result of variations in several non-volitional factors, especially variations in the length of postpartum infecundability associated with differences in infant-feeding practices. Thus information on the average length of birth intervals is insufficient in itself to determine whether or not deliberate attempts at spacing children are present. In addition, even in the absence of deliberate birth control, birth intervals tend to increase with birth rank within given completed family sizes, with a particularly large increase associated with the last interval.[1] The lengthening of intervals with birth rank under conditions of natural fertility is most likely explained by associated differences in fecundability, intrauterine mortality, and the non-susceptible period. Indeed, these components of natural fertility may be more closely related to the age of the mother than to birth rank *per se*. Since the two are very closely associated, it is difficult to distinguish between their effects. A positive association of birth interval length with birth rank within families of a particular size therefore cannot necessarily be assumed to reflect parity-dependent attempts to space births.

One aspect of birth spacing that has received some attention in historical demography studies has been the average length of the last birth interval.[2] However, while the lengthening of the last birth interval is generally seen as an indicator of deliberate fertility control, it is not necessarily a sign of intentional birth spacing. It could instead

---

[1] If couples with different completed family sizes are aggregated together, the association of birth interval with birth rank under conditions of natural fertility is quite different. The mean interval typically increases with rank at first, reaches a plateau, and then decreases at the highest ranks. This results from a compositional effect. When couples with different final family sizes are aggregated together, families of final size *n* contribute only to the calculation of mean intervals up to rank *n* but not to higher ranks. Since the average interval at all ranks tends to decrease with final family size, a substantial compositional impact results (Leridon, *Human fertility*, pp. 110–15). This is not true when birth intervals are calculated by birth rank for families of particular completed family sizes. In this case, the same number of families contribute to each of the separate birth ranks within any given final family size category.

[2] Wrigley, 'Family limitation.'

simply reflect increasing attempts at stopping childbearing. Particularly in populations where the spread of family limitation is at an early stage, as attempts at stopping become more common the last birth interval might be expected to lengthen due to accidental but delayed pregnancies, changes of mind, or desires to replace a child who has died. Thus neither a long last birth interval relative to preceding intervals nor a lengthening of the last birth interval over time can be considered an unambiguous sign of deliberate birth spacing. The first phenomenon could be merely a correlate of the physiology of reproduction or of behavioral patterns not associated with fertility intentions. The second could be a reflection of motivations essentially related to attempts at stopping rather than spacing childbearing.

While there are difficulties in detecting evidence of deliberate birth spacing from family reconstitution data, some basis exists for suspecting that the deliberate postponement of births might have been a feature of reproductive behavior during the period under observation. Contemporary observers in the eighteenth and nineteenth centuries in Europe occasionally expressed the opinion that some women deliberately prolonged breastfeeding to postpone the next birth.[3] The survey of Protestant pastors in rural Germany conducted in the mid-1890s, and described in Chapter 9, elicited comments from several respondents, including one from East Friesland and another from an administrative area not far from Waldeck, explicitly stating that women in their localities deliberately breastfed for long durations to delay conception.[4] More recently, several historical demographers have suggested that birth spacing was an important element of fertility control in the past and may have been an important mechanism contributing to the fertility transition.[5] The relative role of birth spacing and family size limitation has also been at issue in discussions of more recent fertility transitions.[6]

It is useful to begin the analysis of birth-spacing patterns by examining the average interval between confinements by interval order, by groups of families with the same final number of confinements.[7]

---

[3] Pockels, 'Jugendgeschichte,' pp. 104–05; Kull, 'Beitraege zur Statistik,' p. 145; Livi-Bacci, *Italian fertility*, p. 256.

[4] Allgemeine Konferenz der deutschen Sittlichkeitsvereine, *Die geschlechtlich sittlichen Verhältnisse*, Vol. I, Part II, p. 13; Vol. II, pp. 92, 368.

[5] For example, see Flinn, *European demographic system*, pp. 88–89; Gaunt, 'Family planning'; Lachiver, 'Fécondité légitime'; Anderton and Bean, 'Birth spacing and fertility limitation.'

[6] Friedlander *et al.*, 'Family size limitation and birth spacing.'

[7] In this and subsequent tabulations dealing with birth spacing, intervals between confinements rather than births *per se* are analyzed in order to avoid the problems associated with intervals between successive births within a multiple-birth set. Thus

Results for the natural fertility cohorts, defined in the previous chapter as those characterized by values of less than .30 for the *m* index on a village-specific basis, are presented in Figure 12.1 for the combined sample of all villages. Several features are quite prominent. At virtually every confinement rank, the length of interval is inversely associated with the final number of confinements. Within each final family size (defined here in terms of confinements) the length of interval tends to increase with confinement order. Lastly, for all final family sizes for which the comparison can be made, the increase between the next-to-last and last interval is relatively greater than increases between successive intervals at lower orders (such a comparison, of course, cannot be made for final family sizes of two and three). For some family sizes, a greater-than-average increase is also associated with the penultimate interval, although this is less consistent and far more modest than the increases associated with the last interval.

Leridon suggests that longer durations of last intervals, compared to previous ones, in natural fertility populations result from an acceleration of the decline in fecundity preceding the onset of permanent sterility and that this decline is relatively insensitive to the age at which sterility occurs.[8] The general tendency for confinement intervals to increase prior to the last interval probably reflects a progressive decrease in fecundity with increasing age, but at a less precipitous rate than occurs when permanent sterility is near. A decline in coital frequency associated with duration of marriage may also contribute to this effect. While there is a possibility that deliberate spacing contributes to the lengthening of intervals with confinement order, the presence of such a pattern does not necessarily testify to this.

The contribution of attempts to stop childbearing to the lengthening of the last interval should be evident during the period of the onset of family limitation. Given the association between the length of intervals, including the last, and the final number of confinements, it is useful to control for this when examining the course of last birth intervals during the period under observation. Moreover, the extent to which the last interval is affected by stopping behavior might differ according to the final number of confinements, since couples who progress to relatively high parities, and hence end up with a large final number of confinements, are selected disproportionately from among

the interval between the first and second born of a pair of twins is ignored rather than counted as an interval of zero months. In addition, unless specified otherwise, analyses are based on all intervals experienced by married women, including those involving prenuptial births in which the husband is assumed to be the father (see Chapter 8 for a fuller discussion of the definition of prenuptial births).

[8] Leridon, *Human fertility*, p. 160.

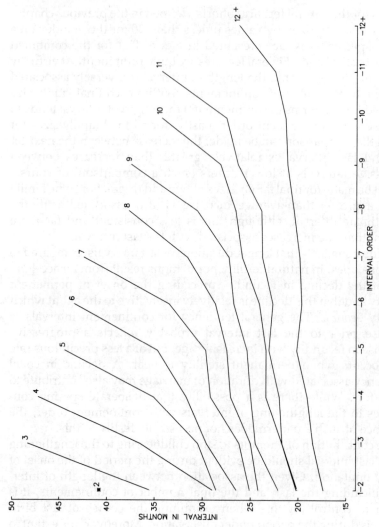

Figure 12.1. Mean interconfinement interval by final number of confinements and interval order, natural fertility cohorts. Results are based on the combined sample of all villages and are subject to restrictions 2, 3 and 6 (see Table A.1). See text for definition of natural fertility cohorts

those who are not attempting to limit family size or are ineffective at it. Trends in the mean last interconfinement interval and the mean of all preceding intervals according to the final number of confinements are provided in Table 12.1 for the combined sample of all villages.

If we focus first on the overall trend without regard for the final number of confinements, it is evident that the last interval increased during the period under observation despite a decrease in the average duration of preceding intervals. However, the trends are irregular and not identical for couples within each of the different categories of final number of confinements. For example, among couples with relatively large final numbers of confinements (the categories 7–10 and 11+), the mean last interval changes little and is actually slightly lower for the cohort married during the last quarter of the nineteenth century compared to the cohort married during the eighteenth century. In contrast, among couples who experience six or fewer confinements, the last interval is typically higher for women who married at the end of the nineteenth century compared to earlier cohorts. Such a pattern is consistent with a possible selection process, referred to in Chapter 11, in which effective attempts to limit family size are concentrated among those couples who experience no more than a moderate number of births.

The mean of intervals preceding the last shows a different pattern of change across successive cohorts. Typically, the average duration of these intervals decreases, not only in terms of the overall trends, but also for most categories of final number of confinements. The trend is less clear among women experiencing small numbers of total confinements, but even in these cases, women married during the last quarter of the nineteenth century experienced shorter average intervals than women married during the eighteenth century. This decrease in intervals preceding the last is probably in part a reflection of the rising level of natural fertility, discussed in Chapter 10. Moreover, the increase in the average length of the last interval may have been moderated to some extent by this phenomenon. If this is so, the evidence would suggest that those features associated with stopping behavior which lengthen the last birth interval more than compensated for a countervailing trend toward increases in the underlying level of natural marital fertility.

Trends in the average interconfinement interval according to the final number of confinements are also of interest with respect to determining whether or not deliberate spacing was part of the strategy to control fertility at early stages of the fertility transition. In the absence of deliberate attempts to either space or stop births, the

Table 12.1. *Mean last interconfinement interval, mean of all preceding intervals, mean age at first confinement, and change in mean of all preceding intervals adjusted for mean age at first confinement, by final number of confinements and marriage cohort*

	Final number of confinements						
	3	4	5	6	7–10	11+	Total
Last interval							
1700–99	46.2	44.7	43.3	44.3	38.3	32.2	40.7
1800–49	51.5	51.7	41.8	41.9	39.7	33.4	42.7
1850–74	49.6	49.6	48.0	41.7	39.7	34.7	43.4
1875–99	48.1	53.1	49.2	48.5	37.6	32.0	44.0
Change[a]	1.9	8.4	5.9	4.2	−0.7	−0.2	3.3
All preceding intervals[b]							
1700–99	34.7	33.8	31.8	31.3	27.8	22.4	29.6
1800–49	37.3	32.7	32.2	30.3	26.7	22.2	29.6
1850–74	33.0	31.3	30.4	29.2	25.3	20.1	28.0
1875–99	33.9	31.2	28.3	27.2	24.3	18.7	27.1
Change[a]	−0.8	−2.6	−3.5	−4.1	−3.5	−3.7	−2.5
Age at first confinement							
1700–99	30.9	29.3	28.1	27.1	24.6	22.2	26.3
1800–49	30.2	28.4	27.8	26.7	24.8	22.7	26.5
1850–74	29.3	27.7	26.6	26.6	25.4	23.2	26.4
1875–99	27.7	27.0	26.6	25.4	25.1	23.9	25.9
Change[a]	−3.2	−2.3	−1.5	−1.7	0.5	1.7	−0.4
Adjusted mean of all preceding intervals[b] [c]							
Change[a]	−4.6	−4.2	−5.2	−5.7	−3.1	−2.6	−2.7

Note: All mean intervals are expressed in months. Results refer to the combined sample of all villages, are subject to restrictions 1, 2, 3 and 4 (see Table A.1), and are limited to couples with at least three confinements.
[a] Based on a comparison of the 1700–99 and 1875–99 marriage cohorts.
[b] The average preceding interval is expressed per woman and thus both the results in the collapsed categories of final number of confinements and the results for the total are weighted by the number of women rather than by the number of intervals involved.
[c] Statistical adjustment for age at first confinement is accomplished through separate multiple regression equations for each category of final number of confinements, in which age at first confinement is entered as a covariate and marriage cohort as a categorical variable.

pattern of child spacing leading up to any specific final number of confinements would presumably reflect the particular combination of non-volitional factors, both biological and behavioral, that determine natural marital fertility. Heterogeneity within the population with respect to these characteristics would lead women to be distributed among a range of different final family sizes. If differences in the time at which childbearing commences are ignored, couples who end up with larger numbers of confinements under conditions of natural fertility experience characteristic intervals that are shorter than those who end up with fewer confinements.

If the initial onset of the transition to family limitation is marked solely by the introduction of effective stopping behavior, and there are no changes either in the components of the underlying level of natural marital fertility or in the age at which couples commenced childbearing, a reduction in the average interconfinement interval within specific categories of final number of confinements would be expected. The reason for this is that, once family limitation begins to spread within a population, the total group of couples achieving a particular final number of confinements would be made up of two types: those who did not deliberately control their fertility and who thus resemble those achieving this number under conditions of natural fertility and those who would have exceeded this number, but chose to deliberately cease childbearing early. The former group would presumably share the same birth intervals characteristic of their counterparts prior to the onset of family limitation. The latter group, however, would be characterized by the shorter birth intervals typical of couples who achieved a higher final number of confinements under natural fertility conditions. The net result would be a reduction in the average interval within a specific category of final number of confinements. The extent of reduction would depend on the proportion of couples within that category who were deliberate family limiters, as well as their distribution with respect to the final number of confinements they would otherwise have had if they had not deliberately practiced control.

In contrast, if couples limited their family size solely by longer spacing, the average interval within a category of final number of confinements would presumably remain unchanged as fertility fell. A decline in fertility for the population as a whole under such circumstances would result through some couples switching from shorter to longer spacing schedules. Since nothing is done to alter the age at which childbearing ceases, and provided the age at which childbearing starts remains unchanged for each category of final number of confinements, the average interval associated with each of these categories should also remain unchanged. What would change is the distribution of couples in terms of final parity: more couples would have few confinements and fewer couples would have large numbers of confinements.

Obviously a number of the conditions specified do not hold in the experience of the village populations under study. The components of natural marital fertility were changing in such a way as to shorten birth intervals, and stopping behavior was not perfect, as is implied by the lengthening of the last interval. Nevertheless, the decline in the average length of interconfinement intervals, excluding the last, within the different categories of final parity for the sample as a whole is generally consistent with expectations of the effect of stopping behavior. However, it might also be expected that the impact would be greatest within the range of moderate final family sizes, where presumably couples deliberately controlling the number of births are concentrated, yet this does not appear to be the case.

Before drawing conclusions from these patterns, account should be taken of the fact that the age at starting childbearing within different categories of final number of confinements was changing during the period under observation. As is also shown in Table 12.1, the age at starting childbearing among women who eventually ended their reproductive life with a moderate number of confinements declined. In contrast, the age at first confinement rose for women in the 7–10 and 11+ categories of final number of confinements.

As long as the age at which reproductive capability ends remains constant, the earlier a woman commences childbearing the longer she has to arrive at a specific final number of confinements and the longer the average birth interval is likely to be within any final parity category. Thus, among women who eventually had four children, someone who began her childbearing at age 30 would have fewer years of fecund life to bear those four children than would someone who started at age 25, provided both lost their childbearing ability at the same time. Hence the earlier the age at which childbearing commences, the longer the average interval is likely to be within any given category of final number of confinements. A statistical adjustment through multiple regression can be made for changes in the age at which women begin childbearing. Once such an adjustment is made, as the results presented in the bottom panel of Table 12.1 indicate, the decline in the average interval, excluding the last, is more pronounced for women with moderate final numbers of confinements and is reduced for women with higher numbers of confinements. Moreover, the statistically adjusted results reveal the expected pattern of a greater decline among women with moderate final numbers of confinements compared to women with large numbers of confinements.

Because of problems associated with a small number of cases, it is difficult to examine extensively the changes in the last and preceding intervals for individual villages while controlling at the same time for the final number of confinements. For this reason, the results are presented in Table 12.2 for two pairs of villages only. By combining villages into pairs rather than treating them individually, the problems associated with small case numbers is reduced to some extent. The particular pairs shown have been chosen to maximize the contrast in the extent to which family limitation characterized their populations during the period under observation. At the same time, the villages are all characterized by relatively similar average birth intervals, particularly once the last interval is excluded. Grafenhausen and Herbolzheim are treated together because their populations experienced the earliest and most extensive increase in family limitation, as indicated by the Coale–Trussell m index (see Table 11.1), while Kappel and Öschelbronn are paired because they represent two villages which are characterized by a relative absence of family limitation even by the end of the nineteenth century, at least as indicated by the Coale–Trussell m index. Cohorts have been grouped, in the case of the village comparisons, into couples who married prior to 1825 and those who married from 1825 through to the end of the nineteenth century, since this division corresponds most closely to the onset of the spread of family limitation in Grafenhausen and Herbolzheim.

Consistent with the assumption that increases in the last birth interval over time are associated with increased attempts at family limitation, the last interval increases in the case of the Grafenhausen and Herbolzheim pair but not in the case of the Kappel and Öschelbronn pair. This holds for almost all categories of final number of confinements. In contrast to the combined sample of all villages, couples with relatively high final numbers of confinements in Grafenhausen and Herbolzheim also experienced an increase in the last interval, raising some doubts about the absence of family limitation attempts among even those who end up with large family sizes. Perhaps this reflects the more advanced stage of the spread of family limitation in these two villages compared to the sample as a whole.

When the final number of confinements is ignored, there is no change in the average of intervals preceding the last in the case of Grafenhausen and Herbolzheim, but a distinct decline in the case of Kappel and Öschelbronn. For the latter pair of villages, this decline characterizes couples regardless of the final number of confinements

Table 12.2. *Mean last interconfinement interval, mean of all preceding intervals, mean age at first confinement, and change in mean of all preceding intervals adjusted for mean age at first confinement, by final number of confinements and marriage cohort for selected villages*

	Final number of confinements						
	3	4	5	6	7–10	11+	Total
Grafenhausen and Herbolzheim							
Last interval							
1700–1824	(42.5)	53.0	42.8	41.5	37.4	30.3	39.9
1825–99	51.0	53.5	45.4	44.3	39.4	32.2	45.2
Change	8.5	0.5	2.6	2.8	2.0	1.9	5.3
All preceding intervals[a]							
1700–1824	(32.9)	30.8	28.6	29.0	26.9	22.4	27.7
1825–99	29.9	31.5	30.1	26.5	24.6	19.5	27.7
Change	−3.0	0.7	1.5	−2.5	−2.3	−2.9	0.0
Age at first confinement							
1700–1824	(31.4)	29.7	29.6	27.8	24.7	22.0	26.4
1825–99	27.8	26.8	26.4	26.1	25.0	23.3	26.1
Change	−3.6	−2.9	−3.2	−1.7	0.3	1.3	−0.3
Adjusted mean of all preceding intervals[a] [b]							
Change	−6.8	−1.1	−2.0	−4.0	−2.0	−2.2	−0.2
Kappel and Öschelbronn							
Last interval							
1700–1824	(48.8)	(49.0)	46.9	(45.1)	40.3	(36.6)	42.9
1825–99	(51.6)	42.8	46.4	43.3	37.2	33.8	40.6
Change	2.8	−6.2	−0.5	−1.8	−3.1	−2.8	−2.3
All preceding intervals[a]							
1700–1824	(38.0)	(32.8)	32.6	(30.2)	27.5	(21.5)	29.4
1825–99	(32.8)	27.9	28.1	28.1	24.1	19.3	25.7
Change	−5.2	−4.9	−4.5	−2.1	−3.4	−2.2	−3.7
Age at first confinement							
1700–1824	(30.3)	(27.2)	26.7	(27.0)	24.2	22.1	(25.5)
1825–99	(29.7)	29.1	27.1	25.9	25.8	24.2	26.5
Change	−0.6	1.9	0.4	−1.1	1.7	2.1	1.0
Adjusted mean of all preceding intervals[a] [b]							
Change	−6.2	−3.7	−4.2	−2.8	−2.6	−1.2	−3.5

Note: All mean intervals are expressed in months. Results are subject to

they achieved. The pattern is irregular for Grafenhausen and Herbolzheim. Declines are evident for some but not for other groupings of
final number of confinements.

Differences are also evident between the two pairs of villages with
respect to changes in the average age at first confinement. For the
Kappel and Öschelbronn pair, a slight increase occurs for most categories of final number of confinements. For the Grafenhausen and
Herbolzheim pair, substantial decreases are evident for categories in
the range of moderate final parity, while slight increases characterize
the higher categories. After statistically adjusting for these changes in
the age at first confinement, declines in the mean interval, excluding
the last, are evident for all categories of final number of confinements
in the Grafenhausen and Herbolzheim pair, as well as in the Kappel
and Öschelbronn pair.

The finding that the average interval, excluding the last, generally
declined within categories of final number of confinements, at least
once adjustment is made for changes in the age at which childbearing
started, does not completely rule out the practice of deliberate spacing
of births as a strategy to control fertility in the sample village populations during the period under observation. Increases in the underlying
level of natural fertility may obscure efforts made to deliberately
postpone the next birth. In addition, deliberate spacing may have
existed during what is assumed to be the natural fertility period that
serves as the basis for comparison when judging change. Nevertheless, the evidence suggests that deliberate birth spacing could have
been of only minimal importance at most, and may well have been
absent, during the initial stages of the fertility transition.

While examining birth intervals according to the final number of
confinements is of considerable analytical value, it is also useful to
summarize trends, especially when dealing with individual villages in
which the number of cases is considerably reduced. In order to

Notes to Table 12.2 – cont.
restrictions 1, 2, 3 and 4 (see Table A.1), and are limited to couples with at least
three confinements. Results in parentheses are based on less than 50 cases.
[a] The average preceding interval is expressed per woman and thus both the
results in the collapsed categories of final number of confinements and the
results for the total are weighted by the number of women rather than by the
number of intervals involved.
[b] Statistical adjustment for age at first confinement is accomplished through
separate multiple regression equations for each category of final number of
confinements, in which age at first confinement is entered as a covariate and
marriage cohort as a categorical variable.

examine whether changes in spacing behavior played a part in the changing reproductive patterns in particular villages, Figure 12.2 displays trends in the average interconfinement interval per married woman.[9] Given the propensity of changes in the last interval to reflect stopping behavior, results are shown separately for the last interval, for intervals excluding the last, and for all intervals together.

The results for the four villages in Baden are particularly interesting. In Grafenhausen, where a continuous fertility decline was evident from early in the nineteenth century and family limitation increased substantially as indicated by a number of measures, the average birth interval follows a slightly irregular trend toward higher levels for successive marriage cohorts from the end of the eighteenth century. This is largely attributable, however, to an increase in the last birth interval. The average birth interval excluding the last shows no consistent tendency to lengthen. In neighboring Rust, where a steady but more modest increase in family limitation was indicated throughout most of the nineteenth century but where marital fertility rose slightly, a (less pronounced) trend toward longer last intervals is also evident. This is accompanied by shorter birth spacing prior to the last interval and thus by a decline in the average of all intervals. In Herbolzheim, where there are also indications of increasing family limitation throughout most of the nineteenth century, the results are somewhat different. An increase in the average last interval apparent for the earlier marriage cohorts levels off for couples married after the first quarter of the nineteenth century. The average interval, excluding the last, shows a little change and thus the average of all intervals, after rising modestly, remains fairly constant for most marriage cohorts during the nineteenth century. In nearby Kappel, where there is little evidence of family limitation and where fertility rose during the nineteenth century, virtually no evidence of a lengthening in the last interval is apparent and the average of all intervals declines.

[9] The average birth interval can be expressed either in terms of a direct mean in which each *interval* receives equal weight or in terms of an average interval per woman in which each *woman* receives equal weight (see Wolfers, 'Birth intervals'). In the first case, women with larger families will contribute more intervals and thus exert a greater influence on determining the average interval than would women with fewer confinements. In the second case, an average interval is first computed per woman and then the average of these intervals is calculated such that each woman receives equal weight. Naturally, in both cases childless women, or women experiencing only one confinement, will not contribute to either measure. In general, averages based on intervals directly are shorter than those expressed per woman, since intervals associated with large numbers of confinements are typically shorter than those associated with smaller completed family sizes. For an examination of interval data for the purpose of detecting signs of deliberate spacing, average intervals per woman seem more appropriate, since birth control is a couple-level phenomenon.

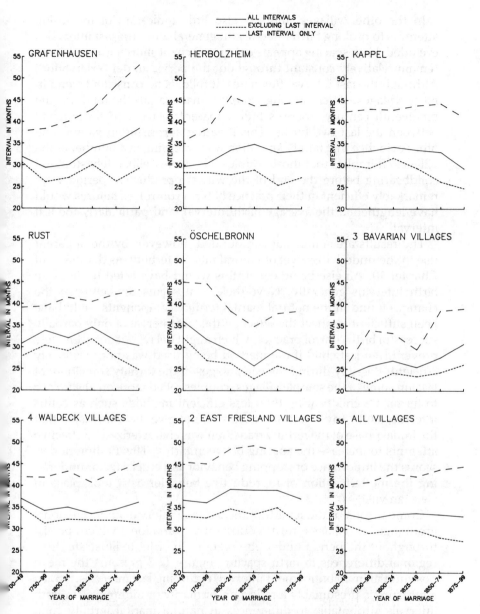

Figure 12.2. *Average interconfinement interval per married woman by village and year of marriage*. Results are subject to restrictions 2, 3 and 4 (see Table A.1). Results for all intervals and last intervals only are based on women with at least two confinements; results for intervals excluding the last are based on women with at least three confinements

In the other villages, there is also little indication of increasing attempts to prolong birth intervals. In general, once the last interval is excluded, birth spacing appears either to occur at shorter intervals or to remain relatively constant throughout the period under observation. Although the last interval fluctuates, it follows no consistent trend in most villages. Even among couples married at the end of the nineteenth century, there is little apparent increase in the interval between the last two births. This is rather surprising in view of the other evidence that family limitation was emerging in a number of the villages. It implies that those couples who were deliberately stopping childbearing before the end of the wife's reproductive period were remarkably efficient in their practice of birth control, as failures would have lengthened the average birth interval, and particularly the last interval.

The results are somewhat confounded, however, by the apparent rise in the underlying level of natural marital fertility, as discussed in Chapter 10. All else being equal, this would have acted to decrease birth intervals generally. Nevertheless, it seems unlikely that the changes found in the natural marital fertility components could have been sufficient to offset the effect on the last interval of only partially successful birth control practice, which might delay, but not ultimately prevent, the last child if the method being used was not reasonably efficient. Possibly during the early stages of the fertility transition, at least in some of the sample villages, couples relied more on abstinence to terminate childbearing than less efficient methods such as coitus interruptus. In any event, the trends do not give the impression that the initial phase of the fertility transition was characterized by effective attempts to increase the spacing between births. This finding underscores the importance of stopping behavior as a crucial factor underlying the modernization of reproductive behavior as it took place in German villages.

Comparisons of the length of the average interval among regional groupings of villages reveal substantial variations which persist throughout the period under observation. In order to illustrate these regional differences in birth spacing, Figure 12.3 presents the mean postnuptial interconfinement interval, excluding last intervals.[10] Such a measure is presumably a reflection primarily of differences in birth intervals attributable to differences in natural marital fertility components. With the exception of the East Frisian populations, there is a general tendency for the interval to decline during the period under

[10] For the purpose of this particular analysis, a direct mean of intervals is taken rather than the average interval per woman.

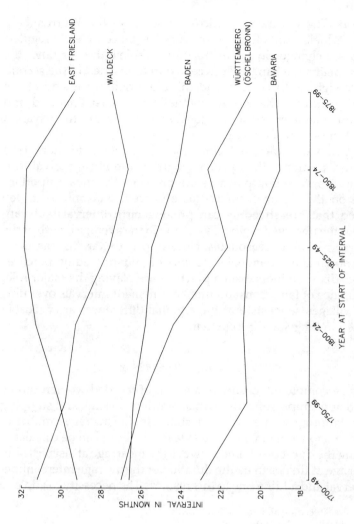

Figure 12.3. *Mean postnuptial interconfinement interval by region and year at start of interval. Last intervals are excluded. Results are subject to restriction 6 (see Table A.1)*

observation. The decline is particularly sharp in the Württemberg village of Öschelbronn, although the trend is not completely regular. Despite these changes in the average interval length over time, the ordering remains unchanged between couples married in the second half of the eighteenth century and those married at the end of the nineteenth century. The village populations in East Friesland and Waldeck are characterized by the longest intervals and the Bavarian villages by the shortest intervals.

Although a wide variety of factors, including deliberate attempts to space births, influence the average length of the birth interval, differences in breastfeeding practices are probably the most important influence on the regional differences observed. Not only is it well established that breastfeeding can prolong birth intervals substantially,[11] but the observed regional variation in the average length of the intervals corresponds reasonably closely to expectations based on what is known about regional differences in infant-feeding practices (see Appendix F). If indeed such practices are playing the major role, the persistence of fairly constant interconfinement intervals over time for most villages suggests that the regional differences are probably entrenched in long-standing custom.

Starting, spacing, and stopping

The average completed fertility of a group of married women can be expressed as a simple function of their starting, spacing and stopping behavior. Ignoring women who are childless, the average number of confinements to women who have at least one birth can be calculated by dividing the duration of time between the mean age at last birth and the mean age at first birth by the duration of the average interconfinement interval and adding one to this result.[12] The necessity to add one

[11] Knodel, 'Breast feeding and population growth.'
[12] More specifically, $C = 1 + (\{\text{ratio } L - F; I\})$ where

> C = mean number of confinements per fertile woman;
> L = mean age at last birth;
> F = mean age at first birth;
> I = mean interconfinement interval among women with at least two confinements.

> This approach is a simplification of one developed by McDonald (*Nuptiality*). In the approach advocated by McDonald, allowance is made for the proportion of women who are childless, and starting behavior is represented by the mean age of marriage in combination with the mean interval between marriage and first birth so that the impact of each of these two components of starting behavior can be investigated. Moreover, he advocates a stepwise standardization approach to presenting results rather than that of estimating the impact of each factor separately. Since there is little

arises because the number of intervals is one less than the number of confinements (given that the calculation does not include the interval between marriage and first birth). This representation incorporates a measure each of starting, stopping, and spacing (the average age at first birth, the average age at last birth, and the average interconfinement interval) in a single relationship.

Thus it is possible within a simple framework to estimate the impact of each separate component on changes in the average number of confinements over time, as well as on differences between villages in the average number of confinements. Note, however, that such a framework ignores several complexities that are likely to be involved in the actual process. On the one hand, changes in the last interval, which may in fact reflect attempts at stopping for the reasons discussed above, are incorporated into the measure of spacing and are thus attributed to the contribution of spacing to the course of fertility decline or to the contrasts between villages. On the other hand, pure spacing behavior, to the extent it lengthened intervals between births, would also lengthen the 'open interval' between last birth and the age at which reproductive ability is lost, thus lowering the age at last birth if the age at loss of reproductive capacity remains constant. Hence some effect of spacing would be attributed to the effect of stopping behavior.[13] Also not taken into account is the fact that the average interconfinement interval per woman would be expected to decrease, as discussed above, if only a stopping strategy was being followed and no attempts to deliberately prolong spacing were being made. These latter two factors operate to understate the role of spacing. Since these

reason to believe that childlessness is voluntary in the village populations under study during the period under observation, and given the high proportion of married couples who either start childbearing before marriage or experience bridal pregnancy, the simpler formulation stated above is used.

[13] The age at last birth will be reduced by about half the amount that the average preceding birth interval is lengthened. Imagine a population in which every woman has a birth every two years and loses her reproductive capability at her 45th birthday. Assuming women can start childbearing at any age, last births will be evenly distributed throughout ages 43 and 44 and the mean age of last birth would be 44.0. Imagine a change in the spacing pattern such that women have a birth every four years rather than every two years, but that there is no change in the age at which reproduction ability is lost. Last births will now be distributed evenly throughout ages 41 and 44 and the mean age of last birth will fall to 43.0. Thus a two-year extension of birth intervals leads to a one-year decline in the age of the mother at last birth. In the case of the German villages under investigation, the effect of any deliberate lengthening of birth intervals must be trivial. For example, if for the sake of argument we made the most extreme assumption – that the entire lengthening of the last interval was due to deliberate spacing rather than failed stopping – the less than four-month increase in the last interval for the sample as a whole would result in a less than two-month reduction in the age at last birth.

various biases do not all operate in the same direction, they will offset each other to some extent.

The estimated effects of changes in starting, spacing and stopping behavior on the total number of confinements, between the marriage cohorts of 1750–99 and each subsequent quarter-century marriage cohort during the nineteenth century, are shown in Table 12.3 for the combined sample of all villages. In addition, the estimated effects of changes between the 1750–99 and 1875–99 marriage cohorts are shown for each village or village set separately. The results indicate the effect that the observed change in one of the components would have on the total number of confinements had the other two components remained as they were for the earlier cohort.[14] It should be pointed out that, due to an interaction effect among the components, the sum of the changes as indicated separately does not necessarily equal the total observed change in the average number of confinements. The magnitude of this interaction effect can be gauged by comparing the sum of the changes indicated by the three components together and the actual observed change. In general, the difference is very small and thus the effect of such interaction can be largely ignored.

For the combined sample of all villages, the results indicate that throughout the nineteenth century changes in the age at last birth had a considerably larger implication for changes in couples' fertility than either of the other two components. Since the age at last birth fell throughout the nineteenth century, changes in stopping behavior had

---

[14] This is done simply by substituting in the equation the changed value of the component whose impact is being estimated, while retaining the unchanged (1750–99) values of the other components, and then comparing the result with the number of confinements when all three unchanged (1750–99) values are retained. For example, for the combined sample of all villages, the following values of the components characterize the 1750–99 and 1875–99 cohorts:

	1750–99	1875–99
L (in years)	40.52	37.86
F (in years)	27.50	26.48
I (in years)	2.473	2.352

The average number of confinements (C) to fertile women in the 1750–99 marriage cohort is 6.26 or $1+[(40.52-27.50)/2.473]$. To determine the impact of the change in age at last birth (L) between the 1750–99 and the 1875–99 cohorts, the 1875–99 value of L is substituted for the 1750–99 value, yielding 5.19 confinements: $5.19 = 1+[(37.86-27.50)/2.473]$. Since $5.19/6.26 = .83$, the amount that the total number of confinements would have declined due to changes in the age at last birth alone is 17 percent. Note that the data used for this calculation are based on all women with at least one confinement and thus values for L and F do not correspond exactly to those shown in Table 12.1 and 12.2, which are based on women with at least three confinements.

Table 12.3. *Estimated effect of changes in age at first birth, interconfinement interval, and age at last birth on the mean total number of confinements among women who experienced at least one confinement*

Basis of comparison, village and marriage cohort	Observed percentage change in total confinements	Percentage change expected due to observed change in		
		Age at first birth	Confinement intervals	Age at last birth
Comparison with all villages, 1750–99				
All villages, 1800–24	−4.2	0.9	−1.9	−3.1
All villages, 1825–49	−9.5	−1.4	−1.1	−7.1
All villages, 1850–74	−8.1	1.0	1.5	−10.4
All villages, 1875–99	−6.8	6.6	4.4	−17.1
Comparison with same village 1750–99				
Grafenhausen, 1875–99	−33.2	15.1	−17.8	−34.5
Herbolzheim, 1875–99	−19.3	0.3	0.4	−20.0
Kappel, 1875–99	−2.0	−0.9	14.1	−12.9
Rust, 1875–99	20.0	15.4	14.6	−10.5
Öschelbronn, 1875–99	−0.6	−11.5	16.2	−2.6
Bavarian villages, 1875–99	−12.0	13.3	−3.3	−22.3
Waldeck villages, 1875–99	−5.9	11.5	1.5	−18.7
Middels, 1875–99	−14.9	0.2	0.2	−14.6

Note: Results are subject to restrictions 1, 2, 3 and 4 (see Table A.1). Werdum is omitted from the individual village comparisons because of insufficient cases for the 1875–99 marriage cohort.

a continuous and increasingly negative impact on the total number of confinements relative to the situation at the end of the eighteenth century. In contrast, the implications of changes in starting and spacing behavior were not consistently in the same direction, although by the end of the nineteenth century changes in either of these would have acted to increase the total number of confinements. Thus, according to this simple accounting framework, for the combined sample of all villages the onset of fertility transition was a matter of increased stopping behavior acting not only to reduce fertility but also to compensate for fertility-enhancing changes in starting and spacing behavior.

Estimates of changes in the total number of confinements for couples married during the last half of the eighteenth century and the last quarter of the nineteenth century are also shown for the individual villages or village sets. The comparison between these particular cohorts was chosen since the earlier cohort presumably represents the situation prior to any sign of the onset of the fertility transition, while the most recent cohort represents the most advanced stage of the fertility transition wherever it had begun.

Of particular interest are those villages in which a substantial decline in the total number of confinements had actually occurred by the end of the nineteenth century. Consistent with the trend in the index of marital fertility presented in Chapter 10, Grafenhausen stands out as experiencing the most extensive fertility decline, with the average number of confinements per fertile couple declining by a third between the last half of the eighteenth century and the end of the nineteenth century. The most important component of the decline in fertility in Grafenhausen is a reduction in the age at last birth. Increases in the interconfinement interval also depressed fertility moderately, but in the case of Grafenhausen this is largely a result of an increase in the length of the last interval, with intervals prior to the last remaining relatively stable (see Figure 12.2). Thus even much of the impact of spacing in Grafenhausen on fertility decline could well be a reflection of attempts to stop childbearing. On the other hand, changes in the age at first birth would have acted to increase fertility had spacing and stopping remained as they were before the transition began.

The overwhelming dominance of stopping behavior in accounting for the decline in the average number of confinements is even clearer in the other villages where substantial reductions in fertility took place. In Herbolzheim, the Bavarian villages, and Middels, where the average number of confinements per couple declined by more than 10 percent, changes in the age at last birth were responsible for virtually all of the change that occurred. In all three cases, changes in spacing behavior had a negligible impact, while changes in the age at first birth were either also negligible or, in the case of the Bavarian villages, changed in a fertility-enhancing direction.

Although the Waldeck villages show only a modest decline in fertility as measured by the average number of confinements, this is a net result of a substantial negative impact attributable to changes in stopping behavior combined with an earlier start to childbearing. Changes in spacing behavior were negligible. Even in the remaining villages, where the average number of total confinements either changed very little or increased substantially (as in the case of Rust), stopping behavior changed in a direction that would by itself depress fertility. Only in Öschelbronn was the change in the age at last birth negligible and hence of little influence. In these cases, the fertility-depressing effect of increased stopping behavior was compensated for by fertility-enhancing changes in birth spacing. In the case of Rust, the age at first birth also declined and, in combination with the reduction in birth spacing, resulted in a substantial increase in the average number of confinements despite the modest impact of changes in the age at last birth.

In brief, the results for the individual villages generally confirm the importance and dominance of stopping behavior at the onset of the fertility transition in rural Germany. Even in those villages where the average number of confinements did not decline, stopping behavior was changing in a direction consistent with lower fertility but was counteracted by changes in either starting or spacing behavior, or both, which acted to negate the depressing effect of the declining age at last birth. Only in Grafenhausen was there any significant fertility-depressing effect of spacing behavior, but even in this case, because the spacing changes were due mainly to a lengthening of last intervals, they can be interpreted largely as a reflection of increased stopping attempts. The fact, however, that the underlying level of natural fertility was changing in such a way as to shorten spacing between confinements should be kept in mind. Nevertheless, even allowing for this, it seems clear that changes in spacing were, at most, an unimportant ingredient in the fertility transition as it emerged in rural Germany.

The simple accounting framework for estimating the impact of starting, spacing, and stopping can also be applied to an analysis of inter-village differences in fertility at different stages of the fertility transition (as opposed to over-time changes in fertility within villages). The results of inter-village comparisons are shown in Table 12.4 for both the 1750–99 and the 1875–99 marriage cohorts. As in the previous

Table 12.4. *Estimated effect of differences between the combined sample and the individual villages in age at first birth, interconfinement interval, and age at last birth in accounting for differences in the mean total number of confinements among women who experienced at least one confinement*

Marriage cohort and village (all comparisons with combined sample of all villages)	Observed percentage difference in total confinements	Percentage difference expected due to observed differences in		
		Age at first birth	Confinement intervals	Age at last birth
1750–99				
Grafenhausen	8.6	0.2	9.0	−0.4
Herbolzheim	8.1	2.7	2.3	3.1
Kappel	2.8	1.2	−2.4	3.9
Rust	−7.6	−3.9	−1.7	−2.0
Öschelbronn	8.8	14.4	3.3	−9.1
Bavarian villages	7.6	−17.1	24.4	4.1
Waldeck villages	−4.5	−1.2	−7.0	4.0
Middels	0.3	14.6	−11.7	−0.7
Werdum	−17.2	−3.7	−8.8	−5.5
1875–99				
Grafenhausen	−22.1	9.5	−13.8	−19.3
Herbolzheim	−6.4	−4.2	−1.5	−0.9
Kappel	8.1	−6.8	6.4	8.3
Rust	19.0	4.5	7.9	5.8
Öschelbronn	16.0	−4.7	14.5	6.0
Bavarian villages	1.5	−14.3	14.9	3.0
Waldeck villages	−3.6	4.7	−9.4	1.8
Middels	−7.7	9.3	−14.9	−0.6

Note: Results are subject to restrictions 1, 2, 3 and 4 (see Table A.1). Werdum is omitted from the 1875–99 marriage cohort comparisons of individual villages with the combined sample of all villages because of insufficient cases.

analysis, these cohorts were chosen because they represent, in the case of the 1750–99 cohort, a clearly pre-transition situation and, in the case of the 1875–99 cohort, the most advanced stage of the fertility transition during the period under observation. In both cases, the standard for comparison is the value of the starting, spacing and stopping parameters characteristic of the combined sample of all villages for the same marriage cohort.

For the 1750–99 cohort, substantial variations in fertility are reflected in the observed differences between the average number of confinements characteristic of couples in a particular village and those characteristic of the overall sample. By far the lowest fertility is found in Werdum; in contrast, no single village stands out with respect to the highest fertility. It should be borne in mind that fertility in this analysis is measured in terms of the average number of confinements to completed families and thus is sensitive not only to the level of marital fertility, as investigated in Chapter 10, but also to the age at first birth, which will closely reflect the differences in average age at marriage and hence nuptiality patterns. Thus the ordering of villages by level of fertility measured in terms of the average number of total confinements to married couples is not necessarily the same as it is when consideration is given to marital fertility alone. The most important component contributing to the relatively low number of confinements in Werdum is longer birth intervals. However, all three components in Werdum act to depress its fertility during the second half of the eighteenth century. Unusually long intervals also depressed fertility in nearby Middels, but these are counteracted by a relatively early starting pattern.

Overall, the least impact among the three components of reproductive behavior for the 1750–99 cohort is inter-village variation in the age at last birth. In most cases, this would account for only a few percentage points difference in the total number of confinements compared to the combined sample. In contrast, both starting and spacing components show considerable inter-village variation in their potential impact. The most extreme case is found for the Bavarian villages, in which the age at first birth is very late but birth intervals are very short, and thus starting behavior has a very substantial fertility-depressing effect, while spacing has a very substantial fertility-enhancing effect. Since these are partially counterbalancing, the net result is only a moderately higher fertility than is found for the combined sample. Indeed, besides Werdum, only in Herbolzheim do all three components operate in the same direction but, unlike Werdum, the result only modestly enhances fertility since the influence of each of the separate components is only minimal. In brief, the pre-transition situation, as represented by couples married during the last half of the eighteenth century, reveals a varied mixture of starting, spacing and stopping patterns which often operate to counteract each other, thus producing a moderating result for the overall inter-village variation in the total number of confinements.

For the marriage cohort at the end of the nineteenth century, considerably greater variation in fertility as measured by the average number of confinements is evident. Moreover, somewhat greater variation is also evident in the impact implied by the separate components, particularly spacing and stopping. Nevertheless, the variations in the impact implied by differences in age at last birth are relatively modest, with the exception of Grafenhausen, where the decline in age at last birth progressed considerably further during the period studied than it did anywhere else. In contrast, variations in spacing behavior have the largest implications for inter-village variations in total confinements. In both Öschelbronn and the Bavarian villages, the spacing patterns by themselves would imply close to 15 percent higher fertility than for the combined sample, while in Grafenhausen and Middels the spacing pattern would imply almost 15 percent lower fertility than that found for the combined sample. In comparison, inter-village variations in the age at last birth imply considerably less than a 10 percent difference, with only the exception of Grafenhausen. Variations in the starting patterns as measured by age at first birth show an intermediate impact on completed fertility.

The relative roles of the starting, spacing and stopping components of reproductive behavior are thus quite different when accounting for inter-village variation than when accounting for the course of fertility during the onset of the fertility transition. Stopping behavior plays the most important role in fertility change as the transition gets under way, but is the least important factor in accounting for inter-village variation at different stages of the fertility transition. In contrast, spacing behavior is a less important component of fertility change but is quite prominent in accounting for inter-village variation, especially for couples married toward the end of the nineteenth century. Finally, starting behavior is moderately important both in accounting for changes over time and in accounting for inter-village variation. The unimportance of stopping behavior in accounting for inter-village variation results from the fact that age at last birth not only varied little among villages prior to the onset of the fertility transition but also changed in the same direction in all villages over the nineteenth century. Thus, although inter-village variation in age at last birth increased somewhat by the end of the nineteenth century, it was moderated considerably by the common trend toward decline.

Proportion of couples effectively stopping

Weir has proposed a technique for estimating the proportion of couples in a given marriage cohort who effectively practice birth control in order to curtail childbearing at an earlier point in the reproductive cycle than would have occurred in the absence of such control. Given the predominant role that stopping behavior appears to have occupied in the initiation of the fertility transition in the sample of German villages, such an estimate is of particular interest and would provide important information on the extent to which family limitation had spread through the population. The technique is relatively simple and straightforward. It is based on changes in the distribution of women by age at last birth. Provided the distribution is known that would prevail in the absence of deliberate stopping, that is with natural fertility, the proportion of women who effectively stop under conditions of deliberate family limitation can be determined by comparing the actually prevailing distribution of age at last birth with the distribution under natural fertility.

As Weir points out, the proportion of women who have not yet had their last birth *before* any given age x is readily apparent from the distribution of ages at last birth.[15] Of this proportion, some fraction can be expected to cease childbearing with a birth at age x without any deliberate effort to control fertility. This proportion can be determined by comparing the observed distribution of ages at last birth to the distribution assumed to represent the appropriate natural fertility situation. If, in the observed distribution, a higher proportion of women have their last birth at a particular given age than is expected in the absence of control, the surplus can be interpreted as those who stop at that age due to effective stopping behavior. By summing the surpluses (and deficits) at each given age over the reproductive age span, the total proportion who are effectively stopping can be determined.[16] An implicit assumption of this technique is that the

---

[15] Weir, 'Fertility transition,' pp. 99–100.

[16] More specifically, the total proportion effectively stopping through deliberate efforts at stopping equals $\{\text{sum } (T\{\text{sub } x\})\}; x=0; x=\infty\}$ and

$$T_x=(1-q_x)\,S_x-S_{x+1}$$

where

T_x=the proportion of all women deliberately stopping at age x;

physiological ability to continue childbearing is similar under conditions of natural fertility and fertility control.

In this study, this technique is applied by using the distribution of ages at last birth for the 1750–99 marriage cohort as the distribution representing natural fertility. Such an assumption seems justified given that there was relatively little inter-village variation in average age at last birth for this cohort despite the substantial differences in marital fertility levels and the fact that, to the extent that any substantial change occurred in age at last birth for subsequent marriage cohorts, it was always toward a lower age. For the purpose of this analysis, effective stopping is arbitrarily defined as having ceased childbearing one year or more before the age that would have been expected under natural fertility conditions.

Estimates of the proportion of couples effectively stopping childbearing due to deliberate fertility control in cohorts married during the nineteenth century are shown in Table 12.5 for the combined sample of all villages and the individual villages or village sets. The analysis is limited to women who started childbearing prior to age 40. In the case of the combined sample of all villages, the results are shown separately for different categories of women according to the age at which they had their first birth. In the case of the results for the individual villages or village sets, calculations were performed separately for each category of women according to age at first birth, but have been aggregated into a single total figure based on a weighted average of these age-at-first-birth groups in order to avoid the problems associated with small numbers of cases. A total figure based on a weighted average of the separate age-at-first-birth groups is also presented for the combined sample of all villages.

For the combined sample, the results point to an increase in the proportion of women effectively stopping childbearing during the nineteenth century for each of the age-at-first-birth categories. Somewhat surprisingly, there is no consistent relationship between the age at first birth and the proportion estimated as deliberately stopping. Assuming that the desired number of children is independent of age at starting childbearing, an inverse relationship

q_x=the expected proportion of women at age x who, under conditions of natural fertility, would not be expected to continue childbearing;

$1-q_x$=the expected proportion of women at age x who would be expected to continue childbearing under conditions of natural fertility;

S_x=the observed proportion of women having last births at ages x and above.

The technique and specifics of the calculations are described in some detail in Weir, 'Fertility transition.'

Table 12.5. *Estimated proportion of couples effectively stopping child-bearing due to deliberate fertility control, by marriage cohort and village, and for the combined sample of all villages by age at first birth*

	Marriage cohort		
	1800–49	1850–74	1875–99
All villages (age at first birth)			
Under 25	7	22	42
25–29	19	28	37
30–34	4	15	29
35–39	30	20	(47)
Total	12	23	39
Village (all ages at first birth under 40)			
Grafenhausen	15	44	58
Herbolzheim	36	50	54
Kappel	18	33	34
Rust	−22	7	28
Öschelbronn	5	1	21
Bavarian villages	37	23	47
Waldeck villages	3	−3	32
Middels	−1	20	46
Werdum	2	34	—

Note: Results refer to women with a first birth prior to age 40 and are subject to retrictions 1, 2, 3 and 4 (see Table A.1). Results in parentheses are based on 20–49 cases; results based on less than 20 cases are omitted.

would have been expected. The reason for this is that a lower proportion of women who begin their childbearing at later ages would presumably achieve any particular family size before reaching the end of their physiological reproductive span than would be true of those who started at an earlier age. One reason for the lack of such a relationship may be the relatively small number of cases on which the results are based for women who had a first birth at ages 35 to 39, particularly given the sensitivity of the technique to the representativeness of the distribution of ages at last birth assumed to characterize the natural fertility situation. It is also possible that desired fertility and age at first birth are not independent. If women who began childbearing at later ages had lower fertility desires than women who began their reproductive careers at earlier ages, the relationship between age at marriage and the proportion stopping would be weakened.

While in some respects the results for the individual villages and village sets conform to a pattern shown by other indicators of family limitation, in particular trends in the Coale–Trussell *m* index, there are also some unexpected results. The negative percentages estimated as effectively controlling fertility for the 1800–49 marriage cohort in Rust and Middels, as well as for the 1850–74 cohort in the Waldeck villages, presumably reflect sampling error due to the small numbers of cases occurring in individual villages. Another reason could be that the distribution for the 1750–99 marriage cohort does not accurately reflect the expected distribution under conditions of natural fertility.

In most villages the proportion estimated to be effective stoppers increased for successive marriage cohorts during the nineteenth century. Consistent with other measures of family limitation, the highest proportions of effective stoppers by the end of the century are found in Grafenhausen and Herbolzheim. Somewhat surprisingly, all villages, including those which lack other signs of family limitation, in particular Kappel and Öschelbronn, appear to be characterized by at least modest proportions of women in the 1875–99 marriage cohort effectively stopping childbearing through deliberate efforts. Also surprisingly, a relatively high proportion of couples are estimated as deliberately stopping in the Bavarian villages, for women married in the first half of the nineteenth century. It would probably be a mistake to take these results literally given the sensitivity of the technique to the accuracy of establishing the distribution of ages at last birth under natural fertility conditions, and the likely sampling variation when only modest numbers of couples are available on which to base the estimates. Nevertheless, the results generally confirm the spread of family limitation in German villages by the end of the nineteenth century and substantiate further the pattern of considerably divergent paths followed in this process by the different villages.

Discussion

In the chapters constituting this section on marital reproduction, a variety of approaches based on indirect evidence have been examined with the aim of detecting the existence and progress of deliberate efforts to control marital fertility. Most attention has been paid to evidence thought to reflect the extent to which couples sought to terminate childbearing before the end of the reproductive span as a way to limit final family size. Some consideration has also been directed toward evidence of deliberate spacing efforts as an alternative strategy for restricting fertility. It is now well recognized that the levels of natural marital fertility can vary substantially and thus little can be inferred about deliberate control from information on the fertility level alone, at least as far as a fairly wide range of levels is concerned.[17] Indeed, the German villages in this study are a good example of this. Even trends in marital fertility levels do not necessarily indicate changes of fertility control: as is evident from Chapter 10, changes in the underlying components of natural marital fertility can counteract and thereby obscure the impact of increasing fertility control on fertility levels. Nevertheless, considerable information can be derived from family reconstitution data to reveal the presence, nature, and extent of marital fertility control.

Various aspects of the age pattern of marital fertility, the age at last birth, and parity progression probabilities can all shed light on the presence, progress, and extent of deliberate family limitation. The fact that prior expectations concerning these aspects of reproductive behavior under conditions of natural fertility can be established permits the detection of deliberate attempts to stop or slow childbearing prior to the end of the reproductive age span. Examination of spacing patterns can also be informative but, given the substantial variation expected even in the absence of control, distinguishing deliberate attempts to delay a subsequent birth from effects of non-volitional determinants of birth intervals is difficult.

These indirect measures should be considered no more than rough indicators of fertility control. Precise and certain identification of the onset and extent of deliberate marital fertility control from information on fertility behavior alone is beyond the present techniques of historical demography, and may well remain so indefinitely. Thus, for the present, the application of a variety of measures and analyses is probably the soundest strategy for research on this topic. The fact that the results will not be completely consistent, as in the case of this study, should be seen as a useful reminder of the imperfections of the data and methods. Nevertheless, the composite picture that emerges is far more informative about reproductive behavior in the past than was imagined possible even a few decades ago.

A number of questions about the behavioral changes involved in the fertility transition, and how they relate to the pre-transition situation, have run through much of this section on marital reproduction. An appropriate way to conclude the section is to summarize briefly these questions and to assess the extent to which they have been answered.

First, were effective attempts at family size limitation through efforts to stop childbearing prior to the end of the reproductive span truly absent among the marriage cohorts labeled as those with natural

[17] Knodel, 'Natural fertility: patterns, levels and trends.'

fertility? While it is not possible to rule out all deliberate stopping behavior, it seems safe to conclude that it was minimal at most. The evidence for this is the similarity of the observed age pattern of marital fertility with the pattern that would be expected under conditions of natural fertility, the high and relatively uniform average ages at last birth characterizing villages with different levels of fertility, and the absence of substantial socio-economic variations in these aspects of reproduction as indicated by the lack of occupational differentials. Some additional evidence relevant to this issue is presented in the following two chapters in connection with analyses of the relationship between marital fertility and age at marriage, and the relationship between reproductive behavior and infant and child mortality.

Second, did couples constituting the natural fertility cohorts deliberately space children? A less confident answer can be provided to this question because of the greater difficulty in detecting the presence or absence of deliberate birth spacing. Inter-village variations in birth intervals fall well within the range that could be explained by differences in non-volitional factors and are roughly consistent with the differences that would be expected from what is known about regional patterns of infant-feeding practices. Detailed analyses of birth intervals by ultimate family size and birth order provide little evidence of deliberate spacing. They also do not rule out this possibility. Perhaps the development of more precise techniques for detecting efforts to postpone births will permit a more definitive judgment on this issue.

Third, were increased efforts at deliberate spacing an important component of the onset of the fertility transition? Here the evidence seems relatively clear. At least during the initial phases of the transition from natural to controlled fertility, couples did not resort to lengthening intervals between births. In general, the average interconfinement interval, especially when the last interval is excluded, either remained relatively constant or declined toward the end of the nineteenth century, a time by which the fertility transition was already under way in most villages. Interpretation of the results is somewhat complicated by the changes in the underlying level of natural fertility and difficulties in interpreting the significance of trends in the last birth interval. Nevertheless, it seems safe to conclude that spacing was not an important part of the early stage of the fertility transition in rural Germany.

Fourth, what was the role of attempts to terminate childbearing prior to the end of the reproductive span in initiating the fertility transition? The evidence here is also relatively clear. Deliberate stopping appears to be the major behavioral means through which marital fertility came under volitional control and is the major feature of reproductive change during the initial phases of the fertility transition. This is evident from the transformation of the age pattern of fertility and the decline in the age at last birth. An algebraic decomposition of changes in the average completed family size during the period under observation underscores the predominant role of stopping behavior as the major behavioral change depressing fertility.

These questions dealing with the relative roles of stopping and spacing in determining reproductive behavior patterns before and during the fertility transition are of some importance because of their bearing on discussions of whether the fertility transition involved an innovation–diffusion dimension, or whether it can be seen solely in terms of an adjustment process involving behavioral mechanisms already well entrenched in the pre-transition demographic regime.[18] The absence of family limitation in the sense of deliberate stopping behavior during the pre-transition period seems reasonably clear from the evidence presented for the sample village populations. It is more difficult, however, to prove that deliberate birth spacing was absent, although its presence is far from firmly established. Thus if the initial stage of the fertility transition is primarily the result of the introduction of family limitation through stopping behavior, and did not include the spread of spacing behavior as an important element, it would seem clear that a new behavioral mechanism was involved. This, then, would be consistent with the view that the process by which the fertility transition spread must be understood involved, at least in part, an important innovation–diffusion element. In contrast, if a substantial part of the fertility transition can be explained in terms of the extended spacing of births, it would be more difficult to deny that couples were simply adjusting their reproductive behavior to changing circumstances, utilizing an approach to controlling fertility that had already been established for some time in the past. While analysis of family reconstitution data cannot completely resolve this issue, at least not if based on the techniques employed in this study, it provides considerably more information than would be available from more conventional macro-level source material.

---

[18] Carlsson, 'Decline in fertility'; Knodel and van de Walle, 'Lessons from the past'; Anderton and Bean, 'Birth spacing and fertility limitation.'

PART V

Interrelationships in demographic behavior

13

Family size, fertility and nuptiality interrelationships

As indicated in Chapter 6, the feature of demographic behavior that most distinguished western Europe from other traditional societies prior to the secular fertility decline was a flexible nuptiality pattern characterized by relatively late ages of marriage for both men and women and substantial proportions who remained single throughout their adult years. Ever since Malthus called attention to the 'preventive check,' most analysts have recognized the central position of nuptiality in the European preindustrial demographic system.[1] Delayed or foregone marriage generally meant delayed or foregone reproduction, which was compensated for only in small part by non-marital reproductive activity. Social controls on entry into marriage, and hence the formation of socially sanctioned reproductive unions, were a crucial force in moderating population growth and provided the major adjustive mechanism through which a community's population and resources were kept in some sort of rough balance. Interrelationships between nuptiality and fertility and their consequences for family size, as they existed within the sample village populations, thus deserve close examination.

Trends and variation in family size

In studies based on family reconstitution data, family size is typically defined as the number of children born to couples whose marriage remained intact throughout the wife's reproductive span. Such marital unions are conventionally referred to as completed families in historical demography. In contrast, unions that are prematurely dissolved by death (or occasionally divorce) before the end of the childbearing years

[1] Wrigley and Schofield, *Population history of England*, Chapter 11; Mackenroth, *Bevölkerungslehre*.

are referred to as incomplete. In this study, completed unions are defined as those remaining intact until the wife reaches age 45. Given the infrequency with which births occur to women past age 45, using this age as a limit probably does little to distort the results, and allows the inclusion of a somewhat larger number of women than would be the case if an older age limit were chosen. It is important to bear in mind that a number of marital unions end before the wife reaches age 45, especially in the past (see Chapter 7), and that these marriages do not figure in the calculation of completed family size considered in the present chapter. Moreover, usually only children to the current marriage (including prenuptial births unless otherwise specified) are considered in the analysis, hence excluding children born to prior marriages of either spouse. When relationships with age at marriage are the focus of the analysis, it is useful to redefine completed family size exclusively in terms of legitimate children. Thus in some analyses, only postnuptial births are considered.

Given the considerable infant and childhood mortality risks that prevailed during the past, defining family size simply in terms of births provides an incomplete picture and exaggerates substantially the actual number of children a couple would rear. To allow for the influence of mortality on child loss, effective family size can also be defined in terms of surviving children. In the present chapter, survival to age 5 is used as the criterion to define surviving children. This age is chosen because it encompasses the age range of most pre-adult mortality and can be measured with reasonable confidence by using the methods of calculating infant and child mortality risks adopted in this study (see Appendix E). However, since the registration of infant and child deaths was deficient in some villages during the earlier part of the period under study, results referring to family size in terms of surviving children must be restricted to those years when death registration is judged to be relatively complete (see Appendix B).

The mean number of children ever born and children surviving to age 5 are shown in Table 13.1 by marriage cohort for the combined sample of all villages and by individual villages for all marriage cohorts combined. The average number of children ever born is shown both for all years and after the exclusion of those periods judged to be characterized by incomplete death registration. In general, the average number of children ever born is very similar whether or not the periods of poor death registration are excluded. For those marriage cohorts or villages that are not characterized by a period of incomplete death registration, the figures are, of course, identical.

The trend in family size across successive marriage cohorts, whether

Table 13.1. *Mean number of children ever born and children surviving to age 5 by year of marriage and by village*

	All years	Excluding periods with incomplete death registration		
	Children ever born	Children ever born	Survivors to age 5	Survivorship ratio
Year of marriage (all villages)				
1700–49	4.95	4.88	3.21	.66
1750–99	5.48	5.51	3.73	.68
1800–24	5.01	4.99	3.49	.70
1825–49	5.01	5.01	3.52	.70
1850–74	5.31	5.31	3.64	.69
1875–99	5.54	5.54	3.87	.70
1700–1899	5.25	5.27	3.63	.69
Village (marriages 1700–1899)				
Grafenhausen	5.11	5.12	3.38	.66
Herbolzheim	5.09	5.04	3.34	.66
Kappel	5.70	5.89	4.25	.72
Rust	5.67	5.76	3.96	.69
Öschelbronn	6.08	6.08	3.75	.62
Anhausen	5.00	5.18	2.84	.55
Gabelbach	5.73	5.66	3.60	.64
Kreuth	4.04	4.06	3.17	.78
Braunsen	5.33	5.33	3.76	.71
Höringhausen	5.28	5.28	3.79	.72
Massenhausen	4.97	5.10	3.62	.71
Vasbeck	5.45	5.45	3.82	.70
Middels	5.31	5.32	4.44	.83
Werdum	4.10	4.12	3.17	.77

Note: Results refer only to children of current marriage and are subject to restrictions 1, 2, 3 and 4 (see Table A.1). The survivorship ratio equals the survivors to age 5 divided by the children ever born.

measured in terms of children ever born or survivors to age 5, is rather irregular, although a distinct tendency to increase during the nineteenth century is evident. Unlike marital fertility, which declines between the last two quarter-century marriage cohorts in the nineteenth century (see Table 10.1), completed family size actually increases, with the highest values for the entire two-century period indicated for the cohort married at the end of the nineteenth century. The reason for this difference, besides the fact that the two measures are based on different subsets of couples, is that family size is influenced by a number of factors other than marital fertility. Changes in the age at first marriage, marital dissolution, remarriage probabilities, and age at remarriage all influence trends in the number of children ever born. The mean number of survivors to age 5 is further influenced by the levels of infant and child mortality. In fact, as indicated by the survivorship ratio, also shown in Table 13.1, the proportion of children ever born who survived to age 5 remained remarkably stable during the period under observation, particularly for the nineteenth century. For this reason, trends in family sizes as measured both by children ever born and by survivors to age 5 are closely parallel. Despite the various factors that could exert an influence, family size remained relatively constant over the entire two-century period under observation, fluctuating between slightly under five to slightly over five and a half children ever born. When mortality under age 5 is taken into account, completed effective family size remained above 3.2 and under 3.9 surviving children during the same period.

Temporal variation in family size is considerably less than inter-village differences, as might be expected given the substantial regional variations in age at marriage, marital fertility, and infant and child mortality risks. The average number of children ever born characteriz-ing the different villages ranges from slightly over 4 for both Kreuth and Werdum to over 6 for Öschelbronn. The number of survivors to age 5 ranges from under 3 for Anhausen to well over 4 for Kappel and Middels. The importance of factors other than marital fertility as determinants of completed family size is reflected in the lack of any substantial association at the village level between the mean number of postnuptial children ever born and the I_g' index of marital fertility. For example, for couples married between the mid-eighteenth and mid-nineteenth centuries, a correlation of only .12 is found between the two measures.

Age at marriage and family size

Individual-level relationships

Since completed family size is the result of a cumulative process over the couple's entire reproductive span, it tends to be closely related to the number of years the couple is exposed to the risk of childbearing. In populations where family limitation is not extensive and non-marital fertility is either negligible or much lower than marital fertility, age at entry into marriage is an extremely important determinant of a woman's completed family size. Even where family limitation prac-tices are widespread, a distinct association between age at first mar-riage and cumulative fertility among individual women can be expected.[2] The younger the age at marriage, the longer the couple's actual reproductive period and the larger the number of births they eventually have. The importance of this relationship in preindustrial Europe has been documented in many studies.

The mean number of postnuptially born children and survivors to age 5 are shown by age at marriage in Table 13.2 for the combined sample of all villages. Given the fact that premarital births to couples were also of some importance in the sample villages during the period under study, it is also of interest to examine family size based on all births to a couple. Thus the mean number of all children ever born and survivors to age 5, including those born prenuptially, are shown according to the mother's age at first birth. The age at which childbearing begins should reflect reasonably accurately the age at the start of sexual activity for a couple, allowing for the fact that the union would have begun an average of a year or two earlier. Childless women are included in the tabulation relating legitimate children to age at marriage, but are necessarily excluded from the results relating all children to age at first birth.

A clear inverse association between age at marriage and completed family size is evident for the village populations. This is true whether measured in terms of children ever born or surviving children, or whether measured in terms of the relationship between postnuptial births and age at marriage, or all births and age at first birth. Without exception, the average completed family size declines with each successive category of age at marriage or age at first birth. Women who married before age 20 had more than twice as many postnuptial births or surviving children as women who married in their early thirties. Because of the exclusion of childless women, the contrast is somewhat reduced when examining the relationship of all births to age at first birth, but even in this case women who had their first birth under age 20 had almost twice as many children ever born or surviving children as those who married in their early thirties.

McKeown has argued that changes in the age at marriage could have had only a negligible effect on population growth rates during the preindustrial past.[3] His reasoning is based on the commonly observed positive association between family size and the risks of infant and child mortality. According to his argument, any increase in the number of children born associated with a lowering of the age at marriage would be offset by an increase in infant and child mortality that would be associated with the resulting larger family sizes. The evidence

[2] van de Walle, 'Age at marriage.'   [3] McKeown, *Rise of populations.*

Table 13.2. *Mean number of postnuptial children ever born and survivors to age 5 by age at marriage, and mean number of total children ever born and survivors to age 5 by age at first birth, marriages 1700–1899*

Age at first marriage Age at first birth	Postnuptial births and survivors by age at marriage (including childless women)				All births and survivors by age at first birth (excluding childless women)			
	All years	Excluding incomplete death registration periods			All years	Excluding incomplete death registration periods		
	Children ever born	Children ever born	Survivors to age 5	Survivor-ship ratio	Children ever born	Children ever born	Survivors to age 5	Survivor-ship ratio
Under 20	7.94	7.96	5.61	.70	8.69	8.72	6.11	.70
20–24	6.78	6.74	4.71	.70	7.41	7.36	5.15	.70
25–29	5.57	5.55	3.77	.68	6.01	5.97	4.13	.69
30–34	3.85	3.87	2.55	.66	4.61	4.61	3.04	.65
35–39	1.92	1.94	1.21	.62	2.85	2.90	1.87	.64
40–49	0.34	0.34	0.21	.62	1.47	1.45	0.87	.60
All ages	5.23	5.23	3.60	.69	6.02	6.00	4.13	.69

Note: Results refer only to children of current marriages and are subject to restrictions 1, 2, 3 and 4 (see Table A.1). The survivorship ratio equals the number of survivors to age 5 divided by the number of children ever born.

presented in Table 13.2 clearly contradicts this argument. Not only does the mean number of survivors to age 5 decline steadily with age at marriage or with age at first birth, but the proportion of children surviving to age 5 is actually higher for women who marry early or who experience their first birth at a young age than it is for women who marry or start childbearing late. This no doubt reflects the fact that, compared to women who marry young or start childbearing at an early age, a much higher proportion of births to women who enter marriage or start childbearing late are born near the end of the mother's reproductive life, when infant mortality risks are highest.

Simple linear regression can be used to estimate the impact of age at marriage on children ever born. Table 13.3 presents the results separately for natural fertility marriage cohorts and family limitation cohorts, as well as for all marriage cohorts combined. The distinction between natural fertility and family limitation cohorts is described in Chapter 11 and utilizes a value of .30 on the Coale–Trussell m index as the dividing point. The impact of age at marriage is expected to be somewhat greater for the natural fertility cohorts than for the family limitation cohorts, since in the latter case couples who marry early would have the option to cease childbearing earlier in order to limit final family size, while in a natural fertility setting such efforts presumably do not occur.

The regression coefficients indicate that the reduction in the final number of children ever born per couple resulting from postponing births by an additional year among women who marry before the age of 50 was approximately one-third of a child for the natural fertility cohorts and somewhat less than this for the family limitation cohorts, when results are based on the combined sample of all villages. Some inter-village variation in the impact is evident as would be expected from the fact that there is considerable inter-village variation in the level of marital fertility. For all cohorts taken together, the impact ranges from approximately one-fourth of a child to almost four-tenths of a child. The least impact is found for Middels and Werdum, the two East Frisian villages, where marital fertility is generally lowest, and the greatest impact is found for the three Bavarian villages, where marital fertility is generally highest (see Table 10.1).

For most villages where the comparison can be made, the impact is lower for the family limitation cohorts than for the natural fertility cohorts. The exceptions are Rust, where the impact is actually slightly higher, and Middels, where the impact remains unchanged. Of particular interest is the case of Grafenhausen since family limitation progressed furthest there. A very substantial reduction in the impact of

Table 13.3. *Regression estimates of the effect of wife's age at marriage on the number of postnuptially born children, by village, and family limitation status of the marriage cohort, marriages 1700–1899*

	Age at marriage under 50			Age at marriage 20–34		
	Natural fertility cohorts	Family limitation cohorts	All cohorts	Natural fertility cohorts	Family limitation cohorts	All cohorts
Grafenhausen	-.34	-.22	-.27	-.41	-.18	-.25
Herbolzheim	-.32	-.27	-.30	-.29	-.26	-.29
Kappel	-.32	—	-.32	-.28	—	-.28
Rust	-.33	-.38	-.34	-.36	-.46	-.40
Öschelbronn	-.33	—	-.33	-.33	—	-.33
3 Bavarian villages	-.40	-.32	-.38	-.37	-.29	-.35
4 Waldeck villages	-.34	-.26	-.33	-.37	-.26	-.35
Middels	-.25	-.25	-.25	-.26	-.16	-.23
Werdum	-.26	—	-.26	-.28	—	-.28
All villages	-.32	-.27	-.31	-.32	-.27	-.30

Note: Results refer only to children of current marriages and are subject to restrictions 1, 2, 3 and 4 (see Table A.1). See text for definition of natural fertility limitation cohorts.

age at marriage on completed family size is evident in Grafenhausen, with the impact being reduced from over a third of a child to slightly over a fifth of a child. In general, then, the results confirm that the link between age at marriage and family size weakens with the onset of family limitation, although it by no means disappears.

Any shift in the mean age of marriage that would have taken place during the period under study would have occurred within the range of 20–34 years of age. Thus results are also presented based only on women within this age range. For the combined sample of all villages, the regression coefficients for this subset are almost identical to those for women married before the end of the entire reproductive span and confirm that delaying marriage on the average by a year would reduce fertility by approximately a third of a child.

Extrapolating from cross-sectional results such as these to the implied effects of a change in the mean age of marriage over time could be misleading, since factors which would produce changes in the average age at marriage might also affect its relationship with fertility. For example, as discussed in Chapter 6, some of the villages are in German states where legislative measures were enacted, during the nineteenth century, to postpone marriage. While such measures may not have affected the relationship of age at marriage with the number of legitimate children ever born, it is likely that they did influence the relationship between age at marriage and the total number of children ever born, by raising premarital fertility.[4] In any event, it is worth noting that the results for the sample German village populations suggest a considerably stronger impact of changing age at marriage on fertility than that estimated by McKeown, who also relied on cross-sectional data for this purpose.[5] He suggests that a rise of one year in the age of marriage would reduce the final number of births per couple by only two-tenths of a child. His estimate, however, based on data for rural Ireland from the 1911 census, appears to be atypical. Evidence from a number of other preindustrial European populations is in considerably closer agreement with the results from the German villages.[6]

Women who marry unusually late in the reproductive span are generally considered to be less likely to practice family limitation than women who marry earlier. Thus it might be expected that estimates of the impact of age at marriage on the number of children ever born, when restricted to ages of marriage from 20 through 34 rather than

[4] Knodel, 'Law, marriage and illegitimacy.'
[5] McKeown, *Rise of populations*, p. 38.
[6] Wrigley, 'Marriage, fertility and growth,' p. 149.

including all ages of marriage, would show a greater contrast in impact between the natural fertility cohorts and the family limitation cohorts. This is clearly the case in Grafenhausen and in Middels. In the latter case, no difference was indicated between natural fertility and family limitation cohorts when the full range of ages of marriage under 50 were considered, but when analysis is limited to the more restricted range of marriage ages, a noticeable reduction is evident with the onset of family limitation. In the other villages, the impact is changed very little and Rust remains an exception, continuing to show the impact increasing with the onset of family limitation. This is a reflection of an unusually large increase in the underlying level of natural fertility in Rust during the period under observation, combined with only a moderate level of family limitation (see Table 10.4).

Community-level and regional associations
While a negative association between age at marriage and completed family size is obvious when the individual couple serves as the unit of analysis, this does not necessarily imply that a similar association will exist at the community level. Populations that have not yet experienced the demographic transition are generally viewed as being broadly characterized by homeostatic, or self-regulatory, demographic regimes. Such regimes represented a particular combination of mortality, fertility and migration patterns which kept population size, density and growth roughly in balance with the available resources. In the case of western European populations, a particularly important mechanism within the homeostatic system was nuptiality. As discussed in Chapter 6, a relatively late but flexible age of entry into marriage, as well as non-universal marriage, helped keep the population's reproductive potential in check. The level of marital childbearing, however, also varied considerably prior to the onset of deliberate family limitation, as discussed in Chapter 10, as a result of different social customs affecting the proximate determinants of natural marital fertility.

Coale has recently argued that in preindustrial populations where homeostatic mechanisms kept births and deaths in a near balance over the long run, there is a societal advantage to achieving this balance through moderate levels of fertility and mortality rather than through very high levels. Thus early and nearly universal marriage, combined with very high marital fertility, would produce a higher than optimal birth rate and would be consistent only with very high mortality levels.[7] For a variety of reasons, such a situation would not be

[7] Coale, 'Fertility in Europe since the eighteenth century.'

advantageous to the welfare, or even survival, of the society. Hence there is reason to expect that among preindustrial societies with high levels of nuptiality and where family limitation is absent, customs and institutions would have evolved that moderated marital fertility. As a result, there would be considerably less intersocietal variation in overall fertility levels, and thus in completed family size, than there would be in marital fertility.

Smith has made a similar point with respect to preindustrial European communities where natural fertility prevailed.[8] He observes that the diversity in the separate components of demographic behavior of communities is misleading in the sense that striking differences in mortality, age at marriage, and marital fertility did not generate equally extreme differences in rates of natural increase among the populations. Instead, a more or less homeostatic pattern in demographic components was common, such that early marriage was associated with both lower natural fertility and higher mortality in childhood. In brief, there was a tendency at the community level for different aspects of demographic behavior to balance each other out.

It is thus of some interest to examine the extent to which such a pattern is evident among the sample of 14 German villages under study. As a first attempt, data for each of the 14 villages are used based on couples married between 1750 and 1849 to minimize the influence of family limitation practices and to maintain the same general historical period. For all of the villages except Grafenhausen and Herbolzheim, these cohorts were characterized by natural fertility as defined by an m value of less than .3. Even in the case of Grafenhausen and Herbolzheim, family limitation is evident only for couples married toward the end of this period, and only at modest levels. Utilizing the village as the unit of analysis, a clear positive association holds between marital fertility and age at marriage. I_g' is correlated .67 with the average age at marriage of women in completed unions. Thus lower average ages at marriage went along with lower marital fertility rates, and higher average ages at marriage were associated with higher rates of marital fertility.

Despite this positive association, complete family size was still negatively related to age at marriage. The number of postnuptial children ever born to completed unions correlated $-.56$ with the wife's age at marriage. Moreover, because marital fertility was positively associated with the risk of a child dying before age 5, as indicated by a correlation of .60, an even stronger association at the village level existed between age at marriage and family size measured in terms of

[8] Smith, Daniel Scott, 'Homeostatic demographic regime.'

surviving children. The age at marriage of women in completed unions correlated $-.81$ with the average number of children surviving to age 5. Nevertheless, some tendency toward a homeostatic pattern among the demographic components is evident from the fact that the effect of age at marriage on family size, as indicated by linear regression analysis, is reduced at the village level compared to the couple level. When the mean number of postnuptial children ever born and the mean number of survivors to age 5 are regressed on age at marriage, with each of the 14 villages serving as an observation, a one-year decrease in age at marriage is associated with only a .17 increase in children ever born and a .18 increase in survivors to age 5. This is considerably lower than implied by the individual-level regressions as presented in Table 13.3.

The mean number of postnuptially born children surviving to age 5 per completed union in a population can be expressed as a function of the proportion of women marrying at the different ages, the mean number of legitimate children ever born to women married at each age, and the probability of surviving to age 5 among legitimate children born to women married at each age.[9] The first of these factors represents the nuptiality pattern (defined, however, solely in terms of age at marriage and thus ignoring differences in the proportions of women who remain single throughout the reproductive age span); the second represents marital fertility; and the third represents infant and child mortality. This relationship provides a simple framework to estimate, through a decomposition procedure, the effect of each of these three separate demographic components on variations in effective family size among different populations.

The results of such an analysis are provided in Table 13.4, based on completed unions to women married only once during their reproductive span. In order to ensure that comparisons are based on an

---

[9] The relationship can be represented as follows:

$$S = \sum_{a=\alpha}^{\omega} M_a \cdot C_a \cdot P_a$$

where

   α = the age at which the childbearing age span begins;
   ω = the age at which the childbearing age span ends;
   M_a = the proportion of women marrying at age a;
   C_a = the mean number of legitimate children ever born to women marrying at age a; and
   P_a = the probability of surviving to age 5 among legitimate children born to women marrying at age a.

In the present analysis, a is defined in terms of six age groups: under 20, 20–24, 25–29, 30–34, 35–39, and 40–49.

Table 13.4. *Estimated effect of differences in the age at marriage distribution, the mean number of children ever born by age at marriage, and the survival rate, on interregional differences on the mean number of legitimate children surviving to age 5*

Marriage cohort and region (all comparisons with combined sample of all villages)	Observed percentage difference in mean survivors to age 5	Percentage difference expected due to observed differences in		
		Marriage age distribution	Children ever born	Survival rate to age 5
Pre-1850				
Baden	+0.6	+0.5	+1.9	−2.0
Württemberg (Öschelbronn)	−3.5	+6.4	+3.4	−12.9
Bavaria	−11.0	−20.6	+24.8	−7.5
Waldeck	−2.2	−3.2	0.0	+1.0
East Friesland	+6.8	+5.8	−12.5	+15.5
1850–99				
Baden	−2.4	+1.7	−1.7	−2.7
Württemberg (Öschelbronn)	+4.4	−4.9	+17.3	−8.2
Bavaria	−9.5	−14.2	+11.4	−12.1
Waldeck	+9.7	−0.3	+0.4	+9.1
East Friesland	+7.1	+4.9	−15.5	+18.4

Note: Results refer to legitimate births to women in first marriages only, and are subject to restrictions 1, 2, 3, 4 and 7 (see Table A.1).

adequate number of cases, results are presented for regional groupings rather than for individual villages. Since nuptiality, marital fertility, and mortality during infancy and childhood vary considerably by region, conducting the analysis at the regional level is still of sufficient interest. Results are also presented separately for cohorts married prior to 1850 and those married during 1850–99, when family limitation was more common. The combined sample of all villages serves as the basis against which all comparisons are made.[10] It should be noted that the sum of the effects of the three separate components will not necessarily equal the total observed difference in the mean number of surviving children.

The fact that regional variations in the mean number of surviving children, as measured by the percentage deviation from the overall mean for the combined sample, are considerably less than the percentage differences that would be implied by the observed differences in any of the three components reflects the tendency for the separate demographic components to balance each other out, both for the pre-1850 and for the 1850–99 marriage cohorts. For example, in Bavaria, family size as measured by surviving children for the pre-1850 cohort is 11 percent below that of the total sample. The marriage age distribution in Bavaria taken alone, however, if combined with the marital fertility

---

[10] In this study, the effect of the difference between the regional value of a specific component and the value for the combined sample is estimated by substituting in the equation the regional value of that component and retaining the values for the other two components from the combined sample. The resulting mean number of surviving children is then compared with the observed value for the combined sample in order to determine the percentage difference attributable to the component in question.

For example, the following values characterize the pre-1850 marriage cohorts for the combined sample and the East Frisian villages:

	Combined sample			East Frisian villages		
	M_a	C_a	P_a	M_a	C_a	P_a
Under 20	.096	8.18	.703	.104	7.03	.831
20–24	.373	6.93	.699	.399	6.24	.799
25–29	.291	5.53	.674	.329	4.60	.781
30–34	.128	3.99	.662	.106	3.64	.772
35–39	.060	1.76	.619	.039	1.27	.714
40–49	.052	.40	.492	.023	.77	.600

Based on the values of M_a, C_a and P_a for the combined sample, the mean number of surviving children (S) is equal to 3.859. To estimate the effect that the difference in the age of marriage distributions between the East Frisian villages and the combined sample would make for the mean number of children, the values of M_a for East Friesland are combined with the values of C_a and P_a for the combined sample, yielding a value of S equal to 4.084. Therefore a difference in the nuptiality pattern alone would result in an additional 5.8 percent surviving children (4.084/3.859=1.058).

and mortality of the combined sample, would result in a considerably lower family size. Mortality risks for children were also relatively high in Bavaria and would have further lowered effective family size. However, these components were contradicted by very high marital fertility, which, if taken alone, would have resulted in considerably more children ever born for any particular age-at-marriage group than for the total sample as a whole.

An opposite pattern is evident for the East Frisian village populations, where effective family size is above average. In this case, the age-at-marriage distribution and survival rates of children both contribute to the larger effective family sizes, but are combined with considerably lower-than-average marital fertility. In none of the regions, for either the pre-1850 or the 1850–99 marriage cohorts, do all three of the demographic components of family size operate simultaneously in the same direction. Thus, despite the substantial regional differences in age at marriage, marital fertility, and infant and child mortality, only moderate differences are evident in actual effective family size.

Age at marriage and age at last birth

As discussed in Chapter 10, in populations where family limitation is common, women cease childbearing earlier than in natural fertility settings. This should be especially true among women who marry at younger ages, since they have been exposed longer to the risks of childbearing and hence have had more time to achieve a given target family size before reaching the end of their reproductive period than would women who married at older ages. Thus, in the absence of attempts at family limitation, little association between age at marriage and age of mother at last birth should be evident. In contrast, once family limitation is common, women marrying at younger ages should cease childbearing earlier than older marrying women. Examination of the relationship between age at marriage and age at last birth is thus a useful way to test further whether family limitation was indeed absent for marriage cohorts thought to be characterized by natural fertility.

The age of mother at last birth according to age at marriage is presented in Table 13.5 for both the natural fertility and the family limitation cohorts. Consideration is limited to women in completed unions. In addition, comparisons are made between women married at different ages who have had at least one birth after a given age. The necessity for making the comparison in this manner stems from the fact that the age at marriage essentially sets a lower limit for the age at last birth (ignoring prenuptial births). Thus a woman who marries at

Table 13.5. *Age of mother at last birth by age at marriage for women with at least one birth after ages 25, 30, 35 and 40*

	At least one birth after age			
	25	30	35	40
Natural fertility cohorts				
Age at marriage				
15–19	39.8	40.5	41.3	43.0
20–24	39.6	40.2	41.1	42.8
25–29		40.7	41.4	43.0
30–34			41.3	43.1
35–39				42.9
Family limitation cohorts				
Age at marriage				
15–19	35.5	37.2	39.2	41.5
20–24	37.0	38.3	40.0	42.6
25–29		39.0	40.2	42.5
30–34			40.6	42.5
35–39				42.9

Note: Results refer to the combined sample of all villages and are subject to restrictions 2, 3 and 4 (see Table A.1). See text for definition of natural fertility and family limitation cohorts.

age 30 would not be able to have her last birth before age 30, while a woman who marries at age 20 would be able to have a last birth at any age after age 20. By limiting comparisons between different age-at-marriage groups to women who marry before a given age but who have at least one birth after that age ensures that the range of ages in which the last birth could occur is identical for each age-at-marriage group. Not to impose such a restriction would bias results such that women marrying younger would generally experience earlier ages at last birth.[11] Thus a series of comparisons, based on the combined

---

[11] For example, the following mean ages at last birth among the natural fertility cohorts (subject to restrictions 1, 3 and 4 – see Table A.1) occur if there is no control on the lower age limit at which the last birth took place:

Age at marriage	Age at last birth
Under 20	39.0
20–24	39.2
25–29	40.3
30–34	41.0
35–39	42.1
40–49	43.3

These results yield a considerably different and necessarily biased impression compared to those presented in Table 13.5.

sample of all villages, are made in Table 13.5 for women with at least one birth after the ages of 25, 30, 35, and 40, respectively.

The results are quite clear. For the natural fertility cohorts, virtually no difference in age at last birth is apparent by age at marriage among women with at least one birth after each of the given ages. For example, among women who have at least one birth after age 30, there is very little difference in the age at which the last birth occurred between women who married at ages 15–19 and those who married at ages 25–29. Likewise, among women who had at least one birth after age 35, the age at last birth is identical for those married at ages 15–19 and those who married at ages 30–34. These results, then, suggest that age at marriage for the natural fertility cohorts had little influence on fertility through the practice of family limitation.

A very different pattern is evident for the family limitation cohorts. For women with at least one birth after ages 25, 30, and 35, respectively, a consistent positive relationship is evident between the age at last birth and age at marriage. Thus, among women who had at least one birth after age 30, those who married at ages 15–19 ceased childbearing almost two years earlier than those who married at ages 25–29. Only for women who had at least one birth after age 40 is the relationship irregular between age at last birth and age at marriage. The lack of a more consistent relationship among this group of women is probably attributable to the fact that, because they have had at least one birth after age 40, they are already self-selected for being ineffective in their practice of family limitation. Nevertheless, even among these women, those who married at the youngest ages experienced the earliest age at last birth, and those who married at the oldest ages experienced the latest age at last birth. In sum, the results in Table 13.5 document the absence of a relationship between age at marriage and age at last birth under conditions of natural fertility and the emergence of such a relationship with the onset of family limitation.

Trends in the age of mother at last birth have already been examined in Chapter 11. The decline in the age at which women cease childbearing, in the combined sample of all villages among successive marriage cohorts during the nineteenth century, has been interpreted as evidence of the increasing practice of family limitation. It is also of interest to examine the trends in the age at last birth according to age at marriage, given the expectation that a trend toward the earlier cessation of childbearing should be more pronounced among women who marry younger than among those who enter marital unions at later ages. The existence of such a pattern would be further evidence that motivations to limit family size underlie the trends toward an earlier termination of childbearing.

Since our interest is in the trends within age at marriage groups, it is not necessary to restrict such an analysis to women who have had at least one birth after a given age. It is of some interest, however, to examine the results separately for women for whom exact birth dates are available in the village genealogy. Such women were typically born in the village and thus an exact birth date was available to the genealogist because it was present in the local birth/baptism register. In some cases of women born outside the village, an exact birth date might be known if it was reported in connection with some other event that was entered into the registers, such as her marriage. In both cases, the birth date will be precise and probably accurate. For other women, the year of birth has been estimated indirectly based on information in the registers about her age, most commonly from the stated age at death. In these cases, the estimated birth date is less precise and may occasionally be biased because of age exaggeration.[12] This would result on average in overstating a woman's age at marriage and age at the birth of each child. Not only would such a tendency bias the relationship between age at marriage and age at last birth, but it could affect the trends in age at last birth by age at marriage if the proportion of women with estimated (and biased) birth dates changed over time. Limiting analysis to women with exact birth dates would eliminate any such bias.

The mean age of mother at last birth by age at marriage for successive marriage cohorts are presented in Table 13.6 for women in completed unions in the combined sample of all villages. Regardless of whether all women in completed unions or only those with exact birth dates were considered, the age of mother at last birth declined within all age-at-marriage categories for successive cohorts married during the nineteenth century. The decline is most pronounced and most regular for women in the youngest age-at-marriage category, and least pronounced and somewhat irregular among women in the oldest age-at-marriage category. Moreover, when consideration is limited to those women with exact birth dates, the amount of decline in the age at last birth shows a consistent and inverse association with age at marriage.

---

[12] In most village genealogies, the compilers followed the convention of placing a birth date in parentheses if it is estimated from a stated age at some later date. Even when the compiler does not follow the convention, it seems reasonable to assume that, when only the birth year or sometimes the month and year are given, the source was a stated age at some later event rather than a direct birth entry. There is some feeling among genealogists and historical demographers who work with parish registers that ages at death are more frequently overestimated than understated, especially when the deceased was fairly elderly (Krausse, *Familiengeschichtsforschung*, p. 142; Hofmann et al., *Von der Kirchenbuchverkartung*, p. 24; Demleitner and Roth, *Volksgenealogie*, p. 32).

Table 13.6. *Age of mother at last birth by age at marriage and year of marriage*

	All women				Women with exact birth dates			
	Under 25	25–29	30–34	35+	Under 25	25–29	30–34	35+
1700–49	39.2	40.9	40.2	42.6	39.2	41.0	(40.1)	(42.5)
1750–99	39.7	40.5	41.2	43.3	39.8	40.3	40.6	42.8
1800–24	39.1	39.7	41.7	42.4	39.2	39.8	41.2	42.2
1825–49	38.0	39.7	40.6	41.7	37.9	39.7	40.4	41.8
1850–74	37.6	39.0	40.4	41.9	37.7	39.0	40.5	41.9
1875–99	36.4	38.9	39.3	41.6	36.4	38.9	39.3	(41.7)
Change[a]	−3.3	−2.0	−2.4	−1.7	−3.4	−2.1	−1.9	−1.1

Note: Results refer to the combined sample of all villages and are subject to restrictions 2, 3, and 4 (see Table A.1). Results in parentheses are based on less than 50 women.
[a] The difference between the marriage cohort with the highest average age at last birth and the 1875–99 cohort.

These results clearly reinforce the impression that increasing attempts at limiting family size were responsible for the general trend toward declining age at last birth.

Age at marriage and marital fertility

Although under a regime of natural fertility a strong inverse relationship between cumulative fertility and age at marriage is to be expected, initial writings on the topic assumed there would be little or no association between duration of marriage and age-specific marital fertility rates, and thus that a positive association indicated the presence of family limitation.[13] Clearly, within populations where family limitation is commonly practiced, there is reason to expect such a relationship. Compared to women who marry at older ages, those marrying younger are likely to be younger when they achieve any particular family size and hence to be more motivated to stop child-bearing or reduce their fertility during later ages in the childbearing span.[14] It is now recognized, however, that there are a number of non-volitional factors operating under conditions of either natural fertility or family limitation that could also produce a positive association between duration of marriage and marital fertility.[15] Thus the existence of a modest association between age at marriage and age-specific marital fertility rates cannot be taken, in and of itself, to signify the presence of family limitation practices.

Age-specific marital fertility rates by mother's age at marriage are presented in Table 13.7 for the combined sample of villages for both the natural fertility and the family limitation cohorts. For both groups, a clear inverse association is apparent between marital fertility for any particular five-year age span and age at marriage. Even for the natural fertility cohorts, the association is quite consistent, with only minor exceptions evident. Thus women who married latest experienced the highest fertility at any given age, and those who married youngest experienced the lowest fertility.

A convenient way to summarize this relationship is to calculate the total marital fertility rate above age 30 (obtained by summing the age-specific rates above age 30 and multiplying by 5). For both natural

---

[13] Henry, *Manuel de démographie historique*, p. 89; Wrigley, 'Family limitation,' pp. 91–92.

[14] This argument assumes that age at marriage is largely independent of target family size and thus that women who marry young desire no more children than women who marry late. To the extent that age at marriage is negatively correlated with the desired number of children, duration effects will be reduced (Weir, 'Fertility transition,' p. 61).

[15] Henry, 'Fécondité naturelle.'

Table 13.7. *Age-specific marital fertility and total marital fertility above age 30 by wife's age at marriage*

Marriage cohort and age at marriage	Births per 1000 married women aged						Total fertility above age 30	
	20–24	25–29	30–34	35–39	40–44	45–49	Rate[a]	Index[b]
Natural fertility cohorts								
Under 20	434	376	331	264	150	17	3.81	.77
20–24	482	419	352	275	146	18	3.95	.80
25–29	—	470	395	307	157	22	4.40	.89
30–34	—	—	454	345	166	24	4.94	1.00
35+	—	—	—	349	180	23	—	—
Family limitation cohorts								
Under 20	492	359	258	158	38	0	2.27	.48
20–24	555	428	297	217	80	7	3.00	.63
25–29	—	514	382	249	98	9	3.69	.78
30–34	—	—	481	331	130	8	4.75	1.00
35+	—	—	—	373	195	11	—	—

Note: Results are subject to restrictions 1, 2 and 3 (see Table A.1). See text for definition of natural fertility and family limitation cohorts.
[a] Total fertility above age 30 equals the sum of the fertility rates for each five-year age group above age 30 multiplied by 5.
[b] Index values of total fertility rate above age 30 are based on a value of 1.00 for women whose age at marriage was 30–34.

fertility and family limitation cohorts, this measure increases steadily with age at marriage. Nevertheless, the association is considerably more pronounced for the family limitation cohorts. For example, in the natural fertility cohorts, total marital fertility above age 30 for women marrying under age 20 is 77 percent as high as it is for women married at ages 30–34, while in the family limitation cohorts it is only 48 percent as high.

The trends in total marital fertility above age 30 by wife's age at marriage are shown in Table 13.8 for the combined sample of all villages. In addition, results are shown for the natural fertility and family limitation cohorts for the individual villages or village sets. In some villages (Kappel, Öschelbronn and Werdum), results for only one cohort are shown because the entire period covered in the particular village was characterized by natural fertility. In the cases of Grafenhausen and Herbolzheim, where the onset of family limitation occurred relatively early, the earliest cohort shown is characterized by natural fertility, while the family limitation cohorts are subdivided into two successive cohorts in order to trace the changing relationship between total marital fertility and age at marriage in greater detail.

As revealed by the index values of the total marital fertility rate above age 30, the positive association between age at marriage and fertility after age 30 became increasingly pronounced over the course of the nineteenth century for the combined sample of all villages. Although a positive association was apparent for couples married during the eighteenth century, the contrast in the total marital fertility rate above age 30 for women married under age 25 compared to those married during ages 30–34 had become considerably greater by the end of the nineteenth century.

In Grafenhausen, the village in which family limitation as measured by the Coale–Trussell m index reached the highest levels, the association between the total marital fertility rate above age 30 and age at marriage became particularly pronounced for couples married toward the end of the nineteenth century. The rate for those married under age 25 for this cohort was only 40 percent as high as the equivalent rate for women married in their early thirties. In each village or village set, the natural marital fertility cohorts exhibited at least some degree of positive association between age at marriage and marital fertility above age 30, with the possible exception of Grafenhausen, where the association is irregular for couples married before 1825. In most others, total fertility after age 30 among women married under age 25 is 20–30 percent below that of women married in their early thirties when natural fertility, as measured by the Coale–Trussell m index, still prevailed.

A positive association between age at marriage and marital fertility has been observed in a number of presumed natural fertility populations.[16] The effects of a number of factors other than family limitation could account for this, including bridal pregnancy, exposure to the risks of sterility associated with complications of childbirth, the effect of a husband's age on fertility, and declines in coital frequency with increasing marriage duration.

Bridal pregnancy shortens intervals between marriage and first birth and thus increases the average fertility rate for women marrying within a particular age interval compared to those who married earlier. For example, marital fertility at ages 30–34 would be inflated by bridal pregnancy for women marrying during the 30–34 age interval, but would be unaffected for women who married below age 30. Sterility associated with complications in childbirth could depress fertility rates at older ages among women marrying early compared to those marrying late, since the former would have had longer exposure to such risks. The age of the husband could also be a contributing factor to a positive association between age at marriage and marital fertility. The difference between husband's and wife's age among women who married at younger ages tends to be greater than for older marrying women. Thus, for married women at any given age, the husbands of those who married young tend to be older than the husbands of those who married late. Finally, a negative association between coital frequency and marriage duration would depress fertility at any given age for younger compared to older marrying women, even if there were no deliberate attempt to reduce family size through less frequent sexual relations. In extreme cases, near-total abstinence due to loss of sexual interest in one's spouse may be associated with marriages of higher duration, completely independently of any desire to reduce the chances of childbearing.

Data from the village genealogies can be used to estimate the influence of all but the last of these factors. The impact of bridal pregnancy can be shown to be relatively minor. Prenuptial pregnancies leading to postnuptial births artificially inflate marital fertility rates because women who are pregnant at marriage are treated as if they were at risk of conceiving only from the start of the marriage. As discussed in Chapter 10, adjusted marital fertility rates devoid of the influence of bridal pregnancies can be readily calculated by attributing approximately one additional year of exposure to the denominator for each pregnant bride. Doing so illustrates that prenuptial pregnancies have only a modest impact on the relationship between

[16] Henry, 'Fécondité naturelle'; Weir, 'Fertility transition,' pp. 60–66; Blake, 'Fertility transition.'

Table 13.8. *Total marital fertility above age 30 by wife's age at marriage, village of residence, and year of marriage*

| | Measure of total fertility above age 30 and age at marriage | | | | | |
| | Rate[a] | | | Index[b] | | |
Village and year of marriage	Under 25	25–29	30–34	Under 25	25–29	30–34
All villages						
1700–99	3.98	4.46	4.82	.83	.93	1.00
1800–49	3.77	4.09	4.94	.76	.83	1.00
1850–74	3.41	4.05	5.16	.66	.78	1.00
1875–99	2.93	4.05	4.62	.63	.88	1.00
Grafenhausen						
Pre–1825	4.20	4.56	4.41	.95	1.03	1.00
1825–49	3.17	3.65	(5.41)	.59	.67	1.00
1850–99	1.94	3.01	(4.85)	.40	.62	1.00
Herbolzheim						
Pre–1825	4.09	4.77	5.22	.78	.91	1.00
1825–49	2.97	3.83	4.78	.62	.80	1.00
1850–99	2.54	3.44	4.16	.61	.83	1.00
Kappel						
1700–1899	3.85	4.63	4.99	.77	.93	1.00

Rust						
1700–1849	4.24	4.59	4.64	.91	.99	1.00
1850–99	3.93	4.30	(4.73)	.83	.91	1.00
Öschelbronn						
1700–1899	3.94	4.71	5.33	.73	.88	1.00
3 Bavarian villages						
Pre-1875	4.60	5.18	5.88	.78	.88	1.00
1875–99	(3.45)	(4.24)	—	—	—	—
4 Waldeck villages						
Pre-1875	4.06	4.27	4.68	.87	.91	1.00
1875–99	2.85	3.48	—	—	—	—
Middels						
Pre-1875	3.32	3.74	4.61	.72	.81	1.00
1875–99	2.75	3.52	—	—	—	—
Werdum						
1700–1899	3.32	3.39	4.55	.73	.75	1.00

Note: Results are subject to restrictions 1, 2 and 3 (see Table A.1). Values in parentheses indicate the results are based on an average of 100–199 woman-years per five-year age group within the 30–49 age range; results based on fewer woman-years are omitted.

[a] Total fertility above age 30 equals the sum of the fertility rates for each five-year age group above age 30 multiplied by 5.

[b] Index values of the total fertility rate above age 30 are based on a value of 1.00 for women whose age at marriage was 30–34.

Table 13.9. *Percent sterile after age 30 and number of births after age 30,*
by age at marriage, natural fertility cohorts only

Age at marriage	Percent sterile after age 30	Number of births after age 30	
		To all women	To women fertile
Under 20	12.9	3.68	4.23
20–24	10.2	3.86	4.30
25–29	8.1	4.40	4.79

Note: Results are based on the combined sample of all villages and are subject to restrictions 2, 3 and 4 (see Table A.1). See text for definition of natural fertility cohorts.

age at marriage and marital fertility. For example, the marital fertility rate at ages 30–34 for women marrying in that age interval in the natural fertility cohorts is reduced from 454 to 424 per 1000 women after adjustment.[17] This is still higher than the rate for all younger age-at-marriage groups (see Table 13.7). Total marital fertility above age 30 for women marrying at ages 30–34 is only reduced from 4.94 to 4.79 births after adjustment. Thus the clear positive relationship between fertility after age 30 and age at marriage remains intact.

Difficult deliveries or infections associated with childbirth can cause definitive sterility or increase the risks of miscarriage, so that, among women of the same age, the proportion already sterile could be higher for women who had been married longer and hence had been exposed to a longer period of risk. Table 13.9 provides some idea of the size of this effect and the extent to which it can account for the association between age at marriage and fertility during later years.

The percentage of women in the natural fertility cohorts that had no children after age 30 is shown by the wife's age at marriage for the combined sample of all villages. From the available data, couples who may have deliberately remained infertile after age 30 cannot be distinguished from those who were physiologically sterile or who were childless after age 30 because of reduced coital frequency not related to fertility intentions. Presumably, few women in the natural fertility cohorts deliberately terminated childbearing before age 30. As expected, the proportion of women infertile after age 30 is generally higher when the wife was younger at the time of marriage rather than when she was older. The differences, however, are modest. Taken collec-

---

[17] For convenience, 12 months of additional exposure have been added for each women who was pregnant at marriage since this is very close to the difference in the interval between marriage and first birth that obtains between pregnant and non-pregnant brides (see Table 10.3).

tively, the experience from the sample villages indicates that the percentage of women who remained childless after age 30 was about 5 percentage points higher for women marrying below the age of 20 than among those marrying at ages 25–29.

One way to estimate whether increased exposure to the risks of sterility associated with earlier marriage may influence the association of age at marriage and fertility at older ages is to examine whether the association is diminished by limiting consideration only to women who are fertile after a given age. To do this, the number of births after age 30 to women in completed unions, according to age at marriage, can be calculated, both including and excluding women who are sterile after age 30. The results are also presented in Table 13.9 for the natural fertility cohorts. While excluding women sterile after age 30 reduces the strength of the association of fertility after age 30 with age at marriage, it by no means eliminates it. When women sterile after age 30 are included, women married at ages 25–29 average an additional .72 births more after age 30 than do women married under age 20. Once women sterile after age 30 are excluded, the difference is reduced to an additional .56 births. These findings agree with the initial results of an inquiry, described by Henry, into French fertility before the Revolution, which indicated that sterility induced by delivery or its effect is insufficient by itself to explain the influence of the duration of marriage on marital fertility.[18]

Another factor that could contribute to the association between age at marriage and fertility at subsequent ages is the husband's age. In several historical studies, the importance of the age of husbands on their wives' fertility has recently been documented for populations in which, presumably, little family limitation was practiced.[19] Results differ with respect to how strong an impact the husband's age is known to have on women's marital fertility rates. The effect of male age on fertility can operate through both physiological factors affecting male reproductive capability and through declining coital frequency associated with age.

The evidence presented in Chapter 6 indicates that there is a clear relationship between the age differences between spouses and the wife's age at marriage. Women who married young tended to marry men considerably older than themselves, while women who married at older ages tended to marry husbands of similar age or even younger. For example, for the combined sample, the husbands of women who

[18] Henry, 'Fécondité naturelle.'
[19] Anderson, 'Male age and fertility'; Houdaille, 'Fécondité des familles souveraines'; Mineau and Trussell, 'Marital fertility'; Charbonneau, 'Jeunes femmes.'

married under age 20 were on average 8.4 years older than their wives, while the husbands of women who married at ages 30–34 were only 1.2 years older (see Table 6.7). Thus, for any given age of wife, husbands of women who married young are older on average than are husbands of women who married at more advanced ages. If the fertility of women of a given age declines with the age of the husband, this could help to account for the association between age at marriage and marital fertility.

Age-specific fertility rates of wives for the natural fertility cohorts of the combined sample of all villages are presented in Table 13.10 according to the wife's age at marriage and the relative age of the husband. When women are grouped together regardless of age at marriage, a clear and consistently negative association between marital fertility at a given age and the relative age of the husband is apparent. The only minor exception occurs for women aged 20–24, for whom those with husbands younger than themselves exhibit lower fertility than those with husbands 0–4 or 5–9 years older than themselves. At all other ages, women with husbands younger than themselves experience the highest fertility. Moreover, at all ages, women with husbands ten or more years older than themselves experienced the lowest fertility and, with the exception of the 20–24 age group, fertility is consistently lower with increasing relative age of husband.

The relative strength of the relationship declines with age, as is indicated by comparing the fertility of women whose husbands were ten or more years older than themselves with the fertility of women whose husbands were younger than themselves. For example, at ages 20–24, the fertility of the former is 94 percent as high as the fertility of the latter, but declines with each successive age group, reaching 40 percent for women 45–49 years old. Total marital fertility above age 30 also declines steadily with the relative age of the husband and is only 75 percent as high for women whose husbands are ten or more years older than themselves compared to women whose husbands are younger than themselves.

A general negative relationship between a woman's marital fertility and her husband's age is also evident, independent of age at marriage. For example, total marital fertility above age 30 declines consistently with the husband's relative age for each age-at-marriage group, with the exception of a minor irregularity in the relationship for women who married at 30–34 years of age. In addition, the relative strength of the relationship generally increases with increasing age of women. Clearly, the negative association between the husband's age and his wife's fertility is not simply a spurious association due to its correlation with the wife's age at marriage.

Also apparent from Table 13.10 is that marital fertility continues to exhibit a positive association with age at marriage, independent of the relative age of the husband. For example, for women whose husband is younger than themselves, those who married at ages 20–24 experienced a total marital fertility above age 30 of 4.26 births compared to 4.75 births for women married at ages 25–29 and 4.97 births for women married at ages 30–34. The same positive association between total marital fertility above age 30 and the wife's age at marriage exists for each category of husband's relative age. Thus, while the age of the husband may account in part for differences in the observed association between marital fertility and marriage duration, it does not account for all of it.

Given that each of the factors examined contributes to a positive association between age at marriage and marital fertility, it is of interest to determine the extent to which their combined impact can account for the overall observed relationship, particularly under conditions of natural fertility. The results of an analysis attempting to eliminate the impact of several factors simultaneously on the relationship between age at marriage and fertility at older ages is provided in Table 13.11, based on the combined sample of villages. Results for both natural fertility and family limitation cohorts are provided to permit comparison. The analysis examines the association between age at marriage and the total number of births born after age 30 to women in completed unions.

To eliminate the impact of bridal pregnancy, the analysis is further limited to women who marry under age 30, since the inflationary impact of bridal pregnancy on their fertility rates would be almost entirely limited to ages before age 30. Moreover, separate results are provided for women who had at least one birth after age 30. These latter results should be free of any impact of longer exposure to the risks of secondary sterility associated with complications due to childbirth prior to age 30 for women who were married at younger ages. Through multiple classification analysis, the number of children born after age 30 to women in different age-at-marriage groups can be adjusted for differences in the husband's relative age and vice versa. Multiple classification analysis is also used to make an additional adjustment for the regional location of villages. This should eliminate possible complications arising from the apparent regional association between differences in marital fertility and differences in age at marriage, discussed earlier in this chapter.

The unadjusted results for the natural fertility cohorts evidence the expected associations between the number of births after age 30 and both the wife's age at marriage and the husband's relative age. Based

Table 13.10. *Age-specific marital fertility and total marital fertility above age 30, by age of wife at marriage and relative age of husband, natural fertility cohorts only*

Age at marriage and husband's relative age	Births per 1000 married women aged							Total fertility above age 30
	20–24	25–29	30–34	35–39	40–44	45–49		
Under 20								
Husband 0–4 years older	467	372	348	288	155	18		4.04
Husband 5–9 years older	430	395	338	271	157	22		3.94
Husband 10+ years older	409	347	295	226	124	9		3.27
20–24								
Husband younger	465	435	364	296	170	22		4.26
Husband 0–4 years older	483	424	358	286	154	20		4.09
Husband 5–9 years older	499	425	361	269	147	16		3.96
Husband 10+ years older	452	397	318	235	100	12		3.32
25–29								
Husband younger	—	475	420	322	179	29		4.75
Husband 0–4 years older	—	468	387	309	152	19		4.33
Husband 5–9 years older	—	477	380	286	150	19		4.17
Husband 10+ years older	—	448	344	269	105	9		3.63

30–34						
Husband younger	—	—	451	353	166	24	4.97
Husband 0–4 years older	—	—	490	367	191	31	5.39
Husband 5–9 years older	—	—	445	312	160	31	4.74
Husband 10+ years older	—	—	427	311	126	6	4.35
35+						
Husband younger	—	—	—	375	178	24	—
Husband 0–4 years older	—	—	—	(366)	189	30	—
Husband 5–9 years older	—	—	—	(284)	197	14	—
Husband 10+ years older	—	—	—	307	164	12	—
All ages at marriage:						
Husband younger	460	457	415	333	175	25	4.74
Husband 0–4 years older	479	430	374	303	159	21	4.28
Husband 5–9 years older	470	426	366	277	154	19	4.08
Husband 10+ years older	433	394	330	256	116	10	3.56

Note: Results refer to the combined sample of all villages, exclude women whose husband's age is unknown, and are subject to restrictions 1, 2 and 3 (see Table A.1). Rates in parentheses are based on 100–199 woman-years per five-year age group; rates based on fewer than 100 woman-years are not known.

Table 13.11. Mean number of births after age 30 to women married before age 30, by age at marriage and by husband's relative age, unadjusted and adjusted statistically for regional grouping of villages and either husband's relative age or wife's age at marriage

	All women			Women fertile after age 30		
	Unadjusted	Adjusted for region	Fully adjusted[a]	Unadjusted	Adjusted for region	Fully adjusted[a]
Natural fertility cohorts						
Age at marriage						
Under 20	3.71	3.77	3.92	4.24	4.30	4.45
20–24	3.87	3.87	3.92	4.30	4.30	4.35
25–29	4.40	4.38	4.28	4.77	4.75	4.65
Eta/beta	.12	.11	.07	.11	.10	.07
Husband's relative age						
Younger than wife	4.61	4.59	4.47	4.96	4.95	4.86
0–4 years older	4.08	4.06	4.07	4.50	4.48	4.50
5–9 years older	3.95	3.97	4.02	4.36	4.38	4.42
10+ years older	3.35	3.38	3.44	3.84	3.87	3.90
Eta/beta	.15	.15	.13	.16	.15	.13

Family limitation cohorts

Age at marriage						
Under 20	2.14	2.19	2.45	2.74	2.81	3.03
20–24	2.91	2.91	2.94	3.51	3.51	3.52
25–29	3.62	3.62	3.54	3.92	3.91	3.87
Eta/beta	.18	.18	.14	.14	.13	.11
Husband's relative age						
Younger than wife	3.80	3.79	3.52	4.01	4.00	3.84
0–4 years older	3.24	3.24	3.23	3.72	3.73	3.72
5–9 years older	2.96	2.96	3.11	3.56	3.56	3.66
10+ years older	2.35	2.37	2.49	2.90	2.91	3.01
Eta/beta	.16	.16	.11	.13	.13	.10

Note: Results refer to the combined sample of all villages, exclude women whose husband's age is unknown, and are subject to restrictions 2, 3 and 4 (see Table A.1). Results are adjusted through multiple classification analysis. See text for definition of natural fertility and family limitation cohorts.

[a] Adjusted for region and the effects of the other variable shown.

on all women, including those sterile after age 30, women married at ages 25–29 averaged almost an additional seven-tenths of a birth more after age 30 than women who married under age 20. Also as expected, the relationship is somewhat less pronounced when only women fertile after age 30 are considered. This is evident from the finding that among these women the difference in the number of births after age 30 between those who married under age 20 and those who married at ages 25–29 was only slightly more than half a birth. Adjustment for the regional location of the village reduces the differences among age-at-marriage groups only slightly.

Adjusting for both husband's relative age and regional location reduces the effect of age at marriage quite substantially. For all women, including those sterile after age 30, there is no difference in the number of births after age 30 between those married under age 20 and those married at ages 20–24. In addition, women married at ages 25–29 averaged only an additional .36 births. When only women fertile after age 30 are considered, the association between fertility after age 30 and age at marriage appears to be irregular after results are adjusted for both regional location and husband's relative age. Nevertheless, women married at ages 25–29 show somewhat higher fertility after age 30 than those in both of the two younger marrying groups, although the differences are not large.

In sum, for the natural fertility cohorts, much of the association between marriage duration and marital fertility can be explained by the factors considered in this analysis. Not taken into account is the possible effect of duration of marriage on coital frequency, since it is not possible to investigate this using family reconstitution data. This remaining factor might account for the weak association that still exists after bridal pregnancy, sterility after age 30, and husband's age are all taken into account. Hence the extent to which the observed association of age at marriage and fertility at older ages is attributable to family limitation practices in the natural fertility cohorts is at most only minimal.

It is of interest to note that a much stronger association between fertility after age 30 and age at marriage is apparent for the family limitation cohorts even after the various factors have been taken into account. Thus, even for women fertile after age 30, and after adjustment for regional grouping and husband's relative age, a consistent and substantial positive association between age at marriage and the number of births after age 30 is still evident. This undoubtedly reflects the additional impact of family limitation on the association between marital fertility and marriage duration. It is also noteworthy that in both the natural fertility and family limitation cohorts, the association between fertility after age 30 and husband's relative age remains substantial even after adjusting for the wife's age at marriage.

Marital dissolution and family size

The duration of exposure to the risk of childbearing for a woman is determined not only by the age at which she enters a sexual union, but also by her age at the time the union ends. Thus, within any given age-at-marriage group, family size should be related to the age at marital dissolution. As indicated in Chapter 7, marital dissolution in the sample of German villages during the eighteenth and nineteenth centuries occurred almost exclusively through the death of one of the spouses. Improvements in adult mortality over the two-century period covered for the present study could potentially contribute to an increase in family size for the average couple, provided family size is calculated to include couples in which marital dissolution occurred prior to the wife reaching the end of the reproductive years.

The proportion of marital unions still intact at the time the wife reaches selected ages within the reproductive age span for different age-at-marriage groups is shown in Table 13.12 for different marriage cohorts for the combined sample of villages. Marital dissolution is defined as occurring at the time of the death of the first spouse to die. No distinction is made with respect to which spouse dies first and thus the timing of marital dissolution is a function of the joint probability of both spouses surviving.

The results make clear that a substantial proportion of marriages throughout the period under investigation terminated before the wife reached the end of her reproductive span. As would be expected, the probability of a marriage still being intact at any given age of the wife is positively related to the wife's age at marriage. Throughout the two-century period under consideration, only about half the marriages in which the wife married under age 20 were still intact by the time she had reached age 45. In contrast, a considerable majority were still intact for women marrying in their thirties. However, in the eighteenth century, even for women who married at ages 30–34, less than two-thirds of their marriages remained intact by age 45, and for the nineteenth century only slightly more than two-thirds did.

The extent to which changes in adult mortality affected the timing of marital dissolution can be judged by comparing the proportion of marriages still intact by the time the wife reaches any particular age for equivalent age-at-marriage groupings across the three successive mar-

Table 13.12. *Proportion of marriages still intact at the time the wife reaches selected ages, by age at marriage and year of marriage*

Year of marriage and age at marriage	Percent still intact when wife reaches age						
	20	25	30	35	40	45	50
1700–99							
Under 20	.98	.90	.80	.69	.59	.51	.39
20–24	—	.96	.87	.77	.66	.54	.42
25–29	—	—	.95	.86	.74	.62	.48
30–34	—	—	—	.90	.76	.63	.49
35–39	—	—	—	—	.89	.74	.61
40–44	—	—	—	—	—	.90	.75
1800–49							
Under 20	.98	.88	.80	.68	.60	.50	.42
20–24	—	.96	.87	.75	.66	.56	.47
25–29	—	—	.93	.84	.71	.60	.49
30–34	—	—	—	.94	.80	.67	.55
35–39	—	—	—	—	.96	.78	.68
40–44	—	—	—	—	—	.92	.79
1850–99							
Under 20	.99	.85	.76	.64	.57	.51	.44
20–24	—	.97	.89	.81	.73	.65	.57
25–29	—	—	.95	.85	.77	.69	.61
30–34	—	—	—	.93	.80	.70	.61
35–39	—	—	—	—	.92	.81	.67
40–44	—	—	—	—	—	.94	.79

Note: Results refer to the combined sample of all villages and are subject to restriction 3 (see Table A.1).

riage cohorts shown. By and large, no consistent trend is evident in the proportions of marriages which were still intact at the time the wife reached particular ages up to age 35. Most of the change appears to be with respect to the proportions of marriages still intact at ages 45 and 50. Hence mortality improvement affected mainly the continuation of marriages through the later years of the wife's childbearing span, when fertility is quite low, and could have had only a relatively minor affect on changes in family size.

The fact that trends in family size were probably only very modestly affected by trends in the timing of marital dissolution should not obscure the fact that a very marked association between the timing of marital dissolution and family size is evident throughout the eighteenth and nineteenth centuries. The mean number of children ever born, as well as the number of children surviving to age 5, is

Table 13.13. *Mean number of children ever born and children surviving to age 5, by age at marriage and age at end of marriage, 1700–1899*

	Age at marriage				
	Under 20	20–24	25–29	30–34	35–39
Children ever born					
Age at end of marriage					
20–24	1.86	1.17	—	—	—
25–29	3.91	2.46	1.23	—	—
30–34	5.78	4.43	2.62	1.12	—
35–39	7.25	5.89	4.30	2.25	0.93
40–49	7.94	6.86	5.33	3.75	1.96
50+	8.05	6.86	5.73	4.00	2.00
Survivors to age 5					
Age at end of marriage					
20–24	1.19	0.62	—	—	—
25–29	2.69	1.50	0.66	—	—
30–34	4.00	2.93	1.61	0.60	—
35–39	4.80	4.11	2.91	1.33	.41
40–49	5.72	4.80	3.69	2.48	1.29
50+	5.75	4.92	3.97	2.73	1.31

Note: Results are based on the combined sample of all villages and are subject to restrictions 1, 2 and 3 (see Table A.1).

shown in Table 13.13 according to the wife's age at marriage and age at marital dissolution for the combined sample of villages. Regardless of which measure is considered, within any age-at-marriage group, a clear positive relationship is evident between family size and age at end of marriage. For example, among women who married at ages 20–24, those whose marriage ended when they were aged 30–34 averaged almost two and a half births less than those whose marriage remained intact until the woman was at least age 50. Generally the impact of age at marital dissolution on survivors to age 5 is somewhat less pronounced in absolute terms than for children ever born because of the higher mortality among children born to women at older ages.

Multiple linear regression can be used to estimate the impact of age at end of union on family size net of the effect of age at marriage. For this purpose, only postnuptial births or postnuptially born survivors to age 5 are considered and the regressions are limited to women married under age 45. Ages of women at the time of marriage dissolution in excess of 45 years of age are treated as if the end of the union occurred at age 45. This is done since there is little reason to expect much impact on family size for increasing ages of the end of union after age 45.

Regressions are calculated separately for the natural fertility and family limitation cohorts for the combined sample of villages. The results indicate that, net of age at marriage, each additional year that the couple remained intact during the wife's reproductive span up until age 45 increased family size by .26 births or .20 survivors to age 5. The impact of marital dissolution on family size for the family limitation cohort is somewhat less, with one extra year of marriage contributing .21 births or .16 survivors to age 5. The effect of age at marital dissolution is weaker than age at marriage (see Table 13.3) because it affects exposure predominantly toward the end of the childbearing span, at which ages fertility is tapering off.

Discussion

In this chapter, a number of aspects of the interrelationships between family size, fertility, and nuptiality have been explored. Clearly, in German village populations of the eighteenth and nineteenth centuries, the age at which a woman first entered into a reproductive union was a very important determinant of the family size which she and her husband eventually achieved. For most women, the start of reproductive activity coincided very closely with marriage although, as discussed in Chapter 8, non-marital fertility was also of some significance. While the link between age at marriage and family size at the level of the couple was somewhat stronger under conditions of natural fertility, it weakened only slightly with the onset of family limitation. Thus, throughout both the eighteenth and nineteenth centuries, relatively late marriage is an effective 'preventive check' on a couple's fertility. Moreover, since mortality risks of children show little relation to the parents' age at marriage, the same association between family size and age at marriage persists after the mortality of infants and young children is taken into account. What cannot be judged from the family reconstitution data is whether couples deliberately took into consideration the implications of age at marriage for their reproductive potential when they were deciding to marry. Indeed, an implicit assumption behind some of the analyses presented in the present chapter is that age at marriage was largely independent of family size intentions, if such intentions were present at all. While there is little evidence in the literature of demographic history to contradict this assumption, it must remain an open question.[20]

Another critical demographic determinant of the eventual family

---

[20] Weir, 'Fertility transition.'

size achieved by a couple was the age of the wife at the time the union dissolved, that is at the time of the death of the first spouse to die. Together with age at marriage, the age at marital dissolution determined the period a woman was at risk of marital childbearing. In eighteenth- and nineteenth-century German village populations, where adult mortality was relatively high, a large proportion of marital unions terminated before the wife had reached the end of the reproductive age span, thus cutting short her potential period of childbearing. Since fertility declines with age during most of the childbearing span, the effect on achieved family size is somewhat less for each year of potential childbearing lost because of marital dissolution brought about by the death of a spouse than it is for postponement of marriage. Nevertheless, the impact of marital dissolution prior to the end of the wife's childbearing age span was substantial.

The relationship between age at marriage and completed family size is less pronounced at the level of village populations than at the level of individual couples. The results from the sample of German villages suggest that younger marrying populations were typically characterized by lower age-specific marital fertility rates than populations in which the age at marriage was relatively late. In some sense, this negative correlation between age at marriage and marital fertility can be seen as part of a pattern of demographic homeostasis through which particular combinations of nuptiality and marital fertility served to moderate the impact of each other on population growth rates.

While it may be unlikely that fertility implications, other than simply a readiness to start having children, served as an important determinant in the decision on when to marry, a plausible argument can be made that, once family limitation was commonly practiced, age at marriage acted as a determinant of fertility during the later years of the childbearing span. Since at any given age of the wife, couples who had been married longer were more likely to have larger family sizes, they would also be more likely to delay or prevent additional births. Thus in populations where family limitation is practiced, an association between age at marriage and both age of the mother at last birth and marital fertility at older ages is to be expected. Results from the German village populations suggest that both of these are indeed the case for the marriage cohorts which were judged to practice family limitation. For the natural fertility cohorts, however, while age at last birth was not related to age at marriage, lower marital fertility at older ages was associated with younger ages at marriage. Indeed, this has been an intriguing finding in a number of historical demographic studies and has been cited recently by Blake as evidence that calls into question the absence of family limitation in populations thought to be in a state of natural fertility.[21]

In the sample of German villages under investigation, much of the observed association between age at marriage and age-specific marital fertility for the cohorts thought to be characterized by natural fertility can be accounted for by factors other than family limitation. In particular, the influences of bridal pregnancies on fertility, complications associated with childbirth leading to secondary sterility, and the fertility effect of the husband's age account for a fair share of the relationship. Moreover, the very modest extent to which an association remains after these factors are controlled for may be attributable to the impact of declining coital frequency with increasing duration of marriage rather than to the impact of some modest degree of family limitation. Thus, in the case of German village populations, it appears that an association between marital fertility and marriage duration prior to the onset of other signs of family limitation is attributable to a number of mechanisms unrelated to deliberate attempts to limit family size. Once the practice of family limitation starts, the association between marriage duration and marital fertility becomes considerably more pronounced and can no longer be accounted for in terms of the same mechanisms.

[21] Blake, 'Fertility transition.'

14

Child mortality and reproductive behavior

The relationship between mortality and fertility has been a matter of interest since the early days of population research. Concern with the nature and extent of the relationship has heightened since the formulation of demographic transition theory, which attributes central importance to the timing and interdependence of the secular declines in birth and death rates in Western demographic experience. Fertility can influence mortality in a variety of ways and in Chapter 4 the impact of the birth interval on infant mortality was examined. Most interest, however, has focused on the effect of mortality, and particularly infant and child mortality, on reproductive behavior. Recent conceptualization of this relationship has identified several different potential effects. These include an insurance (or hoarding) effect whereby couples have extra children in anticipation of child mortality, a replacement effect whereby couples have replacement births in response to their own actual (as opposed to anticipated) experience with child loss, and an involuntary physiological effect on the interval between births attributable to the interruption of breastfeeding and the consequent shortening of the postpartum non-susceptible period. At a different level, a societal effect is sometimes identified which operates indirectly (and presumably unconsciously) through social customs to adjust the community fertility level to the community mortality level.[1]

The present chapter begins with an analysis of the impact of infant mortality on birth intervals. This topic is discussed to a limited extent in

[1] Preston, 'Introduction'; Friedlander, 'Child mortality.' The replacement *effect* is sometimes distinguished from a replacement *strategy*. The former is defined in a broader sense which encompasses all fertility responses, voluntary and involuntary, to child mortality, while the latter refers to the stricter sense of deliberately replacing dead children (see, for example, Preston, 'Introduction'). In the present chapter, the replacement effect is used in the stricter sense of referring to the effect of a replacement strategy and thus excludes non-volitional responses.

Chapter 10 and Appendix F in connection with attempts to measure differences in the extent of breastfeeding, with different villages constituting the sample. Here the relationship is examined in more detail. Particular attention is given to the possibility that a behavioral component is operating beyond the purely physiological effect that would be expected from the curtailment of lactational infecundability associated with an infant death. The analysis then focuses on the replacement effect, examining whether replacement behavior is evidenced when other indications suggest the absence of deliberate attempts to aim for specific family sizes, and whether the evidence suggests the emergence and/or the strengthening of such an effort as family limitation spreads. Finally, the role of infant and child mortality in connection with the fertility transition is assessed, with particular attention being given to the extent that differential experience with child mortality relates to couples' participation in the spread of family limitation practices.

The insurance and societal effects are not directly assessed in the present chapter, in large part because they cannot be appropriately addressed with micro-level data. In contrast, the identification and measurement of birth interval and replacement effects are ideally addressed with family reconstitution data. Most empirical studies examining the link between child mortality and fertility have relied on macro-level data in which the units of analysis are geopolitically defined aggregates.[2] This has been especially true in analyses of the role of mortality change in the secular decline of fertility. The analysis presented in this chapter is of particular importance because it explores evidence of both birth interval effects and replacement attempts based on micro-level data for a period spanning the onset of the fertility transition, helping fill an important gap in the research.

To the extent that improving infant and child mortality operates through volitional responses on the part of the couple, it is important in an analysis of the relationship between reproductive behavior and mortality to distinguish contexts of natural fertility from those where a substantial proportion of couples deliberately limit family size. For example, in situations where volitional control of childbearing is truly absent from marriage, there should also be no evidence of deliberate attempts to replace children who have died. Thus, provided the replacement effect can be distinguished from non-volitional influences, it can serve as an independent test of the existence of family limitation during periods when other measures suggest that natural

---

[2] van de Walle, 'Infant mortality.'

fertility predominates. As in previous chapters, village-specific marriage cohorts characterized by values of the Coale–Trussell *m* index under .30 are treated as natural fertility marriage cohorts, and those characterized by higher values of *m* as family limitation cohorts.

Infant mortality and the birth interval

In previous chapters, substantial contrasts were evident among villages with respect to the length of the mean birth interval. These differences can probably be attributed in the main to differences in prevailing infant-feeding practices. Other factors, including deliberate attempts to space births, may also have played a role, but in general the differences seem to conform moderately well to the pattern that would be expected from the information on regional differences in breastfeeding reviewed in Appendix F and from the indirect evidence from the village genealogies themselves, based on the timing of the first two births (see Estimate B in Table F.1). In particular, the longest birth intervals characterized the East Frisian villages, where breastfeeding was relatively prolonged, while the shortest characterized the Bavarian villages, where breastfeeding was least extensive. Since lactation can prolong birth intervals substantially,[3] it seems likely that much of the difference observed between these two sets of villages can be attributed to differences in their breastfeeding practices. Other factors may have also contributed to the observed differences in the mean length of birth intervals. For example, as shown in Chapter 10, the index of fecundability is considerably higher for the Bavarian than for the East Frisian villages (see Table 10.8). However, fecundability differences are probably only a minor contributor to the total differences observed in the length of the average birth interval.[4] The persistence of fairly constant birth intervals in most of the villages over time, discussed in Chapter 12, suggests that the differences across villages are probably in large part determined by practices entrenched in longstanding custom. Infant-feeding practices are probably among the most important of these.

As discussed previously, the impact of breastfeeding on prolonging the birth interval should be evident from the relationship between the

[3] Knodel, 'Breast feeding and population growth.'
[4] According to Bongaarts ('Natural marital fertility'), the average waiting time to conception (W), expressed in months, that is associated with different levels of fecundability (f) can be estimated by 1.5/f. This would imply that differences in fecundability alone, as represented by the fecundability estimates presented in Chapter 10 (see Table 10.8), could account for about a one-and-a-half-month difference in birth intervals between East Friesland and Bavaria.

length of birth intervals and the age at death of the child born at the onset of the interval. Intervals following the births of children who survived past the age of weaning will reflect the full influence of breastfeeding on the interval, while intervals following births of children who died prior to weaning will be shorter. The sooner an infant dies after birth, the greater the impact of its death should be on shortening the interval. The strength of this relationship in the aggregate depends on the proportion of infants who are breastfed and the average duration (and intensity) of breastfeeding. In situations where breastfeeding is rare and short, the relationship will be far weaker than where breastfeeding is common and of long duration.

The average length of legitimate birth intervals by age at death of the child whose birth began the interval is shown in Figure 14.1 for the sample villages according to regional location. In all regional groupings, except for Bavaria, there is a clear increase in the average length of intervals, during at least the first year and a half, with increasing age at death. The lack of a clear relationship in the Bavarian villages is consistent with the evidence from other sources that breastfeeding was relatively uncommon, and of short duration when practiced. Likewise, the pronounced relationship in the two East Frisian villages conforms to indications that breastfeeding was relatively prolonged in that area. The similarly pronounced relationship in the four Waldeck villages suggests that breastfeeding was common there as well.

In general, the magnitude of the observed relationship between age at death and length of subsequent interval is within the range of what might be expected simply from the physiological effects of curtailing breastfeeding.[5] On the other hand, in some villages the association between longer birth intervals and age at death continues even for infants dying after a year and a half. It is unlikely that breastfeeding could account for this effect; evidence on breastfeeding in Germany generally indicates that even where it was most prolonged, the average duration was approximately a year,[6] making it unlikely that many women breastfed beyond 18 months. While the continued association between length of interval and age at death past this period might be due to random fluctuations in the data, it could also reflect the influence of factors other than breastfeeding.

A number of such factors can be postulated. For example, the survival of an infant might affect coital frequency. The concern with 'overlaying' (smothering a child by lying on top of it while sleeping) in much of Europe in the eighteenth and nineteenth centuries suggests

---

[5] Knodel, 'Breast feeding and population growth'; and 'European populations.'
[6] Kintner, 'Infant mortality'; and 'Breastfeeding in Germany.'

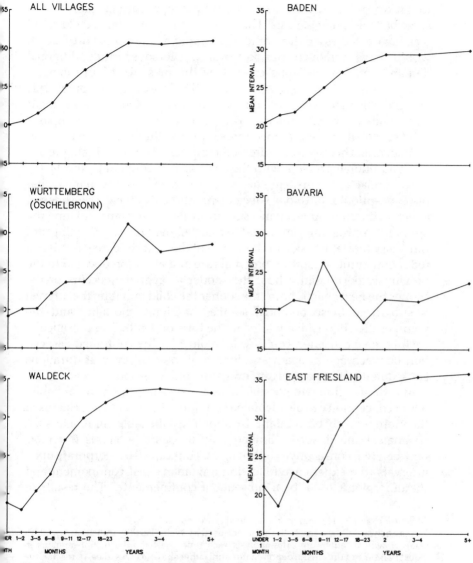

Figure 14.1. *Mean interval between legitimate confinements by age at death of child initiating interval and regional grouping of villages*. Results are based on births to locally married couples during periods of good death registration and are subject to restriction 7 (see Table A.1)

that it was not unusual for infants and young children to sleep in the same bed with their parents. Thus, the presence of a young child could well have acted as a deterrent to intercourse, while a premature death would have removed this constraint. Moreover, the additional demands on parents' time created by the presence of an infant or young child could have acted to reduce the desire for intercourse. It is also possible that a volitional mechanism was involved. Parents might have deliberately attempted to postpone the next birth as long as a child survived, but abandoned these efforts in the event of an infant or child death. This issue is addressed more fully later in this chapter.

An additional problem with the analysis presented in Figure 14.1 is the potential for the presence of a reverse path of causality, namely that the conception or birth of a subsequent infant may have a detrimental effect on the continuing chances of survival for the infant initiating the interval.[7] A pregnancy may lead to a curtailment of breastfeeding and thus raise mortality risks, or the arrival of the next child may result in a reduction in the amount of parental care and attention devoted to the previously born child. Thus, the sooner a pregnancy occurs or the sooner the next child is born, the sooner the child initiating the interval is subject to these potential sources of higher mortality and the younger the child is likely to be at the time of death. The presence of such reverse causation could well account for the continued association between age at death and length of interval, even at durations subsequent to the postpartum non-susceptible period.

In order to eliminate possible reverse causality, monthly probabilities of conception can be calculated conditional on the survival status of the more recently born infant. By applying a life table approach, such an analysis need not be limited only to closed intervals (intervals between two consecutive confinements) but can also incorporate open intervals (the experience following a woman's last confinement and therefore not 'closed' by a subsequent confinement).[8] The results of

---

[7] See, for example, Hobcraft *et al.*, 'Child spacing effects.'

[8] This analysis follows closely the approach used by Weir ('Fertility transition,' pp. 129–36). A woman enters into the analysis each time she has a birth. She remains in observation and thus in the denominator until either she conceives, dies, or reaches the end of the last elapsed month being considered, whichever occurs first. She counts in the numerator for the elapsed month, if any, during which she conceives. Conception is assumed to occur exactly 9 months prior to birth unless this would date it before the previous confinement. In such cases, conception is assumed to occur on the same day as the previous confinement. If the birth beginning the interval is her last birth or if her subsequent birth is conceived after the last elapsed month under observation, then she will remain in the denominator but never contribute to the numerator.

The survival status of the birth initiating the period under observation is determined as of the first day of each elapsed month. For confinements resulting in twins, the death

such an analysis are presented in Figure 14.2 for the total sample and regional groupings of villages. In order to smooth out random fluctuations, three-month weighted moving averages are employed. For this reason, the time series of monthly probabilities in Figure 14.2 begins at the start of the second elapsed month (indicated as month 1) rather than at the start of the first elapsed month (indicated as month 0).

The results clearly point to an initial period following birth during which a woman is at a higher risk of conception if her infant dies than if it survives. For the combined sample of all villages, the higher conception risk following an infant death persists for almost a year and a half following confinement. The differential in conception risk between women whose infant died and those whose infant survived, however, diminishes after the first few months and eventually reverses. Thus, after a year and a half, among those women who have not yet conceived, lower conception risks are associated with child deaths than with child survivals.

The reversal of the differential in conception probabilities at the more extended durations since confinement is probably explained by a selection process. Depending on the extent of breastfeeding, at some point following confinement virtually all women will have passed out of the period of postpartum non-susceptibility and either have conceived another child or remain at risk of conception. At any given duration, however, those still at risk of conception are likely to have been at risk longer if they experienced the loss of their infant than if their most recent birth is still surviving, especially since infant deaths are heavily concentrated in the first two months following confinement. If we assume an inverse correlation between waiting time to conception and fecundability, then at longer durations after confinement, there should be a higher concentration of women who have difficulty conceiving among women whose infant died than among women whose infant is still alive. This could account for the lower conception probability among the former group at longer durations following confinement, when breastfeeding is no longer delaying conception among the latter group. A second selection process may

of the longer-surviving twin is considered. The woman contributes to the probability of conception prior to an infant or child death as long as her most recent birth was alive on the first day of the elapsed month; she contributes to the probability of conception following an infant or child death, starting with the first elapsed month following the death. In cases where a conception and child death both occur on the first day of the elapsed month, the death is treated as if it preceded the conception. Only women whose most recent birth was stillborn or died on the same day that it was born would be treated as being in observation following a death during the first elapsed month after the confinement.

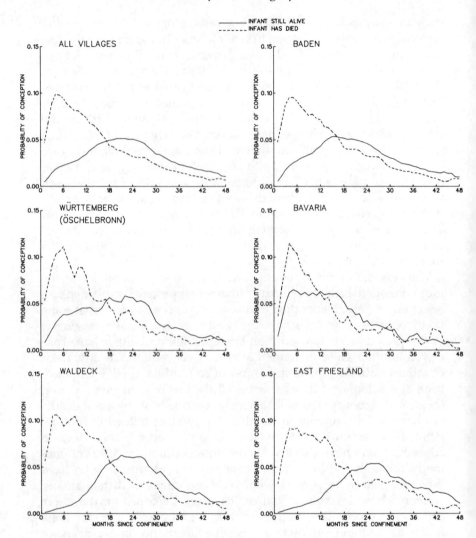

Figure 14.2. *Conditional monthly probability of conception, by survival status of prior birth, months since confinement, and regional grouping of villages.* The monthly probabilities shown represent three-month weighted moving averages. Results refer to legitimate confinements, are based on exact dates, and are subject to restrictions 6 and 7 (see Table A.1)

also be operating. If experience with infant mortality is positively correlated with fetal mortality, which would be unrecorded in the parish registers, the time to conceive, based on recorded births, would be longer on average for women whose infant died. At short durations

Table 14.1. *Unweighted mean conditional monthly probability of conception during the first year after confinement, by survivial status of prior birth and regional grouping of villages*

	Infant still alive	Infant has died	Ratio
4 villages in Baden	.0235	.0748	3.2
Öschelbronn (Württemberg)	.0299	.0839	2.8
3 villages in Bavaria	.0498	.0750	1.5
4 villages in Waldeck	.0058	.0869	15.0
2 villages in East Friesland	.0068	.0716	10.5
All villages	.0189	.0771	4.1

Note: Results refer to legitimate confinements, are based on exact dates, and are subject to restrictions 6 and 7 (see Table A.1).

following confinement, the effect of breastfeeding would more than compensate for this among women whose child is still alive, but such would no longer be the case at longer durations.

Regional differences are also apparent. Perhaps most surprising is the fact that even in the Bavarian villages, where breastfeeding is thought to have been minimal, conception risks following infant deaths are higher than those following survival, for approximately a year after confinement. Given that breastfeeding was not completely absent in the Bavarian villages, this might reflect the same processes at work as in the other villages. It could also reflect factors other than breastfeeding that potentially contribute to the delay in conception when an infant survives. Nevertheless, it is noteworthy that for most elapsed months during this period the *difference* in conception rates in the Bavarian villages is less than that observed in the other regions. Moreover, the reversal of this difference occurs sooner in Bavaria than in the other four regional groupings.

The substantial regional differences are highlighted in Table 14.1, which summarizes the average conditional monthly probability of conception during the first year following a confinement, according to the survival status of the infant, for the different regional groupings of villages. For women in all regions, the probability of conception during the first year following a confinement is greater when the infant dies than when the infant survives. Regional differences in the probability of conception following an infant death during the first twelve months after confinement are quite modest. In contrast, very sharp regional differences are evident in the probability of conception when the infant is still alive. Thus the extent of the differences varies very considerably by region. When the infant is still alive, the monthly probability of conception during the first year is by far the highest in the Bavarian villages, and by far the lowest in the Waldeck and East Frisian villages. Women in both the Baden villages and Öschelbronn are in an inter-mediate position. The ratio of the probability of conception when an infant has died to the probability when an infant is still alive is only one and a half in the Bavarian villages. In contrast, this ratio is over ten in the populations of the villages in East Friesland and Waldeck.

These regional differences conform quite well to what we would expect from the standard evidence about breastfeeding reviewed in Appendix F. Once the influence of breastfeeding is eliminated, as is the case following an infant death, probabilities of conception are remark-ably similar and, indeed, women in the Bavarian villages do not stand out as having unusually high fecundability. The far lower probability of conception in the East Frisian villages compared to the Bavarian villages when an infant is still alive is quite consistent with the suggestion that the postpartum non-susceptible period is significantly extended in East Friesland through prolonged breastfeeding. While the results do not permit us to distinguish the influence of breastfeed-ing from other possible mechanisms, the fact that there are such pronounced regional differences in conception probabilities during the first year when the infant is still alive, but not when the infant has died, suggests that influences other than breastfeeding are far less important in accounting for the impact of an infant death on the birth interval.

Also of interest is the trend over time in the conditional probability of conception by survival status of the child. The results are presented in Table 14.2 for the combined sample of all villages. Several potential problems in interpreting the results should be kept in mind. Some change in the composition of the sample occurs, particularly between the last half of the eighteenth century and the first half of the nineteenth century as a result of the need for exact dates of death for those children who do die and thus of restrictions placed on the analysis which limit results to periods of reliable death registration for infants and children. Thus the Bavarian villages enter the analysis only after 1800 (see Appendix B). Given the relatively small share of the total sample constituted by the Bavarian villages, this compositional shift is unlikely to have a major impact on the comparison between the 1750–99 period and the 1800–49 period. Nevertheless, to the extent it does exert an influence, it could presumably account for some increase in the probability of conception, since the Bavarian villages were charac-terized by unusually high probabilities of conception during the first year for women whose infant remained alive. Compositional shifts are less important during the nineteenth century and thus should have

Table 14.2. *Unweighted mean conditional monthly probability of conception, by survival status of prior birth, months since confinement, and year of marriage*

Elapsed months since confinement	Survival status of prior birth and year of marriage									
	Alive					Dead				
	1750–99	1800–49	1850–74	1875–99	Change index[a]	1750–99	1800–49	1850–74	1875–99	Change index[a]
1–6	.0055	.0076	.0163	.0270	4.90	.0723	.0695	.0711	.0609	.84
7–12	.0173	.0244	.0342	.0407	2.35	.0951	.0872	.0806	.0774	.81
13–18	.0390	.0472	.0467	.0422	1.08	.0759	.0602	.0538	.0541	.71
19–24	.0567	.0547	.0460	.0378	.66	.0470	.0368	.0326	.0386	.82
25–30	.0571	.0464	.0373	.0308	.54	.0350	.0297	.0238	.0268	.77
31–36	.0388	.0314	.0234	.0215	.55	.0216	.0188	.0145	.0177	.82

Note: Results refer to legitimate confinements in the combined sample of all villages, are based on exact dates, and are subject to restrictions 6 and 7 (see Table A.1).
[a] Ratio of the 1875–99 probability to the 1750–99 probability.

only a minimal influence on the time trend during that century. A second potential influence on the trend is the increasing practice of family limitation during the nineteenth century. All else being equal, increases in the practice of birth control should lead to a decreasing probability of conception. Despite these problems, the trend is of considerable interest, revealing a distinctive and suggestive pattern.

The probability of conception during the first six months following confinement for women whose child is still alive increased by almost five-fold between the last half of the eighteenth century and the end of the nineteenth century, as is evident in the change index (the ratio of the 1875–99 probability to the 1750–99 probability). A lesser but also substantial increase is evident for conception probabilities during the second half of the first year following confinement for women whose child is still alive. In both of these cases, increases occur between each two consecutive marriage cohorts, with particularly sharp differences evident during the nineteenth century. Conception probabilities for women whose infant is still alive show a quite different pattern at longer durations after confinement, with steady declines evident for durations after a year and a half. A more irregular trend is evident for conception probabilities when the previously born child has died. Nevertheless, for all durations since confinement, the conception probabilities at the end of the nineteenth century are lower than during the last half of the eighteenth century, although this is generally not the product of a steady trend toward decline. Moreover, the changes in conception probabilities when a child has died are considerably less than when the child is alive.

The results tend to support the suggestion, discussed in Chapter 10, that the extent of breastfeeding, or at least its impact on fertility, was diminishing over the period under study. Such a change would only affect conception probabilities for women whose children were still alive and would have no effect on conception probabilities following the death of a prior infant. Moreover, the effect should be greatest during the earlier durations and have little impact on conception probabilities after more extended durations. The decline in the conception probabilities over time at the more extended durations could well reflect increasing family limitation practice or result from a selection process whereby those women who restrict the number of their children are most likely to reach extended durations and thereby represent a disproportionate share of women at these durations. The impact of family limitation would thus be most evident at the longer durations since last confinement. At shorter durations, the impact of increasing family limitation might well be overwhelmed by the influence of a decreased period of postpartum non-susceptibility resulting from declining breastfeeding, and perhaps also by increased fecundability stemming from other sources (see Chapter 10). An additional impact through selection might also be occurring, with a greater concentration in the longer duration categories of women who have difficulties conceiving. This would result from the higher proportions of women without difficulties in conceiving doing so at the short durations, where the probabilities of conception are increasing.

It is more difficult to interpret the decrease in conception probabilities for women whose infant has already died. Presumably, such probabilities are independent of infant-feeding practices. Moreover, increased practice of birth control would most likely have only a minimal impact on conception risks following an infant death, provided, that is, the parents were interested in replacing the lost child. Such parents would be relatively unlikely to practice birth control at that particular point in their reproductive lives, unless the experience with infant death discouraged further attempts at childbearing. The evidence of declining conception probabilities following an infant or child death probably has little bearing on the plausibility of the argument that changing infant-feeding practices, and particularly a reduction in breastfeeding, is a likely explanation for much of the change observed with respect to changing conception probabilities during the first year following a birth when the infant survives. Moreover, such an argument is consistent with the rise in infant mortality observed during part of the nineteenth century (see Chapter 3). Thus the explanation of the pattern of changing conception probabilities may lie in a combination of increasing family limitation and changing infant-feeding practices.

In brief, the evidence relating infant mortality and birth intervals points clearly to a substantial physiological impact related to breastfeeding and the associated period of postpartum non-susceptibility. In villages located in regions where breastfeeding was moderate or prolonged, the death of an infant or very young child could prematurely curtail lactation and hasten the next conception. Regional differences in this impact conform to expectations based on scattered information about regional differences in infant-feeding practices. Factors other than the physiological impact through breastfeeding may also operate, but these are more difficult to determine and are unlikely to be of major importance.

The child replacement effect

The child replacement effect presumes some form of deliberate fertility control which causes couples to cease childbearing after attaining the number of surviving children they consider sufficient. In the absence of deliberate limitation of family size, there could be no replacement effect since childbearing would continue until the couple was no longer physically capable of reproduction, regardless of their experience with child mortality. While child mortality may also influence the deliberate spacing of births, a replacement strategy is ultimately directed toward the final number of surviving children.

At early stages of the fertility transition, when family limitation is not yet practiced universally and when childbearing within marriage has not previously been considered a matter of deliberate choice, couples with low previous child mortality may react by stopping childbearing before they actually become sterile, while those who have experienced higher mortality may continue to adhere to the traditional pattern of uncontrolled fertility. The behavioral link, therefore, may operate largely through deliberate attempts to limit childbearing in response to child survival, rather than through deliberate attempts at replacement in response to child deaths. Perhaps only at more advanced stages of the demographic transition is deliberate stopping behavior combined with deliberate attempts at replacement. For the sake of convenience, however, the term 'replacement' is used to refer to both situations.

There are several reasons for expecting that replacement will be incomplete. Even when contraception is widespread, a variety of influences may affect the desire to replace children, such as the sex or age of the dead child, or the number of previous child deaths. Multiple child losses might actually encourage a couple to stop childbearing rather than risk yet another disappointment. Even where the desire for replacement is universal, some children will die when their parents are too old to bear additional children. The presence of an insurance effect could also complicate the extent of replacement behavior, since where a child death has been anticipated in advance and protected against, no effort at replacement would be made. An insurance strategy, however, can be made far more efficient when combined with a replacement strategy.[9]

Strategy for analysis

The analytical approach used to detect replacement behavior is to

[9] Olsen, 'Child mortality.'

compare the subsequent reproductive activity of couples who have reached similar stages in the childbearing process, according to their previous experience with child deaths. Attempts are made to control for several factors which might bias or confound the results. Several different indicators of reproductive behavior are used, and all are presumed to be sensitive to attempts at family limitation. These include the number of additional children born after a woman had achieved a given parity, the age of the mother at last birth, and the probability of stopping (measured as the percentage of women who do not continue childbearing). These measures are related to the couple's previous child mortality, defined as the number of children who had died before reaching their fifth birthday. This age was chosen because it encompasses the age range of most pre-adult mortality, while minimizing the chance that the parents will have become sterile by the time of the child's death. In addition, mortality prior to age 5 can be measured with reasonable confidence, based on the methods employed for calculating mortality risks in the present study (see Appendix E).

To reduce or eliminate several factors which could bias or confound the results, several selection criteria are employed. To maximize the chance that only fully observed, reproductively complete unions are included, the analysis is limited to couples whose marriage remained intact until the wife's 45th birthday, whose marriage began and ended in the locality, and for whom the date of the end of union is known with certainty (restrictions 1, 2, 3 and 4 apply – see Table A.1). In addition, only couples who had had no multiple births up to the point at which subsequent fertility is measured were included. The purpose of this control is to avoid the problems which multiple births can create for analyses of this type.[10]

While some ambiguity in the results can be removed by selecting families according to these criteria, other potentially biasing influences can be reduced or eliminated by introducing control variables. By using multiple classification analysis, results are adjusted for four such variables: village of residence, husband's occupational category, age of the wife at the time of a given birth (adjusted for the impact of an infant

---

[10] Since the probability that a subsequent confinement will result in a multiple birth is substantially higher for women who have had a multiple birth previously, and mortality is much higher for multiple births than for single births, their inclusion could lead to an association between the number of subsequent children born and the number of previous child deaths even when no deliberate replacement is present. Multiple births also present a problem since bearing the second birth of a set of twins (or the second and third births of a set of triplets) obviously does not reflect a voluntary continuation of childbearing, and thus confounds measures of subsequent fertility.

death on the postpartum non-susceptible period), and an index of the couple's fecundity (measured either by the interval between marriage and first birth or the interval between the birth of a surviving child and the following birth).

As is evident from the results presented in previous chapters, both village of residence and socio-economic status are related to fertility and child mortality and thus could lead to a spurious association between mortality and fertility at the micro-level. The control variable representing socio-economic status is the broad occupational group of the husband (see Appendix D). But the most important demographic factor which influences a couple's subsequent fertility is the length of the couple's exposure to the risk of additional births, particularly as determined by the age of the wife. The younger a woman is at a given point in the family-building process, the longer she will be exposed to the risk of additional births and the more likely she is to continue childbearing. Since the death of unweaned infants can shorten birth intervals, those who experience infant deaths among women who start childbearing at the same age will tend to reach a given parity when they are younger than those whose infants survive.[11]

Most of the bias that would result from the common association of age at achieving a particular parity with both subsequent fertility and previous child mortality can be avoided by controlling for the age at which that parity is attained. However, this does not take into account that, as a result of the possible interruption of breastfeeding, women whose most recent child had died are more likely to be exposed to the risk of an additional pregnancy sooner than those whose most recent child had survived. While the magnitude of this effect is generally small, it will be largest in populations where breastfeeding is universal and prolonged.[12] To eliminate it, the age of the mother at attaining a given parity has been adjusted on a village-specific basis, according to the fate of the child born at that time. For each village, the additional exposure to risk of a woman whose child had died has been taken as the difference between the average interval to the next birth in these cases and those in which the infant had survived.[13]

[11] A clear negative association between the number of infant deaths and the age at attaining a given parity is apparent in the present sample.

[12] Brass and Barrett, 'Measurement problems.'

[13] To minimize the contribution to this difference of any volitional attempts to space births, last intervals or intervals after the third legitimate confinement were excluded when the correction factor was calculated. The impact of an infant death ranges from approximately one month to a little over one year. The age of the mother was adjusted by letting it stand when the infant survived, but subtracting from it the correction

While it is clear that child mortality can influence the length of birth intervals, closer birth spacing also increases the chances of infant and child deaths and could confound an analysis of replacement behavior (see Chapter 4).[14] If closer birth spacing leads to higher child mortality, women experiencing child deaths would tend to be more fecund, characterized by higher fecundability and/or shorter periods of post-partum non-susceptibility.[15] Because of this possibility, a measure of the couple's fecundity is introduced into the analysis. Two different measures are used. One is based on the interval between marriage and the first legitimate birth (divided into five categories, including separate categories for women whose first birth was illegitimate and for women whose first birth was premaritally conceived). However, this measure is not likely to reflect different characteristic periods of postpartum infertility.[16] The measure does have the advantage that it can be calculated for all fertile married couples.

An alternative index of fecundity is based on the tempo of childbearing as reflected by the average birth interval of women having a birth of a given order. This measure reflects both the woman's characteristic fecundability and her period of postpartum non-susceptibility. To avoid being biased, it must be restricted to intervals that follow surviving children, since the death of a child could lead to the premature interruption of the period of postpartum amenorrhea. The measure, therefore, can only be calculated for women who have had at least one surviving child and a subsequent birth. To interpret this measure as an indicator of fecundity, it is necessary to assume that deliberate birth control was not used for spacing births.

factor for the village in which the woman resided, when the infant died. Thus a woman whose most recent child had died in infancy was treated as if she were somewhat younger at the birth of that child than a woman of the same age whose child survived.

[14] See also, Hobcraft *et al.*, 'Child spacing effects.'

[15] Brass and Barrett, 'Measurement problems.'

[16] Results from the combined sample of 14 German villages indicate that this measure is generally related to fertility in the expected direction. Women with long intervals between marriage and first birth had fewer children ever born and/or ceased child-bearing earlier than women who conceived shortly after marriage (both before and after controlling for age at first birth). Moreover, women with premarital births or conceptions had families which were larger than average and stopped childbearing at later ages. However, the measure showed only a very weak and inconsistent relationship with child mortality and thus is unlikely to have much effect on the relationship between previous child deaths and subsequent fertility. Nevertheless, since there is theoretical justification for controlling for this measure, it is included in the analysis.

Results[17]

If couples attempted to replace children who had died, we would expect a positive relationship between the number of subsequent births to women of a given parity and the number of deaths among the children already born. This relationship is examined in Table 14.3 for the combined sample of 14 villages for the cohorts of natural fertility and for those practicing family limitation, as defined above. The results are shown both unadjusted and simultaneously adjusted for age at attaining a given parity (modified for the fate of the child of that parity as described above), interval to first birth, village of residence, and occupational category of husband. The analysis is repeated five times, starting with women who had their first birth and ending with those who had a fifth birth. The analysis at any particular parity order includes all women who attained that parity, whether or not they had a subsequent birth, but excludes those who stopped childbearing at a lower parity.

Several findings are worth stressing. First, the unadjusted results are consistent with replacement behavior for both types of cohorts at each successive parity. Secondly, adjustment reduces the strength of the relationship among the natural fertility cohorts, particularly for women who attain larger families. In cohorts in which family limitation is practiced, the effect of adjustment is smaller, and at lower parities actually strengthens the association. Thirdly, even after adjustment, a less pronounced but generally positive relationship between the number of additional births and previous child deaths remains for the cohorts with natural fertility. Where family limitation is practiced, the adjusted results also indicate a positive relationship up to and including the fourth birth, but are inconsistent for women attaining a fifth birth. Fourthly, up to and including the third birth, the relationship is more pronounced in cohorts in which family limitation is practiced than in those with natural fertility. The association is weak for both types of cohorts for women who have a fourth birth, but is still consistent with replacement. At the fifth birth, the pattern is irregular in cohorts in which family limitation is practiced, and in those with natural fertility the association is weak.

The stronger association in cohorts in which family limitation was practiced among women who had first, second, or third births,

[17] Results presented in this chapter differ slightly from those previously published in *Population Studies* in July 1982 entitled 'Child mortality and reproductive behavior in German village populations in the past: a micro-level analysis of the replacement effect' because the periods of acceptable infant and child death registration have been respecified (see Appendix B) and because the occupational classification has been revised (see Appendix D).

suggests that efforts to replace children who had died were more common in these cohorts. The association does not, however, hold at higher parities, probably because couples who practice family limitation and whose experience of child mortality was favorable will have ceased reproducing before the wife reached these parities. Thus, among women with low child mortality who have fourth or fifth births, there will be a disproportionate number who do not practice family limitation and are likely to continue reproducing irrespective of their level of child mortality. This contrasts with couples whose child mortality has been high, since they will only have achieved a small family of surviving children. However, as the period of observation relates to the initial stages of the fertility transition, practice of family limitation is probably not very common. The results are consistent with a pattern in which only some couples practice a moderate amount of family limitation, during its initial spread, while others practice none. This conforms to the analysis, in Chapter 12, indicating only a moderate proportion of the family limitation cohorts were effectively stopping childbearing prior to the natural end of the reproductive age span.

The persistence of a positive association between previous child mortality and subsequent fertility for the cohorts with natural fertility, even after adjustment for the four control variables, is intriguing. Two interpretations are possible. The results may genuinely reflect deliberate efforts at replacement and imply that some family limitation was practiced despite the designation of these as cohorts characterized by natural fertility, either because the criterion used to differentiate the two types of cohort was not sufficiently discriminating, or because family limitation may have been practiced even before any change in m took place. In the latter case, we may not be correct in referring to the 'onset' of family limitation. Alternatively, the results may reflect biases which have either been inadequately controlled for or not controlled for at all, and thus yield only a spurious appearance of replacement behavior. As has already been indicated, the interval between marriage and first birth is at best only an imperfect measure of fecundity.

An additional source of bias which may help account for the appearance of a replacement effect and for which no control has been introduced is an intrafamily association between previous and subsequent child mortality. The survivorship histories of infants of the same mother are typically intercorrelated, and this is indeed the case for the present sample. On average, mortality of a woman's subsequent children increases at any parity with the number of deaths that have occurred among previous children. For example, among women

Table 14.3. *Number of additional children born, expressed as deviations from the overall mean, according to the number of deaths before age 5 among children already born, unadjusted and adjusted for modified age at attaining given parity, interval to first birth, village of residence, and occupational category of husband*

Deaths under age 5 up to and including given parity	Natural fertility cohorts				Family limitation cohorts			
		Deviations from mean				Deviations from mean		
	Mean	Unadjusted	Adjusted	N	Mean	Unadjusted	Adjusted	N
Parity 1	5.14				4.66			
0		−.08	−.07	2440		−.16	−.23	1133
1		.19	.16	989		.44	.63	422
Eta/beta		.04	.03			.09	.12	
Parity 2	4.51				3.87			
0		−.26	−.17	1709		−.30	−.34	767
1		.29	.21	1142		.25	.28	574
2		.36	.15	304		.79	.91	110
Eta/beta		.10	.06			.12	.13	

Parity 3	3.90			3.29		
0	−.38	−.19	1144	−.34	−.26	477
1	.11	.06	1133	.05	.00	551
2	.51	.30	479	.41	.44	218
3	.67	.08	102	1.18	.82	38
Eta/beta	.13	.06		.12	.10	
Parity 4	3.37			2.90		
0	−.54	−.26	748	−.35	−.12	279
1	.01	.01	946	.01	−.06	407
2	.46	.20	579	.13	.05	269
3+	.55	.26	237	.55	.43	110
Eta/beta	.16	.08		.10	.06	
Parity 5	2.82			2.54		
0	−.57	−.23	480	−.12	.21	159
1	−.14	−.03	705	−.12	−.07	287
2	.29	.15	602	−.10	−.24	220
3+	.50	.11	390	.40	.21	191
Eta/beta	.16	.06		.09	.08	

Note: Results refer to the combined sample of all villages and are subject to restrictions 1, 2, 3, 4 and 7 (see Table A.1). Results are adjusted by multiple classification analysis. See text for definition of natural fertility and family limitation cohorts.

in the present sample who had a second birth, 29 percent of the subsequent children to women with no previous child mortality died before their fifth birthday, compared to 33 and 42 percent, respectively, for women who had experienced one or two previous child deaths.[18] This association results in the analysis in Table 14.3 being biased in a direction consistent with replacement behavior, since higher mortality among subsequent births can shorten the average length of future birth intervals and can result in large numbers of additional births, even in the absence of any deliberate replacement behavior. In the case of cohorts with natural fertility for whose members the adjusted association between previous child deaths and additional children born is not strong, a substantial proportion of the remaining association could be attributable to the correlation between subsequent and previous child mortality.

A rough estimate suggests that close to half of the observed difference in the number of additional children born, according to previous child mortality after adjustment for other factors, could be attributed to this additional bias for the cohorts with natural fertility.[19]

[18] These results represent the combined experience of the natural fertility and family limitation cohorts and are based on a selection of couples similar to those included in Table 14.3. The only difference is that the calculations were made prior to the respecification of the periods of acceptable infant and child death registration. Since the respecification was quite minor it is unlikely to have any significant effect on the results.

[19] A rough estimate of the size of this bias can be made on the following assumptions: (a) all women, regardless of their previous child mortality, attain a given parity at the average age observed for the cohort with natural fertility; (b) the proportion of these women who have additional births is the same as actually observed; (c) all those who continue childbearing stop at the observed average age at last birth for women who attain that parity and continue childbearing; (d) child mortality among additional births varies according to the mother's previous child mortality as actually observed for the cohort with natural fertility; (e) the average interval at which each group of women classified by previous child mortality bear children will correspond to a weighted average of observed intervals following child death and child survival, with the weights being respectively the observed proportion who die and survive among additional births. The number of additional births to women who continue childbearing will equal the number of years childbearing continues divided by the average interval which characterizes each group of women. These results are then multiplied by the proportion of women who continue childbearing, to allow for the fact that some women have no additional births. The mean birth interval for women none of whose previous children had died will be longer than for women with previous child deaths, since greater weight will have been given to the longer intervals following child survival and less to the shorter intervals following child death. This is a direct result of the positive correlation between previous and subsequent experience with child mortality. These longer intervals translate into a somewhat smaller number of additional births for women with no previous mortality.

For example, based on calculations made prior to the respecification of the periods of acceptable death registration (see note 18), the average age at attaining parity 2 was 29.18 for the natural fertility cohort. Of those reaching parity 2, .921 continued to have

Assuming that the magnitude of this bias is similar for the cohorts practicing family limitation, it would also account for some of the observed association between previous child deaths and subsequent fertility. However, since the observed effect is considerably more pronounced in cohorts in which family limitation is practiced up to and including the third birth, this bias is unlikely to be responsible for more than a small proportion of the observed relationship.

Given the association between a couple's previous and subsequent child mortality, it is useful to consider the effectiveness of any volitional response to child mortality in terms of increasing the number of additional *surviving* children. This question can be treated by an analysis similar to that in Table 14.4, except that only the number of those additional children who survive to their fifth birthday are related to previous child loss. The results presented in Table 14.4 indicate that, if indeed any volitional fertility response to child mortality were being made by the natural fertility cohorts, they were completely frustrated by the higher subsequent child mortality associated with previous child deaths. In the cohorts in which there is family limitation, replacement efforts appear to have been effective, judging by the number of additional surviving children born following the attainment of parities up to and including the third. As expected, the effect is weaker than when expressed in terms only of additional births. The disproportionate concentration of couples not using family limitation among those continuing childbearing in the group with favorable child mortality, and the association between previous and subsequent child loss, eliminates any appearance of replacement in terms of additional surviving children when the analysis refers to women who have a

additional births. The average age at last birth among those continuing childbearing was 40.67. Of those with no prior deaths under age 5, .283 of the additional births died before age 5 compared to .413 for those with two prior child deaths. The average birth interval (excluding last intervals) following the birth of a child who died under age 5 for the natural fertility cohort was 1.82 years, compared to 2.39 years following a child survival. Thus women with no prior child deaths, who continued childbearing, would be expected to bear an additional child every 2.229 years [(.283×1.82)+(.717×2.39)], while women with two prior deaths would bear an additional child every 2.155 years [(.413×1.82)+(.587×2.39)]. Both groups would bear children at these intervals for 11.49 years (40.67−29.18). The average number of additional births expected for women with no prior child mortality would then be 4.75 [.921×(11.49÷2.229)], compared to 4.91 additional children [.921×(11.49÷2.155)] for women with two prior child deaths. This difference of .16 births represents half of the .32 difference in additional births observed between women with no prior child deaths and women with two prior child deaths. Overall, such a set of calculations indicates a difference of .08, .16, .22, .21, and .16 additional births between women none of whose previous children had died and those who had experienced the maximum number of deaths indicated in Table 14.3, for women who had one, two, three, four, or five children respectively.

Table 14.4. *Number of additional children born who survive to age 5, expressed as deviations from the overall mean, according to the number of deaths before age 5 among children already born, unadjusted and adjusted for modified age at attaining given parity, interval to first birth, village of residence, and occupational category of husband*

Deaths under age 5 up to and including given parity	Natural fertility cohorts			Family limitation cohorts		
		Deviations from mean			Deviations from mean	
	Mean	Unadjusted	Adjusted	Mean	Unadjusted	Adjusted
Parity 1	3.54			3.15		
0		.04	.02		-.08	-.14
1		-.10	-.04		.21	.37
Eta/beta		.03	.01		.06	.10
Parity 2	3.07			2.59		
0		-.03	-.01		-.15	-.19
1		.11	.08		.19	.22
2		-.22	-.26		.07	.18
Eta/beta		.05	.04		.08	.10

Parity 3	2.63		2.17	
0	−.08	.01	−.12	−.10
1	.09	.06	.06	.04
2	.03	−.05	.07	.12
3	−.26	−.53	.28	.05
Eta/beta	.05	.06	.05	.04
Parity 4	2.24		1.89	
0	−.15	−.01	−.11	.00
1	.08	.08	.13	.09
2	.13	.01	−.10	−.14
3+	−.17	−.26	.06	.02
Eta/beta	.07	.05	.06	.05
Parity 5	1.86		1.63	
0	−.15	.02	.05	.20
1	.02	.06	−.01	.02
2	.14	.08	.01	−.08
3+	−.07	−.26	−.03	−.10
Eta/beta	.07	.07	.02	.07

Note: Results refer to the combined sample of all villages and are subject to restrictions 1, 2, 3, 4 and 7 (see Table A.1). Results are adjusted by multiple classification analysis. The number of cases is the same as in Table 10.2. See text for definition of natural fertility and family limitation cohorts.

fourth birth. Moreover, the same factors lead to a distinctly negative relationship between previous child loss and additional surviving children born for women who reach their fifth birth.

Effective replacement was far from complete during the early stages of the fertility transition as is apparent from a comparison of the number of additional surviving children born to women who have lost previous children with those born to women all of whose previous children survived. For example, after adjusting for the four control variables among women, in the cohorts in which family limitation was practiced, who had a first birth, those whose first child died averaged .51 (.14+.37) extra additional surviving children compared to women whose first child survived, indicating that replacement net of child mortality was approximately half complete. This is the highest completeness ratio in the entire set of results. Generally the ratio declines for women who attain successively higher parities: similar calculations for women who have a second birth in the cohorts in which family limitation is practiced show that those with one previous child death averaged .41 more surviving children, and those with two previous deaths averaged only .37 more surviving children, than women all of whose children survived, a result which reflects replacement, net of child mortality, that is only 41 and 19 percent complete respectively. For women with three children, the completeness ratios are almost negligible, and for those attaining higher parities either negligible or negative. It should be noted, however, that because of the selection mentioned above, this technique for estimating the completeness of replacement becomes increasingly inappropriate as it is applied to results for women who attain successively higher parities.

As discussed in Chapters 10 and 11, one measure sensitive to couples' attempts to limit family size is the age of the mother at the last birth. In populations with natural fertility, couples would be expected to continue childbearing until either the husband or the wife loses the physiological ability to become a parent. Generally, the wife's reproductive capacity ceases earlier, and it is her age that is the limiting factor. Where family limitation and attempts at replacement are common, couples with favorable child mortality will typically cease childbearing earlier than couples for whom one or more children have died, and we expect a positive relationship between the age of mother at last birth and the number of previous child deaths.

The results of such an analysis are presented in Table 14.5 for the combined sample of all villages. Several points are worth noting. First, there is generally a positive association between age at last birth and the number of previous child deaths in cohorts with natural fertility, although some irregularities are evident in the case of women who have third, fourth, or fifth births. Secondly, the relationship is more pronounced for women who have had between one and three births in cohorts in which family limitation is practiced. In contrast, no consistent pattern appears for women with four or five births. Thirdly, the effect of adjusting for the control variable is small.

The substantially stronger positive association among women in cohorts in which family limitation is practiced, and who have had between one and three births, confirms the strengthening of efforts to replace children who have died, as family limitation spreads. The lack of any consistent association for women of higher parities presumably results from the selection process referred to above.

The impact of adjusting the results for the four control variables is considerably weaker for the relationship between previous child mortality and age at last birth than when the number of additional children was the dependent variable. This is not surprising. The age of mother at last birth, especially for cohorts with natural fertility, differed very little between different villages and occupational categories (see Chapter 11). In addition, the age of mother at last birth is less sensitive to the age at attaining a given parity and to the interval between marriage and first birth than is the number of additional children born.

While the positive relationship, for the cohorts with natural fertility, between age at last birth and the number of previous child deaths suggests deliberate replacement behavior, the possibility exists, as before, that at least part of the observed association results from biases that remain, even in the adjusted results, because of incomplete or omitted controls. For example, the association between subsequent and previous child mortality, discussed above, would bias the results toward the appearance of replacement behavior. The reason is that at any given age of mother the probability that a particular birth will be the last is greater when the child survives than when it dies, independently of any deliberate attempts to stop childbearing. The longer period of postpartum non-susceptibility associated with a surviving child increases the chance that the period of postpartum non-susceptibility will overlap with the onset of secondary sterility.[20]

[20] This bias is undoubtedly small. As an illustration of how it might operate, consider the following example. Two women give birth at exact age 39, but in one case the child survives while in the other the child dies soon after birth. The period of postpartum non-susceptibility for the woman whose child survives is nine months, but only three months for the woman whose child died. Both women become infecund at exact age 39.5. For the woman whose child survived, the period of postpartum non-susceptibility would overlap the end of her reproductive span, thus ending her

Table 14.5. *Age of mother at last birth, expressed as deviations from the overall mean, according to the number of deaths before age 5 among children already born, unadjusted and adjusted for modified age at attaining given parity, interval to first birth, village of residence, and occupational category of husband*

Deaths under age 5 up to and including given parity	Natural fertility cohorts			Family limitation cohorts		
	Mean	Deviations from mean		Mean	Deviations from mean	
		Unadjusted	Adjusted		Unadjusted	Adjusted
Parity 1	40.06			37.81		
0		−.05	−.06		−.33	−.29
1		.13	.14		.88	.77
Eta/beta		.02	.02		.10	.09
Parity 2	40.35			38.03		
0		−.15	−.15		−.43	−.41
1		.18	.17		.42	.39
2		.18	.18		.79	.81
Eta/beta		.04	.04		.10	.09

Parity 3	40.67			38.54		
0		−.17	−.18		−.19	−.21
1		.07	.06		−.06	−.10
2		.30	.31		.48	.61
3		−.24	−.09		.50	.42
Eta/beta		.04	.04		.06	.07
Parity 4	41.05			39.28		
0		−.27	−.30		.10	−.08
1		.03	.03		.06	.04
2		.24	.29		−.19	−.02
3+		.12	.15		−.04	.10
Eta/beta		.05	.06		.03	.01
Parity 5	41.45			39.86		
0		−.34	−.34		.29	.14
1		.06	.04		.20	.16
2		.28	.26		−.46	−.38
3+		−.12	−.04		−.01	−.08
Eta/beta		.07	.06		.08	.06

Note: Results refer to the combined sample of all villages and are subject to restrictions 1, 2, 3, 4 and 7 (see Table A.1). Results are adjusted by multiple classification analysis. The number of cases is the same as in Table 10.2. See text for definition of natural fertility and family limitation cohorts.

Thus it is not possible to conclude definitely that the results indicate a volitional response to previous child mortality. What is evident is that any such volitional response is small, and that a more pronounced association, net of control factors, appears for the cohorts in which family limitation is practiced when the analysis refers to women who have had one, two, or three births.

An additional measure which should be sensitive to attempts to replace children who had died at early ages is the probability of ceasing childbearing after a given parity has been reached. Where replacement behavior is common, we would expect a negative relation between this probability and the number of previous child deaths. Thus a higher percentage of women all of whose children have survived would be expected to stop bearing children at any given parity than women who have experienced previous child loss.[21]

The results presented in Table 14.6 indicate that there is at best a very weak relationship for cohorts with natural fertility between the percentage who stop at a given parity and the number of previous child deaths, especially after the results are adjusted for the four control variables. Indeed, only a negligible or irregular relationship exists for the probabilities of stopping at the first, second, or third birth. For women who are having their fourth or fifth birth, the relationship is more clearly negative although still somewhat irregular, especially for the adjusted results. A different picture emerges for cohorts in which family limitation is practiced. For women who have had between one and four births, the association is more pronounced and regular than for the cohorts with natural fertility. Only for women who had a fifth birth is the pattern irregular, probably because of the confounding influence of the selection process discussed above.

Some differences are found between the results based on stopping

childbearing at age 39.0. In contrast, the period of postpartum non-susceptibility of the woman whose child died would end three months before she loses the ability to conceive and she would thus be able to have another child. If she conceived at any time during the three months remaining to her, she would be over 40 years old at the time of her last birth. Since women with previous child deaths are more likely to experience subsequent child deaths, they are more likely to be in a position of the woman whose child dies and who goes on to have an additional birth, and thus will tend to bear the last child at an older age than a woman with more favorable child mortality experience.

[21] Since, in the present analysis, previous child mortality is measured in terms of child deaths before the fifth birthday, some women among those who have an additional birth may have conceived their next child before the death of one or more of their previous children who died, thus complicating interpretation of the results. However, the number of cases for which this is true must be small since the majority of such deaths occur before the child's first birthday and, indeed, many of these occur within the first few months following birth.

probabilities and those based on additional births or age of mother at last birth. For example, the analysis of stopping probabilities provides even less evidence of replacement behavior among the cohorts with natural fertility than do the previous analyses. The relationship between previous and subsequent child mortality is unlikely to bias the analysis of stopping probabilities since the age at attaining a given parity has already been modified for the fate of the child born, as was described above. The same emergence or strengthening of replacement attempts with the increase of family limitation is apparent in the analysis of stopping probabilities for women who have had between one and three births. Unlike the previous analyses, however, the results for women who have had a fourth birth in cohorts in which family limitation is practiced also show a fairly pronounced pattern consistent with replacement. Despite these differences, the general picture is similar to the impressions gained from the analysis of additional children born and age of mother at last birth.

Another way of examining stopping probabilities for evidence of replacement behavior is to compare the percentage of couples who stop childbearing at the birth following that of some given number of surviving children, according to the fate of that birth. If replacement attempts are common, we would expect, for example, that couples whose second birth followed a first surviving child would be more likely to stop childbearing if that child survived than if it died. This approach has several advantages.

First, since target family sizes are most likely to be formulated in terms of surviving children, by holding the number of previous surviving children constant we are able to compare couples which are at a similar stage in the family-building process in a more meaningful sense than when we compare women at the same parity whose number of surviving children is different. This is important because it should reduce or eliminate differences in the extent to which selection in favor of couples who do not use family limitation affects a comparison between couples with different child mortality.

Second, to the extent that childbearing is under voluntary control, couples who go on to have an additional birth following some given number of surviving children wish to have families larger than the number of surviving children already born. This, in turn, should increase the probability that the couple would want to replace that additional birth if the child died at an early age. Thus a comparison of stopping probabilities according to the fate of that child would be more sensitive to any deliberate attempt at replacement.

Finally, when the analysis is limited to women with at least one

Table 14.6. Percentage of women who stop childbearing at a given parity, expressed as deviations from the overall mean, according to the number of deaths before age 5 among children already born, unadjusted and adjusted for modified age at attaining given parity, interval to first birth, village of residence, and occupational category of husband

Deaths under age 5 up to and including given parity	Natural fertility cohorts			Family limitation cohorts		
	Mean	Deviations from mean		Mean	Deviations from mean	
		Unadjusted	Adjusted		Unadjusted	Adjusted
Parity	6.7			5.4		
0		0.0	0.3		0.2	0.7
1		−0.1	−0.7		−0.4	−1.8
Eta/beta		.00	.02		.01	.05
Parity 2	7.9			9.9		
0		0.7	0.8		2.8	3.1
1		−1.4	−1.4		−2.7	−2.9
2		−1.3	0.8		−5.3	−6.4
Eta/beta		.04	.04		.10	.11

Parity 3	10.9			15.7		
0		0.7	0.0		4.8	4.3
1		-0.3	0.0		-0.1	0.5
2		-0.4	-0.1		-8.9	-9.3
3		-3.0	-0.8		-7.8	-7.7
Eta/beta		.03	.00		.13	.13
Parity 4	11.9			18.2		
0		3.5	2.1		8.0	6.3
1		0.1	0.4		-1.0	-0.1
2		-4.5	-3.1		-3.0	-2.6
3+		-0.5	-0.9		-9.1	-9.0
Eta/beta		.09	.06		.14	.12
Parity 5	17.2			23.6		
0		5.7	3.8		4.1	1.0
1		0.9	0.5		-1.3	-1.4
2		-3.4	-2.4		1.0	3.7
3+		-3.4	-1.8		-2.6	-3.0
Eta/beta		.09	.06		.05	.06

Note: Results refer to the combined sample of all villages and are subject to restrictions 1, 2, 3, 4 and 7 (see Table A.1). Results are adjusted by multiple classification analysis. The number of cases is the same as in Table 10.2. See text for definition of natural fertility and family limitation cohorts.

surviving child and an additional birth, it is possible to calculate an index of fecundity which should reflect not only fecundability, but also any characteristic period of postpartum non-susceptibility. This is done by calculating for each woman a measure of the tempo of childbearing based on the average birth interval following child survivals.[22]

For the purpose of analyzing the percentage who stop childbearing classified by the fate of the child following one of the first four surviving children, only children who survived to at least age 15 were counted as survivors. The fate of the child following surviving children, however, was dichotomized according to survival to fifth birthday in order to increase the chance that the child's death occurred before the end of the couple's reproductive period. The results have been adjusted for the same control variables as previously, except for the measure of the tempo of childbearing, described above, which substitutes for the interval between marriage and first birth.

As is evident in Table 14.7, in both types of cohort a higher proportion of couples stopped childbearing when the child following a given number of survivors survived to its fifth birthday than when it died. The most striking feature for the cohorts with natural fertility is the negligible size of this difference, especially after adjustment for control variables, although the relation that remains is consistent with replacement behavior. For every comparison shown, the impact of a child death on the probability of stopping is substantially greater for the cohorts practicing family limitation than for those with natural fertility. It is worth noting that the survival of children, even of those who follow a third or fourth surviving child in the cohorts in which family

---

[22] For the analysis under discussion (presented in Table 14.7), the index of fecundity is based on the average interval following an infant survival, for each woman, up to the point in the family-building process under consideration. Thus, when the analysis focuses on the fate of the first child following the birth of the first surviving child, the index is of necessity based only on the interval between the birth of the first survivor and the following birth. When the analysis focuses on the fate of the first child born following the birth of the second survivor, the fecundity index is based on the average of the interval following the birth of the first survivor and the interval following the birth of the second survivor, and so on. This measure was then entered into the multiple classification analysis as a categorical variable. A minor problem arose because, when a marriage intervened between two births, the interval between marriage and the succeeding birth was coded rather than the interval between the last illegitimate and first legitimate birth. Thus it was necessary to include a separate category for such cases when the focus of the analysis is on the birth following the first survivor. When the focus is on the fate of the birth following the second or higher-order survivor, such a category is not necessary since there will be at least one interval between a surviving child and a following birth in which marriage did not intervene. Since most couples bore all their children subsequent to marriage, this problem affected only a small number of cases.

Table 14.7. *Percentage of couples who stop childbearing at the birth of the next child according to the fate of that child, unadjusted and adjusted for modified age at the birth of that child, pace of childbearing, village of residence, and occupational category of husband, for women with one, two, three, and four children already born who survive to age 15*

	Natural fertility cohorts			Family limitation cohorts		
	Unadjusted	Adjusted	N	Unadjusted	Adjusted	N
Following 1st survivor						
Survives to 5	8.9	9.2	2234	13.8	13.5	1000
Dies before 5	8.2	7.4	767	6.8	7.6	395
Eta/beta	.01	.03		.10	.08	
Following 2nd survivor						
Survives to 5	12.6	12.5	1835	20.1	19.7	778
Dies before 5	12.2	12.5	687	16.8	17.5	333
Eta/beta	.00	.00		.04	.03	
Following 3rd survivor						
Survives to 5	17.9	17.8	1419	27.3	26.7	568
Dies before 5	15.0	15.0	567	21.3	22.8	211
Eta/beta	.03	.04		.06	.04	
Following 4th survivor						
Survives to 5	24.9	24.0	1043	33.3	31.1	372
Dies before 5	20.6	23.0	398	21.0	27.1	138
Eta/beta	.05	.01		.12	.04	

Note: Results refer to the combined sample of all villages and are subject to restrictions 1, 2, 3, 4 and 7 (see Table A.1). Results are adjusted by multiple classification analysis. See text for definition of natural fertility and family limitation cohorts.

limitation is practiced, shows a positive association with the percentage of couples who stop childbearing. In these cases, the women have had a minimum of four or five births when the birth following the third or fourth survivor occurs. This suggests that, when we focus attention on women achieving higher parities, the biases introduced by selection that favors couples who are not prone to family limitation have been successfully avoided with this particular approach.

It is possible to estimate how complete replacement efforts are by examining stopping probabilities.[23] Since target family sizes differ, only a fraction of couples who achieve a particular stage in the family-building process plan to stop childbearing at that point if their last child survives. Where the most recently born child dies, an additional fraction of these couples will continue childbearing. If we designate the proportion who stop among couples whose most recent child survives as S, and the proportion among those whose most recent child dies as S', the fraction $(S-S')/S$ may be interpreted as the proportion of women who would have stopped but are presumably induced to continue as the result of a child death. From this simple formula, we can estimate the completeness of replacement. For example, using the adjusted results in Table 14.7, the completeness of replacement of a child who died following the birth of the first survivor is .20=[(9.2−7.4)/9.2] for the natural fertility cohorts. In contrast, in cohorts in which family limitation is practiced, the corresponding figure is .44. These are the highest completeness ratios yielded for both types of cohorts. Replacement ratios for a child death following a second, third, or fourth survivor range from .00 to .16 for the natural fertility cohorts and from .11 to .15 for those in which family limitation is practiced. The same calculation may also be used to measure the extent of replacement of a first-born child who dies. Using statistics from Table 14.6, we can calculate that the completeness ratio, based on adjusted results, for replacing the loss of the first-born child is .14 for the natural fertility cohorts and .41 for those in which limitation was practiced. Thus it is clear that replacement, even for the latter cohorts, is far from complete.

The main difference between the results in Table 14.7 and those in the earlier analyses is the indication that couples in cohorts in which family limitation is practiced make some effort at replacement even at a later stage of family building. This finding was apparently obscured in previous analyses of women at higher parities because of the selection

[23] Preston, 'Introduction.'

which disproportionately favored non-limiters among those who had previously experienced lower child mortality. All analyses, however, appear to agree that, at most, only a small amount of replacement behavior is found in the natural fertility cohorts and that replacement efforts become more pronounced with the spread of family limitation.

So far, results have been based on the combined sample of 14 villages. Given the considerable differences between these villages with respect to the timing of the onset and spread of family limitation (as indicated by the index *m*), as well as in fertility and mortality, it is of interest to examine the results for individual villages as well. These results are presented in Table 14.8. In order to reduce the problems associated with smaller numbers, the three Bavarian villages and the four villages in Waldeck have been combined into two subsets. Women who had a second birth and who experienced either one or two previous child deaths, as well as women who had a third birth with two or three previous child deaths, are combined into single categories. Even so, the results for any particular village or subset of villages are based on far fewer cases than for the combined sample of all villages and thus are considerably more vulnerable to random fluctuation.

The results are shown separately for those marriage cohorts for which the *m* index is less than .3 and those characterized by higher values. In Grafenhausen and Herbolzheim, two villages where *m* shows the earliest and largest increase, the marriage cohorts for which *m* is .3 or greater have been further subdivided into two consecutive cohorts in order to make a more detailed examination of the changes in the extent of replacement behavior as family limitation increases. In Kappel, Öschelbronn, and Werdum, villages where *m* remained below .3 during the entire period of observation, the marriage cohorts were not divided. Finally, for economy of presentation, only results adjusted for modified age at attaining a given parity, the interval between marriage and first birth, and occupational category of husband are shown.

The results for Grafenhausen and Herbolzheim, the two villages with the largest increase in family limitation, indicate the absence of a replacement effect for natural fertility cohorts (couples married before 1825) and the emergence and increase of the replacement effect, with the onset and spread of family limitation, among later ones. The experience in Kappel and Rust provides an interesting comparison, since they are located within a few kilometers of Grafenhausen and Herbolzheim. As shown in Chapter 11 (see Table 11.1), little family

Table 14.8. *Number of additional children born, age of mother at last birth, and percent of women having no additional births after attaining parities 2 and 3, according to the number of deaths before age 5 among children already born, by year of marriage and village of residence, adjusted for modified age at attaining given parity, interval to first birth, and occupational category of husband*

Village and fertility measure	Marriage cohort	Child deaths to women attaining parity 2			Child deaths to women attaining parity 3			
		0	1+	Beta	0	1	2+	Beta
Grafenhausen								
Additional births	Pre-1825	5.34	4.95	.06	4.42	4.36	4.64	.04
	1825–59	3.60	4.44	.15	3.26	(2.92)	(4.56)	.25
	1860–99	2.58	3.67	.21	2.15	2.59	(3.00)	.12
Age at last birth	Pre-1825	40.8	40.4	.04	41.2	40.9	41.2	.04
	1825–59	38.7	39.1	.05	39.1	(38.9)	(40.1)	.12
	1860–99	35.5	37.1	.15	36.5	36.7	(38.1)	.12
Percent stopping	Pre-1825	6.1	6.2	.00	3.2	6.1	14.2	.17
	1825–59	11.5	8.9	.04	14.8	(18.3)	(7.0)	.13
	1860–99	17.6	7.5	.15	35.3	29.1	(7.2)	.24
Herbolzheim								
Additional births	Pre-1825	4.60	5.12	.09	3.97	4.40	4.12	.07
	1825–59	3.37	3.63	.05	2.71	2.66	(3.35)	.12
	1860–99	3.30	4.03	.13	2.63	3.25	3.28	.11
Age at last birth	Pre-1825	41.0	41.1	.01	41.1	41.2	41.0	.02
	1825–59	38.1	38.3	.02	38.9	38.0	(38.9)	.11
	1860–99	37.2	38.3	.12	37.7	38.3	38.6	.08

Percent stopping	Pre-1825	6.4	6.3	.00	6.8	5.6	8.3	.04
	1825–59	10.8	5.8	.09	19.3	19.3	(5.6)	.16
	1860–99	13.2	6.7	.11	19.2	17.3	7.1	.13
Kappel								
Additional births	1810–99	4.37	5.13	.12	3.75	4.15	4.36	.08
Age at last birth	1810–99	39.4	40.1	.07	39.8	40.0	40.7	.07
Percent stopping	1810–99	9.2	3.7	.11	11.6	10.5	7.6	.04
Rust								
Additional births	Pre-1850	4.56	4.63	.01	4.03	4.22	(4.09)	.03
	1850–99	4.53	5.28	.11	3.99	4.55	(4.51)	.07
Age at last birth	Pre-1850	40.6	40.5	.01	41.0	41.0	(40.0)	.09
	1850–99	38.8	39.2	.05	39.3	39.6	(39.6)	.03
Percent stopping	Pre-1850	11.8	9.0	.04	12.0	10.5	(18.6)	.09
	1850–99	11.3	4.3	.13	14.7	8.4	(6.4)	.11
Öschelbronn								
Additional births	1700–1899	4.57	5.31	.11	4.12	4.14	5.09	.15
Age at last birth	1700–1899	39.1	39.8	.07	39.7	39.9	40.7	.11
Percent stopping	1700–1899	9.3	7.1	.04	10.7	10.3	5.2	.09
3 Bavarian villages								
Additional births	Pre-1875	5.43	4.68	.11	4.53	4.90	3.83	.13
	1875–99	(3.60)	(5.14)	.23	(3.32)	(4.11)	(4.11)	.12
Age at last birth	Pre-1875	41.2	40.8	.05	40.8	41.7	41.0	.10
	1875–99	(37.8)	(39.0)	.13	(39.1)	(39.1)	(39.1)	.00

Table 14.8 – *cont.*

Village and fertility measure	Marriage cohort	Child deaths to women attaining parity 2			Child deaths to women attaining parity 3			
		0	1+	Beta	0	1	2+	Beta
Percent stopping	Pre-1875	7.2	9.1	.04	13.1	9.6	12.3	.05
	1875–99	(12.9)	(8.4)	.07	(29.0)	(18.6)		.12
4 Waldeck villages								
Additional births	Pre-1875	4.12	4.57	.09	3.49	3.67	3.98	.07
	1875–99	3.62	(3.99)	.07	3.29	(3.02)		.06
Age at last birth	Pre-1875	40.9	41.1	.03	41.2	41.1	41.4	.03
	1875–99	38.0	(38.5)	.05	38.9	(38.8)		.02
Percent stopping	Pre-1875	7.5	6.2	.02	9.9	13.7	12.4	.05
	1875–99	11.7	(7.1)	.07	16.6	(6.7)		.15
Middels								
Additional births	Pre-1875	3.66	4.30	.12	3.06	3.33		.06
	1875–99	(3.28)	(4.25)	.21	(2.76)	(3.52)		.20
Age at last birth	Pre-1875	39.8	40.3	.04	40.2	40.4		.02
	1875–99	(36.7)	(39.7)	.28	(38.0)	(39.2)		.15
Percent stopping	Pre-1875	8.1	5.3	.05	11.8	14.5		.04
	1875–99	(14.1)	(7.5)	.10	(14.6)	(4.4)		.17
Werdum								
Additional births	1710–1874[a]	3.11	3.76	.14	2.43	2.93	(3.46)	.17
Age at last birth	1710–1874[a]	39.3	40.5	.14	39.5	40.6	(41.0)	.15
Percent stopping	1710–1874[a]	11.8	8.9	.05	17.7	16.4	(7.7)	.09

Note: Results are subject to restrictions 1, 2, 3 and 4 (see Table A.1); results in parentheses are based on fewer than 50 cases.
[a] Includes a small number of couples married in 1875 or later.

limitation was indicated for Rust among couples married before 1850, based on the m index, and for couples in Kappel the value of m remained low even among couples married at the end of the nineteenth century. The results for Rust in Table 14.8 are quite consistent with those for both Grafenhausen and Herbolzheim. There is virtually no evidence of replacement behavior in the natural fertility cohorts, while the results for cohorts in which family limitation is practiced are consistent with attempts to replace children who had died. The results for Kappel are more puzzling. Despite the con-sistently low values of m for couples married in that village throughout the nineteenth century, all the results are in a direction indicative of replacement behavior.

Two other villages in the sample, Öschelbronn and Werdum, are also characterized by values of m below .3 throughout the period under observation. In both cases, the results are consistent with replacement behavior. In Öschelbronn, a comparison of couples married before 1850 and those married during the second half of the nineteenth century yields considerably stronger evidence of replacement for the latter group (results not shown). Even the results for couples married before 1850, however, are generally consistent with replacement behavior. A similar comparison cannot be made for Werdum since there is an insufficient number of couples married after 1850.

An interesting comparison with Werdum is provided by the nearby village of Middels. The value of m is low for marriage cohorts in Middels until the third quarter of the nineteenth century, and values exceeding .3 are found only for couples married during the last quarter of the nineteenth century. The results for couples in Middels who were married between 1750 and 1874 are also generally consistent with replacement, except for stopping probabilities for women who have had at least three births. However, the association is noticeably weaker than in Werdum. A much stronger association between previous child deaths and subsequent fertility is found for the couples married in Middels between 1875 and 1899. This result again confirms a strength-ening of the replacement effect with increased family limitation.

The combined subset of the three Bavarian villages provides a relatively clear example of the absence of replacement behavior before m increased beyond .3, and the emergence of such behavior when family limitation became more common. The results for the subset of the four Waldeck villages are much less clear. Values of m in these villages were very close to zero for couples married before 1875, and a sharp increase occurred only in the cohort married during the last quarter of the nineteenth century. Yet the results show a mixed picture relating to replacement behavior, both for couples married before 1875 and for those married between 1875 and 1899.[24]

Stopping probabilities, according to whether the birth following the first and the second child respectively survives to age 15, have also been analyzed for the individual villages. Table 14.9 presents results adjusted for modified age of the mother at the time of the birth, her pace of childbearing based on the length of intervals following surviving children, and the occupational category of the husband. If couples attempt to replace children who die, we would expect the percentage who stop childbearing after losing a child before its fifth birthday to be lower than when the child survives. In addition, the larger the difference in the percentage who stop for reasons associated with the survival status of the child, the more common presumably are efforts at child replacement. The results generally agree with those shown in Table 14.8. In both Grafenhausen and Herbolzheim there is little or no evidence of replacement behavior for the first marriage cohort, but there is a clear emergence or increase of replacement behavior for subsequent marriage cohorts. The results for neighboring Rust are only partially consistent with this pattern, while in Kappel the pattern suggests some effort at replacement even though *m* is less than .3 throughout the period of observation. The results for the three Bavarian villages and Middels again confirm that efforts at replacement become stronger when family limitation begins to be practiced, but the results for the four Waldeck villages are inconsistent in this respect, as before.

In sum, the results for the individual villages show some diversity. In several villages, there is little or no evidence of efforts at child replacement for cohorts for which the value of *m* indicates natural fertility. In others, however, the results for couples in cohorts with low values of *m* are consistent with replacement behavior. The results in still other villages are mixed and do not fit as easily into either of the two patterns just described. However, there is greater consistency in the emergence or strengthening of replacement behavior as family limitation increases. This appears for all villages in which *m* rises above

---

[24] Results not shown indicate that at most only a weak replacement effect is evident for couples in the four Waldeck villages married prior to 1850, while couples married in the period 1850–74 are characterized by results consistent with a much stronger replacement effect. Thus if the 1850–74 cohort had been grouped together with the 1875–99 cohort, a distinct increase in replacement would have been apparent. However, since the 1850–74 cohort is characterized by an *m* index of only .03, it is grouped together with the earlier marriage cohorts. Why a replacement effect should be particularly evident for the 1850–74 marriage cohort but not for the earlier or later ones remains unexplained.

0.3, with the exception of the Waldeck villages. Grafenhausen and Herbolzheim, where family limitation was more widespread than elsewhere by the end of the nineteenth century, provided particularly convincing examples of this process.

The role of child mortality in the fertility transition

The secular decline of fertility on the national level in Germany dates from the end of the nineteenth century.[25] The results in Chapters 10 and 11 have shown local differences in the timing of the fertility transition, particularly when measures sensitive to the increase of family limitation are examined. So far, we have been examining the relationship between fertility and child mortality in order to determine the presence and extent of attempts to replace those children who died prematurely. The same analytical approach can be used to examine whether child mortality influenced couples' participation in the spread of family limitation and the onset of the fertility transition.

In Figure 14.3, we show for the combined sample trends in the number of children ever born, age of mother at last birth, and the percentage who continue childbearing in successive marriage cohorts, according to mortality among their first two or three children. All women who married before 1825 are grouped together since the value of *m*, as well as several other measures, suggest that there was very little family limitation, and little change occurred in cohorts married before the second quarter of the nineteenth century (see Chapters 10 and 11). For economy of presentation, only results adjusted by multiple classification analysis (in this case, applied separately for each of the marriage cohorts) are shown.

Interpretation is complicated somewhat by the apparent increase in the underlying level of natural fertility during the period of observation (see Chapter 10) and by shifts in the age at marriage: in the combined sample the age at marriage (including remarriage) rises from 28.6 years for women married before 1825 to 29.1 for women married between 1825 and 1849 and then falls sharply to 26.5 years for women married during the last quarter of the nineteenth century, with most of the fall occurring between the two marriage cohorts of 1850–74 and 1875–99. Nevertheless, the results seem reasonably clear. The largest declines in the number of children ever born occur among couples with no child deaths among their first two or three births, while there is virtually no consistent trend in children ever born, among successive

[25] Knodel, *Decline of fertility*.

Table 14.9. *Percent of couples stopping childbearing at the birth of the next child, according to the fate of that child, by year of marriage and village of residence, adjusted for modified age at the birth of that child, pace of childbearing, and occupational category of husband, for women with one and two children already born who survive to age 15*

	% stopping at birth after first survivor when birth				% stopping at birth after second survivor when birth			
	Survives to age 5	Dies before age 5	Difference[a]	Beta	Survives to age 5	Dies before age 5	Difference[a]	Beta
Grafenhausen								
Pre-1825	6.8	10.7	−4.0	.07	5.6	(3.5)	(2.0)	.04
1825–59	8.9	(4.9)	(4.1)	.07	20.2	(15.8)	(4.4)	.05
1860–99	23.0	13.5	9.5	.10	30.1	25.4	4.7	.05
Herbolzheim								
Pre-1825	7.0	3.3	3.8	.07	10.7	10.9	−0.2	.00
1825–59	14.1	9.5	4.6	.06	25.4	23.0	2.4	.03
1860–99	12.3	5.3	7.0	.11	19.2	15.7	3.5	.04
Kappel								
1810–99	9.2	5.6	3.6	.05	12.5	9.3	3.3	.05
Rust								
Pre-1850	13.0	14.1	−1.1	.02	14.2	10.0	4.2	.06
1850–99	10.5	4.0	6.5	.11	12.7	13.0	−0.2	.00

Öschelbronn								
1700–1899	9.3	7.4	1.9	.03	14.9	11.9	2.9	.04
3 Bavarian villages								
Pre-1875	9.9	11.9	−2.0	.03	9.1	18.0	−8.9	.13
1875–99	16.4	(5.2)[b]	(11.3)[b]	.15	22.8	(12.8)[b]	(10.0)[b]	.11
4 Waldeck villages								
Pre-1875	8.0	7.1	0.9	.02	11.5	11.0	0.5	.01
1875–99	13.3	(7.3)	(6.1)	.08	14.4	(25.9)[b]	(−11.5)[b]	.11
Middels								
Pre-1875	7.3	(3.2)[b]	(4.1)[b]	.06	13.4	(18.6)[b]	(−5.2)[b]	.05
1875–99	11.7	(6.3)[b]	(5.3)[b]	.07	16.7	(8.1)[b]	(8.7)[b]	.07
Werdum								
1710–1874[c]	11.7	3.6	8.1	.11	17.2	20.2	−3.0	.03

Note: Results are subject to restrictions 1, 2, 3 and 4 (see Table A.1); results in parentheses are based on fewer than 50 cases, or in the case of the difference between two results, at least one result is based on fewer than 50 cases.

[a] Calculated on results to the second decimal place and thus may differ slightly from the difference between figures as shown, due to rounding.

[b] Based on fewer than 20 cases.

[c] Includes a small number of couples married in 1875 or later.

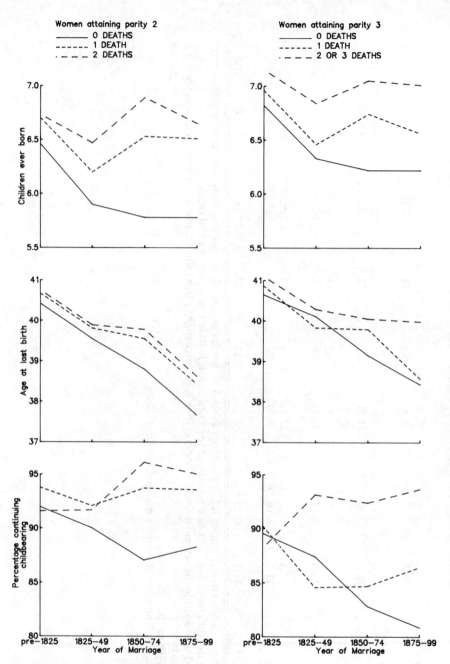

Figure 14.3. *Trends in the adjusted total number of children ever born, age at last birth and percentage continuing childbearing among women attaining parities 2 and 3, according to the number of deaths before age 5 among children already born.* Results refer to the combined sample of all villages and are subject to restrictions 1, 2, 3 and 4 (see Table A.1). Statistical adjustment for modified age at attaining given parity, interval to first birth, occupational category of husband, and village of residence has been made through multiple classification analysis

cohorts, for couples some of whose children had died. The levelling-off of the number of children ever born for couples married during the third and fourth quarters of the nineteenth century, none of whose children had died, may reflect the countervailing effects of increased family limitation on the one hand, and an increased underlying level of natural fertility combined with a lower average age at marriage on the other.

The probable increase in family limitation between cohorts married during the third and fourth quarters of the nineteenth century is illustrated by the decline in the age of mother at last birth, not only for couples whose first two or three children have survived but also among couples with less favorable child mortality. A falling age at last birth for successive marriage cohorts in the nineteenth century is generally evident for women, regardless of their child mortality experience. Among women who have had two or more births, this decline is more pronounced for those women whose first two children both survived. Among women with three or more births, the decline in age at last birth is not very different, whatever their experience with child mortality, although it is more consistent in each successive marriage cohort for women all of whose children survived.

In Figure 14.3, we also show the percentage of couples who continue childbearing after having had two or three births, according to their child mortality experience.[26] In general, the results agree with those based on children ever born. Only among women whose first two children both survived is the proportion who continue childbearing beyond the second birth lower among the cohort married at the end of the nineteenth century than among those married before 1825. Similar results are found for women who have had three or more children. These trends are undoubtedly affected by the increased underlying level of natural fertility and changing age at marriage, particularly the decline in the age at first marriage for women who married during the last quarter of the nineteenth century.

The decline in both the number of children ever born and the percentage who continued childbearing among couples with the most favorable experience of child mortality underscores the point that, during the initial stages of the fertility transition, behavior which appears to conform to the hypothesis of a replacement effect may result from deliberate attempts to limit childbearing when children survive rather than from a deliberate response to child deaths.

---

[26] The percent continuing rather than the percent stopping (its complement) is shown so that, consistent with children ever born and age at last birth, a downward trend would reflect an increase in family limitation or a reduction in fertility.

Given the relatively constant level of child mortality during the nineteenth century, it appears that whatever factors precipitated the onset of family limitation in the present sample of German village populations, a reduction of child mortality from the rather high levels that prevailed was not among them. Yet in a different way, at the level of individual couples, a relationship between child mortality and changing reproductive behavior did exist. As the results in Figure 14.3 indicate, within the context of a relatively unchanging overall child mortality, the individual couple's experience with child mortality appears to have affected their chances of participating in the adoption of family limitation, and the reduction of fertility associated with the early stages of the fertility transition. More specifically, favorable child mortality apparently facilitated a couple's adoption of family limitation, which led them to lower fertility, while unfavorable child mortality seems to have impeded, if not totally prevented, such efforts.

Discussion

In concluding this chapter it will be useful to summarize the evidence with respect to the answers to three questions: (a) Is there any evidence of replacement behavior when other indicators suggest that natural fertility prevailed? (b) Does the replacement effect emerge and/or strengthen as family limitation spreads? (c) Does differential experience with child mortality influence a couple's likelihood to participate in the spread of family limitation during the initial stages of the transition from natural to controlled fertility?

Unfortunately, the results do not permit a decisive answer to the first question. For the combined set of 14 villages, findings for the cohorts with natural fertility were generally consistent with replacement behavior. While the relationship between previous child mortality and subsequent fertility for the natural fertility cohorts was not very pronounced, and could in part have been caused by imprecision in the control variables as well as biases due to variables not taken into account, it seems unlikely that the entire effect could be explained in this manner. The results based on individual villages were even more puzzling. In some, those marriage cohorts for which the value of m was low showed very little, if any, replacement behavior, but in others, sometimes nearby, replacement behavior seemed to be present despite the low values of m. Since m is only an indirect and approximate indicator of family limitation, it is quite possible that some deliberate fertility control in marriage was being practiced and was responsible for the apparent replacement effect. For these same cohorts, however, the age of the mother at last birth was consistently high, supporting the interpretation that little or no family limitation was practiced (see Chapter 11). Perhaps the most that can be said is that if family limitation was being practiced during these earlier periods, it appears only in some villages and not in others. Moreover, even when it was present, it was probably not very extensive, judging from the lack of a stronger replacement response and the generally late age at which women ceased childbearing, even when their previous children all survived.

A much clearer answer can be provided to the second question. For the combined sample, the replacement effect was noticeably more pronounced for the marriage cohorts for which m equalled or exceeded .3 than for cohorts with lower values of m. The results for the individual villages showed that where there was little evidence of replacement behavior initially, efforts to replace children who had died became clearly evident only after the value of m began to exceed .3. Moreover, even in some cases where replacement was already apparent before the value of m increased, it became more pronounced afterward.

The increase of the replacement effect and the appearance of family limitation across successive marriage cohorts provides the answer to the third question – whether an individual couple's experience of child mortality influenced the extent to which they adopted the changing reproduction patterns associated with the onset of the fertility transition. The results from the combined sample of all villages suggest that couples with the most favorable child mortality experience were most likely to adopt family limitation and to reduce their fertility. Unfavorable experience with child mortality seems at least to have impeded, if not totally prevented, efforts either to reduce the number of children ever born or to cease childbearing at an earlier age or at a given parity.

These findings emphasize the importance of micro-level studies for expanding our knowledge of the behavioral processes underlying the demographic transition. The point can be made most forcefully in connection with the last finding reviewed above. The changes in reproductive behavior that occurred among couples with favorable child mortality experience occurred during a period when the general level of child mortality remained moderately high. Thus, on the basis of a macro-level comparison of trends in child mortality and fertility for the sample as a whole or, for that matter, for the separate villages, we can conclude that a reduction in child mortality was clearly not necessary to precipitate the changing reproductive patterns. However, since the data on which the present study is based are reconstituted family histories, it has been possible to go beneath macro-level comparisons and explore the relationship between fertility and mortality at the micro-level. It is at this level that the link between reproductive behavior and child mortality becomes evident. The finding that participation in the early stages of the fertility transition was apparently enhanced by favorable child mortality experience places the macro-level finding that there was little, if any, association in the trends in family limitation and child mortality in quite a different perspective.

PART VI

Conclusion

15

Population dynamics of the past: summing up

The preceding chapters have surveyed demographic behavior in 14 German village populations during the eighteenth and nineteenth centuries, based on reconstituted family histories included in village genealogies. They illustrate the distinctive value of micro-level data derived through family reconstitution for the study of population processes in the past, and in particular for the study of demographic transition. Most of the findings would have been impossible to obtain from conventional sources of demographic data, such as published census tabulations and vital statistics. Not only do such data not exist for much of the period covered, but since such data are already aggregated in the source, they do not permit analyses which interrelate different aspects of demographic behavior at the individual or family level. In addition, much important information known about individuals covered in a family reconstitution study derives from the reconstitution process itself. Thus information often not available from standard demographic sources, such as a child's birth order, the interval between births, or a mother's age at a particular confinement, can be determined through family reconstitution because the vital events of a family have been linked together.

Aggregate analysis of parish records is also much more limited in the extent of information provided and the extent to which such data permits the exploration of interrelationships. While there have been major methodological advances in this approach, as illustrated by the recent study of the population history of England by Wrigley and Schofield,[1] aggregative analysis still provides only the most basic demographic measures for a population.

There are, to be sure, important limitations to family reconstitution

[1] Wrigley and Schofield, 'Population history from family reconstitution.'

studies. In particular, they typically cover only a small number of villages and are inappropriate for the study of several important demographic parameters, including migration, proportions who marry, and adult mortality. Thus family reconstitution should not be viewed as a total approach to demographic history, but as a particularly valuable component that can complement or be complemented by other approaches providing less detailed but broader coverage, as well as estimates of those demographic parameters for which family reconstitution is poorly suited. A review of some of the principal results of the preceding chapters serves to underscore the unique contribution family reconstitution data for local populations can make toward furthering our understanding of population dynamics in the past, including the initial transformation of mortality and reproduction that together constitute the demographic transition.

Mortality

Although family reconstitution data, and thus village genealogies, are ill-suited for studying adult mortality, they can provide detailed and reasonably accurate information on mortality risks during the early years of life. For this reason, the present study had focused primarily on infant and child mortality. One of the most striking findings to emerge is the divergent path followed by infant and child mortality from the mid-eighteenth to the beginning of the twentieth century. The results show that reductions in child mortality above age 1 preceded improvements in infant mortality. While some variation in the trends in infant and child mortality is evident among the different villages, the general pattern of an earlier decline in child than in infant mortality characterized most regional groupings. For the combined sample of villages, infant mortality reached its highest level during the third quarter of the nineteenth century and showed only a modest improvement by the start of the twentieth century. In contrast, both early child mortality (between ages 1 and 5) and later child mortality (between ages 5 and 15) declined almost steadily from the mid-eighteenth century. The combination of somewhat worsening infant mortality and improving early child mortality resulted in a situation in which the probability of dying between birth and age 5 showed little consistent trend, fluctuating around a level of 30 percent during most of the eighteenth and nineteenth centuries.

The fact that reductions in child mortality above age 1 preceded improvements in infant mortality appears to be a general phenomenon of European demographic history and has implications for the assess-

ment of linkages between the changes in mortality and fertility associated with the demographic transition.[2] In particular, these findings
indicate that a rather incomplete and somewhat inaccurate picture of
trends in child survival is provided by focusing exclusively on infant
mortality, as has been common in a number of studies of the demographic transition, including the influential Princeton study of the
European fertility decline.[3] An expanded account of the risks of losing
a child is especially important when assessing the impact of mortality
change on the onset of fertility decline. Nevertheless, it is noteworthy
that throughout the period under observation infant mortality was an
extremely important component of mortality prior to adulthood, often
accounting for over half of all deaths under age 15. The divergent paths
of infant and child mortality also underscore the difficulty of applying
model life tables, which assume a fixed pattern of relations among
mortality rates at different ages, to historical populations over long
periods of time.

In contrast to the similarity in trends, very pronounced differences
in the levels of infant and child mortality are evident for the various
villages and appear to be related to differences in the prevailing infant-
feeding practices. In two of the three Bavarian villages, where breastfeeding was relatively uncommon, mortality claimed the lives of more
than one out of three infants during the first year of life. At the other
extreme, infant mortality was less than half of this level in the two East
Frisian villages, where breastfeeding for at least moderate durations
was common.

Despite the sharp regional differences, socio-economic differences
in infant and child mortality, at least as indicated by the occupation or
village leadership status of the father, show little association with the
mortality risks experienced by the children. The fact that all social
strata within a village appeared to have shared a more or less common
risk of child loss emphasizes the probable role of local or regional
infant-feeding customs, common to all classes, as a key determinant of
infant mortality.

Family reconstitution data also permit a detailed examination of the
risks of infant mortality according to a number of attributes of the
mother or child. For example, a detailed examination of the association
between infant mortality and birth rank is possible and yields interesting results. Within particular sibship sizes, there appears to be little
association between birth order and mortality risk. In contrast, the
total number of children born to a mother is related to infant mortality,

[2] Matthiessen and McCann, 'Mortality.'
[3] See, for example, van de Walle, 'Infant mortality.'

regardless of the child's birth rank. For large families, infant mortality is high for children of all birth orders, while for small families infant mortality is lower, regardless of birth rank. These results illustrate the danger of reaching misleading conclusions that is inherent in the common practice of examining the association between birth order and mortality risk, based on data for families of different sibship sizes aggregated together. They also undermine the view that the greater risk of infant and child death for births of higher orders, observed when sibship size is not taken into account, reflects the existence of 'infanticide by neglect' through underinvestment in the care of children of higher birth ranks.

Maternal deaths are the one aspect of adult mortality that can be investigated relatively easily with family reconstitution data. In German village populations during the eighteenth and nineteenth centuries, there was roughly a 1 percent chance of death for women associated with each confinement. Given that under the prevailing levels of fertility, women averaged about 5 confinements by the end of the reproductive age span, a woman would have had approximately a 5 percent cumulative chance of dying due to childbirth before reaching the end of her childbearing years. Thus not an insignificant proportion of women died as a result of their reproductive efforts. These high mortality risks, especially when combined with the chances of serious but non-fatal complications associated with giving birth under the relatively primitive conditions that prevailed during much of the period under study, could well have contributed to a receptivity to the family limitation practices that eventually were responsible for the fertility transition.

Marriage patterns

It is now well recognized that the prevailing demographic regime in western Europe during the eighteenth and nineteenth centuries was distinguished by an unusual nuptiality pattern. Most striking was the fact that both men and women tended to marry relatively late and a substantial proportion were still single by the end of the reproductive age span. Family reconstitution data are well-suited for studying the age at marriage, although not the proportion who eventually marry, and confirm a pattern of late marriages for both sexes in the sample villages. In most, men first married on average in their late twenties during the two-century period under observation, while women were on average two to three years younger. The fact that women had passed a substantial part of their reproductive age span by the time they initiated marital childbearing is of considerable demographic significance and the crucial feature contributing to the relatively low overall fertility levels of preindustrial Europe when compared to recent fertility in many of the world's less developed countries today.

Some regional variation in age at marriage is evident and needs to be incorporated in any adequate account of regional contrasts in demographic regimes. The major contrast is between unusually late marriages for women in the Bavarian villages and more moderate ages at marriage for those in East Friesland, particularly in one of the two villages studied. Marital fertility was also highest in the Bavarian villages and well below average for the East Frisian villages when compared to the total sample. Thus some tendency is evident for age at marriage and marital fertility to counterbalance each other in terms of their impact on the total number of children ever born per couple, a tendency suggesting a pattern of demographic homeostasis.

There were only modest changes in the age at marriage for the total sample during the two-century period covered and thus this aspect of nuptiality cannot have had a large impact on trends in overall fertility. Both men's and women's age at marriage increased by about a year and a half between the first half of the eighteenth century and the third quarter of the nineteenth. The decline in the average age at first marriage for women, evident at the end of the nineteenth century, acted to counter the effect of declines in marital fertility on family size during that time and thus did not contribute to the onset of the fertility transition in the sample villages.

The pattern of late marriage among the village populations as a whole characterized all major socio-economic groups. Occupational differentials in both levels and trends of age at marriage were not pronounced. A somewhat later-than-average age at marriage for wives of landless laborers, however, contradicts the view, sometimes expressed, that rural proletarianization led to early marriage.

The village genealogies provide compelling evidence for a secular decline in the tendency to remarry. Pronounced age and sex differentials in the likelihood of remarriage were also evident: widows were far less likely to remarry than were widowers, and the probability of remarriage declined rapidly with age, particularly for women. There were, however, no clear differences in either the probability of remarriage or its tendency to decline over time among major occupational groups. The decline in remarriage probabilities was caused in part by declines in adult mortality, which generally raised the ages of surviving spouses to levels at which remarriage has historically been rather unlikely. However, age-specific remarriage probabilities also declined, affecting both men and women and all occupational groups, suggesting the presence of a social change of wide scope that was at most linked only loosely to changes in the economic circumstances of households.

Non-marital births and pregnancies

Although most reproductive behavior in eighteenth- and nineteenth-century German villages took place within marital unions, births born or conceived out of wedlock were not insignificant. A very clear increase in the frequency of illegitimate births took place between the second half of the eighteenth century and the early part of the nineteenth century. For the subset of villages for which calculations can be made, illegitimate births represented as little as 2 percent of all births and less than 10 percent of first births during the early decades of the eighteenth century. By the first third of the nineteenth century, over an eighth of all births and 40 percent of first births were born out of wedlock. A substantial decline in the illegitimacy ratio occurred throughout much of the remainder of the nineteenth century, but it never returned to the low levels that prevailed in the early eighteenth century. Despite considerable variation in the level of illegitimacy among the villages, a rise and later fall in the illegitimacy ratio was a fairly general phenomenon. Moreover, a similar rise and fall of non-marital fertility appears to be a common feature of much of western and northern Europe, as documented in a number of other studies.

Many illegitimate births in the villages were later legitimized through the marriages of the parents and thus were in fact prenuptial rather than totally non-marital. Although measurement problems prevent a precise estimate, the results suggest that at least one-quarter of out-of-wedlock births were eventually legitimized. The chance of a subsequent marriage occurring appears to be greater if the child survived than if it died at an early age, suggesting that the presence of a living illegitimate child acted as an incentive for the parents to wed.

During most of the eighteenth century, the proportion of married couples who started childbearing prior to their marriage was quite low. Prenuptial births became more common during the nineteenth century, involving more than one in eight fertile couples, before declining toward the end of the century. Far more frequent, however, were first postnuptial births conceived prior to marriage. As with illegitimacy, bridal pregnancy increased substantially during the later eighteenth and early nineteenth centuries. Toward the end of the first half of the nineteenth century, almost 30 percent of first legitimate births were conceived prior to marriage. A modest decline in bridal pregnancy occurred thereafter, but it remained relatively high compared to the earlier, eighteenth-century levels. Thus bridal pregnancy, prenuptial births, and illegitimacy increased in concert between the later part of the eighteenth and the middle of the nineteenth centuries, suggesting a major increase in sexual activity outside of marriage. At the time of the peak levels during the second quarter of the nineteenth century, close to 40 percent of married couples began their reproductive careers with a prenuptial birth or conception. Despite some decline, perhaps reflecting the increased use of birth control associated with the onset of the fertility transition, close to a third of married couples still initiated childbearing in this way by the end of the nineteenth century.

Both bridal pregnancy and prenuptial births were clearly most frequent for proletarian occupational groups throughout the two-century period. Nevertheless, the pervasive nature of the major changes in premarital sexual behavior is illustrated by increases in bridal pregnancy and prenuptial births among all the social strata of the villages. While the proletarian strata contributed more than their proportional share, all the major segments of village society were involved in the increased premarital sexual activity implied by the changed levels of bridal pregnancy and prenuptial births.

Non-marital sexual activity in the German village populations undoubtedly took place under a wide range of different circumstances. Much of it appears to have occurred as part of a process leading up to marriage, perhaps linked to engagement or to some more formal commitment to marry. The frequent occurrence of bridal pregnancy by the second quarter of the nineteenth century means that it could hardly have been considered an unusual event at that time. Thus it seems unlikely that out-of-wedlock sex *per se* was considered socially unacceptable behavior. Rather, normative proscriptions were more likely to have been conditional on the context within which such activity took place. Overall, the major changes in premarital sexual activity, evident from family reconstitution data, point to a social change of significant proportions and serve as a precursor to the transformation of marital reproductive behavior associated with the fertility transition.

Natural marital fertility

For the sample as a whole, there is little evidence of any consistent trend in the level of marital fertility. A modest decline is apparent toward the end of the nineteenth century, mirroring the fertility decline evident from conventional demographic sources at the national and provincial level. Very substantial variations in both the levels and trends in marital fertility, however, are evident among the sample villages. In one village, marital fertility fell steadily from the turn of the nineteenth century, while in several others a more or less continuous rise occurred. Even before divergent trends appeared, there were substantial differences in the level of marital fertility. For example, in the second half of the eighteenth century, marital fertility in the Bavarian villages was almost 40 percent higher than marital fertility in the East Frisian villages.

One of the major advantages of family reconstitution data is their suitability for indirectly detecting and measuring the presence and extent of family limitation, defined in terms of deliberate efforts to control family size by stopping childbearing prior to onset of terminal sterility. A situation of natural fertility, defined as the absence of such attempts, can be identified because of relatively clear expectations about the age pattern of fertility, the age of last birth, and parity progression probabilities when deliberate stopping behavior is absent. The evidence from the village genealogies makes clear that natural fertility prevailed in all the villages during the eighteenth century and persisted in many throughout most or all of the nineteenth century. This is indicated by the convex age patterns of marital fertility and the high average ages of mothers at their last birth, both of which were relatively uniform among villages despite quite different levels of marital fertility. There was also little variation by social strata within villages in these aspects of reproductive behavior for marriage cohorts characterized by natural fertility. In addition, at most ages, there was little association between a woman's parity level and the probability that she continued childbearing.

It is far more difficult to determine whether or not couples deliberately spaced children under conditions of natural fertility. The major difficulty stems from the fact that birth intervals can vary substantially even when no deliberate attempts to prolong them are being made. Inter-village differences in average birth intervals fall well within the range that could be explained by variations in non-volitional factors, and are roughly consistent with the differences that would be expected from what is known about regional patterns of infant-feeding practices. Detailed analyses of birth intervals by ultimate family size and birth order provide no conclusive evidence of deliberate spacing in the sample village populations, either during periods of natural fertility or after family limitation is evident, although they also do not conclusively rule out this possibility.

The wide range among the sample villages in the level of natural marital fertility, which in the absence of attempts to stop childbearing is necessarily a function of differences in the average birth interval, emphasizes the importance of societal influences at the local or regional level on reproductive behavior prior to the start of the fertility transition. In the case of Germany, regional differences in infant-feeding practices appear to be a most important factor accounting for much of the observed differences. For example, the relative absence of breastfeeding in the Bavarian villages is associated with unusually high natural marital fertility, while a pattern of more common and extended breastfeeding probably contributed to the lower levels in the East Frisian villages.

The underlying level of natural marital fertility significantly increased in the combined sample of villages between the mid-eighteenth century and the beginning of the twentieth century. Analysis of the proximate determinants responsible for the increase, while not conclusive, is clearest with respect to an increase in fecundability. Some evidence is also suggestive of a reduction in the non-susceptible period following birth. In contrast, there is little evidence that a reduction in primary sterility contributed to this phenomenon.

Both for natural fertility marriage cohorts and those characterized by family limitation, age at marriage was closely associated with family size. Couples who married earlier concluded their reproductive years with a considerably larger average number of births and surviving children than those who married later. Given the longer exposure to chances of childbearing associated with earlier ages at marriage, such a relationship is not surprising.

A particularly interesting finding, also reported in a number of other historical demographic studies, is that women who married later experienced higher age-specific marital fertility rates than those who married younger, even when conditions were otherwise indicative of natural fertility. In the present sample of German villages, this positive association between marriage duration and age-specific fertility for the natural fertility marriage cohorts can be largely accounted for by several non-volitional factors. Once allowance is made for the influence of bridal pregnancy, exposure to risks of sterility associated with complications of childbirth, and the effect of husband's age on fertility, the extent of this association is considerably reduced. The modest relationship that persists can possibly be attributed to a decline in coital frequency with increasing duration of marriage. For cohorts practicing family limitation, a substantial association still remains after the same set of non-volitional influences are taken into account, presumably reflecting the greater proportion of younger marrying women who by any given age have reached a family size they do not wish to exceed, compared to the proportion of older marrying women who have done so.

A more perplexing finding concerning the natural fertility marriage cohorts are behavioral patterns indicative of attempts to alter subsequent fertility in response to the death of previous children. While this relationship could in part have been caused by imprecision in the analysis, it seems unlikely that the entire effect can be explained in this manner. The extent of the relationship between previous child mortality and subsequent fertility, however, was not very pronounced. Even women whose previous children all survived ceased childbearing at a generally late age. In comparison, efforts to replace children who died early were noticeably stronger for the marriage cohorts for which other indicators of family limitation were positive.

The onset of family limitation

Family reconstitution data permit documentation of the shift from natural fertility to family limitation in ways that would be impossible from conventional sources. One of the most striking findings to emerge from the present study is the diversity among the small sample of villages in terms of the timing and emergence of family limitation, as indicated by changing age patterns of marital fertility, declining ages at last birth, and shifts in parity progression probabilities. In some villages, family limitation emerged shortly after the turn of the nineteenth century, while in others, natural fertility persisted until close to or even through to the end of the century. Moreover, differences could be extremely pronounced even between two neighboring villages, emphasizing just how local the process of the fertility transition could be in the past in its early stages. The results demonstrate that cross-sectional or over-time differences in overall levels of marital fertility – the type of information typically available from conventional sources – are not always sensitive to differences in the patterns of reproductive behavior indicative of parity-dependent fertility control. In the case of one sample village, the increasing level of natural marital fertility was sufficient to lead to an increase in observed overall marital fertility despite clear indications that attempts at behavior consistent with family limitation were also increasing.

Family reconstitution data also permit examination of differentials in marital fertility and the extent of family limitation according to the husband's occupational category. The results indicate that such differences were minimal for couples married prior to the mid-nineteenth century, as might be expected in a predominantly natural fertility setting. Occupational differentials in the increase in family limitation among couples married in the second half of the nineteenth century are evident, with the more common pattern pointing to above-average increases among couples in which the husband was a farmer. While occupational differentials in the increase of family limitation practices are reasonably consistent, it is also worth noting that in those villages where at least a moderate increase in family limitation is indicated for the total population, all broad occupational categories participated, at least to some extent, in altering their reproductive behavior in a manner consistent with parity-dependent control.

Examination of average birth intervals reveals that, at least during the initial stages of the fertility transition in rural Germany, couples did not resort to a conscious lengthening of the spacing between births as a way to reduce their fertility. In general, the average interconfinement interval either remained relatively constant or declined toward the end of the nineteenth century, a time by which the fertility transition was already under way in most villages. Rather, the deliberate stopping of childbearing prior to the end of the reproductive age span appears to be the major behavioral change through which marital fertility came under volitional control during the initial phases of the fertility transition in rural Germany.

Although the present analysis extends only into the beginning stage of the fertility transition, it seems safe to infer, based on previous studies, that what has been captured is the start of an irreversible process through which fertility declines to much lower, modern levels.[4] This process involves a change from a situation in which married couples did little to stop childbearing before the end of the reproductive span to one in which it was common for a couple to attempt to terminate childbearing in response to achieving a family size defined by the couple as sufficient. It is this shift from natural fertility to family limitation that constitutes a fundamental break with past patterns of marital childbearing and represents the modernization of reproductive behavior.

Conclusions

Analyses of local, micro-level data can contribute considerably to our understanding of the behavioral processes underlying population phenomena in the past, including both the demographic transition

---

[4] Knodel, 'Family limitation.'

and the preceding reproductive regimes from which it derived. One of the most striking findings to emerge from this study of German village populations during the eighteenth and nineteenth centuries is the central role played by differences in infant-feeding practices in accounting for the substantial regional variation in fertility and mortality patterns. Where prolonged breastfeeding was the norm, both marital fertility and infant mortality tended to be moderate and thus reproduction relatively efficient; where handfeeding at early ages commonly replaced breastfeeding, marital fertility and infant mortality were both typically high, resulting in considerably less efficient reproductive regimes. Moreover, infant-feeding practices were not only a significant determinant of fertility and mortality levels, but also had repercussions on the seasonal pattern of births and infant deaths, as well as the age pattern of mortality early in life.

Recent considerations of preindustrial populations have stressed the contrast between high- and low-pressure demographic regimes, defined in terms of whether the inevitable rough balance between fertility and mortality in preindustrial contexts was brought about by high or only moderate levels of each.[5] While nuptiality has been properly stressed as one crucial determinant of the nature of the reproductive regime, the German example underscores the critical role that differences in infant-feeding customs can play in this respect. Although direct evidence on infant-feeding practices is rarely available for populations in the past, analysis of family reconstitution data permits reasonably firm asessments of their impact based on indirect evidence.

The micro-level study of demographic behavior can clearly serve as a useful complement to macro-level research on population based on conventional demographic sources. The Princeton study of the decline of fertility in Europe, based on provincial-level data from censuses and vital statistics reports, is one of the best-known examples of the macro-level genre of demographic research. A few selective comparisons between the findings on the fertility transition in Germany from this study and those associated with the Princeton study serve both to illustrate this point and to provide an appropriate conclusion to the present analysis of family reconstitution data.

Analysis of fertility trends during the late nineteenth and early twentieth centuries for the 71 administrative areas of Germany as part of the Princeton project led to the conclusion that 'the secular decline in German fertility which culminated in the low levels characteristic of

[5] Wrigley, 'Population history in the 1980s,' pp. 208–09; Coale, 'Fertility in Europe since the eighteenth century'; Perez Moreda and Reher, 'Demographic mechanisms.'

modern times had its temporal origin in the decades immediately following German unification and not earlier. An image of relatively high and constant fertility seems appropriate for at least a century or so preceding 1870.'[6] While this conclusion may be valid for many, even most, areas in Germany, analyses of the sample of German village genealogies suggest that it should be modified in several important ways.

First, there appears to be far more local diversity in the timing of the onset of a sustained decline in marital fertility than would be implied by the relatively homogeneous experience at the provincial level. In at least one of the 14 villages studied, marital fertility began to descend from the beginning of the nineteenth century. Second, at least moderate rises in marital fertility may have been a relatively common feature during the century preceding fertility decline. Third, the crucial change in marital reproductive patterns underlining the fertility decline, namely the onset of family limitation behavior directed at terminating childbearing prior to the end of the reproductive span, appears to have preceded *actual* drops in marital fertility levels in a number of areas, but this has not typically been detected because of the countervailing forces acting to increase marital fertility. Since it is the onset of this pattern of family limitation that represents the distinctive break with past reproductive patterns, the beginning of this transition from natural fertility to controlled fertility can predate the actual onset of fertility decline.

Earlier provincial-level analysis also revealed considerable variation in the level of marital fertility before the start of the decline, although it was noted that it was not possible to determine from the evidence if the substantial geographical differentials in pre-decline marital fertility reflected differences in deliberate family limitation.[7] The evidence from the village genealogies confirms the substantial regional variation in marital fertility levels but also provides far greater insight into the source of these differences, not only in terms of the role that family limitation might have played but also with respect to other proximate determinants of marital fertility levels. Very substantial differences in marital fertility characterized villages in different parts of Germany prior to the onset of family limitation. The evidence strongly suggests that differences in infant-feeding practices underlay much of this variation. The critical information necessary to make this determination, such as data on the length of birth intervals or the parity and age of the mother at the birth of her children, while readily available from

[6] Knodel, *Decline of fertility*, p. 247.
[7] Knodel, *Decline of fertility*.

family reconstitution data, was rarely reported in the conventional data sources in nineteenth-century Europe.

Another important finding of the provincial-level analysis of the fertility decline in Europe was that once such a decline began, it was largely irreversible until far lower levels were reached.[8] Findings from the sample of German villages suggest this may also have been true at a more local level and in terms of the fundamental transformation of natural to controlled fertility. This is evidenced by the progressive change, in those aspects of reproductive behavior indicative of family limitation practices, in the villages where the onset of such practices dates from the start of the nineteenth century.

Initial views of the demographic transition as formulated by Notestein several decades ago envisioned that 'the new idea of the small family arose typically in the urban industrial society.'[9] The findings of the Princeton study were generally consistent with this view of urban areas as leading and rural areas as lagging with respect to the onset of fertility decline.[10] While this pattern may generally be valid for the large part of the population that embarked on the fertility transition toward the end of the nineteenth century, results from the present analysis indicate that pockets of early decline can be found among rural villages and that their inhabitants did not need to wait for an example to be set by their urban counterparts before they started to practice family limitation.

Finally, one central tenet of demographic transition theory that has been challenged by analysis of provincial-level trends in infant mortality and marital fertility for Germany, as well as for other countries,[11] is that prior declines in child mortality are necessary for, or precipitate, declines in fertility and increases in fertility control. Village-level results from the present study provide a more complete perspective on this issue. In those villages where family limitation emerged earliest and proceeded furthest during the nineteenth century, it did so in a context of relatively high child mortality and in advance of any sustained improvements. Thus, based on a macro-level comparison of trends in child mortality and fertility for the sample as a whole, or for the separate villages, results concur with those at the provincial level, namely indicating that a reduction in child mortality was not necessary to precipitate changing reproductive patterns.

[8] Watkins, 'Conclusions,' pp. 420–49; Knodel and van de Walle, 'Lessons from the past.'
[9] Notestein, 'Population change,' pp. 13–31.
[10] Sharlin, 'Historical demography,' pp. 245–62; Watkins, 'Conclusions.'
[11] Knodel, *Decline of Fertility*; van de Walle, 'Infant mortality.'

Exploration of the relationship between fertility and mortality at the micro-level, however, provides a rather different perspective on the link between reproductive behavior and child mortality. While the disposition toward family limitation does not appear to have been prompted by mortality decline, it found expression primarily among families whose mortality was low. Those couples with the most favorable child mortality experience were most likely to adopt family limitation and to reduce their fertility. Unfavorable experience with child mortality appears to have inhibited, if not totally prevented, such efforts. Thus, although changes in reproductive behavior occurred during a period of persistent and high child mortality, participation in the early stages of the fertility transition for the individual couples was apparently enhanced by a favorable experience with child survival. The macro-level finding of little association between fertility and mortality trends is therefore seriously incomplete and potentially misleading in the impression it provides.

A great deal of progress has been made in the last few decades toward establishing the historical record of demographic behavior during the critical period leading up to and encompassing the secular declines in mortality and fertility that constitute the demographic transition. More conventional macro-level approaches, such as that followed by the Princeton European fertility project, have played an important part in reshaping our view of what is surely among the most significant social changes to occur in all of human history. As the few examples just cited illustrate, and as the findings of the preceding chapters more fully document, analyses of family reconstitution data have a crucial role to play in this process. Such micro-level studies can both answer and raise a variety of issues that are not suitably addressed by more conventional macro-level studies. Together, these two complementary approaches can contribute to establishing a broad agenda for future research on the demographic dynamics of the past.

Selection of couples for analysis

The histories of vital events for individual couples are often incomplete and unusable for demographic analysis since the village genealogies include any family (or individual person if he or she cannot be linked to a family unit) that has at least one event entered in the local registers.[1] By coding only couples for whom at least some prespecified minimum amount of information is available, substantial savings in time and effort can be effected at the data preparation stage. For the present study, 6 of the 14 village genealogies in the sample were coded completely (Braunsen, Kappel, Massenhausen, Middels, Öschelbronn, and Rust), while only preselected couples were coded for the remainder. In addition, a more detailed coding scheme was used for the villages in which all couples were coded. In the present study, for the large majority of purposes only those families from the fully-coded villages are included which meet the same minimum tests of completeness that were applied to the villages for which couples were preselected. Thus for most practical purposes the same selection of cases was involved for all 14 villages in the sample.

Criteria for initial selection

Given the considerable attention focused on reproductive behavior in this study, the criteria for selection were chosen such that most couples for whom there was insufficient information to permit their use for

---

[1] For a fuller discussion of the information needed and appropriate restrictions on cases included in specific demographic analyses of family reconstitution data, see Henry, *Manuel de démographie historique*, and 'Fécondité des mariages'; and Wrigley, 'Family reconstitution,' and 'Mortality in pre-industrial England.' The specific rules for the selection of cases included in particular analyses followed in the present study are somewhat less strict in some cases than those suggested by Henry or Wrigley, but conform on the basic logic underlying them.

fertility analyses were excluded. To be included in the initial selection, which was further refined as noted below, a family listed in the genealogy had to meet the following requirements:

1. An exact marriage date (to the day) was given.
2. An exact death date (to the day) of at least one spouse was given, provided that, in cases where only one death date was known, there was no indication that the spouse with the known death date remarried following the current marriage.
3. The marriage did not end in divorce or known separation.
4. The birth date of the wife was known at least within one year.
5. The birth year of every child listed was given and no more than one child lacked a birth day or birth month.
6. The family history contained no unresolvable inconsistencies.

The rules of selection were justified on various grounds. The basic strategy underlying the selection of families was to include only those which could reasonably be considered as exposed to the local registration system during their entire marital reproductive span. A missing marriage date for a couple, or the absence of death dates for both spouses, typically suggests that, in the first case, the couple was married outside the village and, in the second, that the couple moved elsewhere sometime subsequent to marriage. In both cases, since dates of migration are usually not given in the genealogies, determination of their period of risk in terms of calculating fertility rates is not possible. In addition, it would be misleading to assume that the total number of births registered in the local records to couples in either category represents the total number of children they ever had. The very small number of couples who had been divorced or separated were also excluded to avoid ambiguities concerning their period at risk.

Some couples may have married in the village, moved out during part of their reproductive years, and returned later, so that both marriage and death dates of at least one spouse were recorded locally. Such couples would not be present in observation during their entire reproductive span but would not be eliminated through the exact marriage and death date test. The reconstituted family history of such a couple, however, often contains information suggesting that they had children elsewhere. For example, it might include the death date of a child whose birth date is unknown, or reference to a child who later married locally but for whom no birth date is given. Many of these couples can thus be eliminated by excluding family histories in which the birth date of one or more children is missing. Following this procedure, however, risks biasing the selection of couples toward those with fewer births. This is so because the greater the number of children attributed to a couple, the greater the chance that at least one lacks an exact birth date. An exact birth date could be lacking for a child even if the couple resided locally for their entire reproductive span if, for example, the birth entry in the register was illegible or the local priest occasionally failed to record a birth. To minimize this bias and at the same time to eliminate couples who clearly seemed to be out of the parish during some period of their reproductive life, or cases where births were for some other reason not regularly recorded, only couples whose children's birth dates were either all exact, or which included no more than one child whose birth day or month (but not year) was missing were included.

Since much fertility analysis requires knowing women's ages at various events, only couples were included for which at least the birth year of the wife was known. Finally, a small number of family histories contained unresolvable inconsistencies, either due to typographical errors in the village genealogies or incorrect reconstitution, and were judged unsuitable for inclusion. Births spaced only several months apart or occurring after the death of the mother are examples of such inconsistencies.

Additional restrictions for specific analyses

In the actual analyses, additional restrictions are usually applied, resulting in the further exclusion of some initially included couples (or births if the unit of analysis is the child). The rules vary according to the particular tabulation involved. The most common restrictions, along with comments indicating the rationale for imposing them, are listed in Table A.1. The particular combinations of restrictions imposed in obtaining any given set of results are indicated in the notes to tables included in the chapters of this study. For convenience, these most common restrictions are designated in the tables by their reference number. Other, less common restrictions are described when appropriate. In addition, there are also implicit restrictions inherent in particular analyses but not explicitly mentioned in table footnotes as they are assumed to be self-evident. For example, analyses referring to fertility are usually limited to women who are within the reproductive ages (under age 50) at the time of marriage; analyses referring to births or to a characteristic of the mother at the time of birth are limited to couples who have had a birth.

Table A.2 indicates, for couples married during the eighteenth and nineteenth centuries, the proportion in each village genealogy that were initially excluded, the percent of those initially included who

Table A.1. *List of various restrictions imposed on the selection of couples included in specific analyses*

Restriction reference number	Restriction description	Comments
1	Marriage occurred locally	Helps to ensure couple is under observation at start of marriage; unless otherwise specified, 'local' includes both the local village and nearby villages for which a village genealogy was available to check on events occurring there.
2	End of marriage occurred locally	Helps ensure couple is under observation at the time the marriage terminated; see restriction 1 for definition of local.
3	Date of end of marriage certain	Ensures time considered under observation can be terminated at death of first spouse; end of marriage is considered certain if both spouses' death dates are known or if other information indicates that the spouse whose death date is known was the first to die.
4	Wife reached at least age 45 before end of marriage	Ensures that the marriage remained intact until the end of the wife's potentially fertile age span; marital unions meeting this criterion are referred to as 'completed.'
5	Husband's birth date known	A necessary requirement for analyses for which the age difference between husband and wife is relevant.
6	Birth of child occurred locally	This restriction applies only to analyses in which the individual birth is the unit of analysis and helps ensure that the period under observation starts with the birth; see restriction 1 for definition of local.

Table A.1. – *cont.*

Restriction reference number	Restriction description	Comments
7	Birth of child occurred during period when registration of child deaths is judged to be relatively complete	This restriction applies to analyses relating to infant and child mortality and is necessary to ensure that children for whom only a birth date is available can be safely assumed to have survived childhood. See Appendix B for determination of periods when the registration of child deaths is judged to be relatively complete.

meet various common restrictions imposed on various analyses, and the percent meeting several common combinations of restrictions among initially included couples in which the wife was still in the reproductive ages at the time of marriage. Of all premarital unions, the proportion which qualified for initial inclusion varies substantially among the different genealogies, ranging from just over a quarter to three-quarters, with an average of exactly a half for the entire sample combined. Compared to the proportions of reconstituted families meeting similar criteria in other historical demographic studies, the proportions qualifying for inclusion from the village genealogies are reasonably favorable.[2]

For almost all couples (99 percent for the combined sample) meeting the criteria for inclusion, the wife was not yet past her reproductive years at the time of marriage. Since the village genealogies were based largely on local records, dates of events occurring outside the village are generally missed and do not show up in the reconstituted family histories. For a small proportion of couples, dates of the marriage and/ or the end of union (as marked by the death of the first spouse to die) are given even though these events are stated as having occurred outside the village to which the genealogy refers. There is no information in the genealogies as to how the compiler ascertained these dates. In many cases, the events occurred in neighboring villages whose registers were probably accessible to the genealogist. Possibly the genealogist consulted them to supplement the local records. In other cases the dates may have been retrospectively reported by the couple

[2] Knodel and Shorter, 'Family reconstitution data.'

Table A.2. Percent and number of couples in genealogy selected for inclusion, percent of selected couples meeting common restrictions imposed in various analyses, and percent of selected couples in which the wife is under 50 at marriage meeting various combinations of restrictions, for couples married 1700–1899

	Grafenhausen	Herbolzheim	Kappel	Rust	Öschelbronn	Anhausen	Gabelbach	Kreuth	Braunsen	Höringhausen	Massenhausen	Vasbeck	Middels	Werdum	All villages
Of all couples included in genealogy															
Percent selected for analysis[a]	65[b]	66[b]	62	64	66	45[b]	52[b]	46[b]	52	53[b]	55	75[b]	30	27[b]	50[c]
Number of couples selected	1276	2213	1029	1561	842	287	256	210	265	627	460	503	695	1468	11,692
Of couples selected, percent with															
Wife under 50 at marriage	99	99	99	99	99	97	99	99	100	99	99	99	99	99	99
Marriage local	98	96	99	99	90	100	95	97	94	96	97	97	93	93	96
End of union local	97	98	98	98	93	100	95	94	94	95	94	96	90	90	96
End of union certain	93	92	93	91	95	100	92	88	89	87	83	90	90	81	90
Wife 45+ at end of union	68	63	68	63	70	74	67	78	59	66	64	58	66	53	64
Husband's birth date known	89	90	87	85	96	76	88	72	78	78	78	88	86	70	84
Of couples selected in which wife is under 50 at marriage, percent with															
Marriage local and end of union local and certain	90	88	91	90	86	100	87	81	80	80	78	87	80	71	85
Marriage local, end of union local and certain, and wife 45+ at end of union	62	58	61	58	58	76	60	67	49	56	56	54	53	38	55

[a] The year of marriage was estimated when missing to determine the base number of couples married 1700–1899.
[b] Estimated based on a sample consisting of the first 300 couples married 1700–1899 listed in the village genealogy.
[c] Weighted average of the individual villages including those for which the estimate of percentage included is based on the first 300 couples listed in the genealogy.

after they had moved into the village to which the genealogy refers and entered into the local records. In any case, it is uncertain whether all the events which occurred to the family while they were outside the village were recorded in the local records. Thus, for many tabulations, couples for which the marriage or the end of the marital union occurred non-locally are excluded, even though exact dates for these events are given.

It should be noted that in some cases where the marriage or the end of the marital union occurred outside the village, it occurred in another village for which a village genealogy is available. Provided the couple could be found in the other village genealogy, the events occurring in either village were considered local for the purpose of this study since in effect the couple was under observation while in either village. As the results show, the percentage of initially included marital unions in which either the marriage or the end of union was non-local is generally quite low.

There are also differences in the degree of certainty with which the date that a marital union ends is known. When death dates of both spouses are included in the genealogy, the date of the first spouse to die clearly marks the union's end. When only one death date is given but there is an indication that the spouse whose death date is missing remarries, then it is clear that the known death date also marks the end of the union. However, if the spouse whose death date is known also remarries, then the marital union must have ended with the death of the spouse whose death date is unknown. Couples in this particular situation were excluded in the initial selection process. However, couples for whom the death date of only one spouse is known and for whom there is no indication that either spouse remarried were not specifically excluded. In these cases, the known death date probably refers to the first spouse to die and the second death date is lacking because the widow or widower subsequently moved elsewhere, perhaps to remarry or to live with a child or relative. Indications that sometimes this is not the case are provided by instances in the village genealogies mentioned above in which only one death date is given but the spouse whose death date is known also remarried. Thus, for most tabulations in which knowing the date of the end of the marital union is important, only those cases in which the date is known with certainty are included. The proportion of such couples among those initially selected is quite high.

Since mortality was fairly high during the preindustrial period in Germany, a substantial proportion of marriages ended through the death of one of the spouses prior to the end of the wife's reproductive years. The proportion of included couples for whom the marriage remained intact at least until the wife reached age 45 ranged from just over a half to almost four-fifths.

For most analyses of fertility, a combination of restrictions needs to be imposed. For example, it is appropriate to restrict the calculation of age-specific fertility rates to couples for whom marriage and end of marital union occurred locally. By so doing, the probability is increased that all births to the couple during their marital reproductive career were included in the local registers and hence in the village geneal-ogies. For the entire sample, 85 percent of originally included couples in which the wife was under age 50 at marriage meet this combination of restrictions, and in general there is only moderate variation among the individual villages, with the percent falling below 80 percent only in Massenhausen and Werdum. The high percentages are, of course, a result of the original selection, which excluded most couples in the genealogies that would not have met these restrictions.

Other measures, such as completed family size or the extent of permanent childlessness, are more easily interpretable when, in addi-tion to the above-mentioned combination of restrictions, analysis is also limited to couples whose marriage remained intact until the wife reached the close of the childbearing ages (defined for this purpose as age 45). Only 55 percent of originally selected couples in which the wife was under age 50 at the time of marriage, meet all the restrictions for the combined sample. This figure varies considerably from village to village, ranging from less than 40 percent in Werdum to more than three-quarters of the selected couples in Anhausen. If these figures were expressed as a percent of all couples in the genealogy, rather than of selected couples, they would be considerably lower; in all villages such couples would be only a minority, and in some cases a small one.

In family reconstitution studies, most considerations of coverage are based on a determination of the percent of all *couples* present in the village that are included in any particular analysis. Based on this criterion, it is usually evident that for many analyses only a minority of all couples are included, and this is also the case in this study. However, a somewhat different and more favorable picture of coverage is obtained if the percentage of *demographic experience* that is captured in the analyses is considered. This results from the fact that included couples, compared to excluded ones, are more likely to have spent a greater share of their life, and particularly their reproductive career, in the village under study. The lack of information that leads to a couple's exclusion from analysis is typically due to periods during which the couple did not reside in the village. Thus the excluded couples are likely to have experienced some share of their vital events somewhere other than in the village under study, while included couples are likely to have experienced either all or a greater share of their vital events in the village.

To illustrate this point, evidence from the six villages for which all couples in the village genealogy were coded can be used. The number of births to couples selected for analysis as a proportion of *births* to all couples in the genealogy can be compared to the proportion of *couples* selected. Limiting consideration to births to couples married during the eighteenth and nineteenth centuries, the results indicate that the following percent of births were to couples selected for inclusion in the study: 78 in Kappel, 76 in Rust, 82 in Öschelbronn, 65 in Braunsen, 69 in Massenhausen, and 54 in Middels.[3] For all six villages these percentages are higher than the percentage of couples included in the study as shown in Table A.2. Of course the percentage of all births in the genealogy included in any particular analysis for which additional restrictions are imposed will be lower than the percentage selected overall, but they will generally be higher than the equivalent percentages of couples included.

Representativeness of selected families

Given the fact that demographic analyses of family reconstitution data are necessarily based on only a subset of all families in a village, the representativeness of the selected families is an important concern.[4] Assessing the degree of representativeness is complicated by the fact that the subsets of families included in particular analyses differ from each other. The potential for any given subset being unrepresentative increases with the extent to which an analysis is restrictive. For example, limiting consideration to couples in which the wife survived to the end of the childbearing ages will tend to bias the selection of couples in favor of wives who marry later, on the average, than women in general. Among women who marry under age 50 in the combined sample of all villages, the average age at marriage is 26.9 for women initially selected for inclusion. The identical result is found for the more

---

[3] The year of marriage had to be estimated for couples in the genealogy for which it was missing in order to determine if the marriage was likely to have occurred between 1700 and 1899. Births occurring out of wedlock are included in this calculation only to the extent they occur to couples who later marry and who are entered in the genealogy as a married couple.

[4] Schofield, 'Representatives'; Thestrup, 'Methodological problems'; Levine, 'Parochial registration'; Smith, Daniel Scott, 'Homeostatic demographic regime'; Norton, 'Reconstituted families.'

restricted subset whose marriage occurred locally and for whom the end of their marital union was local and certain. However, the average age at marriage increases by almost a year to 27.8 when the calculation is additionally restricted to wives who survive at least to their 45th birthday.

When a comparison is made between families selected for inclusion in the present study and the remainder who are included in the village genealogy but not selected, one important and general difference is that those excluded were more likely to have migrated into or out of the villages to which the genealogies refer, and thus the genealogies are more likely to lack, in these cases, some of the information that was required for inclusion in the analysis. Since the genealogy rarely mentions migration explicitly, this conclusion must rest on inference rather than on direct proof of differences in mobility, but it seems reasonably self-evident.

Occupational designations, available for most husbands in the village genealogies, can serve at least as one source of information by which to judge the representativeness of the couples selected for inclusion. Table A.3 indicates the percent of couples for which the husband's occupation is given, according to inclusion status. Also shown is the percent of all couples in various occupational categories in the genealogy that were selected for inclusion for the six villages for which all couples in the village genealogy were coded. To facilitate comparison across villages, index values of the percent included of each occupational category are provided, with the value for all occupational categories within each particular village set at 100. A discussion of the various occupational categories is provided in Appendix D. The results in Table A.3, however, unlike the occupational classification scheme described in Appendix D, take into account only the first mentioned occupation when more than one occupation was indicated for a particular husband.

With the exception of only the village of Massenhausen, the percent of couples for which occupational information is available is higher for included than for excluded couples. This complicates interpretation of the findings somewhat since the occupational distribution of husbands with no occupational information may differ from that of husbands with information available. Moreover, the results would differ if additional restrictions were imposed on the selection of cases such as is true for various specific analyses. Nevertheless, the results are suggestive and are fairly consistent across villages.

In all six villages, a higher-than-average proportion of husbands designated as farmers were selected for inclusion. This is not surprising since peasants with their own farms would presumably be the least mobile segment of preindustrial society. The proportion of cottagers included is also considerably higher than average in the three villages where they are found, again presumably because of their ties to the land. Similarly, fishermen are more likely to be included than the average of all persons of known occupation, in the two villages where fishermen were in significant numbers. A similar situation is true of weavers in three of the four villages in which they are relatively common.

In all villages except Middels, the small number of husbands classified as professionals were considerably below average in their chances of being selected for inclusion. Even in Middels, professionals are slightly less likely to be included than the average for all husbands for whom occupation is known. A substantial share of the professional category is made up of teachers and administrators and, in Protestant villages, of clergymen, whose ability to earn a livelihood depended on their skills and training rather than on immovable property, and who may have changed assignments over their careers.

Also consistently below average in the proportion selected are husbands in the residual 'Other proletarian' and 'Other occupation' categories. The inclusion of soldiers and others with military occupations in the latter category contributes in part to its underrepresentation among selected couples. Military personnel were highly mobile and most were probably only temporarily stationed in the vicinity of the villages under examination. Interestingly, the proportion selected among husbands listed as day laborers is not consistently below average. Finally, the proportions selected from the artisan and businessmen group seem to be close to average everywhere except, in Middels, where the group is underrepresented.

Table A.4 compares the husbands' occupational distribution in broad groups of couples selected for inclusion with that of all couples in the village genealogies, based on couples married in the eighteenth and nineteenth centuries for whom information on the husband's occupation was given. The composition of broad occupational groups and the rationale behind them are described in Appendix D. In relation to the previous table, the broad group labeled 'Proletarians,' includes the categories of cottagers, day laborers, weavers, and others whose occupation is of a proletarian nature. The 'Artisan and skilled' group includes the artisans, professionals, businessmen and fishermen. Farmers and other occupations remain as groups in themselves.

As expected from the results in the previous table, the proportion of selected couples that are farmers is greater than for all couples, and the

Table A.3. *Percent of couples with occupation of husband given, by inclusion status in present study and percent included in present study and index of percent included in present study by occupation, couples married 1700–1899*

	Kappel	Rust	Öschelbronn	Braunsen	Massenhausen	Middels
Percent with occupation of husband given						
Inclusion status						
Included	99	96	93	89	63	98
Excluded	78	74	79	79	63	90
Per cent included among husbands with given occupation						
Occupation						
Farmers	84	79	81	68	74	43
Cottagers	—	—	—	(83)	73	37
Day laborers	67	75	(61)	81	(69)	15
Weavers	83	79	77	—	—	(31)
Other proletarians	33	47	54	28	41	27
Artisans/businessmen	62	64	69	55	56	16
Professionals	(20)	(25)	(42)	(35)	(12)	31
Fishermen	82	83	—	—	—	—
Other occupations	18	31	31	(38)	50	(7)
All occupations[a]	68	69	69	55	55	32

Index of percent included (all occupations =100)

Occupation						
Farmers	123	114	117	124	134	136
Cottagers	—	—	—	(152)	131	115
Day laborers	99	109	(88)	148	(125)	46
Weavers	122	114	111	—	—	(98)
Other proletarians	48	68	78	51	74	83
Artisans/businessmen	92	92	100	100	101	51
Professionals	(29)	(36)	(60)	(64)	(21)	—
Fishermen	120	121	—	—	—	97
Other occupations	27	45	45	(69)	91	(22)

Note: This table is limited to fully-coded villages. The year of marriage was estimated when missing to determine the base number of couples married 1700–1899. Results refer only to the first-mentioned occupation in village genealogy for any particular husband. Results in parentheses are based on 10–49 cases. Results based on less than 10 cases not shown.
[a] Excluding couples with no occupation given.

Table A.4. *Comparison of the distribution of the husband's occupation for couples included in the present study with that of all couples in the village genealogy, for couples married 1700–1899 with husband's occupation given*

Village and inclusion status	Percent distribution of husbands with known occupations according to broad occupational categories			
	Farmer	Proletarian	Artisans and skilled	Other
Kappel				
Included couples	37	29	33	1
All couples	30	31	35	4
Rust				
Included couples	27	26	45	2
All couples	23	25	47	4
Öschelbronn				
Included couples	40	18	40	2
All couples	34	20	41	5
Braunsen				
Included couples	19	39	37	5
All couples	16	39	38	7
Massenhausen				
Included couples	25	41	24	10
All couples	18	41	29	11
Middels				
Included couples	41	49	10	0
All couples	30	51	17	2

Note: Results refer only to the first-mentioned occupation in the village genealogy for any particular husband.

proportion of couples in the residual 'Other' occupational category is less. However, the proportions classified as proletarians and, except for the village of Middels, as belonging to the artisan and skilled group are quite similar. Moreover, the contrasts among villages in occupational distribution evident for all couples in the genealogies are fairly well preserved among the subset of couples selected for analysis.

In brief, examination of occupational data indicates that the couples selected for analysis are not drawn randomly from the social structure of the village population. Some groups are clearly overrepresented, some underrepresented, and some selected relatively proportional to their size. When the occupational structure is viewed in terms of broader groups, the contrast between all couples and selected couples remains but is not intolerably severe. Moreover, since occupational groups did not differ sharply in a number of key aspects of demographic behavior, the selective nature of the couples included in this study should not greatly distort the overall results.

In addition to questions about representativeness relevant to any study based on family reconstitution data, it is of interest to consider the extent to which the preselection of families in this study might additionally bias results. This issue does not arise in the case of most of the fertility analyses since the preselection criteria were based primarily on eliminating those families which were not suitable for the study of fertility, and thus in any event would not have been included. However, had there been no preselection, the analysis of nuptiality and infant and child mortality could have been based on a larger number of reconstituted families. Relevant comparisons for infant and child mortality based on the six fully-coded villages are presented in Appendix E. They suggest that infant and child mortality rates are largely unaffected by the preselection of families as carried out in the present study.

For the six fully-coded villages, Table A.5 compares the mean age at first marriage based on all couples for whom the requisite data are available with results based only on the preselected couples. In most of the villages, the mean age at first marriage of both men and women based on all couples is very similar to the results based only on the preselected couples. In no village is the difference for men greater than one-tenth of a year of age. For women, a four-tenths of a year's difference is found in Massenhausen and Middels but the direction of the differences is not consistent. Thus there are little grounds for suspecting that the preselection procedures create a substantial systematic bias.

Regardless of the preselection criteria, the calculation of the mean age at first marriage requires knowledge of the marriage date and some indication of birth date, whether obtained directly from an entry in the birth register or estimated based on an age associated with some other registered event, such as age at death. The difference in the number of cases available for calculating age at marriage before and after preselection is largely due to the requirement that the date of the death of at least one spouse be known for the preselected cases. Apparently couples for whom no death date is available differ little in terms of their age at marriage from couples for whom at least one death date is known.

There is, of course, no guarantee that other analyses which could be based on a broader set of reconstituted families than those preselected

Table A.5. *Mean age at first marriage for all couples and for couples included for study, six fully-coded villages,*
1700–1899

| | Men | | | | Women | | | |
| | All couples | | Included couples | | All couples | | Included couples | |
	Mean	N	Mean	N	Mean	N	Mean	N
Kappel	27.7	1003	27.7	818	25.6	1107	25.6	934
Rust	28.2	1498	28.1	1154	26.0	1713	26.1	1401
Öschelbronn	27.9	880	27.8	715	26.0	999	26.0	496
Braunsen	28.6	293	28.7	209	25.8	324	25.6	233
Massenhausen	28.3	482	28.4	357	26.7	552	27.1	422
Middels	28.7	839	28.8	585	24.3	887	23.9	650

for this study would necessarily reveal a similar absence of apparent bias. Nevertheless, it is reassuring that both infant and child mortality rates and the mean age at first marriage appear to be little affected by the preselection process, especially given their importance as aspects of demographic behavior.

Assessment of the quality of demographic data contained in German village genealogies

In any demographic study of the past, the validity of the findings depends on the accuracy and completeness of the source material and, if applicable, on the appropriateness of the techniques employed to overcome known shortcomings in the data. In this study, which is based on analysis of family reconstitution data from German village genealogies, the data are generally treated as if they are accurate although, in the case of data on infant and child mortality, only for specified periods of time for some villages. In this appendix, the quality of the data is assessed and the basis for determining the periods during which mortality data are assumed to be accurate is provided.

Accuracy of transcription and reconstitution

While the data for this study come directly from the village genealogies, those genealogies are in turn based on the parish registers and, in some cases, also the civil registers. Thus the accuracy of the data being used depends both on the completeness with which vital events were reported in the parish and civil registers and on the accuracy with which the genealogist transcribed these events and compiled them into reconstituted family histories. Details of a study have been reported elsewhere in which a sample of entries in the registers of four villages was compared with events recorded in the corresponding village genealogies to see if the events were included and accurately stated. In addition, an effort was made to reconstitute a sample of family units in two villages to check if the compiler made reasonable linkages between vital records.[1] The results are worth summarizing since three of the four village genealogies checked for transcription

---

[1] Knodel and Shorter, 'Family reconstitution data.'

errors (Rust, Braunsen, and Massenhausen) and both of the genealogies checked for their accuracy in family reconstitution (Rust and
Braunsen) are included in the sample used in this study. The fourth
genealogy checked for transcription errors was for an additional village
in the principality of Waldeck but was not incorporated in this study.
The results were quite encouraging with respect to both the transcription and the family reconstitution.

For the four villages combined, a total of 101 legitimate births, 76
illegitimate births, 141 deaths, and 90 marriages entered in the parish
registers (and in the case of Braunsen, also in the civil register) were
chosen in order to determine the completeness and accuracy with
which the entries were included in the village genealogies. Of the total
408 events, only one unambiguous omission was discovered and that
was apparently due to a typographical error in the village genealogy
manuscript. In addition, ten entries in the village genealogies were
inaccurate in one way or another: in three, the day of the event was
incorrectly recorded; in three, the month of the event was incorrect or
left out; and in four, the year of the event was incorrect. In two cases,
some supplemental information found in the register was not included
in the genealogy: in one case the husband's first name was omitted and
in the other case the occupation of the wife's father was omitted.

For both Rust and Braunsen, the quality of family reconstitution was
tested by independently reconstituting a sample of family units in each
village. In all instances, family lines with a common name were chosen
for early periods of time (when the identifying information was often
scanty) in order to make the test a tough one. The results indicated a
very high level of agreement between the reconstitution done by the
genealogists and the sample reconstitution based on the established
rules of historical demography. It is worth adding that for later periods
of time, generally from the late eighteenth century on, the amount of
information provided about each recorded event in the parish registers, and later the civil registers, is typically so extensive that correct
linkages among records for the same individual or among family
members is virtually ensured, although carelessness on the part of the
compiler could lead to an occasional error. This earlier evaluation effort
concluded:

In comparative terms the German parish registers on which the village
genealogies rest are probably superior to the French, on which so much work
has been done to date. They permit a higher degree of confidence in making
links and they allow the reconstitution of a higher proportion of families . . . in
absolute terms the standards of accuracy of the local genealogists meet the
generally established standards of scientific research. Indeed, the genealogists

appear to have been conscientious in the extreme and industrious beyond what most professional historical demographers can manage.[2]

It is of course not possible to generalize from the results of a check of such a small sample of village genealogies to all such genealogies. Nevertheless, it is worth noting that the compiler of the genealogy for Rust was the same person responsible for three other villages included in the sample for this study: Grafenhausen, Herbolzheim (with the aid of co-workers), and Kappel.

Completeness of infant and child death data

While the evidence just reviewed suggests that compilers of village genealogies may well have accurately transcribed events from the registers and have correctly linked them together in reconstituted family histories, the validity of demographic results based on family genealogies also depends on the accuracy and completeness of the registers which serve as their basic source material. Gaps in registers or extremely low frequencies of recorded events relative to surrounding years are obvious indicators of incomplete registration and can be readily identified. Indeed, in selecting the village genealogies which constitute the sample for the present study, those which the compiler indicated in his introductory comments were based on problematic registers, especially ones with long gaps or long periods of obviously defective registration, were avoided. Periods during which the degree of incompleteness is less extreme or affects only certain classes of events were more difficult to identify. Several approaches based on evidence internal to the village genealogies can be helpful in this respect. The remainder of this appendix is devoted to applying several of these approaches.

A detailed study of infant mortality conducted by the Imperial Health Ministry during 1875–77 provides official statistics derived from civil registers on infant mortality at the district level and can thus serve as a basis for comparison with infant mortality indices calculated from the village genealogies.[3] To minimize the problems associated with small numbers of cases, infant mortality based on the village genealogies was calculated for the two-decade period surrounding the years of the official study. The official statistics will suffer from any deficiencies in civil registration that may have existed but these are presumed to be minimal.[4] In some cases, the genealogists had access to

[2] Knodel and Shorter, 'Family reconstitution data,' pp. 151–53.
[3] Würzburg, 'Säuglingssterblichkeit.'
[4] Compare with Knodel, *Decline of fertility*, pp. 19–30.

these same records, and in these circumstances the comparison serves as a check on the completeness with which events were covered by the genealogist in the course of the compilation. In cases where the genealogist relied only on parish registers, or on parish registers for part of the two-decade period used for comparison, the results reflect both the completeness of parish registers (assuming the civil registers to be complete) as well as the completeness of coverage in the genealogy of those events recorded in the parish registers.

The comparison between the results for the villages and the official infant mortality statistics for the districts in which the villages are located is presented in Table B.1. Given the fact that the district-level statistics referred to a considerably larger population than that of the particular village or villages to which they are being compared, and the fact that there is a difference in the time periods to which the results refer, only a rough correspondence between village and district-level infant mortality should be expected. In addition, the official statistics refer to all births, while the results for the villages are based only on the preselected families and exclude non-legitimized children born out of wedlock, whose mortality is usually higher (see Appendix E). In general, the mortality rates from the official statistics and those calculated from the village genealogies agree rather well.

The events which would seem logically to be most likely to be left out of family histories (or the parish registers on which they were based) are stillbirths and deaths of children dying very early in infancy. For the two decades under observation, all the village genealogies, with the exception of Kreuth, included at least some stillbirths. In most cases, the level of stillbirths is below that reported in the official statistics for the districts. It is difficult to know how to interpret the data on stillbirths since even today such statistics are frequently beset by problems of definition. In some sense, it is encouraging that stillbirths were included at all since they would seem to have little genealogical relevance *per se*.

Infant death rates during the first week of life correspond more closely with the official statistics than do the levels of stillbirths. The main differences are found for the two Bavarian villages in the district of Augsburg, which show somewhat lower mortality rates during the first week of life than for the district, and for the four villages in Waldeck, which show a higher death rate than the district-level statistics. Likewise, death rates during the first year of life based on village genealogies correspond rather closely to those provided in the official statistics for the corresponding districts. The largest discrepancy in this case is for Kreuth. It is worth noting that the results for

Table B.1. *Stillbirth and first-week mortality rates, infant mortality rates, and percentage of infant deaths occurring in the first month as calculated from village genealogies for 1866–85, compared with official statistics for 1875–77 for district in which the village is located*

Village or district	Per 1000 births[a]		Deaths under age 1 per 1000 births		% of all deaths under age 1 occurring in first month	
	Stillborn	Died in 1st week[b]	Including stillbirths[c]	Excluding stillbirths[d]	Including stillbirths[c]	Excluding stillbirths[d]
Grafenhausen	24	26	286	268	36	30
Herbolzheim	12	34	298	289	37	34
Kappel	18	34	223	208	44	39
Rust	29	37	286	265	38	31
Combined	21	33	278	262	38	33
District (Freiburg)	34	35	249	224	43	34
Öschelbronn	32	33	326	303	46	40
District (Waiblingen)	48	—	302	268	44	35
Anhausen	47	38	435	408	38	31
Gabelbach	12	32	433	426	37	35
Combined	27	35	434	418	37	33
District (Augsburg)	26	49	467	454	42	38

Kreuth	0	39	136	136	79	79
District (Miesbach)	28	37	274	254	49	44
Braunsen	30	16	152	125	35	19
Höringhausen	37	38	222	192	50	40
Massenhausen	41	17	177	142	49	33
Vasbeck	38	26	204	172	55	44
Combined	37	28	199	168	50	38
District (Waldeck)	43	17	176	140	47	31
Middels	29	19	132	106	51	38
Werdum	19	15	120	103	44	33
Combined	26	18	128	105	49	36
District (Aurich)	47	19	154	114	55	37

Note: Results for villages are limited to births occurring locally to couples selected for analysis.

[a] Including stillbirths.

[b] Excluding stillbirths from numerator.

[c] Both numerator and denominator include stillbirths.

[d] Both numerator and denominator exclude stillbirths.

Source: The official statistics for the districts are derived from Arthur Würzburg, 'Die Säuglingssterblichkeit im Deutschen Reiche während der Jahre 1875 bis 1877,' Part II in, *Arbeiten aus dem Kaiserlichen Gesundheitsamte*, Vol. II (1887), pp. 343–446.

Kreuth are based on the fewest births (slightly more than 100), corresponding to the small size of the village, and thus are particularly susceptible to random fluctuation. The infant mortality rate for Kreuth for the full 50-year period 1850–99, based on a larger number of births, is 206 per 1000 births, which is considerably closer to the district-level figure than is the rate for the shorter 20-year period used for comparison.

Another indication of how completely infant deaths (and to a lesser extent, births) were included in the village genealogies is provided by the distribution of deaths within the first year of life. Infant deaths are typically concentrated in the first several weeks of life when 'endo-genous' mortality resulting from an intrinsic non-viability of some infants plays an important part, although the extent of concentration depends on a variety of factors including the level of mortality.[5] At the same time, infants dying soon after birth seem to be the most likely candidates for omission from the birth and death registers or from the genealogies. In general, the proportion of all deaths under age 1 occurring during the first month of life and recorded in the village genealogies is similar to the proportion indicated by the official stat-istics for the corresponding districts. The largest discrepancy is again found for the village of Kreuth, but in this case the difference is in the opposite direction from what would be expected if underregistration of early infant deaths was common.

While the foregoing comparison suggests that the village geneal-ogies and the sources on which they were based accurately represent mortality experience at the end of the nineteenth century, such may not have been the case for earlier periods. Indeed, a detailed examina-tion of infant mortality reveals problems of underregistration of deaths for some periods in some villages.

Table B.2 presents for each decade of the eighteenth century and for the first three decades of the nineteenth century the percentage of all births that result in a death before age 1, as well as the percentage for which no information other than a birth date is provided, for each of the individual villages included in the present study. Even when registration is complete and accurately reflected in the genealogies, out-migration will result in some persons from whom no information is recorded other than a birth date. However, higher than usual proportions of such cases can be symptomatic of incomplete death registration.

Unrealistically low percentages of children dying in infancy are

[5] Knodel and Kintner, 'Breast feeding patterns.'

Table B.2. *Percent of births to couples selected for analysis indicated as dying before age 1 and percent with no information other than a birth date, by village and year of birth*

	1700–09	1710–19	1720–29	1730–39	1740–49	1750–59	1760–69	1770–79	1780–89	1790–99	1800–09	1810–19	1820–29
Grafenhausen													
% infant deaths	0	0	0	2	28	20	29	28	21	27	24	23	26
% fate unknown	53	68	54	46	17	7	10	8	8	7	7	5	9
N of births	53	50	90	169	133	133	239	213	232	278	368	404	334
Herbolzheim													
% infant deaths	7	5	7	19	23	20	13	21	17	20	22	22	26
% fate unknown	45	49	33	10	11	11	26	8	10	5	5	8	11
N of births	133	175	239	237	299	361	383	463	523	527	558	618	602
Kappel													
% infant deaths	—	0	0	11	11	0	0	1	4	0	2	19	16
% fate unknown	—	43	38	21	37	49	44	35	45	52	39	12	19
N of births	2	28	92	100	128	190	188	155	231	262	297	341	308
Rust													
% infant deaths	0	0	1	1	15	8	22	22	23	23	21	17	18
% fate unknown	45	42	38	40	16	27	15	8	6	4	6	5	5
N of births	64	81	169	154	143	199	188	242	297	335	473	428	448
Öschelbronn													
% infant deaths	23	24	22	26	30	24	31	25	25	27	29	35	36
% fate unknown	12	12	3	1	1	1	3	3	1	1	1	0	1
N of births	86	109	99	107	127	157	188	153	181	217	251	211	231

Table B.2. – cont.

	1700–09	1710–19	1720–29	1730–39	1740–49	1750–59	1760–69	1770–79	1780–89	1790–99	1800–09	1810–19	1820–29
Anhausen													
% infant deaths[a]	53	21	11	11	48	58	15	45	59	41	42	31	26
% fate unknown	20	35	53	66	38	21	25	13	13	13	13	19	21
% of deaths marked only by †[b]	31	0	25	100	90	100	33	80	81	57	5	3	0
N of births	45	43	38	35	21	19	20	56	114	104	96	80	89
Gabelbach													
% of infant deaths[a]	17	7	15	26	19	18	30	38	49	43	34	35	23
% fate unknown	58	68	63	33	50	50	35	17	15	25	5	9	11
% of deaths marked only by †[b]	100	100	100	100	86	100	100	100	100	100	74	4	14
N of births	12	28	27	42	36	38	46	60	68	51	64	65	56
Kreuth													
% infant deaths	—	—	—	—	—	14	23	22	20	29	25	20	28
% fate unknown	—	—	—	—	—	10	23	15	26	21	22	26	18
N of births	0	0	0	0	4	52	57	54	54	73	59	46	39
Braunsen													
% infant deaths	—	17	16	5	28	24	13	17	29	15	18	8	14
% fate unknown	—	14	16	14	12	6	15	10	9	15	23	21	17
N of births	1	29	31	21	25	48	46	63	58	73	65	76	69

Höringhausen													
% of infant deaths	—	—	—	18	14	15	14	13	12	18	15	17	10
% fate unknown	—	—	—	7	21	20	18	13	19	25	22	32	29
N of births	0	0	1	39	97	142	152	126	132	147	170	130	140
Massenhausen													
% infant deaths	6	13	14	12	4	22	15	7	14	20	14	22	25
% fate unknown	29	15	30	47	40	15	13	24	24	11	12	16	21
N of births	34	52	76	43	53	75	78	54	78	104	113	109	126
Vasbeck													
% infant deaths	17	19	19	9	13	14	26	24	19	32	28	28	22
% fate unknown	15	16	19	3	10	12	9	8	14	8	6	11	19
N of births	48	90	97	77	102	83	65	120	139	123	111	127	151
Middels													
% infant deaths	—	—	—	0	13	13	14	17	14	10	18	12	10
% fate unknown	—	—	—	27	30	25	26	17	23	15	9	13	12
N of births	2	6	6	11	23	71	109	122	149	144	148	172	182
Werdum													
% infant deaths	—	33	23	19	20	21	17	20	17	12	14	16	11
% fate unknown	—	0	14	14	13	23	24	17	23	23	27	23	14
N of births	0	36	143	249	249	336	399	365	336	380	369	351	316

Note: Results are based on local births only. Infant deaths include stillbirths. Results not shown if number of local births is fewer than 10.
[a] Including deaths indicated by a cross only without an exact date of death, some of which almost certainly occurred to children past age 1.
[b] Deaths indicated by a cross only as a percentage of deaths under age 10 as calculated from birth and death dates plus deaths indicated by a cross only.

evident in a number of villages for at least part of the eighteenth century. Furthermore, the same decades that are characterized by low or even non-existent infant mortality are generally associated with high proportions of births for which no further information is available. For example, it is evident in Grafenhausen that serious under-registration of infant deaths was present during the first four decades of the eighteenth century. These were the same decades for which very high proportions of children have no information about them indicated in the genealogy other than their date of birth.

Examination of the results for a number of the other villages indicates a similar pattern. The worst case is Kappel, where serious underregistration appears to persist through to the beginning of the nineteenth century. On the other hand, there are several villages for which no obvious problem in death registration is evident. In Öschelbronn, for example, infant mortality remains at plausible levels for all decades and the percentage of births with an unknown fate is consistently low. Likewise, there appears to be no serious problem with death registration in Kreuth, Braunsen, Höringhausen, Vasbeck, and Werdum; and for Middels the problematic period includes only the earliest decades, for which there are very few events in any case.

In villages where problems are evident, typically there is a point at which infant mortality shows a significant increase and the percentage of births of an unknown fate shows a significant decrease, followed by relatively stable, non-problematic levels thereafter, especially if allowance is made in the cases of the smaller villages for a certain amount of random fluctuation. One notable exception is Herbolzheim, for which the information is based on a sizable number of births throughout the period of observation. After an improvement evident between the second and third decades of the eighteenth century, the infant mortality rate falls temporarily to a level that appears suspiciously low for the decade of the 1760s. At the same time there is a rise in the proportion of births whose fate is unknown.

Evidence of deficiencies in the registration of child deaths does not necessarily imply that adult deaths were also underregistered during the same periods. A separate assessment of the completeness of adult mortality data in the genealogies has not been carried out, both because it is less central to the present study and because it would be considerably more difficult to do, given the nature of family reconstitution data and the manner in which such data have been coded for the present study. Noteworthy, however, is that the rates of maternal mortality in Rust and Kappel were not unusually low, indeed were above average, during the periods when infant and child deaths were clearly unreported in the genealogies. The reason that infant and child deaths were particularly vulnerable to omission during the early periods, at least in Catholic parishes, is probably related to the practice of treating the registration of deaths to persons prior to their first communion (about age 12 or 13) differently from deaths to persons who had already experienced their first communion. At least in some parishes in Baden during earlier periods, special registers were kept for such deaths, while in other parishes these deaths were simply not registered at all.[6] In cases where a separate register was kept, if it were lost but the regular death register were not, only death dates for adults would be available and those for infants and children would be missing. This might have been the case in Kappel for the period before 1810.[7]

A related problem with death registration is apparent in the geneal-ogies for the two Bavarian villages of Anhausen and Gabelbach. In both villages throughout the eighteenth century, and in the case of Gabelbach during the early nineteenth century, deaths of infants and young children were often not entered into the burial register but rather indicated only by a cross next to the entry in the baptismal register.[8] An examination of the distribution of deaths by age in both Gabelbach and Anhausen during the period when this practice was followed reveals very few deaths to anyone in either infancy or childhood. The compiler of the Anhausen village genealogy notes that infants and small children who died, unlike adults, did not receive the sacrament of extreme unction and that burials of infants and children in the past did not usually involve a church service, and possibly not even the assistance of a priest.[9] Likewise, according to the compiler of the Gabelbach genealogy, before the nineteenth century, priests there only entered in the register deaths of persons who had received their first holy communion and thus would include only persons past age 12 or 13.[10]

The practice of indicating infant and child deaths only by a cross in the baptism register ended around the turn of the nineteenth century, as is evident from the percentage of presumed child deaths that were indicated in this manner, shown in Table B.2, for the villages in question. The change in this practice is probably a result of the

---

[6] Personal communication from Albert Köbele.
[7] Personal communication from Ernest Benz.
[8] Scheuenpflug, *Ortssippenbuch Anhausen*, pp. 6–7; personal communications from Lorenz Scheuenpflug and Franz Hauf; discussed also in Knodel, 'Demographic history.'
[9] Personal communication from Lorenz Scheuenpflug.
[10] Personal communication from Franz Hauf.

government regulations that were imposed on the content of parish registers early in the nineteenth century in Bavaria and the introduction of registers with a uniform format specifying the exact information to be recorded.[11] Thus in the case of these two Bavarian villages, there is a gap between the time when most infant and child deaths are indicated in the registers (and hence the village genealogies) and the time when information on the actual date of the death (and thus the age at which it occurs) becomes available.

Another indicator of changes in the completeness of registration of infant and child deaths can be obtained by examining entries in the genealogy for children with the same given name within the same family unit. It was common in the past to name a later child after an earlier sibling who died.[12] When death registration of infants and children is complete, we would expect to find a death date associated with the first of any specific pair of children within the same family which had the same given name. Moreover, that death date should occur prior to the birth of the second child in the pair. If the compiler of the genealogy incorporated a hard-and-fast rule forbidding links of children with the same name to the same family unless the death of the first child in the pair was indicated in the registers, then such evidence cannot be used to measure the completeness of the death register. This is clearly not the case, however, for at least some of the village genealogies on which this study is based.

Other problems with this approach stem from the fact that insufficient cases are available for some places to determine very precisely the year in which death registration completeness changes. In addition, there was some limited number of cases in which the genealogy clearly indicated that the earlier child survived past the birth date of the second child of the pair. This was not very common, however, and could arise from several circumstances: incorrect linkages made by the compiler; incomplete recording of given names such that the two siblings actually had different names but that their full names were not completely specified; or the actual practice by some parents of giving more than one child the same name even when an earlier child was still alive.

Table B.3 shows, for the four villages in Baden, the percent of first siblings with the same name as a later sibling for whom the death date is indicated. In most cases, examination of the annual series of this measure shows a clear breaking point, and the time periods indicated in the table reflect these breaking points. They correspond very closely

---

[11] Personal communication from Lorenz Scheuenpflug.
[12] Krausse, *Familiengeschichtsforschung*, p. 140.

Table B.3. *Percent of first of two siblings with the same name for whom an exact death date is provided in village genealogies, by year of death (or year of birth if death date not provided) and village of residence, for four villages in Baden*

Village	Time period	% of first sibling with same name for whom death date is indicated	N of cases
Grafenhausen	prior to 1740	0	11
	1740–59	90	10
Herbolzheim	prior to 1726	28	57
	1726–59	92	77
	1760–66	54	24
	1767–80	94	31
Kappel	1790–1809	11	47
	1810–29	86	37
Rust	1750–63	42	12
	1764–79	100	22

Note: For families with more than two children with the same name, each sibling with that name except the last is included in this analysis. Cases in which there is explicit evidence that the first of two siblings with the same name survived past the date of birth of the second of the pair are excluded from the analysis.

with the breaking points indicated, from examination of the annual series, of the percentage of infant deaths and percentage of births of unknown fate, for these villages. Through examination of the annual series of information presented in Tables B.2 and B.3, it is possible to pinpoint with a reasonable degree of certainty the year in which inclusion of child deaths becomes relatively complete in the genealogy, presumably reflecting the comparable situation in parish registers.

In the villages where infant mortality levels and the percentage of births of unknown fate suggested there was little problem with death registration during the period covered by the genealogies, examination of siblings with the same name also suggests no serious problems in death registration. For each of the villages (Öschelbronn, Kreuth, Braunsen, Höringhausen, Vasbeck, Middels, and Werdum), death dates were indicated for virtually all of the same-named pairs. In the remaining villages, where problems in death registration were indicated from evidence in Table B.2 (Anhausen, Gabelbach, and Massenhausen), the death of the first born of same-named sibling pairs was almost always indicated throughout the entire period covered, but for each village the number of such cases, especially for periods of presumed poor registration, was very small. Thus little can be con-

Table B.4. *The year the extant parish records begin and the year infant and child death registration starts to be complete*

	Year extant parish registers begin	Year death registration considered complete
Grafenhausen	1690	1740
Herbolzheim	1596	1726 (excluding 1760–66)
Kappel	1700	1810
Rust	1654[a]	1764
Öschelbronn	1610[b]	1610
Anhausen	1692	1765 (1798)[e]
Gabelbach	1648	1766 (1811)[e]
Kreuth	1746	1746
Braunsen	1707[c]	1707
Höringhausen	1731	1731
Massenhausen	1651	1749
Vasbeck	1662	1662
Middels	1743[d]	1743
Werdum	1662	1710

[a] Baptism register began in 1652.
[b] Baptism register began in 1558, marriage register in 1561, and burial register in 1610.
[c] Some records date from 1642 but, due to large gaps and lost portions, for practical purposes the registers begin in 1707.
[d] Baptism register began in 1672, marriage register in 1704, and burial register in 1742. Due to incompleteness, for practical purposes the registers begin in 1743.
[e] The year in parentheses indicates when the practice ceased of indicating an infant death by a cross in the baptismal register rather than by a full entry in the burial register, including death date.

cluded from this evidence for these particular villages. Quite likely, the compilers of these genealogies only linked two children of the same name to the same family when they felt they had evidence that the earlier one had died.

Table B.4 indicates the beginning of the extant parish records on which the village genealogies were based, along with the first year for which infant and child death registration is judged to be relatively complete. In general, the starting year for complete infant and child death registration could be determined in a relatively straightforward manner, based on combined information for annual series of the proportion of births for which an infant death was indicated, the proportion of births of unknown fates and, in the case of the four villages in Baden, the information on the proportion of first-born siblings in pairs with the same name that had death dates given.

For most villages where the start of complete death registration is judged to postdate the start of the parish registers, the beginning of improved death registration corresponds closely to a change in the tenure of the local clergyman. In Grafenhausen, a new priest started in 1739; in Herbolzheim, in 1725; in Kappel, in 1809; in Rust, in 1764; in Anhausen, in 1765; and in Massenhausen there was a change in ministers in 1748. Such close correspondence in these cases lends indirect support to the conclusion drawn from the data just reviewed that a change in the completeness of registration occurred more or less at the times indicated. In the case of Kappel, however, probably more important was the establishment of new laws regarding civil registration in Baden.

In some populations, completeness of birth and death registration differs by sex of the deceased, with female events typically less completely registered than male events. Such distortions are generally attributed to the greater importance given to the registration of one sex (usually male) in populations where children (or adults) of that sex are, for whatever reason, more highly valued.[13] To test for the possibility of differential completeness of death registration for boy and girl infants for the period after overall registration of infant and child deaths became relatively complete, we can examine the distribution of infant deaths by age at death.

Assuming that the deaths most likely to be omitted are deaths in the first month of life, a comparison can be made of the proportion of all infant deaths (i.e. deaths under age 1) that occur in the first month, by sex of infant. Results of such a comparison are shown in Table B.5 and indicate that similar proportions of male and female infant deaths occurred in the first month for most villages, although in several a noticeably lower proportion characterized female than male infant deaths. This is consistent with greater underregistration of female infant deaths. Interpretation, however, is complicated since other reasons may underlie the observed differences. In particular, the larger average size of males at birth could result in disproportionately higher male stillbirth and neonatal mortality rates, for the risks of death associated with parturition would be increased. Thus while some differential female death underregistration remains a possibility, it is by no means a certainty.

The last problem concerning the quality of the infant death data deals with the treatment of stillbirths. As Table B.6 indicates, the level of stillbirths, as recorded in the village genealogies, varies considerably

---

[13] van de Walle, *Female population*, pp. 49–55; Livi-Bacci, *Portuguese fertility*, p. 2; United Nations, *Methods of appraisal*, p. 19.

Table B.5. *Deaths under one month as proportion of deaths under age 1 by sex of child and village*

	Male	Female	Difference
Grafenhausen	.472	.478	−.006
Herbolzheim	.428	.395	.033
Kappel	.470	.451	.019
Rust	.489	.410	.079*
Öschelbronn	.537	.487	.050
Anhausen[a]	.483	.491	−.008
Gabelbach[a]	.419	.316	.103
Kreuth	.663	.583	.080
Braunsen	.474	.517	−.043
Höringhausen	.451	.450	.001
Massenhausen	.489	.446	.043
Vasbeck	.556	.576	−.020
Middels	.530	.534	−.004
Werdum	.579	.533	.046
All villages	.488	.457	.031*

Note: Stillbirths are included. Results subject to restrictions 6 and 7 (see Table A.1). Differences that differ from zero at a .05 level of statistical significance are marked by an asterisk (*).
[a] Excluding periods when a cross without an exact date of death was commonly used to indicate a child death.

Table B.6. *Stillbirths and deaths in first three days of life as percent of all births, by village*

	Stillbirths	Deaths in first 3 days
Grafenhausen	2.4	3.2
Herbolzheim	1.1	3.1
Kappel	1.1	3.9
Rust	3.2	2.9
Öschelbronn	5.7	1.9
Anhausen	2.8	3.7
Gabelbach	0.6	2.8
Kreuth	0.8	6.1
Braunsen	4.0	0.9
Höringhausen	2.7	1.0
Massenhausen	3.8	2.1
Vasbeck	5.2	1.9
Middels	3.7	0.9
Werdum	4.4	1.3
All villages	3.0	2.5

Note: Results subject to restrictions 6 and 7 (see Table A.1).

from village to village. There is little reason to believe that the true inter-village variation in stillbirths is accurately reflected in these figures. In many cases, the levels are much too low to be plausible.

A more likely explanation for the inter-village variation would be that there were differences in the extent to which stillbirths were recorded in the parish registers, as well as differences in the way in which stillbirths were defined. While it is also possible that the compilers of the genealogies differed in the extent to which they transcribed stillbirths, the fact that all genealogies included at least some stillbirths suggests that the compilers simply followed the indications in the parish registers. Given the difficulty in arriving at a uniform and practical definition of stillbirths even today,[14] it seems likely that there was enough latitude on the local level for differing definitions and treatments of stillbirths to occur in the past.

There is considerable evidence that in Germany, differing definitions of stillbirth were applied, in practice, in Catholic and Protestant areas, with the result that stillbirths were artificially depressed in the Catholic areas. For example, in the 1870s, every large administrative area (*Regierungsbezirk*) with less than 3 percent of the births registered as stillbirths was predominantly Catholic.[15] Likewise, official statistics for Baden show considerably lower stillbirth rates for Catholics than for Protestants for various periods during the second half of the nineteenth century. In discussing the frequency of stillbirths in Bavaria, Grassl has commented that, given the extreme religious importance in Catholicism of baptizing a child before it dies, there is a tendency in Catholic populations to report some stillbirths as live births in order to permit a baptism to be performed.[16] It is thus notable that among the sample villages, the five with the lowest stillbirth rates are all Catholic and that the two other Catholic villages show only moderate stillbirth rates. Moreover, all the Protestant villages show stillbirth rates above the average for the combined sample, with the exception of Höringhausen, which is only slightly below average.

It is difficult to determine conclusively whether low stillbirth rates reflect an omission of stillbirths from the parish registers and hence from the village genealogies, or whether they simply reflect a transference of stillbirths into very early infant deaths. That the latter is the case, however, is strongly suggested by the fact that infant death rates during the first three days of life, also shown in Table B.6, are generally higher where stillbirth rates are low. All seven Catholic villages show death rates during the first three days of life that are

---

[14] United Nations, *Population trends*, p. 122.
[15] Knodel, *Decline of fertility*.   [16] Grassl, *Gebärfähigkeit*, pp. 283–84.

higher than the average for the combined sample, and all seven Protestant villages show below-average rates. Moreover, in some Protestant villages there is the possibility that some children dying immediately after birth may have been treated as stillbirths. For example, in Öschelbronn stillbirths average close to 6 percent, a quite high rate even for relatively primitive conditions.

Completeness of birth data

Assessing the completeness of the registration of marriages and births is more difficult than in the case of deaths. The frequency of marriage, which in any event is difficult to determine with family reconstitution data, is not a subject of this study. Thus the completeness of marriage registration is of less relevance. While the frequency of remarriage is examined, there are special problems associated with it beyond the completeness of registration (see the discussion in Chapter 7). However, given the substantial attention paid to fertility analysis, it is important that birth registration be relatively complete during the periods for which such data are used.

For two villages in Bavaria, Anhausen and Gabelbach, it is possible to compare the number of births recorded in the genealogy with the number reported by civil authorities for the three years (1876–78) following the establishment of the civil registry, when the birth data were published separately for each village (*Gemeinde*).[17] In the case of Anhausen, the official count included 39 legitimate and 5 illegitimate births for the three-year period, while there are 38 legitimate and 5 illegitimate births included in the genealogy for the same period. Thus one more legitimate birth is included in the official statistics than could be found in the genealogical material.[18] For Gabelbach, the official statistics indicated 42 legitimate live births and 2 illegitimate live births during the period 1876–78. The village genealogy also indicated two illegitimate live births but one less legitimate live birth. However, the official statistics indicated 3 stillbirths during the period, while none were included in the genealogy. This confirms the deficiency in stillbirths for the Gabelbach genealogy previously suggested by the results in Table B.1.

Examination of sex ratios at birth can provide clues to incomplete

---

[17] The official statistics are found in Bavaria, Statistisches Landesamt, *Beiträge zur Statistik*, Vols. 37, 38, 43. A similar check is not possible in the case of the third Bavarian village, Kreuth, because of a lack of correspondence in the boundaries between the parish, to which the genealogy refers, and the *Gemeinde*.

[18] Knodel, 'Infant mortality and fertility,' p. 306.

Table B.7. *Sex ratios at birth (males per 100 females) by year of birth and village*

	Pre-1800	1800–49	1850+	Total
Grafenhausen	106.8	100.6	106.3	104.5
Herbolzheim	107.6	109.6	107.8	108.2
Kappel	100.3	105.9	94.9*	99.7*
Rust	95.6*	109.3	109.9	106.1
Öschelbronn	110.6	103.4	104.9	106.2
Anhausen	(116.9)	(114.7)	(96.3)	108.6
Gabelbach	(116.5)	(104.8)	(106.0)	108.9
Kreuth	(97.3)	(102.6)	(124.5)	(107.0)
Braunsen	(104.7)	(114.0)	(108.1)	108.7
Höringhausen	(105.4)	(99.7)	107.2	104.6
Massenhausen	(97.5)	(115.0)	(96.1)	102.4
Vasbeck	(104.1)	(97.3)	(99.5)	100.7
Middels	(100.9)	(111.6)	104.6	105.8
Werdum	101.4	107.2	(112.2)	104.9
All villages	104.1	106.7	105.2	105.3

Note: Results in parentheses are based on fewer than 100 births. Results are subject to restriction 6 (see Table A.1). Sex ratios deviating from 105.5 at a .05 level of statistical significance are marked by an asterisk (*).

birth registration if the degree of underregistration is greater for one sex than for the other. The sex ratio at birth for Caucasian populations generally falls between 104 and 107 males per 100 females and most frequently is in the 105 to 106 range.[19] For Germany as a whole, the annual sex ratio at birth during the 25 years following 1875, the first year for which civil registration data were available for the entire country, varies between 105.1 and 105.9, averaging 105.3 for the entire quarter century. Deviations from this range, when not a result of random fluctuations associated with small numbers of cases, usually reflect sex-selective underreporting of births. Indeed, in historical and contemporary populations where birth registration is poor, it is not unusual to find 'distorted' sex ratios at birth (usually showing an excessive predominance of males).

The sex ratios at birth for our sample villages are presented in Table B.7. For births in the combined sample of villages for the period under study taken as a whole, the sex ratio falls within the expected 105 to 106 range. There is considerable variation in the sex ratios among the separate data sets, especially when broken down further by marriage cohort. Tests of statistical significance, however, suggest these vari-

[19] Visaria, 'Sex ratio.'

ations are most likely the result of random fluctuation; in only a few instances does the sex ratio deviate from the hypothetical 105.5 level by an amount greater than would be expected by chance 1 out of 20 times. In those cases, however, the ratio is lower rather than higher than expected. Moreover, no particular pattern appears to dominate any one of the data sets. In brief, sex ratios at birth in our sample villages appear normal and suggest that if there was underregistration, it was apparently not sex-selective.

Evidence of deficiencies in the registration of infant and child deaths for earlier periods for some of the villages does not necessarily mean that birth registration was also incomplete. The fact that during the periods when infant mortality rates were implausibly low the proportion of births for which the fate is not known is high suggests that at least a substantial proportion of those children whose deaths were not recorded were included in the baptismal registers. It is notable that, of the eight villages in which death registration becomes complete after the beginning of the extant parish registers, six are Catholic, while of the remaining six villages, only one is Catholic. While the sacrament of extreme unction may not have been commonly administered to children or thought necessary for them, the sacrament of baptism, especially in Catholic villages, was considered essential by priests and parishioners, based on the belief that an upbaptized person cannot go to heaven. Thus, while it may have been considered unimportant to register the death and burial of a child, it still could have been considered important to register the birth and baptism.

In order to test whether the improvement in death registration was associated with a corresponding improvement in birth registration, the following measures thought to be sensitive to completeness of birth registration were selected: the mean interval to first birth, the proportion of marriages with no birth in the first five years, the mean interconfinement interval, and the proportion of interconfinement intervals at least 48 months long. Under conditions of incomplete birth registration, we would expect to find longer intervals indicated between marriage and first birth and between confinements than during periods of more complete registration. The reason for this is that during periods of incomplete registration, some intervening births would be omitted and longer apparent intervals would result. This would increase both the average length of intervals and the proportion of intervals that were unusually long.

It should be noted that the interconfinement interval and the length of the interval between marriage and first birth are sensitive to factors other than the underregistration of births. For example, both could be influenced by the extent of birth control. Interconfinement intervals are also influenced by infant-feeding practices since breastfeeding extends the non-susceptible period following a birth. As is evident from analyses in Chapter 11, deliberate birth control was largely absent during the periods in question, and unless abrupt changes in infant-feeding practices occurred, the length of the interconfinement interval should not change abruptly. Thus, while inter-village differences in interconfinement intervals can be substantial, over-time differences within villages should be modest in the absence of changing registration completeness. Considerably greater inter-village consistency is to be expected in the average length of the interval to first birth, but even in this case it is not possible to state an unambiguously narrow range for plausible values of this measure.

For each village where death registration was incomplete for at least some period of time subsequent to the start of the parish registers, the four measures discussed above are compared, in Table B.8, for the 25-year period prior to and subsequent to the improvement in death registration. In addition, for Herbolzheim the seven-year period during the 1760s when death registration was judged to have deteriorated seriously is also shown. Results for Werdum are omitted since only one couple selected for analysis was married prior to the year indicated for the improvement of death registration.

In general, marked decreases in the mean interval to first birth and the mean interconfinement interval, and marked increases in the proportion of such intervals that were particularly long, do not seem to be associated with the improvement in death registration. Only Anhausen and Massenhausen show this pattern with some consistency across measures. For both villages, however, the number of cases on which the calculations are based is relatively small, especially for those calculations associated with the interval to first birth. Moreover, when longer time spans are examined, thus embracing larger numbers of cases, the differences are far less marked. For example, the average interconfinement interval in Anhausen for the entire pre-1760 period is 24.0 months compared to 23.2 months for the remaining decades of the eighteenth century. Likewise in Massenhausen, the pre-1750 interconfinement interval is 34.5 months compared to 34.3 months for the second half of the eighteenth century. Although there may have been some problem with birth registration for at least part of the earlier period for these two villages, the problem appears to be far less severe than in the case of death registration. Therefore none of the available periods is excluded from the fertility analysis. Analyses focusing on mortality, however, are generally

Table B.8. *The mean interval between marriage and first birth, the proportion of couples with no births within the first five years of marriage, the mean interval between confinements, and the proportion of interconfinement intervals that are 48 months or longer, for the 25 years before and after improvement in death registration, by village*

	Mean interval to first birth[a]		Proportion with no birth during first five years of marriage[b]		Interconfinement intervals[c]		
	Mean (in months)	N	Proportion	N	Mean (in months)	Proportion 48 months or longer	N
Grafenhausen							
Before (1714–39)	17.1	56	.085	59	28.8	.067	298
After (1740–64)	17.6	76	.105	76	27.0	.050	360
Herbolzheim							
Before (1701–25)	17.1	89	.048	84	28.1	.047	449
After (1726–50)	18.0	135	.049	122	27.7	.057	575
1760–66[d]	17.0	33	.029	34	30.7	.092	185

Kappel							
Before (1785–1809)	17.6	105	.082	122	30.5	.095	558
After (1810–34)	14.4	106	.079	140	30.1	.100	637
Rust							
Before (1739–63)	17.8	60	.105	76	28.3	.053	338
After (1764–88)	17.2	121	.055	128	28.9	.059	615
Anhausen							
Before (1740–64)	31.8	12	.200	15	28.1	.087	46
After (1765–89)	17.1	29	.057	35	21.6	.043	185
Gabelbach							
Before (1741–65)	22.9	14	.125	16	21.9	.000	93
After (1766–90)	12.6	18	.136	22	20.9	.027	112
Massenhausen							
Before (1724–48)	24.0	26	.212	33	38.3	.226	93
After (1749–73)	16.3	35	.103	39	35.7	.157	134

[a] Restricted to women with no prenuptial birth or pregnancy.
[b] Restricted to women under age 40 at marriage.
[c] Restricted to intervals between local confinements.
[d] Temporary period of poor death registration.

limited to those periods in which death registration is judged to be complete.

One additional potential source of error, especially concerning information on the date of birth, deserves mention. The primary purpose of the records kept by the parish was presumably to record baptisms rather than births *per se*. Converting baptism dates to birth dates, and adjusting for omission of births that died before baptism, has been a significant problem for scholars utilizing parish registers in England for historical demographic analysis.[20] The problem seems to be much less severe in the case of German parish registers. During much of the past, baptism frequently took place very soon after birth; in Catholic areas, baptism often took place on the same day as the birth, and elsewhere by the following day.[21] In the case of the village genealogies serving as the basis for the present study, with only rare exceptions, the information provided explicitly gives birth rather than baptism dates. The genealogists used different symbols to distinguish a baptism date from a birth date when the latter was not available. During the period covered in this study, virtually all the dates for the birth are indicated as birth dates rather than baptism dates. Typically both dates are recorded in the parish records, at least for much of the eighteenth and nineteenth centuries, and the compilers of the village genealogies apparently chose to take the birth date. While some problem may exist with children dying prior to baptism not being recorded, this was clearly not the general rule, as is indicated by the fact that stillbirths were included and that a number of the genealogies also include children that were never named. In addition, at least in Catholic areas, baptisms were performed on an emergency basis by laypersons when there was a danger that the child would die before it could be brought to a clergyman. Births of children receiving such baptisms are also frequently found in the parish registers, designated as *Nottaufe*, although it is not possible to determine if all such cases were included.

[20] Wrigley, 'Births and baptisms'; Wrigley and Schofield, *Population history of England*.
[21] Krausse, *Familiengeschichtsforschung*, p. 141.

Local village conditions

The genealogies for all the villages in the sample contain at least some introductory material about the village, although in the cases of Öschelbronn, Kreuth, Vasbeck, and especially the two East Frisian villages, the information is quite minimal. Based primarily on the descriptive material contained in the introductory sections, some of the more salient features of the villages' history and then social and economic characteristics can be summarized.

The villages in Baden

Given the close proximity of the four villages in Baden, it is useful to start their description with some information on the general history of the local area. The strategic position between the Rhine and the Black Forest meant that the villages are located in a corner of Germany that was regularly overrun and held by competing armies during the many wars of the past centuries. At various times, soldiers of Sweden, France, Austria, and Prussia were quartered in the area, creating considerable hardship through looting and demands for provisions. There was some respite from war during the middle of the eighteenth century but the area again became a battleground following the outbreak of the French Revolution and in the Wars of the First Coalition. Not until the Napoleonic period was there any extended period of peace again. The degree of seigniorial control varied across villages and over time. Grafenhausen and Kappel fell largely under the jurisdiction of the Bishop of Strasbourg, a local lord was in control in Rust, and Herbolzheim was part of the Hapsburg Monarchy (Austria) up until the time it was transferred to Baden in the early nineteenth century. A variety of instances recounted in the village histories in the genealogies indicate that relations between villagers and their seignior were not always harmonious. In the early nineteenth century, the area under the jurisdiction of the grand dukes of Baden was expanded, encompassing the area in which the four villages are located and placing them under the control of the state.

Both Protestant and Catholic villages coexisted on the Upper Rhine Plain, although the four sample villages were all Catholic. Social contact with nearby Protestant villages was apparently hampered by religious differences. The sharing of the Catholic faith, in combination with being located near each other, undoubtedly facilitated contact among them, although it is also claimed that there were fairly strong feelings of community among village inhabitants which separated them from people outside the village community. Moreover, rivalries between villages, for example between Rust and Kappel with regard to fishing rights on the Rhine, may have hindered relations between the two villages at times.

All four of the villages apparently experienced a sense of population pressure during the eighteenth century, as indicated in Chapter 2. Substantial emigration began fairly early in the nineteenth century, spurred by a series of crop failures in 1817–19, and persisted more or less throughout the remainder of the century.

In addition to being on the path of armies as they marched back and forth to war, the area was also located on an active trade route along the Rhine Valley which passed through Herbolzheim and near the other villages. One of the earliest railroad lines in Germany was built in the early 1840s from Mannheim to Freiburg and passed through Herbolzheim; a branch line to the Rhine constructed in 1893 passed through Grafenhausen and Kappel. Thus in a number of respects the area was less isolated than many others.

The Upper Rhine Plain was favorable to agriculture, which was the mainstay of the economy of most of the area during the eighteenth and nineteenth centuries. The economy of Herbolzheim, as a small town, was somewhat more diversified than the other three more purely agricultural villages. In both Kappel and Rust, located on the banks of the Rhine, fishing was an important activity during much of the period. Due to the practice of partible inheritance, farms were generally small, although considerable differences in the size of holdings and the wealth of farmers within each of the villages is noted.

Agriculture was apparently fairly stable, with the imposition of the three-field system extending into the nineteenth century. Cattle and pigs were free to forage on pastureland and in the woodlands. Beginning in the second half of the eighteenth century, substantial changes occurred which led to the intensification of agriculture in all four villages. Stall-feeding was introduced for livestock. Hemp and flax, important in all four villages, were early cash crops and contributed to the local weaving industry. A great deal of the preparation of hemp, including spinning, was women's work. The production and trade of linen was particularly important in Herbolzheim, which depended for its source of supply on the surrounding villages. The area was one of the earliest known for tobacco production, with significant cultivation of tobacco starting in the eighteenth century. The growing of tobacco and chicory increased substantially from the late eighteenth century through to the end of the nineteenth century. The increasing importance of tobacco as a cash crop is mentioned in connection with all the villages and was associated with the decline in hemp and flax cultivation. As with the cultivation and preparation of hemp and flax, tobacco cultivation required intensive labor input. Starting in the 1840s, workshops for the tobacco industry were set up in the countryside to take advantage of cheap labor. The production of cigars was primarily women's work and provided employment for a number of women in the area, including in each of the villages, at least throughout the remainder of the nineteenth century.

Several characteristics of the four sample villages in Baden are indicated in Table C.1, based on selected socio-economic indicators derived from village-level information occasionally published by the state statistical office for Baden. The predominance of Catholics in all four villages is apparent both in the mid-nineteenth century and at the turn of the twentieth century. The village of Rust had a small Jewish community which declined substantially during the latter half of the nineteenth century and thus represented a smaller proportion of the village population in 1900 than half a century earlier.[1]

As a small town, Herbolzheim experienced the development of some small industry and attracted migrants from outside. This is reflected in the small change in religious composition indicated by the reduction in the percent Catholic over the last half of the nineteenth century. It is also reflected in the noticeably higher percent of residents who were not born in the village, according to the 1900 census, compared to the other three villages. Indeed, the fact that the other three villages were relatively self-contained is suggested by the very low percentage of residents, even in 1900, that were born outside the village.

Comments in the village genealogies suggest that, of the three

---

[1] Jewish families are included in the village genealogy and in the present study, although because few met the selection criteria described in Appendix A, the actual number included in the data set for Rust is quite small.

Table C.1. Selected socio-economic indicators from official state statistics for the four villages in Baden

Socio-economic indicators	Year	Grafenhausen	Herbolzheim	Kappel	Rust
% Catholic (Jewish)	1852	100	100	99	87(13)
	1900	100	93	99	95(4)
% of agricultural households					
Owning livestock	1873	87	75	83	69
With less than 1 acre (*Morgen*) of land	1873	1	4	3	9
With more than 5 acres (*Morgen*) of land	1873	71	48	57	48
% of all households					
With some agricultural undertaking	1925	93.7	46.2	92.1	85.4
% of agricultural operations					
With more than 2 ha. of land	1925	54	24	50	33
% of residents not born in village	1900	7	27	10	11
% voting for the Catholic Party	1925	29	71	81	78
	1927	52	73	71	75

neighboring villages, the population of Rust was poorest on the average, with the fewest wealthy farmers, Grafenhausen the best off, and Kappel in between. This ranking is substantiated to some extent by the lower percentage of households that reported owning livestock in 1873 and by the distributions of holdings by size both in 1873 and later in 1925. The heavily agricultural nature of the three villages is indicated by the high proportion of households in each that reported having some agricultural undertaking in the 1925 census. The more urban character of Herbolzheim is reflected in this information as well as in that on land holdings. The difference between Herbolzheim and the other villages during most of the period under study, however, is probably considerably less than indicated by the 1925 statistics. Even toward the end of the nineteenth century, a large majority of households contained at least one member who pursued agriculture or forestry (94 percent in 1882 and 87 percent in 1895). Moreover, while a decline in the proportion is evident at this time, it came about mainly from an increase in new non-agricultural households, rather than from a decrease in agricultural activity among traditional practitioners. The 1925 census results thus probably represent a trend that took place primarily in the preceding several decades.[2]

Also indicated in Table C.1 is the percentage of the population in two elections during the 1920s that voted for the Catholic Party (*Zentrumspartei*). This is intended as a measure of the degree of secularization in the villages: higher proportions voting for the Catholic Party presumably reflect greater traditionalism and less secularization. While the data referred to years after the period under consideration in the study, there is considerable evidence that political attitudes and value orientations persist over fairly long periods of time, and indeed that voting patterns years later may show a very high correlation with demographic behavior in the past, particularly fertility.[3] On this measure, Grafenhausen stands out as having a lower proportion voting for the Catholic Party than any of the other villages.

While the four villages in Baden share certain common features in their historical development and in their social and economic context, they also have their own local histories. A few comments on each village are thus in order.

Grafenhausen
While considerable land in Grafenhausen was leased from the church

---

[2] Personal communication from Ernest Benz, December 16, 1986.
[3] Lesthaeghe and Wilson, 'Production, secularization and fertility decline'; Livi-Bacci, *Portuguese fertility*.

and the nearby cloister which held title to it, the right to lease land was usually hereditary and was passed on from father to son. Following the introduction of stall-feeding and the cultivation of the fallow toward the end of the eighteenth or in the early nineteenth century, large areas of woodland controlled by the village were converted into arable land.

There has been a school in Grafenhausen at least since the middle of the seventeenth century. Nevertheless, up until the middle of the eighteenth century, there were many inhabitants who could not write their names, as is indicated by their inability to sign the parish registers. A count of students in 1819 indicated that there were 200 enrolled in the school which, given the size of the village at the time, would suggest fairly universal enrollment. During the course of the nineteenth century, a considerable improvement in the standard of education and the training of the teachers occurred.

Herbolzheim
The right to hold a market was gained by Herbolzheim toward the end of the sixteenth century. Its economic activities, spurred by its location on a major trade route, led to its gaining official status as a city in 1810, shortly after coming under the control of Baden. Prior to the construction of the railroad in the 1840s, the town was an important rest stop, with both travellers and commercial traffic creating a lively business for the large number of local inns. Linen weaving and cigar production were particularly important as local industries. Cultivation of grapes for wine was also of some importance. Around 1800 there were 40 independent weaving operations of varying sizes in Herbolzheim.

Two large and four small trade enterprises concerned themselves with business in hemp and hemp products, with outlets in Switzerland, Alsace, and France. With the mechanization of weaving during the nineteenth century, the small weaving enterprises disappeared. Mention is made of a linen factory employing 50 people in 1857.

During the nineteenth century, the importance of tobacco cultivation replaced that of hemp and in 1854 a firm was founded to produce cigars. Soon after, several other merchants started their own tobacco firms, and this led to a significant cigar industry. A large number of families in the mid-nineteenth century were involved in one way or another with the economic activities associated with the tobacco industry. In 1873, the most important cigar manufacturer in south Baden established his firm in Herbolzheim.

Kappel
The location of Kappel on the Rhine has had an important influence on its history. Damage was often done in the village due to flooding,

which was a serious problem, especially prior to the nineteenth-century projects controlling the river. As a result of these projects, it was possible to reclaim a fair amount of land that had previously been swampy. Prior to this, it was not infrequent for crops to be destroyed by floods, resulting in hunger crises and poverty.

A crossing of the Rhine dating from an early period is located at Kappel. During the second half of the nineteenth century, there was an increase in trade and traffic between Alsace and the villages in Baden, further stimulated no doubt by the annexation of Alsace–Lorraine by Germany following the Franco-Prussian War and the building of a bridge across the Rhine at Kappel.

In earlier times, fishing was an extremely important part of the village economy. A fishermen's guild developed quite early. As fishing started to decline, fishermen tended to improve their situation by relying more heavily on farming small plots of land. Some were eventually forced to become day laborers or farmhands, working for larger farmers, or to become artisans. The regulation of the Rhine in the nineteenth century, perhaps combined with overfishing and pollution, more or less wiped out commercial fishing, resulting in a large number of fishermen and their descendants either working in the local industries or emigrating. The transformation of Kappel from a fishing to a primarily agricultural village reached its peak in the second half of the nineteenth century. The greater part of the landed property at that time was in the hands of relatively few rich farmers, and social differentiation of the various social strata within the village population was perhaps even more pronounced than previously. Fishermen and their descendants were in a particularly unfavorable position. The development of local industry helped alleviate the situation considerably.

Rust

The local history of Rust is distinguished from that of the other villages in that it was under the control of a local noble family. This had an important influence on the economic development and social conditions of the village. Discontent about the burden of obligations due to the lord was apparently pervasive during much of the period. Starting in 1806 when Baden gained control of Rust, the seigniorial rights of the local lord over the peasantry were considerably modified and feudal obligations abolished. While this had some beneficial consequences for the villagers, especially in the form of reduced taxation, it also resulted in the local lord reclaiming some land and thus in a reduction of land available to the villagers, land that had been formerly available on a sharecropping basis.

As in Kappel, the location of Rust on the Rhine meant that fishing was an important activity and that fish were an important part of the diet. A fishermen's guild was established quite early. The fee for joining the guild was increased substantially in 1768, probably reflecting considerable population growth during the eighteenth century and the fact that more new people were trying to enter the guild than the members thought would be to their advantage. As in Kappel, the decline of fishing associated with the regulation of the Rhine in the nineteenth century resulted in impoverishment for the fishermen and their descendants. The poverty was exacerbated by the seigniorial dues owed the local lord and later by the engrossment of the seigniorial demesne.

During the early nineteenth century, the local government was forced to allow part of the forest to be cleared to make available arable land for particularly needy residents. This piece of newly won agricultural land was named *Amerika* as a commemoration of the dire times for which emigration to the New World was an important symptom. Among all the villages in the district, Rust rated highest in terms of the number of emigrants in the early to mid-nineteenth century. In the years 1831–34, 33 families, or about 160–80 persons left, representing an eighth of the entire population. In 1832 alone, 122 persons were sent to America, largely at the expense of the community, as a way of getting rid of the poorer people.

For those who did not emigrate, there was little choice but to make a living through some connection with agriculture. But there was considerable social differentiation at this time among the village population. Some of the farmers who had control over their own plots were protected from the worst miseries, and crop yields are said to have increased during the nineteenth century. The landless, however, were particularly poor and thus compelled from very early in their lives to be farmhands. The sharp inequality within the village is evident in the contrast between the farmhouses and the much smaller houses of fishermen, day laborers, and smallholders. The village had a considerable number of weavers, especially during the second half of the eighteenth century and the first half of the nineteenth century.

In 1870, a cigar factory was established in Rust by a firm in Herbolzheim. This provided a number of opportunities for the less well-off families. Other workshops were established in 1882 and around the turn of the century. These were an important part of the economy at that time and employed a number of women. The small farmers were able to take advantage of this by having their wives and daughters work. Few women, at least until the time of marriage, did not work at some time in the cigar factory. Thus in the course of a few decades in the latter part of the nineteenth century factory work came to play an important part in shaping the character of the village.

It is not known when schools were first established in Rust. Reference to a schoolmaster dates back to the middle of the seventeenth century. The school operated initially only in the winter. The first record of a special school house existing dates from 1770.

A small Jewish community existed in Rust. It is not known when they originally settled there, but the first reference to Jews is from the first half of the eighteenth century. The Jewish community reached a peak in the mid-nineteenth century and then declined substantially through migration to cities. Formerly, the Jewish population had its own school and teacher.

Öschelbronn

Öschelbronn is the only village in the sample located in the former Kingdom of Württemberg. It became Protestant very early in the Reformation, some time between 1534 and 1536. Cattle-raising was important in earlier times, but as the population grew and there was a greater need for human consumption of grain, there was a switch to stall-feeding for cattle and much of the pastureland was converted into cultivated land. As a result of partible inheritance, farm plots became small. Industry and factories were non-existent in Öschelbronn until quite recently and there were apparently few economic opportunities outside of agriculture. As early as the middle of the eighteenth century, entire families emigrated to Pennsylvania.

The Bavarian villages

Anhausen

This small village is situated about 13 kilometers west-southwest of Augsburg in the Swabian area of Bavaria. During much of the eighteenth and nineteenth centuries, the population of Anhausen shows very little growth, with the number of houses changing little between 1728 and 1859, two years for which such information is given. Agriculture, stock-farming, and forest industries were the chief means of livelihood. Records of school instruction are available since the end of the seventeenth century.

The nearness of a large city, Augsburg, which could be reached in about two hours by a footpath, exerted an influence on Anhausen, for it served as a main market for the agricultural products and raw materials produced in the surrounding communities. In addition, it was a source of important commercial goods, including tools and, later, industrial products. In 1853 a railway was constructed which connected Augsburg and Diedorf, a village one and a half kilometers from Anhausen. A main road to Augsburg also ran through Diedorf. In the middle of the nineteenth century much industry sprang up in Augsburg and attracted many of the farmers' sons into the city thereafter. In addition, the spinning and weaving mills drew female workers from the countryside. Nevertheless, the lack of direct connections between Augsburg and Anhausen, and the natural barriers in the landscape, were sufficient to permit Anhausen to maintain an essentially rural character well into the twentieth century.

Gabelbach

This village in the Swabian area of Bavaria is located about 25 kilometers west of Augsburg and about 20 kilometers from Anhausen. It was an overwhelmingly agricultural village relying mainly on grain production. The cultivation of all available arable land within village jurisdiction was completed at an early period. In combination with impartible inheritance, this meant there was little capacity to absorb population increases. The number of houses increased from 3 in 1677 to only 39 in 1770, with no further change until the middle of the nineteenth century. A testimony to the strong population pressure experienced was the immediate establishment of nine new cottager-type holdings immediately after 1848, when the restrictions of manorial control were lifted and farmers were free to dispose of their land as they wished. During the last third of the nineteenth century, both the number of houses and the population remained fairly stable.

With the exception of the quartering of troops in the early part of the eighteenth century, the first seven decades were ones of relatively quiet development. However, harvest failures, combined with an epidemic among the cattle, led to particularly difficult years between 1768 and 1772. Following these bad years, the farmers began to cultivate potatoes and some of the commons were divided. The village was again affected by war at the end of the eighteenth century. At the beginning of the nineteenth century, feudal obligations were abolished as a result of the Napoleonic Wars and the transfer of jurisdiction over land to the state of Bavaria. These new regulations did not mean great relief for the peasants since taxes and fees had to be paid in approximately the same amount to the Bavarian state as to the manorial lord. Only half a century later, in 1848, did a true abolition of these obligations occur.

In the early 1850s, a railroad line was built through the province which passed through Gabelbach. This is the same line that passed near Anhausen and it connected both villages to Augsburg. During the construction period, workers from outside the area were quartered in the village and some land was confiscated for the purpose of building the railroad. This had a devastating effect on several of the small farmers. The new railroad was economically useful for agriculture and made the city of Augsburg more accessible. The first schools are already mentioned in the seventeenth century.

Kreuth
This village is located in the Alpine area of Upper Bavaria and was on a route through which considerable traffic passed. This put it in touch with the wider world but also meant that it frequently suffered during wars, particularly those between Austria and Bavaria. Thus in the early eighteenth century, the village was adversely affected by the Spanish War of Succession, and the Austrian War of Succession, in 1743, again resulted in plundering and loss of life. There were also disturbances during the Napoleonic Wars.

The last enlargement of the settlement area was made around 1700. The manorial rights of the area belonged to a cloister which gave the land over to the residents to cultivate at a fairly early date, while still maintaining some control. Despite impartible inheritance, some division of the farmsteads occurred in response to population growth. There was never much growing of grains or other crops because of the nature of the landscape. Instead, there was considerable pasturage and dairy farming, with production of butter and cheese. Forestry was also important. There was an early tourist industry based on mineral water baths.

The villages in Waldeck

Modern industry began in Waldeck only at the start of the twentieth century.[4] The most decisive reason for the exclusion of Waldeck in the general development associated with industrialization in the latter part of the nineteenth century was its isolation with respect to the transportation network associated with the construction of railroads. Not until the 1890s was the principality connected to the main railroad network. The industrialization elsewhere in the nineteenth century, however,

---

[4] The general overview of conditions in the principality of Waldeck during the period under study is based largely on an essay by Karl Englehard, entitled 'Entwicklung der Kulturlandschaft.'

made itself felt in Waldeck by contributing to the decline of the mining and smith industries, as well as the home textile industries, forcing out-migration of the landless and some of the small farmers, who were attracted to the Rhineland Westphalian industrial area. The decline in the iron industry helped to contribute to a large emigration early in the nineteenth century to the New World.

There was substantial social differentiation both among farmers and among the cottager class. During the eighteenth century a new, essentially landless group (*Beiwohner*) emerged and grew. The increase in the number of this class was related to prohibitions on the division of property and on the clearing of new land.

The three-field system which had dominated agriculture for much of the time from the sixteenth century resulted in limiting the main fields to the most important grains. Vegetables and beets were grown only in small gardens in locations near the village where good soil existed. Reforms in agriculture and forestry, however, started in the middle of the eighteenth century, progressed throughout the first half of the nineteenth century. Root crops were introduced about the middle of the eighteenth century and were important in this process. Potatoes grew well in some areas and became an essential food for the poorer classes.

By the mid-nineteenth century a situation prevailed that was substantially different to that prevailing earlier. Small-farm operations became more dominant, permitting the cultivation of potatoes to spread substantially in some communities. The cultivation of clover as green fallow increased, contributing to the development of stall-feeding for livestock. Improved agricultural techniques, including an increase in the amount of manure used, helped to increase the harvest yields, a trend which was already evident by the mid-nineteenth century. This is thought to have led to an improvement in the nutrition of the population of some communities. Stock-farming also seems to have improved during the first half of the nineteenth century.

A variety of laws weakened the obligations of the peasants to the seigniors during the nineteenth century. By mid-century the laws requiring impartibility, which were apparently adhered to only in part, were repealed temporarily. This led to a number of cottagers, and others with relatively small holdings, acquiring additional land. Substantial changes in the property holdings of individuals occurred in the years immediately following. Traditional impartibility nevertheless continued to be an important influence and the splitting of holdings occurred only out of fairly severe economic necessity.

Braunsen

This village is located only a few kilometers outside of Arolsen, the small town where the prince maintained his residence in Waldeck. The numbers of farmers and cottagers remained relatively stable for quite some time prior to the mid-nineteenth century. In 1852, following the substantial relaxation of restrictions on the disposal of property, an additional 34 small agricultural operations were created, permitting those who were formerly landless or almost landless to obtain at least a small agricultural plot. This is but one indication of the population pressure that apparently characterized the village and led to emigration to America in the nineteenth century. There is evidence that in the eighteenth century there was also pressure on non-inheriting children of farmers and cottagers to leave the village. Some of the young men in the 1760s and 1770s became mercenaries in Holland.

Potato cultivation was known relatively early in Braunsen, with at least one widow growing potatoes in 1742. This is several decades earlier than potato cultivation was thought to have begun in most other villages in Waldeck. The earliest schoolteacher known in Braunsen came in the second half of the seventeeth century. A water main was not installed until the twentieth century. A number of earlier deaths were thought to have been attributed to contaminated water.

Höringhausen

Although Höringhausen was an enclave within the area of Waldeck and not administratively a part of it, there was a close connection through common customs, language, and tradition.

Farmers during much of the period under study did not own property outright but rather had hereditary rights to property for which a fee was paid to the manorial landlord. The various fees and obligatory duties due to the seignior were seen as oppressive and were a source of hardship for many of the farmers. The Seven Years War, in the mid-eighteenth century, resulted in plundering and led to considerable misery within the village.

Following the Napoleonic Wars, the obligatory service of the farmers to the lords was repealed and seigniorial fees were reduced in various stages. The law insisting on impartibility of holdings was also weakened and some division of large holdings into smaller ones occurred. Some subdivision had apparently also occurred during the eighteenth century despite the general rule of primogeniture and impartibility. In the mid-nineteenth century, when restrictions on the disposal of property were relaxed, there was a considerable amount of property exchanged in various transactions. This gave the persons with small holdings an opportunity to enlarge them. Consolidation of fragmented land parcels took place during the period 1877–81.

In the mid-nineteenth century grain cultivation, especially rye and oats, represented the most important use of land. Very little was used for wheat, and this was mainly to fulfill the needs of the farmers themselves. Potato and beet cultivation were not very extensive. In general, the population lived close to the subsistence level and was particularly vulnerable during years of poor harvest.

Not until the second half of the nineteenth century did an adequate road system connecting Höringhausen with other places develop. Just before mid-century, the road connecting Höringhausen with two small towns was built. Other than footpaths, road connections between Höringhausen and other villages generally developed later.

There was little mechanization of agriculture until the turn of the twentieth century, although some use of machinery by large farmers in the second half of the nineteenth century occurred. A steam-run threshing machine was brought to Höringhausen in 1885 and used not only there but in neighboring villages. A water main was built only after the turn of the twentieth century.

Children are said to have often helped in agricultural work. Both male and female youths, even those of the wealthier farmers, worked as agricultural servants for some years. There was an annual fair where servants were exchanged and hired out.

Schools existed in the seventeenth century. They were reorganized after the Thirty Years War. In 1669, guidelines were issued indicating that schools should not be oriented only toward religious life but should instruct in such a manner that students would be fluent in writing, reading, and arithmetic. Children from the ages of 5 through 12 were supposed to attend school both in summer and winter. Nevertheless, in the seventeenth and eighteenth centuries, there was a close connection between the school and the church, with the schoolmaster typically serving as sexton and organist. Only in the mid-nineteenth century were church and school obligations officially separated, and only then did teachers receive special training. At this time illiteracy was minimal although not completely eliminated.

A Jewish community had existed in Höringhausen since at least the first half of the eighteenth century and is included in the village genealogy. Only after 1750 did a substantial number of Jews move into the village. The size of the Jewish community reached a maximum in the third quarter of the nineteenth century, when it represented slightly over a fifth of the total population. Around the middle of the nineteenth century, the Jewish community started their own school.

Massenhausen

Obligations to the manorial lord imposed considerable hardships on the peasants and, when combined with bad harvests, led some to emigrate. While impartibility was the rule during the period of seigniorial control, it was possible, with the permission of the lord, to divide a larger farmstead, and this apparently occurred occasionally. Nevertheless, there was difficulty in absorbing the population increase and opportunities were sought elsewhere. One outlet was as mercenary soldiers during the Seven Years War. In 1818, a road was built which connected Massenhausen to the town of Arolsen, which was only five kilometers away, and made it easier for persons to seek employment there. As a result, poorer couples, including wives, no longer needed to work as day laborers for farmers in the village and were able to improve their living standards through employment in Arolsen. Farmers were thus forced to rely more on their own family as a source of labor.

During the early 1770s, there was an outbreak of dysentery which caused considerable hardship and resulted in the abandonment of several farmsteads. Ten new farmsteads were created and settled by the sons of farmers from neighboring villages. This considerable change in the population at this time is thought to have contributed to the more individualistic character of the residents of Massenhausen as opposed to the stronger sense of community found in other Waldeck villages.

With the repeal of the manorial lords' control over farmsteads and the relaxation of restrictions on the disposal of land, in the mid-nineteenth century, considerable amounts of land changed hands. The economically more astute residents were able to expand their holdings, and opportunities were available for the landless to acquire land and improve their situation. The less astute lost out in these dealings and their position within the economy of the village became worse. Improvements in agriculture during the second half of the nineteenth century followed the emancipation of the peasants as the incentives increased to introduce other crops such as clover, legumes, and barley. Consolidation of fragmented land parcels in the mid- and later nineteenth century also helped improve the agricultural situation and made the use of farm machinery economical. Dairy-farming became important.

Some sort of schooling had existed since the seventeenth century at least, but the content of the education was more a form of religious indoctrination than of teaching basic reading and writing skills. The instruction was the responsibility of the sexton. There was no mandatory school attendance. Gradually school teaching became a full-time profession, with special training required. This occurred about the middle of the nineteenth century.

Vasbeck

This is a village neighboring Massenhausen, located a few kilometers further in the direction away from Arolsen. By the beginning of the eighteenth century, the village had so recuperated from its almost total devastation during the Thirty Years War that new land was being cultivated. A series of bad harvests and epidemics caused difficult times for the village in the eighteenth century. As a result, a number of the young men in the village left to become mercenary soldiers, most of whom did not return. Substantial emigration occurred to the New World around 1820 following bad harvests and a major fire which placed some inhabitants in serious debt. In the mid-nineteenth century, considerable exchange of property occurred in association with the freeing of peasants from their obligations to the manorial lord. A number of farmsteads were sold or divided. Few remained intact in the course of the many transfers. This resulted in the emergence on the one hand of several large farmsteads, and on the other in the acquisition of at least a small plot by those who were formerly landless.

The East Frisian villages

East Friesland is in the northwest corner of Germany adjacent to the Dutch province of Friesland. The area first became part of Prussia in 1744. Following the Congress of Vienna, East Friesland was incorporated into the kingdom of Hanover but again became part of Prussia in 1866, when all of Hanover was annexed by Prussia. The East Frisian countryside is divided into three types of land zones: fenland (*Marsch*), peatbog (*Moor*), and sandy dry soil (*Geest*). Colonization of the area occurred over a long period of time. It was spurred on by official Prussian policy in the mid-eighteenth century, which promoted ambitious reclamation and settlement programs. At that time, persons were settled on previously uncultivated land, especially on the marginal areas around villages. These settlers were drawn from landless rural laborers and discharged soldiers. The amount of land they received was often small and of poor quality. In many cases, settlers were unable to produce sufficient food to feed their families and pay for taxes.[5] A more favorable policy toward settlers was followed in the first half of the nineteenth century.

[5] Mayhew, *Rural settlement and farming*, p. 168.

Limited economic opportunities in the area led to considerable seasonal or permanent migration to Holland during the late seventeenth and early eighteenth centuries. When this outlet dried up in the nineteenth century, population problems led to large numbers leaving for America, especially during the second half of the century.[6]

A system of canals in the area, modeled after Holland, substantially increased the opportunities for transportation and trade. Some shipping industry developed, initially branching out from the shipping of peat. Thus contact was possible within the relatively wide area covered by the usual boat trips. In the second half of the nineteenth century, as communications systems overland were improved through roads and railroads, this network of canals lost its importance.

Very little information specific to the two sample villages is provided in the introductions of the genealogies. Mention is made that in Middels housing was extremely primitive, with the walls of housing in the past made of mud or loam. There were apparently many houses in which no stones were used and the floors were typically mud. Usually there was only a kitchen and a small unheated room, with no separate sleeping rooms but rather alcoves with beds in them. Prior to the division and distribution of the commons in the mid-nineteenth century, a considerable common area was available for farmers to graze their cattle, which were always brought back into the stalls at night, with their manure collected and used for fertilizer.

The genealogy for Werdum indicates that the parish encompassed a relatively large area which was made up of scattered farmsteads and little groups of houses. Because of temporary leases held by many of those working the land, there was considerable movement back and forth from one village to another in the search for available plots to rent. The compiler of the genealogy indicates that this created problems for the reconstitution and may account for the low percentage of families which had sufficient information to qualify them for inclusion in this study (see Appendix A).

[6] Mayhew, *Rural settlement and farming*, pp. 153–54.

Appendix D

The occupational and status classification schemes

While the reconstituted family histories contained in the village genealogies are rich in information documenting demographic behavior, only limited information is typically available to indicate the social or economic standing of the couple in the community. Such information is usually limited to the mention of the husband's occupation. For some families even this information is lacking. Occasionally there is mention of the husband's legal status in the community, some honorary position, or position in the village leadership, but such information is far less common than occupational designations. No similar information is provided for the wife. In some cases the occupation, legal status, or honorary position of the husband's and wife's fathers are available, although less frequently than for the husband himself. In this study, only information on the husband's occupation or related designation and, to a much lesser extent, status as a village leader is used to differentiate socio-economic groups within the villages.

The purpose of this appendix is to describe in some detail the construction of the occupational and village leader classification employed. Note should be taken that the occupational classification used in the present study is a revised version of the scheme used in previous analyses of the sample villages and thus the occupational differentials in demographic behavior differ from those published in earlier articles.[1]

Occupational classification scheme

Constructing meaningful occupational groupings for past populations from the limited information derived from parish registers is an

[1] For a description of the earlier scheme, see Knodel, 'Natural fertility in preindustrial Germany.'

extremely difficult task. Some of the occupational titles refer to occupations which no longer exist or are local expressions which are difficult
to interpret. The social significance of any particular designation may
vary from area to area or have changed considerably over time.[2] Even
within the same village and time period, the same designation can
encompass a variety of situations. The fact that some persons change
occupations during their lives creates additional difficulties, since the
occupational designation in the genealogy, which is frequently
derived from the marriage or burial entry in the parish register, may
not represent a lifetime occupation for that person. For 20 percent of
husbands married in the eighteenth and nineteenth centuries, more
than one occupation was listed in the genealogies, presumably in most
cases because different occupations were attributed to him in connection with different entries in the parish register, although single entries
could also mention more than one occupation.[3] Part of the difficulty in
devising an occupational scheme lies in the need to establish some set
of rules to deal with such cases.

For all of the reasons stated, any classification based only on
occupational designations as given in the village genealogies will
necessarily be imprecise and incorporate a variety of ambiguities.
Despite these difficulties, an attempt has been made to group occupations to enable at least an initial exploration of occupational differentials in demographic behavior. The fact that differentials based on the
proposed scheme are evident for at least several important aspects of
demographic behavior suggests that the scheme is not totally devoid of
relevance for this purpose. No claim, however, is intended that the
particular classification proposed here is the most meaningful of the
many possible alternatives. Moreover, the classification of couples into
socio-economic groups could no doubt be improved substantially by
linking relevant data from other sources to those in the village
genealogy. Such an endeavor would clearly require considerable
additional effort and is beyond the scope of this study. Given the
importance of examining differences among socio-economic subgroups in the study of demographic behavior in the past, a scheme has
been devised based on the information available in the genealogies.

Over 1000 different occupational designations were included in the
14 village genealogies comprising the sample. These designations have
been coded into 12 categories, including 1 residual category for all
those occupations which did not fit conveniently into the other 11.
Categories were selected either because they correspond to an occupational grouping that is expected to be meaningfully associated with

---

[2] Mayhew, *Rural settlement and farming*, p. 123.
[3] Personal communication from Ernest Benz.

demographic behavior on the basis of theoretical considerations or previous empirical research, or because they correspond to frequently mentioned occupations or occupational clusters in the genealogies. Moreover, they were chosen in such a way that they could be combined into three broader groups thought to reflect, at least to some extent, common social and economic circumstances.

The broad groups and the occupational categories (referred to as subcategories) that constitute them are indicated in Table D.1 along with some examples of the specific occupations included in each. While every *occupation* mentioned in the village genealogies fits into one and only one of the 12 original categories, a *person* with two or more occupations would not if the occupations listed belonged to different categories. The scheme is thus expanded to permit it to accommodate persons for whom more than one occupation was stated by adding several mixed categories to the classification. When more than one occupation is mentioned for an individual, only the first two listed are considered. Attempts to take more than two occupations into consideration simultaneously would inordinately complicate the classification for the sake of only a very small minority of cases. In cases where the two occupations fell in different subcategories but within the same broad group, the person was assigned to the subcategory of the first-mentioned occupation. When the two occupations fell in subcategories which were not in the same broad group, the person was placed in a mixed category representing a combination of the two broad groups, with the exception of cases where one of the occupations was in the residual 'other' category. In those specific cases, the person was assigned to the non-residual subcategory.

Four broad groupings of the separate subcategories are distinguished: farmers; proletarians; artisans and skilled occupations; and mixed, other, and unknown. Given the imprecise nature of many of the occupational designations and the sometimes arbitrary decisions required for assigning specific occupations to a particular subcategory, there is clearly some variation within the subcategories or broad groups with respect to social and economic standing.

Farmers form both a single subcategory and a broad group in themselves. Farmers are presumed to differ from persons in other occupations in that they earn their livelihood primarily through agricultural pursuits on land which is essentially under their control. In most European villages of the time there were considerable differences in the size of holdings, and associated wealth, power, and privilege, between individual farmers.[4] The sample villages are unlikely to be an

---

[4] Blum, *Old order*.

Table D.1. *List of major occupational groups and component subcategories with selected examples*

Major groups and subcategories	Examples of occupations included in subcategory
A. *Farmers*	
1. Farmers	Primarily Ackermann, Bauer, Landwirt, Ökonom, Pächter and, in Ostfriesland, Hausmann, Heuermann
B. *Proletarians*	
2. Cottager	Primarily in Bavaria, Söldner; in Waldeck, Kötter and Kötner; in Ostfriesland, Warfsmann
3. Day laborer	Exclusively Taglöhner; in Ostfriesland, Arbeiter
4. Other unskilled	Arbeiter (outside Ostfriesland), Gemeindediener, Knecht, Schütz, Strassenwart, and many others
5. Sailor[a]	Primarily Matrose, Schiffer, Seefahrer, Steuermann
6. Weaver	Exclusively Weber or some variant
7. Other home industry	Hafner, Hutmacher, Korbmacher, Säckler, Seifensieder, and many others
C. *Artisans and skilled occupations*	
8. Artisan	Küfer, Maurer, Sattler, Schmied, Schneider, Schuhmacher, Tischler, and many others
9. Fisherman[b]	Exclusively Fischer or some variant
10. Businessman	Brauer, Kaufmann, Krämer, Metzger, Müller, Wirt, and many others
11. Professional	Arzt, Bader, Förster, Lehrer, Pfarrer, Schulmeister, and many others
D. *Mixed, other and unknown*	
12. Farmer–artisan, etc.	—
13. Farmer–proletarian	—
14. Proletarian–artisan, etc.	—
15. Other (difficult to classify)	Jäger, Küster, Mesner, Musikant, and many others
16. Unknown	—

Note: In the treatment of cases with two occupations coded but in different subcategories, if the two subcategories were within the same major group, the first-mentioned occupation prevailed. If the two occupations were in different major groups, the person was placed in the appropriate mixed subcategory, with one exception: if one of the occupations was in a subcategory 'other,' the other subcategory prevailed regardless of the major group it was in.

[a] Coded only for Werdum; the small number of cases elsewhere coded as 'other.'

[b] Coded only for Kappel and Rust; the small number of cases elsewhere coded as 'other.'

exception. Thus this category undoubtedly incorporates a considerable variety of different situations, even among persons with identical occupational designations. Occasionally, different terms are indicated which imply differences in the size of the farmer's property; in the majority of cases, however, the occupational designation for particular farmers provides no clue to either his wealth or the amount of land and livestock under his control. Thus, without additional information from sources other than the village genealogies, and the parish records on which they are based, it is not feasible to differentiate systematically among persons designated as farmers.

The problem is reduced to some extent in villages where farmers and cottagers are distinguished and both can be assigned to different categories (see below). No attempt was made to distinguish leaseholders from farmers who owned their own land. Land ownership in the past was a more complex matter than it is now, with all kinds of intricate tenurial relations possible, such that tenant farmers and leaseholders were not necessarily at a disadvantage compared to owner-occupiers.[5] In most villages, leaseholders were rarely specifically designated as such. The two East Frisian villages, Middels and Werdum, especially the latter, are exceptions. However, while separate terms for a farmer (*Hausmann*) and for a leaseholder (*Heuermann*) appeared frequently, quite commonly a person designated as one was also designated as the other (*Hausmann und Heuermann*). According to Rudolf Manger, one of the compilers of the Werdum genealogy, such persons both owned and leased land.[6] Thus the distinction does not appear, in the case of these villages, to provide a meaningful basis for distinguishing one type of farmer from another. A distinction is made, however, between persons who are indicated as farmers and those who are indicated as farmers with some occupation outside of farming. Such persons are placed in the appropriate mixed category.

It seems safe to assume that considerable differences existed between villages as well as within villages with respect to the social and economic position of individual farmers. The inter-village differences are undoubtedly related, among other factors, to the locally prevailing inheritance system. In areas of exclusively partible inheritance, such as the four villages in Baden on the Rhine Plain and the village in Württemberg, the farms were generally small and cottagers absent, while in areas of impartible inheritance, such as in the areas where the Bavarian villages are located, farms could be large and cottagers with small holdings would be present.[7]

[5] Slicher van Bath, 'Agriculture,' p. 106; Blum, *Old order*, Chapter 5.
[6] Personal communication from Rudolf Manger.
[7] Mayhew, *Rural settlement and farming*, pp. 125–35.

The second broad grouping refers to those who can perhaps be most conveniently labeled as proletarians. The term is used fairly broadly, in the sense recently stressed by Tilly, as embracing workers dependent for survival on the sale of their labor power and who do not have extensive control over property or the means of production.[8] We have included in this broad grouping persons designated as cottagers. Such persons generally lived in a cottage surrounded by a small tract of land which they put to agricultural use. While they may also have owned some livestock, their houses, land, and livestock holdings are assumed to have been less extensive than those of farmers and in many, perhaps most, cases would not be sufficient to provide entirely for the family subsistence.[9] Thus it seems likely that many cottagers needed to supplement their income either by selling their services as agricultural laborers to farmers or in some other way. Indeed, about a quarter of persons designated as cottagers were also specifically designated in the genealogies as having a second occupation in one of the other categories of the proletarian grouping, mainly as laborers. Nevertheless, there is probably substantial inter- and intra-village variation in the position of cottagers, with some controlling moderate amounts of land and others almost none.[10]

A second subcategory under the proletarian group refers to persons specifically designated as day laborers (*Taglöhner* outside of East Friesland and *Arbeiter* in East Friesland). Day laborer was a common designation in a number of the villages. Presumably many persons so designated were engaged in agricultural labor, although the term does not specifically exclude non-agricultural work such as construction, ditch-digging and the like. Other persons indicated as laborers (including those designated as *Arbeiter* outside of East Friesland), as well as those with any of a variety of occupations judged to require little skill, such as minor civil servants and farmhands, are grouped together in another subcategory.

Persons indicated as sailors in the East Frisian village of Werdum, located on the North Sea coast, where they were relatively common, were included as a separate subcategory under proletarians. Although a description of their activities is not available in the village geneal-

---

[8] Tilly, *Sociology meets history*, Chapter 7.

[9] Mayhew, *Rural settlement and farming*, p. 129.

[10] Some indication of the size of holdings controlled by cottagers is provided in the village genealogies of Gabelbach, Braunsen, and Massenhausen which include listings of inhabitants and their property, in the case of Gabelbach for 1834, Braunsen for 1748, and Massenhausen for 1856. They confirm that persons designated as cottagers in those village genealogies had holdings that were in the order of a quarter to a half that of persons classified as farmers. According to Rudolf Manger (personal communication), a cottager (*Warfsmann*) in East Friesland had very little land and only a small house.

ogies, they may have been more likely than persons in other occupations to have spent prolonged periods of time away from home and may thus exhibit unusual demographic behavior. Finally, persons engaged in home production requiring minimal skill or capital were included within the proletarian grouping. Weaving was by far the most common such activity, and thus there are sufficient cases to separate out weavers from persons engaged in other home industry.

The third broad grouping places together artisans and persons with occupational titles implying that they required more skill or capital. Frequently the decision of whether a particular occupation qualified a person as an artisan or as being engaged in some less skilled home industry requiring a smaller investment in capital was arbitrary. Moreover, it was not possible to distinguish systematically and with precision those persons who became masters in their craft and those who remained journeymen. Presumably most of the persons designated as artisans possessed at least some degree of skill and capital to carry out their trade and perhaps controlled the right to pass on a craft shop to a son.

A separate category under the same broad group in which the artisans are placed was designated for fishermen in the villages of Kappel and Rust. Both villages are located on the Rhine and a substantial number of persons in the genealogies of each were designated as fishermen. In both villages, there were longstanding fishermen's guilds, suggesting a similarity between the social standing of this occupation and those of artisans.[11] Moreover, fishermen presumably possessed a certain amount of capital in the form of their equipment and boats. In addition, in a private census conducted in 1770 in Rust for the local lord, the compiler of the results generally classified men's occupations as either farmers, artisans, or day laborers; fishermen were included with artisans.[12] It is also somewhat reassuring that the contemporary census compiler used three categories closely resembling the broad categories employed in this study and grouped fishermen with artisans.

Separate subcategories are indicated for businessmen and professionals. The former was reserved for occupations that were less likely to involve the production of goods as such, as would be the case for artisans, but that involved instead the selling of goods or services. The latter subcategory included a variety of service occupations which implied some sort of higher status and, in a number of cases, greater education than most other occupations. With the exception of

[11] Köbele, *Dorfsippenbuch Kappel am Rhein*, pp. 42–46; *Ortssippenbuch Rust*, pp. 84–90.
[12] Personal correspondence from Ernest Benz.

fishermen, the other subcategories forming this third broad grouping are perhaps less well delineated, incorporating a larger number of specific designations than most of the other subcategories. Thus, this third broad grouping may be even less homogeneous than the previous two.

The fourth broad grouping is a residual one and includes persons for whom the given occupation did not seem to fit into one of the other subcategories, persons with two occupations which fell in subcategories under different broad groupings, and persons for whom no occupational information was provided in the genealogy. While of little substantive interest *per se*, this group is necessary to make the classification exhaustive.

As a result of the rules used to classify a man with two occupations, some proportion of most subcategories is made up of men with a second occupation within a different subcategory under the same broad grouping, or a second occupation falling in the residual 'other' category. The distribution of each subcategory in this respect is shown, in Table D.2, for husbands married in the eighteenth and nineteenth centuries. Two points are evident. First, the vast majority of husbands classified in any particular occupational subcategory were not designated in the genealogies as having a second occupation in any other category. This is largely a result of the fact that most husbands had only one occupation designated in the village genealogy and is only secondarily due to the fact that some persons with two occupations listed were placed in the separate mixed categories. Second, most persons classified within particular subcategories but with a second occupation in a different subcategory generally had second occupations which were in subcategories within the same broad grouping rather than in the residual 'other' category.

Table D.2 also shows the distribution of the broad occupational groupings and subcategories within the total sample, as well as the distribution of subcategories with each broad grouping. Less than a fifth of husbands fell in the broad residual grouping of 'mixed, other, and unknown.' Of these about half were in the three subcategories of 'mixed' occupations, with most of the remainder in the 'unknown' category. Only a very small percentage were classified as having an occupation in the residual 'other' subcategory. The rest of the sample is fairly evenly divided among the three occupational groupings of farmers, proletarians, and artisans and skilled. No subcategories have been designated for the farmer grouping. Within the other two broader groupings, however, the size of subcategories is quite variable. While most of the analysis of occupational differentials in demographic

Table D.2. Percent of men with more than one occupation according to occupational subcategory assigned, percent of total sample by major occupational groups and subcategory, and percent of major occupational group by subcategory, husbands married 1700–1899, combined sample of 14 villages

	Percent (across) of subcategory with a second occupation				Percent (down) of total in		Percentage (down) of major group in subcategory
	No other occupation	In same group	In residual 'Other' category	Total percent	Major group	Subcategory	
Farmers	98.5	—	1.5	100	25.5	25.5	100.0
Proletarians					27.9		100.0
Cottager	81.0	16.9	2.1	100		6.0	21.4
Day laborer	78.9	17.7	3.4	100		10.6	37.9
Other unskilled	77.9	16.7	5.4	100		3.8	13.7
Sailor	87.6	6.6	5.8	100		1.0	3.7
Weaver	83.0	15.9	1.0	100		4.9	17.7
Other home industry	87.5	11.4	1.1	100		1.6	5.6
Artisans and skilled					28.0		100.0
Artisan	96.1	2.5	1.4	100		18.1	64.5
Fisherman	91.5	1.3	7.1	100		1.9	6.8
Businessman	97.0	1.7	1.3	100		6.1	21.5
Professional	90.6	2.6	6.9	100		2.0	7.1
Mixed, other, and unknown					18.6		100.0
Farmer–artisan, etc.	—	—	—	—		2.8	15.2
Farmer–proletarian	—	—	—	—		3.4	18.5
Proletarian–artisan, etc.	—	—	—	—		2.9	15.5
Other	94.7	—	5.3	100		1.5	7.9
Unknown	100.0	—	—	100		8.0	43.0
					100.0	100.0	

Note: Results refer to the combined sample of all villages.

behavior in the present study is directed toward the broader group-ings, occasionally more detailed differentials are examined. When this is done, the smaller of the subcategories are typically insufficient in size to permit reliable differentials to be calculated for them, and thus are either omitted or combined with one or more other subcategories.

The percentage of couples for which the husband's occupation is known, as well as the distribution of couples according to husband's occupation for those for whom the occupational group is known, is shown for each of the separate villages, in Table D.3, for the eighteenth and nineteenth centuries separately, as well as for the two centuries combined. Occupational information is available for the majority of husbands, often the vast majority, for every village in the sample. In almost every case, information is more complete for the nineteenth than for the eighteenth century. For several villages, only a minority of husbands included in the analysis married during the eighteenth century have occupational information provided, but even in these villages the large majority of couples who married in the nineteenth century have some occupational information included.

Since it is unlikely that husbands for whom occupational data are missing, as well as the husbands in couples that did not meet the criteria necessary for inclusion in the present study (see Appendix A), are randomly distributed with respect to the overall occupational distribution of the village, the occupational data contained in Table D.3 must be considered as only a rough indicator of the occupational distribution of the entire village populations. Nevertheless, it seems reasonably safe to assume that the diversity in occupational structures evident in Table D.3 reflects a genuine diversity among the villages included in the sample. Moreover, the relative stability in the occupational structure evident for the sample as a whole, while masking some inter-village differences, is probably reflective of a relatively stable situation in most cases.

Village leader status

In every village, the information about husbands included for a small number of them a designation indicating that they held some position of leadership in the village administration or in the local Church. Presumably these positions were not full-time jobs but rather largely honorific positions. Some positions clearly indicated that the man was the equivalent of the mayor (e.g. *Bürgermeister, Schultheiss, Gemeinde-vorsteher*, and in the Waldeck villages before the mid-nineteenth cen-tury, *Dorfrichter*), while in others they indicated that the man was a

Table D.3. *Percent of couples with husband's occupation known and percent distribution of couples with husband's occupation known, by occupational group and subcategory, by year of marriage*

	Grafenhausen			Herbolzheim			Kappel			Rust			Öschelbronn		
	1700–99	1800–99	Total	1700–99	1800–99	Total	1700–99	1800–99	Total	1700–99	1800–99	Total	1700–99	1800–99	Total
N of all couples	381	895	1276	726	1487	2213	333	696	1029	485	1076	1561	294	548	842
% of all couples with occupations known	97	100	99	93	98	97	98	100	99	89	96	94	88	96	93
Occupational group and sub-category (excluding unknown)															
Total percent	100	100	100	100	100	100	100	100	100	100	100	100	100	100	100
Farmers	41	48	46	29	20	23	28	30	29	19	19	19	30	35	33
Proletarians	25	18	20	17	31	27	30	25	27	31	22	25	20	14	16
Cottager	0	0	0	0	0	0	0	0	0	0	0	0	0	0	0
Day laborer	19	12	14	3	10	7	18	16	17	21	11	14	3	4	3
Other unskilled	0	2	1	1	7	5	2	3	2	0	2	2	3	3	3
Sailor	0	0	0	0	0	0	0	0	0	0	0	0	0	0	0
Weaver	4	3	3	10	9	9	10	6	7	10	8	8	14	6	9
Other home industry	1	2	2	4	6	5	0	0	0	1	2	1	0	1	0
Artisans, businessmen and professionals	30	28	28	38	41	40	34	26	28	38	42	41	32	36	35
Artisan	21	20	20	27	27	27	17	16	16	17	22	21	23	26	25
Fisherman	0	0	0	0	0	0	12	5	7	15	8	10	0	0	0
Businessman	5	6	6	9	12	11	3	5	4	5	11	9	7	6	7
Professional	4	2	3	2	2	2	1	1	1	2	1	1	2	4	3
Mixed and other	5	6	6	16	8	10	9	19	16	11	17	15	18	15	16
Farmer–artisan, etc.	2	3	3	7	2	4	1	6	4	3	5	4	7	4	5
Farmer–proletarian	2	2	2	5	3	4	6	8	8	6	7	7	4	6	5
Proletarian–artisan, etc.	0	1	0	4	2	3	1	4	3	2	4	3	5	4	4
Other occupation	1	0	0	0	0	0	0	0	0	0	0	0	2	1	2

	Anhausen			Gabelbach			Kreuth			Braunsen			Höringhausen		
	1700–99	1800–99	Total	1700–99	1800–99	Total	1700–99	1800–99	Total	1700–99	1800–99	Total	1700–99	1800–99	Total
N of all couples	109	178	287	83	173	256	67	143	210	104	161	265	209	418	627
% of all couples with occupations known	68	95	85	41	95	77	36	95	76	75	98	89	38	78	65
Occupational group and sub-category (excluding unknown)															
Total percent	100	100	100	100	100	100	100	100	100	100	100	100	100	100	100
Farmers	12	14	14	6	9	9	13	31	28	18	22	20	18	25	24
Proletarians	45	54	51	27	50	46	33	27	28	28	34	32	16	31	28
Cottager	5	33	25	0	27	22	29	20	21	14	2	6	1	2	2
Day laborer	4	11	9	3	8	7	0	1	1	4	27	19	1	17	14
Other unskilled	12	4	7	0	6	5	4	6	6	10	6	7	14	12	13
Sailor	0	0	0	0	0	0	0	0	0	0	0	0	0	0	0
Weaver	22	6	11	18	8	10	0	0	0	0	0	0	0	0	0
Other home industry	1	0	0	6	2	3	0	0	0	0	0	0	0	0	0
Artisans, businessmen and professionals	35	15	21	62	32	37	21	22	22	33	33	33	47	36	38
Artisan	31	12	18	32	24	26	13	8	9	23	29	27	34	26	28
Fisherman	0	0	0	0	0	0	0	0	0	0	0	0	0	0	0
Businessman	3	4	3	18	4	7	0	10	9	4	3	3	5	5	5
Professional	1	0	0	12	4	5	8	4	4	6	1	3	8	4	5
Mixed and other	8	16	14	6	9	8	33	20	22	21	11	14	19	8	10
Farmer–artisan, etc.	0	0	0	0	2	2	0	5	4	1	1	1	0	0	0
Farmer–proletarian	1	2	2	0	0	0	4	5	5	3	5	4	0	1	1
Proletarian–artisan, etc.	4	12	9	6	4	5	17	7	8	6	3	4	1	1	1
Other occupation	3	2	2	0	2	2	13	3	4	10	2	5	18	6	9

Table D.3 – cont.

	Massenhausen			Vasbeck			Middels			Werdum			All villages		
	1700 -99	1800 -99	Total	1700 -99	1800 -99	Total	1700 -99	1800 -99	Total	1700 -99	1800 -99	Total	1700 -99	1800 -99	Total
N of all couples	188	272	460	224	279	503	159	536	695	747	721	1468	4109	7583	11,692
% of all couples with occupations known	38	78	62	89	92	91	99	98	98	93	99	96	85	96	92
Occupational group and sub-category (excluding unknown)															
Total percent	100	100	100	100	100	100	100	100	100	100	100	100	100	100	100
Farmers	13	25	22	49	43	46	44	31	34	28	19	24	29	27	28
Proletarians	25	39	36	20	25	23	34	47	44	46	55	51	29	31	30
Cottager	7	13	12	13	11	12	32	33	33	23	9	16	8	6	6
Day laborer	1	13	10	0	4	2	1	8	6	10	30	20	9	13	11
Other unskilled	17	13	14	7	9	8	0	4	3	1	6	3	2	5	4
Sailor	0	0	0	0	0	0	0	0	0	10	7	9	2	1	1
Weaver	0	0	0	0	0	0	1	2	1	1	2	1	6	5	5
Other home industry	0	0	0	0	0	0	0	0	0	1	1	1	1	2	2
Artisans, businessmen and professionals	34	23	25	20	23	22	10	8	8	18	20	19	30	31	30
Artisan	31	20	23	14	18	16	1	4	3	11	14	12	19	20	20
Fisherman	0	0	0	0	0	0	0	0	0	0	0	0	3	2	2
Businessman	0	1	1	2	2	2	3	2	2	6	5	5	6	7	7
Professional	3	1	2	4	3	3	6	2	3	1	2	2	3	2	2
Mixed and other	28	13	17	11	9	10	12	14	14	8	5	7	12	11	12
Farmer–artisan, etc.	1	0	1	2	2	2	3	4	4	1	1	1	3	3	3
Farmer–proletarian	0	5	4	1	0	0	3	6	5	1	0	1	3	4	4
Proletarian–artisan, etc.	0	3	2	0	1	1	6	4	5	5	3	4	3	3	3
Other occupation	27	4	10	9	6	7	0	1	0	1	1	1	2	1	2

Note: Percentages do not always add to exactly 100 due to rounding.

Table D.4. *Village leaders: absolute number of all husbands in sample, and distribution by type of leader, by village, couples married 1700–1899*

| | Village leaders | | % distribution of village leaders | | | | |
	Number	As % of all husbands	Village head	Councilman	Other official	Church leader	Total
Grafenhausen	51	4.0	49	16	33	2	100
Herbolzheim	82	3.7	20	63	13	4	100
Kappel	47	4.6	30	57	9	4	100
Rust	53	3.4	42	34	21	4	100
Öschelbronn	116	13.8	17	75	3	4	100
Anhausen	8	2.8	25	25	25	25	100
Gabelbach	5	2.0	100	0	0	0	100
Kreuth	4	1.9	100	0	0	0	100
Braunsen	14	5.3	100	0	0	0	100
Höringhausen	36	5.7	36	28	19	17	100
Massenhausen	19	4.1	68	32	0	0	100
Vasbeck	25	5.0	68	0	0	32	100
Middels	64	9.2	23	0	41	36	100
Werdum	32	2.2	13	3	72	13	100
All villages	556	4.8	33	38	19	10	100

member of the village council (e.g. *Gemeinderat, Gemeindsmann, Rats-verwandter, Ratsherr*). A number of other men were indicated as having miscellaneous titles that appeared to imply some role in the village leadership other than that of mayors or councilmen (e.g. *Gemeinderech-ner, Gerichtsschreiber, Armenvorsteher, Schulvorsteher*). Finally, some men were indicated as having positions of lay leadership in the Church (e.g. *Kirchenälster, Kirchenvorsteher, Kirchenrat, Dekan*).

Since it appears likely that these men were the most prominent and respected members of the village community, some analyses in this study examine the experience of this particular group of villagers. As indicated in Table D.4, their numbers are not large in any particular village. For the overall sample, approximately 5 percent of husbands had some such status attached to their entry in the genealogy, although this varied considerably from village to village. In only one village, Öschelbronn, are more than 10 percent of the men designated as village leaders. Undoubtedly this reflects differences in the structure of administration in the villages, as well as differences in the extent to which such titles were transcribed into the village genealogy. In a number of cases, lists of at least the different mayors, and occasionally men in other leadership positions over the history of the village, are included in the introduction to the genealogy and can be linked to the reconstituted family histories. Thus for some men, even when infor-mation was not indicated in their entry in the family history sections, it could be added to that entry during data-processing.

Also indicated in Table D.4 is the distribution of the village leaders according to the type of status associated with them. Again, there is considerable variation among villages in this respect. In several vil-lages, only men holding the position equivalent to mayor were designated, while in others a variety of designations were available, including Church leadership roles or official positions other than mayor or councilman.

While the classification of husbands as village leaders is no doubt incomplete, it should be relatively pure in the sense that those who are so classified will be limited to leading citizens. At least some of the husbands of greater power and status within the village will be included. Thus the category is a potentially useful supplement to the occupational classification scheme.

Calculation of infant and child mortality risks

In all the analyses of infant and child mortality, calculations are limited to locally born children during periods when registration of child deaths are judged to be relatively complete (restrictions 6 and 7 as defined in Appendix A). The reason for limiting mortality analysis to periods of reliable death registration is self-evident. Requiring that the child be born locally helps ensure that the period under observation starts with the birth.

In order to calculate infant and child mortality risks, all children for whom a birth date but no death date was given in the reconstituted families selected from the genealogies for analysis were assumed to survive to at least age 15. Presumably, missing death dates signified that the person left the village and died elsewhere. In effect, the assumption is made that in these cases no child who left the village died before age 15. In most cases this assumption is probably reasonable since the sample includes only families in which at least one parent's death date was known, generally indicating that the family was in the village until the union was broken by death. Moreover, when calculating death risks for analyses including or focusing on mortality risks through ages past infancy, usually only children born to couples whose union ended locally and for whom the date of the end of union is known with certainty are included. It seems unlikely that children under age 15 would leave the village independently of their parents. There is, however, the possibility that in cases where the union ends before all children reached age 15, some of the children were either sent to live with families outside the village or went away with the surviving parent and died outside the village before reaching age 15. Under these circumstances, the estimates of mortality risks would be biased downward, especially at older childhood ages.

In order to check if the estimates were seriously biased downward, mortality risks were calculated based on identical sets of families, both using the procedure followed in the present study and using a program (developed by the Cambridge Group for the History of Population and Social Structure) which incorporates the stricter rules for determining how long a child is 'present in observation' that are generally recommended when calculating child mortality from family reconstitution data.[1] The results are shown in Table E.1.

Since the Cambridge Group's program excluded stillbirths from that calculation and limited consideration only to postnuptially born children, similar restrictions are imposed for this comparison. In addition, in the case of the Bavarian villages, the Cambridge Group program excluded infant and child deaths which were indicated in the genealogy with a cross but without a date of death. Thus for this comparison, calculations for the Bavarian villages also exclude deaths indicated in this way and are restricted to children to marriages in the period 1800–99, for whom exact death dates were usually provided. Non-local births are also included in these comparisons since the Cambridge Group program did not exclude them. For these various reasons, estimates of infant and child mortality presented in the tables in the main text differ from those shown in Table E.1. Since the data for Herbolzheim, Kappel, and Rust were not yet processed at the time the other villages were run through the Cambridge Group program, they cannot be included in this comparison.

The comparison reveals that quite similar rates result from both procedures and that the simpler procedure actually yields slightly *higher* estimates in general than the stricter procedure at younger ages and, in some cases, even at older childhood ages. Except for the infant mortality rates shown in parentheses, results for the simplified procedure are restricted to children born to couples whose union ended locally and for whom the date of end of union is known with certainty. These restrictions are generally not imposed on calculations of infant mortality in this study when the analysis focuses on infant mortality

---

[1] See, for example, Henry, *Manuel de démographie historique*, Chapter 6; Wrigley, 'Mortality in pre-industrial England.' For the purpose of studying infant and child mortality, a family enters into observation from the date when the marriage is contracted or, in its absence, from the date of birth of the earliest child. It passes from observation with the death of the first of the two parents to die where dates of death for both parents are known. If the death date of only one parent is known, but it is also known that the other parent survived, this date marks the passage from observation of the family. If the death date of only one parent is known, but it is not clear whether the other parent died earlier or later, and also when the death date of neither parent is known, the family passes from observation on the date of birth of the youngest child in the family. The limits of observation defined in this way apply to all the children in a family.

Table E.1. *Comparison of mortality risks as calculated by standard procedure and simplified procedure used in present study*

	Estimated mortality risk					
	$_1q_0$	$_4q_1$	$_5q_5$	$_5q_{10}$	$_5q_0$	$_{10}q_5$
Grafenhausen						
Standard	.231	.119	.038	.014	.323	.052
Simplified	.233 (.232)	.122	.037	.015	.327	.052
Öschelbronn						
Standard	.263	.113	.030	.019	.346	.046
Simplified	.266 (.265)	.115	.029	.019	.350	.048
3 Bavarian villages[a]						
Standard	.301	.065	.028	.009	.347	.037
Simplified	.307 (.303)	.070	.029	.008	.355	.037
4 Waldeck villages						
Standard	.151	.127	.036	.018	.259	.053
Simplified	.157 (.155)	.133	.039	.020	.269	.059
Middels						
Standard	.085	.060	.034	.010	.140	.044
Simplified	.085 (.091)	.066	.034	.013	.146	.046
Werdum						
Standard	.108	.091	.035	.028	.189	.062
Simplified	.117 (.111)	.102	.041	.028	.207	.068

Note: All calculations exclude stillbirths and prenuptial births and are based on births to couples married 1750–1899, except for Bavarian villages, which are based on children to marriages 1800–99. Results based on the standard procedure were obtained through use of a program made available by the Cambridge Group for the History of Population and Social Structure. Results based on the simplified procedure are subject to restrictions 2 and 3 (see Table A.1), except the values of $_1q_0$ in parentheses, which are not subject to any restrictions.

[a] Excluding child deaths marked only by a cross without an exact death date.

alone. Thus infant mortality rates are also shown (in parentheses) based on children without these restrictions.

There is little difference between the two sets of infant mortality rates. The relaxation of the restrictions leads to slightly lower rates than when they are imposed, for all villages except Middels, but in all cases the simplified procedure still yields rates higher than the standard procedure. Of course had couples been included for which the death dates of both spouses are unknown, the simpler procedure undoubtedly would have seriously underestimated mortality risks, particularly for later years. Given our prior selection of couples for analysis, however, the simpler procedure for calculating infant and childhood mortality seems justified, even preferable.

One possible explanation why the simpler procedure yields somewhat higher mortality estimates may have to do with an association between deaths of parents and deaths of children. In the Cambridge Group program, children pass out of observation at the death of the first parent to die. Thus young children who die shortly after the death of a parent are excluded. Since parental deaths are likely to be related to infant and possibly child deaths (for example, if infant and maternal mortality are closely associated), the Cambridge Group program would tend to underestimate infant and child mortality. In contrast, our simpler procedure would be unaffected, as such infant and child deaths would be included in the calculations. Indeed, in recognition of this problem, the Cambridge Group has recently modified their program.[2]

While the *method* of calculating infant and child mortality risks used in the present study does not appear to introduce perceptible biases into the analysis, some downward bias probably arises from the *selection* of couples for analysis, since the selection criteria result in the exclusion of illegitimate births other than those attributable as premarital births to marital unions (i.e. illegitimate births followed by the marriage of the parents). It is possible to roughly estimate mortality differentials by legitimacy status for the six fully-coded villages, since for these villages all births were coded, including those to non-marital unions. Determining how long a child born out of wedlock remains present in observation, however, is even more problematic than in the case of legitimate children. Indeed, the conventional rules for dealing with the calculation of infant and child mortality based on family reconstitution data are designed only to deal with children from postnuptial births; children from illegitimate births are usually ignored.

To estimate roughly if infant mortality risks differ according to legitimacy status at birth, it is probably adequate to include simply all infants resulting from local births without imposing any further restrictions, and to assume that children without death dates given survive infancy. While this procedure will underestimate mortality, unless many women left the village in which the birth occurred immediately after giving birth, infant mortality risks would not be severely underestimated by such a procedure. This assumption can be partially verified by comparing mortality for infants – excluding illegitimate

---

[2] Wrigley and Schofield, 'Population history from family reconstitution.'

births not later legitimized – based only on the preselected couples with the mortality rates for the comparable infants when calculated in the absence of any restrictions. As argued above, there is reason to expect that children born to the preselected couples can by and large be considered in observation for at least some years following birth. Thus a small or negligible difference would suggest that only a minimum number of infants are lost to observation soon after birth, even when no restrictions are imposed. Unfortunately, a similar check cannot be made for illegitimate infants that are not later legitimized by a marriage, since the data for preselected couples excludes them.

Mortality risks by legitimacy status of birth are provided in Table E.2 for the six fully-coded villages for all infants and for those born to the preselected couples. In addition, for the complete sample of 14 villages, mortality for prenuptially and postnuptially born infants is shown.

For all infants in the six fully-coded villages, mortality risks for illegitimately born infants are in general substantially higher than they are for legitimately born infants. For the combined two-century period, illegitimate infant mortality is approximately 30 percent higher than legitimate infant mortality. These results may even underestimate the actual difference, since mothers of illegitimate children appear more likely to have left the village than mothers of legitimate children, with the result that illegitimate children are presumably more likely to have been lost to observation soon after birth than are legitimate children. However, the loss of children to observation during the first year of life is probably not great in either case. It does not appear to affect substantially the calculation of mortality for the combined categories of prenuptial and legitimate infants, even when no restrictions are placed on the births included in the calculation. This is evident from the fact that infant mortality for the combined eighteenth and nineteenth centuries is only modestly lower in the six fully-coded villages when no selection of couples is imposed than when it is based only on preselected couples (.216 versus .221).

Within the illegitimate birth group, a very striking difference in the level of mortality is apparent for prenuptial births and those which do not appear to be followed by the marriage of the parents. Indeed, prenuptially born infants show far lower mortality than even legitimate infants, both in the 6 fully-coded villages and in the complete sample of 14 villages. As discussed in Chapter 8 and Appendix G, there are probably two reasons for such low infant mortality among the prenuptially born. First, a couple may be more likely to marry following an illegitimate birth if the infant survives than if it dies early.

Table E.2. *Estimated risks of mortality before age 1 ($_1q_0$) according to legitimacy status of birth and selection of couples on which calculations are based*

	Year of birth		
	1700–1899	1700–99	1800–99
6 fully-coded villages			
All births (no preselection of couples)			
Total	.223	.215	.225
Legitimate (postnuptial)	.218	.213	.219
Illegitimate	.282	.274	.283
Prenuptial[a]	.121	(.229)	.112
Non-prenuptial[b]	.342	.286	.349
Pre- and postnuptial	.216	.213	.216
Births to preselected couples			
Total	.221	.217	.221
Prenuptial[a]	.136	(.200)	.131
Postnuptial	.223	.218	.224
Complete sample of 14 villages			
(preselected couples only)			
Total (pre- and postnuptial)	.225	.211	.230
Prenuptial[a]	.141	.134	.142
Postnuptial	.227	.212	.233

Note: All results are subject to restriction 7 (see Table A.1). Results referring to preselected couples are subject to restriction 6, while results referring to all births (no preselection of couples) are restricted to births occurring in the village itself. Results in parentheses are based on fewer than 50 births.
[a] Followed by marriage of parents.
[b] Not followed by marriage of parents.

Second, for particular villages and periods for which the name of the father of an illegitimate birth was not routinely given in the register, the genealogist probably found it more difficult to link births of children who died soon after birth to any subsequent marriage of the parents than he did in cases in which the child survived.

Thus, even if the birth actually were prenuptial, if it resulted in an early death, it could easily be attributed to a non-marital union in the genealogy rather than appear as prenuptial. Both of these reasons suggest that a strong selectivity bias is operating through which births of surviving illegitimate children are far more likely actually to become, or at least to appear as, prenuptial births than births of illegitimate children dying at an early age. The fact that infant and child mortality rates for the complete sample of 14 villages are based only on preselected couples, and thereby exclude out-of-wedlock births not linked to subsequent marriages, biases downward somewhat the resulting mortality estimates in comparison to the ones which would have resulted had the analyses also included illegitimate births that were not followed by marriage.

Prevailing infant-feeding patterns

Infant-feeding practices, particularly the prevalence and duration of breastfeeding, are an important determinant of infant mortality in situations where modern hygienic conditions are lacking, and an important determinant of fertility where deliberate birth control is not practiced.[1] Fortunately some information is available on breastfeeding for a number of areas in Germany, at least for the end of the period covered by the present study.[2] There can be no question that sharp regional differences in breastfeeding existed around 1900. Moreover, there is some limited evidence that many of the regional patterns had existed for a considerable period in the past. While the quantity and quality of information varies for the areas in which the sample villages are located, at least some indication of the pattern prevailing around 1900 is available for all. In addition, indirect evidence can be derived from the reproductive histories of couples in the village genealogies. In brief, the evidence indicates that the three Bavarian villages are located in areas where it was not common to breastfeed at all or to breastfeed for only very short durations. In all the areas where the other sample villages are located, breastfeeding appears to have been the general rule, although differences with respect to duration were probably substantial. Fairly prolonged breastfeeding appears to have been most common in Waldeck and East Friesland, while more moderate breast-feeding characterized the areas of Baden and Württemberg where the sample villages are located.

---

[1] Knodel, 'Breast feeding and population growth'; Bongaarts, 'Framework.'
[2] Knodel and van de Walle, 'Breast feeding, fertility, and infant mortality'; Kintner, 'Infant mortality,' and 'Breastfeeding in Germany.'

Direct evidence

The most extensive direct evidence on breastfeeding is available for Bavaria. A detailed survey of mothers bringing children to vaccination centers was conducted in 1904–07 by the Bavarian Statistical Bureau. The results were tabulated on the basis of districts (*Amtsbezirke*, called today *Kreise*) or even smaller subdivisions of the districts (*Amtsgerichtsbezirke*), rather than at the village level.[3] Detailed evidence for several districts indicates a high degree of homogeneity among the villages within them. Moreover, breastfeeding customs appear to have followed distinct regional patterns, so that neighboring districts tended to show similar results. Thus it is reasonable to assume that the results for a district or subdistrict are representative of at least most of the villages within it.

Findings of the survey are available for each of the districts or subdistricts in which the three Bavarian villages in the sample are situated. At the time of the study, Anhausen was part of the rural district of Augsburg, and Gabelbach belonged to the neighboring district of Zumarshausen. In Augsburg district, 69 percent of mothers reported never breastfeeding their infants and an additional 19 percent reported weaning by one month. Only one percent reported breastfeeding six months or more. In the district of Zumarshausen, 66 percent reported never breastfeeding, an additional 8 percent weaning by one month, and only 3 percent breastfeeding for at least six months. In the subdistrict of Tegernsee, which included Kreuth, 84 percent of children were reported as never breastfed and only 2 percent breastfed for more than six months. Thus in all three areas the average duration of breastfeeding was less than a month.

The custom of avoiding breastfeeding appears to have been a long-established tradition in parts of Bavaria, dating back at least several centuries.[4] Summaries of annual reports recording the impressions of doctors and midwives about infant feeding were published for Bavaria from 1857 on and indicate that breastfeeding customs did not change greatly, at least not during the last half of the nineteenth century in the areas where the three sample villages are located. In the first report, feeding infants meal pap rather than breast milk is said to be usual throughout the entire regions of Oberbayern and Oberschwaben, which encompass the sample villages.

In Baden, statistics on breastfeeding by district based on reports from midwives were published for several decades, beginning in the

---

[3] Groth and Hahn, 'Säuglingsverhältnisse.'
[4] Knodel, 'Infant mortality and fertility.'

1880s, in the *Statistisches Jahrbuch für das Grossherzogthum Baden*. They indicate the method of feeding in the first one or two weeks after confinement but do not provide information on the duration of breastfeeding. During the time period covered by the statistics, Herbolzheim was located in the district of Emmendingen, while the other three villages belonged to the district of Ettenheim. The statistics indicated only a small difference between the two districts. An unweighted average indicates that 86 percent of the infants in the two districts were ever breastfed in 1882–83, the earliest years for which such statistics were published, while in 1904–05 the percent ever breastfed was also 86 percent. Only minor fluctuations are evident during the intervening years.

No information is available on breastfeeding practices for the district in which the Württemberg village of Öschelbronn is located. However, reports from local health officials from the early 1900s from several villages in the neighboring districts of Calw and Nagold uniformly indicate that mothers breastfed at least a quarter of a year and that there had been no apparent decline in breastfeeding over the previous 20 years.[5] The same study on rural nutrition in Germany from which this information comes indicates that 'in East Friesland, the custom of breastfeeding, as in earlier times, is almost a universal practice.'[6] Although information was not reported for the two East Frisian districts in which the sample villages are located, in the district of Norden, which borders on both, 88 percent of mothers reported ever breastfeeding in 1906, and 87 percent in 1907.[7] A survey of school children around 1900 in villages in two other East Frisian districts, Emden and Weener, indicated respectively average durations of breastfeeding of 9.7 and 10.4 months, with 23 and 22 percent never breastfed.[8] It is noteworthy that in an unusual survey of Protestant pastors in the mid-1890s that included an inquiry about birth control practices, one respondent from East Friesland wrote: 'To hinder conceptions, mothers keep children on the breast very long, up to 3 years.'[9]

Data on breastfeeding in Waldeck are not available, but reports for the rural part of the administrative area (*Regierungsbezirk*) of Kassel, in which Waldeck was later incorporated, indicate that breastfeeding was usual and often prolonged.[10] In addition, the compiler of the

[5] Kaup, *Ernährung und Lebenskraft*, p. 448.
[6] *Ibid.*, p. 209.　　　　[7] *Ibid.*, p. 209.
[8] Röse, 'Wichtigkeit der Mutterbrust.'
[9] Allgemeine Konferenz der deutschen Sittlichkeitsvereine, *Die geschlechlich sittlichen Verhältnisse*, p. 92.
[10] Kaup, *Ernährung und Lebenskraft*, p. 240.

Höringhausen genealogy comments in regard to past customs, perhaps based on his memory, that children were nursed by their mothers 'even outside during work in the fields.'[11]

These scattered data refer largely to the period around 1900, with occasional information indicating that similar patterns existed during the previous few decades. Equivalent information about earlier periods appears to be lacking. There is evidence that in other areas, especially cities, and most notably Berlin, infant-feeding practices were changing and that breastfeeding was declining by the end of the nineteenth century.[12] It is thus possible that the patterns observed around 1900 for the areas in which the sample villages are located were not characteristic of these areas during earlier periods. Nevertheless, it is encouraging that the limited information on trends, available in the studies reviewed, at least suggests little change during the last decades of the nineteenth century.

Indirect evidence

Indirect indications of breastfeeding patterns in the individual villages during the period under study can be derived through examination of information on birth intervals contained in the reproductive histories in the village genealogies. The rationale is based on the well-established finding that breastfeeding typically postpones the resumption of ovulation in women following birth, and thus extends the postpartum period when a woman is not susceptible to conception.[13] As a result, breastfeeding lengthens the average interval to the next birth. Two types of intervals, however, are totally or largely unaffected by breastfeeding: intervals between marriage and first birth and intervals following the birth of a child that dies very early in infancy. The difference between these intervals and intervals which are affected by breastfeeding, in contexts where deliberate birth spacing or other possible confounding influences are absent or minimal, should reflect the extent of breastfeeding in the population.

Table F.1 presents the results of two different comparisons for each village, which are intended to indicate the impact of breastfeeding on the length of the non-susceptible period. The first comparison, referred to as Estimate A, contrasts the average interconfinement interval following the birth of a child dying within one month with the average interval following the birth of a child who survives at least one

[11] Sauer, *Höringhausen*, p. 75.
[12] Bluhm, 'Stillhäufigkeit und Stilldauer.'
[13] McCann *et al.*, 'Breastfeeding.'

Table F.1. *Two indirect approaches to derive measures reflecting the extent of breastfeeding, by village*

Village	Estimate A: comparisons of interconfinement intervals according to survival of child[a]			Estimate B: comparisons between interval to 1st birth and 1st inter-confinement interval		
	Child dies in 1st month	Child survives at least 1 year	Difference[b]	Interval to 1st birth	1st to 2nd confinement[c]	Difference[b]
Grafenhausen	19.0	26.6	7.6	14.9	26.6	11.6
Herbolzheim	17.3	26.0	8.7	15.0	25.9	10.9
Kappel	17.8	26.1	8.3	15.4	25.1	9.7
Rust	17.0	25.8	8.7	15.0	26.6	11.6
Öschelbronn	17.3	25.2	7.9	15.4	24.5	9.1
Anhausen	17.4[d]	18.1[d]	0.7[d]	17.1	19.9	2.8
Gabelbach	(16.5)[d]	20.5[d]	(4.0)[d]	13.6	18.5	4.9
Kreuth	(18.2)	22.4	(4.2)	16.4	22.6	6.2
Braunsen	(18.3)	30.7	(12.5)	15.1	29.1	14.0
Höringhausen	16.4	30.7	14.2	17.1	30.7	13.6
Massenhausen	15.9	30.7	14.8	16.8	31.0	14.2
Vasbeck	17.1	29.5	12.4	16.3	29.1	12.8
Middels	17.0	32.3	15.3	17.2	31.0	13.9
Werdum	19.3	31.8	12.6	17.2	32.7	15.5
All villages	17.6	27.7	10.1	15.7	27.3	11.6

Note: All figures in months. Estimate A is based on intervals following the first through third legitimate confinements during periods of good death registration. Intervals which are the last interval recorded to the couple or that follow a non-local confinement are excluded. Estimate B is based on women with no prior illegitimate births, whose interval to marriage and first confinement is at least 9 months, and whose marriage and first confinement occurred locally. Results in parentheses are based on fewer than 50 cases.

[a] In cases where the confinements marking the start of the interval resulted in multiple births, the survival status of the longest surviving birth is considered.

[b] Difference may vary slightly from the difference of the results as shown due to rounding.

[c] Excluding cases in which the first birth resulted in an infant death.

[d] Excluding periods when infant and child deaths were indicated by a cross after the birth date.

year.[14] The difference indicates the extent to which breastfeeding extends the non-susceptible period. In order to minimize the contribution to this difference of any volitional attempts to space births, only intervals following the first through the third legitimate confinement were considered. Moreover, if the interval was the last interval in the woman's reproductive history, it was also excluded because last intervals tend to be longer than others for reasons unrelated to breastfeeding processes (see the discussion in Chapter 12).

The second comparison, referred to as Estimate B, contrasts the average interval between marriage and first birth (excluding intervals involving a premarital pregnancy) with the first interconfinement interval (excluding cases in which the first birth resulted in an infant death). The difference between these two intervals should theoretically measure the average length of the period of postpartum non-susceptibility. While the results of both of these comparisons can be considered rough approximations, they nevertheless should reflect differences among villages in the prevailing breastfeeding patterns.

The two different ways of estimating the extent to which breastfeeding lengthened the period of postpartum non-susceptibility are only approximate. Thus it is particularly encouraging that for the combined sample of all villages, the estimates differ by one and a half months, which is about the length of time that would be expected given that Estimate B should reflect the entire non-susceptible period, while Estimate A reflects only the extent to which the non-susceptible period is extended by breastfeeding (i.e. net of the two months of non-susceptibility that occurs on average in the absence of breastfeeding).[15] Agreement between the two estimates for individual villages, after allowing for the fact that Estimate B should be about two months longer than Estimate A, is not perfect but is nevertheless reasonably close.

Both sets of estimates confirm that breastfeeding was least extensive in the three Bavarian villages (and particularly in Anhausen), inter-

---

[14] Intervals between confinements differ from birth intervals in that they treat a multiple birth as a single event. In the present study, stillbirths are also included and count as confinements.

[15] Estimate B does not exclude cases in which the first interconfinement interval was also the last interval, since it seems reasonable to assume that failed efforts to stop childbearing were particularly unlikely to occur before the second confinement. However, last intervals tend to be longer even when they are the first interconfinement interval. Thus if Estimate B were limited to women with at least three confinements, the estimated length of the postpartum non-susceptible period would be 10.1 rather than 11.6 months and thus be the same as Estimate A. Since Estimate B should be about two months longer, the lack of such a difference must be attributable to the differing extent to which biases and random error affect the two estimates.

mediate in the four villages in Baden and in Öschelbronn, and most extensive in the four villages in Waldeck and the two East Frisian villages. According to both estimates, the most extensive breastfeeding occurred in an East Frisian village, although according to the first estimate Middels ranked highest, while according to the second Werdum ranked highest. Moreover, in both of the comparisons, the interval reflecting the impact of breastfeeding, that is the interval following cases where the child survives in Estimate A and the interval between first and second births in Estimate B, are longest for the two East Frisian villages. Thus breastfeeding might have been slightly more extensive in East Friesland than in Waldeck, although the differences do not appear to be large.

Several aspects of the results in Table F.1 support the idea that they reflect differences in breastfeeding as manifested in the length of the non-susceptible period. There is a remarkable similarity in the length of interconfinement intervals following cases where the child dies early in infancy. For no village is the average interval under these circumstances as long as 20 months or much shorter than 16 months. In addition, there is considerable similarity in the interval between marriage and first birth, which ranges from just under 14 to just over 17 months on average for the different villages. Thus intervals that theoretically should be totally or largely unaffected by breastfeeding are quite uniform.

In contrast, the average interval following child survival, or between the first and second confinements, both of which should reflect the impact of breastfeeding, vary considerably from village to village, as would be expected if breastfeeding patterns also varied. Moreover, the results agree relatively well with the direct evidence on breastfeeding available for around 1900 with regard to the ranking of the different regional groupings of villages. Thus it seems fairly safe to conclude that the differences in breastfeeding patterns that have been identified for the regions in which the villages are located generally characterize at least most of the period covered by the study.

The results do not rule out the possibility that changes in breastfeeding patterns were occurring and indeed, as results in Chapter 10 indicate, there is some suggestion that breastfeeding may have declined during the nineteenth century. This may help explain why the estimated impact on the non-susceptible period of breastfeeding in the two East Frisian villages and in two of the three Bavarian villages, as indicated in Table F.1, is longer than the durations of breastfeeding around 1900 as indicated in the various sources reviewed above. Generally speaking, we would expect the opposite to be the case since the duration of breastfeeding usually exceeds the postpartum non-susceptible period, at least in populations where breastfeeding is of moderate or longer duration. However, if by 1900 breastfeeding had declined somewhat in East Friesland, the average duration of breast-feeding over the eighteenth and nineteenth centuries may have been considerably longer. Alternatively, the indirect estimates may over-state the impact of breastfeeding on the non-susceptible period, or the 1900 data may be inaccurate, or may not be representative of the experience in the sample villages.[16]

[16] Various biases possibly affecting the indirect estimates are discussed in Chapter 10.

Evidence of biases in the determination of legitimization status

The number of births born out of wedlock that were eventually followed by the marriage of the parents, and hence should be classified as legitimate according to the definition used in the present study, is probably biased downward due to two problems. First, some mothers of illegitimate births might marry the father outside the village and hence not have the marriage recorded in the parish registers on which the village genealogy is based. Second, during periods when the name of the father of the illegitimate child is not given in the parish register, the genealogist might not know that the father was the eventual husband of the child's mother, especially if the child died before the marriage or no further mention of the child is found in the parish registers subsequent to the parents' marriage.

The possibility that a number of subsequent marriages of unwed parents could have taken place outside the village is suggested by the fact that a substantial proportion of unwed mothers whose child appears as non-legitimized in the genealogy did not remain permanently in the village where the birth occurred and thus did not remain under observation as far as the local records were concerned. While the departure of someone from the village is only occasionally noted explicitly in the village genealogies, it can be inferred from the lack of a death date or from a mention of the death occurring elsewhere. Based on the combined results for the six fully-coded villages, over half (56 percent) of women whose first birth was not legitimized left the village before death. This compares to only 31 percent of women whose first birth appears as legitimized, and 19 percent of women whose first birth was postnuptial. If some of these women eventually married their child's father after leaving the village, the genealogist would probably be unable to deduce it from the records available to him.

It is worth noting that while women who die outside the village have clearly migrated from the village – at least this was the case during earlier times, when the terminally ill were not sent to hospitals to die – death in the village does not ensure that out-migration never occurred, since return migrants would also die in the village. Thus the percentage who die outside the village is a conservative estimate of out-migration. Nevertheless, this is a particularly relevant measure for estimating the extent to which out-migration could lead to an underestimate of the proportion of out-of-wedlock births that were later legitimized. The reason for this is that death entries of women who had married typically mentioned the name of the husband, regardless of where their marriage occurred. Thus the genealogist would be in as equally favorable a position to determine if an unwed mother married the child's father in cases of returning migrants who married outside the village as he would be in cases of women who remained and married in the village. The problem is created instead by those women who migrate out of the village, marry the child's father, and do not return.

Some women who die in the village do so soon after birth and thus may have had little chance to migrate out or, in the case of an unwed mother, to marry the child's father. However, in any absolute sense, the number of women who fall into this situation is quite small. For example, in the six fully-coded villages, slightly over 2 percent of women with known death dates died within a year of their first birth. This figure surely overstates the risk since women with unknown death dates are excluded from the denominator and are far less likely to have died soon after birth than women for whom death dates are known. This point is discussed in Chapter 5, as are maternal mortality risks more generally. When women who are known to have died within the first year following their first birth are excluded, the resulting figures are almost identical to those cited in the text.

There is also some limited evidence that the absence of the father's name in records concerning an illegitimate birth made it more difficult for the genealogist to be able to link genuinely prenuptial births to the subsequent marital union of the parents. The problem is presumably greatest in cases where the illegitimate child died before the couple married, and perhaps also in cases where the only event recorded in the local registers was the child's birth. If this is the case, during periods when the father's name was routinely excluded, the proportion indicated as legitimized among illegitimate infants would be expected to be particularly low for those dying soon after birth and for those for whom only the birth date is known.

Since the periods during which the exclusion of the father's name was usual can be inferred from village genealogies by examining if the father's name is missing in non-marital unions, the expectations just outlined can be tested with data for the six fully-coded villages. The results are presented in Table G.1. Survival status is defined in terms of survival to age 1. Given that most infant deaths occurred during the first few months and that most unwed parents waited at least that long before marrying (see Chapter 9), infants not surviving to age 1 will usually have died before the marriage took place. The number of comparisons that can be made is unfortunately quite limited due to a lack of sufficient cases (resulting in part from the necessity of limiting the analysis to only those periods when the registration of child deaths is judged to be relatively complete – see Appendix B). Nevertheless, several interesting findings emerge.

Even when the father's name was routinely included, the proportion of out-of-wedlock births that were legitimized is greater in cases where the child survived infancy than in cases where the child died. Only in Rust and Öschelbronn is it possible to compare periods of routine exclusion and inclusion of the father's name from the entries of illegitimate births. The results for Öschelbronn are particularly consistent with the expectation that the likelihood a genealogist could link the birth of a non-surviving illegitimate infant to the parents' marriage increased with the frequency with which the father's name was included in the register. The proportion legitimized among non-surviving infants decreases in Öschelbronn as the inclusion of the father's name becomes less frequent. This occurs despite the fact that over the same period of time legitimization of children surviving to age 1 increased substantially. The results for Rust are less clear. The proportion of illegitimate infants dying before age 1 that were legitimized is actually slightly higher during the period when the father's name was routinely excluded than when it was included. However, because the proportion legitimized among surviving infants was far higher in that period, the *difference* in the percentage legitimized according to survival status is considerably more pronounced when the father's name is absent and in this respect is consistent with expectations.

Results are rather ambiguous with regard to the percentage legitimized among children for whom only a birth date is available in the genealogy. In Middels, contrary to expectations, a somewhat higher proportion of those with only the birth date given appear as legitimized, even though the father's name was apparently excluded in entries of illegitimate births throughout. While in all other villages, the reverse is true, this is the case whether or not the father's name

Table G.1. *Percent legitimized among out-of-wedlock births, by village, inferred frequency of inclusion of father's name in register, and survival status, and among survivors by amount of information available for survivors*

Village and inferred frequency of father's name in register	Survival status of birth		Among survivors	
	Dies before age 1	Survives to age 1	Only birth given	Other information given
Kappel				
Mostly excluded (1810–99)	20	37	27	43
Rust				
Mostly included (1764–1809)	(03)	18	(12)	20
Mostly excluded (1810–99)	07	42	39	43
Öschelbronn				
Mostly included (1700–1812)	24	25	(14)	(32)
Mixed (1813–73)	15	30	(27)	31
Mostly excluded (1874–99)	11	36	27	—
Braunsen and Massenhausen				
Mostly included (before 1875)	13	29	23	34
Mostly excluded (1875–99)	—	(16)	(04)	(32)
Middels				
Mostly excluded (1743–1899)	—	34	(38)	(29)
All villages				
Mostly included	13	27	21	31
Mostly excluded	11	38	32	41

Note: Results refer to the six fully-coded villages and are restricted to births occurring in the village for which an exact birth date is known during periods when the registration of child deaths is judged to be relatively complete. Legitimized births refer to illegitimate births which are attributed to a couple who subsequently married. Results in parentheses are based on 20–49 births; results based on fewer than 20 births are omitted.

appears to be excluded in the entries. Indeed, the *difference* in the percentage legitimized between these two categories does not seem to be greater during periods when the father's name is excluded. One possible reason for a lower proportion of children with only a birth date given generally appearing as legitimized is that these children are more likely to have been born to women who migrated from the village and thus are more likely to have had parents who, if they married, did so outside the jurisdiction of the records available to the genealogist.

Results based on preselected couples from the combined sample of all 14 villages provided additional evidence that the absence of the father's name in records of illegitimate births hindered their linkage to the parents' subsequent marriage in cases where the infant died under age 1. For those villages and periods when the father's name was routinely included, the mortality difference between prenuptial and postnuptial births was far less than for those villages and periods when the father's name was excluded. In the former case, 19 percent of prenuptial versus 24 percent of postnuptial births are indicated as dying before reaching age 1; in the latter case, only 13 percent of prenuptial births compared to 21 percent of postnuptial births died in infancy. Part of the differential in mortality between prenuptially and postnuptially born infants probably reflects a genuinely greater likelihood for unwed parents to marry if their child survives. However, this would not explain why the difference was greater when the father's name was excluded from illegitimate birth entries in the parish registers. Rather, such a finding is consistent with a lower likelihood that genealogists were able to link a prenuptial birth to a subsequent marital union if the infant died before the marriage, for periods when the father's name was unknown.

Results for the combined sample of all villages do not indicate any particular problem in linking illegitimate children for whom only a birth date is available to the subsequent marriage of the parents during periods when the father's name was not included in the records of an illegitimate birth. For surviving infants, the proportion for whom only a birth date is known is actually slightly higher for prenuptially born than for postnuptially born children, whether or not the father's name was routinely included in the registers.

An example from the village genealogy of Rust, shown in Table G.2, illustrates particularly clearly the nature of the problem of linking likely prenuptial births to the marriage of the parents when the births do not survive until the marriage.[1] The example refers to Monika Baumann,

---

[1] I am grateful to Ernest Benz for calling my attention to this example.

Table G.2. A listing of births to Monika Baumann in Rust

Birth order	Birth date of child	Death date of child	Union number	Father according to genealogy	Status of birth according to genealogy
1	9 Mar. 1830	11 Mar. 1830	168	Not given	Illegit.
2	23 Dec. 1831	After 1872	1681	George Hirsche	Illegit.
3	26 Nov. 1835	30 Apr. 1907	192	Landolin Baumann	Prenup.
4	11 Nov. 1841	20 Apr. 1845	168	Not given	Illegit.
5	17 Jan. 1843	30 Apr. 1843	168	Not given	Illegit.
6	26 May. 1845	Unknown	192	Landolin Baumann	Prenup.
7	1 June 1847	6 Oct. 1847	192	Landolin Baumann	Postnup.
8	16 Oct. 1849	3 Nov. 1849	192	Landolin Baumann	Postnup.
9	27 Dec. 1850	20 May 1852	192	Landolin Baumann	Postnup.

who is represented in the village genealogy by two non-marital unions (numbers 168 and 1681) and one marital union (number 192). A total of nine births are attributed to her in the genealogy. She married Landolin Baumann on 21 October 1846 after giving birth the sixth time and died shortly after giving birth the last time.

Note that of the six children born before her marriage, the three children who died at early ages are attributed to a non-marital union with an unknown partner or partners. Two of the remaining three, both of which apparently survived past the date of her marriage, are attributed as prenuptial births to her marital union with Landolin Baumann. The remaining one, which also survived past her marriage date, is attributed to a non-marital union with George Hirsche. Apparently in these three cases, information about the father was available in entries in the parish records other than the birth register. Although there is no direct evidence of who was the father of the fourth- and fifth-born children, it is quite plausible that it was Landolin Baumann, given that he was the father of the previously born child and all subsequently born children, including an additional one born prior to the marriage. Thus the lack of a father's name in the birth register for the fourth and fifth children prevented the genealogist from linking them to the subsequent marriage of the mother, even though it is likely that they were in fact prenuptial births to her and her subsequent husband. This particular case is rather extreme and potentially complicated by the fact that the mother's maiden name is the same as the surname of her eventual husband, perhaps creating an added difficulty for proper identification of the eventual husband as the father of the illegitimate children. Nevertheless, it illustrates the types of problems that can give rise to biases in the analyses of prenuptial childbearing. If, in fact, the fourth and fifth children were prenuptial births to Monika and Landolin, then analyses of the number of prenuptial births and the intervals between them will be in error. Thus there is clearly potential for some error in the analyses of prenuptial births, although the exact extent is unknown.

Bibliography

Allgemeine Konferenz der deutschen Sittlichkeitsvereine. 1895 and 1896. *Die geschlechtlich sittlichen Verhältnisse der evangelischen Landbewohner im Deutschen Reiche*, Vols. I and II. Leipzig: Reinhold Werther.

Anderson, Barbara A. 1975. 'Male age and fertility: results from Ireland prior to 1911.' *Population Index*, 41: 561–67.

Anderson, Barbara A. and James L. McCabe. 1977. 'Nutrition and the fertility of younger women in Kinshasa, Zaire.' *Journal of Development Economics*, 4: 343–63.

Anderton, D. and Lee Bean. 1985. 'Birth spacing and fertility limitation: a behavioral analysis of nineteenth century frontier populations.' *Demography*, 22: 169–83.

Andorka, Rudolph. 1979. 'Family reconstitution and types of household structures.' In Jan Sundin and Erik Söderland (eds.), *Time, space, and man*: 4–33. Atlantic Highlands: Humanities Press.

Bakketeig, Leiv and Howard Hoffman. 1979. 'Perinatal mortality by birth order within cohorts based on sibship size.' *British Medical Journal*, 2: 693–96.

Baulant, Micheline. 1976. 'The scattered family: another aspect of seventeenth century demography.' In R. Foster and D. Ranum (eds.), *From family to society*. Baltimore: Johns Hopkins Press.

Bean, Lee L., Geraldine Mineau, Mark Skolnick, Klancy de Nevers, and Dean May. 1978. 'The introduction of family limitation in a natural fertility population.' Paper presented at the annual meetings of the Population Association of America, Atlanta, Georgia, April 13–15, 1978.

Berdahl, Robert. 1979. 'Christian Garve on the German peasantry.' *Peasant Studies*, 8: 86–102.

Berry, L. G. 1977. 'Age and parity influences on maternal mortality: United States 1919–1969.' *Demography*, 14: 297–310.

Bideau, Alain. 1980. 'A demographic and social analysis of widowhood and remarriage: the example of the castellany of Thoissey-en-Dombes, 1670–1840.' *Journal of Family History*, 5: 28–43.

1981. 'Accouchement "naturel" et accouchement d'haut risque.' *Annales de démographie historique 1981*: 49–66.

1986. 'Fécondité et mortalité après 45 ans: l'apport des recherches en démographie historique.' *Population*, 41(1): 59–72.

557

Blake, J. 1985. 'The fertility transition: continuity or discontinuity with the past.' In *International Population Conference, Florence 1985*, Vol. IV: 393–405. Liège: International Union for the Scientific Study of Population.

Bluhm, A. 1912. 'Stillhäufigkeit und Stilldauer.' In A. Grotjahn and J. Kaup (eds.), *Handwörterbuch der sozialen Hygiene*, Vol. II: 570–91. Leipzig: F. C. W. Vogel.

Blum, J. 1971a. 'The European village as community: origins and functions.' *Agricultural History*, 45: 157–78.

— 1971b. 'The internal structure and polity of the European village community from the fifteenth to the nineteenth century.' *Journal of Modern History*, 43: 541–76.

— 1978. *The end of the old order in rural Europe*. Princeton: Princeton University Press.

Bongaarts, John. 1975. 'A method for the estimation of fecundability.' *Demography*, 12: 645–60.

— 1978. 'A framework for the proximate determinants of fertility.' *Population and Development Review*, 4: 105–32.

— 1980. 'Does malnutrition affect fecundity?' *Science*, 208(9): 564–79.

— 1983. 'The proximate determinants of natural marital fertility.' In R. A. Bulatao and R. D. Lee (eds.), *Determinants of fertility in developing countries: a summary of knowledge*, Vol. I: 103–38. New York: Academic Press.

Bongaarts, John and Robert G. Potter. 1983. *Fertility, biology and behavior: an analysis of the proximate determinants*. Studies in Population Series. Orlando: Academic Press.

Bonte, J. T. P. and H. P. Verbrugge. 1967. 'Maternal mortality: an epidemiological approach.' *Acta Obstetricia et Gynecologica Scandinavica*, 46: 445–74.

Bourgeois-Pichat, Jean. 1952. 'An analysis of infant mortality.' *Population Bulletin of the United Nations* (New York), 2: 1–14.

Brändström, Anders and Jan Sundin. 1981. 'Infant mortality in a changing society: the effects of child care in a Swedish parish 1820–1894.' In Anders Brändström and Jan Sundin (eds.), *Tradition and transition*. Umeå: The Demographic Data Base.

Brass, W. and J. C. Barrett. 1978. 'Measurement problems in the analysis of linkage between fertility and child mortality.' In Samuel Preston (ed.), *The effects of infant and child mortality on fertility*: 209–33. New York: Academic Press.

Brezing, Karl. 1963. *Dorfsippenbuch Öschelbronn*. No publisher given.

Cabourdin, G. 1978. 'Le remariage.' *Annales de démographie historique, 1978*: 305–36.

— 1981. 'Le remariage en France sous l'Ancien Régime (seizième–dix-huitième siècles.' In J. Dupâquier, E. Hélin, P. Laslett, M. Livi-Bacci, and S. Sogner (eds.), *Marriage and remarriage in populations of the past*. New York: Academic Press.

Carlsson, Gosta. 1966. 'The decline in fertility: innovation or adjustment process.' *Population Studies*, 20: 149–74.

Cassen, R. H. 1978. *India: population, economy, society*. New York: Holmes and Meier.

Charbonneau, Hubert. 1970. *Tourouvre-au-Perche aux XVIIe et XVIIIe siècles*. Institut National d'Études Démographiques, cahier 55. Paris: Presses Universitaires de France.

1980. 'Jeunes femmes et vieux maris: la fécondité des mariages précoces.' Population, 35: 1101–20.

Chen, L. C., Emdadul Huq, and Stan D'Souza. 1981. 'Sex bias in the family allocation of food and health care in rural Bangladesh.' Population and Development Review, 7: 55–70.

Coale, Ansley J. 1967. 'Factors associated with the development of low fertility: an historic summary.' In United Nations, World Population Conference, Vol. 2: 205–09. New York: United Nations.

1969. 'The decline of fertility in Europe from the French Revolution to World War II.' In S. J. Behrman, Leslie Corsa Jr., and Ronald Freedman (eds.), Fertility and family planning. Ann Arbor: University of Michigan Press.

1981. 'Introduction to Part III.' In J. Dupâquier, E. Hélin, P. Laslett, M. Livi-Bacci, and S. Sogner (eds.), Marriage and remarriage in populations of the past: 151–56. New York: Academic Press.

1986. 'The decline of fertility in Europe since the eighteenth century as a chapter in human demographic history.' In Ansley J. Coale and Susan Watkins (eds.), The decline of European fertility: 1–30. Princeton: Princeton University Press.

Coale, Ansley J. and Paul Demeny. 1966. Regional model life tables and stable populations. Princeton: Princeton University Press.

1983. Regional model life tables and stable populations, 2nd edn. New York: Academic Press.

Coale, Ansley J. and T. James Trussell. 1974. 'Model fertility schedules: variations in the age structure of childbearing in human populations.' Population Index, 40: 185–258. (See also 'Erratum.' Population Index, 41: 572.)

1978. 'Technical note: finding the two parameters that specify a model schedule of marital fertility.' Population Index, 44: 203–13.

Coale, Ansley J. and Susan Watkins (eds.). 1986. The decline of fertility in Europe. Princeton: Princeton University Press.

Curlin, George T., L. C. Chen, and S. B. Hussain. 1975. Demographic crisis: the impact of the Bangladesh civil war (1971) on births and deaths in a rural area of Bangladesh. Dacca: The Ford Foundation.

deMause, Lloyd. 1976. 'The formation of the American personality through psychospeciation.' Journal of Psychohistory (Summer): 1–30.

Demleitner, Josef and Adolf Roth. 1937. Der Weg zur Volksgenealogie, 3rd edn. Munich: R. Oldenbourg.

Dobbie, B. M. Wilmott. 1982. 'An attempt to estimate the true rate of maternal mortality, sixteenth to eighteenth centuries.' Medical History, 26: 79–90.

Doring, G. K. 1969. 'The incidence of anovular cycles in women.' Journal of Reproductive Fertility, Supplement 6: 256–63.

Dupâquier, J. and M. Lachiver. 1969. 'Sur les débuts de la contraception en France ou les deux malthusianismes.' Annales: économies, sociétés, civilisations, 24: 1391–406.

Dyrvik, Stale. 1981. 'Gagne-pain ou sentiments? Trait du remariage en Norvège au dix-neuvième siècle.' In J. Dupâquier, E. Hélin, P. Laslett, M. Livi-Bacci, and S. Sogner (eds.), Marriage and remarriage in populations of the past. New York: Academic Press.

Dyson, Tim and Mike Murphy. 1985. 'The onset of fertility transition.' Population and Development Review, 11: 399–440.

El-Badry, M. A. 1969. 'Higher female than male mortality in some countries of

South Asia: a digest.' *Journal of the American Statistical Association*, 64: 1234–44.

Englehard, Karl. 1971. 'Entwicklung der Kulturlandschaft.' In B. Martin and R. Wetekam (eds.), *Waldeckische Landeskunde*. Arolsen: Waldeckischer Geschichtsverein.

Eriksson, Ingrid and John Rogers. 1978. *Rural labor and population change*. Studia Historica Upsaliensia 100. Stockholm: Almqvist and Wiksell.

Festy, Patrick. 1980. 'On the new context of marriage in Western Europe.' *Population Development Review*, 6: 311–15.

Flandrin, Jean-Louis. 1976. *Families in former times: kinship, household and sexuality*. Cambridge: Cambridge University Press.

Fleury, Michel and Louis Henry. 1965. *Nouveau manuel de dépouillement et d'exploitation de l'état civil ancien*. Paris: Institut National d'Études Démographiques.

Flinn, Michael. 1981. *The European demographic system, 1500–1820*. Baltimore: Johns Hopkins University Press.

Friedlander, D. 1977. 'The effect of child mortality on fertility: theoretical framework of the relationship.' In *International Population Conference, Mexico 1977*. Vol. I: 183–203. Liège: International Union for the Scientific Study of Population.

Friedlander, D., Zvi Eisenbach, and Calvin Goldscheider. 1980. 'Family size limitation and birth spacing: the fertility transition of African and Asian immigrants in Israel.' *Population and Development Review*, 6: 581–93.

Frinking, G. A. B. and F. W. A. von Poppel. 1979. *Een sociaal-demografische analyse van de Huwelijkssluiting in Nederland*. 1971 Census Monograph 6. The Hague: Staatsuitgeverij.

Frisch, Rose. 1978. 'Population, food intake, and fertility.' *Science*, 199: 22–30. 1982. 'Malnutrition and fertility.' *Science*, 215 (March 5, 1982): 1272–73.

Gaunt, David. 1973. 'Family planning and the preindustrial society: some Swedish evidence.' In Kurt Ågren *et al.* (eds.), *Aristocrats, farmers, and proletarians*. Uppsala: Almqvist and Wiksell Informationindusri.

Gautier, Etienne and Louis Henry. 1958. *La population de Crulai, paroisse normande: étude historique*. Institut National d'Études Démographiques, cahier 33. Paris: Presses Universitaires de France.

Golde, Günter. 1975. *Catholics and Protestants: agricultural modernization in two German villages*. New York: Academic Press.

Golding, Jean. 1980. 'The analysis of completed reproductive histories: a cautionary tale.' Paper delivered at the meeting on Developments in the Analysis of Infant and Foetal Mortality sponsored by the British Society for Population Studies, London, January 11, 1980.

Goldstein, Alice. 1981. 'Some demographic characteristics of village Jews in Germany: Nonnenweier, 1800–1931.' In P. Ritterband (ed.), *Modern Jewish fertility*. Leiden: E. J. Brill.

1984a. 'Aspects of change in a nineteenth century German village.' *Journal of Family History*, 9: 145–57.

1984b. *Determinants of change and response among Jews and Catholics in a nineteenth century German village*. New York: Conference on Jewish Social Studies.

Goody, Jack. 1983. *The development of the family and marriage in Europe*. Cambridge: Cambridge University Press.

Grassl, Josef. 1904. *Die Gebärfähigheit der bayerischen Frauen*. Allgemeines Statistisches Archiv, 6: 282–93.

Groth, Alfred and Martin Hahn. 1910. 'Säuglingsverhältnisse in Bayern.' *Zeitschrift des bayerischen statistischen Landesamtes*, 42: 78–164.

Hair, P. E. H. 1966. 'Bridal pregnancy in rural England in earlier centuries.' *Population Studies*, 20: 233–43.

1970. 'Bridal pregnancy in earlier rural England further examined.' *Population Studies*, 24: 59–70.

Hajnal, John. 1953. 'Age at marriage and proportions marrying.' *Population Studies*, 7: 111–36.

1965. 'European marriage patterns in perspective.' In D. V. Glass and D. E. C. Eversley (eds.), *Population in history*. London: Edward Arnold.

1982. 'Two kinds of pre-industrial household formation systems.' *Population Development Review*, 8: 449–94.

Hauf, Franz. 1975. *Ortssippenbuch Gabelbach*. Frankfurt: Zentralstelle für Personen- und Familiengeschichte.

Hazzi, Joseph. 1801–08. *Statistische Aufschlüsse über das Herzogthum Baiern*, 11 Vols. Nürnberg.

Henry, Louis. 1953. 'Fondements théoriques des mesures de la fécondité naturelle.' *Revue Institut International de Statistique*, 21(3): 135–51.

1956. *Anciennes familles génévoises, étude démographique: 16ᵉ–20ᵉ siècle*. Institut National d'Études Démographiques, cahier 26. Paris: Presses Universitaires de France.

1961. 'Some data on natural fertility.' *Eugenics Quarterly*, 8: 81–91.

1967. *Manuel de démographie historique*. Geneva: Librairie Droz.

1976. 'Étude de la fécondité des mariages à partir de la reconstitution des familles.' *DH: Bulletin d'information*, 19: 2–25.

1979. 'Concepts actuels et résultats empiriques sur la fécondité naturelle.' In H. Leridon and J. Menken (eds.), *Natural fertility*. Liège: Ordina.

Himes, Norman E. 1963. *Medical history of contraception*. New York: Gamat Press.

Hindelang, Hans. 1909. *Die eheliche und uneheliche Fruchtbarkeit mit besonderer Berüksichtigung Bayerns*. Beiträge zur Statistik Bayern 71. Munich.

Hobcraft, John, John McDonald and Shea Rutsein. 1983. 'Child spacing effects on infant and early mortality.' *Population Index*, 49: 585–618.

Hochstadt, Steve. 1982. 'Appendix: demography and feminism.' In Priscilla Robertson, *An experience of women*. Philadelphia: Temple University Press.

Hofmann, Manfred, Albert Köbele and Robert Wetekam. 1957. *Von der Kirchenbuchverkartung zum Ortssippenbuch. Aktuelle Themen zur Genealogie*, Vol. II. Glücksburg, Ostsee: C. A. Starke.

Hollingsworth, T. H. 1969. *Historical demography*. Ithaca: Cornell University Press.

Houdaille, J. 1976. 'Fécondité des familles souveraines du XVIᵉ au XVIIIᵉ siècle: influence de l'âge du père sur la fécondité.' *Population*, 31: 961–70.

Hughes, E. C. 1972. *Obstetric–gynecologic terminology with section on neonatal mortality and glossary of congenital abnormalities*. American College of Obstetrics and Gynecology. Philadelphia: F. A. Davis.

Imhof, Arthur. 1975a. 'Die namentliche Auswertung der Kirchenbücher.Die Familien von Giessen 1631–1730 und Heuchelheim 1691–1900.' In Arthur Imhof (ed.), *Historische Demographie als Sozialgeschichte*: 279–516. Darmstadt and Marburg: Selbstverlag der Hessischen Historischen Kommission Darmstadt und der Historischen Kommission für Hessen.

1975b. 'Die Illegitimät in Giessen und Umgebung.' In Arthur Imhof (ed.), *Historische Demographie als Sozialgeschichte*: 517–58. Darmstadt and Marburg: Selbstverlag der Hessischen Historischen Kommission Darmstadt und der Historischen Kommission für Hessen.

1976. *Aspeckte der Bevölkerungsentwicklung in den nördischen Ländern 1720–1750*. Bern: Franke.

1977. *Einführung in die historische Demographie*. Munich: C. H. Beck.

1981a. 'Remarriage in rural population and in urban middle and upper strata in Germany from the sixteenth to twentieth century.' In J. Dupâquier, E. Hélin, P. Laslett, M. Livi-Bacci, and S. Sogner (eds.), *Marriage and remarriage in populations of the past*. New York: Academic Press.

1981b. 'Unterschiedliche Säuglingssterblichkeit in Deutschland, 18. bis. 20. Jahrhundert – Warum?' *Zeitschrift für Bevölkerungswissenschaft*, 7: 343–82.

1981c. 'Women, family, and death: excess mortality of women in childbearing age in four communities in nineteenth-century Germany.' In R. Evans and W. R. Lee, *The German family*: 148–74. London: Croom Helm.

Janssen, Ludwig. 1966. *Die Familien der Kirchengemeinde Middels*. Aurich: Verlag Ostfriesische Landschaft.

1971. *Die Familien der Kirchengemeinde Werdum*, Part I. Aurich: Verlag Ostfriesische Landschaft.

Janssen, Ludwig and Hans Rudolf Manger. 1975. *Die Familien der Kirchengemeinde Werdum*, Part II. Aurich: Verlag Ostfriesische Landschaft.

Kaup, J. 1910. *Ernährung und Lebenskraft der ländlichen Bevölkerung*. Schriften der Zentralstelle für Arbeiter=Wohlfahrtseinrichtungen. Berlin: Carl Henmanns.

Kennedy, Robert E. Jr. 1973. *The Irish emigration, marriage, and fertility*. Berkeley: University of California Press.

Kintner, Hallie. 1982. 'The determinants of infant mortality in Germany from 1871 to 1933.' Ph.D. dissertation, Department of Sociology, University of Michigan.

1985. 'Trends and regional differences in breastfeeding in Germany from 1871 to 1937.' *Journal of Family History*, 10: 163–82.

Knodel, John. 1967. 'Law, marriage and illegitimacy in nineteenth century Germany.' *Population Studies*, 20: 279–94.

1968. 'Infant mortality and fertility in three Bavarian villages: an analysis of family histories from the 19th century.' *Population Studies*, 22: 297–318.

1970. 'Two and a half centuries of demographic history in a Bavarian village.' *Population Studies*, 24: 353–76.

1974. *The decline of fertility in Germany, 1871–1939*. Princeton: Princeton University Press.

1975. 'Ortssippenbücher als Quelle für die historische Demographie.' *Gesellschaft und Geschichte*, 1: 288–324.

1977a. 'Family limitation and the fertility transition: evidence from the age patterns of fertility in Europe and Asia.' *Population Studies*, 31: 219–49.

1977b. 'Breast feeding and population growth.' *Science*, 198: 1111–15.

1978a. 'Natural fertility in preindustrial Germany.' *Population Studies*, 32: 481–510.

1978b. 'European populations in the past: family-level relations.' In Samuel

Preston (ed.), *The effects of infant and child mortality on fertility*. New York: Academic Press.

1983. 'Natural fertility: patterns, levels and trends.' In R. A. Bulatao and R. D. Lee (eds.), *Determinants of fertility in developing countries: a summary of knowledge*, Vol. I: 61–102. New York: Academic Press.

Knodel, John and T. Espenshade. 1972. 'Genealogical studies as demographic data.' In I. Husain (ed.), *Population analysis and studies*. Bombay: Somaiya Publications.

Knodel, John and Steven Hochstadt. 1980. 'Urban and rural illegitimacy in imperial Germany.' In Peter Laslett, Karla Oosterveen and Richard M. Smith (eds.), *Bastardy and its comparative history*. London: Edward Arnold.

Knodel, John and Hallie Kintner. 1977. 'The impact of breast feeding patterns on the biometric analysis of infant mortality.' *Demography*, 14: 391–409.

Knodel, John and Mary Jo Maynes. 1976. 'Urban and rural marriage patterns in imperial Germany.' *Journal of Family History*, 1: 129–68.

Knodel, John and Edward Shorter. 1976. 'The reliability of family reconstitution data in German village genealogies (Ortssippenbücher).' *Annales de démographie historique 1976*: 115–54.

Knodel, John and E. van de Walle. 1967. 'Breast feeding, fertility, and infant mortality: an analysis of some early German data.' *Population Studies*, 21: 109–32.

1979. 'Lessons from the past: policy implications of historical fertility studies.' *Population and Development Review*, 5: 217–45.

Knodel, John and Chris Wilson. 1981. 'The secular increase in fecundity in German village populations: an analysis of reproductive histories of couples married 1750–1899.' *Population Studies*, 35: 53–84.

Köbele, Albert. 1967. *Sippenbuch der Stadt Herbolzheim*. Grafenhausen bei Lahr: private publication of the compiler.

1969a. *Dorfsippenbuch Kappel am Rhein*, 2nd edn. Grafenhausen bei Lahr: private publication of the compiler.

1969b. *Ortssippenbuch Rust*. Grafenhausen bei Lahr: private publication of the compiler.

1971. *Ortssippenbuch Grafenhausen*. Grafenhausen bei Lahr: private publication of the compiler.

Kopf, Ernst. 1938. 'Von Wesen und Ziel des Dorfsippenbuches.' *Der Lebensquell*, 1: 26–30.

Krausse, Johannes. 1951. *Taschenbuch für Familiengeschichtsforschung*. Schellenberg bei Berchtesgaden: Degener.

Kull. 1875. 'Beiträge zur Statistik des Königsreichs Württemberg.' *Württembergische Jahrbücher für Statistik und Landeskunde, 1874*, Part I. Stuttgart: K. Statistisch-Topographischen Bureau.

Lachiver, Marcel. 1973. 'Fécondité légitime et contraception dans la région parisienne.' In *Sur la population française au XVIIIe et au XIXe siècle. Hommage à Marcel Reinhard*: 383–401. Paris: Société de Démographie Historique.

Langer, William L. 1974. 'Infanticide: a historical survey.' *History of Childhood Quarterly*, 1: 354–66.

Laslett, Peter. 1977a. 'Characteristics of the Western family considered over time.' *Journal of Family History*, 2: 89–116.

1977b. *Family life and illicit love in earlier generations*. Cambridge: Cambridge University Press.

1980a. 'Introduction: comparing illegitimacy over time and between cultures.' In Peter Laslett, Karla Oosterveen and Richard M. Smith (eds.), *Bastardy and its comparative history*. London: Edward Arnold.

1980b. 'The bastardy prone sub-society.' In Peter Laslett, Karla Oosterveen and Richard M. Smith (eds.), *Bastardy and its comparative history*. London: Edward Arnold.

Laslett, Peter, Karla Oosterveen and Richard M. Smith. 1980. *Bastardy and its comparative history*. London: Edward Arnold.

Lee, Ronald D. 1977. 'Introduction.' In Ronald D. Lee (ed.), *Population patterns in the past*: 1–17. New York: Academic Press.

Lee, W. R. 1977. *Population growth, economic development and social change in Bavaria 1750–1850*. New York: Arno Press.

1979. 'Germany.' In W. R. Lee (ed.), *European demography and economic growth*: 144–95. London: Croom Helm.

1980. 'The mechanism of mortality change in Germany, 1750–1850.' *Medizin historisches Journal* 15: 244–68.

1981. 'Family and modernization: the reasons for family and social change in nineteenth-century Bavaria.' In R. J. Evans and W. R. Lee (eds.), *The German family*. London: Croom Helm.

Leridon, Henri. 1977a. 'Sur l'estimation de la stérilité.' *Population*, 32 (special edn): 231–45.

1977b. *Human fertility*. Chicago: University of Chicago Press.

Lesthaeghe, Ron and Chris Wilson. 1986. 'Modes of production, secularization and the pace of fertility decline in western Europe, 1870–1930.' In A. J. Coale and Susan Watkins (eds.), *The decline of European fertility*. Princeton: Princeton University Press.

Levine, D. C. 1976. 'The reliability of parochial registration and the representativeness of family reconstitution.' *Population Studies*, 30: 107–22.

Lévy, Claude and Louis Henry. 1960. 'Ducs et pairs sous l'Ancien Régime: caractéristiques démographiques d'une caste.' *Population*, 5: 807–30.

Lindner, Friederich. 1900. *Die unehelichen Geburten als Sozialphänomen*. Leipzig: A. Deichert.

Lithell, Ula-Britt. 1981. 'Breastfeeding, infant mortality, and fertility.' *Journal of Family History*, 6: 182–94.

Livi-Bacci, Massimo. 1971. *A century of Portuguese fertility*. Princeton: Princeton University Press.

1977. *A history of Italian fertility during the last two centuries*. Princeton: Princeton University Press.

1981. 'On the frequency of remarriage in nineteenth century Italy: methods and results.' In J. Dupâquier, E. Hélin, P. Laslett, M. Livi-Bacci, and S. Sogner (eds.), *Marriage and remarriage in populations of the past*. New York: Academic Press.

McCann, M. F., L. S. Liskin, P. T. Piotrow, W. Rinehart, and G. Fox. 1981. 'Breastfeeding, fertility, and family planning.' *Population Reports*, J(24).

McDonald, Peter. 1984. *Nuptiality and completed fertility: a study of starting, stopping and spacing behavior*. Comparative studies 35. World Fertility Survey.

Macfarlane, Alan. 1980. 'Illegitimacy and illegitimates in English history.' In Peter Laslett, Karla Oosterveen and Richard M. Smith (eds.), *Bastardy and its comparative history*. London: Edward Arnold.

Mackenroth, Gerhard. 1953. *Bevölkerungslehre: Theorie, Soziologie und Statistik der Bevölkerung*. Berlin: Springer.

McKeown, Thomas. 1976. *The modern rise of populations*. New York: Academic Press.

Maine, Deborah. 1981. *Family planning: its impact on the health of women and children*. New York: Columbia University, Center for Population and Family Health.

Malthus, T. R. 1830. *A summary view of the principle of population*. London: John Murray.

Matthiessen, Paul and James McCann. 1978. 'The role of mortality in the European fertility transition: aggregate-level relations.' In Samuel Preston (ed.), *The effects of infant and child mortality on fertility*: 47–68. New York: Academic Press.

Matz, Klaus-Jürgen. 1980. *Pauperismus und Bevölkerung*. Stuttgart: Klett-Cotta.

Mayhew, Alan. 1973. *Rural settlement and farming in Germany*. London: B. T. Batsford.

Menken, Jane, James Trussell, and Susan Watkins. 1981. 'The nutrition fertility link: an evaluation of the evidence.' *Journal of Interdisciplinary History*, 11 (Winter): 425–41.

Mineau, G. P., L. L. Bean, and M. Skolnick. 1979. 'Mormon demographic history II: the family life cycle and natural fertility.' *Population Studies*, 33: 429–46.

Mineau, G. and J. Trussell. 1982. 'A specification of marital fertility by parents' age, age at marriage, and marriage duration.' *Demography*, 19: 335–49.

Mitterauer, M. and R. Sieder. 1982. *The European family*. Oxford: Basil Blackwell.

Myrdal, Alva. 1941. *Nation and family*. New York: Harper and Brothers.

Naeye, Richard, L. S. Burt, D. L. Wright, W. A. Blanc, and D. Tatter. 1971. 'Neonatal mortality: the male disadvantage.' *Pediatrics*, 48: 902–06. New York: Academic Press.

Nag, Moni. 1983. 'The impact of sociocultural factors on breastfeeding and sexual behavior.' In R. A. Bulatao and R. D. Lee (eds.), *Determinants of fertility in developing countries: a summary of knowledge*, Vol. I: 163–98.

Netting, Robert. 1981. *Balancing on an Alp*. Cambridge: Cambridge University Press.

Noonan, John T. 1966. *Contraception*. Cambridge, Mass.: Harvard University Press.

Nortman, Dorothy. 1974. *Parental age as a factor in pregnancy outcome and child development*. Reports on population – family planning 16. New York: Population Council.

Norton, Susan L. 1980. 'The vital question: are reconstituted families representative of the general population?' In B. Dyke and W. Morrill (eds.), *Genealogical demography*. New York: Academic Press.

Notestein, Frank W. 1953. 'Economic problems of population change.' In *Proceedings of the Eighth International Conference of Agricultural Economics*: 13–31. London: Oxford University Press.

Olsen, Randall J. 1980. 'Estimating the effects of child mortality on the number of births.' *Demography*, 17: 429–43.

Oosterveen, Karla, Richard M. Smith and Susan Stewart. 1980. 'Family reconstitution and the study of bastardy: evidence from certain English parishes.' In Peter Laslett, Karla Oosterveen and Richard M. Smith (eds.), *Bastardy and its comparative history*. London: Edward Arnold.

Perez Moreda, V. and David Reher. 1985. 'Demographic mechanisms and long-term swings in population in Europe, 1200–1850.' In *International Population Conference, Florence 1985*, Vol. IV: 313–29. Liège: International Union for the Scientific Study of Population.

Phayer, J. Michael. 1977. *Sexual liberation and religion in nineteenth century Europe*. London: Croom Helm.

Pockels, C. F. 1786. 'Schock Fluurs Jugendgeschichte.' *Magazin für Erfahrungs-seelenkunde*, 4(2): 96–127.

Pressat, Roland. 1972. *Demographic analysis: methods, results, applications*. Chicago: Aldine-Atherton.

Preston, Samuel H. 1976. *Mortality patterns in national populations*. New York: Academic Press.

   1978. 'Introduction.' In Samuel Preston (ed.), *The effects of infant and child mortality on fertility*: 1–80. New York: Academic Press.

Rechenbach, Horst. 1938. 'Aufgaben und Ziele des Vereins für bäuerliche Sippenkunde und bäuerliches Wappenwesen.' *Der Lebensquell*, 1: 2–6.

Rindfuss, Ronald and Larry Bumpass. 1976. 'How old is too old? Age and the sociology of fertility.' *Family Planning Perspectives*, 8: 226–30.

Robinson, W. S. 1950. 'Ecological correlations and behavior of individuals.' *American Sociological Review*, 15: 351–57.

Rodriguez, G. and J. N. Hobcraft. 1980. *Illustrative analysis: lifetable analysis of birth intervals in Columbia*. Scientific reports 16. World Fertility Survey.

Roller, Otto Konrad. 1907. *Die Einwohnerschaft der Stadt Durlach im 18. Jahrhundert in ihren wirtschaftlichen und kulturgeschichtlichen Verhältnissen dargestellt aus ihren Stammtafeln*. Karlsruhe: G. Braunschen.

Röse, C. 1905. 'Die Wichtigkeit der Mutterbrust für die körperliche und geistige Entwicklung des Menschen.' *Deutsche Monatsschrift für Zahn-heilkunde*, 23: 129–76.

Rotberg, Robert I. and Theodore K. Rabb (eds.). 1980. *Marriage and fertility: studies in interdisciplinary history*. Princeton: Princeton University Press.

Sabean, David. 1978. 'Small peasant agriculture in Germany at the beginning of the nineteenth century: changing work patterns.' *Peasant Studies*, 7(4): 218–24.

Sauer, Friederich. 1975. *Höringhausen*. Arolsen: Waldeckischer Geschichts-verein.

Schaub, Walter. 1975. 'Dorfsippenbücher–Ortssippenbücher.' In W. Ribbe and E. Henning (eds.), *Taschenbuch für Familiengeschichtsforschung*. Neustadt an der Aisch: Degener.

Scheuenpflug, Lorenz. 1961. *Ortssippenbuch Anhausen*. Frankfurt am Main: Deutsche Arbeitsgemeinschaft geneologischer Verbände.

Schofield, Roger. 1972. 'Representativeness and family reconstitution.' *Annales de démographie historique 1972*: 121–25.

   1973. 'Statistical problems.' *International Population Conference, Liège 1973*, Vol. III: 45–57. Liège: International Union for the Scientific Study of Population.

   1976. 'The relationship between demographic structure and environment in pre-industrial Europe.' In W. Conze (ed.), *Sozialgeschichte der Familie in der Neuzeit Europas*: 147–60. Stuttgart: Ernst Klett.

1986. 'Did mothers really die? Three centuries of maternal mortality in the World We Have Lost.' In Lloyd Bonfield, Richard M. Smith, and Keith Wrightson (eds.), *The world we have gained: histories of population and social structures*. Oxford: Basil Blackwell.

Schofield, Roger and E. A. Wrigley. 1979. 'Infant and child mortality in England in the late Tudor and early Stuart periods.' In C. Webster (ed.), *Health, medicine, and mortality in the sixteenth century*: 61–96. Cambridge: Cambridge University Press.

1981. 'Remarriage intervals and the effect of marriage on fertility.' In J. Dupâquier, E. Hélin, P. Laslett, M. Livi-Bacci, and S. Sogner (eds.), *Marriage and remarriage in populations of the past*. New York: Academic Press.

Scrimshaw, Susan C. M. 1978. 'Infant mortality and behavior in the regulation of family size.' *Population and Development Review*, 4: 383–404.

Segalen, Martine. 1981. 'Mentalité populaire et remariage en Europe occidentale.' In J. Dupâquier, E. Hélin, P. Laslett, M. Livi-Bacci, and S. Sogner (eds.), *Marriage and remarriage in populations of the past*. New York: Academic Press.

Sharlin, Allan. 1977. 'Historical demography as history and demography.' *American Behavioral Scientist*, 21: 245–62.

1986. 'Urban–rural differences in fertility in Europe during the demographic transition.' In Ansley J. Coale and Susan Watkins (eds.), *The decline of European fertility*: 234–60. Princeton: Princeton University Press.

Shorter, Edward. 1975. *The making of the modern family*. New York: Basic Books.

1978. 'The evolution of maternal mortality, eighteenth to twentieth centuries.' Unpublished manuscript.

1981. 'L'âge des premières règles en France, 1750–1950.' *Annales: économies, sociétés, civilisations*, 36(3): 495–511.

1982. *A history of women's bodies*. New York: Basic Books.

1986. 'Die grosse Umwälzung in den Mutter–Kind Beziehungen vom 18. bis zum 20. Jahrhundert.' In Jochen Martin and August Nitschke (eds.), *Zur Sozialgeschichte der Kindheit*. Freiburg: Karl Alber.

Shorter, Edward, John Knodel and E. van de Walle. 1971. 'The decline of non-marital fertility.' *Population Studies*, 25: 371–93.

Sieder, R. and M. Mitterauer. 1983. 'The reconstruction of the family life course: theoretical problems and empirical results.' In R. Wall. J. Robin and P. Laslett (eds.), *Family forms in historic Europe*: 309–45. Cambridge: Cambridge University Press.

Skolnick, M., L. L. Bean, V. Arbon, K. de Nevers, and P. Cartwright. 1978. 'Mormon demographic history I: nuptiality and fertility of once-married couples.' *Population Studies*, 35: 5–19.

Slicher van Bath, B. H. 1977. 'Agriculture in the vital revolution.' In E. E. Rich and C. H. Wilson (eds.), *The economic organization of early modern Europe*. *Cambridge Economic History of Europe*, Vol. V. Cambridge: Cambridge University Press.

Smith, Daniel Scott. 1977. 'A homeostatic demographic regime: patterns in west European family reconstitution studies.' In Ronald D. Lee (ed.), *Population patterns in the past*. New York: Academic Press.

Smith, Richard M. 1979. 'Some reflections on the evidence for the origins of the European marriage pattern in England.' In C. C. Harris (ed.) *The sociology of the family: new directions for Britain. Sociological Review* monograph 28. Keele: University of Keele.

Spagnoli, Paul. 1977. 'Population history from parish monographs: the problems of local demographic variations.' *Journal of Interdisciplinary History*, 3: 427–52.

Taucher, Erica. 1982. 'Effects of declining fertility on infant mortality levels: a study based on data from five Latin American countries.' Unpublished report to the Ford Foundation and the Rockefeller Foundation.

Teuteberg, H. J. 1975. 'The general relationship between diet and industrialization.' In E. Forster and R. Forster (eds.), *European diet from pre-industrial to modern times*. New York: Harper Torch.

Thestrup, P. 1972. 'Methodological problems in Danish family reconstitution.' *Scandinavian Economic Review*, 20: 1–26.

Tilly, Charles. 1978. 'The historical study of vital processes.' In Charles Tilly (ed.), *Historical studies of changing fertility*: 3–55. Princeton: Princeton University Press.

    1981. *As sociology meets history*. New York: Academic Press.

    1984. 'Demographic origins of the European proletariat.' In David Levine (ed.), *Proletarianization and family history*: 1–85. New York: Academic Press.

Trussell, James and Chris Wilson. 1984. 'Sterility in a natural fertility population.' Paper delivered at the 1984 annual meeting of the Population Association of America, Minneapolis, May 1984.

United Nations. 1954. *Foetal, infant, and early childhood mortality*, Vol. I. Population Studies 13. New York: United Nations.

    1955. *Methods of appraisal of quality of basic data for population estimates*, Manual II. New York: Department of Economic and Social Affairs.

    1973. *The determinants and consequences of population trends*, Vol. I. New York: United Nations.

van de Walle, Etienne. 1968. 'Marriage and marital fertility.' *Daedalus*, 97: 486–501.

    1973. 'Age at marriage and fertility.' *IPPF Medical Bulletin*, 7(3): 1-2.

    1974. *The female population of France in the nineteenth century*. Princeton: Princeton University Press.

    1980. 'Illegitimacy in France during the nineteenth century.' In Peter Laslett, Karla Oosterveen and Richard M. Smith (eds.), *Bastardy and its comparative history*. London: Edward Arnold.

van de Walle, Etienne and John Knodel. 1980. 'Europe's fertility transition: new evidence and lessons for today's developing world.' *Population Bulletin*, 34(6): 1–43.

van de Walle, Francine. 1986. 'Infant mortality and the European demographic transition.' In A. J. Coale and Susan Watkins (eds.), *The decline of fertility in Europe*: 201–33. Princeton: Princeton University Press.

van Ginneken, Jeroen K. 1978. 'The impact of prolonged breastfeeding on birth intervals and on postpartum amenorrhea.' In W. Henry Mosley (ed.), *Nutrition and Human Reproduction*: 179–98. New York: Plenum Press.

Verein für bäuerliche Sippenkunde und bäuerliches Wappenwesen. 1938. *Dorfsippenbuch Kreuth*. Goslar: Blut und Boden Verlag.

    1939. *Dorfsippenbuch Vasbeck*. Goslar: Blut und Boden Verlag

Visaria, Pravin M. 1967. 'Sex ratio at birth in territories with a relatively complete registration.' *Eugenics Quarterly*, 14: 132–42.

von Ungern-Sternberg, Roderich and Hermann Schubnell. 1950. *Grundriss der Bevölkerungswissenschaft (Demographie)*. Stuttgart: Piscator.

Wall, Richard. 1981. 'Inferring differential neglect of females from mortality data.' *Annales de démographie historique 1981*: 119–40.

Watkins, Susan. 1981. 'Regional patterns of nuptiality in western Europe, 1870–1960.' *Population Studies*, 35: 199–215.

1986. 'Conclusions.' In Ansley J. Coale and Susan Watkins (eds.), *The decline of European fertility*: 420–49. Princeton: Princeton University Press.

Weir, David. 1983. 'Fertility transition in rural France, 1740–1829.' Ph.D. dissertation, Stanford University.

Wetekam, Robert. 1956. *Massenhausen*. Arolsen: Waldeckischer Geschichtsverein.

1971. *Braunsen*. Arolsen: Waldeckischer Geschichtsverein.

Wickman, K. Rob. V. 1937. 'Die Einleitung der Ehe.' In *Acta Academiae Aboensis*, Vol. II, Part I: 1–384. Abo: Abo Akademi.

Wilson, C. 1984. 'Natural fertility in pre-industrialized England.' *Population Studies*, 38: 225–40.

Winberg, Christer. 1978. 'Population growth and proletarianization. The transformation of social structures in rural Sweden during the agrarian revolution.' In Sune Akerman *et al.* (eds.), *Chance and change: social and economic studies in historical demography in the Baltic area*. Odense: Odense University Press.

Wolfers, D. 1968. 'The determinants of birth intervals and their means.' *Population Studies*, 22: 253–62.

Wray, Joe D. 1971. 'Population pressure on families: family size and child spacing.' In National Academy of Sciences, *Rapid population growth*. Baltimore: Johns Hopkins Press.

Wrigley, E. A. 1961. *Industrial growth and population change*. Cambridge: Cambridge University Press.

1966a. 'Family reconstitution.' In E. A. Wrigley (ed.), *An introduction to English historical demography*. New York: Basic Books.

1966b. 'Family limitation in pre-industrial England.' *Economic History Review*, 19: 82–109.

1968. 'Mortality in pre-industrial England: the example of Colyton, Devon, over three centuries.' *Daedalus*, 97: 546–80.

1969. *Population and history*. New York: McGraw-Hill.

(ed.) 1973. *Identifying people in the past*. London: Edward Arnold.

1976. 'The significance of appropriate source material to the progress of historical population studies.' *Archives*, 12: 109–15.

1977. 'Births and baptisms: the use of Anglican baptism registers as a source of information about the numbers of births in England before the beginning of civil registration.' *Population Studies*, 31(2): 281–312.

1978. 'Fertility strategy for the individual and the group.' In Charles Tilly (ed.), *Historical studies of changing fertility*: 135–54. Princeton: Princeton University Press.

1981a. 'Population history in the 1980s.' *Journal of Interdisciplinary History*, 12: 207–26.

1981b. 'Marriage, fertility and population growth in eighteenth-century England.' In R. B. Outhwaite (ed.), *Marriage and society*: 137–85. London: Europa Publications.

Wrigley, E. A. and R. S. Schofield. 1981. *The population history of England 1541–1871*. Cambridge, Mass.: Harvard University Press.

1983. 'English population history from family reconstitution: summary results 1600–1799.' *Population Studies*, 37: 157–84.

Wülker, Ludwig. 1944. 'Dorfsippenbücher.' *Archiv für Landesvolkskunde von Niedersachsen*, 21: 273–77.

Würzburg, Arthur. 1887, 1888. 'Die Säuglingssterblichkeit im deutschen Reich während der Jahre 1875 bis 1877.' *Arbeiten aus dem kaiserlichen Gesundheitsamt*, 2: 208–22, 343–446, 4: 28–108.

Index